Geologic Evolution of the Mojave Desert and Southwestern Basin and Range

Edited by

Allen F. Glazner
Department of Geological Sciences
CB 3315 University of North Carolina
Chapel Hill, North Carolina 27599
USA

and

J. Douglas Walker
Department of Geology
University of Kansas
Lawrence, Kansas 66045
USA

and

John M. Bartley
University of Utah
Department of Geology and Geophysics, 717WBB
Salt Lake City, Utah 84112-1183
USA

THE
GEOLOGICAL
SOCIETY
OF AMERICA

Memoir 195

3300 Penrose Place, P.O. Box 9140 ▪ Boulder, Colorado 80301-9140 USA

2002

Published by The Geological Society of America, Inc.
3300 Penrose Place, P.O. Box 9140, Boulder, Colorado 80301
www.geosociety.org

Printed in U.S.A.

GSA Books Science Editor Abhijit Basu
Cover design by Margo Good

Library of Congress Cataloging-in-Publication Data

Geologic evolution of the Mojave Desert and southwestern basin and range / edited by
Allen F. Glazner, J. Douglas Walker and John M. Bartley.
        p. cm. — (GSA Memoir ; 195)
      Includes bibliographical references and index.
      ISBN 0-8137-1195-9
          1. Geology—California—Mojave Desert Region. I. Glazner, Allen F. II. Walker, J.
  Douglas, 1958 III. Bartley, John M. IV. Memoir (Geological Society of America) ; 195.

QE90.M64 G46 2002
557.94'95—dc21   2002024238

Cover: View to northwest from the summit of the Waterman Hills, near Barstow, California. The red-on-green contact in the foreground is the Waterman Hills detachment fault (Chapter 2) that separates an upper plate of brecciated and potassically altered early Miocene rhyolite from a lower plate of shattered mylonite derived from the early Miocene Waterman Hills granodiorite. Weakly deformed Waterman Hills granodiorite, also unroofed by the detachment, underlies the northern Waterman Hills in the distance behind the red truck (see inside flap). Black Mountain, the rounded basaltic mountain on the skyline behind the truck, is an anticline formed by late Cenozoic dextral transpression across the Harper Lake fault. Fremont Peak, the pointed summit to the left of Black Mountain (back cover), is underlain by Mesozoic granitoids and migmatites (Chapter 8). In the distance between Black Mountain and Fremont Peak lies Red Mountain, Miocene volcanic rocks near the Garlock fault (Chapter 9).

10 9 8 7 6 5 4 3 2 1

Contents

Geological Society of America
Memoir 195
2002

Preface

Allen F. Glazner
Department of Geological Sciences, CB 3315 University of North Carolina, Chapel Hill, North Carolina 27599, USA
J. Douglas Walker
Department of Geology, University of Kansas, Lawrence, Kansas 66045, USA
John M. Bartley
University of Utah, Department of Geology and Geophysics, 717WBB, Salt Lake City, Utah 84112-1183, USA

The Mojave Desert region of southern California has long been a geologic puzzle. The broad outlines of its geologic history have been clear for decades (e.g., Burchfiel and Davis, 1981), but details of how it relates to bordering geologic provinces such as the Basin and Range and Sierra Nevada and how it has responded to plate-boundary effects during the Phanerozoic are less certain.

All major developmental phases of the Cordilleran orogen are recorded in the Mojave Desert, including Neoproterozoic rifting and Paleozoic passive-margin development (e.g., Miller and Cameron, 1982; Martin and Walker, 1992); Mesozoic arc magmatism and subduction-related deformation (e.g., Karish et al., 1987; Walker et al., 1990a; Schermer and Busby, 1994; Jacobson et al., 1996); mid-Tertiary volcanism and crustal extension (e.g., Glazner and Supplee, 1982; Dokka, 1989; Glazner et al., 1989; Walker et al., 1995); and dextral shear and transpression related to the modern Pacific-North American plate boundary (e.g., Dibblee, 1961; Garfunkel, 1974; Dokka, 1983; Bartley et al., 1990; Luyendyk, 1991). Contributions in this volume address diverse aspects of this history, with particular emphasis on the tectonics of the Jurassic-Cretaceous magmatic arc and on magmatism and regional tectonic deformation over the past 25 m.y.

In spite of this well-established general picture, a paucity of detailed geologic studies has made it convenient to interpret that major structures pass through the Mojave area to solve geologic problems that were defined outside its boundaries. For example, the Mojave-Sonora megashear (Anderson and Silver, 1979), the Permian-Triassic truncation boundary (Burchfiel and Davis, 1975; Walker, 1988), and the Mojave-Snow Lake fault (Schweickert and Lahren, 1990) are all hypothesized to pass through the Mojave Desert region, but whether the geology of the region actually permits these structures has remained uncertain. The Salinian block west of the San Andreas fault has been hypothesized to represent a nappe formed by thrust decapitation of the Mojave block (Silver, 1982), but again, evaluation of this hypothesis has been hampered by a lack of fundamental geologic data.

Although each editor of this volume earlier worked on various aspects of Mojave geology, our three-way collaboration began in the mid-1980s with recognition of the Waterman Hills detachment fault, a large-displacement, early Miocene extensional fault complex that crops out near Barstow. Recognition of this structure followed on the work of Greg Davis, Steve Reynolds, and many others in the Colorado River trough-southern Arizona extensional corridor, which showed that such faults are common in the Basin and Range and can accumulate up to several tens of kilometers of displacement. Recognition that the Waterman Hills detachment fault shuffled pre-Miocene geology (Walker et al., 1990b) led to several breakthroughs in understanding the pre-Cenozoic geology of the Mojave Desert region. In particular, removing Miocene slip across the detachment restores several pre-Cenozoic markers to understandable configurations (Martin et al., 1993).

Unraveling the geology of the Mojave Desert region was advanced by integration with ongoing research north of the Garlock fault arising from the U.S. Navy's Geothermal Program at China Lake. As both chief administrator of the USN Geothermal Program Office and an active participant in some of the research reported in this volume, Frank Monastero played key roles in advancing understanding of Mojave tectonics. Access to the China Lake Naval Weapons Center and also to Fort Irwin helped to tie the Mojave Desert region to surrounding geologic provinces and to solve several long-standing enigmas.

This volume summarizes collaborative work over the past 15 years involving scientists from many institutions including the universities of North Carolina, Kansas, Utah, California at Santa Barbara, and Nevada at Las Vegas, as well as the USN Geothermal Program Office and U.S. Geological Survey. We particularly acknowledge selfless collaboration by several USGS scientists, notably Keith Howard, Jane Nielson, Dave Miller, and Howard Wilshire.

Glazner, A.F., Walker, J.D., and Bartley, J.M., 2002, Preface, *in* Glazner, A.F., Walker, J.D., and Bartley, J.M., eds., Geologic Evolution of the Mojave Desert and Southwestern Basin and Range: Boulder, Colorado, Geological Society of America Memoir 195, p. v–vi.

These studies were advanced greatly by several outstanding Ph.D. and M.S. students, most of whom have contributed to papers in the volume. It is clear that many of the major leaps in understanding came from their studies. Although many of the students have published summary articles of their work, much of the important basic data that reside in theses remain difficult to access. This is particularly true for geologic maps (of both students and other workers). For that reason, we have made available on an accompanying CD-ROM many of the new geologic maps that cover parts of the Mojave Desert region and adjacent Basin and Range province. The maps are in geographic information system (GIS) format as well as graphical formats.

In addition, we have taken this new work, along with other published studies, and created a 1:250 000 compilation map that incorporates new geologic studies for the area. This color map is included in paper form (Plate 1) with this volume as well as being on the CD-ROM in GIS format. This compilation was modeled on the California Division of Mines and Geology Geologic Portfolio series. Maps of this series have been indispensable in our studies.

Please see the final two papers in this volume for more information concerning the maps on the CD-ROM. Of these two papers, the first details how the disparately scaled maps were processed to compile Plate 1. The second of the pair explains how the map files are organized and presented.

We dedicate this volume to the outstanding scientists who laid the groundwork for our geologic studies in the Mojave Desert: Tom Dibblee, Jr., whose geologic maps made our work possible; Greg Davis, Clark Burchfiel, Warren Hamilton, and Tanya Atwater, whose imaginative syntheses of the tectonic history of the southwestern United States set the stage for our work; and Bruce Luyendyk and his students, who showed that translation along strike-slip faults is not the only sort of mobility that crustal terranes can exhibit. Finally, we acknowledge Roy Dokka as an important catalyst for our research. Disagreements about the Cenozoic geology of the Mojave Desert stimulated much of the work presented here, and the need to address alternative views put forward by Roy and his students encouraged us always to consider more than one possible interpretation of our observations.

REFERENCES CITED

Anderson, T.H., and Silver, L.T., 1979, The role of the Mojave-Sonora megashear in the tectonic evolution of northern Sonora, *in* Anderson, T.H., and Roldan-Quintana, J., eds., Geology of northern Sonora: Boulder, Colorado, Geological Society of America, 1979 Annual Meeting Guidebook, p. 59–68.

Bartley, J.M., Glazner, A.F., and Schermer, E.R., 1990, North-south contraction of the Mojave block and strike-slip tectonics in southern California: Science, v. 248, p. 1398–1401.

Burchfiel, B.C. and Davis, G.A., 1975, Nature and controls of Cordilleran orogenesis, western United States: extensions of an earlier synthesis: American Journal of Science, v. 275-A, p. 363–396.

Burchfiel, B.C. and Davis, G.A., 1981, Mojave Desert and environs, *in* Ernst, W.G., ed., The geotectonic development of California, Rubey Volume 1: Englewood Cliffs, New Jersey, Prentice-Hall, p. 217–252.

Dibblee, T.W., Jr., 1961, Evidence of strike-slip movement on northwest-trending faults in Mojave Desert, California: U.S. Geological Survey Professional Paper 424-B, p. B197–B199.

Dokka, R.K., 1983, Displacements on late Cenozoic strike-slip faults of the central Mojave Desert, California: Geology, v. 11, p. 305–308.

Dokka, R.K., 1989, The Mojave extensional belt of Southern California: Tectonics, v. 8, p. 363–390.

Garfunkel, Z., 1974, Model for the late Cenozoic tectonic history of the Mojave Desert, California, and for its relation to adjacent regions: Geological Society of America Bulletin, v. 85, p. 1931–1944.

Glazner, A.F. and Supplee, J.A., 1982, Migration of Tertiary volcanism in the southwestern United States and subduction of the Mendocino fracture zone: Earth and Planetary Science Letters, v. 60, p. 429–436.

Glazner, A.F., Bartley, J.M., and Walker, J.D., 1989, Magnitude and significance of Miocene crustal extension in the central Mojave Desert, California: Geology, v. 17, p. 50–53.

Jacobson, C.E., Oyarzabal, F.R., and Haxel, G.B., 1996, Subduction and exhumation of the Pelona-Orocopia-Rand schists, Southern California: Geology, v. 24, p. 547–550.

Karish, C.R., Miller, E.L., and Sutter, J.F., 1987, Mesozoic tectonic and magmatic history of the central Mojave Desert: Arizona Geological Society Digest, v. 18, p. 15–32.

Luyendyk, B.P., 1991, A model for Neogene crustal rotations, transtension, and transpression in Southern California: Geological Society of America Bulletin, v. 103, p. 1528–1536.

Martin, M.W., Glazner, A.F., Walker, J.D., and Schermer, E.R., 1993, Evidence for right-lateral transfer faulting accommodating en echelon Miocene extension, Mojave Desert, California: Geology, v. 21, p. 355–358.

Martin, M.W. and Walker, J.D., 1992, Extending the western North American Proterozoic and Paleozoic continental crust through the Mojave Desert: Geology, v. 20, p. 753–56.

Miller, E.L., and Cameron, C.S., 1982, Late Precambrian to Late Cretaceous evolution of the southwestern Mojave Desert, California, *in* Cooper, J.D., et al., eds., Geology of selected areas in the San Bernardino Mountains, western Mojave Desert, and southern Great Basin, California: Shoshone, CA, Death Valley Publishing Co., p. 21–34.

Schermer, E.R. and Busby, C., 1994, Jurassic magmatism in the central Mojave Desert: Implications for arc paleogeography and preservation of continental volcanic sequences: Geological Society of America Bulletin, v. 106, p. 767–790.

Schweickert, R.A. and Lahren, M.M., 1990, Speculative reconstruction of the Mojave-Snow Lake Fault; implications for Paleozoic and Mesozoic orogenesis in the Western United States: Tectonics, v. 9, p. 1609–1629.

Silver, L.T., 1982, Evidence and a model for west-directed early to mid-Cenozoic basement overthrusting in Southern California: Geological Society of America Abstracts with Programs, v. 14, no. 7, p. 617.

Walker, J.D., 1988, Permian and Triassic rocks of the Mojave Desert and their implications for timing and mechanisms of continental truncation: Tectonics, v. 7, p. 685–709.

Walker, J.D., Martin, M.W., Bartley, J.M., and Coleman, D.S., 1990a, Age and kinematics of deformation in the Cronese Hills, California, and implications for Mesozoic structure of the Southern Cordillera: Geology, v. 18, p. 554–557.

Walker, J.D., Bartley, J.M., and Glazner, A.F., 1990b, Large-magnitude Miocene extension in the central Mojave Desert; implications for Paleozoic to Tertiary paleogeography and tectonics: Journal of Geophysical Research, v. 95, p. 557–569.

Walker, J.D., Fletcher, J.M., Fillmore, R.P., Martin, M.W., Taylor, W.J., Glazner, A.F., and Bartley, J.M., 1995, Connection between igneous activity and extension in the central Mojave metamorphic core complex: Journal of Geophysical Research, vol. 100, p. 10477–10494.

MANUSCRIPT ACCEPTED BY THE SOCIETY MAY 9, 2001

Geological Society of America
Memoir 195
2002

Late Paleozoic to Mesozoic development of the Mojave Desert and environs, California

J. Douglas Walker
Department of Geology, University of Kansas, Lawrence, Kansas 66045, USA
Mark W. Martin
Department of Earth, Atmospheric, and Planetary Sciences, Massachusetts Institute of Technology,
Cambridge, Massachusetts 02139, USA
Allen F. Glazner
Department of Geology, University of North Carolina, Chapel Hill, Chapel Hill, North Carolina 27599, USA

ABSTRACT

The Mojave Desert region displays a relatively unusual tectonic history in that it went from an inboard to an outboard position during latest Paleozoic time. This change was accomplished by strike-slip truncation of the continental margin. Following truncation, the newly formed margin became the site of east-directed subduction as recorded by arc-affinity igneous rocks of Late Permian–Early Triassic age. Sedimentation was relatively continuous during this time in the eastern Mojave Desert. Farther west, events over this time period are less well understood owing to the scarcity of rocks and structures of this age.

The development of the Mojave Desert region in Middle to Late Jurassic time was dominated by arc activity. Middle to Late Jurassic volcanic rocks are preserved in the footwalls of Jurassic thrusts that carry Jurassic plutons and their pendant rocks. Volcanic rocks are also preserved in calderas and volcano-tectonic depressions. The thrusts are organized into a relatively continuous belt that probably represents the southern continuation of the East Sierran thrust system.

The main Cretaceous structure in the area is the Rand thrust of Late Cretaceous age. This structure is exposed in the northern Mojave Desert, but rocks of the footwall presumably underlie most of the western Mojave Desert. Other minor structures are present, but their tectonic significance is less certain.

Although the Mojave Desert region went from an inboard to an outboard tectonic position, the region still preserved aspects of both geologic settings. The locus of arc magmatism mostly paralleled the newly formed margin. The late Paleozoic truncation structures and not the thermal structure of the arc, on the other hand, in part controlled contractional deformation.

INTRODUCTION

The Mojave Desert is coincident with one of the geologically most diverse and complex regions of the southwestern North American Cordillera. The area forms the southwestern-most extent of Precambrian continental North America (Martin and Walker, 1992) and rests at the present plate edge formed by the San Andreas transform fault. Because an oceanic plate has bordered the western part of North America since late Precambrian time (Burchfiel and Davis, 1972), the Mojave Desert

Walker, J.D., Martin, M.W., and Glazner, A.F., 2002, Late Paleozoic to Mesozoic development of the Mojave Desert and environs, California, *in* Glazner, A.F., Walker, J.D., and Bartley, J.M., eds., Geologic Evolution of the Mojave Desert and Southwestern Basin and Range: Boulder, Colorado, Geological Society of America Memoir 195, p. 1–18.

and environs have undergone most styles of continental-margin tectonism through the Phanerozoic.

We define the Mojave Desert as that area bordered by the Garlock fault to the north, the San Andreas fault to the southwest, and the southern extension of the Death Valley fault zone to the east (Fig. 1). This definition is primarily tectonic in scope. In this paper we limit our discussion to that part of the Mojave Desert that is north of the eastern Transverse Ranges. Over the past 600 m.y., the region has had a complex geologic history that includes extension, contraction, and plutonism.

The geologic history of the Mojave Desert divides nicely into Cenozoic events overprinting Paleozoic and Mesozoic tectonism. We present two companion papers on this region (this paper and Glazner et al., this volume): one dealing with geologic events of the past 60 Ma and one that discusses late Paleozoic and Mesozoic development. Deciphering the geologic history necessarily involves using both young and old markers to understand the strain significance of various deformational events. In this paper we give a brief geologic setting and history for the region. This description is followed by detailed discussions of important tectonic, magmatic, and depositional events. A simplified geologic map for the northern Mojave Desert and southwestern Basin and Range province is included (Plate 1—a 1:250 000 scale map prepared from the California Division of Mines and Geology 1:250 000 Geologic Portfolio Series and from compilation of more recent published and unpublished mapping). In addition, a series of previously unpublished maps is also included with this volume (see additional maps on CD-ROM in pocket). The last two papers by Walker et al. in this volume describe the compilation of Plate 1 and the sets of maps on the CD-ROM.

GEOLOGIC SETTING

Rocks of Precambrian to late Cenozoic age are exposed across the greater Mojave Desert region (Fig. 1 and Plate 1). Precambrian basement rocks are generally either ca. 1700 Ma or ca. 1400 Ma (Anderson et al., 1993) and are widely distributed across the southern and eastern Mojave Desert (Martin and Walker, 1992; Anderson et al., 1993). Precambrian rocks of other ages, such as ca. 1.1 Ga diabase sills, have relatively minor exposure. Upper Precambrian–Lower Permian miogeoclinal-cratonal strata overlie the basement rocks (Figs. 1 and 2; Burchfiel and Davis, 1972, 1975; Stewart and Poole, 1975; Martin and Walker, 1992). Detrital zircons from upper Precambrian clastic rocks in the Marble Mountains (eastern Mojave Desert) suggest locally derived 1.1 Ga zircons from granitic source(s) (Gehrels, 2000). The miogeoclinal strata generally have southwest- to south-trending facies patterns. Deposits related to the Devonian–Mississippian Antler orogeny are not present in any of the Mojave miogeoclinal-cratonal sections (Walker, 1988).

Paleozoic rocks of eugeoclinal affinity (e.g., continental-slope and -rise deposits) are present in the northern Mojave

Desert from the Alvord Mountain area to Pilot Knob Valley and across the Garlock fault in the El Paso Mountains (Figs. 1 and 2; Burchfiel and Davis, 1972, 1975). Facies are mismatched, therefore, across the central Mojave Desert: eugeoclinal rocks crop out to the north, and miogeoclinal rocks are found to the south. As discussed later in this paper, this mismatch has been a locus of repeated tectonic activity. The eugeoclinal section is capped by Late Permian andesite (U-Pb zircon, Martin and Walker, 1995), and Permian–Triassic plutonic rocks intrude both the eugeoclinal section and the miogeoclinal-cratonal sections (Miller and Sutter, 1982; M.D. Carr et al., 1984; Martin and Walker, 1995; Miller et al., 1995).

Mesozoic strata consist of Lower Triassic (and possibly Middle Jurassic) marine sedimentary rocks and Middle (?) Triassic–Upper Jurassic volcanic and epiclastic strata (Walker, 1987, 1988; Schermer, 1993; Schermer and Busby, 1994). In addition, the Mojave Desert region resides in the heart of the Jurassic–Cretaceous magmatic arc (Fig. 1 and Plate 1; Kistler, 1974; Barton et al., 1988). Facies and magmatic patterns in these Mesozoic strata generally follow northwest trends across the Mojave Desert region (Hamilton and Myers, 1966; Hamilton, 1969; Burchfiel and Davis, 1981; Walker, 1987, 1988), indicating that the continental margin had a northwest to north trend during this time. Orientation of the continental margin probably changed in late Paleozoic time owing to truncation of the continental margin accompanied by late-stage contractional deformation and igneous activity (Davis et al., 1978; Burchfiel and Davis, 1981; Walker, 1988, Stone and Stevens, 1988).

Paleogene rocks are confined to the northernmost Mojave Desert and southwestern Basin and Range province (Goler Formation; Cox, 1982; Cox and Diggles, 1986) whereas Neogene to Holocene rocks are widely exposed. Most Neogene sections include earliest Miocene (or possibly latest Oligocene) volcanic rocks overlain by lower to middle Miocene sedimentary, volcanic, and epiclastic sections that were deposited in basins formed by extensional faulting associated with metamorphic core complex activity (Fillmore and Walker, 1996). Extensional activity began at ca. 23 Ma in areas around the Colorado River to the central Mojave Desert (Fig. 1; Dokka, 1989; Walker et al., 1990a, 1995a). Starting in late Miocene time, the Mojave Desert region was transected by northwest-trending, right-lateral strike-slip faults with local areas of east-trending, left-lateral strike-slip faults (Dibblee, 1961; Garfunkel, 1974; Dokka and Travis, 1990). Cumulative slip on these faults has been small. Important contractional faulting and folding (Bartley et al., 1990) has accompanied this extensional and strike-slip faulting across most of the region.

PERMIAN–TRIASSIC TRUNCATION

The passive margin that dominated the geology of the western Cordillera throughout most of the Paleozoic was disturbed by tectonic activity in late Paleozoic time. The Mojave Desert region was dramatically affected by these changes and went from an inboard tectonic position in middle Paleozoic time to a plate-margin position in latest Paleozoic time. This change is reflected in the character of stratigraphic sequences, in the deformation of some of these sequences, and in local magmatic activity.

Stratigraphic sequences across much of the region record Pennsylvanian–middle Permian platform sedimentation conformable with older miogeoclinal-cratonal strata. This pattern is broken for sections in the western Death Valley area and into the central and northeastern Mojave Desert (the Soda Mountains and Shadow Mountains; Martin and Walker, 1991; Walker and Wardlaw, 1989) where Pennsylvanian–middle Permian rocks consist of turbidites and other deep-water strata apparently deposited in a continental-borderland setting (Stone and Stevens, 1988; Walker, 1988; Stevens et al., 1998). Areas underlain by Mojave eugeoclinal sections, which were displaced from the Antler belt of Nevada and eastern California, (as described later in this section) also show evidence for similar active basin formation in Pennsylvanian and especially Early Permian time (M.D. Carr et al., 1984).

Late Permian deformation and magmatism are recorded locally in ranges in the western Mojave Desert and are best understood for eugeoclinal rocks in the El Paso Mountains (Figs. 1 and 3). There, Guadalupian (early Late Permian) debris-flow deposits are overlain by Late Permian volcaniclastic and andesitic rocks (M.D. Carr et al., 1984), the latter of which have been dated at ca. 260 Ma (U-Pb zircon; Martin and Walker, 1995). (All radiometric ages given in this paper were determined by U-Pb on zircon unless otherwise stated.) These rocks are deformed into west-vergent folds and west-directed faults that involve a gneissic pluton, dated at 260 Ma (Miller et al., 1995), which is interpreted to be synkinematic (M.D. Carr et al., 1984). Deformed rocks in the El Paso Mountains are cut by postkinematic plutons as old as 246 Ma (Miller et al., 1995). Hence, deformation and magmatism in this area are Late Permian–Early Triassic in age (using the time scale of Bowring et al., 1998).

Miogeoclinal-cratonal sections also record late Paleozoic deformation, although geologic relationships are less clear. In the Victorville area, at Black Mountain, rocks as young as Mississippian are deformed and intruded by a pluton dated at 243 Ma (Fig. 3; Miller, 1981; Walker, 1988; Miller et al., 1995). In addition, structures predate deposition of the Mesozoic Fairview Valley Formation. East-vergent folding of lower Paleozoic rocks at Quartzite Mountain is approximately the same age on the basis of similarity of deformation style and the presence of the overlying Fairview Valley Formation (Miller, 1981, p. 52–53).

In the Shadow Mountains, undated volcaniclastic strata similar to those in the El Paso Mountains cap the miogeoclinal Paleozoic section (Martin and Walker, 1991, 1995). In addition, all strata in the Shadow Mountains are folded into a large-scale west-vergent anticline. The timing of this deformation is bracketed between late Paleozoic and late Middle Jurassic (Martin and Walker, 1995; Martin et al., this volume).

These data suggest that the eugeoclinal succession of the northern Mojave Desert was juxtaposed (by one of two means described next) against the miogeoclinal-cratonal sequences to the south by latest Permian time. The igneous activity present in these areas serves to stitch these sequences together. Previous interpretations that Lower Triassic rocks provided an overlap for this juxtaposition are less compelling because of uncertainties about the exact ages of Triassic rocks (compare Walker [1987, 1988] to Schermer et al. [this volume], and the subsequent discussion here).

There are conflicting hypotheses about the mechanism of late Paleozoic juxtaposition. Late Paleozoic, left-lateral strike-slip truncation of the continental margin and some of the craton has been proposed for the western Mojave Desert (Hamilton, 1969; Davis et al., 1978; Stone and Stevens, 1988; Walker, 1988). This interpretation is consistent with changes in late Paleozoic facies patterns and characteristics of miogeoclinal-cratonal and eugeoclinal sections from the Death Valley area to the Mojave Desert region. Alternatively, extreme telescoping by thrust faulting along a preexisting continental margin has been considered as the mechanism of juxtaposition (Poole, 1974; Dickinson, 1981; Snow, 1992). We prefer the former mechanism and timing for several reasons: (1) known and probable late Paleozoic shortening in the Mojave Desert is both east and west directed rather than solely east directed as proposed for the Death Valley area; (2) Late Permian–Early Triassic igneous activity in the western Mojave Desert probably indicates that this area shifted to a position nearer to the continental margin during late Paleozoic time; and (3) isotopic data for Permian and Triassic plutons in the eugeoclinal sections lack evidence for involvement of ancient continental crust, which would be necessary for the telescoping model (Miller et al., 1995). Hence, we interpret strike-slip truncation of the western margin of the Mojave Desert region and associated juxtaposition of miogeoclinal and eugeoclinal sections to be the first major event to modify the region. Truncation started in Pennsylvanian time as recorded in the sections in the Death Valley area and the El Paso Mountains. The Mojave Desert region then became active as a subduction margin starting in Late Permian–Early Triassic time.

TRIASSIC–MIDDLE JURASSIC STRATA

The record of Triassic–Middle Jurassic events in the Mojave Desert region is uncertain because of the scarcity and generally poor dating of rocks of this age. In general, Triassic–Middle Jurassic rocks consist of shallow-marine strata overlain by Middle Jurassic quartzite and Middle to Upper Jurassic volcanic rocks.

Rocks unambiguously determined to be Lower Triassic (based on biostratigraphy) are exposed in the eastern Mojave Desert in the Soda Mountains (Silver Lake Formation). These

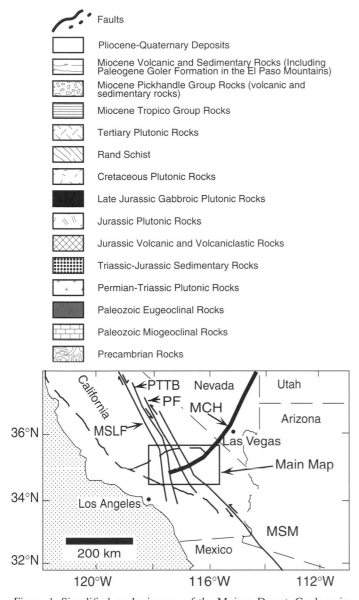

Faults

Pliocene-Quaternary Deposits

Miocene Volcanic and Sedimentary Rocks (Including Paleogene Goler Formation in the El Paso Mountains)

Miocene Pickhandle Group Rocks (volcanic and sedimentary rocks)

Miocene Tropico Group Rocks

Tertiary Plutonic Rocks

Rand Schist

Cretaceous Plutonic Rocks

Late Jurassic Gabbroic Plutonic Rocks

Jurassic Plutonic Rocks

Jurassic Volcanic and Volcaniclastic Rocks

Triassic-Jurassic Sedimentary Rocks

Permian-Triassic Plutonic Rocks

Paleozoic Eugeoclinal Rocks

Paleozoic Miogeoclinal Rocks

Precambrian Rocks

Figure 1. Simplified geologic map of the Mojave Desert. Geology is generalized from Dibblee (1968). Main figure: BM—Black Mountain, CM—Cady Mountains, MH—Mud Hills, NM—Newberry Mountains, NTM—North Tiefort Mountain, OM—Ord Mountain, QM—Quartzite Mountain, SM—Soda Mountains, STM—South Tiefort Mountain, WHMR—Waterman Hills and Mitchel Range. Only ranges mentioned in the text are labeled. Legend for location map: MCH—miogeoclinal-cratonal hinge line, MSLF—Mojave-Snow Lake fault, MSM—Mojave-Sonora megashear, PF—Pinenut fault, PTTB—Permian-Triassic truncation boundary. Dot pattern indicates locus of arc plutonic rocks.

rocks consist of calcareous shale, limestone, conglomerate, sandstone, and their metamorphic equivalents (Walker and Wardlaw, 1989). Similar strata (although lacking conglomerate) are exposed farther east in the Providence Mountains and New York Mountains (Moenkopi Formation; Hazzard, 1954; Burch-

fiel and Davis, 1977). The Lower Triassic rocks rest paraconformably to unconformably on Permian rocks in the eastern Mojave Desert.

Fairview Valley Formation

Lithologically similar strata are exposed in pendants across the Mojave Desert region to the west. Some of the most extensive outcrops expose the Fairview Valley Formation in the Victorville area of the western Mojave Desert. These rocks have been interpreted to be Early Triassic in age (Walker, 1987, 1988). Although the rocks are isoclinally folded and metamorphosed to greenschist facies, conodonts were recovered from two beds of the lower part of the formation. One bed contained a mixed-age fauna (the youngest being Early Triassic), but the other bed contained an assemblage of Smithian age (Walker, 1987, p. 7; B.R. Wardlaw, 1984, personal communication).

There are two possible problems with this age assignment for the Fairview Valley Formation. (1) The unit rests on and incorporates detritus from a monzonite pluton (Black Mountain Monzonite; Miller, 1981) dated at 243 ± 2 Ma by Miller et al. (1995) and at 241 ± 2 Ma by Barth et al. (1997). If the Permian-Triassic boundary is placed at ca. 251 Ma and the Early Triassic is about 6.5 m.y. in duration (Gradstein et al., 1995), then the pluton should be Middle Triassic in age. (Walker [1987, 1988] previously used the time scale of P.F. Carr et al. [1984] to support an Early Triassic age for the Fairview Valley Formation. These authors placed the Permian-Triassic boundary at 237 Ma, making the Black Mountain Monzonite Late Permian in age.) But a Middle Triassic age is inconsistent with the conodont data and may indicate that all conodonts recovered were reworked. (In metamorphosed sections, the assessment of reworking of conodonts can be ambiguous.) (2) The other potential problem with an Early Triassic age for the Fairview Valley Formation is the reported interfingering of the upper Fairview Valley Formation with overlying Middle Jurassic volcanic rocks (Schermer et al., this volume). This stratigraphic relationship indicates that the age of the upper part of the Fairview Valley Formation cannot be Early Triassic and is permissively as young as Middle Jurassic.

Although we consider the Fairview Valley Formation likely to be younger than Early Triassic, the evidence just given for a younger age is not definitive. The age of the Black Mountain Monzonite is not strictly inconsistent with an Early Triassic age for the Fairview Valley Formation. Conodonts in the lower Fairview Valley Formation consist of the assemblage *Neospathodus* sp. and *Ellisonia* sp.—a Smithian Subage assemblage. Hongfu (1994) reported the age of the Smithian to be between 246 and 243 Ma (Hongfu used 251 Ma as the age of the base of the Triassic, which is consistent with the more recent work of Bowring et al. [1998]). The underlying pluton may be as old as 245.4 Ma according to the upper limit on the Pb-Pb age of the oldest, most concordant zircon grain analyzed (Miller et al., 1995). (Zircons from this rock have undergone Pb loss, so that

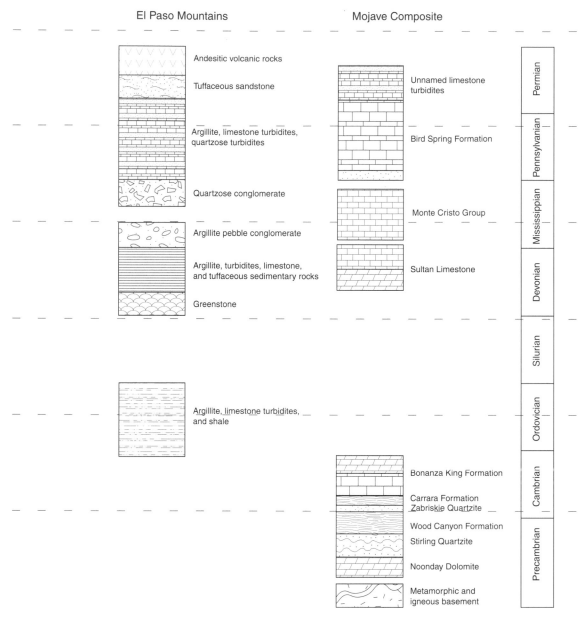

Figure 2. Stratigraphic columns from miogeoclinal-cratonal and eugeoclinal terranes in the greater Mojave Desert region. Eugeoclinal column is for the El Paso Mountains (modified from M.D. Carr et al., 1984). Mojave composite is from Stewart (1970), Stewart and Poole (1975), Miller (1981), and Walker and Wardlaw (1989). For this section, the lower part of the upper Precambrian strata may differ from east to west across the Mojave Desert. Ages from M.D. Carr et al. (1984), Poole and Sandberg (1977), Poole et al. (1977), Rich (1977), Stevens (1977), and Walker and Wardlaw (1989).

this age must be considered a minimum.) Hence the Fairview Valley may be as much as 2–3 m.y. younger than the underlying pluton.

The stratigraphic arguments also have some uncertainty. Evidence for interfingering and/or gradational contacts can be difficult to interpret for deformed and metamorphosed sections. For example, the Triassic–Jurassic section in the Inyo Mountains exhibits many characteristics similar to the Fairview Valley Formation and Sidewinder volcanic rocks (compare Schermer et al. [this volume] to Dunne et al. [1998], and ref-

erences therein). In exposures of the Mesozoic section in the southern Inyo Mountains, the transition from well-dated Lower Triassic marine rocks to Middle Jurassic volcanic rocks appears to be locally gradational, whereas in the northern Inyo Mountains, this contact is clearly unconformable. This detailed understanding of a complex contact zone is possible because the rocks are exposed over 30 km along strike in the Inyo Mountains, yielding sufficient exposure to permit differentiation between interfingering or transitional sections and those sections that contain similar rocks above and below major breaks in

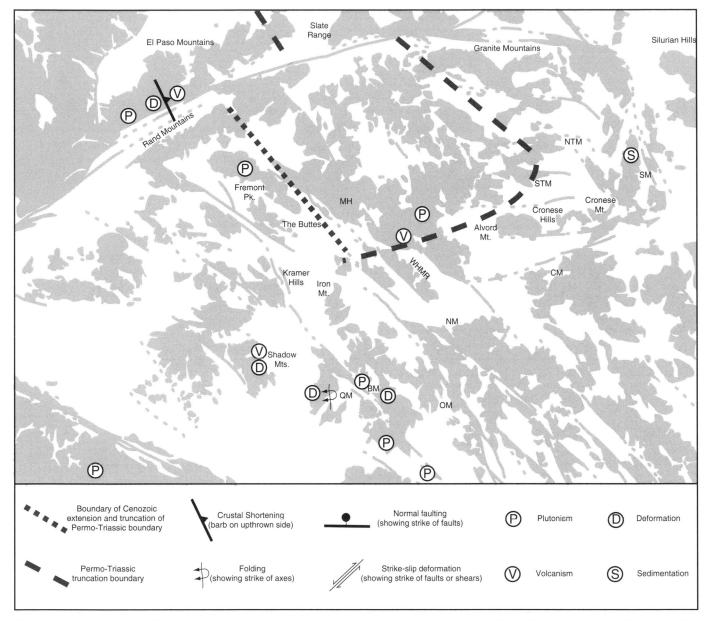

Figure 3. Map highlighting Permian-Triassic structures and rocks and plutonic rocks of Permian-Early Jurassic age. D—deformation, P—plutonism, V—volcanism. Line with barb shows area affected by crustal shortening; line strikes parallel to structures, and barb is on upthrown side. Dashed gray line is approximate location of Permian-Triassic truncation boundary. Dotted line is where this boundary is truncated by Miocene extensional faults. Ranges are in gray. Labels as in Figure 1.

the section. In contrast, over any given 1 km segment (e.g., the strike length of the Fairview Valley–Sidewinder contact), the precise interpretation of the contact in the Inyo Mountains can be unclear.

In summary, we agree with Schermer et al. (this volume) that the Fairview Valley Formation is probably (but not definitively) Early Jurassic in age. However, if the Fairview Valley Formation is Early Jurassic, the presence of Triassic conodonts indicates that some Lower Triassic marine rocks must have been present in this area. This interpretation helps to set limits

on at least some aspects of the Early Triassic paleogeography of the Mojave Desert region, such as that interpreted by Walker (1988).

Strata in other areas

Schermer et al. (this volume) have correlated similar strata in the Fry and Rodman Mountains and at Cave Mountain with the Fairview Valley Formation. Walker (1987) correlated these rocks, as well as strata at Lane Mountain and the Cronese Hills, with the Fairview Valley Formation *and* with the Silver Lake Formation and assigned all these rocks an Early Triassic age. We no longer consider any of these correlations compelling.

Dated Middle Triassic to Lower Jurassic stratified rocks are unknown from the Mojave Desert region, whereas Middle to Upper Jurassic rocks are voluminous. These are best represented by rocks of the Sidewinder Volcanic Series and have been thoroughly discussed by Schermer (1993) and Schermer and Busby (1994). These rocks consist of intermediate to felsic volcanic rocks with intercalated quartzite. In addition, if the upper Fairview Valley Formation and adjacent strata are Early Jurassic in age (Schermer et al., this volume), then shallow-marine strata and conglomerate are also a component of the Middle to Late Jurassic section.

On the basis of the preceding discussion, we interpret there to be two principal ages of Triassic and Jurassic sedimentary rocks in the Mojave Desert region. The older strata of the pair are mainly Early Triassic in age and consist of shallow-marine rocks such as those exposed in the Soda Mountains. The younger strata—quartzite and possible marine rocks interbedded with Early to Late Jurassic volcanic rocks—include rocks exposed in the upper part of the Fairview Valley Formation and the Cowhole Mountains (Wadsworth et al., 1995).

TRIASSIC PLUTONISM AND DEFORMATION

Triassic plutonic rocks are present in the central and southwestern Mojave Desert (Miller, 1978; Barton et al., 1988; Miller et al., 1995; Barth et al., 1997). These plutons range in age from 245 Ma to ca. 210 Ma and have been interpreted to represent early magmatic activity in the Cordilleran arc. Plutonic rocks of similar age are exposed northward into the Death Valley area and into the Walker Lane region (Dilles and Wright, 1988; Snow et al., 1991). No deformational events have been identified in the Mojave Desert region as Triassic–Early Jurassic in age. Deformation in the Clark Mountains previously considered to be pre-200 Ma (Burchfiel and Davis, 1971, 1981, 1988) is now considered to be Late Jurassic in age (Walker et al., 1995b). Other structures, such as a thrust fault in the Cowhole Mountains (Burchfiel and Davis, 1981; Wadsworth et al., 1995), are not definitively dated. Although structures in the region may turn out to be Middle Triassic–Early Jurassic age, none have yet been definitively dated.

MIDDLE JURASSIC–EARLY LATE JURASSIC ARC ROCKS

Middle Jurassic (175–165 Ma) magmatic arc activity and associated sedimentation are widespread in the Mojave Desert and environs. Rocks of the lower Sidewinder Volcanic Series are widely exposed from the Victorville area to the Cady Mountains and consist of intermediate to felsic volcanic rocks with intercalated quartzose sandstone (Fig. 4; Schermer, 1993). This sequence is typically 1 km thick, but increases locally to 4 km

in thickness where intracaldera facies are present. The Sidewinder unit is divided into lower and upper subunits. The age of this sequence is estimated by U-Pb zircon dating at 179 ± 3 Ma (Schermer et al., this volume) and 171 ± 9 Ma (Graubard et al., 1988) at the base to ca. 167 Ma in the upper part of the lower subunits (Schermer et al., this volume). Similar-age rocks, grouped with the Delfonte Volcanics whose type section is in the Mescal Range (discussed subsequently), are present in the Cowhole Mountains (Busby-Spera et al., 1987). Possibly coeval rocks are also present in the Soda Mountains (Grose, 1959), Cronese Hills area (Walker et al., 1990b), Providence Mountains (Hazzard, 1954), and New York Mountains (Burchfiel and Davis, 1977). Volcanic rocks are commonly associated with quartzose sedimentary rocks in these areas. Walker (1987, 1988) interpreted the quartzose sedimentary rocks at the base of the volcanic sequences to be Middle Triassic in age, but more recent work indicates that an age assignment of Middle Jurassic is more consistent with known ages and regional stratigraphic relationships (Schermer et al., this volume). Older volcanic rocks are exposed to the east in southern Arizona, with some sequences as old as Early Jurassic (Tosdal et al., 1989). These older sequences are absent, however, across most of the Mojave Desert region.

Middle Jurassic plutons are also common throughout the region; a significant number are dated between 165 and 170 Ma (Miller and Glazner, 1995). These plutons form the southern continuation of the Sierra Nevada batholith into the Mojave Desert region. This belt continues southeastward into southeast California and Arizona (Tosdal et al., 1989).

Middle Jurassic–early Late Jurassic structural development

The structural development of the Jurassic arc was complex and both contractional and extensional in character. Normal faults cut the lower Sidewinder Volcanic Series, resulting in ~15% north-south extension across the area where the lower Sidewinder section is exposed (Schermer, 1993). Extension occurred between ca. 167 Ma, the end of the magmatism that formed the early Sidewinder volcanic rocks, and 150 Ma, the age of dikes that cut the extensional faults (Schermer, 1993). Busby-Spera (1988), on the other hand, interpreted the lower part of the Sidewinder Volcanic Series to have been deposited in an arc-related graben depression that stretched the length of the Early and Middle Jurassic arc. However, little direct evidence for graben structures is present, and the Sidewinder Volcanic Series in the Mojave Desert region owes its preserved thickness largely to caldera activity (Schermer, 1993). Hence, extensional deformation happened after the lower part of the Sidewinder was erupted rather than being synvolcanic and occurring during the interval 167 to 150 Ma. By comparison, coeval volcanism along the east side of the Sierra Nevada batholith within the East Sierran thrust system (Dunne and Walker, 1993; Dunne et al., 1998) was preserved in the footwall of Late Jurassic thrust faults.

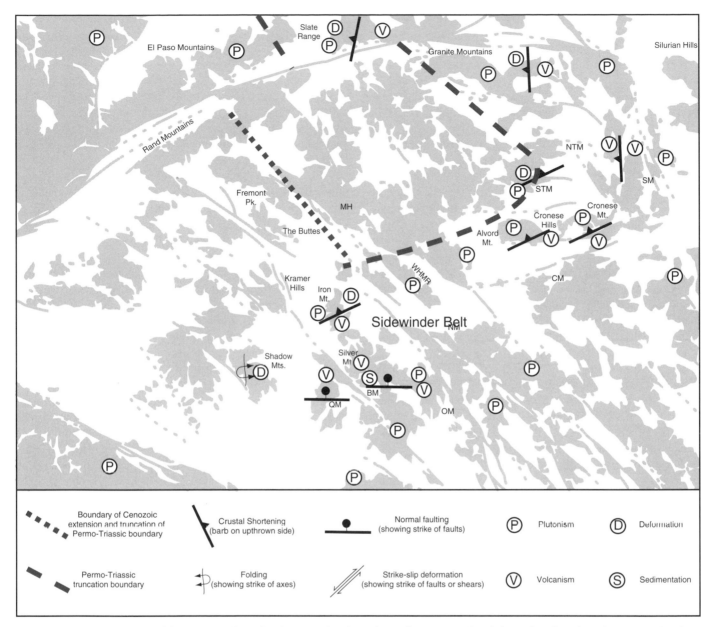

Figure 4. Map highlighting Middle to Late Jurassic plutons, volcanic rocks, and structures. D—deformation, P—plutonism, V—volcanism. Lines with barb show areas affected by crustal shortening; lines strike parallel to structures, and barbs are on upthrown side. Lines with ball show locations of crustal extension. Labels as in Figure 1.

In contrast to this apparently localized extensional deformation, regional shortening is present to the north and west of the Sidewinder exposure belt (Fig. 4). Deformation is typified by folds, mylonitic shear zones, thrusts faults, and probable thrusts that are directed to the east and northeast (Davis and Burchfiel, 1973; Walker et al., 1990b; Miller et al., 1991; Stephens et al., 1993; Boettcher and Walker, 1993; Schermer et al., 2001), except in the Shadow Mountains to the west where thrusts dip generally to the east (Martin et al., this volume). The shear zones and thrust faults generally place Jurassic plutonic rocks over Mesozoic sedimentary and volcanic strata. Hence,

the zones place structurally lower rocks over structurally higher ones. Deformational fabrics developed under prograde metamorphic conditions to greenschist or amphibolite facies (Walker et al., 1990b; Boettcher and Walker, 1993; Martin et al., this volume). Timing relationships for this contractional deformation are best bracketed in the Cronese Hills area. Prekinematic plutonic rocks are dated at 166 ± 3 Ma, and postkinematic granite is dated at 155 ± 1 Ma, giving a possible age range of 169 to 154 Ma (Walker et al., 1990b). Timing relationships in other areas are consistent with this age range and are certainly bracketed between ca. 170 and 148 Ma (Miller et al., 1991;

Boettcher and Walker, 1993; Stephens et al., 1993, Martin et al., this volume). Walker et al. (1990b) considered this deformational belt to be continuous with the East Sierran thrust system exposed north of the Garlock fault. Timing of major activity in the east Sierran belt is bracketed between 170 and 148 Ma (Dunne and Walker, 1993), although older and younger structural elements are also present (Dunne et al., 1978, 1983; Dunne, 1986).

The amount of crustal shortening represented across this belt of deformation in the Mojave Desert region is uncertain. Shear zones indicate dominantly thrust senses of shear, but fabrics are typically annealed, making quantitative estimates of shortening highly speculative. Walker et al. (1990b) concluded that a few kilometers of shortening had been taken up by the shear zone in the Cronese Hills. Offsets across all of the contractional structures are difficult to determine owing to the presence of abundant plutonic rocks and the lack of appropriate strain markers such as a coherent (or even identifiable) stratigraphic succession of pendant rocks across the hanging walls or footwalls of thrusts and shear zones. Shortening is best considered small; a probable minimum cumulative offset is 10 km.

The magnitude of shortening, however, may be larger. Glazner et al. (1989) inferred that, on the basis of restoration of Tertiary extensional faulting, eugeoclinal rocks were stacked by thrusting above miogeoclinal rocks in the central Mojave Desert, which would indicate that thrusting may have been on the order of tens of kilometers. Some of this overlap, however, may have occurred in Triassic or Early Jurassic time (discussed subsequently). In addition, the overall width of the belt of contractional deformation is at least 20 km or so, indicating that cumulative shortening could be large. Also, this width implies that the zone represents a fundamental crustal feature and not one associated only with pluton emplacement.

Reconciling the evidence for essentially coeval contractional and extensional deformation across this region (bracketed between 169 and 154 Ma, and 167 and 150 Ma, respectively—see previous discussion) is crucial to understanding the late Middle Jurassic development of the area. Perhaps one of the most critical relationships is exposed from the Iron Mountain area southward to the northern part of Silver Mountain (Figs. 1 and 4). At Iron Mountain, rocks equivalent to the lower part of the Sidewinder Volcanic Series (Hodge volcanic rocks) were deformed under greenschist-facies metamorphic conditions during an episode of contractional deformation (Boettcher and Walker, 1993). The deformational fabrics are cut by a 151 ± 11 Ma pluton. Lower Sidewinder rocks at Silver Mountain, only about 10 to 15 km to the south of Iron Mountain, are affected only by extensional deformation. Hence, it is clear that the lower part of the Sidewinder section was deformed by both contraction and extension and that these deformation events may not be completely isolated in areal extent.

The close association in time and space of extension and contraction was attributed by Saleeby and Busby-Spera (1992) to plate-margin activity within a sinistral, oblique subduction

setting. Schermer (1993) considered this interpretation likely but with a possible contribution from the effects of basement rocks (extension in areas underlain by thick crust), position within the arc, and differences allowed by the loose brackets on the ages of the individual deformations. The plate-margin and crustal effects are important, but are only germane if the deformations are essentially coeval. We explore here the possibilities that the timing of these events differs by a few million years and that such a difference in age is consistent with other Cordilleran tectonic events.

We can liken the deformational history and general timing relationships of the Mojave Desert region to developments in the western part of the Sierran magmatic arc. Development of the Josephine, Coast Range, and Smartville ophiolites is spatially and temporally associated with extensional deformation within the arc region that is dated between 172 and 162 Ma followed by a further major pulse of extension (Saleeby and Busby-Spera, 1992, p. 152). This extensional event was immediately succeeded by some contractional phases of the Nevadan orogeny including thrust faults in the Smartville complex that are cut by 158 Ma plutons (Saleeby and Busby-Spera, 1992, p. 158). Hence, an abrupt transition from extension to contraction at ca. 160 Ma is indicated along the Cordilleran margin to the north.

Given the timing constraints available for the Mojave rocks, an analogy with the Sierra Nevada magmatic arc can be made: Sidewinder Volcanic Series rocks of 170 to 166 Ma age could have been deformed by normal faults and subsequently shortened over the 10 m.y. interval permitted by the bracketing ages. No evidence for extensional deformation is present in the contractional belt, but such structures could be completely overprinted or obliterated by the strong mylonitic fabrics. Hence, although there is only very limited (and local) direct evidence for Middle to Late Jurassic extension, the close association of contractional and extensional structures presents no great quandary in our interpretation of the Mojave Desert region. In fact, rapid switching between extension and contraction should be expected in an area that resided within the Cordilleran magmatic arc.

Isotopic evidence for a cryptic Triassic–Jurassic thrusting event

As previously described herein, Permian–Triassic plutonic rocks that intrude the eugeoclinal sections show no isotopic evidence for involvement of Precambrian continental crust (Miller et al., 1995). Middle Jurassic plutons (175 Ma), on the other hand, contain Pb, Sr, and Nd isotopic values that show strong involvement of Precambrian crust in their genesis (Miller and Glazner, 1995; Miller et al., 1995). This difference indicates that stacking of eugeoclinal rocks onto miogeoclinal rocks and their Proterozoic basement may have occurred between Early Triassic and Middle Jurassic time (235 to 180 Ma). The presence of miogeoclinal strata structurally beneath eugeoclinal rocks is also required in reconstruction of Miocene deformation (Glazner et al., 1989). No structural features in the Mojave Desert region have yet been associated with this time interval. This said, the East Sierran thrust system to the north has abundant evidence for some pre-180 Ma deformation (Dunne et al., 1978; Dunne, 1986), so if these structures continued southward into the region, they have been obliterated by later deformation and plutonism.

LATE JURASSIC ARC

Limited plutonism and volcanism of Late Jurassic age followed the late Middle to early Late Jurassic deformation. Late Jurassic granitic rocks are exposed in the Cronese Hills, Iron Mountain area, and Shadow Mountain (Fig. 4; Walker et al., 1990b; Boettcher and Walker, 1993; Martin et al., this volume). Other such rocks, if present, await identification.

The most widespread Late Jurassic igneous rocks are those related to the Independence dike swarm. (For a review of the Independence dike swarm, see Carl and Glazner, this volume.) The Independence dike swarm consists of a suite of west-northwest–striking mafic to felsic dikes that run from the eastern wall of the Sierra Nevada southward into the Eagle Mountains of the eastern Transverse Ranges (Chen and Moore, 1979; James, 1989; Carl et al., 1998; Glazner et al., 1999). The age of these dikes is commonly given as 148 Ma (Chen and Moore, 1979; James, 1989; Carl and Glazner, this volume). Coeval mafic plutons are locally exposed in the Shadow Mountains, Goldstone area, and probably at Iron Mountain (Fig. 4). The Independence dike swarm apparently fed lava flows of the upper part of the Sidewinder Volcanic Series (Karish et al., 1987; Schermer and Busby, 1994).

The tectonic setting of the Independence dike swarm is in debate. Previous studies have interpreted the swarm to have formed in a variety of settings, including (1) extension perpendicular to the swarm (e.g., Chen and Moore, 1979; Karish et al., 1987; James, 1989), (2) tectonic activity associated with the Nevadan orogeny (e.g., Page and Engebretson, 1984), (3) dilation of plutons associated with the Jurassic arc (Hopson, 1988), (4) sinistral transtension (Saleeby and Busby-Spera, 1992), and (5) sinistral transpression (Carl et al., 1996; Carl, 1999). Glazner et al. (1999) showed that Independence dikes in the Sierra Nevada opened obliquely, in a north-south direction, and proposed that the dikes are magma-filled tension gashes that formed at high levels of the Sierra Nevada batholith when the direction of absolute North American plate motion changed dramatically at the end of Jurassic time. Therefore, we do not consider the Independence dike swarm to represent a time of any significant extension within the arc.

Clear evidence for Late Jurassic–Early Cretaceous contraction is present for the Pechalka Spring thrust in the Clark Mountains in the easternmost Mojave Desert. This thrust places mylonitic Mesozoic plutonic rocks over miogeoclinal strata (Burchfiel and Davis, 1971, 1988; Walker et al., 1995b).

Hanging-wall rocks are dated at 146 ± 2 Ma (Walker et al., 1995b). Footwall rocks are highly folded, and the folds are kinematically coordinated with the thrust. These folds are cut by a pluton dated at 142 ± 7 Ma (Walker et al., 1995b). This time brackets thrust deformation to the latest Jurassic or earliest Cretaceous (with errors, between 148 and 135 Ma).

CRETACEOUS DEVELOPMENT

Voluminous plutonism and deformation occurred across the Mojave Desert during Cretaceous time. Cretaceous plutonic rocks are common in the western and eastern parts of the Mojave Desert and scattered across the rest of the region (Fig. 5). Most of the dated Cretaceous rocks are latest Early to Late Cretaceous in age (105 to ca. 80 Ma; Miller et al., 1996; Schermer et al., 2001; Fletcher et al., this volume; Miller and Walker, this volume). Cretaceous volcanic rocks are only locally exposed in the eastern Mojave Desert where they are preserved beneath thrust faults (Fleck and Carr, 1990; Fleck et al., 1994).

Cretaceous deformation is present across the Mojave Desert. Mylonitic shear zones of Cretaceous age are exposed from Ord Mountain to North Tiefort Mountain (Fig. 5). The zones have a north strike at Ord Mountain and a shallowly plunging lineation (Karish, 1983). At Iron Mountain, these zones are steep and strike northeast. Shear sense indicators yield both dextral and sinistral results, with dextral somewhat more common. These shear zones are post-148 Ma and pre-83 ± 1 Ma (Boettcher and Walker, 1993). At Ticfort Mountain, similar steep zones cut a ca. 105 Ma pluton but are intruded by ca. 82 Ma dikes (Schermer et al., 2001). In addition, Sidewinder rocks at Ord Mountain and areas to the west are deformed by upright folds whose axial planes strike northwest.

Rand thrust and related features

One of the most profound events to disrupt the crust of the Mojave Desert region was the emplacement of the Rand Schist in Late Cretaceous time. During this underthrusting event, the lower crust of the western Mojave Desert was removed and replaced by high-pressure metamorphic rocks of the Rand Schist. This event is reflected in the thermal and structural evolution of rocks in the northern Mojave Desert and the southern Sierra Nevada batholith (Dumitru et al., 1991; Wood and Saleeby, 1998; Fletcher et al., this volume).

High-grade metamorphic rocks and migmatites of Cretaceous age are exposed from The Buttes to the Fremont Peak area (Fig. 5), where mineral assemblages record temperatures up to 850 °C and pressures on the order of 6 to 8 kbar (Henry and Dokka, 1992; Glazner et al., 1994; J.M. Fletcher, 2000, personal communication). Metamorphism was accompanied by deformation. Ages of synkinematic plutons in this area range from ca. 105 to 91 Ma, and monazite and zircon from leucosomes of syn- to late-kinematic migmatite yield ages of ca.

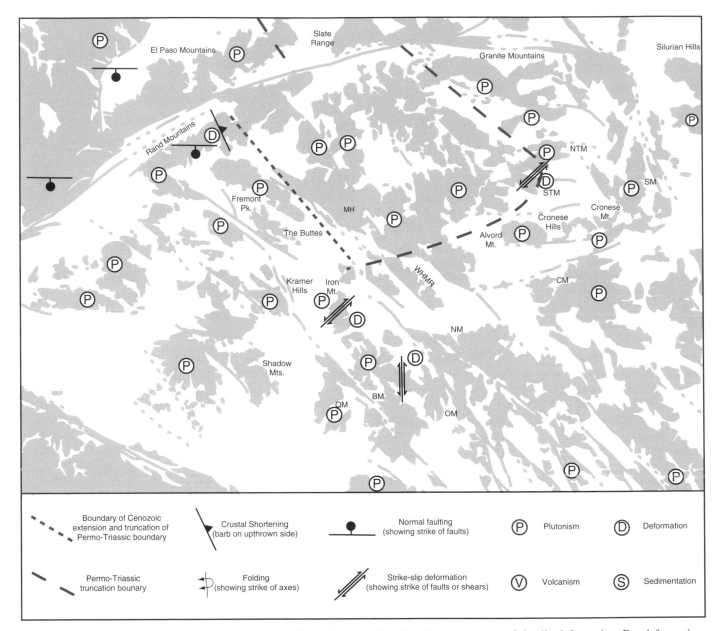

Figure 5. Map highlighting Cretaceous plutons and possible volcanic rocks. Also shown are areas of ductile deformation. D—deformation, P—plutonism, V—volcanism. Line with barb shows area affected by crustal shortening; line strikes parallel to structures, and barb is on upthrown side. Lines with ball show location of crustal extension. Lines with opposing arrows show areas with strike-slip deformation with no particular preferred sense of motion. Shortening in the northern area was along the Rand thrust. Labels as in Figure 1.

95–93 Ma (Fletcher et al., this volume). Hence, deformation and high-grade metamorphism occurred in the area during middle to Late Cretaceous time. Deformation was associated with north-south contraction and dextral shear and had ceased probably by ca. 83 Ma (Fletcher et al., this volume).

The Rand thrust is exposed in the northwestern part of the Mojave Desert (Fig. 5). This thrust places North America miogeoclinal and related rocks (called the Johannesburg Gneiss by Hulin, 1925) over the Rand Schist, a complex of Mesozoic rocks related to the Franciscan Complex (e.g., Burchfiel and

Davis [1981] and Crowell [1981]) or Great Valley Group (Barth and Schneiderman, 1996). The timing of this structure is best estimated as Late Cretaceous. The Rand Schist contains detrital zircons as young as ca. 80 Ma (Grove et al., 2000) and is cut by a postkinematic pluton dated at 79 ± 1 Ma (Silver and Nourse, 1986). The hanging wall of the thrust contains the Cretaceous migmatite complex of The Buttes (95–93 Ma; U-Pb on monazite—see Fletcher et al., this volume, for discussion) and granodiorite in the Rand Mountains dated at ca. 87 Ma (Silver and Nourse, 1991). Although neither of these is strictly cut by the Rand thrust, we interpret thrusting to postdate migmatization in the hanging wall in the adjacent area comprising The Buttes and Fremont Peak. All models for the Rand thrust involve replacing lower batholithic crust with low-temperature, high-pressure rocks of the Rand Schist. This process should cause cooling of the upper-plate rocks, which is incompatible with the area comprising The Buttes and Fremont Peak remaining at very high temperatures.

Late Cretaceous deformation also affected the southern Sierra Nevada. The main elements of Late Cretaceous deformation are the eastern Tehachapi shear zone, the proto–Kern Canyon fault, and related structures (Wood and Saleeby, 1998). The proto–Kern Canyon fault was active at ca. 85 Ma and records dextral strike-slip deformation (Busby-Spera and Saleeby, 1990). This fault ties southward into the eastern Tehachapi shear zone, which is a south-southwest-directed, shallowly northeast-dipping ductile shear zone that is inferred to be related to emplacement of the Rand Schist under the southern Sierra Nevada (Wood and Saleeby, 1998). In addition, large-scale, dextral oroclinal folding occurred in the area between 100 and ca. 85 Ma; the resulting structures record Late Cretaceous dextral transpression (Wood and Saleeby, 1998).

Hence, timing and styles of deformation are consistent from the Sierra Nevada into the Mojave Desert region. Dextral transpression occurred between 100 and 85 Ma in the southern Sierra Nevada and between 105 and 83 Ma in the Mojave Desert. Emplacement of the Rand Schist occurred in both regions at ca. 80 Ma. Although detrital zircons in the schist are as young as ca. 80 Ma, thrusting probably started as early as ca. 85 Ma (e.g., the age of the eastern Tehachapi shear zone).

Intrusion of northeast-striking dikes and activity on northeast-striking shear zones across the Mojave Desert region (see previous discussion) are roughly coeval with this deformation. These rocks and structures are probably related to emplacement of the Rand Schist. Deformation is related to adjustments in the North American plate due to underthrusting of the Rand Schist during dextral transpression. Generation of the dikes may be related to dewatering of the underlying schist, similar to interpretations made for areas of southeastern California (e.g., Hoisch and Hamilton, 1988).

Emplacement of the Rand Schist was followed by extensional deformation. In the Rand Mountains, south-southwest-directed faults that exhumed the high-pressure metamorphic rocks have been identified (Postlethwaite and Jacobson, 1987; Nourse, 1989). This deformation is interpreted to be bracketed between 87 and 79 Ma (similar to the age of the Rand thrust) by Nourse (1989). In addition, muscovite and hornblende cooling ages for the Rand Schist are between 74 and 72 Ma (Jacobson, 1990). These results indicate that the Rand Schist was substantially unroofed by ca. 70 Ma. A similar unroofing also occurred in the southern Sierra Nevada–Tehachapi area (Malin et al., 1995; Wood and Saleeby, 1998), but the timing of this deformation is less well determined than in the Rand Mountains: deformation is bracketed between 85 and 50 Ma (Wood

and Saleeby, 1998). The Paleogene Witnet and Goler Formations may have been deposited in basins created by extensional faulting (Wood and Saleeby, 1998), possibly related to unroofing of the Rand Schist.

Restoration of ~65 km of slip on the Garlock fault aligns the Rand Schist in the Tehachapi Mountains north of the Garlock fault to the west of similar rocks in the Rand Mountains south of the Garlock fault (Fig. 6); high-grade gneisses bound the Rand Schist to the north and south. In this restored view, metamorphic grade and exposure depth of batholithic rocks decrease both northward and southward.

The northward decrease in depth of exposure has been well documented by many authors (see Wood and Saleeby, 1998, for a summary). The southward decrease is more complex because of the adjacent Miocene Central Mojave metamorphic core complex. Conditions of metamorphism of rocks in the hanging

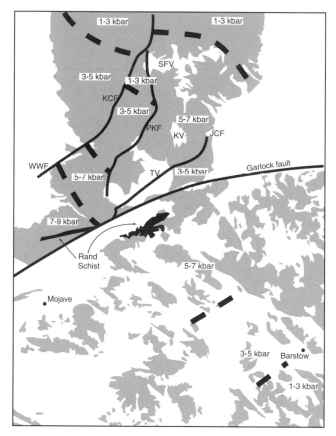

Figure 6. Southern Sierra Nevada and northwestern Mojave Desert region with 65 km of slip restored on the Garlock fault. Pressures recorded in metamorphic rocks are indicated. Ranges are shown in gray and Rand Schist in black. Note the increase in exposure depth as reflected by metamorphic pressures southward through the Sierra Nevada. A southward decrease in exposure depth is inferred for the Mojave Desert (see text for explanation). Geology of the southern Sierra Nevada from Wood and Saleeby (1998). Locations in the Sierra Nevada: JCF—Jawbone Canyon fault, KCF—Kern Canyon fault, KV—Kelso Valley, PKF—proto-Kern Canyon fault, SFV—South Fork Valley, TV—Tehachapi Valley, WWF—White Wolf fault.

wall of the Rand thrust in the Rand Mountains are uncertain. The degree of recrystallization of marbles and quartzites in the Johannesburg Gneiss is similar to that found in The Buttes where pressures of 6 kbar or more were recorded during Cretaceous metamorphism. Hence areas adjacent to the Rand Schist appear to have resided at relatively deep crustal levels. Farther southward, in the Victorville and Barstow areas, Jurassic volcanic rocks are only weakly metamorphosed. In addition, K/Ar cooling ages for biotite in these areas generally give Jurassic ages (Miller and Morton, 1980), indicating that exposed rocks were probably at shallow crustal depths (1–3 kbar pressure) during Cretaceous time. Intervening areas, such as Iron Mountain, expose rocks that were exhumed from intermediate depths (amphibolite-grade, sillimanite-bearing assemblages; Boettcher and Walker, 1993). For this reason, the change in crustal exposure depth seems to be roughly symmetrical north to south across the Rand Schist. This pattern is consistent with previous interpretations (e.g., Malin et al. [1995] and Wood and Saleeby [1998]) that extensional faulting uplifted the Rand Schist. In this model, the schist is essentially a metamorphic core complex uplifted in the footwall of a dominantly down-to-the-south fault system.

The Rand Schist is part of a belt of a subduction zone-related rocks thrust under the western edge of North America during the Late Cretaceous and early Tertiary. A confusing aspect of the Rand Schist and related rocks is that underthrusting must be diachronous between northern and southern exposures. Northern exposures (the Rand Schist) were emplaced in the Late Cretaceous and uplifted soon thereafter, apparently by southwest-directed extension (Postlethwaite and Jacobson, 1987; Wood and Saleeby, 1998). Schists exposed farther south (e.g., the Orocopia Schist) have zircon provenance ages as young as 70 Ma, indicating younger emplacement (Jacobson et al., 2000). They also appear to have been extensionally unroofed, but at a later time than those to the north and by northeast-directed extension. In addition, on a pre-San Andreas reconstruction, the northern schists are spatially distinct from southern ones (Fig. 1B in Jacobson et al., 2000). This geometry may suggest that the underthrusting of the schists may have been accomplished by two temporally and spatially distinct events.

Thrust faults in the eastern Mojave Desert

Thrust faults of Cretaceous age are present in the eastern Mojave Desert (east of most areas discussed in this paper), from the Clark Mountains southward into the Big Maria Mountains. The former is part of the Sevier thrust belt whereas the latter is part of the Maria fold-and-thrust belt that extends well into Arizona. The Sevier belt contains west-dipping thrust faults and east-vergent folds that cut the miogeoclinal-cratonal Paleozoic section and locally involve Precambrian basement rocks (Burchfiel and Davis, 1988). Activity on frontal thrusts of the Sevier belt is dated as post–98 Ma (Fleck and Carr, 1990),

Structurally higher thrusts are somewhat older. Rocks of the Delfonte Volcanics in the Mescal Range are Early Cretaceous (Fleck et al., 1994) and involved in thrust faulting and folding; thrusts are cut by parts of the Teutonia batholith. Hence, many of the structures may date to the interval 118 to 95 Ma (R.J. Fleck, 1993, personal communication). This deformation continues southward into the Old Woman Mountains area where structures are dominated by somewhat younger ductile thrusts (ca. 85 Ma or somewhat younger) of Late Cretaceous age (Fletcher and Karlstrom, 1990; Karlstrom et al., 1993).

The Maria fold-and-thrust belt of southeastern California and western Arizona is also an important area of Cretaceous contractional deformation. Thrusts in the Maria belt typically cut into Proterozoic basement rocks as well as a thin Paleozoic and Mesozoic section. Timing of deformation is generally confined to the Late Cretaceous, with ca. 85 Ma plutons quite deformed and 71 Ma dikes undeformed (Reynolds et al., 1986; Knapp and Walker, 1989). The Sevier and Maria deformational belts, although regionally important, do not affect areas in the central and western Mojave Desert.

DISCUSSION

An important observation about the late Paleozoic-Jurassic development of the Mojave Desert region is that deformation seems to be localized along the boundary between miogeoclinal and eugeoclinal rocks. This boundary was created in late Paleozoic time by truncation of the continental margin and southward displacement of eugeoclinal rocks. To the south, this boundary cuts across Paleozoic facies trends such that in the Mojave Desert region, rocks of miogeoclinal-cratonal facies were juxtaposed against eugeoclinal rocks. The margin outboard of the eugeoclinal rocks became active as a subduction margin in Permian time. As far as is evident, there was no telescoping of eugeoclinal and miogeoclinal rocks at that time. The first evidence for telescoping is recorded in the isotopic compositions of Middle Jurassic plutons that intrude the eugeoclinal sections, although no structures related to this deformation are clearly identified. Later Middle to Late Jurassic structures, however, roughly coincide with the boundary between eugeoclinal and miogeoclinal rocks.

The East Sierran thrust system, a roughly north-northwest-trending zone exposed north of the Garlock fault, follows closely the eastern margin of Jurassic batholithic rocks. The eastern margin of the batholith through this region is roughly parallel to and coincident with the miogeoclinal-eugeoclinal boundary. The relationship of this belt of deformation to the Jurassic batholith is less clear to the south in the Mojave Desert region where Miocene core complex-related extension obscures these older relationships. First appearances suggest that this belt of deformation cuts westward across the batholith trend through the Mojave Desert region (e.g., to the Cronese Hills and Iron Mountain), whereas the batholithic belt continues uninterrupted southeastward. However, structures in the Cronese Hills and at

Iron Mountain are located immediately west of Middle to Late Jurassic volcanic rocks and therefore occupy a position, relative to the Jurassic volcanic arc, similar to that in the East Sierran thrust system. Although it can be argued that the East Sierran thrust system north of the Garlock fault was controlled by the thermal structure of the batholith, this condition may not have applied in the Mojave Desert region. We suggest that the spatial coincidence of the Permian-Triassic truncation boundary with the zone of Jurassic contractional deformation indicates that the truncation boundary was a fundamental lithospheric weakness that was exploited by Jurassic thrusting in the west-central Mojave Desert. Cretaceous and later deformations were not influenced by this boundary, indicating to us that the lithosphere was essentially healed following Jurassic deformation and magmatism.

Late Paleozoic and early Mesozoic depositional patterns were strongly influenced by the truncation boundary and by the tectonic transition from a strike-slip borderland setting to subduction at the leading edge of the plate margin. Middle to Late Jurassic depositional patterns in the Mojave Desert region were controlled by a low-standing to moderately high standing convergent magmatic arc. It is unclear at present what role intra-arc extension versus contraction played in controlling depositional patterns during this time period—e.g., were basins created by normal faults or thrust faults? Except for the easternmost Mojave Desert where sedimentation patterns were controlled by thrust faults of the Sevier thrust belt, there is no record of Cretaceous sedimentation, suggesting that at this time the arc was relatively high standing.

Unlike Cretaceous deformation in the eastern Mojave Desert, which was characterized by west-dipping thrust faults of the southern Sevier belt, deformation in the central and western Mojave Desert is much more cryptic. The most obvious expression of deformation during this interval is the preservation of the Rand Schist and associated structures. This assemblage was underplated to the continental margin and exhumed during the middle to Late Cretaceous during a period of oblique convergence.

The studies presented in this volume suggest that the overall picture of the late Paleozoic and Mesozoic tectonic development of the Mojave Desert region is reasonably well understood; however, in the details remain the insights required to obtain a more complete understanding of fundamental processes of crustal growth at continental margins. Plutonism, volcanism, sedimentation, deformation, and metamorphism are cornerstone processes in arcs at continental margins. Their spatial relationships to one another are, in general, well understood; it is the temporal relationships that must be better understood before significant new insights can be achieved in this arena.

ACKNOWLEDGMENTS

This paper recounts over a decade of work, and the individuals who contributed in one way or another are far too numerous to acknowledge here. Several, however, deserve special mention. Thomas W. Dibblee, Jr., made our studies possible by his masterful reconnaissance mapping of much of the Mojave Desert. In areas that he had not already mapped, our studies proceeded far more slowly. Discussion and/or mapping by John Fletcher, Jonathan Miller, Elizabeth Schermer, David Miller, Bruce Wardlaw, and Stefan Boettcher greatly helped this effort. This work was supported by National Science Foundation grants (EAR) 8219032, 8817076, 8816941, 8917291, 8917300, and 9204961 (to Glazner) and 8816628 and 8916802 (to Walker); by grants from the Petroleum Research Fund, administered by the American Chemical Society (to Glazner and Walker); by the University of North Carolina Research Council and the University of Kansas Endowment. This paper is part of a regional compilation project on Mojave Desert and Basin and Range geology funded by the Geothermal Program Office of the U.S. Navy.

REFERENCES CITED

Anderson, J.L., Wooden, J.L., and Bender, E.E., 1993, Mojave Province of southern California and vicinity: The Geology of North America, Precambrian: Coterminous U.S.: Boulder, Colorado, Geological Society of America, p. 176–188.

Barth, A.P., and Schneiderman, J.S., 1996, A comparison of structures in the Andean orogen of north Chile and exhumed midcrustal structures in southern California, USA: An analogy in tectonic style?: International Geology Review, v. 38, p. 1075–1085.

Barth, A.P., Tosdal, R.M., Wooden, J.L., and Howard, K.A., 1997, Triassic plutonism in southern California: Southward younging of arc initiation along a truncated continental margin: Tectonics, v. 16, p. 290–304.

Bartley, J.M., Glazner, A.F., and Schermer, E.R., 1990, North-south contraction of the Mojave block and strike-slip tectonics in southern California: Science, v. 248, p. 1398–1401.

Barton, M.D., Battles, D.A., Debout, G.E., Capo, R.C., Christensen, J.N., Davis, S.R., Hanson, R.B., Michelsen, C.J., and Trim, H.E., 1988, Mesozoic contact metamorphism in the western United States, *in* Ernst, W.G., ed., Metamorphism and crustal evolution of the western United States: Englewood Cliffs, New Jersey, Prentice Hall, p. 110–178.

Boettcher, S.S., and Walker, J.D., 1993, Geologic evolution of Iron Mountain, central Mojave Desert, California: Tectonics, v. 12, p. 372–386.

Bowring, S.A., Erwin, D.H., Jin, Y.G., Martin, M.W., Davidek, K., and Wang, W., 1998, U/Pb zircon geochronology and tempo of the end-Permian mass extinction: Science, v. 280, p. 1039–1045.

Burchfiel, B.C., and Davis, G.A., 1971, Clark Mountain thrust complex in the Cordillera of southeastern California: Geologic summary and field trip guide, *in* Elders, W.A., ed., Geological excursions in Southern California: Riverside, California, University of California, p. 1–28.

Burchfiel, B.C., and Davis, G.A., 1972, Structural framework and evolution of the southern part of the Cordilleran Orogen, western United States: American Journal of Science, v. 272, p. 97–118.

Burchfiel, B.C., and Davis, G.A., 1975, Nature and controls of Cordilleran orogenesis, western United States: Extensions of an earlier synthesis: American Journal of Science, v. 275-A, p. 363–396.

Burchfiel, B.C., and Davis, G.A., 1977, Geology of the Sagamore Canyon-Slaughterhouse Spring area, New York Mountains, California: Geological Society of America Bulletin, v. 88, p. 1623–1640.

Burchfiel, B.C., and Davis, G.A., 1981, Mojave Desert and environs, *in* Ernst, W.G., ed., The geotectonic development of California [Rubey Symposium. V.1]: Englewood Cliffs, New Jersey, Prentice Hall, p. 217–252.

Burchfiel, B.C., and Davis, G.A., 1988, Mesozoic thrust faults and Cenozoic low-angle normal faults, eastern Spring Mountains, Nevada, and Clark Mountains thrust complex, California, *in* Weide, D.L., and Faber, M.L., eds., This extended land: Geological journeys in the southern Basin and Range: Las Vegas, Nevada, University of Nevada Department of Geoscience, p. 87–106.

Busby-Spera, C.J., 1988, Speculative tectonic model for the early Mesozoic arc of the southwest Cordilleran United States: Geology, v. 16, p. 1121–1125.

Busby-Spera, C.J., and Saleeby, J., 1990, Intra-arc strike-slip fault exposed at batholithic levels in the southern Sierra Nevada, California: Geology, v. 18, p. 255–259.

Busby-Spera, C.J., Mattinson, J.M., and Riggs, N.R., 1987, Lower Mesozoic extensional continental arc, Arizona and California: A depocenter for Craton-Derived Quartz Arenites: Geology, v. 19, p. 607.

Carl, B.S., 1999, Structure, intrusion, and tectonic origin of the Independence dike swarm, eastern California [Ph.D. dissertation]: Chapel Hill, North Carolina, University of North Carolina, 269 p.

Carl, B.S., Bartley, J.M., and Glazner, A.F., 1996, Mechanical model for syn-intrusive Nevadan deformation in the eastern Sierra: Eos (Transactions, American Geophysical Union), v. 77, p. F641.

Carl, B.S., Glazner, A.F., Bartley, J.M., Dinter, D.A., and Coleman, D.S., 1998, Independence dikes and mafic rocks of the eastern Sierra: Guidebook and roadlog, *in* Behl, R.J., ed., Guidebook to Field Trip #4: Long Beach, California, California State University Department of Geological Sciences, Geological Society of America Cordilleran Section Meeting Field Trip Guidebook, 26 p.

Carr, M.D., Christiansen, R.L., and Poole, F.G., 1984, Pre-Cenozoic geology of the El Paso Mountains, southwestern Great Basin, California—A summary, *in* Lintz, J., Jr., ed., Western geologic excursions: Reno, Nevada, p. 84–93.

Carr, P.F., Jones, B.G., Quinn, B.G., and Wright, A.J., 1984, Toward an objective Phanerozoic time scale: Geology, v. 11, p. 274–277.

Chen, J.H., and Moore, J.G., 1979, Late Jurassic Independence dike swarm in eastern California: Geology, v. 7, p. 129–133.

Cox, B.F., 1982, Stratigraphy, sedimentology, and structure of the Goler Formation (Paleocene), El Paso Mountains, California: Implications for Paleogene tectonism in the Garlock fault [Ph.D. dissertation]: Riverside, California, University of California, 248 p.

Cox, B.F., and Diggles, M.F., 1986, Geologic map of the El Paso Mountains wilderness study area, Kern County, California: U.S. Geological Survey Miscellaneous Field Studies Map, MF-1827, 1:24 000.

Crowell, J.C., 1981, An outline of the tectonic history of southeastern California, *in* Ernst, W.G., ed., The geotectonic development of California, Rubey Symposium, Volume 1: Englewood Cliffs, New Jersey, Prentice Hall, p. 583–600.

Davis, G.A., and Burchfiel, B.C., 1973, Garlock fault: An intracratonic transform structure, southern California: Geological Society of America Bulletin, v. 84, p. 1407–1422.

Davis, G.H., Monger, J.W.H., and Burchfiel, B.C., 1978, Mesozoic construction of the Cordilleran "collage," central British Columbia to central California, *in* Howell, D.G., and McDougall, K.A., eds., Mesozoic paleogeography of the western United States: Los Angeles, California, Pacific Section, Society of Economic Paleontologists and Mineralogists, p. 1–32.

Dibblee, T.W., Jr., 1961, Evidence of strike-slip movement on northwest-trending faults in Mojave Desert, California: U.S. Geological Survey Professional Paper 424-B, p. 197–198.

Dibblee, T.W., Jr., 1968, Geology of the Fremont Peak and Opal Mountain quadrangles, California: California Division of Mines Geological Bulletin, v. 188, 64 p.

Dickinson, W.D., 1981, Plate tectonics and the continental margin of California, *in* Ernst, W.G., ed., The geotectonic development of California, Rubey Volume 1: Englewood Cliffs, New Jersey, Prentice-Hall, p. 1–28.

Dilles, J.H., and Wright, J.E., 1988, The chronology of early Mesozoic arc magmatism in the Yerington district of western Nevada and its regional implications: Geological Society of America Bulletin, v. 100, p. 644–652.

Dokka, R.K., 1989, The Mojave extensional belt of southern California: Tectonics, v. 8, p. 363–390.

Dokka, R.F., and Travis, C.J., 1990, Late Cenozoic strike-slip faulting in the Mojave Desert, California: Tectonics, v. 9, p. 311–340.

Dumitru, T.A., Gans, P.B., Foster, D.A., and Miller, E.L., 1991, Refrigeration of the western Cordilleran lithosphere during Laramide shallow-angle subduction: Geology, v. 19, p. 1145–1148.

Dunne, G.C., 1986, Geologic evolution of the southern Inyo Range, Darwin Plateau, and Argus and Slate Ranges, east-central California: An overview, *in* Dunne, G.C., ed., Mesozoic and Cenozoic structural evolution of selected areas, east-central California: Los Angeles, Geological Society of America Cordilleran Section Field Trip Guidebook, p. 3–21.

Dunne, G.C., and Walker, J.D., 1993, Age of Jurassic volcanism and tectonism, southern Owens Valley region, east-central California: Geological Society of America Bulletin, v. 105, p. 1223–1230.

Dunne, G.C., Gulliver, R.M., and Sylvester, A.G., 1978, Mesozoic evolution of the White, Inyo, Argus, and Slate Ranges, eastern California, *in* Howell, D.G., and McDougall, K.A., eds., Mesozoic paleogeography of the western United States: Pacific Coast Section, Society of Economic Paleontologists and Mineralogists, Pacific Coast Paleogeography Symposium 2, p. 189–207.

Dunne, G.C., Moore, S.C., Gulliver, R.M., and Fowler, J., 1983, East Sierran thrust system, eastern California: Boulder, Colorado, Geological Society of America, Abstracts with Programs, v. 15, no. 5, p. 322.

Dunne, G.C., Garvey, T.P., Oborne, M., Schneidereit, D., Fritsche, A.E., and Walker, J.D., 1998, Geology of the Inyo Mountains volcanic complex: Implications for Jurassic paleogeography of the Sierran magmatic arc in eastern California: Geological Society of America Bulletin, v. 110, p. 1376–1397.

Fillmore, R.P., and Walker, J.D., 1996, Evolution of a supradetachment extensional basin: The Early Miocene Pickhandle Basin, central Mojave Desert, California: Boulder, Colorado, Geological Society of America Special Paper 303, p. 107–126.

Fleck, R.J., and Carr, M.D., 1990, The age of the Keystone thrust: Laser fusion $^{40}Ar/^{39}Ar$ dating of foreland basin deposits, southern Spring Mountains, Nevada: Tectonics, v. 9, p. 467–476.

Fleck, R.J., Mattinson, J.M., Busby, C.J., Carr, M.D., Davis, G.A., and Burchfiel, B.C., 1994, Isotopic complexities and the age of the Delfonte volcanic rocks, eastern Mescal Range, Southeastern California: Stratigraphic and tectonic implications: Geological Society of America Bulletin, v. 106, p. 1242–1253.

Fletcher, J.M., and Karlstrom, K.E., 1990, Late Cretaceous ductile deformation, metamorphism, and plutonism in the Piute Mountains, eastern Mojave Desert: Journal of Geophysical Research, v. 95, p. 487–500.

Garfunkel, Z., 1974, Model for the late Cenozoic tectonic history of the Mojave Desert, California, and its relation to adjacent regions: Geological Society of America Bulletin, v. 5, p. 141–188.

Gehrels, G.E., 2000, Mid-Proterozoic to mid-Mesozoic sediment dispersal in western North America: Geological Society of America Abstracts with Programs, v. 32, no. 7, p. A-46.

Glazner, A.F., Bartley, J.M., and Walker, J.D., 1989, Magnitude and significance of Miocene crustal extension in the central Mojave Desert, California: Geology, v. 17, p. 50–54.

Glazner, A.F., Walker, J.D., Bartley, J.M., Fletcher, J.M., Martin, M.W., Schermer, E.R., Boettcher, S.S., Miller, J.S., Fillmore, R.P., and Linn, J.K., 1994, Reconstruction of the Mojave Block, *in* McGill, S.F., and Ross, T.M., eds., Geological investigations of an active margin: Redlands, California, San Bernardino County Museum Association, Geological Society of America Cordilleran Section Guidebook, p. 3–30.

Glazner, A.F., Bartley, J.M., and Carl, B.S., 1999, Oblique opening and noncoaxial emplacement of the Independence dike swarm, California: Journal of Structural Geology, v. 21, p. 1275–1283.

Gradstein, F.M., Agterberg, F.P., Ogg, J.G., Hardenbol, J., Van Veen, P., Thierry, J., and Huang, Z., 1995, A Triassic, Jurassic and Cretaceous time scale: SEPM (Society for Sedimentary Geology) Special Publication 54, p. 95–126.

Graubard, C.M., Mattinson, J.M., and Busby-Spera, C.J., 1988, Age of the lower Sidewinder volcanics and reconstruction of the Early Mesozoic Arc in the Mojave Desert: Geological Society of America Abstracts with Programs, v. 20, no. 7, p. A274.

Grose, L.T., 1959, Structure and petrography of the northeast part of the Soda Mountains, San Bernardino County, California: Geological Society of America Bulletin, v. 70, p. 1509–1548.

Grove, M., Jacobson, C.E., and Barth, A.P., 2000, Temporal and spatial trends of Late Cretaceous-early Tertiary underplating beneath southern California and southwest Arizona: Geological Society of America Abstracts with Programs, v. 32, no. 7, p. A46.

Hamilton, W., 1969, Mesozoic California and the underflow of the Pacific mantle: Geological Society of America Bulletin, v. 80, p. 2409–2430.

Hamilton, W., and Myers, W.B., 1966, Cenozoic tectonics of the western United States: Review of Geophysics, v. 4, p. 509–549.

Hazzard, J.C., 1954, Rocks and structure of the northern Providence Mountains, San Bernardino County, California, *in* Jahns, R.H., ed., Geology of Southern California: Sacramento, California, California Division of Mines and Geology, p. 27–35.

Henry, D.J., and Dokka, R.K., 1992, Metamorphic evolution of exhumed middle to lower crustal rocks in the Mojave extensional belt, southern California, USA: Journal of Metamorphic Geology, v. 10, p. 347–364.

Hoisch, T.D., and Hamilton, W.B., 1988, Latest Cretaceous crustal metamorphism in southeastern California by fluids from subducted schist: Geological Society of America Abstracts with Programs, v. 20, no. 3, p. 169.

Hongfu, Y., 1994, Synthetic regional stratigraphic charts of south China: Albertiana, no. 14, p. 79.

Hopson, C.A., 1988, Independence dike swarm: origin and tectonic significance: Eos (Transactions, American Geophysical Union), v. 69, p. 1479.

Hulin, C.D., 1925, Geology and ore deposits of the Randsburg quadrangle, California: California Mining Bureau Bulletin, v. 95, 152 p.

Jacobson, C.E., 1990, The $^{40}Ar/^{39}Ar$ geochronology of the Pelona Schist and related rocks, southern California: Journal of Geophysical Research, v. 95, p. 509–528.

Jacobson, C.E., Barth, A.P., and Grove, M., 2000, Late Cretaceous protolith age and provenance of the Pelona and Orocopia Schists, southern California: Implications for evolution of the Cordilleran margin: Geology, v. 28, p. 219–222.

James, E.W., 1989, Southern extension of the Independence dike swarm of eastern California: Geology, v. 17, p. 587–590.

Karish, C.R., 1983, Mesozoic geology of the Ord Mountains, Mojave Desert [M.S. thesis]: Stanford, California, Stanford University, 112 p.

Karish, C.R., Miller, E.L., and Sutter, J.F., 1987, Mesozoic tectonic and magmatic history of the central Mojave Desert: Arizona Geological Society Digest, v. 18, p. 15–32.

Karlstrom, K.E., Miller, C.F., Kingsbury, J.A., Wooden, J.L., 1993, Pluton emplacement along an active ductile thrust zone, Piute Mountains, southeastern California: Interaction between deformation and solidification processes: Geological Society of America Bulletin, v. 105, p. 213–230.

Kistler, R.W., 1974, Phanerozoic batholiths in western North America: A summary of some recent work on variations in time, space, chemistry, and isotopic compositions: Annual Reviews Earth and Planetary Sciences, v. 2, p. 403–418.

Knapp, J.H., and Walker, J.D., 1989, Mesozoic and Tertiary magmatism in the Mesquite and Moon Mountains areas, western Arizona: Implications for tectonic development: Geological Society of America Abstracts with Programs, v. 21, no. 5, p. 103.

Malin, P.E., Goodman, E.D., Henyey, T.L., Li, Y.G., Okaya, D.A., and Saleeby, J.B., 1995, Significance of seismic reflections beneath a tilted exposure of deep continental crust, Tehachapi Mountains, California: Journal of Geophysical Research, v. 100, p. 2069–2087.

Martin, M.W., and Walker, J.D., 1991, Upper Precambrian-Paleozoic Paleogeographic Reconstruction of the Mojave Desert, California, *in* Cooper, J.D., and Stevens, C.H., eds., Paleozoic paleogeography of the western United States—II: Pacific Section SEPM (Society for Sedimentary Geology), p. 167–192.

Martin, M.W., and Walker, J.D., 1992, Extending the western North American Proterozoic and Paleozoic craton through the Mojave Desert: Geology, v. 20, p. 753–756.

Martin, M.W., and Walker, J.D., 1995, Stratigraphy and paleogeographic significance of metamorphic rocks in the Shadow Mountains, Western Mojave Desert, California: Geological Society of America Bulletin, v. 107, p. 354–366.

Miller, C.F., 1978, An early Mesozoic alkalic magmatic belt in western North America, *in* Howell, D.G., and McDougall, K.A., eds., Mesozoic paleogeography of the western United States: Los Angeles, California, Pacific Section, Society of Economic Paleontologists and Mineralogists, p. 163–173.

Miller, E.L., 1981, Geology of the Victorville Region, California: Parts I and II: Geological Society of America Bulletin, v. 92, p. 160–163; 554–608.

Miller, J.S., and Glazner, A.F., 1995, Jurassic plutonism and crustal evolution in the central Mojave Desert, California: Contributions to Mineralogy and Petrology, v. 118, p. 379–395.

Miller, F.K., and Morton, D.M., 1980, Potassium-Argon geochronology of the eastern Transverse Ranges and southern Mojave Desert, southern California: U.S. Geological Survey Professional Paper 1152, 30 p.

Miller, E.L., and Sutter, J.F., 1982, Structural geology and $^{40}Ar/^{39}Ar$ geochronology of the Goldstone-Lane Mountain area, Mojave Desert, California: Geological Society of America Bulletin, v. 93, p. 1191–1207.

Miller, J.S., Walker, J.D., Orell, S.E., Martin, M.W., and Harrison, S.E., 1991, Stratigraphy and Mesozoic contractile deformation at Alvord Mountain, central Mojave Desert, California: Geological Society of America Abstracts with Programs, v. 23, no. 2, p. 79.

Miller, J.S., Walker, J.D., Glazner, A.F., and Martin, M.W., 1995, Geochronologic and isotopic evidence for Triassic-Jurassic emplacement of the eugeoclinal allochthon of the Mojave Desert region, California: Geological Society of America Bulletin, v. 107, p. 1441–1457.

Miller, J.S., Glazner, A.F., and Crowe, D.E., 1996, Muscovite-garnet granites in the Cretaceous arc: Relation to crustal structure of the Mojave Desert: Geology, v. 24, p. 335–338.

Nourse, J.A., 1989, Geologic evolution of two crustal scale shear zones [unpublished Ph.D. thesis]: Pasadena, California, California Institute of Technology, 394 p.

Page, B.M., and Engebretson, D.C., 1984, Correlation between the geologic record and computed plate motions for central California: Tectonics, v. 3, p. 133–155.

Poole, F.G., 1974, Flysch deposits of the Antler Foreland Basin, western United States: Society of Economic Paleontologists and Mineralologists Special Publication 22, p. 58–82.

Poole, F.G., and Sandberg, C.A., 1977, Mississippian paleogeography and tectonics of the western United States, *in* Stewart, J.H., et al., eds., Paleozoic paleogeography of the western United States: Los Angeles, California, Pacific Section, Society of Economic Paleontologists and Mineralogists, p. 67–85.

Poole, F.G., Sandberg, C.A., and Boucot, A.J., 1977, Silurian and Devonian paleogeography of the western United States, *in* Stewart, J.H., et al., eds., Paleozoic paleogeography of the western United States: Los Angeles, California, Pacific Section, Society of Economic Paleontologists and Mineralogists, p. 39–65.

Postlethwaite, C.E., and Jacobson, C.E., 1987, Early history and reactivation of the Rand thrust, southern California: Journal of Structural Geology, v. 9, p. 195–205.

Reynolds, S.J., Spencer, J.E., Richard, S.M., and Laubach, S.E., 1986, Mesozoic structures in west-central Arizona: Arizona Geological Society Digest, v. 16, p. 35–51.

Rich, M., 1977, Pennsylvanian paleogeographic patterns in the western United States, *in* Stewart, J.H., et al., eds., Paleozoic paleogeography of the western United States: Los Angeles, California, Pacific Section, Society of Economic Paleontologists and Mineralogists, p. 87–111.

Saleeby, J.B., and Busby-Spera, C., 1992, Early Mesozoic tectonic evolution of the western U.S. Cordillera, *in* Burchfiel, B.C., et al., eds., The Cordilleran orogen: Conterminous U.S.: Boulder, Colorado, Geological Society of America, Geology of North America, p. 107–168.

Schermer, E.R., 1993, Mesozoic structural evolution of the west-central Mojave Desert, *in* Dunne, G., and McDougall, K., eds., Mesozoic paleogeography of the western United States—II: p. 307–322.

Schermer, E.R., and Busby, C.J., 1994, Jurassic magmatism in the central Mojave Desert: Implications for arc paleogeography and preservation of continental volcanic sequences: Geological Society of America Bulletin, v. 106, p. 767–790.

Schermer, E.R., Stephens, K.A., and Walker, J.D., 2001, Continental margin tectonic evolution, Tiefort Mountains, northern Mojave Desert, California: Geological Society of America Bulletin v. 113, p. 920–938.

Silver, L.T., and Nourse, J.A., 1986, The Rand Mountains "thrust" complex in comparison with the Vincent thrust-Pelona Schist relationship, southern California: Geological Society of America Abstracts with Programs, v. 18, no. 2, p. 185.

Silver, L.T., and Nourse, J.A., 1991, Timing of the Rand thrust and implications for late Cretaceous tectonics in southern California: Geological Society of America Abstracts with Programs, v. 23, no. 5, p. A480.

Snow, J.K., 1992, Large magnitude Permian shortening and continental margin tectonics in the southern Cordillera: Geological Society of America Bulletin, v. 104, p. 80–105.

Snow, J., Asmeron, Y., and Lux, D., 1991, Permian-Triassic plutonism and tectonics, Death Valley region, California and Nevada: Geology, v. 19, p. 629–632.

Stephens, K.A., Schermer, E.R., and Walker, J.D., 1993, Mesozoic intra-arc tectonics in the northeast Mojave Desert, California: Geological Society of America Abstracts with Programs, v. 25, no. 5, p. 150.

Stevens, C.H., 1977, Permian depositional provinces and tectonics, western United States, *in* Stewart, J.H., et al., eds., Paleozoic paleogeography of the western United States: Los Angeles, California, Pacific Section, Society of Economic Paleontologists and Mineralogists, p. 113–135.

Stevens, C.H., Stone, P., Dunne, G.C., Greene, D.C., Walker, J.D., and Swanson, B.J., 1998, Paleozoic and Mesozoic evolution of east-central California, *in* Ernst, W.G., and Nelson, C.A., eds., Integrated earth and environmental evolution of the southwestern United States: The Clarence A. Hall, Jr., Volume: Columbia, Maryland, Bellwether Publishing, p. 119–160.

Stewart, J.H., 1970, Upper Precambrian and Lower Cambrian strata in the southern Great Basin, California and Nevada: U.S. Geological Survey Professional Paper 620, 206 p.

Stewart, J.H., and Poole, F.G., 1975, Extension of the Cordilleran miogeosynclinal belt to the San Andreas Fault, southern California: Geological Society of America Bulletin, v. 86, p. 205–212.

Stone, P., and Stevens, C.H., 1988, Pennsylvanian and Early Permian paleogeography of east-central California: Implications for the shape of the continental margin and the timing of continental truncation: Geology, v. 16, p. 330–333.

Tosdal, R.M., Haxel, G.B., and Wright, J.E., 1989, Jurassic geology of the Sonoran Desert region, southern Arizona, southeastern California, and northernmost Sonora: Construction of a continental-margin magmatic arc, *in* Jenney, J.P., and Reynolds, S.J., eds., Geologic evolution of Arizona: Tucson, Arizona, p. 397–434.

Wadsworth, W.B., Ferriz, H., and Rhodes, D.D., 1995, Structural and stratigraphic development of the Middle Jurassic magmatic arc in the Cowhole Mountains, central-eastern Mojave Desert, California, *in* Miller, D.M., and Busby, C., eds., Jurassic magmatism and tectonics of the North American Cordillera: Boulder, Colorado, Geological Society of America Special Paper 299, p. 327–349.

Walker, J.D., 1987, Permian to Middle Triassic rocks of the Mojave Desert: Arizona Geological Digest, v. 18, p. 1–14.

Walker, J.D., 1988, Permian and Triassic rocks of the Mojave Desert and their implications for timing and mechanisms of continental truncation: Tectonics, v. 7, p. 685–709.

Walker, J.D., and Wardlaw, B.R., 1989, Implications of Paleozoic and Mesozoic rocks in the Soda Mountains, northeastern Mojave Desert, California, for late Paleozoic and Mesozoic Cordilleran orogenesis: Geological Society of America Bulletin, v. 101, p. 1574–1583.

Walker, J.D., Bartley, J.M., and Glazner, A.F., 1990a, Large-magnitude Miocene extension in the central Mojave Desert: Implications for Paleozoic to Tertiary paleogeography and tectonics: Journal of Geophysical Research, v. 95, p. 557–569.

Walker, J.D., Martin, M.W., Bartley, J.M., and Coleman, D.S., 1990b, Timing and kinematics of deformation in the Cronese Hills, California, and implications for Mesozoic structure of the southwestern Cordillera: Geology, v. 18, p. 554–557.

Walker, J.D., Fletcher, J.M., Fillmore, R.P., Martin, M.W., Taylor, W.J., Glazner, A.F., and Bartley, J.M., 1995a, Connection between igneous activity and extension in the central Mojave metamorphic core complex: Journal of Geophysical Research, v. 100, p. 10477–10494.

Walker, J.D., Burchfiel, B.C., and Davis, G.A., 1995b, New age controls on initiation and timing of foreland belt thrusting in the Clark Mountains, southern California: Geological Society of America Bulletin, v. 107, p. 742–750.

Wood, D.J., and Saleeby, J.B., 1998, Late Cretaceous-Paleocene extensional collapse and disaggregation of the southernmost Sierra Nevada Batholith, *in* Ernst, W.G, and Nelson, C.A., eds., Integrated Earth and environmental evolution of the southwestern United States: The Clarence A. Hall, Jr., Volume: Columbia, Maryland, Bellwether Publishing, p. 289–325.

MANUSCRIPT ACCEPTED BY THE SOCIETY MAY 9, 2001

Geological Society of America
Memoir 195
2002

Cenozoic evolution of the Mojave block of southern California

Allen F. Glazner
*Department of Geological Sciences, CB 3315, University of North Carolina, Chapel Hill,
North Carolina 27599-3315, USA*
J. Douglas Walker
Department of Geology, University of Kansas, Lawrence, Kansas 66045, USA
John M. Bartley
University of Utah, Department of Geology and Geophysics, Salt Lake City, Utah 84112-0111, USA
John M. Fletcher
*Departamento de Geologia, CICESE (Centro de Investigación Científica y de Educación Superior de Ensenada),
P.O. Box 434843, San Diego, California 92143-4843, USA*

ABSTRACT

The recorded Cenozoic history of the Mojave Desert region of southern California began in the latest Oligocene, when intense volcanism and tectonism interrupted a long early Tertiary silence. Volcanism commenced across the region in an east-west band ca. 24–22 Ma. Northwest of Barstow, volcanism was accompanied by intense crustal extension and development of a metamorphic core complex. Outside of this relatively restricted area, extension was minor or absent. After extension ceased ca. 18 Ma, volcanism shifted to small-volume eruptions of basalt. Post-extensional deformation has largely been by strike-slip faulting along northwest-striking dextral faults and west-striking sinistral faults, and total dextral slip across the Mojave Desert region since the early Miocene is ~45–60 km. Strike-slip deformation has been overprinted locally by intense north-south contraction that is the dominant style of deformation in the western Mojave block.

Paleomagnetic data indicate that parts of the Mojave block were rotated clockwise, although the magnitude and timing of this rotation are poorly determined. The best evidence for large (>45°) rotation comes from the area east of Barstow, where large clockwise declination anomalies and Mesozoic and Cenozoic dikes with anomalous strikes may reflect early Miocene clockwise deflection along the Mojave River fault.

Volcanism and tectonism in the Mojave block resulted from interactions among the North American, Pacific, and various oceanic plates. Patterns of volcanism and tectonism do not correlate with growth of slab windows beneath the continent, but do correlate with the position of the subducted Mendocino fracture zone. Plate-circuit reconstructions suggest that the driving force for extension was divergence between the Pacific and North American plates along the transform margin that separated the two. This hypothesis accounts for the direction, magnitude, and rate of extension in the Mojave block.

Glazner, A.F., Walker, J.D., Bartley, J.M., and Fletcher, J.M., 2002, Cenozoic evolution of the Mojave block of southern California, *in* Glazner, A.F., Walker, J.D., and Bartley, J.M., eds., Geologic Evolution of the Mojave Desert and Southwestern Basin and Range: Boulder, Colorado, Geological Society of America Memoir 195, p. 19–41.

INTRODUCTION

The Mojave Desert region of southern California (Figs. 1, 2) occupies a key position in southwestern North America because it is located at the junction of several geologic provinces. The region includes the wedge-shaped Mojave block that lies between the Big Bend segment of the dextral San Andreas fault and the sinistral Garlock fault, adjoining the narrow junction between the northern and southern segments of the Basin and Range province and straddling the transition from the Basin and Range to the transform plate boundary between the North American and Pacific plates. It also lies in the gap between the Sierra Nevada and Transverse Ranges physiographic provinces and between the Sierra Nevada and Peninsular Ranges batholiths. The geologic history of the Mojave Desert region records elements of the diverse histories of these adjoining provinces and therefore provides important information about relationships among them.

We define the Mojave Desert region as that area bounded by the Garlock fault to the north, the San Andreas fault to the southwest, and the Colorado River to the east (Fig. 1). The Mojave block is that part of the Mojave Desert region that lies west of the southern extension of the Death Valley fault zone. The eastern limit of the Mojave block is a prominent but poorly understood geologic boundary that separates a geologically stable region of abundant Paleozoic rocks and basin-and-range topography on the east from an area of disorganized topography, sparse Paleozoic rocks, and active strike-slip faulting on the west.

This paper summarizes current thought regarding the Cenozoic evolution of the Mojave block. This paper, a companion paper (by Walker, Martin, and Glazner, this volume), and a guidebook (Glazner et al., 1994) provide a reconstruction of the Phanerozoic history of the Mojave block. Although the broad outlines of Mojave geologic history are well known, several key issues remain controversial and are discussed herein. These include the nature and areal extent of Miocene crustal extension, the character of late Cenozoic strike-slip deformation, and the ultimate causes and controls of Cenozoic tectonism and magmatism.

PREVIOUS WORK

In spite of its key position, relatively little work had been done in the Mojave Desert region until the past few decades. Early reports (e.g., Thompson, 1929; Hewett, 1954) laid out the general stratigraphy and structure and established that the Mojave Desert region was distinct from the Basin and Range province. Much of our knowledge of Mojave geology comes from the astounding volume of quadrangle mapping accomplished by T.W. Dibblee, Jr. (see dibblee.geol.ucsb.edu.) His maps and accompanying reports form an excellent base for interpreting the tectonic evolution of the region and were invaluable in our work. Dibblee (1961) also was first to recognize the importance of strike-slip faulting in the Mojave Desert region.

Starting in the 1970s, academic and U.S. Geological Survey geologists turned their attention to the Mojave Desert region in an effort to understand its resources and relationships to surrounding provinces. Continued regional mapping and geochemical and geochronologic studies, including dozens of M.S. and Ph.D. theses, have resulted in a much clearer under-

Figure 1. Locations of the Mojave Desert region and the Mojave block. Also shown are several important faults that are either observed (solid lines) or inferred (dashed lines). Black blobs are outcrops of Pelona, Rand, and Orocopia Schists. Diagonal-ruled area is the Mojave block. The Mojave Desert region encompasses this area and eastward to the Colorado River. DVFZ—Death Valley fault zone; CL—China Lake; E—Edwards; FI—Fort Irwin, Goldstone, and China Lake South Range; TP—Twentynine Palms.

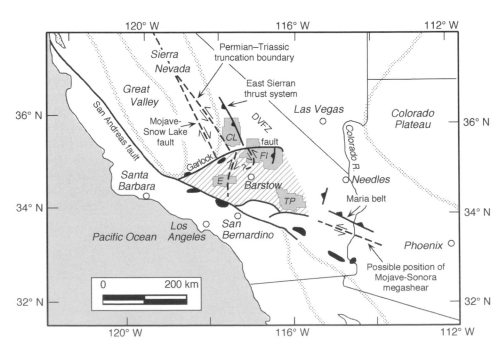

standing of the region's geology. The recognition of late Cenozoic strike-slip faulting (Dibblee, 1961) and Miocene low-angle normal faulting in the Colorado River trough (Davis et al., 1980) provided a framework for understanding regional Cenozoic deformation in the Mojave Desert region and how it relates to surrounding regions.

SUMMARY OF THE CENOZOIC HISTORY OF THE MOJAVE BLOCK

Early Tertiary: A meager record

The recorded Cenozoic history of the Mojave block begins around the Oligocene–Miocene boundary. The early Tertiary was apparently a time of quiescence in the Mojave block; few rocks and fewer structures younger than Late Cretaceous and older than late Oligocene have been identified. This circumstance suggests that the region was a tectonically static area that was drained efficiently and externally (Hewett, 1954; Nilsen, 1977; Howard, 1996).

Locally, Oligocene, Eocene, and probable Upper Cretaceous strata are known around the margins of the Mojave block. At least 4 km of the Paleocene and Eocene Goler Formation accumulated in a basin immediately north of the Garlock fault (Cox, 1987). This sequence is largely nonmarine but includes a thin marine interval (Cox, 1987; McDougall, 1987). No equivalent rocks are known in the Mojave block, and the tectonic significance of this sequence is unclear. In the Death Valley region, a thick sequence of nonmarine Oligocene strata of the Titus Canyon Formation (Schweickert and Caskey, 1990; Saylor and Hodges, 1991) may have accumulated in an extensional basin at the southern end of a north-trending extensional belt that runs from eastern California to northern Nevada (Axen et al., 1993). In Cajon Pass, a thin, enigmatic sequence of marine strata depositionally overlies pre-Tertiary basement. These strata contain plesiosaur remains and are probably Late Cretaceous in age (Lucas and Reynolds, 1991).

Hewett (1954) estimated early Tertiary unroofing of more than 4 km, on the basis of the thickness of pre-Mesozoic strata on the Colorado Plateau and their absence within the Mojave block. New data indicate that this estimate is tenuous at best. Such strata are present within the Mojave block, but they have been fragmented and obscured by intense Mesozoic and Cenozoic tectonism and plutonism (Kiser, 1981; Miller and Cameron, 1982; Boettcher and Walker, 1993). The eastern boundary of the Mojave block is thus analogous to Owens Valley to the north; preplutonic strata west of Owens Valley are engulfed by plutons of the Sierra Nevada batholith.

Early Miocene return of magmatism

The Oligocene–Miocene boundary marked a dramatic return of magmatism, sedimentation, and tectonism to the Mojave block. At ca. 24–22 Ma, volcanic rocks were erupted along an east-trending belt that stretched from the westernmost Mojave Desert region inland to the Whipple Mountains and beyond (Glazner and Bartley, 1984; Glazner, 1990). The onset of magmatism was accompanied by the onset of extensional faulting, as both swept northwestward out of Arizona (Glazner and Supplee, 1982; Glazner and Bartley, 1984). Abundant coarse-clastic sedimentation accompanied volcanism and deformation (Fillmore and Walker, 1996).

The northwestward sweep of volcanism is evident within the Mojave Desert region from the stratigraphic data compiled by Sherrod and Nielson (1993). Late Oligocene volcanism was predominant in the southern part of the region and adjacent Arizona, early Miocene volcanism was prevalent at the latitude of the central part of the region, and late early Miocene to middle Miocene volcanism dominated farther north, at the latitude of the northern Mojave Desert region and southernmost Nevada.

In the central Mojave block, 24–20 Ma volcanic strata are widespread in the ranges southeast of Barstow (Glazner, 1990; Walker et al., 1995) and extend west in scattered outcrops to the very western edge of the Mojave block (e.g., Armstrong and Higgins, 1973; Matthews, 1976; Dokka and Baksi, 1989). Volcanic rocks north of the latitude of Barstow are younger, predominantly 20–14 Ma, with scattered outcrops of late Miocene and younger basalts (Burke et al., 1982; Schermer et al., 1996; Sabin et al., 1994; Smith et al., this volume).

Volcanism, which locally produced piles up to several kilometers thick, was calc-alkalic and spanned the compositional range from basalt to rhyolite. Composite volcanoes have been identified locally (Glazner, 1988; Sabin et al., 1994). Some areas are dominated by intermediate-composition and silicic rocks, whereas others are bimodal accumulations of basalts and basaltic andesites with silicic tuffs (Glazner, 1990; Miller and Miller, 1991). East of Barstow, mafic flows and silicic tuffs typically overlie thick sequences of andesite and dacite lavas, but geochronologic data indicate that these lithologically correlative sequences are not strictly time correlative (Gardner, 1940; Glazner, 1988; Glazner et al., 2000).

Volcanic rocks of the Mojave block are broadly calc-alkalic, but the mafic end of the spectrum is typically high in titanium and mildly alkalic, unlike typical subduction-related suites such as the Cascades (Glazner, 1990). In a given area, the most mafic rocks are typically basaltic andesites. Petrographic and isotope data clearly indicate that these rocks are basalts that were contaminated by assimilation of crustal material (Glazner, 1990; Miller and Miller, 1991; Miller et al., 2000), in contrast to similar widespread basaltic andesites in Arizona and northern Mexico, which Cameron et al. (1989) interpreted to be uncontaminated.

Isotopic data indicate that magmatism involved significant recycling of preexisting crust. For example, $^{87}Sr/^{86}Sr$ increases and ε_{Nd} decreases with both SiO_2 and with distance from the coast (Glazner and O'Neil, 1989; Miller et al., 2000). The increase of $^{87}Sr/^{86}Sr$ with SiO_2 is caused by a greater proportion

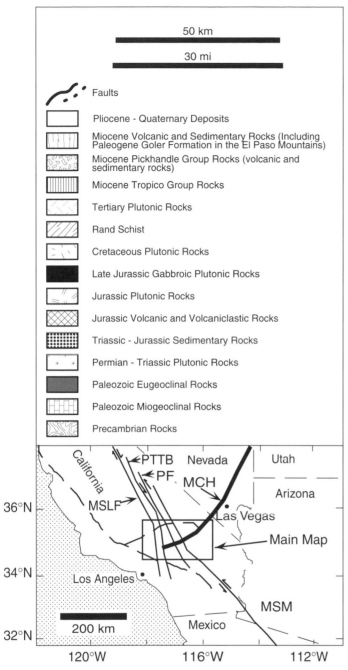

Figure 2. Geologic map of the Mojave block. Modified, on the basis of our work, from Dibblee (1968a) and other sources. AM—Azucar Mine, BH—Bissell Hills, BM—Black Mountain, CM—Cady Mountains, CaM—Calico Mountains, HH—Hinkley Hills, LR—Leuhman Ridge, MH—Mud Hills, NM—Newberry Mountains, NTM—North Tiefort Mountain, OM—Ord Mountain, QM—Quartzite Mountain, RM—Rodman Mountains, SM—Soda Mountains, STM—South Tiefort Mountain, WHMR—Waterman Hills and Mitchel Range. Only ranges mentioned in the text are labeled. Location map with legend: MCH—miogeoclinal-cratonal hinge line; MSLF—Mojave-Snow Lake fault; MSM—Mojave-Sonora megashear; PF—Pine Nut fault; PTTB—Permian-Triassic truncation boundary; dot pattern indicates locus of arc plutonic rocks.

of old crust in more silicic rocks. The correlation with position probably reflects both an eastward increase in the proportion of Proterozoic rocks in the crust and changes in the underlying mantle lithosphere. Rocks from the north-central Mojave block have uniformly low $^{87}Sr/^{86}Sr$ and high ε_{Nd}, consistent with derivation from oceanic lithosphere (Keith et al., 1994; Miller et al., 2000).

Early Miocene extension

Evidence for large-magnitude extension. Dokka (1986) and Dokka and Woodburne (1986) first proposed that the lithosphere of the central Mojave Desert region was greatly extended in the early Miocene, on the basis of relationships in the Newberry Mountains, which lie 20 km east of Barstow. New work in the Newberry Mountains calls the existence of a detachment fault there into question (see Discussion). Unequivocal evidence for large-scale extension was first provided by Glazner et al. (1989; also see Dokka, 1989; Walker et al., 1990), who showed that the area north and northwest of Barstow (Waterman Hills, Mitchel Range, and Hinkley Hills) contains a classic detachment fault system with a well-exposed low-angle normal fault, a chloritic, ultramylonitic footwall with synkinematic intrusions, and a highly extended hanging wall of early Miocene volcanic and coarse clastic rocks (Figs. 3, 4). The most intensely extended rocks (as indicated by mylonitization of footwall rocks and extreme distension and tilting of upper-plate rocks) are only found in the area from the Mitchel Range to The Buttes, roughly coincident with the areal extent of the Waterman Hills granodiorite (Fletcher et al., 1995; Walker et al., 1995; Fig. 3). The detachment fault system is regionally folded into a dome-and-basin geometry typical of Cordilleran metamorphic complexes (Fletcher et al., 1995). Correlations of upper- and lower-plate lithologic assemblages and offset pre-Miocene markers indicate 40–60 km of northeast-directed displacement across this fault system (Glazner et al., 1989; Walker et al., 1990; Martin et al., 1993).

The mylonitic shear zone is thickest and most penetrative in the Mitchel Range where all rock types of the heterogeneous pre-Tertiary basement—dominated by plutonic rocks ranging from hornblende diorite to leucogranite with minor calcite and dolomite marbles and quartzite—form ultramylonites (Fletcher and Bartley, 1994; Fletcher et al., 1995). Although the base of the shear zone is not exposed, the mylonitic sequence is at least 1000 m thick, and ultramylonites are found at the structurally lowest level exposed. Relative to the Mitchel Range, the Hinkley Hills lie structurally up the dip of the detachment, along the direction of transport. Here, mylonitization is distinctly less penetrative. The shear zone forms anastomosing strands, generally <100 m in thickness, and only the weakest rock types (calcite marble and quartzite) were mylonitized (Fletcher et al., 1995). The Buttes region contains the westernmost exposures of mylonitic footwall; the shear zone there reaches ~200 m thick (Fletcher et al., 1995).

Figure 3. Tectonic map of the Central Mojave metamorphic core complex (CMMCC). The zone of ductile deformation is largely coextensive with outcrops of the Waterman Hills granodiorite (diagonal-line pattern). Locations: B—The Buttes, CM—Calico Mountains, FP—Fremont Peak, GH—Gravel Hills, HH—Hinkley Hills, IM—Iron Mountain, L—Lead Mountain, LCM—Lynx Cat Mountain, LM—Lane Mountain, MH—Mud Hills, MR—Mitchel Range, WH—Waterman Hills. Abbreviations in inset map: GF—Garlock fault, SAF—San Andreas fault; location of main map is shown. Modified from Fletcher et al. (1995).

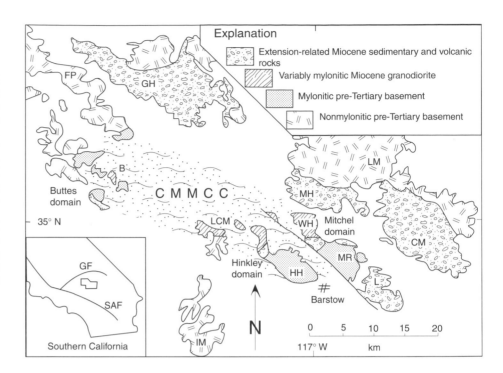

Age and relationship of extension and magmatism.

Near Barstow, magmatism and intense crustal extension were synchronous. The oldest volcanic rocks in this area were erupted at ca. 24–23 Ma, about the same time that the Waterman Hills granodiorite was intruded into what is now the footwall of the Waterman Hills detachment fault (Walker et al., 1995). Extensional-basin development and accumulation of the Pickhandle Formation began at about the same time (Fillmore, 1993; Fillmore and Walker, 1996).

Field observations from the Central Mojave metamorphic core complex indicate that magmatism and mylonitic deformation were closely linked (Walker et al., 1995; Fletcher et al., 1995). The spatial distributions of Miocene dikes and plutons and of the brittle-ductile detachment coincide. Although all Miocene intrusions demonstrably were emplaced during slip across the detachment, there are important variations in crosscutting relationships in different areas of the core complex. In The Buttes, mylonite is restricted to close proximity to Miocene intrusions. Thin mylonitic margins are common along the walls of most dikes (Fletcher et al., 1995). It is interesting that dikes in the Hinkley Hills ubiquitously cut the mylonitic shear zone but not the brittle detachment, which suggests that they were emplaced synkinematically at a time when their wall rocks resided at a level above the brittle-ductile transition (Fletcher et al., 1995). In contrast, dikes in the Mitchel Range ubiquitously display and are transposed into parallelism with the mylonitic fabric, which suggests that they were emplaced at a time when their wall rocks resided at a level below the brittle-ductile transition (Fletcher et al., 1995). Although crosscutting relationships in the Mitchel Range indicate either pre- or synkinematic emplacement, we infer that the dikes were likely to have been

emplaced after some period of ductile shear, as can be observed in the Hinkley Hills.

Sedimentation.

Sedimentary rocks deposited during the early Miocene vary greatly depending on their position relative to the extensional basin. Strata deposited west of Barstow are typically fine grained and tuffaceous (Tropico Group of Dibblee, 1967a). These strata host the huge boron deposits near the town of Boron (Gale, 1946) and attest to deposition in relatively quiet water. In contrast, strata deposited near Barstow are predominantly conglomerates, breccias, megabreccias, and pyroclastic rocks assigned to the Pickhandle and Mud Hills Formations (Fillmore and Walker, 1996; Ingersoll et al., 1996). These rocks clearly record intense tectonism. Strata deposited east of the highly extended region include a mixture of coarse- and fine-grained clastic sedimentary rocks (e.g., Hector Formation of Woodburne et al., 1974; Clews Formation of Byers, 1960).

Fillmore et al. (1994) interpreted these stratal assemblages in terms of three basin types developed during extension: (1) the intrarift Pickhandle basin, which received a thick section of coarse clastic and volcanic detritus; (2) the extrarift Tropico basin, which lay to the southwest, involved quiet-water deposition, and may have formed by flexure of the footwall during extension; and (3) intra–hanging-wall basins to the east, including the Clews basin at Alvord Mountain and the Hector basin in the Cady Mountains. Ingersoll et al. (1996) further demonstrated the complex interplay of sedimentation and tectonism in the Mud Hills.

Offset of paleogeographic markers.

The Mojave block has been difficult to fit into regional geologic syntheses because many regional paleogeographic patterns lose continuity within

Figure 4. Photographs of deformation styles in the Mojave block. (A) Waterman Hills detachment fault exposed at the summit of the Waterman Hills north of Barstow. Light-colored rocks are early Miocene granodiorite of the footwall that have undergone cataclasis, chloritization, and mylonitization; darker rocks above are brecciated and potassium-metasomatized early Miocene rhyolite flows and plugs. Automobile and roads give scale. The detachment fault is warped into a culmination here, but is regionally gently dipping. (B) Typical fault style in hanging-wall strata of the Waterman Hills detachment fault. Here, near the Waterman Mine, sandstone, conglomerate, and siltstone layers are cut by domino-style faults that accommodate extension of the hanging wall. (C) Contractional deformation style that characterizes the western Mojave block: complex refolded folds in fine-grained Tropico Group rocks, Bissell Hills (northwest of Edwards Air Force Base). This style of deformation is common throughout the western Mojave block, including in the Kramer Hills.

it. For example, many Mesozoic features of the Sierra Nevada and eastern California—such as the Independence dike swarm, Mesozoic thrust faults, and isotopic boundaries—can be tracked southward to or across the Garlock fault, but then are lost.

Much of this pattern complexity is simplified when extension near Barstow is removed (Glazner et al., 1989). Martin et al. (1993) demonstrated that several important paleogeographic markers—including the Independence dike swarm, a belt of Mesozoic volcanic rocks, the Mesozoic thrust belt, and the Paleozoic miogeoclinal-cratonal hinge line—can be aligned by restoring 50–70 km of right-lateral displacement across a postulated fault, designated the Mojave Valley fault (see subsequent section on Displacement Transfer in the Extensional Systems). They proposed that this fault formed the southeastern

boundary of the highly extended region. Although the Mojave Valley fault has not been located in the field, recent mapping in the Newberry and Rodman Mountains (see subsequent section on Reinterpretation of the Newberry Mountains, and Glazner et al. [2000]) reinforces the need for such a structure along which extension in the Barstow area was transferred to the coeval extensional belt in the Colorado River trough.

Late Neogene–Holocene sedimentation, faulting, transpression, and volcanism

Following early Miocene extension, which was over by the time of eruption of the Peach Springs Tuff (18.5 Ma; Nielson et al., 1990), the central Mojave Desert region was the site of fluviolacustrine deposition of the lower Barstow Formation, upper Tropico Group, and upper Hector Formation. The Barstow Formation sits in angular unconformity upon Pickhandle and Mud Hills strata in the Mud Hills (Dibblee, 1968a; Ingersoll et al., 1996) and records quieter deposition and less volcanism. Silicic tuffs are common in the Barstow Formation, although their sources are unknown. They may have been derived from the Eagle Crags area to the north (Burke et al., 1982; Sabin et al., 1994). A similar transition is recorded at Alvord Mountain to the east, where the Barstow Formation overlies deformed lower Miocene Clews Formation strata that were deposited in a hanging-wall basin (Fillmore, 1993). We attribute this sedimentation to filling of extensional and flexural basins, coupled with thermal subsidence.

Volcanism continued its northward migration during the middle Miocene. Volcanism at the latitude of Barstow shut off at ca. 18 Ma, although some of the undated silicic plugs around Barstow could be younger. Post–18 Ma volcanism was concentrated in the northern Mojave block, northwest of Barstow (Burke et al., 1982), on the China Lake and Fort Irwin military bases (Schermer et al., 1996), and in the far-eastern part of the Mojave Desert region (Turner and Glazner, 1991; Sherrod and Nielson, 1993). Post–18 Ma volcanic rocks in the northern Mojave block are predominantly mafic or bimodal (Keith et al., 1994), sit nonconformably on pre-Tertiary basement, and have not been affected by extension.

Locally, basaltic volcanism continued throughout the Miocene and into the Quaternary. For example, tilted 20 Ma volcanic rocks near Ludlow are overlain unconformably by basalt flows that are relatively flat lying (basalt of Ash Hill of Dibblee, 1967c). Two samples of this unit and a sample from the nearby Sunshine Peak cinder cone were dated by K/Ar at 15.6, 4.9, and 0.4 Ma, respectively (H.G. Wilshire, personal commun., 1994). These ages indicate persistent alkalic volcanism over a 20 m.y. time span.

Elsewhere in the Mojave Desert region, alkali basalt cinder cones and lava flows sit in angular unconformity on tilted lower Miocene strata (Wise, 1969). K/Ar dating indicates that most of these lavas were erupted within the past 10 m.y. (Glazner and Farmer, 1993). They bear little relationship to current structure in the region, and some were erupted through areas undergoing active crustal shortening (Glazner and Bartley, 1994).

The dominant post–early Miocene deformation comprised strike-slip faulting and related transpression (Dibblee, 1961; Garfunkel, 1974; Dokka and Travis, 1990). Transpressional structures are ubiquitous across the Mojave block and are overprinted on extended rocks in the eastern part of the area (Bartley et al., 1990). Although it is commonly assumed that strike-slip faulting began when the Gulf of California opened at 5–4 Ma, there is evidence that it began at least locally in the early Miocene immediately following the major extensional phase (Bartley et al., 1990). For example, the Lenwood anticline west of Barstow is an active transpressional structure related to the Camp Rock–Harper Lake fault system. Lower Miocene strata

exposed in the core of the Lenwood anticline are much more tightly folded than overlying Miocene-Pliocene alluvial-fan deposits (Dibblee, 1967a; Glazner et al., 1994), implying that most of the growth of the structure predated the fan deposits. Early Miocene volcanic and volcanogenic strata on the southeast side of the Newberry Mountains are folded into a west-trending south-vergent asymmetric anticline. We interpret the fold be a hanging-wall anticline above a north-dipping reverse-slip segment of the Calico fault system (Bartley et al., 1990). Nearby exposures of the Peach Springs Tuff are flat lying and thus imply that the anticline formed before 18.5 Ma.

DISCUSSION

Key controversies and enigmas

Although the general outlines of the Mojave block's Cenozoic history, as just discussed, are well known, several controversies remain. These are discussed here and include the following: (1) How much vertical-axis rotation occurred during Cenozoic extension and strike-slip faulting? (2) How widespread was Cenozoic extension? (3) How much strike-slip faulting has taken place, and how is this deformation areally distributed? (4) How widespread is late Cenozoic transpression? (5) What are the relative roles of extension, transpression, and strike-slip faulting in producing the topography of the Mojave block? (6) What was the driving mechanism for extension? (7) How are these events tied to the region's plate-tectonic history?

Vertical-axis rotation

Paleomagnetic studies in southern California commonly indicate clockwise rotation of fault blocks during the Miocene (e.g., Luyendyk, 1991). However, such studies in the Mojave Desert region have produced a bewildering variation in paleomagnetic declinations, with studies in neighboring areas commonly giving contradictory results, and studies in the same area yielding both clockwise and counterclockwise declination anomalies over brief stratigraphic intervals (e.g., Valentine et al., 1993; Dokka et al., 1998).

There are two basic types of paleomagnetic studies on Tertiary rocks from the Mojave block. In the first type, data have been collected from several lava flows in a given structural area and averaged to smooth out secular variation and structural correction errors (e.g., Ross et al., 1989; Valentine et al., 1993). Strata involved in the studies usually are tilted to dips of $>20°$ (e.g., the average dip of strata at 68 sites measured by Ross [1988] is 30°), at least locally in the limbs of plunging folds. The studies typically show significant clockwise (and locally counterclockwise) declination anomalies, but are hampered by significant scatter (both within and between areas) and by lack of evidence that secular variation was adequately averaged (e.g., data are typically unipolar, or nearly so; Ross, 1988). The second type involves analysis of sedimentary strata (e.g., MacFadden et al., 1990a, 1990b) or the Peach Springs Tuff, a widespread ignimbrite that blanketed most of the eastern Mojave Desert region (Wells and Hillhouse, 1989). Strata analyzed in these studies are typically postkinematic and relatively flat lying. These studies solve the secular-variation problem by either more effective averaging (sedimentary-rock studies) or by examining deflection relative to a reference section of the paleomagnetic pole in a single rapidly cooled unit (in this case, the Peach Springs Tuff on the Colorado Plateau).

Results from studies of sedimentary strata and the Peach Springs Tuff typically show relatively small or negligible declination anomalies. For example, MacFadden et al. (1990b) determined ~20° of clockwise rotation of the lower Miocene Hector Formation in the Cady Mountains, and MacFadden et al. (1990a) found no significant rotation of the middle Miocene Barstow Formation near Barstow. Data from Wells and Hillhouse (1989) indicate no rotation in much of the Mojave Desert region since eruption of the 18.5 ± 0.2 Ma Peach Springs Tuff.

Significant declination anomalies are confined to areas of tilted volcanic rocks. This restriction could indicate that the anomalies result from inadequate structural corrections and/or inadequate averaging of secular variation, but several lines of evidence indicate that the anomalies record at least some amount of true vertical-axis rotation. First, the declination anomalies are overwhelmingly clockwise (Ross et al., 1989). Second, analysis of data from Ross (1988) indicates no correlation between average declination anomaly and either average or maximum bedding dip in a given structural subblock. Such a correlation would be expected if the anomalies resulted from either incorrect structural correction or wrench faulting (e.g., Miller, 1998). Third, the tilted strata are at least slightly older than the weakly rotated, less-deformed strata, allowing for the possibility that significant rotation occurred before deposition of the weakly rotated strata.

This last point implies that significant block rotations could only have occurred in the early Miocene either during or immediately following crustal extension and, therefore, cannot be related to late Miocene and younger dextral faulting. This timing relationship, the consistent clockwise-rotation sense, and the spatial correlation between declination anomalies and stratal tilting led Bartley and Glazner (1991) to propose that the declination anomalies reflect dextral shearing that transferred displacement between the Central Mojave metamorphic core complex and the coeval Colorado River trough extensional corridor.

Dike orientation. Orientations of Mesozoic dikes provide another test of block-rotation models. The northwest-striking Independence dike swarm (Moore and Hopson, 1961; Smith, 1962; Carl and Glazner, this volume, Chapter 7) crosses eastern California and provides a structural datum. For example, Ron and Nur (1996) concluded that dikes in the northeastern and southern Mojave block are rotated clockwise, whereas dikes in the central Mojave block are not significantly rotated. They

concluded that the block-rotation model of Luyendyk et al. (1985) best matched available data. Hopson et al. (2000) looked at a more complete set of dikes and found that dike orientations are roughly concordant with paleomagnetically determined rotations in those few places where both types of study have been done.

Figure 5 is a compilation of dike orientations in the Mojave block, based on the compilation of Carl and Glazner (this volume, Chapter 7) and supplemented by published geologic maps of T.W. Dibblee, Jr. We have included dikes of all ages, because Jurassic, Cretaceous, and Cenozoic dikes are subparallel across the region (e.g., Coleman et al. [2000] showed that Jurassic and Cretaceous dikes are interleaved in the type locality of the Independence dike swarm) and few of the dikes have been dated. Most of the dikes in Figure 5 are probably Jurassic. Figure 5 shows that most of these dikes strike northwest, but that there is significant scatter. In several ranges there are conjugate(?) sets, one striking north and the other northwest. A conspicuous region east of Barstow (oval in Fig. 5) contains dikes that only strike north or northeast (however, the number of such dikes is curiously small, given the widespread area over which declination anomalies are reported). This region contains some of the largest declination anomalies found by Ross et al. (1989), as well as the trace of the proposed Mojave Valley fault (see the previous section on Offset of Paleogeographic Markers). We infer that these rotations may have been caused by dextral movement across this northeast-striking fault (Martin et al., 1993).

Counterclockwise anomalies. Bidirectional declination anomalies occur in some areas. Valentine et al. (1993) and Dokka et al. (1998) argued that such anomalies represent vertical-axis rotations caused by drag along, or decoupled rotation between, faults that are inferred to separate subblocks with different anomalies. This interpretation is possible, but structural and stratigraphic complexities render it debatable and current data are inadequate to test it. For example, many of the units sampled by these authors have been affected by intense noncylindrical folding, which makes standard structural corrections inadequate (Bartley et al., 1990; Walker et al., 1990). The Kramer Hills study reported by Dokka et al. (1998), for example, was performed in rocks that were strongly folded, locally isoclinally, in the late Cenozoic (Fig. 4; Linn et al., this volume, Chapter 10). The data from the study by Dokka et al. have not been published; therefore these concerns cannot be evaluated. The Valentine et al. (1993) study of volcanic strata near Barstow revealed several declination anomalies of varying magnitude and sense. However, some of these units have anomalously shallow magnetic inclinations that are inconsistent with nearby units and would require large northward transport relative to North America; such transport is inconsistent with geologic and other paleomagnetic data. We therefore suspect that these declination anomalies at least partly reflect eruption during a magnetic excursion and are not reliable indicators of structural deformation.

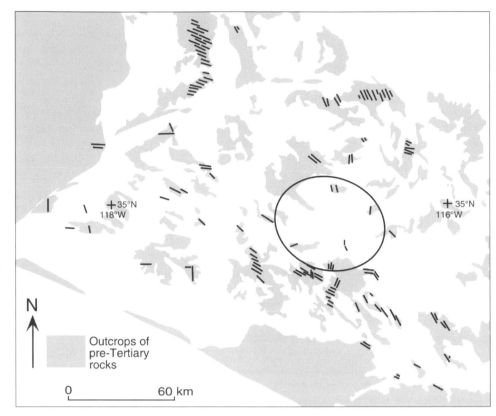

Figure 5. Summary of dike orientations in the Mojave block, modified from Carl and Glazner (this volume). Although conjugate dike sets are not uncommon, in an area (oval) east of Barstow, mapped dikes strike only north or northeast, consistent with large paleomagnetic declination anomalies in Miocene volcanic rocks. These rotations may record deformation along a transfer fault that bounds the highly extended area near Barstow (see Fig. 6).

Schermer et al.'s (1996) study of the structure and paleomagnetism of volcanic rocks in the northeastern Mojave block bears on this question. Faults in this area are well exposed and well mapped, and Schermer and coworkers carefully noted the relationship of paleomagnetic samples to these structures. They concluded that Independence dikes and Miocene volcanic rocks have similar rotations, ~25° clockwise. Larger clockwise rotations are present, but mostly come from areas around fault terminations where larger strains are probable (Schermer et al., 1996). A modest rotation of 25° clockwise is consistent with most models of strike-slip deformation in the Mojave block (see Schermer et al., 1996, for discussion). Schermer et al. found no evidence for counterclockwise rotations near left-lateral faults that accommodate rotation within the larger subblock, as predicted by the Dokka et al. (1998) hypothesis.

Summary. In summary, we find evidence—i.e., the consistent relationship between older Mesozoic structural markers and paleomagnetic measurements on younger Cenozoic rocks—for moderate rotation (~25°) of fault subblocks in the northeastern Mojave block. The mechanism for rotation is deflection of east-trending fault subblocks in an overall right-lateral shear system (e.g., Garfunkel, 1974; Schermer et al., 1996). Rotations proposed for the western and southern parts of the Mojave block are possible but unverified. Although some paleomagnetic data from Cenozoic rocks (e.g., Golombek and Brown, 1988) suggest similar clockwise rotations, these observations are at odds with older structural markers such as dikes. Without more data,

the hypothesized rotations are impossible to evaluate. Data from the eastern Mojave block east of Barstow indicate significant clockwise rotation, probably along the Mojave Valley fault, but the precise structural mechanism of this rotation is undetermined.

Extension direction

Kinematic indicators such as tilt direction, mylonitic lineation, and synkinematic dikes require that hanging-wall rocks moved to the northeast in present coordinates. However, Dokka (1989) and Ross (1995) interpreted paleomagnetic data to indicate that extension originally occurred with the hanging wall moving to the north and that the current northeast orientation of extension vectors results from clockwise rotation. We view this interpretation as unlikely for several reasons.

First, northeast-directed extension parallels that in much of the rest of southern California and western Arizona (Wust, 1986; Bartley and Glazner, 1991) and particularly parallels the displacement vector of coeval extension in the Colorado River extensional corridor that we interpret to be kinematically linked to extension in the central part of the Mojave Desert region. As Ingersoll (1982) noted, the extension vector pointed toward the position of the Mendocino triple junction throughout the Neogene, indicating that space-making processes at the continental margin control how and where extension occurred (Glazner and Bartley, 1984; Bohannon and Parsons, 1995). North-directed extension in the Mojave Desert region would have been highly discordant to this trend.

Second, structural markers across the Mojave Desert region, including the dike swarms already noted, maintain a consistent northwest strike (Fig. 5). Although the factors that produced this consistent orientation are not well known, their parallelism over a 120 m.y. span and their general parallelism to the continental margin indicate that plate-boundary orientation exerts a major control.

Finally, Ross's (1995) study of the western Cady Mountains is consistent with an original north-south orientation of extension in that local area but does not require it. Ross found large clockwise declination anomalies in Miocene strata. Extension orientation was inferred on the basis of a single fault of unknown kinematics that he assumed to be a large-displacement normal fault. Other interpretations of this poorly exposed fault clearly are possible.

Given these considerations, we interpret the present northeast-southwest orientation of early Miocene kinematic indicators to be close to their original orientation. Extension was probably coupled with the evolving plate margin in the manner proposed by Ingersoll (1982) and Glazner and Bartley (1984), such that extension is a response of the plate margin to the divergent component of Pacific–North American plate interaction (see the subsequent section on Plate-Tectonic Setting).

Areal extent of extension

The fraction of the Mojave Desert region that was affected by mid-Tertiary extension is highly controversial (Fig. 6). Dokka (1989) and Tennyson (1989) proposed that much of the region, including virtually all of the western and most of the eastern Mojave block, was significantly extended in the Miocene. However, field observations indicate that much of the area included by these authors probably was unaffected by extension and that the dominant form of Cenozoic deformation was crustal shortening.

Dokka (1989) proposed that steeply dipping Miocene strata in the Kramer Hills (western Mojave block) were tilted above a shallow extensional detachment fault that surfaces near Leuhman Ridge on Edwards Air Force Base. However, Dokka's (1989) cross section is incompatible with geologic relationships exposed in these hills. Field data clearly demonstrate that these strata and their basal nonconformity are tightly folded (Dibblee, 1967a; Bartley et al., 1990; Linn et al., this volume). Leuhman Ridge consists of shattered basement rocks and is probably the core of a denuded late Cenozoic anticline. Isoclinal folds are spectacularly exposed in nearby ranges (Fig. 4; Bartley et al., 1990). Our reconnaissance of Cenozoic strata in most of the hills of the western part of the Mojave block corroborates Dibblee's (1967a) observation that this style of deformation is common and that most contacts between basement and cover rocks in the area are depositional.

Stratigraphic data also are inconsistent with significant extension in the western part of the Mojave block. Lower Miocene strata there are predominantly fine-grained lake deposits and tuffs, unlike the conglomerates and breccias that were deposited during extension in the central part of the Mojave Desert region. These strata are consistent with an origin outside the area of significant extension (Fillmore et al., 1994).

In the eastern Mojave block, many ranges that lie within the Daggett terrane (see Fig. 6) of Dokka (1989) are essentially devoid of Cenozoic deformation (Dibblee and Bassett, 1966, 1967b, 1967c; Glazner and Bartley, 1990). Closer to Barstow, modest amounts of extension are expressed by homoclinally tilted strata in the Newberry and Cady Mountains (Dokka, 1986; Glazner, 1988; see subsequent discussion), but aggregate extension in these areas is likely to have been small, on the order of a few kilometers. Field relationships in the Rodman Mountains indicate no evidence for significant extension and, in fact, that tilting there results from late Cenozoic transpression (Dibblee, 1990; Glazner et al., 2000). We conclude that significant extension in the Mojave block was restricted to the area near and northwest of Barstow (Fig. 6).

Reinterpretation of the Newberry Mountains

The Newberry Mountains occupy a key area in the Mojave block between highly extended rocks in the area northwest of Barstow and weakly to unextended rocks in the Rodman Mountains and ranges to the south and east. Dokka (1986, 1989) and Dokka and Woodburne (1986) proposed that the Newberry Mountains are underlain by a major extensional structure, the Newberry Mountains detachment fault. However, our reexamination of most of the exposures of the proposed Newberry Mountains detachment fault yielded no evidence for low-angle faulting. The contacts interpreted to be the Newberry Mountains detachment fault and related low-angle normal faults are high- to moderate-angle faults, intrusive contacts, or nonconformities.

Geologic maps of two key areas are displayed in Figure 7. Contacts between basement and cover rocks southwest of Newberry Springs were described as spectacular examples of a low-angle normal fault (e.g., Figs. 24 and 25 in Dokka and Woodburne, 1986; Fig. 12 in Dokka, 1986). However, the contact shown in these figures is intrusive and dips 50° to the north (Fig. 7A). The contact between basement and Tertiary rocks on the north side of the same hill is a nonconformity with Miocene tuffaceous rocks deposited on Mesozoic granitic rocks. Dikes emanating from the plug cut both the tuffaceous rocks and granitic rocks, demonstrating no displacement across the contact between basement and Tertiary rocks. Other such contacts in the area southwest of Newberry Springs are depositional, intrusive, or high-angle faults.

Figure 7B is a geologic map of the north-central Newberry Mountains. Much of the contact between basement and Tertiary rocks in this region was interpreted to be the Newberry Mountains detachment fault (Figs. 4 and 11 in Dokka, 1986). How-

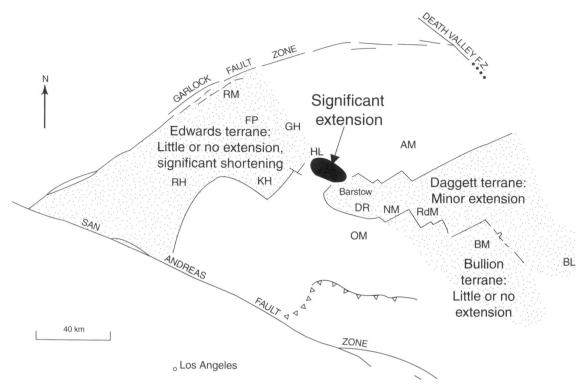

Figure 6. Interpretation of the area affected by extension. Patterned areas outline the extensional domains of Dokka (1986). Data presented herein indicate that significant extension was confined to a small area northwest of Barstow; see also Figure 10. Locations: AM—Alvord Mountain, BL—Bristol Lake, BM—Bullion Mountains, DR—Daggett Ridge, FP—Fremont Peak, GH—Gravel Hills, HL—Harper Lake, KH—Kramer Hills, NM—Newberry Mountains, OM—Ord Mountains, RdM—Rodman Mountains, RH—Rosamond Hills, RM—Rand Mountains.

ever, our mapping shows that this contact is defined by an array of intersecting east-striking and northwest-striking high-angle faults that put Tertiary strata on the south against brecciated granite. Kinematic data from a 5 km reach of this fault are shown in Figure 8; these indicate predominantly oblique-normal displacement (Fig. 9). None of the exposed faults dips shallowly and most dip >50°. In several areas, outcrops of brecciated granitic rocks north of the fault rise up steeply 20–75 m above adjacent Tertiary rocks (Fig. 7), precluding a low-angle fault contact with Tertiary rocks in the hanging wall as shown by Dokka (1986, his Fig. 11).

Several other lines of evidence argue against exposure of a large-displacement, low-angle normal fault in the Newberry Mountains. For example, the northwest- to north-striking dacite dike swarm mapped by Dibblee and Bassett (1966) intrudes both cover rocks and basement. Individual dikes are subperpendicular to bedding in cover rocks regardless of bedding attitude, showing that dike injection predated tilting. Because the dikes are tilted and cut contacts between basement and Tertiary rocks, they demonstrate that there has been no significant movement across proposed strands of the Newberry Mountains detachment fault in the vicinity of the dike swarm. Conversely, basement and cover exposures west of the swarm lack dikes, indicating that there has been no significant relative movement

between cover and basement since the early Miocene dike swarm was emplaced.

Another argument against major extension in the Newberry Mountains is the character of the proposed Newberry Mountains detachment fault. Where not intrusive or depositional, contacts between basement and cover rocks are steeply to moderately dipping faults that differ from well-studied detachment faults in other parts of the southwestern United States (e.g., Davis et al., 1980, 1986; Glazner et al., 1989) in the following ways: (1) The contacts rarely dip less than ~50°, and footwall rocks typically stand topographically well above hanging-wall rocks. (2) Footwall rocks lack the distinctive structures and minerals of detachment-fault footwalls (e.g., chlorite breccia and mylonite). (3) Kinematic indicators (generally grooved and striated fault surfaces) typically rake steeply in the fault plane at a high angle to the proposed transport direction on the Newberry Mountains detachment fault (Fig. 9), precluding these fault surfaces from being the upturned edges of an otherwise low-angle fault. (4) Mesozoic granitic rocks near the Azucar Mine, which were described by Dokka (1986) as lying immediately below the Newberry Mountains detachment fault, are undeformed and unbrecciated.

Moderate extension of perhaps a few kilometers across moderately to steeply dipping domino-style normal faults, most

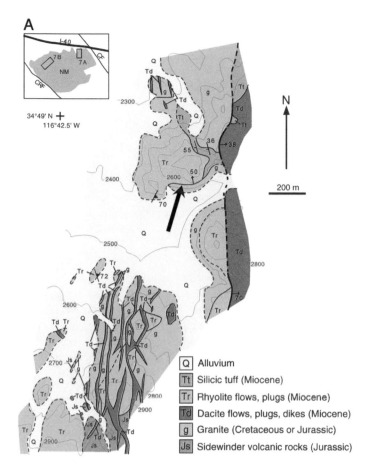

A

34°49' N
116°42.5' W

N

200 m

Figure 7. (A) Geologic map of the area southwest of Newberry Springs; contour interval is 100 m. The contact between rhyolite (Tr) and granite in the northern part of this area (bold arrow), mapped as the Newberry Mountains detachment fault by Dokka (1986), is here interpreted as an intrusive contact that dips 50° to the north. Inset map: CF—Calico fault, CRF—Camp Rock fault, NM—Newberry Mountains; locations of maps A and B are shown. (B) Geologic map of the north-central Newberry Mountains; contour interval is 100 m. Much of the contact between Tertiary rocks and granite was mapped as a detachment fault by Dokka (1986). We interpret the contact as an intersecting set of high- to moderate-angle faults, as shown.

Q Alluvium
Tt Silicic tuff (Miocene)
Tr Rhyolite flows, plugs (Miocene)
Td Dacite flows, plugs, dikes (Miocene)
g Granite (Cretaceous or Jurassic)
Js Sidewinder volcanic rocks (Jurassic)

B

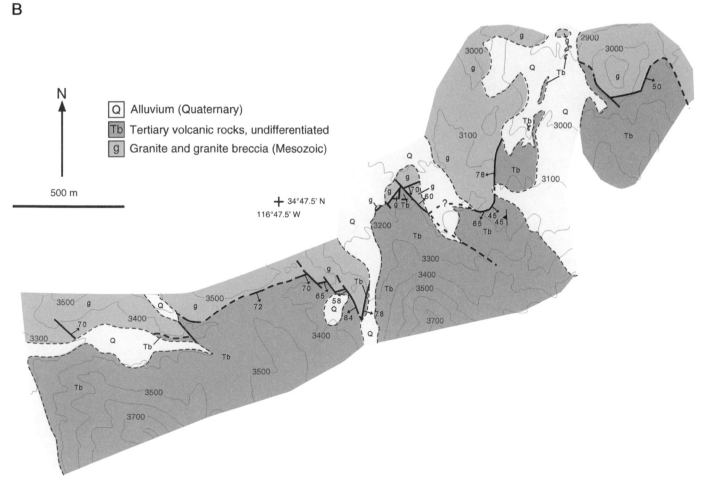

N

Q Alluvium (Quaternary)
Tb Tertiary volcanic rocks, undifferentiated
g Granite and granite breccia (Mesozoic)

500 m

34°47.5' N
116°47.5' W

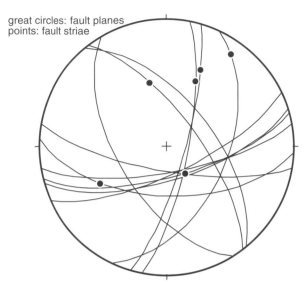

great circles: fault planes
points: fault striae

Figure 8. Kinematic data from the faults in the north-central Newberry Mountains (Fig. 7B). None of the measured faults dips less than 50°; most are steep, and slickenlines and grooves are consistent with oblique extension of the area.

Figure 9. View to west of grooves along a planar fault surface in the north-central Newberry Mountains. Grooves on this fault, which strikes 011° and dips 76° toward the camera, indicate left-normal displacement.

of which were recognized by Dokka (1986, 1989) and assigned postdetachment ages, clearly affected the Newberry Mountains. Whether these normal faults root into an unexposed detachment is unknown. The Peach Springs Tuff (18.5 Ma; Nielson et al., 1990) was deposited in angular unconformity across tilted lower Miocene strata in the Newberry Mountains (Bartley et al., 1990; Buesch, 1992); therefore, modest extensional tilting in the Newberry Mountains probably overlapped in time with formation of the metamorphic core complex to the northwest.

Many outcrops of orange- and red-stained, cavernous,

brecciated granitic rocks in the northwestern Newberry Mountains are landslide sheets and megabreccias. This can be seen in the area northwest of the Azucar Mine, where conglomeratic rocks are interbedded with granite megabreccia. Although complicated by later faults, the megabreccias appear to grade upward and laterally northward into highly brecciated granitic rocks. Many of the rocks were mapped as granite breccia by Dibblee (1970), and some were mapped as intact basement. Sedimentary interbeds are generally lacking, but the breccias are crudely stratified on the 1 to 10 m scale. The general appearance and continuity of the brecciated rocks leads us to interpret most of these outcrops as landslide deposits (e.g., Fillmore, 1993). The landslide deposits must have been shed off a significant topographic escarpment, probably the northeast-striking fault system mapped in Figure 7B.

We therefore conclude that extension is relatively modest in the Newberry Mountains and that the southern limit of highly extended crust in the Mojave block is located north of the Newberry Mountains. Relative uplift across the southern boundary of the extended domain may have provided the source for the granite landslides in the northern Newberry Mountains.

Displacement transfer in the extensional systems

Extension was probably accommodated laterally by various transfer mechanisms (Fig. 10). Bartley and Glazner (1991) proposed that early Miocene extension in the Colorado River trough is kinematically linked to extension near Barstow by distributed dextral shear and clockwise rotation of a weakly extended area in the central part of the Mojave block. Martin et al. (1993) proposed that the highly extended region near Barstow is bounded on the southeast by a cryptic right-lateral fault that runs under the Mojave River valley and separates an extended terrane to the northwest from modestly extended crust to the southeast.

The northwestern limit of extension is less well defined. It is tempting to invoke Miocene extension to unroof the Rand Schist in the northern Mojave block, but late Mesozoic biotite Ar cooling ages are widespread across the area; therefore, unroofing of the Rand Schist is not related to Miocene extension (Jacobson, 1990). Mapping in the northern Mojave block (e.g., Fletcher et al., this volume, Chapter 8; Sabin et al., 1994) has not yielded evidence for significant Cenozoic extension, consistent with the Ar studies. Goodman and Malin (1992) and Tennyson (1989) presented evidence for extension in the southern San Joaquin Valley, to the west-northwest of the Mojave block, but it is not clear whether this deformation was linked to that near Barstow.

Transpression, extension, and the origin of Mojave block topography

Transpression and strike-slip faulting have shaped much of the present-day topography of the Mojave block (Bartley et al.,

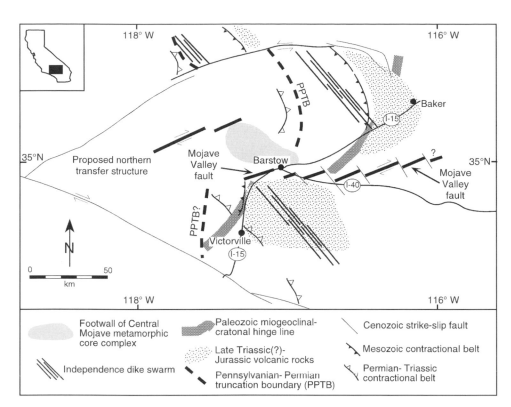

Figure 10. Map showing pre-Tertiary structural and stratigraphic features that are offset along the Mojave Valley fault, an inferred transfer fault that bounds the Central Mojave metamorphic core complex on the south. Modified from Martin et al. (1993).

1990; Glazner and Bartley, 1994; Glazner et al., 1994). This view is in sharp contrast to that of Dokka and Travis (1990), who proposed that much of the region's topography is controlled by transtension, which produced several large pull-apart basins.

There are several problems with their interpretation, the most important of which is that many of the basins that they consider to be pull-aparts are bounded by or contain contractional structures. Specific examples of this geometry include (1) the Mojave River valley south of the Calico Mountains, which is bounded by steep dextral-reverse faults (Glazner and Bartley, 1994; Glazner et al., 1994); (2) valleys in the southern Mojave block, east of the San Bernardino Mountains, where Dibblee (1967b, 1968b) mapped contractional structures in Quaternary alluvium; and (3) most of the northeastern Mojave block, where Schermer et al. (1996) reported that most of the east-trending faults have a significant component of reverse slip. Thus, although some basins in the Mojave block may be transtensional in origin, contraction caused by transpressional faulting has produced much of the current topography in the region.

Strike-slip faulting

Perhaps the most apparent structural features of the Mojave Desert region are the Miocene–Holocene strike-slip faults that cut across it (Fig. 11). In fact, the Mojave block is defined in terms of the bounding strike-slip faults that serve to isolate it

from surrounding areas (e.g., Davis and Burchfiel, 1973). These faults and their slip histories have been the subject of numerous investigations (e.g., Dibblee, 1961; Garfunkel, 1974; Dokka, 1983; Dokka and Travis, 1990; Luyendyk, 1991; Schermer et al., 1996).

There are two basic domains of strike-slip faults in the Mojave block: (1) northwest-striking, right-lateral faults throughout much of what is referred to as fault domain 1 in Figure 11 and (2) west-striking, left-lateral faults that are mainly found in the northeastern Mojave block (fault domain 2 in Fig. 11). Other significant left-slip faults include the Garlock fault and faults bounding the eastern Transverse Ranges in the southern part of the Mojave block. The first attempt to relate these strike-slip fault domains was made by Garfunkel (1974), and his model still forms the basic framework being tested at present.

Our interpretation for the development of the strike-slip faults combines interpretations made by Schermer et al. (1996) for the northeastern Mojave block, Dokka (1983) for the western Mojave block, and Richard (1993) for the eastern Transverse Ranges and the southeastern Mojave block. These interpretations of kinematics are fairly complete, honor geologic relationships, and are consistent with most of the paleomagnetic data and geologic markers. Slip along the eastern boundary is less certain (see later description). We discuss the faulting by dividing structures into four fault domains (Fig. 11) on the basis of location and kinematics. We summarize our interpretation by summing up the amount of northwest-directed shear accumulated across the Mojave block.

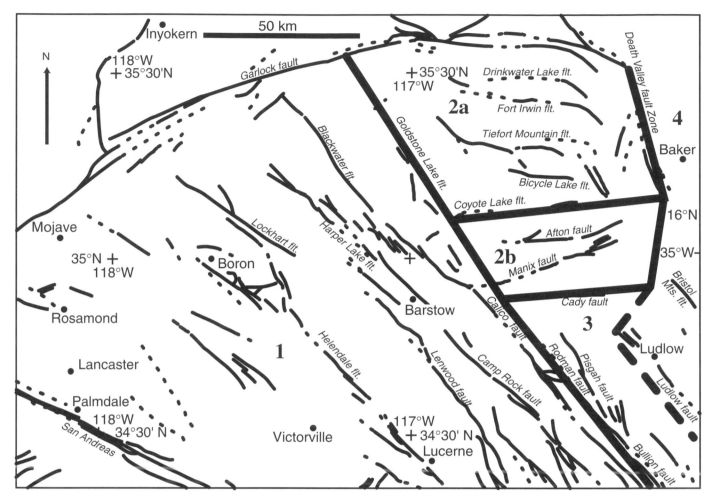

Figure 11. Fault domains 1–4 discussed in text.

Schermer et al. (1996) presented the results of detailed mapping and paleomagnetic studies for the northeastern Mojave block (Fig. 11, domain 2a). Their conclusion was that displacement is distributed across roughly east-striking faults that bound structural subblocks roughly 50 km long and 7 to 10 km wide. The eastern boundary of this fault array is the southern Death Valley fault zone (Soda-Avawatz fault zone of Schermer et al., 1996); the western boundary is the Goldstone Lake fault; the northern boundary is the Garlock fault; the southern boundary is the Coyote Lake fault. Clockwise block rotation accomplished by field-documented sinistral slip results in ~22 km of dextral shear across the region (~23° of clockwise rotation). An additional ~11 km may result from rigid-body rotation of the area as a whole according to paleomagnetic results (an added 15° of rotation; Fig. 14 in Schermer et al., 1996). This deformation results in 33 km of dextral shear across a roughly northwest-striking plane (Fig. 11).

Faults in domain 2b give similar results for rotation. Assuming subblocks ~7 km wide with ~5 km of slip (on the Afton and Manix faults; mapping by J.D. Walker; Meek and

Battles, 1990) gives ~22° of clockwise rotation for this subblock (by using the method of Ron et al., 1984). This value is very similar to that derived by Schermer et al. (1996). Movements on these faults do not, however, add to the total documented slip in domains 2a and 2b (e.g., ~22 km).

This displacement must be balanced by slip across faults between the Calico and Ludlow faults (domain 3). The best estimate for slip across these faults, 20 km, comes from Richard (1993), who estimated ~30 km of cumulative slip across faults from the Camp Rock to the Ludlow fault. Subtracting 13 km for the Camp Rock and Calico faults (e.g., Dokka and Travis, 1990) leaves ~17 km to feed into the southern part of domain 2, ~13 km less than the estimate that is given by Schermer et al. (1996). We see two possible causes for this discrepancy: (1) there is deformation in domain 2b that results in an increase in the amount of right shear from south to north or (2) the paleomagnetic results in domain 2a do not reflect actual vertical-axis rotations. At present, we take 21 km as the best estimate of right slip across domains 2a, 2b, and 3 (average of Schermer et al. [1996] without rigid-body rotation, and Richard [1993]).

The next component we consider is slip between domains 2 and 4. Faults that accommodate this deformation are the Death Valley fault zone to the north and the Ludlow, Broadwell Lake, Bristol Mountains, and Granite Mountains faults (hereafter, Ludlow–Granite Mountains fault system) to the south (Fig. 11; Granite Mountains fault is not shown, but is located immediately east of the Bristol Mountains fault). Davis (1977) and Davis and Burchfiel (1993) estimated ~8 km of right slip across the southern Death Valley fault zone on the basis of offset of pre-Cenozoic rocks and the inferred continuation of the Garlock fault. Alternatively, Brady (1984) reported ~20 km of slip from the distance between alluvial-fan deposits and their probable source. Richard (1993) reported a maximum of 16 km of right slip based on relationships in southeastern California; no minimum was given. We take 8 km as the minimum and 20 km for the maximum estimates of dextral slip across this zone.

Dokka and Travis (1990) estimated a combined slip of 37.5 km across the Ludlow–Granite Mountains fault system based on palinspastic restoration of fault-bounded subblocks. Their interpretation requires ~20 km of slip across the Granite Mountains fault, but Howard and Miller (1992) estimated significantly less slip across this fault (0–10 km of strike slip, with a significant reverse component) on the basis of geologic relationships. We take right slip across the Death Valley fault zone to be between 8 and 20 km. We are unsure exactly how to distribute the slip among the various faults within the Ludlow–Granite Mountains fault system, but an average slip of ~4 km across each fault does not violate any geologic relationships of which we are aware.

The discrepancy between Dokka and Travis's (1990) estimate and ours for net slip across the Ludlow–Granite Mountains fault system appears to be explained by differing assumptions. Dokka and Travis assumed little or no slip across faults now known to have accommodated significant right slip (e.g., Harper Lake fault). Also, Dokka and Travis assumed that misfits between fault subblocks in the western and central Mojave block were accommodated by opening of pull-apart basins between rigid subblocks, whereas we interpret the field evidence to favor north-south intrablock contraction as a major mechanism for accommodating misfits. These differing assumptions lead us to infer a substantially larger amount of deformation in the western Mojave block and forced Dokka and Travis to transfer an equivalent amount of displacement eastward to the Ludlow–Granite Mountains fault system.

The last region to consider is domain 1, the western Mojave block. Net-slip values across the main faults are relatively well known and include Helendale, 3 km (Miller and Morton, 1980); Camp Rock–Harper Lake, 3 km (Bartley et al., 1992; Glazner et al., 1994); and Calico–Blackwater, 10 km (Garfunkel, 1974). The only regionally extensive fault with unknown slip is the Lockhart-Lenwood fault. There is fault-zone deformation associated with the Lenwood fault (e.g., the Lenwood anticline west of Barstow), but no clearly offset markers. Hence, right

slip across the western Mojave block is ~16 km, with the possibility of significant addition from the Lenwood fault.

Summing geologically demonstrated slips across the Mojave block yields a minimum of ~44 km and a maximum of ~72 km of right shear (Table 1). Most of the strain is concentrated in the band from the southern Death Valley fault zone to the Calico fault. This result makes sense if strike-slip in the Mojave block balances Basin and Range extension (i.e., Davis and Burchfiel, 1973; Walker and Glazner, 1999): dextral shear is greatest in the region south of the area stretching from Death Valley to the Panamint Valley, where extension has been most active over the past 12 m.y. This estimate is similar in magnitude but different in detail to the 65 km value given by Dokka and Travis (1990).

Plate-tectonic setting

The early Miocene episode of volcanism and deformation in the Mojave Desert occurred during the changeover from subduction to transform-fault motion at the continental margin (Ingersoll, 1982; Glazner and Bartley, 1984). The kinematics of this process have been refined in a series of papers (Atwater, 1970; Nicholson et al., 1994; Bohannon and Parsons, 1995; Atwater and Stock, 1998). Initial contact of the Pacific and North American plates occurred in the late Oligocene, forming two triple junctions separated by a transform fault that evolved into the San Andreas system. The northern triple junction (the Mendocino triple junction) migrated past southern California from late Oligocene to middle Miocene time.

Several studies have linked volcanism and tectonism in the Mojave Desert region to migration of the Mendocino triple junction. For example, Glazner and Supplee (1982) and Glazner and Bartley (1984) showed that volcanism and tectonism migrated northward through the Mojave Desert region, tracking the triple junction. They proposed that volcanism and tectonism were triggered by two effects: flexure of the North American plate above the subducted part of the Mendocino Fracture Zone, and extension of the North American plate into the Mendocino triple junction, which was unstable and migrated away from the

TABLE 1. NORTHWEST-DIRECTED DEXTRAL SHEAR ACROSS THE MOJAVE BLOCK

Domain	Minimum	Maximum
Domain 1	16 km	19 km
Domain 2a	20 km	33 km
Domain 3	10 km	20 km
Domain 4	8 km	20 km
Total	44 km	72 km

Note: Slips in domains 2 and 3 do not contribute to the total displacement. Minimum and maximum slips for domain 1 and domain 2a are inferred from Richard (1993) and taken from Schermer et al. (1996), respectively. Slip in domain 2b (not listed) is consistent with that in domain 2a. The maximum slip for domain 1 assumes that the Lenwood-Lockhart fault has 3 km of right slip, similar to that of the Helendale and Camp Rock faults.

North American plate (Ingersoll, 1982; Atwater and Stock, 1998). Stratigraphic studies (Glazner and Loomis, 1984; Glazner et al., 2000) support this flexure model. Dickinson (1997) and Atwater and Stock (1998) related volcanism and tectonism in southern California to development of slab windows inboard of the transform margin and south of the Mendocino Fracture Zone.

Correlating geologic events in the Mojave block with the plate-tectonic record requires knowing the location of the Mojave block relative to stable North America in the late Oligocene and early Miocene. The plate reconstruction of Atwater and Stock (1998) locates points on the Pacific plate with respect to stable North America, but the Mojave block lies in the deformed western margin of North America and must be restored.

Atwater and Stock (1998) used the reconstruction of Wernicke and Snow (1998) to restore the Sierran block to an early Miocene position significantly south of its present location. Northwestward movement of the Sierran block from 8 Ma to the present in this reconstruction drags the Mojave block to the northwest. Thus, in the early Miocene, this reconstruction places the Mojave block ~100 km south and 150 km east of its present position relative to the Colorado Plateau. However, uncertainties in the reconstruction (Wernicke et al., 1988) allow that the northward shift could have been significantly smaller.

We see two significant problems with 100 km of northward translation of the Mojave block relative to stable North America. First, this shift requires 100 km of dextral displacement since 8 Ma across a fault or set of faults between the western Mojave block and the Colorado Plateau. Northwest-striking dextral faults in the Mojave block have observed slips of about half this amount (as previously described), and no significant faults of appropriate age and kinematics are known between the Mojave block and the Colorado Plateau. Second, if this reconstruction is followed, then there is little correlation between plate-tectonic events and geologic events in the Mojave block and areas north (discussed subsequently). However, if the Mojave block is interpreted to have remained at its present latitude since the early Miocene, then the correlation is excellent.

These concepts are presented in Figure 12. In the Atwater and Stock reconstruction, at 28 Ma the subducted part of the Mendocino Fracture Zone was under the middle of the Mojave block, but there are no geologic events that record its passage. At 24 Ma, the Mendocino triple junction and subducted part of the Mendocino Fracture Zone were well north of the Mojave block at about the latitude of the southernmost Sierra Nevada. As a result, a slab window would have underlain the southern San Joaquin basin, and most of the Mojave block would have been underlain by the subducted Farallon plate. There are no known late Oligocene–early Miocene events (volcanism, faulting, basin formation) in the southern Sierra Nevada or Owens Valley region that record these events, and the intense extension and magmatism that began in the Mojave block at ca. 24 Ma are inconsistent with the placement of these slab windows. Subsidence of the southernmost San Joaquin basin in the late Oli-

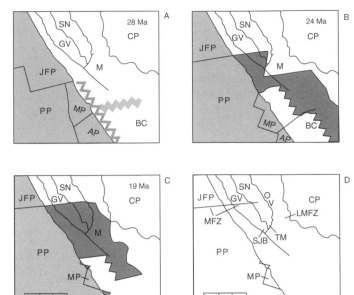

Figure 12. Slab-window reconstruction of Atwater and Stock (1998). Lighter gray marks oceanic plates; darker gray marks slab windows; zigzags indicate incipient breaks in subducted slabs. Arguello, Juan de Fuca, and Monterey plates are remnants of the Farallon plate. This reconstruction of the Mojave Desert region and the Sierra Nevada is not entirely consistent with geologic events in detail (see text). In particular, at 19 Ma, most of the southern Sierra Nevada and Owens Valley would have been underlain by slab windows, but there is no geologic record of such geometry. Panel D gives locations of features discussed in text superimposed on 19 Ma reconstruction. AP—Arguello plate, BC—Baja California, CP—Colorado Plateau, GV—Great Valley, JFP—Juan de Fuca plate, LFMZ—Lake Mead fault zone, M—Mojave block, MFZ—Mendocino Fracture Zone, MP—Monterey plate, OV—Owens Valley, PP—Pacific plate, SJB—San Joaquin basin, SN—Sierra Nevada.

gocene may be related to passage of the Mendocino triple junction, but the restored locations of this area and the Tehachapi Mountains are especially in doubt owing to uncertainties in how to restore the southern tail of the Sierra Nevada (Atwater and Stock, 1998). At 19 Ma, the Mendocino triple junction was well north of the southern Sierra Nevada, and the predicted slab windows underlay most of the southern half of California. Growth of the slab windows in this analysis would lead to eastward expansion of the volcanic fields, inconsistent with observation.

We therefore favor an alternative reconstruction in which early to middle Miocene motion of the Sierra Nevada relative to the Colorado Plateau was more toward southwest than west. This extension vector lies within the uncertainties of the Wernicke and Snow (1998) reconstruction, and it has at least three advantages over the reconstruction in which the Mojave block moved significantly northward. First, it positions the Mojave block in the early Miocene at a more northern latitude where its geologic history correlates well with the position of the Mendocino triple junction and associated slab window. Second, the

Lake Mead fault zone, which forms the southeastern sidewall of the extensional domain analyzed by Wernicke and Snow (1998), strikes southwest. It is likely that the Garlock fault, which forms a similar lateral boundary farther to the west, had a similar southwestern strike prior to late Cenozoic transpressional modification (e.g., Garfunkel, 1974; Dokka and Travis, 1990; Bartley et al., 1990). Third, southwest-directed Miocene extension required by this reconstruction matches the middle Tertiary extension vector throughout the southwestern United States.

Figure 13 demonstrates that volcanism in the Mojave Desert region was not triggered by the enlarging slab window, but may have been triggered by the northern edge of the slab window and the subducted Mendocino Fracture Zone. It is apparent that the fit between the inception of volcanism and the position of the Mendocino Fracture Zone would be improved if the Mojave Desert region was restored somewhat southward in the Miocene relative to stable North America—perhaps 50 km, about half the distance used by Atwater and Stock (1998) and

well within the uncertainties of the Wernicke and Snow (1998) reconstruction.

The kinematics of extension calculated from the Atwater and Stock (1998) reconstruction match observations in the Mojave block well (Fig. 14). From their reconstruction (Atwater and Stock, 1998, their Table 2 and Figure 3), in the early Miocene (20–15 Ma), the Pacific plate was moving away from the North American plate at 35 mm/yr along a vector oriented 300°. The orientation of the Pacific-North American boundary (the evolving San Andreas transform) was ~323°. This geometry resolves into 32 mm/yr parallel to the plate boundary and 14 mm/yr perpendicular to it (azimuth 053°). This azimuth is close to the observed extension direction of ~045°, and the rate of extension would require ~4 m.y. to accumulate the observed extension of ~60 km, consistent with the geochronologic data (ca. 23–18 Ma) presented by Walker et al. (1995).

CONCLUSIONS

The Cenozoic geology of the Mojave Desert region is dominated by three tectonic regimes. Prior to late Oligocene time, the region was a tectonically quiescent, externally drained plateau that left little geologic record. This condition ended in the late Oligocene when the North America–Farallon subduction zone encountered the Farallon–Pacific spreading ridge. This ridge-trench encounter formed the unstable Mendocino trench-fault-fault triple junction, the proto–San Andreas dextral transform plate boundary, and one or more slab windows beneath

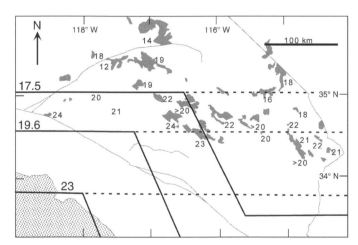

Figure 13. Evolving slab windows according to the reconstruction of Dickinson (1997). In this reconstruction, plate boundaries are plotted on an unrestored base map of southern California. For each time (23, 19.6, and 17.5 Ma), the corresponding slab window is delimited on its north and east by solid lines. The east-west line along the northern boundary of each window represents the Mendocino Fracture Zone; the dashed extension represents the Mendocino Fracture Zone in the subducted plate. Gray areas are outcrops of early Miocene volcanic rocks; numbers are ages of inception of volcanism in each field. Note that volcanism began simultaneously across the Mojave Desert region in the early Miocene. If volcanism was triggered by development of the slab window, then the volcanic activity should have migrated inland to the northeast, a pattern that is inconsistent with observation (although coastal volcanism may have been triggered by the slab window; Dickinson, 1997). The pattern of inception of volcanism is consistent with triggering by subduction of the Mendocino Fracture Zone (Glazner and Bartley, 1984). Sources for inception of volcanism: Armstrong and Higgins, 1973; Burke et al., 1982; Cox and Diggles, 1986; Davis and Fleck, 1977; Dokka and Baksi, 1989; Glazner, 1988; Glazner et al., 2000; McCurry, 1988; Sabin et al., 1994; Sherrod and Nielson, 1993; Smith et al. (this volume); Walker et al., 1995; Weigand, 1982.

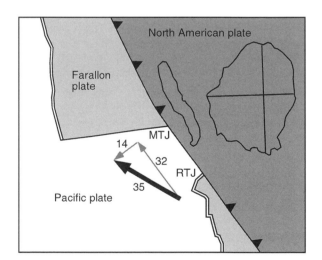

Figure 14. Early Miocene plate kinematics of the Mojave Desert region, from Atwater and Stock (1998). Relative motion of 35 mm/yr between the Pacific plate and stable North America can be resolved into 32 mm/yr parallel to the transform plate margin and 14 mm/yr perpendicular to it. Black teeth indicate remnant subduction zones north and south of the transform margin. Slip partitioning like this explains the direction, magnitude, and rate of extension in the Mojave block. Outlines of the Colorado Plateau and Sierra Nevada shown for reference. MTJ—Mendocino triple junction; RTJ—Rivera triple junction.

the North American plate. These three plate-tectonic features governed later evolution of the Mojave Desert area.

Instability of the triple junction, transtensional obliquity of the Pacific plate-North American plate relative-motion vector, and the slab window all probably contributed to a wave of lithospheric extension and magmatism that migrated northwestward across the southwestern United States. Early Miocene crustal extension mainly affected the Basin and Range province to the east of the Mojave Desert region, but 40–60 km of early Miocene extension took place to form the Central Mojave metamorphic core complex in a restricted area that is surrounded by areas of little or no extension.

We interpret this pattern of highly localized large-magnitude extension to record an east-northeast-trending belt of dextral transtension that linked the northern end of early Miocene extension in the Colorado River trough southwestward to the active proto-San Andreas transform. The inferred Mojave Valley fault linked the Colorado River extensional corridor to the Central Mojave metamorphic core complex. No specific structure has yet been identified that links the northwestern termination of the Central Mojave metamorphic core complex westward to the early Miocene plate boundary, but the absence of evidence for significant early Miocene extension in the northern Mojave block indicates that such a structure must trend westward from a location between The Buttes and Fremont Peak. The estimated extension rate across the Central Mojave metamorphic core complex, ~15 mm/yr, is compatible with extension being driven by partitioning of the divergent component of the Pacific-North America relative plate motion into intracontinental extension.

Northward migration of the Mendocino triple junction away from the Mojave Desert area correlated with the change from transtensional to transpressional deformation that has dominated Mojave geology from the middle or late Miocene to the present. About 50 km of dextral shear have accumulated across a complexly branching array of northwest-striking right-slip and west-striking left-slip faults that transfer motion from the San Andreas fault system to the Walker Lane belt. Sporadic but locally intense folding and reverse faulting accompanied late Cenozoic dextral shear and accommodated a yet-undetermined amount of north-south transpression across the Mojave block.

ACKNOWLEDGMENTS

This work was supported by the Geothermal Program Office of the U.S. Navy and by National Science Foundation grants (EAR) 8219032, 8817076, 8816941, 8917291, 8917300, and 9204961 (to Glazner), 8816628 and 8916802 (to Walker), and 8816944 and 8916838 (to Bartley). Ray Ingersoll and Elizabeth Schermer provided critical reviews that significantly improved the presentation. Our work was greatly aided by Tom Dibblee's maps and discussions and field trips with our colleagues, including Frank Monastero, David Miller, Jane Nielson, Keith Howard, Drew Coleman, and many, many others.

REFERENCES CITED

Armstrong, R.L., and Higgins, R.E., 1973, K-Ar dating of the beginning of Tertiary volcanism in the Mojave Desert, California: Geological Society of America Bulletin, v. 84, p. 1095–1100.

Atwater, T., 1970, Implications of plate tectonics for the Cenozoic tectonic evolution of western North America: Geological Society of America Bulletin, v. 81, p. 3513–3536.

Atwater, T., and Stock, J., 1998, Pacific-North America plate tectonics of the Neogene southwestern United States: An update: International Geology Review, v. 40, p. 375–402.

Axen, G.J., Taylor, W.J., and Bartley, J.M., 1993, Space-time patterns and tectonic controls of Tertiary extension and magmatism in the Great Basin of the western United States: Geological Society of America Bulletin, v. 105, p. 56–76.

Bartley, J.M., and Glazner, A.F., 1991, En echelon Miocene rifting in the southwestern United States and model for vertical-axis rotation in continental extension: Geology, v. 19, p. 1165–1168.

Bartley, J.M., Glazner, A.F., and Schermer, E.R., 1990, North-south contraction of the Mojave block and strike-slip tectonics in southern California: Science, v. 248, p. 1398–1401.

Bartley, J.M., Glazner, A.F., Fletcher, J.M., Martin, M.W., and Walker, J.D., 1992, Amount and nature of dextral offset on Neogene faults near Barstow, California: Eos (Transactions, American Geophysical Union), v. 73, p. 363.

Boettcher, S.S., and Walker, J.D., 1993, Geologic evolution of Iron Mountain, central Mojave Desert, California: Tectonics, v. 12, p. 372–386.

Bohannon, R.G., and Parsons, T., 1995, Tectonic implications of post-30 Ma Pacific and North American relative plate motions: Geological Society of America Bulletin, v. 107, p. 937–959.

Brady, R.H., 1984, Neogene stratigraphy of the Avawatz Mountains between the Garlock and Death Valley fault zones, southern Death Valley, California: Implications as to late Cenozoic tectonism: Sedimentary Geology, v. 38, p. 127–157.

Buesch, D.C., 1992, Incorporation and redistribution of locally derived lithic fragments within a pyroclastic flow: Geological Society of America Bulletin, v. 104, p. 1193–1207.

Burke, D.B., Hillhouse, J.W., McKee, E.H., Miller, S.T., and Morton, J.L., 1982, Cenozoic rocks in the Barstow Basin area of southern California—Stratigraphic relations, radiometric ages, and paleomagnetism: U.S. Geological Survey Bulletin, v. 1529-E, p. 1–16.

Byers, F.M., Jr., 1960, Geology of the Alvord Mountain quadrangle, San Bernardino County, California: U.S. Geological Survey Bulletin, v. 1089-A, 71 p.

Cameron, K.L., Nimz, G.J., Kuentz, D., Niemeyer, S., and Gunn, S., 1989, Southern Cordilleran basaltic andesite suite, southern Chihuahua, Mexico: A link between Tertiary continental arc and flood basalt magmatism in North America: Journal of Geophysical Research, v. 94, p. 7817–7840.

Coleman, D.S., Glazner, A.F., Bartley, J.M., and Carl, B.S., 2000, Cretaceous dikes within the Independence dike swarm in eastern California: Geological Society of America Bulletin, v. 112, p. 504–511.

Cox, B.F., 1987, Stratigraphy, depositional environments, and paleotectonics of the Paleocene and Eocene Goler Formation, El Paso Mountains, California: Geologic summary and roadlog, in Cox, B.F., ed., Basin analysis and paleontology of the Paleocene and Eocene Goler Formation, El Paso Mountains, California: Los Angeles, Pacific Section, Society of Economic Paleontologists and Mineralogists, Book 57, p. 1–29.

Cox, B.F., and Diggles, M.F., 1986, Geologic map of the El Paso Mountains wilderness study area, Kern County, California: U.S. Geological Survey Miscellaneous Field Studies Map MF-1827, scale 1:24 000.

Davis, G.A., 1977, Limitations on displacement and southeastward extent of the Death Valley fault zone, California: California Division of Mines and Geology Special Report 129, p. 27–33.

Davis, G.A., and Burchfiel, B.C., 1973, Garlock fault: An intracratonic transform structure, southern California: Geological Society of America Bulletin, v. 84, p. 1407–1422.

Davis, G.A., and Burchfiel, B.C., 1993, Tectonic problems revisited: The eastern terminus of the Miocene Garlock Fault and the amount of slip on the southern Death Valley fault zone: Geological Society of America Abstracts with Programs, v. 25, p. 28.

Davis, G.A., and Fleck, R.J., 1977, Chronology of Miocene volcanic and structural events, central Owlshead Mountains, eastern San Bernardino County, California: Geological Society of America Abstracts with Programs, v. 9, p. 409.

Davis, G.A., Lister, G.S., and Reynolds, S.J., 1986, Structural evolution of the Whipple and South mountains shear zones, southwestern United States: Geology, v. 14, p. 7–10.

Davis, G.A., Anderson, J.L., Frost, E.G., and Shackelford, T.J., 1980, Mylonitization and detachment faulting in the Whipple-Buckskin-Rawhide Mountains terrane, southeastern California and western Arizona: Geological Society of America Memoir, v. 153, p. 79–129.

Dibblee, T.W., Jr., 1961, Evidence of strike-slip movement on northwest-trending faults in Mojave Desert, California: U.S. Geological Survey Professional Paper, v. 424-B, p. 197–198.

Dibblee, T.W., Jr., 1967a, Areal geology of the western Mojave Desert, California: U.S. Geological Survey Professional Paper 522, p. 1–153.

Dibblee, T.W., Jr., 1967b, Geologic map of the Deadman Lake quadrangle, San Bernardino County, California: U.S. Geological Survey Miscellaneous Geologic Investigations Map I-488, scale 1:62 500.

Dibblee, T.W., Jr., 1967c, Geologic map of the Ludlow quadrangle, San Bernardino County, California: U.S. Geological Survey Map I-477, scale 1:62 500.

Dibblee, T.W., Jr., 1968a, Geology of the Fremont Peak and Opal Mountain quadrangles, California: California Division of Mines and Geology Bulletin, v. 188, 64 p.

Dibblee, T.W., Jr., 1968b, Geologic map of the Twentynine Palms quadrangle, San Bernardino and Riverside counties, California: U.S. Geological Survey Miscellaneous Geologic Investigations Map I-561, scale 1:62 500.

Dibblee, T.W., Jr., 1970, Geologic map of the Daggett quadrangle, San Bernardino County, California: U.S. Geological Survey Map I-592, scale 1:62 500.

Dibblee, T.W., Jr., 1990, Mid-Tertiary volcanic and sedimentary rocks of the Newberry Mountains and vicinity, central Mojave Desert: Unconformable on, or detached from, pre-Cenozoic crustal basement?, in Foster, J.F., and Lewis, L.L., eds., Lower Colorado River extensional terrane and Whipple Mountains guidebook: Santa Ana, California, South Coast Geological Society, p. 62–88.

Dibblee, T.W., Jr., and Bassett, A.M., 1966, Geologic map of the Newberry quadrangle, San Bernardino County, California: U.S. Geological Survey Miscellaneous Geologic Investigations Map I-461, scale 1:62 500.

Dickinson, W.R., 1997, Overview: Tectonic implications of Cenozoic volcanism in coastal California: Geological Society of America Bulletin, v. 109, p. 936.

Dokka, R.K., 1983, Displacements on late Cenozoic strike-slip faults of the central Mojave Desert, California: Geology, v. 11, p. 305–308.

Dokka, R.K., 1986, Patterns and modes of early Miocene crustal extension, central Mojave Desert, California: Geological Society of America Special Paper 208, p. 75–95.

Dokka, R.K., 1989, The Mojave extensional belt of southern California: Tectonics, v. 8, p. 363–390.

Dokka, R.K., and Baksi, A.K., 1989, Age and significance of the Red Buttes Andesite, Kramer Hills, Mojave Desert, California, in Reynolds, R.E., ed., The west-central Mojave Desert: Quaternary studies between Kramer and Afton Canyon, Redlands, California, San Bernardino County Museum Association, p. 51.

Dokka, R.K., and Travis, C.J., 1990, Late Cenozoic strike-slip faulting in the Mojave Desert, California: Tectonics, v. 9, p. 311–340.

Dokka, R.K., and Woodburne, M.O., 1986, Mid-Tertiary extensional tectonics and sedimentation, central Mojave Desert, California: Louisiana State University Publications in Geology and Geophysics, Tectonics and Sedimentation, v. 1, 55 p.

Dokka, R.K., Ross, T.M., and Lu, G., 1998, The trans Mojave-Sierran shear zone and its role in early Miocene collapse of southwestern North America, in Holdsworth, R.E., Strachan, R.A., and Dewey, J.F., eds., Continental transpressional and transtensional tectonics: Geological Society [London] Special Publication 135, p. 183–202.

Fillmore, R.P., 1993, Sedimentation and extensional basin evolution in a Miocene metamorphic core complex setting, Alvord Mountain, central Mojave Desert, California, USA: Sedimentology, v. 40, p. 721–742.

Fillmore, R.P., and Walker, J.D., 1996, Evolution of a supradetachment extensional basin: The lower Miocene Pickhandle Basin, central Mojave Desert, California, in Beratan, K.K., ed., Reconstructing the history of Basin and Range extension using sedimentology and stratigraphy: Geological Society of America Special Paper 303, p. 107–126.

Fillmore, R.P., Walker, J.D., Bartley, J.M., and Glazner, A.F., 1994, Development of three genetically related basins associated with detachment-style faulting: Predicted characteristics and an example from the central Mojave Desert, California: Geology, v. 22, p. 1087–1090.

Fletcher, J.M., and Bartley, J.M., 1994, Constrictional strain in a noncoaxial shear zone: Implications for fold and rock fabric development, central Mojave metamorphic core complex, California: Journal of Structural Geology, v. 16, p. 555–570.

Fletcher, J.M., Bartley, J.M., Martin, M.W., Glazner, A.F., and Walker, J.D., 1995, Large-magnitude continental extension: An example from the central Mojave metamorphic core complex: Geological Society of America Bulletin, v. 107, p. 1468–1483.

Gale, H.S., 1946, Geology of the Kramer borate district, Kern County, California: California Journal of Mines and Geology, v. 42, p. 325–378.

Gardner, D.L., 1940, Geology of the Newberry and Ord Mountains, San Bernardino County, California: California Journal of Mines and Geology, v. 36, p. 257–292.

Garfunkel, Z., 1974, Model for the late Cenozoic tectonic history of the Mojave Desert, California, and its relation to adjacent regions: Geological Society of America Bulletin, v. 5, p. 141–188.

Glazner, A.F., 1988, Stratigraphy, structure, and potassic alteration of Miocene volcanic rocks in the Sleeping Beauty area, central Mojave Desert, California: Geological Society of America Bulletin, v. 100, p. 424–435.

Glazner, A.F., 1990, Recycling of continental crust in Miocene volcanic rocks from the Mojave block, southern California: Geological Society of America Memoir 174, p. 147–168.

Glazner, A.F., and Bartley, J.M., 1984, Timing and tectonic setting of Tertiary low-angle normal faulting and associated magmatism in the southwestern United States: Tectonics, v. 3, p. 385–396.

Glazner, A.F., and Bartley, J.M., 1990, Early Miocene dome emplacement, diking, and limited tectonism in the northern Marble Mountains, eastern Mojave Desert, California, in Foster, J.F., and Lewis, L.L., eds., Lower Colorado River extensional terrane and Whipple Mountains guidebook: Santa Ana, California, South Coast Geological Society, p. 89–97.

Glazner, A.F., and Bartley, J.M., 1994, Eruption of alkali basalts during crustal shortening in southern California: Tectonics, v. 13, p. 493–498.

Glazner, A.F., and Farmer, G.L., 1993, Evolution of late Cenozoic basaltic volcanism in the Mojave Desert, California: Geological Society of America Abstracts with Programs, v. 25, p. 42.

Glazner, A.F., and Loomis, D.P., 1984, Effect of subduction of the Mendocino fracture zone on Tertiary sedimentation in southern California: Sedimentary Geology, v. 38, p. 287–303.

Glazner, A.F., and O'Neil, J.R., 1989, Crustal structure of the Mojave Desert, California: Inferences from Sr- and O-isotope studies of Miocene volcanic rocks: Journal of Geophysical Research, v. 94, p. 7861–7870.

Glazner, A.F., and Supplee, J.A., 1982, Migration of Tertiary volcanism in the southwestern United States and subduction of the Mendocino fracture zone: Earth and Planetary Science Letters, v. 60, p. 429–436.

Glazner, A.F., Bartley, J.M., and Sanner, W.K., 2000, Nature of the southern boundary of the central Mojave Tertiary province, Rodman Mountains, California: Geological Society of America Bulletin, v. 112, p. 34–44.

Glazner, A.F., Bartley, J.M., and Walker, J.D., 1989, Magnitude and significance of Miocene crustal extension in the central Mojave Desert, California: Geology, v. 17, p. 50–53.

Glazner, A.F., Walker, J.D., Bartley, J.M., Fletcher, J.M., Martin, M.W., Schermer, E.R., Boettcher, S.S., Miller, J.S., Fillmore, R.P., and Linn, J.K., 1994, Reconstruction of the Mojave block (guidebook and roadlog), *in* McGill, S.F., and Ross, T.M., eds., Geological investigations of an active margin: Geological Society of America Cordilleran Section Guidebook, Redlands, California, San Bernardino County Museum Association, p. 3–30.

Golombek, M.P., and Brown, L.L., 1988, Clockwise rotation of the western Mojave Desert: Geology, v. 16, p. 126–130.

Goodman, E.D., and Malin, P.E., 1992, Evolution of the southern San Joaquin Basin and mid-Tertiary "transitional" tectonics, central California: Tectonics, v. 11, p. 478–498.

Hewett, D.F., 1954, General geology of the Mojave Desert region, California: California Division of Mines and Geology Bulletin, v. 170, p. 5–20.

Hopson, R.F., Hillhouse, J.W., and Howard, K.A., 2000, Rotation of the Late Jurassic Independence dike swarm, southern California: Geological Society of America Abstracts with Programs, v. 32, p. 173.

Howard, J.L., 1996, Paleocene to Holocene paleodeltas of ancestral Colorado River offset by the San Andreas fault system, southern California: Geology, v. 24, p. 783–786.

Howard, K.A., and Miller, D.M., 1992, Late Cenozoic faulting at the boundary between the Mojave and Sonoran blocks: Bristol Lake area, California, *in* Richard, S.M., ed., Deformation associated with the Neogene eastern California shear zone, southeastern California and southwestern Arizona: Proceedings of the workshop on the Eastern California shear zone, southeastern California and southwestern Arizona, Redlands, California, San Bernardino County Museum Association Special Publication 92-1, p. 37–47.

Ingersoll, R.V., 1982, Triple-junction instability as cause for late Cenozoic extension and fragmentation of the western United States: Geology, v. 10, p. 621–624.

Ingersoll, R.V., Devaney, K.A., Geslin, J.K., Cavazza, W., Diamond, D.S., Heins, W.A., Jagiello, K.J., Marsaglia, K.M., Paylor, E.D., II, and Short, P.F., 1996, The Mud Hills, Mojave Desert, California: Structure, stratigraphy, and sedimentology of a rapidly extended terrane, *in* Beratan, K.K., ed., Reconstructing the history of basin and range extension using sedimentology and stratigraphy: Geological Society of America Special Paper 303, p. 61–83.

Jacobson, C.E., 1990, The ^{40}Ar/^{39}Ar geochronology of the Pelona Schist and related rocks, Southern California: Journal of Geophysical Research, v. 95, p. 509–528.

Keith, L., Miller, J.S., Glazner, A.F., and Schermer, E.R., 1994, Geochemistry of Miocene volcanism on Fort Irwin, northern Mojave Desert, California: Geological Society of America Abstracts with Programs, v. 26, p. 62–63.

Kiser, N.L., 1981, Stratigraphy, structure and metamorphism in the Hinkley Hills, Barstow, California [M.S. thesis]: Stanford University, Stanford, California, 70 p.

Lucas, S.G., and Reynolds, R.E., 1991, Late Cretaceous(?) plesiosaurs from Cajon Pass, California, *in* Woodburne, M.O., Reynolds, R.E., and Whistler, D.P., eds., Inland southern California: The last 70 million years: San Bernardino County Museum Association Quarterly: San Bernardino, California, San Bernardino County Museum, p. 52–53.

Luyendyk, B.P., 1991, A model for Neogene crustal rotations, transtension, and transpression in southern California: Geological Society of America Bulletin, v. 103, p. 1528–1536.

Luyendyk, B.P., Kamerling, M.J., Terres, R.R., and Hornafius, J.S., 1985, Simple shear of southern California during Neogene time suggested by paleomagnetic declinations: Journal of Geophysical Research, v. 90, p. 12454–12466.

MacFadden, B.J., Swisher, C.C.I., Opdyke, N.D., and Woodburne, M.O., 1990a, Paleomagnetism, geochronology, and possible tectonic rotation of the middle Miocene Barstow Formation, Mojave Desert, southern California: Geological Society of America Bulletin, v. 102, p. 478–493.

MacFadden, B.J., Woodburne, M.O., and Opdyke, N.D., 1990b, Paleomagnetism and Neogene clockwise rotation of the northern Cady Mountains, Mojave Desert of southern California: Journal of Geophysical Research, v. 95, p. 4597–4608.

Martin, M.W., Glazner, A.F., Walker, J.D., and Schermer, E.R., 1993, Evidence for right-lateral transfer faulting accommodating en echelon Miocene extension, Mojave Desert, California: Geology, v. 21, p. 355–358.

Matthews, V., III, 1976, Correlation of Pinnacles and Neenach volcanic formations and their bearing on San Andreas fault problems: American Association of Petroleum Geologists Bulletin, v. 60, p. 2128–2141.

McCurry, M., 1988, Geology and petrology of the Woods Mountains volcanic center, southeastern California: Implications for the genesis of peralkaline rhyolite ash flow tuffs: Journal of Geophysical Research, v. 93, p. 14835–14855.

McDougall, K., 1987, Foraminiferal biostratigraphy and paleoecology of marine deposits, Goler Formation, California, *in* Cox, B.F., ed., Basin analysis and paleontology of the Paleocene and Eocene Goler Formation, El Paso Mountains, California: Los Angeles, Pacific Section, Society of Economic Paleontologists and Mineralogists, p. 43–67.

Meek, N., and Battles, D.A., Evidence for approximately 5.2 km of left-lateral displacement on the Manix fault, central Mojave Desert, California: Geological Society of America Abstracts with Programs, v. 22, no. 3, p. 68.

Miller, D.D., 1998, Distributed shear, rotation, and partitioned strain along the San Andreas fault, central California: Geology, v. 26, p. 867.

Miller, E.L. and Cameron, C.S., 1982, Late Precambrian to Late Cretaceous evolution of the southwestern Mojave Desert, California, *in* Cooper, J.D., Troxel, B.W., and Wright, L.A., eds., Geology of selected areas in the San Bernardino Mountains, western Mojave Desert, and southern Great Basin, California: Shoshone, California, Death Valley Publishing Co., p. 21–34.

Miller, F.K., and Morton, D.M., 1980, Potassium-argon geochronology of the eastern Transverse Ranges and southern Mojave Desert, southern California: U.S. Geological Survey Professional Paper 1152, p. 1–30.

Miller, J.S., and Miller, C.F., 1991, Tertiary extension-related volcanism, Old Woman Mountains area, eastern Mojave Desert, California: Journal of Geophysical Research, v. 96, p. 13629–13643.

Miller, J.S., Glazner, A.F., Farmer, G.L., Suayah, I.B., and Keith, L.B., 2000, Middle Tertiary magmatism across the Mojave Desert and southeastern California: A Sr, Nd, and Pb isotopic study of mantle domains and crustal structure: Geological Society of America Bulletin, v. 112, p. 1264–1279.

Moore, J.G., and Hopson, C.A., 1961, The Independence dike swarm in eastern California: American Journal of Science, v. 259, p. 241–259.

Nicholson, C., Sorlien, C.C., Atwater, T., Crowell, J.C., and Luyendyk, B.P., 1994, Microplate capture, rotation of the western Transverse Ranges, and initiation of the San Andreas transform as a low-angle fault system: Geology, v. 22, p. 491–495.

Nielson, J.E., Lux, D.R., Dalrymple, G.B., and Glazner, A.F., 1990, Age of the Peach Springs Tuff, southeastern California and western Arizona: Journal of Geophysical Research, v. 95, p. 571–580.

Nilsen, T.H., 1977, Early Tertiary tectonics and sedimentation in California, *in* Nilsen, T.H., ed., Late Mesozoic and Cenozoic sedimentation and tectonics in California: Bakersfield, California, San Joaquin Geological Society, p. 86–98.

Richard, S.M., 1993, Palinspastic reconstruction of southeastern California and southwestern Arizona for the middle Miocene: Tectonics, v. 12, p. 830–854.

Ron, H., Freund, R., and Garfunkel, Z., 1984, Block rotation by strike-slip faulting: Structural and paleomagnetic evidence: Journal of Geophysical Research, v. 89, p. 6256–6270.

Ron, H., and Nur, A., 1996, Vertical axis rotations in the Mojave: Evidence from the Independence dike swarm: Geology, v. 24, p. 973–976.

Ross, T.M., 1988, Neogene tectonic rotations in the central Mojave Desert, California, as indicated by paleomagnetic directions [M.A. thesis]: Santa Barbara, University of California, 242 p.

Ross, T.M., 1995, North-south directed extension and timing of extension and vertical-axis rotation in the southwest Cady Mountains, Mojave Desert, California: Geological Society of America Bulletin, v. 107, p. 793–811.

Ross, T.M., Luyendyk, B.P., and Haston, R.B., 1989, Paleomagnetic evidence for Neogene clockwise tectonic rotations in the central Mojave Desert, California: Geology, v. 17, p. 470–473.

Sabin, A.E., Monastero, F.C., and Katzenstein, A.M., 1994, Middle to late Miocene age stratovolcano on the South Ranges, Naval Air Weapons Station, San Bernardino County, California, *in* McGill, S.F., and Ross, T.M., eds., Geological investigations of an active margin: Geological Society of America Cordilleran Section Guidebook: Redlands, California, San Bernardino County Museum Association, p. 293–301.

Saylor, B.Z., and Hodges, K.V., 1991, The Titus Canyon Formation: Evidence for early Oligocene extension in the Death Valley area, CA: Geological Society of America Abstracts with Programs, v. 23, p. 82.

Schermer, E.R., Luyendyk, B.P., and Cisowski, S., 1996, Late Cenozoic structure and tectonics of the northern Mojave Desert: Tectonics, v. 15, p. 905–932.

Schweickert, R.A., and Caskey, S.J., 1990, Pre-middle Miocene extensional history of the Nevada Test Site (NTS) region, southern Nevada: Geological Society of America Abstracts with Programs, v. 22, p. 81.

Sherrod, D.R., and Nielson, J.E., 1993, Tertiary stratigraphy of highly extended terranes, California, Arizona, and Nevada: U.S. Geological Survey Bulletin 2053, 250 p.

Smith, G.I., 1962, Large lateral displacement on the Garlock fault, California, as measured from an offset dike swarm: American Association of Petroleum Geologists Bulletin, v. 46, p. 85–104.

Tennyson, M.E., 1989, Pre-transform early Miocene extension in western California: Geology, v. 17, p. 792–796.

Thompson, D.G., 1929, The Mohave Desert region, California: U.S. Geological Survey Water-Supply Paper 578, 759 p.

Turner, R.D., and Glazner, A.F., 1991, Miocene volcanism, folding, and fault-ing in the Castle Mountains, southern Nevada and eastern California: Geological Society of America Memoir 176, p. 23–35.

Valentine, M.J., Brown, L.L., and Golombek, M.P., 1993, Cenozoic crustal rotations in the Mojave Desert from paleomagnetic studies around Barstow, California: Tectonics, v. 12, p. 666–677.

Walker, J.D., and Glazner, A.F., 1999, Tectonic development of the southern California deserts: Geological Society of America Special Paper 338, p. 375–380.

Walker, J.D., Bartley, J.M., and Glazner, A.F., 1990, Large-magnitude Miocene extension in the central Mojave Desert: Implications for Paleozoic to Tertiary paleogeography and tectonics: Journal of Geophysical Research, v. 95, p. 557–569.

Walker, J.D., Fletcher, J.M., Fillmore, R.P., Martin, M.W., Taylor, W.J., Glazner, A.F., and Bartley, J.M., 1995, Connection between igneous activity and extension in the central Mojave metamorphic core complex, California: Journal of Geophysical Research, v. 100, p. 10477–10494.

Weigand, P.W., 1982, Middle Cenozoic volcanism of the western Transverse Ranges, *in* Fife, D.L., and Minch, J.A., eds., Geology and mineral wealth of the California Transverse Ranges: Santa Ana, California, South Coast Geological Society, p. 170–188.

Wells, R.E., and Hillhouse, J.W., 1989, Paleomagnetism and tectonic rotation of the lower Miocene Peach Springs Tuff: Colorado Plateau, Arizona, to Barstow, California: Geological Society of America Bulletin, v. 101, p. 846–863.

Wernicke, B., and Snow, J.K., 1998, Cenozoic tectonism in the central Basin and Range: Motion of the Sierran-Great Valley block: International Geology Review, v. 40, p. 403–410.

Wernicke, B., Axen, G.J., and Snow, J.K., 1988, Basin and Range extensional tectonics at the latitude of Las Vegas, Nevada: Geological Society of America Bulletin, v. 100, p. 1738–1757.

Wise, W.S., 1969, Origin of basaltic magmas in the Mojave Desert area, California: Contributions to Mineralogy and Petrology, v. 23, p. 53–64.

Woodburne, M.O., Tedford, R.H., Stevens, M.S., and Taylor, B.E., 1974, Early Miocene mammalian faunas, Mojave Desert, California: Journal of Paleontology, v. 48, p. 6–26.

Wust, S., 1986, Regional correlation of extension directions in Cordilleran metamorphic core complexes: Geology, v. 14, p. 828–830.

MANUSCRIPT ACCEPTED BY THE SOCIETY MAY 9, 2001

Geological Society of America
Memoir 195
2002

Timing of Middle to Late Jurassic ductile deformation and implications for paleotectonic setting, Shadow Mountains, western Mojave Desert, California

Mark W. Martin*
J. Douglas Walker
Department of Geology, University of Kansas, Lawrence, Kansas 66044, USA
John M. Fletcher
Departamento de Geologia, CICESE (Centro de Investigación Científica y de Educación Superior de Ensenada),
P.O. Box 434843, San Diego, California 92143-4843, USA

ABSTRACT

Detailed mapping (1:12 000) in the Shadow Mountains, western Mojave Desert, California, indicates that upper Proterozoic and Paleozoic miogeoclinal-cratonal rocks, upper Paleozoic continental-borderland assemblages, and upper Paleozoic–lower Mesozoic(?) arc-derived sedimentary rocks are ductilely transposed and record at least three generations of north-trending, dominantly west-vergent folds. We favor the interpretation that the evolution of these structures is related to progressive east-west shortening; however, an alternative interpretation is that they formed by an early phase of contraction followed by extensional collapse. Ductile deformation was accompanied by amphibolite-grade metamorphism that occurred at ca. 153 Ma on the basis of U-Pb geochronology on metamorphic zircon. Deformation predates intrusion of a bimodal igneous complex that ranges in age from 148 to 141 Ma (U-Pb geochronology).

On the basis of similar styles of folding and similar grade of coeval metamorphism, as well as permissive timing constraints, ductile deformation in the Shadow Mountains is broadly correlative with Middle to Late Jurassic contractional deformation in the central and northeastern Mojave Desert and, except for grade of metamorphism, along the east side of the Sierra Nevada batholith. On the basis of (1) the distribution of known Middle to Late Jurassic igneous rocks and (2) the kinematics of the belt of contraction to the northeast, we suggest that the Shadow Mountains resided slightly west of or near the central axis of the Middle to Late Jurassic magmatic arc.

INTRODUCTION

Understanding the Paleozoic and Mesozoic structural development of the central and western Mojave Desert is hindered by the paucity of pre-Cenozoic exposures and lack of continuity of rocks of appropriate age and character that record structural information. In general, Cretaceous and Tertiary igneous rocks, Tertiary deformation, and Quaternary alluvium obscure Paleo-

---

*Present address: Department of Earth, Atmospheric and Planetary Sciences, Massachusetts Institute of Technology, Cambridge, Massachusetts 02139, USA.

Martin, M.W., Walker, J.D., and Fletcher, J.M., 2002, Timing of Middle to Late Jurassic ductile deformation and implications for paleotectonic setting, Shadow Mountains, western Mojave Desert, California, *in* Glazner, A.F., Walker, J.D., and Bartley, J.M., eds., Geologic Evolution of the Mojave Desert and Southwestern Basin and Range: Boulder, Colorado, Geological Society of America Memoir 195, p. 43–58.

zoic and Mesozoic sedimentary rocks and the structures they record. Our present knowledge of Paleozoic and Mesozoic structural history in this region is based on a handful of detailed geologic mapping studies and limited geochronology. These areas include (Fig. 1) the El Paso Mountains (Carr et al., 1984), the Goldstone-northern Lane Mountain area (Miller and Sutter, 1982), Cronese Hills (Walker et al., 1990), Iron Mountain (Boettcher and Walker, 1993), the Ord and Fry Mountains (Karish et al., 1987), Quartzite Mountain (Miller, 1981; Schermer and Busby, 1994), the San Bernardino Mountains (Miller and Cameron, 1982; Brown, 1991), and the Shadow Mountains (Martin and Walker, 1995). For a review of this history, see Walker et al. (this volume, Chapter 1).

The Shadow Mountains display the largest exposure of metasedimentary rock in the central and western Mojave Desert and as such offer an excellent opportunity to study the deformation recorded in pre-Cenozoic rocks. Furthermore, understanding the timing of this deformation is critical for paleotectonic reconstructions of the region. Previous workers suggested that siliciclastic rocks, calc-silicate rocks, and marbles in the Shadow Mountains had eugeoclinal affinity and were allochthonous (Poole, 1974; Burchfiel and Davis, 1975, 1981; Dickinson, 1981); however, these rocks are now interpreted to belong to autochthonous upper Proterozoic–Mesozoic(?) miogeoclinal-cratonal facies (Brown, 1983; Martin and Walker, 1992, 1995).

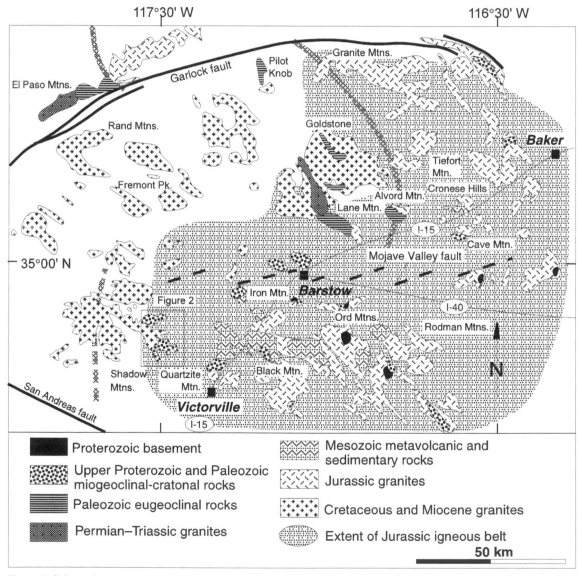

Figure 1. Schematic geologic map of pre-Tertiary rocks in the central and western Mojave Desert. Shaded line represents Pennsylvanian–Permian truncation boundary. Mojave Valley fault shown offset by known Holocene right-lateral strike-slip faults. Shaded background is known extent of Jurassic igneous belt in the central and western Mojave Desert. Modified after Martin and Walker (1992), Martin et al. (1993), and Miller et al. (1995).

Although a substantial amount of geologic work has been conducted in the Shadow Mountains (Dibblee, 1967; Troxel and Gunderson, 1970; Miller and Cameron, 1982; Brown, 1983), the details of the extent, magnitude, style, kinematics, or timing of deformation or metamorphism in this range have not been formally published (Martin, 1992). Therefore, the regional context of the structural history in the Shadow Mountains is unknown. Previous studies in the region indicate that late Paleozoic–Jurassic deformation may have affected rocks in the Shadow Mountains. Therefore understanding the style and timing of deformation recorded in the Shadow Mountains further aids our understanding of the paleotectonic environment of the region and the southwestern Cordillera in general. The purpose of this paper is to summarize the salient structural and metamorphic features in the Shadow Mountains and to present new U-Pb geochronology that provides estimates of the timing of these deformational features.

REGIONAL OVERVIEW

Contractional structures in allochthonous Paleozoic eugeoclinal rocks exposed in the El Paso Mountains (Carr et al., 1981, 1984; Miller et al., 1995) record the oldest deformation in the western Mojave Desert. Equivalent rocks are exposed in the north-central Mojave Desert that have been offset across the Garlock fault, although deformation of Antler age has not been clearly demonstrated in these areas (Miller and Sutter, 1982). The rocks of the Antler belt were tectonically juxtaposed to transitional miogeoclinal-cratonal rocks in the greater Mojave Desert region during late Paleozoic modification of the southwestern part of the Cordilleran margin (Burchfiel and Davis, 1981; Carr et al., 1981, 1984; Miller and Sutter, 1982; Walker, 1988; Stone and Stevens, 1988; Snow, 1992; Martin and Walker, 1995). Permian–Early Triassic contractional deformation and magmatism have been documented in the El Paso Mountains (Carr et al., 1984; Miller et al., 1995), Goldstone–Lane Mountain area (Miller and Sutter, 1982), Quartzite Mountain, (Miller, 1981), and the San Bernardino Mountains (Miller and Cameron, 1982). This deformation is thought to be associated with the onset of subduction that closely followed modification of the southwestern North American continental margin.

There is considerable speculation concerning the importance of extension versus contraction in the greater Mojave Desert region during the Triassic and Jurassic. Busby-Spera (1988) proposed that Late Triassic(?)–Middle Jurassic sedimentation and volcanism in the region and within the southwestern Cordillera in general, occurred in an arc that was primarily extensional in character. Schermer and Busby (1994) cited preservation of the Middle Jurassic Sidewinder Volcanic Series in the Victorville area as evidence for an intra-arc graben. The Shadow Mountains would have been adjacent to or within the area of extensional deformation. In contrast, Walker et al. (1990) proposed that late Middle to early Late Jurassic (169-

154 Ma) contractional deformation at the Cronese Hills (Fig. 1) and similar deformation northward to the Garlock fault is the southern extension of the East Sierran thrust system (Dunne, 1986). Farther south at Iron Mountain (Fig. 1), contractional deformation similar to that seen in the Cronese Hills is bracketed between 164 and 151 Ma (Boettcher and Walker, 1993). Therefore, a belt of Middle to Late Jurassic contractional deformation can be traced from the east side of the Sierra Nevada batholith, southward across the Garlock fault, into the Mojave Desert, and then southwestward toward the Shadow Mountains.

Evidence for Cretaceous deformation in the central and western Mojave Desert is sparse. In the Black Mountain area (Fig. 1), Schermer (1993) reported cleavage formation and folding of the Jurassic Sidewinder Volcanic Series of probable Cretaceous age. At Iron Mountain, steep mylonitic shear zones containing a subhorizontal mineral lineation are bracketed in age by pre- and postkinematic igneous rocks dated at 151 Ma and 83 Ma, respectively (Boettcher and Walker, 1993). In the Buttes–Fremont Peak area, migmatite formation occurred at 95 Ma (Glazner et al., 1994; Fletcher et al., this volume). In the Rand Mountains (Fig. 1), the Rand thrust is responsible for underplating the Rand Schist beneath Paleozoic and Mesozoic North America and is intruded by a 79 Ma granite (Silver and Nourse, 1986; Jacobsen, 1990). Although the timing of underplating is not well determined in the Rand Mountains, correlative schist bodies (Orocopia and Pelona) distributed throughout southern California and southwestern Arizona were underplated to the southwestern Cordillera during Late Cretaceous to Paleocene subduction (Ehlig, 1981; Haxel and Dillon, 1978; Jacobsen et al., 1988; Barth et al., 1991). In addition, Lahren and Schweickert (1989) have proposed that movement of ~400 km occurred on the inferred Cretaceous Mojave–Snow Lake right-lateral fault according to the offset of the upper Proterozoic–Cambrian miogeoclinal rocks in the western Mojave Desert and in the central Sierra Nevada.

AGE AND CORRELATION OF METASEDIMENTARY ROCKS IN THE SHADOW MOUNTAINS

Detailed discussion of the stratigraphy in the Shadow Mountains has been presented by Martin (1992) and Martin and Walker (1995). The following is a brief description of the metasedimentary rocks exposed in the Shadow Mountains and discussion of their age assignments. Three lithologic packages are present. Package 1 comprises quartzite, biotite schist, dolomite marble, and calc-silicate rocks and is correlated with upper Proterozoic and Cambrian rocks of miogeoclinal affinity. Also present in package 1 is calcite marble that possibly correlates with Devonian–Mississippian transitional cratonal-miogeoclinal strata. Package 2 contains calcite marble, calc-silicate rocks, and meta-arkose of probable Pennsylvanian–Permian age. These rocks are interpreted to have been deposited in a strike-slip borderland setting associated with modification of the southwestern continental margin during late Paleozoic time.

Package 3 is composed of mica $\pm$ sillimanite $\pm$ andalusite $\pm$ amphibole schists and hornfels intercalated with and overlain by calc-silicate rocks and calcite marble. Though speculative, these rocks are inferred to have been deposited in a late Paleozoic–Middle Jurassic arc. On the basis of considerations of internal stratigraphic relationships and the regional stratigraphy, Martin and Walker (1995) concluded that the Shadow Mountains stratigraphy represents an upper Proterozoic–Mesozoic sequence autochthonous to cratonal North America, not a series of autochthonous and allochthonous sequences.

DUCTILE DEFORMATION

The Shadow Mountains record at least three periods of Paleozoic and Mesozoic tectonism. The two older periods are represented only by apparent unconformities; one is between Pennsylvanian–Permian rocks and middle to lower Paleozoic transitional miogeoclinal-cratonal rocks, and the other is between Permian–Jurassic rocks and Pennsylvanian–Permian strata (Martin and Walker, 1995). The last period of tectonism affected the entire stratigraphic section in the Shadow Mountains and resulted in development of a transposition foliation and at least three generations of coaxial folds. Ductile deformation and folding predated emplacement of a Late Jurassic–Early Cretaceous bimodal igneous complex. Folding also predated relatively minor high-angle brittle faulting that was either associated with emplacement of the igneous complex or with younger Cretaceous or Tertiary deformation. We next present a summary of the structural observations that define the last major period of ductile deformation in the Shadow Mountains.

The area can be divided into distinct structural domains that are separated by both the igneous complex and a large expanse of Quaternary alluvium (Fig. 2). Rocks in the northern domain record the highest strain and deformational fabrics and can be divided into three groups on the basis of style and orientation. Because of strong domain partitioning of deformation, relative timing relationships between the three groups were difficult to establish at the mesoscopic scale. Therefore the descriptive order need not correspond to the temporal development of fabrics. Deformational events and structures or fabrics inferred to have formed during these events are signified by D_1, F_1, and S_1 and are considered first generation, whereas D_2, F_2, and S_2 are considered second generation.

The first group is defined by a strong subhorizontal foliation (S_1) that has fully transposed the original compositional layering. The S_1 foliation is typically best developed in the overturned limbs of two major west-vergent recumbent anticlines that dominate the macroscopic structure of the northern domain (Figs. 2 and 3; see also the map of the Shadow Mountains area ["SHADOW"] included on the CD-ROM accompanying this volume). The northern and southern anticlines are here termed the Silver Peak and Shadow Valley anticlines, respectively. Both folds plunge shallowly to the south, and strata in the hinge become younger to the west. In the overturned limb

of the Silver Peak anticline, quartzite clasts of the Zabriskie Quartzite show oblate shapes with aspect ratios of 5–10 on structural faces perpendicular to foliation. However, in the hinge region of the folds, clasts have prolate shapes and thus indicate significant extension parallel to the north-trending hinge lines.

The second and third group of deformational fabrics are defined by folds and cleavages that do not transpose compositional layering. F_2 folds are west vergent, whereas F_3 folds are upright. Both F_2 and F_3 folds are coaxial with the south-plunging F_1 nappes, and both sets have an axial-planar cleavage that is most commonly manifested as a siliceous pressure-solution cleavage in carbonate rocks. In general, folds and cleavages of the second and third groups are best developed in the upright limb of the F_1 recumbent anticlines. Although warps observed in the overturned limb are somewhat congruent with F_2 folds in the upright limb, only the subhorizontal S_1 foliation was observed in the overturned limb. Therefore, strict timing relationships between the deformational groups cannot be fully documented.

The juxtaposition of the Shadow Valley and the Silver Peak anticlines, without an apparent intervening syncline (Fig. 3), is interpreted as the consequence of attenuation and ductile faulting associated with high-strain deformation. In addition, there is a large competency contrast between the Bonanza King Formation (dolostone) and surrounding limestone units. Therefore, the high strain recorded on the limbs of these tight to isoclinal folds is inferred to have left the Bonanza King Formation stranded in a rootless parasitic anticline-syncline pair above the Carrara Formation on the upright limb of the Silver Peak anticline (Fig. 3). This interpretation explains (1) why the Bonanza King Formation is not present around the nose or on the overturned limb of the Silver Peak anticline, (2) the apparent hidden intervening syncline, and (3) the pinching out of units along the Carrara–Bonanza King contact in both the along- and across-strike directions.

Rocks in the southern domain record less overall strain compared to those in the northern domain. F_1 folds are not represented in the southern domain. This observation and the metamorphic evidence discussed in the next section support the conclusion that the southern domain is structurally higher than the northern domain. Two generations of north-trending folds with associated axial-planar cleavage are recorded in the southern domain. On the basis of similarities in style and geometry, these two generations of folds are correlated with F_2 and F_3 folds in the northern domain. F_2 folds in the southern domain, however, are both east and west vergent. In the eastern half of the southern domain are minor, east-vergent, brittle D_3 thrust faults.

We consider two scenarios to be possible to explain the evolution of these structures in the Shadow Mountains. The first, which we favor, relates the three groups of structures to a progressive contractional event that produced bulk east-west shortening and crustal thickening. The initial stages of such a

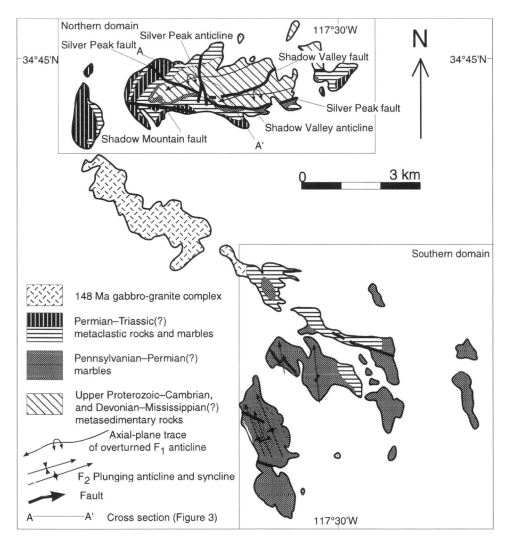

Figure 2. Simplified tectonic map of the Shadow Mountains (see Fig. 3 for cross section A-A').

Map legend:

- 148 Ma gabbro-granite complex
- Permian–Triassic(?) metaclastic rocks and marbles
- Pennsylvanian–Permian(?) marbles
- Upper Proterozoic–Cambrian, and Devonian–Mississippian(?) metasedimentary rocks
- Axial-plane trace of overturned F₁ anticline
- F₂ Plunging anticline and syncline
- Fault
- A———A' Cross section (Figure 3)

Map labels: Northern domain, Silver Peak fault, Silver Peak anticline, Shadow Valley fault, Silver Peak fault, Shadow Valley anticline, Shadow Mountain fault, Southern domain; 34°45'N, 117°30'W; 0 3 km; N

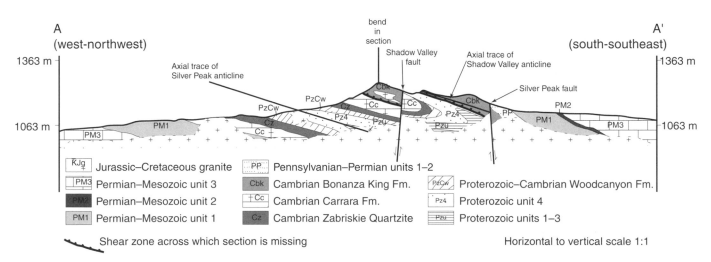

Figure 3 labels:

A (west-northwest) ... A' (south-southeast)

1363 m ... 1363 m
1063 m ... 1063 m

Axial trace of Silver Peak anticline; bend in section; Shadow Valley fault; Axial trace of Shadow Valley anticline; Silver Peak fault

Cbk, PzCw, Cc, Cc, Cbk, Cz, PzCw, Pz4, Pzu, Pz4, PP, PM2, PM1, Cc, PM1, PM3, PM3

Cross-section legend:

- KJg Jurassic–Cretaceous granite
- PM3 Permian-Mesozoic unit 3
- PM2 Permian-Mesozoic unit 2
- PM1 Permian-Mesozoic unit 1
- PP Pennsylvanian–Permian units 1–2
- Cbk Cambrian Bonanza King Fm.
- Cc Cambrian Carrara Fm.
- Cz Cambrian Zabriskie Quartzite
- PzCw Proterozoic–Cambrian Woodcanyon Fm.
- Pz4 Proterozoic unit 4
- Pzu Proterozoic units 1–3

Shear zone across which section is missing   Horizontal to vertical scale 1:1

Figure 3. Cross section across Silver Peak and Shadow Valley anticlines in the northern Shadow Mountains (see Fig. 2 for location of line of section).

history would likely be dominated by layer-parallel shortening of the sedimentary sequence, followed by stronger buckling and overthrusting to form the recumbent nappes. Alternatively, the upright and horizontal fabrics could have developed episodically as a result of initial contraction to produce the upright fabrics and later extensional collapse to produce the horizontal fabrics.

METAMORPHISM

Metamorphism associated with deformation

The following discussion focuses on the northern domain, because it contains pelitic assemblages suited for determining metamorphic conditions associated with deformation. However, where appropriate, relationships in the southern domain are also discussed. Unfortunately, dynamothermal metamorphism in the Shadow Mountains is overprinted by lower-grade contact metamorphism associated with emplacement of the Late Jurassic igneous complex. As a result, primary mineral assemblages and fabrics associated with mineral growth have been statically recrystallized and retrograded.

In the northern domain, prograde textures and mineral assemblages associated with the development of S_1 fabric are most common in biotite + staurolite + fibrolitic sillimanite schists and local biotite + hornblende schists of the Wood Canyon Formation in the core of the Silver Peak anticline. Although these mineral assemblages are strongly retrograded by chlorite and white mica, limited petrographic textural relationships suggest that biotite and fibrolitic sillimanite that grew during S_1 formation overprinted porphyroblasts of garnet and sillimanite, some of which contain opaque-mineral trains that define a relict fabric discordant to the S_1 fabric in which the porphyroblasts reside, thus indicating the possible presence of a pre-S_1 regional metamorphic event. Garnet and sillimanite porphyroblasts were subsequently rigidly rotated during development of S_1 as shown by (1) the obliqueness of opaque-mineral trains within the porphyroblasts to the S_1 fabric surrounding the porphyroblasts and (2) asymmetries in the S_1 biotite foliation around the porphyroblasts. North-trending crenulations fold the S_1 schistosity composed of biotite and sillimanite and are therefore considered F_2 structures.

Petrographically, dolomite marbles of the Bonanza King Formation contain rare forsterite; unfortunately, because this dolomite is so coarsely recrystallized, the timing of forsterite growth could not be related to any fabric development. However, the subvertical S_3 pressure-solution spaced-cleavage structures in the Bonanza King Formation contains forsterite (now mostly retrograded to talc or serpentine), which is attributed to the concentration of silica and magnesium during the partial remobilization of dolomite during dynamothermal metamorphism. Elsewhere, pressure-solution axial-planar cleavage (S_2-S_3) associated with calc-silicates throughout the study area is defined petrographically by the concentration of silica, the result of remobilization of calcite during dynamothermal metamorphism.

Locally, metamorphic conditions reached conditions of migmatite formation in some of the pelitic rocks. This occurrence is suggested by a small intrusion of intermediate composition exposed within the core of the Silver Peak anticline (Fig. 3; see also the map of the Shadow Mountains area ["SHADOW"] included on the CD-ROM accompanying this volume). This intrusion has gradational contacts with migmatitic biotite schists of the Wood Canyon Formation. We infer from this textural relationship that the schists were engulfed and incorporated into an igneous body in the subsurface; however, in situ partial melting of the pelitic schists during peak metamorphism is an alternative interpretation. In most exposures, this migmatite contains a deformational fabric that is subparallel to S_1 foliation in the country rock (see the map of the Shadow Mountains area ["SHADOW"] included on the CD-ROM accompanying this volume); however, it is locally undeformed. On the basis of these observations, this igneous body is interpreted to be synkinematic to late-kinematic with respect to D_1 contractional deformation.

Because of extensive retrograde contact metamorphism of earlier mineral assemblages, precise thermobarometric determinations were not attempted. However, approximate pressure and temperature estimates can be made. Sillimanite in the pelitic assemblages is characteristic of temperatures in excess of 500°C. The presence of andalusite with sillimanite but without kyanite indicates that pressures were less than 4.0 kbar (Baldwin et al., 1997). The growth of forsterite associated with D_3 spaced-cleavage development in the Bonanza King Formation suggests that CO_2 and H_2O fluids had to be present locally for this paragenesis. Field relationships previously discussed indicate that limited partial melting of pelitic assemblages occurred locally. If aqueous fluids were present during metamorphism (derived from devolatilization of pelitic and carbonate rocks), then temperatures necessary for minimum-temperature melt formation (wet granite solidus) may have been attained in the study area. For most crustal pressures, this temperature lies between 620 and 700°C (Miyashiro, 1973). In addition, U-Pb zircon geochronology from pelitic assemblages in the northern domain (discussed subsequently) suggests that temperatures were high enough to partially reset the U-Pb system in detrital zircon and to grow new metamorphic zircon.

The metamorphic history of the southern domain is less informative than that of the northern domain. Sillimanite was never observed in pelitic rocks from the southern domain. Pre-S_1 textures similar to those already discussed from the northern domain are observed petrographically in relict andalusite porphyroblasts in retrograded biotite + andalusite schists. In addition, forsterite in dolomites in the southern domain was not observed although tremolite and diopside are present in dolomite and calc-silicate lithologies.

On the basis of the preceding discussion, dynamothermal metamorphism in the northern domain is inferred to have taken place at temperatures greater than 500°C and at pressures less than 4.0 kbar (~13 km depth based on average lithostatic pressures). Associated with the apparent decrease in strain from the northern to the southern domain is an apparent decrease in overall metamorphic grade (lack of sillimanite and forsterite in appropriate assemblages). This relationship is supporting evidence that higher structural levels are exposed in the southern domain.

Contact metamorphism

Static contact metamorphism is ubiquitous throughout the entire study area. In pelitic assemblages, it is characterized by fine- to medium-grained hornfels texture that overprints older dynamothermal textures. In relatively pure carbonate assemblages (calcite and dolomite), older dynamic recrystallization textures are obliterated by coarse calcite and dolomite hornfels texture, and in calc-silicate assemblages, static metamorphism is characterized by garnet hornfels. Contact-metamorphic assemblages that have overprinted greenschist-facies to lower-amphibolite-facies assemblages are characterized by chlorite + muscovite + andalusite in pelitic assemblages, tremolite and diopside in pure marbles, and garnet + tremolite + diopside with local wollastonite in calc-silicates.

TIMING CONSTRAINTS ON D1–D3 DUCTILE DEFORMATION AND COEVAL METAMORPHISM

In order to bracket the age of contractional deformation and amphibolite-facies metamorphism and also to date igneous activity in the Shadow Mountains, U-Pb geochronology was performed on representative samples from several igneous phases and amphibolite-facies pelitic assemblages from the study area (Table 1 and Appendix). Some of these results have been presented in Martin and Walker (1995); however, here we present the underlying data and our interpretations.

Amphibolite-facies dynamothermal metamorphism

To determine the age of D_1 deformation and coeval regional metamorphism in the Shadow Mountains, samples of various amphibolite-facies pelitic rocks as well as a sample from the Zabriskie Quartzite were collected from the northern domain in hopes of finding metamorphic minerals suitable for U-Pb geochronology. Zircons were recovered from pelite samples SP-1, SP-2, Sh-3.7.11, and Sh-4.5.16 of the Zabriskie Quartzite (Table 1 and Appendix).

Samples SP-1, SP-2, Sh-3.7.11, and Sh-4.5.16 all show evidence for strong resetting of an older zircon U-Pb system and new zircon growth. The lower intercepts of these samples are indistinguishable within error (Fig. 4, A–E, and Appendix). All the zircon analyses from these samples are plotted together in Figure 4F. Given the range of stratigraphic ages for these units, the upper intercept of the well-defined discordia array

suggests that these metasedimentary rocks had a common source region composed of 1.7 Ga basement, consistent with basement ages known locally (Martin and Walker, 1992) and from southern California and Arizona (Wooden and Miller, 1990). The lower intercept of 161 ± 10 Ma (revised from the 165 ± 11 Ma reported by Martin and Walker, 1995) suggests that the U-Pb zircon system in these samples was subjected to a Jurassic thermal resetting event. This trajectory represents a long-protracted history that involves Pb loss during Proterozoic–Paleozoic sedimentation and Mesozoic deformation, as well as an admixture of older inherited zircon and new metamorphic zircon growth. A linear regression through the youngest five analyses, which belong to sample Sh-3.7.11 (see Appendix), yields a lower-intercept age of 153 ± 3 Ma (see Fig. 4D). Because the youngest zircons from sample Sh-3.7.11 are interpreted to be predominantly metamorphic in origin (see Appendix for discussion), the age of 153 ± 3 Ma is taken as the best estimate of the timing of peak metamorphism and D_1 deformation in this area. The strong disturbance of the U-Pb system in the study area during the Late Jurassic amphibolite-facies metamorphism is inferred to be related to regional metamorphism associated with the emplacement of the Sierra Nevada batholith at this time.

Postkinematic igneous rocks

The following discussion of the postkinematic igneous rocks describes relationships within the central igneous complex (Fig. 2). Because of the widespread static metamorphic overprint throughout the study area, postkinematic igneous rocks exposed in the complex are inferred to expand downward and underlie the entire Shadow Mountains. Where postkinematic igneous rock and country rock were observed in contact, transposition foliation and folds in the country rock are discordant to the igneous contact, and the igneous rocks contain no deformational fabric. Locally, xenoliths of the country rock are engulfed by these igneous rocks and contain transposition foliation. On the basis of these observations, the igneous complex in the Shadow Mountains is interpreted to be completely postkinematic.

The oldest postkinematic igneous rocks are gabbro and diorite, which range from coarse-grained hornblendite to medium-grained quartz diorite. In most thin sections, the hornblende has clinopyroxene cores. Commonly, these mafic phases are well layered. Along pluton margins, igneous layering is subvertical, whereas at the center of the igneous complex, layering is subhorizontal (Smith, 1983; Martin, 1992). The gabbro and diorite are interpreted to have crystallized at 148 ± 1.5 Ma on the basis of U-Pb analyses of zircon from a quartz diorite (sample Sh-2.27.3, Fig. 4G and Appendix).

Other major components of the igneous complex are hornblende granite and biotite granite. Locally, the hornblende quartz diorite and hornblende granite are commingled: this processes is shown by cuspate-lobate textures and hornblende

TABLE 1. U-Pb DATA FROM METAMORPHIC AND IGNEOUS ZIRCON, RUTILE, AND MONAZITE FROM THE SHADOW MOUNTAINS

Sample fractions	Weight (mg)	Concentration		Measured ratios[‡]			Radiogenic ratios			Age (Ma)		
		U (ppm)	Pb* (ppm)	$\frac{^{206}Pb*}{^{204}Pb}$	$\frac{^{207}Pb}{^{208}Pb}$	$\frac{^{208}Pb}{^{206}Pb}$	$\frac{^{206}Pb}{^{238}U}$	$\frac{^{207}Pb}{^{235}U}$	$\frac{^{207}Pb}{^{206}Pb}$	$\frac{^{206}Pb}{^{238}U}$	$\frac{^{207}Pb}{^{235}U}$	$\frac{^{207}Pb[†]}{^{206}Pb}$
SP-1												
nm(+2)>240e	0.21	682	42	5929	0.08797	0.1234	0.07177	0.84820	0.08571	446.8	623.6	1331.6 (1)
nm(+1)>240e	0.21	584	38	11774	0.08717	0.1239	0.07593	0.90120	0.08609	471.8	652.4	1340.1 (1)
nm(0)<240e	0.07	599	40	364	0.12561	0.2217	0.07762	0.93080	0.08697	481.9	668.0	1359.7 (8)
nm(−1)<240e	0.04	560	30	387	0.11534	0.2139	0.06342	0.68500	0.07834	396.4	529.8	1155.5 (5)
nm(−1)<240b	0.75	447	34	7259	0.09025	0.1313	0.08731	1.06460	0.08843	539.6	736.1	1391.9 (1)
nm(−1)<240ab	0.51	456	36	3941	0.09260	0.1363	0.09298	1.14320	0.08917	573.1	774.0	1407.9 (1)
Rutile												
nm(+5)<240b	0.78	288	6	888	0.06404	0.0451	0.02276	0.14920	0.04753	145.1	141.2	76.0 (12)
nm(+5)<240a	0.29	283	6	528	0.07908	0.0767	0.02337	0.16570	0.05141	148.9	155.6	259.3 (13)
>200b	0.79	436	8	2256	0.05510	0.0193	0.02260	0.15160	0.04864	144.1	143.3	130.9 (5)
>200a	0.35	409	8	792	0.06595	0.0471	0.02307	0.15090	0.04744	147.0	142.7	71.2 (15)
Zabriskie Quartzite												
nm(0)>240b	1.20	1060	108	460	0.12096	0.1881	0.08694	1.08910	0.09085	537.4	748.1	1443.4 (8)
nm(−1)>240b	1.27	701	93	1152	0.10906	0.1404	0.12142	1.62720	0.09719	738.7	980.8	1571.0 (3)
nm(−2)>240ab	1.45	700	99	2397	0.10304	0.1142	0.13483	1.81040	0.09739	815.3	1049.2	1574.7 (2)
nm(−2)<240e	0.04	1209	215	313	0.14154	0.2223	0.14638	1.97360	0.09779	880.7	1106.5	1582.3 (13)
nm(−1)<240e	0.08	516	81	839	0.11360	0.1509	0.14614	1.96350	0.09744	879.3	1103.1	1575.7 (2)
nm(2)>240a	0.73	1673	104	1294	0.09088	0.1322	0.05829	0.64400	0.08012	365.3	504.8	1200.0 (2)
nm(2)>240b	1.39	1513	90	900	0.09390	0.1453	0.05475	0.59160	0.07837	343.6	471.9	1156.4 (3)
Sh-3.7.11 (Elm Sequence)												
nm(0)>200a,e	0.37	204	5	1458	0.06337	0.2046	0.02611	0.19220	0.05339	166.1	178.5	345.5 (7)
nm(−1)>200a	0.13	213	7	1799	0.07682	0.1628	0.03811	0.36380	0.06924	241.1	315.1	906.0 (3)
nm(0)>240e	0.32	299	10	892	0.08379	0.1750	0.03703	0.34620	0.06779	234.4	301.8	862.2 (4)
nm(−2)<240e	0.12	282	13	183	0.15485	0.3209	0.05391	0.57760	0.07771	338.5	462.9	1139.4 (17)
nm(−1)<240e	0.14	310	8	489	0.09032	0.2178	0.02995	0.25100	0.06077	190.3	227.4	631.0 (9)
nm(0)<240e	0.12	334	7	439	0.08465	0.2279	0.02498	0.17680	0.05130	159.0	165.2	254.3 (22)
nm(−2)<240b	0.87	305	18	2470	0.09281	0.1321	0.06879	0.82750	0.08724	428.9	612.2	1365.8 (2)
nm(−1)<240b	1.02	329	19	918	0.10243	0.1608	0.06689	0.80510	0.08730	417.4	599.7	1367.1 (3)
nm(0)<240b	0.61	358	21	2003	0.09272	0.1439	0.06894	0.81570	0.08581	429.8	605.7	1334.0 (2)
SP-2 (Tonalite)												
>100a	0.05	214	17	799	0.11085	0.1534	0.09058	1.16910	0.09361	559.0	786.2	1500.2 (7)
nm(0)<100ba	0.20	646	35	6512	0.08458	0.1364	0.06328	0.71200	0.08252	395.5	550.7	1257.9 (1)
nm(+1)<100a	0.21	785	39	4683	0.08560	0.1211	0.05841	0.66610	0.08270	366.0	518.3	1262.2 (1)
monazite < 200	1.39	3843	108	3995	0.07037	2.8581	0.03267	0.30110	0.06685	207.2	267.3	833.1 (2)
Sh.2.27.3 (Quartz Diorite)												
nm(0) > 200b	1.08	1296	25	938	0.06374	0.3261	0.02258	0.14980	0.04813	143.9	141.8	105.7 (11)
nm(−1) > 200b	1.75	1228	24	6246	0.05089	0.3176	0.02299	0.15400	0.04859	146.5	145.4	127.9 (2)
nm(−2) > 200b	1.78	886	18	4635	0.05193	0.2961	0.02300	0.15480	0.04881	146.6	146.1	138.7 (2)
nm(−2) > 200a	0.86	855	17	5515	0.05146	0.3056	0.02329	0.15680	0.04884	148.4	147.9	140.3 (2)
nm(−1) > 200a	1.47	963	19	5031	0.05196	0.3334	0.02329	0.15760	0.04909	148.4	148.6	152.2 (4)

(continued)

enclaves reacting with more leucocratic rocks. Because the hornblende granite is virtually always gradational with the biotite granite, they were mapped as a single undifferentiated unit. Locally, however, both hornblende granite and biotite granite intrude gabbros and diorites, and the biotite granite intrudes the hornblende granite. A sample of the hornblende granite (Sh-29.3.9, Fig. 4H) and one of the biotite granite (Sh-4.20.12, Fig. 4I) each yielded interpreted U-Pb zircon crystallization ages of ca. 144–143 Ma (see Appendix). Late-phase tourmaline + garnet + muscovite peraluminous pegmatite dikes cut all older igneous units within the igneous complex. A sample of the pegmatite yielded a U-Pb monazite crystallization age of 141.5 ± 1.0 Ma (Fig. 4J and Appendix).

Postemplacement deformation within the igneous complex is minor. Local, laterally discontinuous, north-striking, sub-

vertical ductile shear zones (<1 m thick) cut gabbroic and granitic phases along the western margin of the igneous complex. Where observed, kinematic indicators in mylonitic fabrics show dip slip. These shear zones continue along strike for several meters before dying out within the igneous phases. On the basis of this observation, these structures are attributed to local adjustments during cooling of the igneous complex. The U-Pb data from the posttectonic igneous complex indicate that these zones may have been active over ~7 m.y.

Dikes and small bodies of dacite porphyry were not found in the igneous complex or in the northern domain, but are relatively common in the southern domain. This rock type is distinguished by large K-feldspar, resorbed quartz, and biotite phenocrysts. Locally, xenoliths and hornblende phenocrysts are common. These dacitic intrusions truncate contractional struc-

TABLE 1. U-Pb DATA FROM METAMORPHIC AND IGNEOUS ZIRCON, RUTILE, AND MONAZITE FROM THE SHADOW MOUNTAINS (continued)

Sample fractions	Weight (mg)	Concentration U (ppm)	Pb* (ppm)	Measured ratios‡ $\frac{206Pb^*}{204Pb}$	$\frac{207Pb}{208Pb}$	$\frac{208Pb}{206Pb}$	Radiogenic ratios $\frac{206Pb}{238U}$	$\frac{207Pb}{235U}$	$\frac{207Pb}{206Pb}$	Age (Ma) $\frac{206Pb}{238U}$	$\frac{207Pb}{235U}$	$\frac{207Pb†}{206Pb}$
Sh-29.3.90 (Hornblende Granite)												
nm(0) < 240b	2.27	389	8	1813	0.05708	0.2007	0.02271	0.15360	0.04905	144.7	145.1	150.1 (4)
nm(0) < 240a	0.82	330	7	3071	0.05422	0.2334	0.02343	0.15990	0.04950	149.3	150.6	171.8 (3)
nm(−1) > 240b	0.68	310	6	1231	0.06103	0.1992	0.02295	0.15530	0.04916	146.3	146.8	155.4 (8)
monazite > 100	0.60	122	2	47	0.35755	1.6972	0.02352	0.15730	0.04853	149.8	148.4	125.1 (33)
monazite > 200	0.26	129	3	81	0.23183	1.3752	0.02286	0.16570	0.05256	145.7	155.6	310.0 (50)
monazite < 200	0.27	123	2	67	0.26550	1.6267	0.02321	0.14880	0.04649	147.9	140.9	23.2 (48)
Sh-4.20.12 (Biotite Granite)												
nm(+2) < 240b	5.43	1609	30	1695	0.05745	0.1810	0.02186	0.14726	0.04885	139.4	139.5	140.5 (3)
nm(+1) < 240b	1.77	2592	50	1640	0.05794	0.2006	0.02258	0.15270	0.04905	144.0	144.3	150.0 (4)
nm(0) < 240b	1.25	991	20	1130	0.06098	0.2093	0.02301	0.15240	0.04803	146.6	144.0	100.7 (6)
nm(−1) < 240b	0.90	533	11	439	0.08234	0.2329	0.02354	0.15880	0.04892	150.0	149.6	144.0 (11)
nm(+1) < 240a	0.87	1250	24	7490	0.05099	0.1932	0.02269	0.15360	0.04909	14.6	145.1	152.2 (2)
nm(+1) > 200a	1.96	1208	24	4845	0.05169	0.2175	0.02328	0.15640	0.04871	148.3	147.5	134.1 (2)
Sh-4.16.3 (Peraluminous Granite)												
monazite > 140	0.67	4148	79	603	0.07326	2.5212	0.02222	0.15000	0.04896	141.7	141.9	145.9 (8)
monazite < 140	1.39	5953	116	638	0.07391	2.2340	0.02268	0.15960	0.05104	144.6	150.3	242.6 (7)
monazite < 240	1.53	5613	109	1609	0.05713	2.5747	0.02268	0.15030	0.04805	144.6	142.2	101.8 (4)
Shadow Hills (Dacite)												
nm(0) > 240b	1.09	394	6	1022	0.07830	0.2002	0.01916	0.16980	0.06428	122.4	159.3	751.0 (5)
nm(0) < 240b	0.66	439	7	967	0.07571	0.1933	0.01892	0.15870	0.06081	120.8	149.5	632.7 (6)
nm(−1) < 240b	0.41	332	6	548	0.09293	0.2210	0.02049	0.18880	0.06682	130.8	175.6	832.3 (11)
nm(−1) < 240e	0.07	356	5	76	0.23960	0.6247	0.01506	0.09650	0.04646	96.4	93.5	21.3 (59)

Note: nm(#) = nonmagnetic on Frantz separator at angle of tilt # degrees; >240 = size in standard mesh; a = air-abraded fraction; b = bulk fraction; e = handpicked, euhedral fraction. Zircon dissolution followed the methods of Krogh (1973) and Parrish (1987). Elemental separation was done with HBr anion column chemistry for lead and HCl column chemistry for uranium. Air abrasion followed the methods of Krogh (1982). Decay constants used were $^{238}U = 0.15513 \times 10^{-9}\ yr^{-1}$ and $^{235}U = 0.98485 \times 10^{-9}\ yr^{-1}$ (Steiger and Jäger, 1977). Isotopic analyses were determined on a VG Sector multicollector thermal-ionization mass spectrometer. A mass-fractionation correction of 0.10%/amu, as determined by standard runs on NBS 981 (common-lead) and NBS 982 (equal-atom lead), was applied to the lead data. Errors on $^{206}Pb/^{204}Pb$ were minimized by use of a Daly multiplier.

Common-lead corrections were made by using values determined from Stacey and Kramers (1975) for the crystallization age. For zircons analyses that are reversely discordant and have low $^{206}Pb/^{204}Pb$ (≪1000), the data were also reduced by using common-Pb values more typical of Mesozoic granites of the western and central Mojave Desert, most of which lie above average crustal growth curve of Stacey and Kramers (Wooden et al., 1988). Whole-rock common-Pb values for granites of similar composition and age from the western Mojave Desert were taken from Miller and Glazner (1995) in these reductions. These analyses were not sensitve to the range of Pb values used in the common-Pb correction.

*Radiogenic component. Total Pb procedural blanks ranged from 50 to 20 pg.

‡Ratios corrected for spike and mass fractionation.

†Numbers in parentheses are analytical errors on age (in m.y., 2σ). Errors were computed by using data reduction program PBDAT of Ludwig (1989).

tures, but crosscutting relationships with other igneous units or high-angle brittle faults were not observed. A dacite porphyry dike from the Shadow Hills yielded a U-Pb zircon age of 98.5 ± 8.7 Ma (Fig. 4K and Appendix).

DISCUSSION

Correlation of deformation

Middle to Late Jurassic contractional deformation is present northeast of the Shadow Mountains at Iron Mountain (Boettcher and Walker, 1993) and in the Cronese Hills (Walker et al., 1990). In the Cronese Hills (Fig. 1), northwest-dipping mylonitic shear zones and folds, both associated with green-schist metamorphism, placed Middle Jurassic metaplutonic and metavolcanic rocks over Triassic and Jurassic metasedimentary, volcanic, and plutonic rocks (Walker et al., 1990). On the basis of U-Pb geochronology on pre- and postkinematic igneous bodies, contractional deformation occurred between 169 and 154 Ma (Walker et al., 1990). These authors suggested that late Middle to Late Jurassic deformation in the Cronese Hills represents the southern continuation of the East Sierran thrust system (Dunne et al., 1978, 1983; Dunne, 1986; Dunne and Walker, 1993). Similar styles of deformation and metamorphism are present at Alvord Mountain (Miller et al., 1991) and in the Tiefort Mountain area (Fig. 1; Schermer et al., 2001). At Iron Mountain (Fig. 1), contractional deformation involves upper Proterozoic, miogeoclinal-affinity metasedimentary rocks and Middle to Late Jurassic igneous rocks (Boettcher and Walker, 1993). Ductile deformation is bracketed by prekinematic 164 Ma Hodge volcanic series (Sidewinder Volcanic Series) rocks and a postkinematic 151 Ma granite (U-Pb geochro-

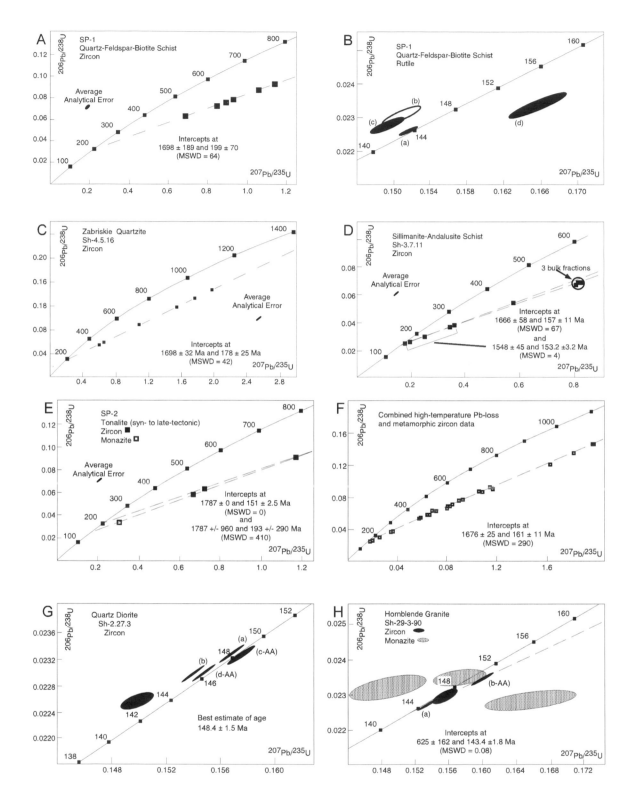

nology; Boettcher and Walker, 1993). Sillimanite-grade regional metamorphism recorded in the Hinkley Hills (Kiser, 1981) and Iron Mountain predate intrusion of an undeformed 148 Ma gabbro complex in the Iron Mountains (Boettcher and Walker, 1993).

On the basis of broadly permissive timing constraints and similar styles of deformation, folding and coeval metamorphism in the Shadow Mountains are considered to be correlative with deformation and regional metamorphism at Iron Mountain and the Cronese Hills. Thus, contractional deformation in the

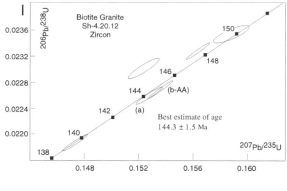

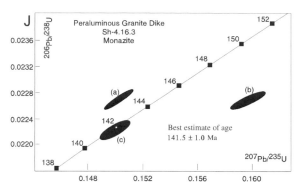

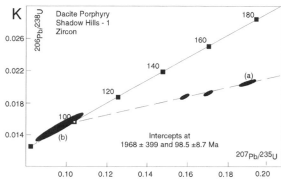

Figure 4 (on this and previous page). U-Pb concordia diagrams for metamorphic rocks, and syn- to late- and posttectonic igneous rocks. See the Appendix for further information. MSWD—mean square of weighted deviates.

Shadow Mountains extends the belt of Middle to Late Jurassic deformation outlined by Walker et al. (1990) and Boettcher and Walker (1993) farther to the southwest. This correlation is especially obvious once Tertiary extensional deformation has been restored in the central Mojave Desert (e.g., Martin et al., 1993). Contractional deformation in the East Sierran thrust system extends from the Inyo Mountains south along the east side of the Sierra Nevada batholith to the Garlock fault where it is offset eastward to the Granite Mountains and extends southward into the Cronese Hills (Fig. 1). South of the Cronese Hills, this belt of contraction is interpreted to be offset along the Mojave Valley fault (Martin et al., 1993) westward to Iron Mountain where it extends south through the Shadow Mountains.

The significance of local west-vergent deformation in the Shadow Mountains within this belt composed predominantly of east-vergent structures is uncertain. Broadly coeval west-vergent thrust faults and folds are known from the White Mountains (Hanson et al., 1987) from the northern part of the East Sierran thrust system. The Shadow Mountain deformation may represent a zone of local backthrusting aided by high heat flow associated with local plutons in an east-vergent system of deformation. Alternatively, this deformation may have resided within the central axis of the arc during the Middle to Late Jurassic and the vergence of structures was a function local strain partitioning near plutons in the arc during east-west shortening. A discussion of the arc paleogeographic setting of the Shadow Mountains is expanded upon in the following section.

Correlation of magmatism

To better understand the paleogeographic setting of Late Jurassic deformation in the Shadow Mountains relative to the active arc, a brief discussion of the position of the arc is necessary. Dunne et al. (1998) divided volcanic provinces associated with the Middle to Late Jurassic arc into different transverse paleogeographic and paleotectonic realms. In the region north of the Garlock fault and south of the White Mountains, these authors distinguished between marine volcanic centers of the western part of the arc, arc-core volcanic complexes, and arc-flank complexes of the eastern part of the arc. South of the Garlock fault, such distinctions are not obvious. Restoration of left-lateral offset along the Garlock fault suggests that Middle to Late Jurassic volcanic rocks and deformation in the Cronese Hills likely correlate with either arc-core or arc-flank complexes north of the Garlock fault. Restoration of right-lateral offset along the Mojave Valley fault (Martin et al., 1993) places (1) the Jurassic Sidewinder Volcanic Series in the Victorville area and (2) the Hodge volcanic rocks and Jurassic deformation at Iron Mountain into a position immediately south of the Cronese Hills. This reconstruction suggests that the Sidewinder and Hodge volcanic rocks likely correlate with arc-core to arc-flank volcanic rocks in the Cronese Hills. Dunne et al. (1998) proposed that the Sidewinder Volcanic Series are correlative with arc-core volcanic rocks in the Sierra Nevada batholith, consistent with work by Schermer and Busby (1994) who placed the

Sidewinder Volcanic Series in an intra-arc setting during Middle to Late Jurassic time.

Compared with the volcanic rocks, the position of the Middle to Late Jurassic arc as defined by intrusive bodies is less well defined owing to the lack of geochronology. Middle Jurassic intrusions are not known west of the Iron Mountains, but are known in the Cronese Hills to the east; it is uncertain how far east they extend. Late Jurassic intrusions are not known west of the Shadow Mountains, but do extend eastward into the Rodman Mountains (Schermer and Busby, 1994) and Cronese Hills (Walker et al., 1990) and to the north at Iron Mountain (Boettcher and Walker, 1993) and Lane Mountain (Miller and Sutter, 1982).

These volcanic correlations suggest that the Shadow Mountains and deformation recorded there resided either slightly west of or in an intra-arc setting during the Late Jurassic. We therefore speculate that Late Jurassic metamorphism and deformation in the Shadow Mountains is broadly coeval with the belt of east-vergent deformation present along the East Sierran thrust system (Dunne et al., 1983; Walker et al. 1990). However, unlike the East Sierran thrust system, deformation in the Shadow Mountains appears to have occurred within or west of the central axis of the arc; as yet distinguishing between these two settings is not possible.

One observation that is rather enigmatic is the close proximity of (1) Late Jurassic west-vergent deformation and coeval amphibolite-grade metamorphism, which formed at shallow- to middle-crustal levels in the Shadow Mountains, to (2) coeval, but relatively undeformed, mildly metamorphosed volcanic rocks of the upper Sidewinder Volcanic Series to the east (Fig. 1). If these two areas have not undergone significant lateral displacements since their formation, for which there is no field evidence, how they attained their present-day relative position is not clear. We can envision several possible mechanisms that might have led to this relationship.

The first relies on reverse or normal dip-slip kinematic processes proposed to operate in arc settings. Tobisch et al. (1986) described Jurassic–Cretaceous subvertical to shallowly dipping volcanic rocks juxtaposed to coeval shallow- to middle-crustal intrusions in the central Sierra Nevada batholith. These authors attributed the subvertical to shallow-dipping orientations of volcanic rocks along the margins of granitic plutons to be due to a combination of protracted regional extension and downward flow of host rocks along pluton margins during pluton emplacement. Because the western Mojave Desert was within the Jurassic–Cretaceous magmatic arc and because the model proposed by Tobisch et al. (1986) can result in the juxtaposition of low- and high-grade rocks (i.e., Sidewinder Volcanic Series and Shadow Mountain rocks), such a model could explain this relationship. However, except for minor normal faults found within the Sidewinder Volcanic Series (Schermer and Busby, 1994) and the Late Jurassic Independence dike swarm, there is no demonstrable evidence for significant extension during the Jurassic Period in the western Mojave Desert.

In contrast, as discussed previously, there is ample evidence for regional contraction during this time frame. Relationships described by Boettcher and Walker (1993) at Iron Mountain and Walker et al. (1990) in the Cronese Hills indicate that deformation is similar to deformation along the East Sierran thrust system (Dunne and Walker, 1993) where both Jurassic plutonic and volcanic rocks can be found in hanging-wall positions. In these areas, burial of Middle to Late Jurassic volcanic rocks by thrust faulting occurred either during the final phases of volcanism or immediately after volcanism but prior to 151-148 Ma. In this scenario, west-vergent kinematics in the Shadow Mountains may be associated with backthrusting above a west-dipping thrust fault that lies covered between the Shadow Mountains and the Sidewinder Volcanic Series. This structure might be the southern equivalent of the structure that separates Neoproterozoic metasedimentary rocks from Hodge volcanic rocks in the Iron Mountains (Boettcher and Walker, 1993).

A third possibility is that the Shadow Mountains and the Sidewinder Volcanic Series are not separated by a structure with any significant vertical dip-slip offset. In this scenario, high heat flow associated with arc plutonism thermally weakened the country rock, permitting strain to be concentrated locally in the Shadow Mountains whereas areas to the east, where the Sidewinder Volcanic Series rocks were extruded, were cooler and perhaps dryer.

Of these scenarios, we favor the interplay of east-west shortening and plutonism that allowed strain to be concentrated in the area of the Shadow Mountains. The prevalence of Late Jurassic intrusions in the Shadow Mountains and broadly coeval contractional deformation across the western and central Mojave Desert supports this conclusion.

CONCLUSIONS

We interpret much of the west-vergent deformational and coeval metamorphic fabric recorded in the Shadow Mountains to be related to a progressive, possibly protracted, contractional deformation that is Late Jurassic in age. This deformation is the southward continuation of coeval east-vergent contractional deformation recorded in the East Sierran thrust system that continues south from the White-Inyo Mountains into the north-central Mojave Desert. Whereas deformation in the East Sierran thrust system occurred paleogeographically along the eastern margin of the Middle to Late Jurassic arc, deformation in the Shadow Mountains appears to have been located nearer the central axis of the arc, according to our present understanding of the distribution of broadly coeval arc volcanism and plutonism. A satisfactory explanation for west-vergent deformation in the Shadow Mountains is lacking; however, we favor two possibilities or a combination of the two: (1) During east-west shortening within the central part of the Late Jurassic arc, strain was partitioned in hot country rock near plutons in such a manner as to yield west-vergent structures, or (2) deformation was associated with a zone of backthrusting within a belt of east-vergent deformation correlated with the East Sierran thrust system.

ACKNOWLEDGMENTS

We thank G. Dunne, A. Glazner, and D. Tosdal for careful and critical reviews of the manuscript. This study was supported by funds from the National Science Foundation (grants EAR-8816628 and EAR-8916802 to Walker) and from a Sigma Xi research grant and Shell Oil Company Graduate Fellowship (to Martin).

Appendix. U-PB geochronology

Metamorphic rocks

SP-1. SP-1 is coarse-grained biotite schist collected from a small schist body within the westernmost exposures of the Bonanza King Formation (Fig. 2). Because of the intensity of deformation, either a clastic sedimentary or igneous protolith for this sample is possible. SP-1 yielded numerous zircons, most of which display zircon overgrowths. A few of these zircons, however, are clear and euhedral with no visual sign of cores. Although all analyses are strongly discordant, the euhedral, clear, populations without cores are the youngest fractions (Fig. 4A). Fractions containing cores yielded older ages, and air-abraded fractions with cores yielded the oldest ages. On the basis of these results, the overgrowths are interpreted to have grown during amphibolite-facies metamorphism in the study area, and the clear, euhedral zircons apparently lacking cores are inferred to have grown during this metamorphic event but with less core material. The lower intercept of the linear regression with concordia, 199 ± 70 Ma, is representative of the age of this event. Given the field relationships and the old, strongly discordant zircons yielded by this sample, it is assumed that the protolith was sedimentary (clastic), though a granitic protolith cannot be excluded; this assumption is further corroborated by an identical upper-intercept age for detrital zircons from the Zabriskie Quartzite (see later description). On the basis of this assumption, the upper intercept, ca. 1700 Ma, represents the gross average age of the provenance area from which these zircons were derived, which agrees with the age of Proterozoic basement in the region (Wooden and Miller, 1990; Martin and Walker, 1992)

Rutile was also recovered from SP-1. Three of the four fractions analyzed display reverse discordance (Fig. 4B). Reverse discordance, although commonly observed in monazite (Scharer, 1984; Parrish, 1990), has not been reported in rutile. Reverse discordance is generally attributed to excess ^{206}Pb derived from initially incorporated ^{230}Th, an intermediate decay product of ^{238}U (Scharer, 1984). However, because the $^{208}Pb/^{206}Pb$ ratio is not elevated, this explanation probably does not explain the rutile data. Studies by Mezger et al. (1989) indicate that U-Pb ages on metamorphic rutile can be utilized to understand cooling histories in high-grade terranes. Mezger et al. (1989) also determined that the closure temperature for U-Pb diffusion in rutile is ~420–380°C and is dependent on grain size (i.e., controlled by volume diffusion): smaller grains have younger ages. Air-abrasion of fractions a and b gave rise to c and d, respectively. Although the results for these rutile fractions are enigmatic, the nearly concordant behavior of three of the fractions, although reversely discordant, suggest that rutile in SP-1 closed to U-Pb diffusion (~400°C) at ca. 144 Ma. As will be shown later, this age corresponds well with the last stages of development of the igneous complex.

Sh-4.5.16 (zabriskie quartzite). As with the previous sample, zircons retrieved from Sh-4.5.16, which was collected in the nose of the Silver Peak anticline (Fig. 2), also contain cores. However, euhedral fractions without apparent cores were not systematically the youngest populations. On these grounds it cannot be argued that the zircons without cores are metamorphic zircon. However, air-abraded bulk zircon fractions containing cores move up discordia toward older ages, indicating that the zircon overgrowths are a young feature (Table 1, Fig. 4C). As with SP-1, the lower intercept of the linear regression (178 ± 25 Ma) is interpreted to represent the age during which the U-Pb system was disturbed and new zircon growth occurred. The upper intercept (ca. 1700 Ma) is interpreted to represent the average age of the source region for these detrital zircons.

Sh-3.7.11. Sh-3.7.11 is a retrograded, sillimanite + andalusite + biotite schist. This sample was collected from the transition from unit 1 to unit 2 in package 3 on the nose of the Silver Peak anticline (Fig. 2). This sample yielded numerous zircons, the majority of which are euhedral to subhedral, with very few rounded zircons, all bearing metamorphic zircon overgrowths. However, abundant euhedral, acicular zircons without apparent cores are also present. Three bulk, non-air-abraded fractions of different magnetic properties are the most discordant and plot essentially on top of each other (Fig. 4D), suggesting that the bulk population is composed of a mixture of detrital zircons of various ages. The remaining analyzed fractions were all handpicked to consist of clear, euhedral zircons without cores, and it is these that yield the youngest U-Pb ages. On the basis of these systematics, the zircons from these young analyses are interpreted to be predominantly new metamorphic zircon containing a minor inherited component. A linear regression through all the analyses yields a lower-intercept age of 157 ± 11 Ma, whereas a linear regression through the five youngest analyses yields a lower-intercept age of 153 ± 3 Ma (Fig. 4D). The best estimate for the minimum age of this resetting event and new zircon growth is represented by the lower intercept of the linear regression (153 ± 3 Ma).

Pre- to synkinematic igneous rocks

SP-2. Zircons from the syn- to late-kinematic tonalite have diverse morphologies (rounded to euhedral), suggesting that most of these zircons are xenocrystic. Zircon overgrowths are also prevalent on a majority of the zircons. As with the previous samples, the diverse morphologies, the presence of overgrowths, and the strongly discordant results displayed by the zircons from this sample suggest that xenocrystic zircons (Fig. 4E) underwent partial thermal resetting and new zircon growth. The age of this event is represented by the lower intercept (193 ± 290 Ma). (The error about this age is not realistic and is a side affect of the reduction program, in which the *t*-multiplier is 12.5 for *n* = 3 at 2σ.) These observations corroborate the field relationships that indicate that large amounts of biotite schist from the Wood Canyon Formation was either engulfed and incorporated into an intruding magma at depth or that the schist itself underwent partial melting related to peak amphibolite-facies metamorphism. The single monazite analysis is also discordant, indicating the presence of inherited and partially reset monazite. The U-Pb system of monazite is generally more susceptible to thermal resetting than zircon (Parrish, 1990). The monazite more accurately defines the age of the thermal event represented by the lower intercept of the zircon regression. Because only one monazite was analyzed, a linear regression through the monazite data forced through an upper intercept of 1787 Ma was performed (the gross average xenocrystic Pb component from this sample is represented by the upper intercept of the zircon regression). The lower intercept of this regression is 151 ± 2.5 Ma. A linear regression through the monazite and three zircon fractions yields a lower-intercept age of 158 ± 84 Ma (Fig. 4E). It can be argued that the age obtained by a regression using two different U-Pb systems is equivocal because, for example, the monazite could have been subject to a significantly longer cooling interval than the zircon. However, this age (158 ± 84 Ma) is consistent with the field relationships and with the metamorphic ages of the previous samples (Sh-3.7.11, Sh-4.5.16, and SP-1).

Postkinematic igneous rocks

Sh-2.27.3. A sample of quartz diorite (Sh-2.27.3) was collected from an exposure that has a prominent igneous layering. Five zircon fractions were analyzed from this sample (Fig. 4G). Four of the five fractions are slightly reversely discordant. Fractions a and b were air-abraded, moving their positions to c and d, respectively. In this case, air abrasion only changed the 207Pb/235U ratios whereas the 206Pb/238U ratios were virtually unchanged. Reverse discordance in zircons, though rare, has been reported from elsewhere in the Sierra Nevada batholith (see Mattinson et al., 1996, for discussion). Although these zircons (sample Sh-4.20.12 also) were not imaged nor were leaching experiments performed, we attribute reverse discordance to be associated with submicrometer Pb transport from high-U zones to low-U zones in oscillatory-zoned zircon, as described by Mattinson et al. (1996). On the basis of the near concordance of fractions a and c, the age of this sample is interpreted to be the weighted mean of those fractions' 206Pb/238U dates, 148.4 ± 1.5.

Sh-29.3.90. Sample Sh-29.3.90 is a hornblende granite, which locally displays commingled textures with more mafic phases of the complex (e.g., Sh-2.27.3), but is also observed intruding those phases. Three zircon and monazite fractions were analyzed (Fig. 4H). The zircon analyses are normally discordant with Pb/Pb dates ranging from 172 to 150 Ma (Table 1), suggesting that they incorporated a small amount of xenocrystic zircon during crystallization. This interpretation is corroborated by air-abraded fraction a, which moved toward an older age (fraction b). A linear regression through the zircon analyses yields a lower-intercept age of 143.4 ± 1.8 Ma, which is interpreted as the age of this sample. The three monazite fractions display both reverse and normal discordance (Fig. 4H). However, the low 206Pb/204Pb ratios (Table 1) lead to large errors in both 206Pb/238U and 207Pb/235U ages. Although these monazite analyses were not used for determining the age of this sample, their age is consistent with the zircon data.

Sh-4.20.12. A sample was taken of biotite granite (Sh-4.20.12) that intrudes both the hornblende granite and older mafic phases, yet locally the biotite granite shares a gradational contact with the hornblende granite. Six zircon fractions were analyzed (Fig. 4I). Three of these fractions are reversely discordant and generally give slightly older ages than the three fractions that are nearly concordant. After air-abrading, fraction a moved toward a more discordant, slightly older age (fraction b), implying that some xenocrystic zircon was incorporated during crystallization of these zircons. The Pb/Pb ages of these two fractions (150–152 Ma, Table 1) also imply a slightly older Pb component. Because of the scatter along concordia of these data, the significance of inheritance versus Pb-loss behavior cannot be accurately determined. We interpret the age of this sample to be best estimated by the weighted mean of the 206Pb/238U dates of fractions a and b, 144.3 ± 1.5 Ma, which is consistent with the field relationships and the interpreted ages of the previous two samples (Sh-29.3.90 and Sh-2.27.3).

Sh-4.16.3. A peraluminous, tourmaline- and garnet-bearing granitic dike yielded sample Sh-4.16.3. The dike strikes north-northeast and cuts across the core of the Silver Peak anticline (NW¼ sec. 32—see the map of the Shadow Mountains area ["SHADOW"] included on the CD-ROM accompanying this volume). This dike was barren of zircon, but yielded monazite. Fraction c is concordant and fraction a is re-

versely discordant, but both have similar 207Pb/235U dates (Fig. 4J). The third fraction is normally discordant, indicating that it contains some inherited xenocrystic component. Because the 207Pb/235U ages of fractions a and c are within error of one another (Table 1), the age of this sample is interpreted to be 141.5 ± 1.0 Ma.

Shadow hills-1. A dacite porphyry dike is exposed on the western side of the Shadow Hills in the southeastern Shadow Mountains. The majority of the zircons in this sample (Shadow Hills-1) had obvious overgrowths on both euhedral and rounded grains. The morphology of these zircons suggests that most are xenocrystic with igneous overgrowths. This interpretation is corroborated by field and petrographic observations that indicate that this sample is undeformed and not metamorphosed, but contains numerous embayed quartz phenocrysts (possibly xenocrysts) and locally small xenoliths. Three bulk zircon fractions were analyzed and are normally discordant (Fig. 4K), verifying the inherited zircon component. From fraction a, euhedral, inclusion-free zircons without overgrowths were analyzed. Fraction b zircons are nearly concordant at 95 Ma (Fig. 4K). A linear regression through the four fractions yields a lower-intercept age of 98.5 ± 8.7 Ma, which is interpreted as the age of this sample.

REFERENCES CITED

Baldwin, J.A., Whitney, D.L., and Hurlow, H.A., 1997, Metamorphic and structural evidence for significant vertical displacement along the Ross Lake fault zone, a major orogen-parallel shear zone in the Cordillera of western North America: Tectonics, v. 16, p. 662–681.

Barth, A.P., Jacobsen, C.E., and May, D.J., 1991, Mesozoic basement terranes of the San Gabriel Mountains, southern California: Summary and field-guide, *in* Wallawender, M.J., and Hanan, B.B., eds., Geologic excursions in southern California and Mexico: Geological Society of America Field-trip Guidebook, San Diego, p. 186–198.

Boettcher, S., and Walker, J.D., 1993, Geologic evolution of the Iron Mountains, central Mojave Desert, California: Tectonics, v. 12, p. 373–386.

Brown, H.J., 1983, Possible Cambrian miogeoclinal strata in the Shadow Mountains, western Mojave Desert, California: Geological Society of America Abstracts with Programs, v. 15, p. 413.

Brown, H.J., 1991, Stratigraphy and paleogeographic setting of Paleozoic rocks in the San Bernardino Mountains, California, *in* Cooper, J.D., and Stevens, C.H., eds., Paleozoic paleogeography of the western United States. 2: Pacific Coast Section, Society of Sedimentary Geologists, v. 67, p. 193–207.

Burchfiel, B.C., and Davis, G.A., 1975, Nature and controls of Cordilleran orogenesis, western United States: Extensions of an earlier synthesis: American Journal of Science, v. 275-A, p. 363–396.

Burchfiel, B.C., and Davis, G.A., 1981, Mojave Desert and environs, *in* Ernst, W.G., ed., The geotectonic development of California: Englewood Cliffs, New Jersey, Prentice-Hall, p. 217–252.

Busby-Spera, C.J., 1988, Speculative tectonic model for the early Mesozoic arc of the southwest Cordilleran United States: Geology, v. 16, p. 1121–1125.

Carr, M.D., Poole, F.G., Harris, A.G., and Christiansen, R.L., 1981, Western facies Paleozoic rocks in the Mojave Desert, California: U.S. Geological Survey Open-File Report 8 1–503, p. 15–17.

Carr, M.D., Christiansen, R.L., and Poole, F.G., 1984, Pre-Cenozoic geology of the El Paso Mountains, southwestern Great Basin, California: A summary, *in* Lintz, J., Jr., ed., Western geological excursions: Reno, Nevada, Cordillera Section, Geological Society of America Fieldtrip Guidebook 7, v. 4, p. 84–93.

Dibblee, T.W., Jr., 1967, Areal geology of the western Mojave Desert, California: U.S. Geological Survey Professional Paper 522, 153 p.

Dickinson, W.R., 1981, Plate tectonics and the continental margin of California, in Ernst, W.G., ed., The geotectonic development of California: Englewood Cliffs, New Jersey, Prentice-Hall, p. 1–28.

Dunne, G.C., 1986, Geologic evolution of the southern Inyo Range, Darwin Plateau, and Argus and Slate Ranges, east-central California: An overview: Los Angeles, Cordilleran Section, Geological Society of America Fieldtrip Guidebook, p. 3–21.

Dunne, G.C., and Walker, J.D., 1993, Age of Jurassic volcanism and tectonism, southern Owens Valley region, east central California: Geological Society of America Bulletin, v. 105, p. 1223–1230.

Dunne, G.C., Gulliver, R.M., and Sylvester, A.G., 1978, Mesozoic evolution of the White, Inyo, Argus and Slate Ranges, eastern California, in Stewart, J.H., Stevens, C.H., and Fritsche, A.E., eds., Paleozoic paleogeography of the western United States: Pacific Coast Section, Society of Economic Paleontologists and Mineralogists, Pacific Coast Paleogeography Symposium 2, p. 189–207.

Dunne, G.C., Moore, S.C., Gulliver, R.M., and Fowler, J., 1983, East Sierran thrust system, eastern California: Geological Society of America Abstracts with Programs, v. 15, p. 322.

Dunne, G.C., Garvey, T.P., Osborne, M., Schneidereit, D., Fritsche, A.E., and Walker, J.D., 1998, Geology of the Inyo Mountains volcanic complex: Implications for Jurassic paleogeography of the Sierran magmatic arc in eastern California: Geological Society of America Bulletin, v. 110, p. 1376–1397.

Ehlig, P.L., 1981, Origin and tectonic history of the basement terrane of the San Gabriel Mountains, central Transverse Ranges, in Ernst, W.G., ed., The geotectonic development of California: Englewood Cliffs, New Jersey, Prentice-Hall, p. 153–283.

Glazner, A.F., Walker, J.D., Bartley, J.M., Fletcher, J.M., Martin, M.W., Schermer, E.R., Boettcher, S.S., Miller, J.S., Fillmore, R.P., and Linn, J.K., 1994, Reconstruction of the Mojave Block, in McGill, S.F., and Ross, T.M., eds., Geological investigations of an active margin: Geological Society of America Cordilleran Section Guidebook 27: Tulsa, Oklahoma, Geological Society of America, p. 3–30.

Hanson, R.B., Saleeby, J.B., and Fates, D.G., 1987, Age and tectonic setting of Mesozoic metavolcanic and meta-sedimentary rocks, northern White Mountains, California: Geology, v. 15, p. 1074–1078.

Haxel, G., and Dillon, J., 1978, The Pelona-Orocopia schist and Vincent-Chocolate Mountain thrust system, southern California, in Howell, D.G., and McDougall, K.A., eds., Mesozoic paleogeography of the western United States: Pacific Coast Section, Society of Economic Paleontologists and Mineralogists, Pacific Coast Paleogeography Symposium 2, p. 453–469.

Jacobsen, C.E., 1990, The $^{40}Ar/^{39}Ar$ geochronology of the Pelona Schist and related rocks, southern California: Journal of Geophysical Research, v. 95, p. 509–528.

Jacobsen, C.E., Dawson, M.R., and Postlethwaite, C.E., 1988, Structure, metamorphism, and tectonic significance of the Pelona, Orocopia, and Rand Schists, in Ernst, W.G., ed., Metamorphism and crustal evolution of the western United States: Englewood Cliffs, New Jersey, Prentice-Hall, p. 976–997.

Karish, C.R., Miller, E.L., and Sutter, J.F., 1987, Mesozoic tectonic and magmatic history of the central Mojave Desert, in Dickinson, W.R., and Klute, M.A., eds., Mesozoic rocks of Arizona and adjacent areas: Arizona Geological Society Digest, v. 18, p. 15–32.

Kiser, N.L., 1981, Stratigraphy, structure and metamorphism in the Hinkley Hills, Barstow, California [M.S. thesis]: Palo Alto, California, Stanford University, 70 p.

Krogh, T.E., 1973, A low-contamination method for hydrothermal decomposition of zircon and extraction of U and Pb for isotopic age determination: Geochimica et Cosmochimica Acta, v. 37, p. 485–494.

Krogh, T.E., 1982, Improved accuracy of U-Pb ages by creation of more concordant systems using an air abrasion technique: Geochimica et Cosmochimica Acta, v. 46, p. 637–649.

Lahren, M.M., and Schweickert, R.A., 1989, Proterozoic and Lower Cambrian miogeoclinal rocks of the Snow Lake pendant, Yosemite-Emigrant Wilderness, Sierra Nevada, California: Geology, v. 17, p. 156–160.

Ludwig, K.R., 1989, PBDAT for MS-DOS, a computer program for IBM-PC compatibles for processing raw Pb-U-Th isotope data version 1.06: U.S. Geological Survey Open-File Report 88–542, p. 40.

Martin, M.W., 1992, Stratigraphic and structural evolution of the Shadow Mountains, western Mojave Desert, California: Implications for the tectonic development of the central and western Mojave Desert [Ph.D. thesis]: Lawrence, Kansas, University of Kansas, 225 p.

Martin, M.W., and Walker, J.D., 1992, Extending the western North American Proterozoic and Paleozoic continental crust through the Mojave Desert: Geology, v. 20, p. 753–756.

Martin, M.W., and Walker, J.D., 1995, Stratigraphy and paleogeographic significance of metamorphic rocks in the Shadow Mountains, western Mojave Desert, California: Geological Society of America Bulletin, v. 107, no. 3, p. 354–366.

Martin, M.W., Glazner, A.F., Walker, J.D., and Schermer, E.R., 1993, Evidence for right-lateral transfer faulting accommodating en echelon Miocene extension, Mojave Desert, California: Geology, v. 21, p. 355–358.

Mattinson, J.M., Graubard, C.M., Parkinson, D.L., and McClelland, W.C., 1996, U-Pb reverse discordance in zircons: The role of fine-scale oscillatory zoning and submicron transport of Pb, in Basu, A., and Hart, S., eds., Earth processes: Reading the isotopic code: American Geophysical Union Geophysical Monograph 95, p. 355–370.

Mezger, K., Hanson, G.N., and Bohlen, S.R., 1989, High-precision U-Pb ages of metamorphic rutile: Application to the cooling history of high-grade terranes: Earth and Planetary Science Letters, v. 96, p. 106–118.

Miller, E.L., 1981, Geology of the Victorville region, California: Part I and II: Geological Society of America Bulletin, v. 92, p. 160–163; 554–608.

Miller, E.L., and Cameron, C.S., 1982, Late Precambrian to Cretaceous evolution of the southwestern Mojave Desert, California, in Cooper, J.P., Troxel, B.W., and Wright, L.A., eds., Geology of selected areas in the San Bernardino Mountains, western Mojave Desert, and southern Great Basin, California: Fresno, California, Cordillera Section, Geological Society of America Fieldtrip 9, p. 5–20.

Miller, E.L., and Sutter, J.F., 1982, Structural geology and $^{40}Ar/^{39}Ar$ geochronology of the Goldstone-Lane Mountain area, Mojave Desert, California: Geological Society of America Bulletin, v. 93, p. 1191–1207.

Miller, J.S., and Glazner, A.F., 1995, Jurassic plutonism and crustal evolution in the central Mojave Desert, California: Contributions to Mineralogy and Petrology, v. 118, p. 379–395.

Miller, J.S., Glazner, A.F., Martin, M.W., and Walker, J.D., 1991, Age relations, chemical and isotopic signature, and tectonic implications of Middle to Late Jurassic plutonism in the central and western Mojave Desert: Geological Society of America Abstracts with Programs, v. 23, no. 5, p. 249.

Miller, J.S., Glazner, A.F., Walker, J.D., and Martin, M.W., 1995, Geochronologic and isotopic evidence for Triassic-Jurassic emplacement of the eugeoclinal allochthon in the Mojave Desert region, California: Geological Society of America Bulletin, v. 107, n. 12, p. 1441–1457.

Miyashiro, A., 1973, Metamorphism and metamorphic belts: London, George Allen and Unwin, 492 p.

Parrish, R.R., 1990, U-Pb dating of monazite and its application to geological problems: Canadian Journal of Earth Sciences, v. 27, p. 1431–1450.

Parrish, R.R., 1987, An improved micro-capsule for zircon dissolution in U-Pb geochronology: Chemical Geology, v. 66, p. 99–102.

Poole, F.G., 1974, Flysch deposits of the Antler foreland basin, western United States: Society of Economic Paleontologists and Mineralogists Special Publication 22, p. 58–82.

Scharer, U., 1984, The effect of initial ^{230}Th disequilibrium on young U-Pb ages: The Makalu case, Himalaya: Earth and Planetary Science Letters, v. 67, p. 191–204.

Schermer, E.R., 1993, Mesozoic structural evolution of the west-central Mojave Desert, in Dunne, G., and MacDougall, K.A., eds., Mesozoic paleogeography of the western United States II: Pacific Section, Society of Economic Paleontologists and Mineralogists, p. 307–322.

Schermer, E.R., and Busby, C., 1994, Jurassic magmatism in the central Mojave Desert: Implication for arc paleogeography and preservation of continental volcanic sequences: Geological Society of America Bulletin, v. 106, p. 767–790.

Schermer, E.R., Stephens, K.A., and Walker, J.D., 2001, Continental margin tectonic evolution, Tiefort Mountains, northern Mojave Desert, California: Geological Society of America Bulletin, v. 113, p. 920–938.

Silver, L.T., and Nourse, J.A., 1986, The Rand Mountains "thrust" complex in comparison with the Vincent thrust–Pelona Schist relationship, southern California: Geological Society of America Abstracts with Programs, v. 18, p. 185.

Smith, D.K., 1983, Mesozoic alkaline and calc-alkaline igneous rocks, north-central San Bernardino Mountains, California: Geological Society of America Abstracts with Programs, v. 15, p. 281.

Snow, J.K., 1992, Large-magnitude Permian shortening and continental-margin tectonics in the southern Cordillera, Geological Society of America Bulletin, v. 104, p. 80–105.

Stacey, J.S., and Kramers, J.D., 1975, Approximation of terrestrial lead isotope evolution by a two-stage model: Earth and Planetary Science Letters, v. 26, p. 207–221.

Steiger, R.H., and Jäger, E., 1977, Subcommission on geochronology: Convention on the use of decay constants in geo- and cosmochronology: Earth and Planetary Science Letters, v. 36, p. 359–362.

Stone, P., and Stevens, C., 1988, Pennsylvanian and Early Permian paleogeography of east-central California: Implications for the shape of the continental margin and the timing of continental truncation: Geology, v. 16, p. 330–333.

Tobisch, O.T., Saleeby, J.B., and Fiske, R.S., 1986, Structural history of continental volcanic arc rocks, eastern Sierra Nevada, California: A case for extensional tectonics: Tectonics, v. 5, p. 65–94.

Troxel, B.W., and Gunderson, J.N., 1970, Geology of the Shadow Mountains and northern part of the Shadow Mountains southeast quadrangles, western San Bernardino County, California: California Division of Mines and Geology, Sacramento, Preliminary Report 12, 21 p.

Walker, J.D., 1988, Permian and Triassic rocks of the Mojave Desert and their implications for timing and mechanisms of continental truncation: Tectonics, v. 7, p. 685–709.

Walker, J.D., Martin, M.W., Bartley, J.M., and Coleman, D.S., 1990, Timing and kinematics of deformation in the Cronese Hills, California, and implications for Mesozoic structure of the southwestern Cordillera: Geology, v. 18, p. 554–557.

Wooden, J.L., and Miller, D.M., 1990, Chronologic and isotopic framework for the Early Proterozoic crustal evolution in the eastern Mojave Desert region, SE California: Journal of Geophysical Research, v. 95, p. 20 113–20 146.

Wooden, J.L., Stacey, J.S., Robinson, A.C., Kistler, R.W., Tosdal, R.M., Whitehouse, M.J., 1988, Pb isotopic characteristics of Mesozoic intrusive magmatism along the craton margin in the Western U.S., *in* Bartholomew, M.J., et al., eds, 8th international conference on basement tectonics; Characterization and comparison of ancient and Mesozoic continental margins: Proceedings: International Conference on Basement Tectonics, p. 741–742.

Manuscript Accepted by the Society May 9, 2001

Geological Society of America
Memoir 195
2002

Mesozoic geologic evolution of Alvord Mountain, central Mojave Desert, California

Jonathan S. Miller
Department of Geology, San Jose State University, San Jose, California 95192-0102, USA
J. Douglas Walker
*Department of Geology and Isotope Geochemistry Laboratory, University of Kansas,
Lawrence, Kansas 66045, USA*

ABSTRACT

The pre-Cenozoic geology of Alvord Mountain, located in the central Mojave Desert of California, records a complex history of deformation, magmatism, and metamorphism related to development of the southern North American Cordilleran arc. Paleozoic schist and marble are the main preintrusive rocks. The rocks are correlated with either lower Paleozoic displaced eugeoclinal rocks that are part of the Antler allochthon and/or with uppermost Permian(?)–Lower Triassic continental-borderland rocks. These rocks were intruded by a monzodiorite to quartz monzonite pluton (mainly quartz monzodiorite) during the early Middle Jurassic. Both the metamorphic rocks and the quartz monzodiorite pluton were subsequently metamorphosed, folded during northeast-southwest contraction, and sheared along northwest-striking, steeply dipping shear zones. The timing of deformation is bracketed between 179 Ma (the age of the quartz monzodiorite) and an undeformed 149 Ma gabbro. Both the prekinematic and postkinematic plutons are parts of larger regionally recognized suites of Jurassic plutonic rocks. Northwest-striking hornblende diabase dikes are correlated with the 148 Ma gabbro and are interpreted to belong to the regional Late Jurassic Independence dike swarm. Metapsammites in the schist record conditions of upper-greenschist-lower-amphibolite facies, but the age of metamorphism is uncertain. Peak metamorphic conditions were probably attained during Jurassic time closely associated with intrusion of the main Jurassic quartz monzodiorite. However, petrographic observations and $^{40}Ar/^{39}Ar$ data from biotite from the 179 Ma pluton indicate that Late Cretaceous plutons and dikes (ca. 85 Ma), which crop out in the southern part of the range, probably produced a static thermal overprint. Northwest-striking Late Cretaceous granodiorite porphyry dikes crop out for several kilometers along strike and approach thicknesses of 10 m. The dikes cut all pre-Tertiary rocks and correlate with a newly recognized Late Cretaceous dike swarm that is oriented roughly parallel to the Late Jurassic Independence dike swarm.

The style and timing of deformation at Alvord Mountain are similar to those seen in the nearby Cronese Hills and Tiefort Mountains, where structures have been correlated with the Jurassic–Cretaceous East Sierran thrust system. Unlike the reverse-sense, mostly downdip shear zones in the Cronese Hills and Tiefort Mountains, small-scale shear zones at Alvord Mountain primarily show evidence of strike slip. A

Miller, J.S., and Walker, J.D., 2002, Mesozoic geologic evolution of Alvord Mountain, central Mojave Desert, California, *in* Glazner, A.F., Walker, J.D., and Bartley, J.M., eds., Geologic Evolution of the Mojave Desert and Southwestern Basin and Range: Boulder, Colorado, Geological Society of America Memoir 195, p. 59–77.

sinistral, obliquely convergent tectonic setting during the Middle and Late Jurassic is consistent with close spatial and temporal association of contractional and strike-slip structures.

Dike azimuth data suggest that proposed Miocene vertical-axis rotation at Alvord Mountain appears not to have drastically reoriented Mesozoic structures, but the data allow some variable rotation as inferred from previous paleomagnetic data.

INTRODUCTION

Alvord Mountain is located in the central Mojave Desert of California (Fig. 1) in the vicinity of several important Paleozoic and Mesozoic paleogeographic and tectonic boundaries. The boundaries include (1) the southern and eastern limits of known occurrences of lower Paleozoic eugeoclinal rocks,

which are thought to be correlative with displaced Antler belt rocks (Carr et al., 1984, 1992; Walker, 1988; Martin and Walker, 1991); (2) the inferred miogeoclinal-eugeoclinal transition boundary (Martin and Walker, 1991); and (3) the (Jurassic–Cretaceous) East Sierran thrust system (Walker et al., 1990) (Fig. 1). The purposes of this study are (1) to describe the major Paleozoic and Mesozoic rock units and structures and discuss

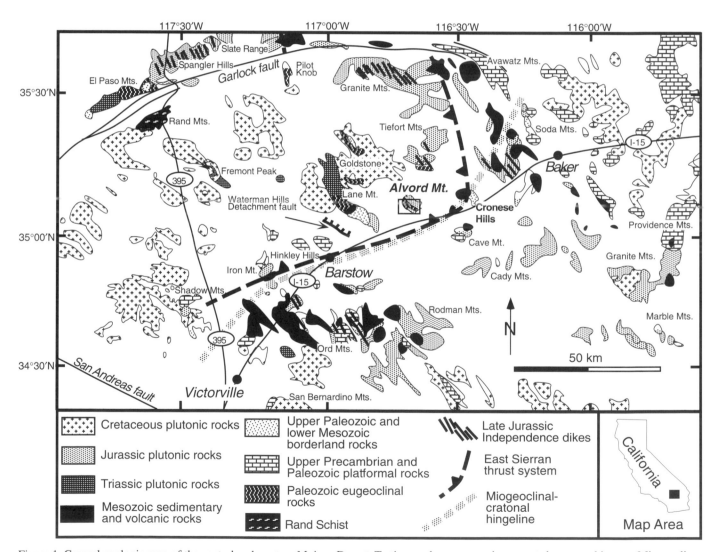

Figure 1. General geologic map of the central and western Mojave Desert. Tertiary and younger rocks are not shown on this map. Miogeocline-cratonal hinge line from Martin and Walker (1992). East Sierran thrust system is after Walker et al. (1990). Note that the continuation of the thrust system is offset ~40 km left laterally across the Garlock fault and continues northward from the Slate Range at the north edge of the map. Box enclosing Alvord Mountain shows area of Figure 2.

their relationship to the tectonic and paleogeographic elements just mentioned and (2) to correlate them with surrounding areas. We particularly focus on how the metamorphic and plutonic rocks involved in deformation at Alvord Mountain can provide additional insight into the timing and regional extent of Jurassic deformation in the Mojave Desert.

Alvord Mountain can be conveniently divided into eastern and western halves on the basis of exposed geology. Pre–Tertiary metamorphic and plutonic rocks, exposed mainly in the western half of the range (Byers, 1960), are the subject of this study (Fig. 2). The Paleozoic–Mesozoic(?) metamorphic rocks have sedimentary protoliths that correlate with surrounding strata in the vicinity of Alvord Mountain, but they have been intensely deformed and metamorphosed. Mesozoic plutons and several generations of dikes of variable age have intruded the metamorphic rocks.

The eastern half of Alvord Mountain is composed mainly of Tertiary volcanic and sedimentary rocks deposited nonconformably on Mesozoic plutonic basement (Byers, 1960; Fill-

more, 1993). The Tertiary rocks are not discussed here, but some of our work bears on proposed tectonic vertical-axis rotations of the Alvord Mountain area during the Tertiary. We discuss the implications of our work for vertical-axis rotation and the possible effects of rotation on Mesozoic structures at the end of this paper.

METAMORPHIC ROCKS

Metamorphic rocks at Alvord Mountain crop out in a northwest-trending linear belt bounded by and also cut by plutonic rocks (Fig. 2) on the southwest and northeast. Two main metamorphic rock types are exposed at Alvord Mountain, biotite schist and marble, both of which have sedimentary protoliths. The contact between these units is relatively sharp but is not obviously faulted. Hence we infer that the contact is stratigraphic, although it could be disconformable. No facing indicators are preserved in the units owing to the relatively high grade of metamorphism. Thus it is not possible to determine

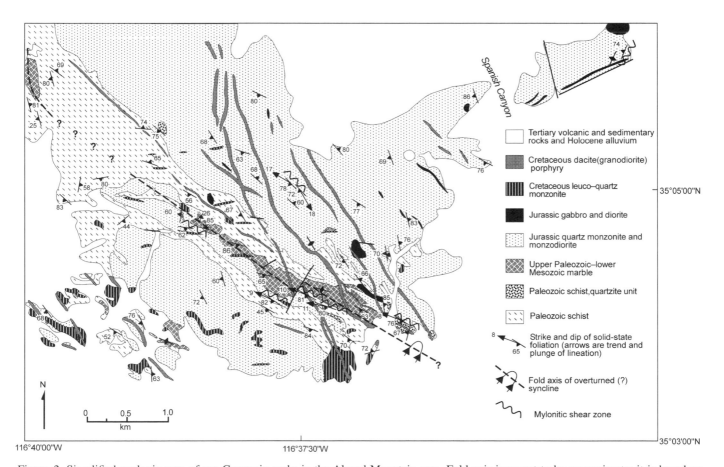

Figure 2. Simplified geologic map of pre-Cenozoic rocks in the Alvord Mountain area. Fold axis is meant to be approximate; it is based on the map pattern of metamorphic rocks and the overall foliation pattern. The fold appears upright to slightly overturned toward the northeast and steeply plunging to the southeast. Note that foliation patterns appear to close to the southeast and northwest, so the fold may be doubly plunging. Interpretation as a synclinal fold depends primarily on the age assignment of metamorphic units. Note that shear zones (squiggles) are developed only in the oldest pluton and the metamorphic rocks. Also note northeast trend of diabase dikes in fault-bounded block on east side of Spanish Canyon. See text for further discussion.

definitively whether the sequence is upright. The marble currently sits structurally above the schist. Similar metamorphic rocks have been mapped in the Fort Irwin–Tiefort Mountains area (Byers, 1960; Yount et al., 1994; Schermer et al., 2001), in the Lane Mountain–Goldstone area (McCulloh, 1954; Miller and Sutter, 1982; Fig. 1), and in the Cronese Hills area (Walker et al., 1990).

Biotite schist

The most widespread of the two main metamorphic units at Alvord Mountain is biotite schist (Fig. 2; see also accompanying Plate 1). The main rock type is quartz + biotite schist, consisting mainly of quartz and biotite, with lesser amounts of plagioclase, K-feldspar, epidote, chlorite, and white mica. Total original stratigraphic thickness is impossible to determine, but the structural thickness of the schist ranges from ~200 to 300 m. Lenses and bands of quartz-pebble conglomerate, impure quartzite, mafic to intermediate-composition metavolcanic rocks, banded argillite, and minor calc-silicate rocks also crop out within this unit. These rocks are lumped with the biotite schist for mapping purposes because of their limited vertical thickness and lateral extent. The layers of subordinate rock types range from less than 1 m to a maximum of 5 m thick and can be traced a few tens of meters to ~100 m along strike. Near pluton contacts, the schist has a hornfelsic texture. Locally, the schist is injected and has a migmatitic gneiss texture. Especially along the northern contact with adjacent plutonic rocks, migmatitic texture is so prevalent that the rock would be better termed a gneiss or possibly an injection gneiss (Fig. 3A). Minor more pelitic and psammitic layers that contain muscovite and andalusite are also interlayered in the biotite schist. Andalusite in these layers occurs as either small subhedral crystals or as relict crystals that are corroded and mantled in fine-grained white mica. Quartzite is relatively uncommon at Alvord Mountain (Fig. 2). Several relatively small, isolated exposures of quartzite are present toward the southeastern end of the metamorphic belt, and one small hill underlain by nearly pure vitreous orthoquartzite is found adjacent to the contact between the schist and the pluton in the northwestern part of the map area (Fig. 2).

In addition to the main biotite foliation, small (meter width and a few to tens of meters long), discontinuous ductile shear zones are also present in this unit (Fig. 2). These are discussed further in subsequent sections.

Marble

The predominant rock type in the marble unit (Fig. 2) is gray to white, medium- to coarse-grained calcite marble. The marble unit varies in thickness from <2 to 200 m at its thickest. Several layers of banded marble with thin (1–5 cm) siliceous interlayers, ranging in thickness from one to several meters, can be traced for as much as ~100 m along strike, particularly

toward the southeastern end of the marble band. Folding is most prevalent and well developed in these calc-silicate layers (Fig. 3B). Minerals present in the calc-silicate layers include epidote, garnet, tremolite, scapolite, plagioclase, diopside, wollastonite, and quartz. In the southeastern area, skarn-type mineralization is prevalent; massive skarn garnets are locally up to 1 m in diameter, and iron mineralization (siderite, hematite, and jasper) is also widespread in this area. At the northwestern limit of the main band of marble (Fig. 2), two small (several meters wide) outcrops of distinctive calcareous metaconglomerate are present. The conglomerate has a calcareous matrix and contains clasts that are compositionally identical to the matrix. Some siliceous interlayers are also present. It has been recrystallized to medium-grained to coarse-grained marble, siliceous marble, and calc-silicate, but nevertheless preserves the relict conglomeratic texture (Fig. 3C).

PLUTONIC ROCKS

Byers (1960) originally lumped all intrusive rocks into a single map unit but recognized that several different intrusive units were present at Alvord Mountain. The most widespread intrusive rock at Alvord Mountain is a conspicuously dark-weathering monzodiorite to quartz monzonite pluton. The pluton is weakly to strongly deformed and cut by numerous smaller intrusions and several generations of dikes that range from gabbro to granite compositionally. These smaller intrusions lack any internal deformation.

Monzodiorite and quartz monzonite

The largest and oldest exposed pluton at Alvord Mountain is an early Middle Jurassic (179 Ma) monzodiorite–quartz monzonite (Miller et al., 1995). The unit grades from more mafic (monzodiorite) along the southern edge of the range to more felsic (quartz monzonite) toward the north and east. The margins of the pluton are not exposed, and it probably extends into surrounding areas (Byers, 1960). Quartz monzodiorite is the most widespread rock type in this pluton, so for the purposes of this discussion, we hereafter refer to this unit as Jurassic quartz monzodiorite. The rock is coarse grained and porphyritic with 0.5–2-cm-sized K-feldspar crystals. In addition to K-feldspar, minerals present in this unit include clinopyroxene, hornblende, biotite, plagioclase, quartz, titanite, accessory apatite, zircon, and allanite and secondary epidote and sericite. Ellipsoidal mafic enclaves are present throughout the pluton. Enclave minerals are similar to those present in the host pluton, but the enclaves have a higher color index and fine to medium grain size. Centimeter-sized K-feldspar crystals are sometimes contained within the enclaves. The most mafic monzodiorite has a higher percentage of biotite relative to hornblende than the quartz monzodiorite. Clinopyroxene is present only in the monzodiorite and occurs as isolated subhedral ragged crystals and as anhedral crystals within hornblende.

A

B

Figure 3. (A) Mesoscopic fold in migmatitic injection gneiss. Small anticline-syncline pairs to left of pencil plunge moderately to the southeast and are slightly overturned to the northeast; they mimic range-scale structure. However, folding in migmatite can be variable in orientation. Pencil for scale is ~15 cm. (B) Recumbent fold in banded siliceous marble. Fold is overturned toward the northeast. Hammer for scale is ~35 cm. (C) Calcareous metaconglomerate in marble unit. Note large elongate clast ~10 cm to left of pocket knife. Clasts are lighter-colored carbonate or banded calc-silicate. A few darker marble clasts are also seen in this outcrop. Pocket knife for scale is ~8 cm long.

C

A pervasive north- to northwest-striking, steeply west-dipping to vertical biotite and hornblende foliation is present throughout the entire pluton. Mylonitic shear zones, like those in the biotite schist, are also present (Fig. 2) in the quartz monzodiorite pluton and are subparallel with the biotite foliation. Byers (1960) noted gneisses at Alvord Mountain but lumped these with the biotite schist and marble and assumed that they were Precambrian. However, Byers (1960) did note that the gneiss fabric grades into weakly deformed quartz monzodiorite with the same mineral assemblage as the gneiss.

Hornblende gabbro and hornblende diabase dikes

Several small plutons of hornblende gabbro and/or diorite are present in several areas (Fig. 2). These crosscut the older quartz monzodiorite, the biotite schist, and the marble unit. The gabbros consist predominantly of hornblende and plagioclase and are coarse grained. Clinopyroxene is also present as discrete subhedral crystals and as ragged cores within hornblende. Other minor minerals present include biotite, sphene, apatite, and zircon. Secondary sericite and muscovite replace plagioclase in some samples. The gabbros generally have ophitic textures. In one small pod on the west side of Spanish Canyon, the gabbro has mineral layering formed by centimeter-scale alternating bands of hornblende and plagioclase (Miller and Glazner, 1995). Layering orientations in this area range from near vertical to moderately west dipping, and cross-bedded layers can also be observed. No enclaves are present in the gabbros, and they lack any discernible subsolidus deformational fabric.

Fine- to medium-grained diabasic dikes with a mineral assemblage similar to that of the gabbro plutons also cut the quartz monzodiorite in the basement on the west and east side of Spanish Canyon (Fig. 2). The orientations of the dikes vary. On the west side of Spanish Canyon, the dikes are northwest-striking with subvertical dips. The mean azimuth of Late Jurassic diabase dikes west of Spanish Canyon is 319° ± 11° (number of measurements [*n*] = 16) (Fig. 4A). On the east side of Spanish Canyon, they have variable orientations ranging from nearly north-striking to northeast-striking with subvertical dips (Fig. 2). The mean azimuth is 25° ± 34° (*n* = 10), but the dikes cluster into two populations. Five dikes have orientations of 350° ± 1°, and five dikes have a mean of 53° ± 11° (Fig. 4B). Because they are mineralogically similar to the gabbro pods and are undeformed, we tentatively correlate the diabase dikes with the gabbros.

Leucocratic quartz monzonite pluton

A leucocratic quartz monzonite pluton (hereafter referred to as leuco–quartz monzonite) and several smaller pods of this igneous rock cut the biotite schist and the older quartz monzodiorite along the southern perimeter of the range (Fig. 2). The north edge of this pluton is exposed in this area, but the pluton may extend farther to the south beneath the alluvium. Scattered

exposures in the southwest part of the map area also suggest that this pluton may encompass a larger area than present exposures reveal (Fig. 2). The pluton is deeply weathered, heavily jointed, and has a pervasive sericitic alteration. Minerals present in the pluton are plagioclase, K-feldspar, quartz, and biotite, accessory apatite, zircon, and monazite, and secondary sericite

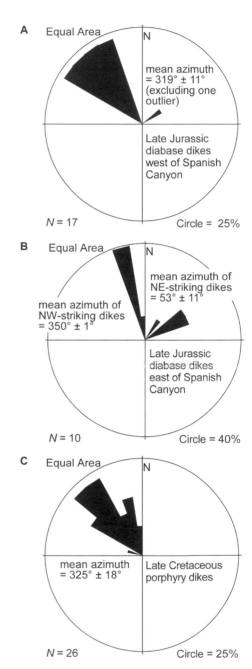

Figure 4. Dike-azimuth rose diagrams for Late Jurassic diabase dikes (A) east and (B) west of Spanish Canyon and (C) Late Cretaceous porphyry dikes. Mean azimuths also given for populations of dikes. Note that Jurassic diabase dikes west of Spanish Canyon have a mean azimuth that is the same as the mean azimuth of Independence dikes north of the Garlock fault. Dikes east of Spanish Canyon cluster into two groups. See text for further discussion.

and muscovite. The leuco–quartz monzonite is easily distinguished from the older quartz monzonite pluton because it is medium grained and equigranular, lacks hornblende, and has a lower color index. Mafic enclaves are absent in the pluton.

Several east-striking, vertical to moderately north-dipping leucocratic quartz monzonite dikes cut the older plutonic and metamorphic units but not the leuco–quartz monzonite itself (Fig. 2). The dikes are somewhat finer-grained than the leuco–quartz monzonite but have the same mineral assemblage as the pluton and may therefore be related. However, several dikes are composite and contain quenched pillow-like enclaves of basalt, whereas the leuco–quartz monzonite pluton lacks any mafic enclaves. One quartz monzonite dike cuts one of the diabase dikes, indicating that the quartz monzonite dikes are younger than the diabase dikes. Neither the leuco–quartz monzonite pluton nor the dikes are deformed. In some areas, the leuco–quartz monzonite contains a barely discernible to weak biotite foliation, but this fabric is not pervasive, and quartz has not been dynamically recrystallized.

Dacite (granodiorite) porphyry dikes

A conspicuous swarm of dacite (granodiorite) porphyry dikes cuts all of the pre-Tertiary units in the western part of Alvord Mountain (Fig. 2). The porphyry dikes are resistant to erosion and form prominent ridges that shed extensive talus slopes in some areas. Dike thicknesses vary from 1 m to greater than 10 m. Some of these dikes can be traced nearly continuously for nearly 3 km along strike. The dikes grade texturally from aphanitic porphyritic dacite to phaneritic porphyritic granodiorite in the interiors of thick dikes. Along the margins, some dikes have a remarkably fresh but devitrified glassy groundmass. Minerals in the porphyry dikes include quartz, plagioclase, K-feldspar, biotite, hornblende, sphene, iron-titanium oxides, and accessory zircon, although in thin dikes, plagioclase and sparse biotite are commonly the only phenocrysts visible in hand specimen. K-feldspars are commonly mantled with plagioclase in many of the thicker dikes (rapakivi). We hereafter refer to these as granodiorite porphyry dikes. Except for the few exposures of Tertiary rocks, these dikes are the youngest rocks in the western half of Alvord Mountain.

Dike orientations are variable, ranging from northwest-striking to north-striking with a mean azimuth of 325° (*n* = 26; standard deviation [s.d.] = 18°) (Fig. 4C). Dips are subvertical. Several dikes curve from northwest strikes in the southern part of Alvord Mountain to north strikes in the northern part of the area (Fig. 2).

GEOCHRONOLOGY

In order to help determine the time of deformation and the subsequent cooling and metamorphic history at Alvord Mountain, several igneous units were dated by using the U-Pb zircon method (Table 1; Fig. 4). Fission-track and $^{40}Ar/^{39}Ar$ dates

(Figs. 5 and 6; Data Repository Table DR1)[1] were obtained from one sample (AL-8).

Zircon dating

A U-Pb zircon age of 179 Ma has been previously reported for the main Jurassic quartz monzodiorite pluton from Alvord Mountain (Miller et al., 1995). We noted that zircons from this sample are severely complicated by Pb loss and Proterozoic inheritance (Miller et al., 1995). One concordant fraction with an appreciable error was obtained at 179 Ma. Most fractions for this pluton give U-Pb ages close to ca. 170 Ma, and it is possible that the pluton is slightly younger (see Miller et al., 1995). Zircons from other Jurassic plutonic rocks in the Mojave Desert typically show inheritance and Pb loss, and these factors have complicated efforts to determine the timing of plutonism and deformation elsewhere (e.g., Walker et al., 1990; Gerber et al., 1995; Howard et al., 1995; Miller et al., 1995).

Zircons from one of the hornblende gabbro bodies (Al-26; Table 1) were dated for this study (Table 1; Fig. 5A). Multiple populations of zircons—including low-aspect ratio (~2:1), simple tetragonal crystals; longer euhedral, tetragonal crystals; and highly faceted equant crystals—characterize the zircon separates. Handpicking from these different populations failed to yield a concordant age. One fraction of tiny (<74 μm), elongated euhedral zircons is nearly concordant at 147 Ma (Fig. 4), although this sample also has the largest error. Two other fractions of the least magnetic, >74 μm zircons are slightly discordant with U-Pb ages and errors that fall within the error of the most concordant fraction. These two fractions have slightly older Pb-Pb ages (150 to 152 Ma; Table 1). The two most discordant fractions probably contain appreciable inherited zircon as indicated by their Pb-Pb ages (Table 1). One of these fractions is also the most magnetic fraction and has also probably lost an appreciable amount of Pb. If we omit these two discordant points and assume that only recent Pb loss has affected the remaining fractions, a maximum age of 151 ± 2 Ma is given by a discordia line forced through a zero intercept. Omitting the most magnetic fraction, which likely has inheritance and Pb-loss problems, a minimum age for the sample is 147.4 ± 0.5 Ma, based on the weighted average $^{206}Pb/^{238}U$ ages of all the other fractions (Table 1) and assuming that only inheritance has affected these fractions. Considering this minimum age of 147 Ma, the three nearly concordant fractions, and allowing for some inheritance and minor Pb loss, we estimate the age to be 149 ± 3 Ma.

Three zircon fractions were analyzed from one porphyry dike (Alvo-6). An unforced (model 1 York fit) discordia regression on these three points gives a lower intercept of 82.7 ± 1.1 Ma (Fig. 5B; MSWD [mean square of weighted deviates]

[1]GSA Data Repository item 2002098, $^{40}Ar/^{39}Ar$ and fission-track data and electron-microprobe analyses, is available on request from Documents Secretary, GSA, P.O. Box 9140, Boulder, CO 80301-9140, USA, editing@geosociety.org, or at www.geosociety.org/pubs/ft2002.htm.

TABLE 1. ZIRCON ANALYTICAL DATA FOR ALVORD MOUNTAIN

Sample fraction	Size (mg)	U (ppm)	Pb* (ppm)	206Pb/204Pb (meas.)	207Pb/206Pb (meas.)	208Pb/206Pb (meas.)	207Pb*/235U	206Pb*/238U	±2s (%)	207Pb*/206Pb*	Correl. Coeff. (rho)	±2s (%)	206Pb*/238U Age (Ma)	±2s (Ma)	207Pb*/235U Age (Ma)	±2s (Ma)	207Pb/206Pb* Age (Ma)	error 2s (Ma)	comm. Pb (pg)
Hornblende gabbro (AL-26)																			
nm/–1/+74	2.963	674	16.89	2952	0.05401	0.2266	0.15685	0.02317	0.48	0.04909	0.985	0.08	147.4	0.7	147.9	0.7	152.0	2.0	312
nm/0;+74	1.380	708	17.76	2164	0.05578	0.2286	0.15636	0.02312	0.50	0.04905	0.983	0.09	147.3	0.7	147.5	0.7	150.3	2.2	330
nm/0;'+74/hp	0.357	743	18.59	1497	0.05925	0.2284	0.15803	0.02316	0.54	0.04949	0.938	0.19	147.6	0.8	149.0	0.8	171.3	4.4	450
nm/0;'–74/hp	0.204	694	18.31	840.7	0.06639	0.3160	0.15584	0.02309	1.03	0.04896	0.531	0.87	147.1	1.5	147.1	0.8	145.7	20.0	153
nm/1;'+74/hp	0.050	619	15.36	1593	0.05844	0.2415	0.15435	0.02272	0.49	0.04927	0.966	0.13	144.8	0.7	145.8	0.7	160.8	3.0	362
Granodiorite porphyry dike (Alvo-6)																			
nm/0;'–174	2.380	434	6.20	521.8	0.07744	0.2631	0.09058	0.01330	0.68	0.04939	0.736	0.47	85.2	0.6	88.0	0.6	166.2	11.0	629
nm/–1/–174	0.516	449	6.27	397.5	0.08535	0.2800	0.08736	0.01308	0.86	0.04844	0.721	0.58	83.8	0.5	85.0	0.7	120.9	14.0	634
nm/0;'–74	1.000	330	4.96	242.0	0.11049	0.3357	0.09253	0.01343	1.55	0.04997	0.510	1.34	86.0	0.5	89.9	1.4	193.8	31.0	780
Leuco-quartz monzonite (AL-27)																			
nm/0;'+74	0.951	565.0	11.59	1030	0.07187	0.1979	0.15570	0.01952	0.51	0.05784	0.929	0.50	124.7	0.6	146.9	0.7	523.6	4.1	559
nm/0;'–74	0.813	515.1	7.78	892.5	0.06769	0.2633	0.09729	0.01374	0.55	0.05135	0.916	0.50	88.0	0.4	94.3	0.5	256.6	5.0	359
nm/1/–74	0.288	692.7	9.70	517.4	0.07788	0.2884	0.08738	0.01278	0.64	0.04957	0.788	0.39	81.9	0.4	85.1	0.5	175.0	9.2	682

Note: nm(#)/# = nonmagnetic on Frantz separator at side tilt angle of # degrees and less than (–) or greater than (+) # in micrometers. Dissolution followed standard procedures, and elemental separation utilized HBr anion-column chemistry for Pb and HCl column chemistry for U. Decay constants after Steiger and Jäger (1977). All ratios corrected for fractionation and blank except $^{206}Pb/^{204}Pb$ (measured). Samples were analyzed with $^{206}Pb/^{235}U$ spike at the University of North Carolina or University of Kansas. Total procedural blank ≤150 ± 50 pg. All analyses were measured by static multicollector analysis on a Micromass Sector 54 mass spectrometer equipped with Daly ion counting at either the University of North Carolina or University of Kansas. Replicate splits of identical fractions of AL-26 run at Kansas and North Carolina yield the same age within measurement errors. Data were reduced with PbDat of Ludwig (1989). Common-lead corrections used Stacey and Kramers (1975) model lead for the estimated crystallization age.

= 0.23). The upper intercept is ca. 1700 Ma but with a large error. Three zircon fractions from the undeformed leuco–quartz monzonite (AL-27; Table 1) were also analyzed. These three fractions give a discordia (also unforced regression; model 1 York fit) with a lower-intercept age of 75.2 ± 0.6 Ma and a Proterozoic upper-intercept age of 972 ± 13 Ma (Fig. 5C; MSWD = 0.83). Both intrusions clearly have appreciable Proterozoic inheritance. However, the regressions are three-point discordia, and the high degree of fit (as indicated by the low MSWD) does not necessarily indicate that the ages are geologically meaningful.

We regard the lower intercept for the porphyry dike as the crystallization age for the dike and a minimum age for the leuco–quartz monzonite for several reasons. (1) The analyzed porphyry dike (Alvo-6) cuts the leuco–quartz monzonite (AL-27) in the field and must therefore be younger (perhaps only slightly younger) than the leuco–quartz monzonite. (2) Upper-intercept ages of 1000 Ma have not been reported from any other Mesozoic plutonic rocks or Precambrian rocks in the Mojave Desert, to our knowledge. Thus we are skeptical that the upper intercept for the leuco–quartz monzonite is meaningful. Zircon ages of Proterozoic basement and discordia upper intercepts for Mesozoic zircons of 1700-1600 Ma are common (e.g., Wooden and Miller, 1990; Miller et al., 1990; Martin and Walker, 1991; Howard et al., 1995). Thus, the upper intercept for the granodiorite porphyry dike may be more reasonable. Demonstrable Proterozoic inheritance with an anomalous upper intercept in the leuco–quartz monzonite suggests that the zircons have likely lost some Pb. Consequently, the lower intercept for the leuco–quartz monzonite is probably erroneous. (3) The leuco–quartz monzonite has undergone considerable hydrothermal alteration as indicated by the presence of abundant sericitic and/or muscovitic alteration, whereas the porphyry dikes are remarkably fresh and probably have undergone minimal low-temperature Pb loss, i.e., less than the leuco–quartz monzonite.

Biotite and apatite dating

One sample (AL-8) from the main Jurassic quartz monzodiorite pluton from Alvord Mountain was also dated by using $^{40}Ar/^{39}Ar$ and fission-track methods. The $^{40}Ar/^{39}Ar$ age was obtained on a bulk separate of biotite. Step heating failed to yield a plateau age (Fig. 6). The total gas age of 103.2 ± 1.2 Ma and an isotope correlation diagram age of 105.3 ± 0.8 Ma suggest that biotite cooled through Ar closure at ca. 105-103 Ma (Fig. 5). However, partial resetting of this sample may have occurred during Late Cretaceous plutonism. Resetting could also account for an apparent initial $^{40}Ar/^{36}Ar$ component that is appreciably lower than atmospheric argon (Fig. 6; Table DR1 [see footnote 1]). We consider this further in the subsequent discussion of metamorphism.

Apatite fission-track data for this same sample yield a pooled age of 65 ± 2.4 Ma and a mean etchable track length

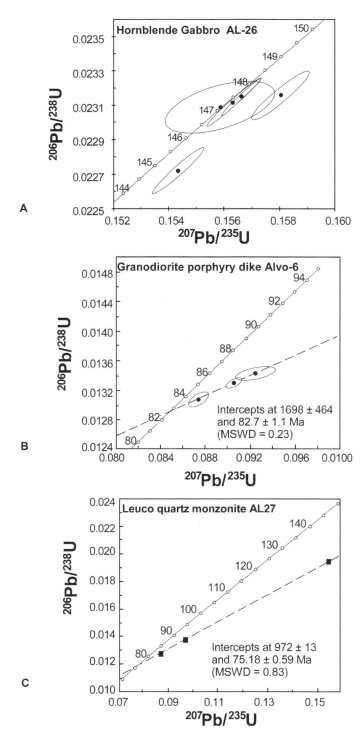

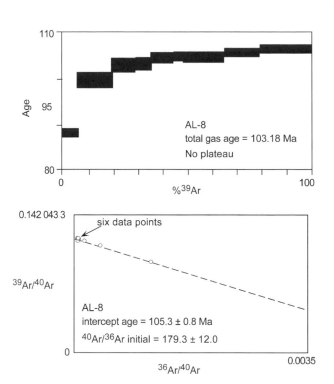

Figure 6. Ar-release spectrum and isotope-correlation diagram for $^{40}Ar/^{39}Ar$ data from sample AL-8 (Jurassic monzodiorite-quartz monzonite). Sample failed to yield a plateau age. Note that the lowest-temperature increment is close the age of the Late Cretaceous plutons and dikes at Alvord Mountain. Isotope-correlation diagram also gives an initial Ar intercept significantly below atmospheric Ar (295.5). Sample was probably degassed during Cretaceous plutonism. Individual degassing steps reported in Table DR1 (see footnote 1).

Figure 5. U-Pb concordia diagrams for samples from Alvord Mountain. (A) Undeformed, postkinematic hornblende gabbro (AL-26). Clustering of ages and minimum ages for least magnetic samples with slight inheritance (Table 1) indicate an age of 149 ± 3 Ma for the gabbro. Data show minor inheritance and minor Pb loss. The gabbro is inferred to correlate with the diabase dikes. (B) Granodiorite porphyry dike (Alvo-6) and (C) leuco-quartz monzonite (AL-27); both have appreciable Precambrian inheritance, and the leuco-quartz monzonite also shows Pb loss. The minimum age for the leuco-quartz monzonite is given by the lower intercept for the granodiorite porphyry dike, which cuts the leuco-quartz monzonite. The lower intercept of the granodiorite porphyry dike is interpreted as the crystallization age for the dike and similar dikes in the swarm. See text for more detailed explanation. Concordia plots, error ellipses, and discordia regressions calculated with Isoplot/Ex of Ludwig (1998).

of 11.36 ± 1.55 µm (Fig. 7; Table DR1 [see footnote 1]). We interpret the data as indicating that the sample cooled through 110° ± 20°C during the Late Cretaceous. The relatively old age and lack of nearly full-length tracks (>14 µm) may indicate that the sample cooled below 50°C more recently (post-middle Miocene?) according to trial thermal models (S. Boettcher, 1999, personal communication). Although the fission-track data are intriguing, more such data are required to better understand the late Mesozoic and Cenozoic thermal and unroofing history of the basement at Alvord Mountain. We will not discuss these data further.

DISCUSSION

Correlation of metasedimentary rocks

Correlation of the metasedimentary rocks at Alvord Mountain to stratigraphic packages of the region is difficult because the rocks have been deformed and recrystallized to the extent that recovery of fossils for biostratigraphic age control is probably impossible. Nevertheless, some assessment of likely correlative strata is imperative in evaluating tectonic models and timing of deformation in the Alvord Mountain area. Miller et al. (1991) tentatively correlated these strata with middle to upper Paleozoic rocks in the Goldstone–Lane Mountain area on the basis of gross lithologic similarity, but did not give a detailed discussion of this correlation. We therefore discuss correlation of the metasedimentary rocks at Alvord Mountain in detail here. Our correlation is made by comparison with better-known and less metamorphosed stratigraphic units in the Mojave Desert and environs.

Byers (1960) speculated that the metasedimentary rocks at Alvord Mountain were Precambrian–early Paleozoic but did not formally correlate the rocks with any regional strata of Precambrian–early Paleozoic age. Latest Precambrian-early Paleozoic cratonal and transitional miogeoclinal-cratonal strata are found regionally in the Providence and Marble Mountains and ranges in their vicinity (Fig. 1) (Hazzard, 1954; Stewart, 1970; Stone et al., 1983), in the Death Valley area (Wright et al., 1974; not shown in Fig. 1), and in scattered exposures south, west, and northeast of Alvord Mountain (Stewart and Poole, 1975; Boettcher and Walker, 1993; Martin and Walker, 1995; Schermer et al., 2001; Fig. 1). Continental-margin strata in all these areas are dominantly terrigenous clastic rocks with abundant quartzites and dolomites.

The oldest rocks recognized regionally are the Pahrump Group rocks in the Death Valley area (Crystal Spring Formation, Beck Spring Dolomite, and Kingston Peak Formation). However, these strata are confined to the Death Valley area and have not been previously identified in the western and central Mojave Desert or in ranges surrounding Alvord Mountain (e.g., Burchfiel and Davis, 1981). We therefore consider it unlikely that the Alvord Mountain rocks can be correlated with strata in the Pahrump Group.

Late Precambrian (post–Pahrump Group) strata include the Noonday Dolomite, Johnnie Formation (interlayered shales, sandstones, dolomite, and limestone), and Stirling Quartzite (Wright et al., 1974). Cambrian continental-margin rocks elsewhere in the Mojave Desert include (from oldest to youngest) the Wood Canyon Formation (probably partly Precambrian, boundary is uncertain), Zabriskie Quartzite, Carrara Formation, Bonanza King Formation, and Nopah Formation (Hazzard, 1954; Stewart, 1970; Burchfiel and Davis, 1981; Stone et al., 1983).

Boettcher and Walker (1993) correlated dolomitic marble and interlayered quartzite and muscovite + biotite schist in the Iron Mountain area (Fig. 1) with the upper Noonday Dolomite and lower Johnnie Formation, which also predominantly contains dolomite of variable thickness. However, no dolomite is present at Alvord Mountain, quartzite is volumetrically minor, and muscovite schist is rare. Therefore, Alvord Mountain metasedimentary rocks probably do not correlate with the Noonday Dolomite and lower Johnnie Formation.

Schermer et al. (2001) have speculated that a marble unit and feldspathic quartz + biotite schists with intercalated marbles and abundant quartzites in the Tiefort Mountains (Fig. 1) may be correlative with the upper Johnnie Formation, which

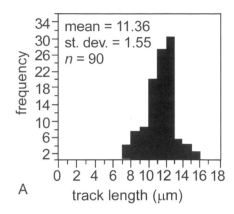

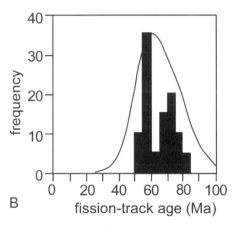

Figure 7. (A) Apatite fission-track length distribution and (B) age histogram for sample AL-8 from the main Jurassic quartz monzodiorite pluton from Alvord Mountain. Note the low abundance of near full-length tracks (>14 μm), indicating that the sample remained above ~50 °C well after cooling through 110 ± 20 °C in the latest Cretaceous (65 Ma). Table DR1 (see footnote 1) contains count data pertaining to this age determination.

does contain a thick calcite limestone, and/or with the Stirling Quartzite and overlying Wood Canyon Formation. The Tiefort Mountains rocks are also in contact with 1400 Ma augen gneiss (Schermer et al., 2001).

Although we cannot completely rule out a correlation with continental-margin strata, we do not think that the Alvord Mountain metasedimentary rocks correlate with these units for four reasons. (1) The Wood Canyon Formation and Zabriskie Quartzite are dominated by quartzite and arkosic quartzite with locally preserved cross-bedding, even in amphibolite-grade rocks (Stone et al., 1983). Where exposed, the Wood Canyon Formation and Zabriskie Quartzite sit on Precambrian basement (including in the Tiefort Mountains). Precambrian gneiss has not been identified at Alvord Mountain, and quartzites are volumetrically minor at Alvord Mountain (although quartz is an important component of the biotite schist unit). (2) The schists of the metamorphosed Carrara Formation are generally more pelitic than the biotite schist at Alvord Mountain (including abundant muscovite; Stone et al., 1983), and the carbonate units are much thinner and contain appreciable dolomite, in contrast to the marble at Alvord Mountain. (3) The Bonanza King and Nopah Formations are also dominated by gray and tan dolomite (and dolomitic marble where metamorphosed) and are therefore unlikely to be present at Alvord Mountain. (4) Metavolcanic rocks are not intercalated with the continental-margin strata in any of the Mojave Desert stratigraphic sections. The Cambrian continental-margin sequence in the Mojave Desert is overlain unconformably by the Devonian Sultan Limestone, which is also dolomite and thus not present at Alvord Mountain.

Abundant calcite limestones with interbedded siliceous beds (and their metamorphosed equivalents) (calcite marble and calc-silicates) make up the Mississippian–Lower Permian continental-margin strata in the Mojave Desert (Monte Cristo Limestone and Bird Spring Formation) (Hazzard, 1954; Stewart, 1970; Stone et al., 1983; Walker and Wardlaw, 1989). Possibly, the marble unit at Alvord Mountain may be correlated with some of these strata, although thick intervals of siliciclastic rocks are not present in these late Paleozoic rocks, making correlation of the biotite schist unit to continental-margin strata difficult.

Of the surrounding potentially correlative strata, the Alvord Mountain rocks are most similar to rocks exposed in the Goldstone and possibly the Lane Mountain areas (Fig. 1; McCulloh, 1952, 1960; Miller and Sutter, 1982; Walker, 1988). Rocks in Goldstone area have been correlated with lower Paleozoic eugeoclinal rocks (displaced Antler belt rocks) and upper Paleozoic–lower Mesozoic basinal facies and continental-borderland strata (Miller and Sutter, 1982; Walker, 1988; Martin and Walker, 1991).

Consideration of the Alvord Mountains rocks in relation to the Goldstone rocks leads to two possibilities. In the first interpretation, the biotite schist and marble units at Alvord Mountain may correlate with units 2 and 3, respectively, of Miller and Sutter (1982) at Goldstone. Unit 2 of Miller and Sutter (1982) comprises several hundred meters (structural thickness) of siliceous argillite ("black phyllite"), interbedded with mafic (volcanic?) stretched-pebble conglomerate, impure quartzite, argillaceous chert, vitreous orthoquartzite, and minor andalusite schist and calc-silicate. Gray limestone and marble and impure silty limestone composing the lower part of unit 3 are in sharp contact on unit 2 in the Goldstone area (Miller and Sutter, 1982). However, much of the lower part of unit 3 is covered in the Goldstone area, and the total thickness of the lower marble unit is unknown. Argillaceous chert layers have not been recognized at Alvord Mountain, but the combination of siliceous argillite, impure quartzite, mafic metavolcanic rocks, vitreous orthoquartzite, minor andalusite schist, and calc-silicate is somewhat similar to the rocks composing the biotite schist at Alvord Mountain. The contact between the marble unit and underlying phyllites and quartzites at Goldstone is sharp and therefore similar to the contact between the biotite schist

and marble at Alvord Mountain, except that at Goldstone, quartzites predominate in the upper part of unit 2. In general, the rocks at Alvord Mountain appear to be metamorphosed to somewhat higher grades, making definitive correlation difficult.

In a second interpretation, all of the rocks at Alvord Mountain could be part of unit 3 of Miller and Sutter (1982). A thick sequence (several hundred meters) of pelitic hornfels and schist intercalated with volcanic flows, calc-silicate layers, and several sandy limestones comprises the middle and upper part of unit 3 of Miller and Sutter (1982). This hornfels unit overlies the basal marble, but the contact is covered. The biotite schist at Alvord Mountain may correlate with part of the pelitic hornfels and schist of the middle and upper part of unit 3 of Miller and Sutter (1982). If so, the biotite schist at Alvord Mountain would be stratigraphically above the marble at Alvord Mountain, if it is assumed that the marble correlates with the lower part of unit 3 at Goldstone. Miller and Sutter (1982) reported andalusite and white mica as primary constituents in the hornfels of unit 3 at Goldstone, whereas at Alvord Mountain, andalusite and white mica are rare. Thus the second interpretation is less favored. We permissively correlate the biotite schist and marble units at Alvord Mountain with either units 2 and 3 or just unit 3 of Miller and Sutter (1982) on the basis of overall gross lithologic similarity.

Miller and Sutter (1982) correlated rocks of unit 2 in the Goldstone area with lower Paleozoic displaced Antler allochthon rocks in the El Paso Mountains and Pilot Knob Valley (Fig. 1; Carr et al., 1984, 1992). Miller and Sutter (1982) correlated unit 3 rocks with Permian basinal-facies rocks overlying the lower Paleozoic eugeoclinal rocks in the El Paso Mountains and with the Coyote Group (McCulloh, 1954) in the Lane Mountain area. Martin and Walker (1991) correlated the unit 3 strata at Goldstone with parautochthonous borderland-basin strata of Late Permian–Early Triassic age (Fairview Valley Formation). The presence of sandy limestone clast conglomerate within the marble unit at Alvord Mountain may also be evidence that the marble correlates with Lower Triassic continental-borderland strata because sandy, limestone-clast-rich conglomerates and calc-silicates occur within Triassic overlap assemblages throughout the central and western Mojave Desert (Walker, 1988). Furthermore, if the biotite schist unit correlates with eugeoclinal assemblages at Goldstone, then it suggests a sharp transition between the eugeoclinal strata at Alvord Mountain and continental-margin strata in the Tiefort Mountains area (Fig. 1) (see also Schermer et al., 2001).

Correlation of igneous rocks

As already mentioned, the edges of the main deformed Jurassic monzonite pluton are not exposed at Alvord Mountain. Therefore, this pluton must be part of a larger body buried by the alluvium and possibly exposed in other ranges surrounding Alvord Mountain. However, ages of ca. 180-170 Ma have not been widely reported in the vicinity of Alvord Mountain.

Scattered plutonic rocks in the eastern part of the Larrea Complex in the Lane Mountain area (McCulloh, 1960; Fig. 1) are mineralogically similar to the main Middle Jurassic quartz monzodiorite at Alvord Mountain (Byers, 1960; Miller et al., 1991), but the ages of these rocks are not well established. Intrusive relationships require the similar quartz monzonites in the Lane Mountain area to be younger than 240 Ma (age of Lane Mountain diorite; Miller et al., 1995) and older than 148 Ma (age of hornblende gabbros; Miller and Sutter, 1982).

Schermer et al. (2001) have dated Jurassic quartz monzo-diorite and diorite gneisses in the Tiefort Mountains (Fig. 1) area that are similar to the deformed quartz monzodiorite at Alvord Mountain; they reported minimum ages between 164 and 160 Ma. These dates are also severely hampered by Pb loss and inheritance; thus they could be older by several million years.

In the eastern El Paso Mountains (Fig. 1), the Laurel Canyon pluton (Carr et al., 1984) has been tentatively dated at 171 Ma (Miller et al., 1995). The Laurel Canyon pluton is minera-logically, chemically, and isotopically similar to the quartz monzonite at Alvord Mountain (Miller et al., 1995) but, because of Pb loss and inheritance, the pluton could be slightly younger or slightly older than 171 Ma (Miller et al., 1995). From our observations, plutonic rocks in the Spangler Hills and south-ernmost Argus Range east of the El Paso Mountains (Fig. 1) resemble the Laurel Canyon pluton and the Alvord Mountains quartz monzodiorite. Dated (U-Pb zircon) Late Jurassic Inde-pendence dikes also cut the eastern Spangler Hills and eastern El Paso Mountains quartz monzonites (Chen and Moore, 1979; Fig. 1), and restoration of ~60 km of left-lateral slip (e.g., Carr et al., 1992) aligns the dikes and similar occurrences of Jurassic quartz monzonite and monzodiorite north (El Paso Mountains, Spangler Hills, southern Argus Range) and south (Granite Mountains, Tiefort Mountains, Alvord Mountain) of the Gar-lock fault.

We thus speculate that the Jurassic quartz monzodiorite at Alvord Mountain may be part of a contiguous or semicontig-uous plutonic terrane that was emplaced within a relatively nar-row time interval (5–10 m.y.?) during the early Middle Jurassic. However, more and better geochronology and more detailed field work and petrology are required to resolve whether such a batholith exists and was indeed emplaced within 5–10 m.y.

The age of the Alvord Mountain gabbros is similar to ages reported for other isolated occurrences of layered gabbro plu-tons in the Shadow Mountains (Martin, 1992; Fig. 1) and Gold-stone area (Miller and Sutter, 1982). However, Late Jurassic gabbros have not been reported in the Tiefort Mountains, El Paso Mountains, Spangler Hills, or Argus Range. Crosscutting relationships suggest that other undated layered gabbros in the Iron Mountain area (Boettcher and Walker, 1993) and Fremont Peak area (Fletcher et al., this volume) also have Late Jurassic ages.

The 148 Ma age reported for the Alvord Mountain gabbro in this paper is also the widely accepted age for the Indepen-dence dike swarm (Chen and Moore, 1979; James, 1989; Carl and Glazner, this volume). If the hornblende diabase dikes are age correlative with the hornblende gabbros at Alvord Moun-tain, then they would be considered Independence dikes. Dia-base dikes west of Spanish Canyon also have approximately N40°W orientations (Fig. 4), similar to the predominant re-gional orientation of the Independence dikes (Moore and Hop-son, 1961; Carl and Glazner, this volume). Dikes east of Span-ish Canyon have likely been affected by Tertiary rotation, as discussed in a subsequent section.

The ages and extent of Cretaceous plutonic rocks in the central and western Mojave Desert, particularly surrounding Alvord Mountain, are not well known. Miller and Sutter (1982) reported a preferred $^{40}Ar/^{39}Ar$ age of ca. 82 Ma on an unde-formed, porphyritic K-feldspar granodiorite in the Paradise Range (Goldstone area). Similar plutonic rocks are exposed in the Tiefort Mountains area but are deformed and have a U-Pb zircon age of ca. 105 Ma (Schermer et al., 2001). Undeformed Late Cretaceous equigranular granites and quartz monzonites are also present in the Tiefort Mountains, but the ages are un-known, except from crosscutting relationships.

A number of ages have been reported for Cretaceous dikes that suggest regionally significant diking between ca. 85 and 82 Ma. Schermer et al. (2001) reported an age of ca. 82 Ma on pegmatite dikes in the Tiefort Mountains area. An age of 83 Ma for muscovite + garnet granite dikes has also been reported in the Iron Mountain area (Boettcher and Walker, 1993). Miller and Sutter (1982) reported a preferred $^{40}Ar/^{39}Ar$ age of 77 Ma for granodiorite porphyry dikes at Goldstone. These dikes are identical to the Alvord porphyry dikes and are probably cor-relative. The age that Miller and Sutter (1982) reported is prob-ably a minimum age as the sample failed to yield a plateau.

The Alvord Mountain dikes and the Goldstone dikes are especially significant because they are thick dikes with an over-all northwest strike that is similar to the regional orientation of the Independence dike swarm. The age reported here for the Alvord dikes, and for correlative dikes at Goldstone, further extends the regional distribution of dated Cretaceous northwest-striking dikes within the area encompassed by the Late Jurassic Independence dike swarm. Coleman et al. (2000) reported two Cretaceous U-Pb mineral ages (one monazite, one zircon) for dikes in the eastern Sierra Nevada, within the type locality of the Independence dike swarm, although the ages obtained by these authors were slightly older (ca. 90 Ma). The dike dated by Schermer et al. (2001) in the Tiefort Mountains area strikes northeast and has probably been rotated by Late Cenozoic clockwise vertical-axis rotation.

Deformation

The major structure at Alvord Mountains is a southeast-plunging syncline (Fig. 2), assuming that our stratigraphic cor-relation is correct and the marble is younger than the schist. Toward the northwest end of the map area, dips in the schist on either side of a small blob of the marble, although steep, generally dip toward the marble, consistent with a synform. The fold is defined primarily by biotite schistosity and layering in the marbles. Although somewhat variable, most foliations in the schist and marble dip steeply southwest. This dip implies that the fold is slightly inclined (overturned?) toward the northeast with a steeply southwest-dipping hinge surface. The hinge of the fold is poorly defined in the field. There is a hint in the foliation that the structure may be doubly plunging with closure both to the northwest and southeast (Fig. 2), but this geometry is difficult to verify because of poor exposure. Poles to foliations in the marble and schist (Fig. 8A) also suggest a generally northwest-striking hinge surface with a weakly defined, moderately southeast-plunging fold axis. Mesoscopic folds in the banded marble and schist are generally tight and upright or overturned toward the northeast with steeply southwest-dipping hinge surfaces and moderate plunge, generally southeast (Fig. 8A). Less commonly, mesoscopic folds in the marble unit are recumbent.

Foliations in the quartz monzodiorite are concordant with foliations in the schist and marble (Fig. 8B). Some of the foliation may have formed before the pluton reached the solidus, particularly in the northern part of the map area, where samples show little grain-size reduction and only minor recrystallization of quartz, but possess a moderate to strong biotite and hornblende foliation. Toward the south, and particularly along the northern contact between the metamorphic rocks and the quartz monzodiorite, solid-state fabrics in the pluton indicate dynamic recrystallization and dynamic recovery. Within the gneissic layers, quartz and plagioclase show subgrain development with serrated grain boundaries. More commonly, quartz and feldspar occur as small grains (much reduced in size from the centimeter-sized grains in the weakly deformed protolith) with polygonal grain boundaries and uniform extinction. Biotite is commonly strongly aligned but shows little internal strain.

Solid-state ductile deformation is most strongly manifested as discrete, narrow mylonitic shear zones (meter-wide and less than 50 m in length) (Fig. 2). These are present locally in the schist and in the quartz monzodiorite. The shear zones generally strike northwest and are subparallel with the dominant range-scale foliation. Dips are steep (70°–80°SW) (Fig. 8C), but stretching lineations are shallow (8°–17°) (Fig. 9C), plunging northwest predominantly (Fig. 8C). Shear-sense indicators are rare ($n = 6$) but indicate sinistral top-to-the-southeast shear (Fig. 9B). Sinistral S-C fabric was noted in three outcrops. Fabrics are similar to those already described for the gneissic quartz monzodiorite, but show more pronounced grain-size reduction.

We interpret the deformation history as follows: (1) formation of the original metamorphic foliation; (2) folding of the original metamorphic foliation and deformation of the pluton, which produced steeply southwest-dipping solid-state fabrics and mesoscopic folds with southwest-dipping hinge surfaces; and (3) formation of southwest-dipping discrete mylonitic shear zones.

It is not possible to determine when the original metamorphic foliation formed, but it must predate folding, although it is possible that all of the deformation stages represent a single progressive deformation. Metamorphic fabric formation may have accompanied emplacement of the main quartz monzodiorite; subsequently, this fabric was folded and a coplanar solid-state fabric was developed in the quartz monzodiorite during shortening. Because the small mylonitic shear zones are parallel to the main foliation and developed primarily in foliated rocks and not in younger nonfoliated rocks, the mylonitic shear zones are probably part of the same general episode of deformation. We infer that they postdate folding because the shear zones are not folded. However, the steep dips and shallowly plunging stretching lineations indicate that strike-slip deformation accompanied formation of these shear zones.

Metamorphism

The metamorphic mineral assemblages for several bulk schist compositions is summarized in Table 2. The metamorphic mineral assemblages are inferred on the basis of textural evidence to be in equilibrium and are generally consistent with metamorphism at upper-greenschist or lower-amphibolite facies (Table 2 and DR2 [see footnote 1]). The best temperature estimates come from samples of metapsammitic rocks from the schist and give temperatures of 480 ± 50 °C. Pressure is difficult to estimate from the metamorphic mineral assemblages, because no assemblages containing garnet have been found, except for grossular in the calc-silicates. Phengite geobarometry (Massonne and Schreyer, 1987) from coarse-grained white mica gives 200 to 250 MPa pressure estimates, but the lowest Si contents measured for white micas are out of the range of the calibration. Pressure could have been as high as 375 MPa at a temperature of 500 °C, which is close to the aluminosilicate triple-point estimate of Holdaway and Mukhopadhyay (1993). Relatively low pressures are consistent with the presence of andalusite and not kyanite in the metapsammites and the relatively low Na content of amphiboles in the mafic metavolcanic rocks.

The timing of peak metamorphism relative to deformation is uncertain, and definitive textural evidence (e.g., porphyroblast and inclusion relationships) is lacking or ambiguous. In a few samples from the folded biotite schist, metamorphic micas are bent slightly around adjacent grains, suggesting that mica growth occurred prior to folding. However, in most other samples, metamorphic biotite grains that define mesoscopic folds show no internal strain, suggesting that metamorphic recrystallization was synkinematic with or outlasted folding. This interpretation would also be consistent with the textural relationships in the gneissic quartz monzodiorite previously mentioned. The presence of skarn in the carbonates, the local formation of migmatitic injection gneiss along the margins of the Jurassic quartz monzodiorite (Fig. 3A), and the low-pressure environment suggest that peak metamorphic conditions are related to

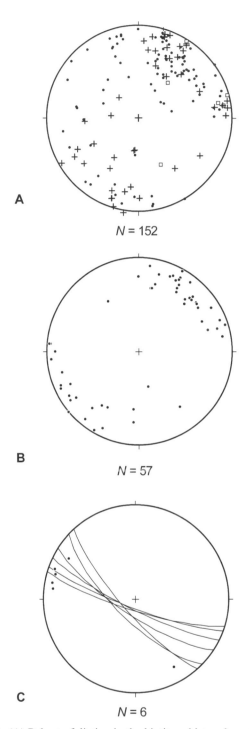

Figure 8. (A) Poles to foliation in the biotite schist and marble units. Symbols: Small solid circles—biotite foliation in schist; crosses—layering in marble, boxes—poles to axial surfaces of mesoscopic folds. (B) Poles to biotite and hornblende foliation (predominantly subsolidus) in the Jurassic monzodiorite-quartz monzonite. Although variable, most foliations and axial surfaces of mesoscopic folds indicate steep southwest dips. (C) Strike and dip of mylonitic shear-zone foliation. Small solid circles give trend and plunge of lineation. Note the steep dip of shear zones that are approximately parallel to the main range-scale solid-state foliation but uniformly shallow, with a predominantly northwest-plunging lineation.

intrusion of the Jurassic quartz monzodiorite, although the calculated temperatures may not represent peak temperatures. The low-pressure and moderate- to high-temperature metamorphism recorded in these rocks is typical of regional metamorphism associated with magmatism elsewhere in the western Cordillera (cf. Barton et al., 1988). However, it is not possible to rule out an earlier metamorphic event on the basis of available evidence.

Some evidence for local static recrystallization well after peak metamorphism is found in the southern part of the map area, where medium-grained biotite schist is overprinted locally by randomly oriented sprays of fine-grained white mica. Heating in the aureole of the Cretaceous pluton may thus have overprinted some of the older Jurassic metamorphic fabric. The $^{40}Ar/^{39}Ar$ loss spectrum from biotite in the Jurassic quartz monzodiorite (Fig. 6) also suggests that the pluton was subjected to some later reheating. The lowest-temperature increment yielded an age of ca. 88 Ma (Fig. 6; Table DR1 [see footnote 1]). This lowest-temperature increment is close to the best age estimate of the leuco–quartz monzonite and the age of the porphyry dikes.

Timing and style of deformation and relationship to regional events

The prekinematic quartz monzodiorite and the postkinematic hornblende gabbros bracket the age of deformation at Alvord Mountain. Thus deformation occurred between 179 Ma and 149 Ma. Walker et al. (1990) reported middle- to upper-greenschist–facies Jurassic contractional deformation and metamorphism in the Cronese Hills that is bracketed between 169 and 154 Ma. Miller et al. (1996) and Schermer et al. (2001) reported greenschist–facies to upper-amphibolite–facies Jurassic contractional deformation and metamorphism in the Tiefort Mountains–Fort Irwin area. However, peak pressures (600–700 MPa) are higher than the pressures estimated at Alvord Mountain (Miller et al., 1996). In the Tiefort Mountains, deformation is bracketed between ca. 164 and 148 Ma (Schermer et al., 2001).

Walker et al. (1990) and Schermer et al. (2001) correlated deformation in the Cronese Hills and Tiefort Mountains with the Jurassic–Cretaceous East Sierran thrust system (Dunne et al., 1978; Dunne, 1986; Dunne and Walker, 1993) and Walker et al. (1990) speculated that the deformation at Alvord Mountain could also be correlative. The age overlap, similarity in style, similar grade of metamorphism, and close proximity of Alvord Mountain to the Cronese Hills and Tiefort Mountains support this interpretation.

In the Cronese Hills area, the main contractional structure is a northwest-dipping thrust fault (moderately west-dipping mylonitic shear zone) that places metavolcanic and metaplutonic rocks on east-vergent folds in lower Mesozoic metasedimentary rocks cut by west-dipping thrust faults (Walker et al., 1990). In the Tiefort Mountains area, west-dipping Middle Jurassic ductile shear zones cut Middle Jurassic plutons and

A

B

Figure 9. (A) Shear zone in biotite schist. Pencil points in direction of shallowly plunging lineation in plane of foliation. Lineation is defined by quartz ribbons and chlorite and plunges ~8°NW. Pencil for scale is ~15 cm long. (B) Shear zone in banded injection gneiss. Surface is perpendicular to foliation and parallel to lineation. Lineation plunges less than 8°NW in this outcrop. Shear-sense indicators are ambiguous in parts of this outcrop. Fold trains in lighter layers above pencil show sinistral (top-to-the-southeast) motion. Pencil for scale is ~15 cm long.

metasedimentary rocks and were the sites of southeast to south vergence (Schermer et al., 2001). The geometry of folding at Alvord indicates northeast-southwest shortening with northeast-vergent folding; sparse shear indicators give a top-to-the-southeast sense of shear. Thus all Middle Jurassic deformation in the area was broadly east vergent.

Deformation at Alvord Mountain (and at these other areas) differs from deformation in the Cronese Hills and Tiefort Mountains in that lineations in the mylonitic shear zones in the Cronese Hills and Tiefort Mountains plunge downdip or strongly oblique to strike, whereas at Alvord Mountain, mylonitic shear zones are steeply dipping with shallowly plunging lineations. Unfortunately the age brackets on deformation at Alvord are relatively large compared with the more tightly bracketed deformation in the Cronese Hills and the Tiefort Mountains. Thus the strike-slip shear zones at Alvord Mountain

TABLE 2. METAMORPHIC MINERALS AND CONDITIONS FROM SAMPLES WITHIN BIOTITE SCHIST

Protolith or bulk composition (sample numbers)	Mineral assemblage	Relevant geothermometers	Relevant geobarometers
Mafic to intermediate-composition metavolcanic rock (AVM-90-20; AM4-17)	cpx + hb + bi + Ksp + pl + qz + ep + Fe-oxide	hornblende-plagioclase*	
Intermediate-composition metavolcanic rock (1-3-90C)	qz + Ksp + pl + bi + mu + ch + il + hm	biotite-muscovite[†], muscovite-plagioclase[§]	Si content in white mica[#]
Psammite and pelite (AVM90-006; AVM90-12)	qz + pl + bi + ms + il ± ch ± hm ± ap ± rt ± andalusite	biotite-muscovite[†], muscovite-plagioclase[§]	Si content in white mica[#], maximum P stability of andalusite**

Calculated temperatures: 480 ± 50°C. Calculated pressures: 250–375 MPa. Mineral abbreviations follow Kretz (1983).
*Spear (1981); Blundy and Holland (1990).
[†]Hoisch (1989).
[§]Green and Udansky (1987).
[#]Massonne and Schreyer (1987), pressure calculated at reference temperature of 500°C.
**Maximum pressure stability of andalusite at reference temperature of 500 °C using aluminosilicate phase diagram of Holdaway and Mukhopadhyay (1993).

may not be strictly age correlative with the mostly dip-slip shear zones in the Cronese Hills and Tiefort Mountains. Nevertheless, they imply a fairly close spatial and temporal association of contractional and strike-slip deformation within the East Sierran thrust system. Such close association of contractional and strike-slip deformation is generally compatible with a sinistral, obliquely convergent subduction setting, which is thought to have existed during the time this deformation occurred (e.g., Ave Lallemant and Oldow; 1988; May et al., 1989; Saleeby and Busby-Spera, 1992; Schermer, 1993; Schermer and Busby, 1994; Wolf and Saleeby, 1995).

Tertiary structural complications: Miocene extension and vertical-axis rotation

A number of fairly recent studies have suggested that Miocene and younger deformation may have affected the Alvord Mountain area (Ross et al., 1989; Walker et al., 1995; Schermer et al., 1996; Ron and Nur, 1996). The Cenozoic deformation could have disrupted the original orientation of Mesozoic structures at Alvord Mountain. Thus it is prudent to briefly examine the possible effects of Tertiary deformation in this area and also to examine these studies in light of this work.

Early Miocene extension occurred in parts of the central Mojave Desert (Dokka, 1989; Glazner et al., 1989; Walker et al., 1995; Glazner et al., this volume). However, large-magnitude displacement along normal faults occurred west of Alvord Mountain (see Glazner et al., this volume). Alvord Mountain occupied a hanging-wall position within the Central Mojave metamorphic core complex (Fillmore, 1993; Walker et al., 1995), and early Miocene extensional faulting does not appear to have severely disrupted Mesozoic structures. Numerous small, high-angle Tertiary faults are present mainly in the eastern part of Alvord Mountain, east of Spanish Canyon (Byers, 1960). The Tertiary faults show dip-slip or strike-slip displacement of meters to perhaps hundreds of meters. Stratal tilts on fault-bounded blocks are ≤40° in most areas, except locally

where fault drag has steepened dips. West of Spanish Canyon, and just north of the map area shown in Figure 2, lower Miocene sedimentary rocks and mafic volcanic flows sit nonconformably on deformed quartz monzodiorite and generally dip less than 5° northeast. Thus we infer that there has been no appreciable Cenozoic tilting west of Spanish Canyon and that Mesozoic structures have not been markedly affected by early Miocene extension.

Some variability in the vergence of Mesozoic structures might be explained by Cenozoic rotation about a vertical axis. Schermer et al. (2001) speculated that rocks in the Tiefort Mountains could have been rotated between 25° and 40° clockwise about a vertical axis, on the basis of paleomagnetic data from Miocene basalts in the Fort Irwin area (Schermer et al., 1996). However, they noted that allowing this much clockwise rotation does not dramatically change the overall east to southeast vergence of Jurassic structures in the Tiefort Mountains.

At Alvord Mountain, ~50° degrees of post-early Miocene clockwise vertical-axis rotation has also been proposed from paleomagnetic data (Ross et al., 1989) and from statistical analysis of the azimuths of presumed Independence dikes taken from aerial photographs in the Fort Irwin area (Ron and Nur, 1996).

Ron and Nur (1996) included 16 dikes from Alvord Mountain in their analysis of dike orientations and inferred 43° ± 5° of clockwise rotation (*n* = 16) from a mean azimuth of ~315° for unrotated Independence dikes north of the Garlock fault. However, both Jurassic Independence-age dikes (the diabase dikes) and Cretaceous porphyry dikes are exposed at Alvord Mountain. The large Cretaceous porphyry dikes are most easily picked out on aerial photographs and presumably weighed preferentially in Ron and Nur's (1996) analysis. The Cretaceous dikes cannot be used to determine rotation because they are not age correlative with the Late Jurassic Independence dikes north of the Garlock fault, which were used to establish the unrotated Independence dike mean. Furthermore, the mean azimuth of Cretaceous porphyry dikes in our study (Fig. 4C) is ~20° more toward the west than the mean obtained by Ron and Nur (1996) and overlaps the Independence dike mean within error.

If we assume that the Late Jurassic diabase dikes are correlative with the Independence dikes, as proposed herein, then these could potentially be used to examine rotation of Alvord Mountain. The Late Jurassic dike orientations suggest that the amount of rotation that might be inferred at Alvord Mountain is nonuniform. Azimuth data from west of Spanish Canyon would seem to suggest little if any vertical-axis rotation because the mean azimuth of diabase dikes west of Spanish Canyon is 319° ± 11° (n = 16) (Fig. 4B)—statistically the same as the unrotated Independence dike mean. The data further imply that Mesozoic structures west of Spanish Canyon have been rotated little if at all during the Cenozoic. However, east of Spanish Canyon, half the diabase dikes have azimuths that are ~35° clockwise from the Independence dike mean of 315°, and the other half have azimuths that are ~95° clockwise from the Independence dike mean. Because of the variable orientations of Late Jurassic diabase dikes measured in this study, it is thus not completely clear that the Jurassic dikes can be used to determine rotation reliably. It may be that the orientation of the diabase dikes at Alvord Mountain is at least partly controlled by local stresses associated with emplacement of the gabbro plutons.

Paleomagnetic data presented by Ross et al. (1989) also suggest that Alvord Mountain has been rotated. Ross et al. (1989) obtained a stable site mean (n = 9) for individual lava-flow sites at and immediately east of Alvord Mountain. The site mean reported by Ross et al. (1989) has a declination of ~48° clockwise from the Miocene reference direction of Calderone et al. (1990) and would seem to indicate rotation of Alvord Mountain. Most of their data are from nearly flat lying flows south and east of Spanish Canyon and thus may be compatible with variable rotation at Alvord Mountain.

Regardless of how the paleomagnetic data and dike-azimuth data are interpreted, some clockwise rotation of Alvord Mountain on the order of 40°–45° does not dramatically alter the main conclusions of our study with regard to Mesozoic deformation.

SUMMARY

The results of this study can be summarized as follows:

1. Metasedimentary rocks at Alvord Mountain are correlated with either the displaced Antler allochthon or uppermost Paleozoic–lower Mesozoic parautochthonous borderland-basin rocks. Marbles and siliceous marbles that structurally overlie the schists are probably borderland-basin strata. These strata formed during inception of the active continental margin of the western Cordillera. Correlative strata of slightly lower metamorphic grade are found just to the west in the Goldstone–Lane Mountain area.

2. Multiple plutons and dikes, ranging from 179 Ma to 82 Ma, intruded the metasedimentary rocks. The largest and oldest

exposed pluton at Alvord Mountain is a relatively mafic biotite monzodiorite to quartz monzonite. This pluton may correlate with similar Middle Jurassic rocks to the north of the Alvord Mountain area and therefore may be part of a larger coeval plutonic terrane. Hornblende gabbros and diorites and associated northwest-striking diabasic dikes were intruded in the Late Jurassic during the time of the regional emplacement of Independence dikes. The gabbros form part of a Late Jurassic gabbro-diorite suite that can be found throughout the central Mojave Desert. The remaining intrusions are Late Cretaceous and include a biotite leuco–quartz monzonite pluton and possibly associated east-striking composite dikes, and northwest-striking dacite (granodiorite) porphyry dikes. The Late Cretaceous age reported here for the large northwest-striking porphyry dikes further emphasizes the need for caution when using undated northwest-striking Mesozoic dikes for Jurassic tectonic models based on the regional strike and emplacement of the Independence dikes (see Coleman et al., 2000).

3. Range-scale fabric development, contractional folding, and shear-zone development occurred between intrusion of the deformed 179 Ma quartz monzodiorite and the undeformed 149 Ma hornblende gabbros. Foliation fabrics in the quartz monzodiorite (near solidus and subsolidus) and the metamorphic rocks, hinge surfaces of mesoscopic folds, and discrete mylonitic shear zones are all approximately coplanar and probably part of the same deformational episode. An earlier metamorphic and deformational event cannot be ruled out.

4. Metamorphic conditions reached upper-greenschist–lower-amphibolite facies, but the timing of peak metamorphism is uncertain. Contact metamorphism associated with intrusion of the younger Cretaceous pluton and dikes accounts for some of the local static recrystallization in the schists.

5. Deformation at Alvord Mountain is correlated regionally with the Jurassic–Cretaceous East Sierran thrust system, which is known to have affected the immediate vicinity of Alvord Mountain in the Cronese Hills and in the Tiefort Mountains.

6. Alvord Mountain was affected by Tertiary extension, but minor tilting associated with Tertiary extension did not reorient Mesozoic structures to any appreciable degree.

7. Vertical-axis rotation of Mesozoic structures may have occurred, but the data used to infer this are conflicting. Some rotation is inferred from previous paleomagnetic studies. Cretaceous porphyry dike azimuths obtained via remote sensing cannot be used to measure rotation because the dikes were assumed to have Late Jurassic ages and to correlate with Independence dikes north of the Garlock fault. On the basis of the azimuths of more reliably inferred Late Jurassic (Independence) diabase dikes in this study, Mesozoic structures at Alvord Mountain would appear not to have been appreciably reoriented by vertical-axis rotation west of Spanish Canyon. However, it is not clear that the diabase dikes can be reliably used to infer or eliminate rotation because the dikes have variable orientations, particularly east of Spanish Canyon where the dikes cluster into two populations.

ACKNOWLEDGMENTS

We especially thank Allen Glazner for support and assistance during completion of this work. Support for this project was provided by National Science Foundation grants EAR 89-17300 (to Glazner) and EAR 89-16802 (to Walker). Most of this project was done during the senior author's doctoral work at the University of North Carolina. Insightful discussions with and/or field assistance from Allen Glazner, Mark Martin, George Dunne, Stefan Boettcher, Dave Miller, Elizabeth Schermer, John Bartley, Sue Orrell, Richard Tosdal, Brian Carl, Drew Coleman, and Donna Whitney were important to the ideas presented herein. Critical reviews by Dave Miller, Liz Schermer, and John Bartley substantially improved the manuscript. The original mapping efforts at Alvord Mountain began with the Advanced Field Camp class run jointly by the University of North Carolina and the University of Kansas in the winter of 1990. Stefan Boettcher provided the fission-track analysis, Wanda Taylor provided the $^{40}Ar/^{39}Ar$ analysis, and Sue Orrell provided the microprobe data and helped with determination of metamorphic grade. Curtis Manley, Justin Hodge, Aaron Ferris, and John Mitsdarfer digitized the Alvord geologic map for inclusion in this memoir. To all these individuals we are grateful. Liz Schermer graciously provided a preprint.

REFERENCES CITED

Avé Lallemant, H.G., and Oldow, J.S., 1988, Early Mesozoic southward migration of Cordilleran transpressional terranes: Tectonics, v. 7, p. 1057–1088.

Barton, M.D., Battles, D.A., Bebout, G.E., Capo, R.C., Christensen, J.N., Davis, S.R., Hanson, R.B., Michelsen, C.J., and Trim, H.E., 1988, Mesozoic contact metamorphism in the western United States, *in* Ernst, W.G., ed., Metamorphism and crustal evolution of the western United States, Rubey Volume VII: Englewood Cliffs, New Jersey, Prentice-Hall, p. 110–178.

Blundy, J.D., and Holland, T.J.B., 1990, Calcic amphibole and a new amphibole-plagioclase thermometer: Contributions to Mineralogy and Petrology, v. 104, p. 208–224.

Boettcher, S.S., and Walker, J.D., 1993, Mesozoic tectonic history of Iron Mountain, central Mojave Desert, California: Tectonics, v. 12, p. 861–862.

Burchfiel, B.C., and Davis, G.A., 1981, Mojave Desert and environs, *in* Ernst, W.G., ed., The geotectonic development of California: Engelwood Cliffs, New Jersey, Prentice-Hall, p. 217–252.

Byers, F.M., Jr., 1960, Geology of the Alvord Mountain quadrangle, San Bernardino County California: U.S. Geological Survey Bulletin 1089-A, 71 p.

Calderone, G.J., Butler, R.F., and Acton, G.D., 1990, Paleomagnetism of Middle Miocene volcanic rocks in the Mojave-Sonora Desert region of western Arizona and southeastern California: Journal of Geophysical Research, v. 95, p. 625–648.

Carr, M.D., Poole, F.G., and Christiansen, L., 1984, Pre-Cenozoic geology of the El Paso Mountains, southwestern Great Basin, California: A summary, *in* Lintz, J., ed., Western geological excursions, Volume 4: Reno, Nevada, Department of Geological Sciences, Mackay School of Mines, p. 84–93.

Carr, M.D., Harris, A.G., Poole, F.G., and Fleck, R.J., 1992, Stratigraphy and structure of Paleozoic outer continental-margin rocks, *in* Pilot Knob Valley, north-central Mojave Desert: U.S. Geological Survey Bulletin 2015, 33 p.

Chen, J.H., and Moore, J.G., 1979, Late Jurassic Independence dike swarm in eastern California: Geology, v. 7, p. 129–133.

Coleman, D.S., Carl, B.S., Glazner, A.F., and Bartley, J.M., 2000, Cretaceous dikes within the Jurassic Independence dike swarm in eastern California: Geological Society of America Bulletin, v. 112, p. 504–511.

Dokka, R.K., 1989, The Mojave extensional belt of southern California: Tectonics, v. 8, p. 363–390.

Dunne, G.C., 1986, Mesozoic evolution of the southern Inyo Mountains, Darwin Plateau, and Argus and Slate ranges, *in* Dunne, G.C., compiler, Mesozoic and Cenozoic structural evolution of selected areas, east-central California: Geological Society of America Cordilleran Section meeting guidebook, field trips 2 and 14: Los Angeles, California State University, p. 3–43.

Dunne, G.C., and Walker, J.D., 1993, Age of Jurassic volcanism and tectonism, southern Owens Valley region, east-central California: Geological Society of America Bulletin, v. 105, p. 1223–1230.

Dunne, G.C., Gulliver, R.M., and Sylvester, A.G., 1978, Mesozoic evolution of rocks of the White, Inyo, Argus and Slate Ranges, eastern California, *in* Howell, D.G., and McDougall, K.A., eds., Mesozoic paleogeography of the western United States: Pacific Coast Paleogeography Symposium 2: Los Angeles, Society of Economic Paleontologists and Mineralogists, Pacific Section, p. 189–207.

Fillmore, R.P., 1993, Sedimentation and extensional basin evolution in a Miocene metamorphic core complex setting, Alvord Mountain, central Mojave Desert, California, USA: Sedimentology, v. 40, p. 721–742.

Gerber, M.E., Miller, C.F., and Wooden, J.L., 1995, Plutonism at the interior margin of the Jurassic magmatic arc, Mojave Desert, California, *in* Miller, D.M., and Busby, C.J., eds., Jurassic magmatism and tectonics of the North American Cordillera: Boulder, Colorado, Geological Society of America Special Paper 299, p. 351–374.

Glazner, A.F., Bartley, J.M., and Walker, J.D., 1989, Magnitude and significance of Miocene crustal extension in the central Mojave Desert, California: Geology, v. 17, p. 50–53.

Green, N.L., and Udansky, S.I., 1986, Toward a practical plagioclase-muscovite geothermometer: American Mineralogist, v. 71, p. 1109–1117.

Hazzard, J.C., 1954, Rocks and structure of the northern Providence Mountains, San Bernardino County, California, *in* Jahns, R.H., ed., Structural features: Geology of southern California: California Division of Mines and Geology Bulletin 170, p. 27–35.

Hoisch, T.D., 1989, A muscovite-biotite geothermometer: American Mineralogist, v. 74, p. 565–572.

Holdaway, M.J., and Mukhopadhyay, B., 1993, A reevaluation of the stability relations of andalusite: Thermochemical data and phase diagram for the aluminum silicates: American Mineralogist, v. 78, p. 298–315.

Howard, K.A., McCaffrey, K.J.W., Wooden, J.L., Foster, D.A., and Shaw, S.E., 1995, Jurassic thrusting of Precambrian basement over Paleozoic cover in the Clipper Mountains, southeastern California, *in* Miller, D.M., and Busby, C.J., eds., Jurassic magmatism and tectonics of the North American Cordillera: Boulder, Colorado, Geological Society of America Special Paper 299, p. 375–392.

James, E.W., 1989, Southern extension of the Independence dike swarm of eastern California: Geology, v. 17, p. 587–590.

Kretz, R., 1983, Symbols for rock-forming minerals: American Mineralogist, v. 68, p. 277–279.

Ludwig, K.R., 1989, PBDAT for MS-DOS: A computer program for IBM-PC compatibles for processing raw Pb-U-Th isotope data, version 1.06: U.S. Geological Survey Open-File Report 88-542, 40 p.

Ludwig, K.R., 1998, Isoplot/Ex: A geochronological toolkit for Microsoft Excel, version 1.00b: Berkeley Geochronology Center Special Publication No. 1, 44 p.

Martin, M.W., 1992, Stratigraphic and structural evolution of the Shadow Mountains, western Mojave Desert, California: Implications for the tectonic development of the central and western Mojave Desert [Ph.D. thesis]: Lawrence, Kansas, University of Kansas, 196 p.

Martin, M.W., and Walker, J.D., 1991, Upper Precambrian to Paleozoic paleogeographic reconstruction of the Mojave Desert, California, *in* Cooper,

J.D., and Stevens, C.H., eds., Paleozoic paleogeography of the western United States-II: Pacific Section, SEPM (Society for Sedimentary Geology), v. 67, p. 167–192.

Martin, M.W., and Walker, J.D., 1992, Extending the western North American Proterozoic and Paleozoic continental crust through the Mojave Desert: Geology, v. 20, p. 753–756.

Martin, M.W., and Walker, J.D., 1995, Stratigraphy and paleogeographic significance of metamorphic rocks in the Shadow Mountains, western Mojave Desert, California: Geological Society of America Bulletin, v. 107, p. 354–366.

Massonne, H-J., and Schreyer, W., 1987, Phengite geobarometry based on the limiting assemblage with K-feldspar, phlogopite, and quartz: Contributions to Mineralogy and Petrology, v. 96, p. 212–224.

May, S.R., Beck, M.E., Jr., and Butler, R.F., 1989, North American apparent polar wander, plate motion, and left-oblique convergence: Late Jurassic-Early Cretaceous orogenic consequences: Tectonics, v. 8, p. 443–452.

McCulloh, T.H., 1952, Geology of the southern half of the Lane Mountain quadrangle, California [Ph.D. thesis]: Los Angeles, University of California, 180 p.

McCulloh, T.H., 1954, Problems of the metamorphic and igneous rocks of the Mojave Desert: Geology of southern California: California Division of Mines and Geology Bulletin, v. 170, p. 13–24.

McCulloh, T.H., 1960, Geologic map of the Lane Mountain quadrangle, California: U.S. Geological Survey Open-File Map, scale 1:48000.

Miller, J.S., and Glazner, A.F., 1995, Jurassic plutonism and crustal evolution in the central Mojave Desert: Contributions to Mineralogy and Petrology, v. 118, p. 379–395.

Miller, E.L., and Sutter, J.F., 1982, Structural geology and ^{40}Ar-^{39}Ar geochronology of the Goldstone-Lane Mountain area, Mojave Desert, California: Geological Society of America Bulletin, v. 93, p. 1191–1207.

Miller, C.F., Wooden, J.L., Bennet, V.C., Wright, J.E., Solomon, G.C., and Hurst, R.W., 1990, Petrogenesis of the composite peraluminous-metaluminous Old Woman-Piute Range Batholith, southeastern California; isotopic constraints, *in* Anderson, J.L., ed., The nature and origin of Cordilleran magmatism: Boulder Colorado, Geological Society of America Memoir 174, p. 99–109.

Miller, J.S., Walker, J.D., Orrell, S.E., Martin M.W., and Harrison, S.E., 1991, Stratigraphy and Mesozoic contractional deformation at Alvord Mountain, central Mojave Desert California: Geological Society of America Abstracts with Programs, v. 23, no. 2, p. 79.

Miller, J.S., Walker, J.D., Glazner, A.F., and Martin, M.W., 1995, Geochronologic and isotopic evidence for Triassic-Jurassic emplacement of the eugeoclinal allochthon in the Mojave Desert region, California: Geological Society of America Bulletin, v. 107, p. 1441–1457.

Miller, D.M., Wooden, J.L., Hoisch, T.D., Schermer, E.L., and Walker, J.D., 1996, Intra-arc juxtaposition of cratonal and eugeoclinal rocks, north-central Mojave Desert, California: Geological Society of America Abstracts with Programs, v. 28, no. 5, p. 91.

Moore, J.G., and Hopson, C.A., 1961, The Independence dike swarm in eastern California: American Journal of Science: v. 259, p. 241–259.

Ron, H., and Nur, A., 1996, Vertical axis rotations in the Mojave: Evidence from the Independence dike swarm: Geology, v. 24, p. 973–976.

Ross, T.M., Luyendyk, B.P., and Haston, R.B., 1989, Paleomagnetic evidence for Neogene clockwise rotations in the central Mojave Desert, California: Geology, v. 17, p. 470–473.

Saleeby, J.B., Busby-Spera, C., Oldow, J.S., Dunne, G.C., Wright, J.E., Cowan, D.S., Walker, N.W., and Allmendinger, R.W., 1992, Early Mesozoic tectonic evolution of the western U.S. Cordillera, *in* Burchfiel, B.C., et al., eds., The Cordilleran Orogen: Conterminous U.S.: Boulder, Colorado, Geological Society of America, Geology of North America, v. G-3, p. 107–168.

Schermer, E.L., 1993, Mesozoic structural evolution of the west-central Mojave Desert *in* Dunne, G., and McDougall, K., eds., 1993, Mesozoic paleogeography of the western United States-II: Pacific Section Guidebook, Society of Economic Paleontologists and Mineralogists, Book 71, p. 307–322.

Schermer, E.L., and Busby, C., 1994, Jurassic magmatism in the central Mojave Desert: Implications for arc paleogeography and preservation of continental volcanic sequences: Geological Society of America Bulletin, v. 106, p. 767–790.

Schermer, E.L., Luyendyk, B.P., and Cisowski, S., 1996, Late Cenozoic structure and tectonics of the northern Mojave Desert: Tectonics, v. 15, p. 905–932.

Schermer, E.L., Stephens, K.A., and Walker, J.D., 2001, Paleogeographic and tectonic implications of the geology of the Tiefort Mountains, northern Mojave Desert, California: Geological Society of America Bulletin, v. 113, no. 7, p. 920–938.

Spear, F.S., 1981, Amphibole-plagioclase equilibria; an empirical model for the relation albite + tremolite = edenite + 4quartz: Contributions to Minerology and Petrology, v. 77, p. 355–364.

Stacey, J.S., and Kramers, J.D., 1975, Approximation of terrestrial lead by a two-stage model: Earth and Planetary Science Letters, v. 26, p. 207–221.

Steiger, R.H., and Jäger, E., 1977, Subcommission on geochronology: Convention on the use of decay constants in geo- and cosmochronology: Earth and Planetary Science Letters, v. 1, p. 369–371.

Stewart, J.H., 1970, Upper Precambrian and Lower Cambrian strata in the Southern Great Basin, California and Nevada: U.S. Geological Survey Professional Paper 620, p. 1–51.

Stewart, J.H., and Poole, F.G., 1975, Extension of the Cordilleran miogeosynclinal belt to the San Andreas fault, southern California: Geological Society of America Bulletin, v. 86, p. 205–212.

Stone, P., Howard, K.A., and Hamilton, W., 1983, Correlation of metamorphosed strata of the southeastern Mojave Desert region, California and Arizona: Geological Society of America Bulletin, v. 94, p. 1135–1147.

Walker, J.D., 1988, Permian and Triassic rocks of the Mojave Desert and their implications for timing and mechanisms of continental truncation: Tectonics, v. 7, p. 685–709.

Walker, J.D., and Wardlaw, B.R., 1989, Implications of Paleozoic and Mesozoic rocks in the Soda Mountains, northeastern Mojave Desert, California, for late Paleozoic and Mesozoic Cordilleran orogenesis: Metamorphosed strata of the southeastern Mojave Desert region, California and Arizona: Geological Society of America Bulletin, v. 101, p. 1574–1583.

Walker, J.D., Martin, M.W., Bartley, J.M., and Coleman, D.S., 1990, Timing and kinematics of deformation in the Cronese Hills, California, and implications for Mesozoic structure of the southern Cordillera: Geology, v. 18, p. 554–557.

Walker, J.D., Fletcher, J.M., Fillmore, R.P., Martin, M.W., Taylor, W.J., Glazner, A.F., and Bartley, J.M., 1995, Connection between igneous activity and extension in the central Mojave metamorphic core complex: Journal of Geophysical Research, v. 100, p. 10477–10494.

Wolf, M.B., and Saleeby, J.B., 1995, Late Jurassic dike swarms in the southwestern Sierra Nevada foothills terrane, California: Implications for the Nevadan orogeny and North American plate motion, *in* Miller, D.M., and Busby, C., eds., Jurassic magmatism and tectonics of the North American Cordillera: Geological Society of America Special Paper 299, p. 203–228.

Wooden, J.L., and Miller, D.M., 1990, Chronologic and isotopic framework for Early Proterozoic crustal evolution in the eastern Mojave Desert region, SE California: Journal of Geophysical Research, v. 95, p. 20133–20146.

Wright, L.A., Troxel, B.W., Williams, E.G., Roberts, M.T., and Deihl, P.E., 1974, Precambrian sedimentary environments of the Death Valley region, eastern California: Death Valley Region, California and Nevada, Field Trip 1: Geological Society of America Field Trip Guidebook, Shoshone, California, Death Valley Publishing Co., p. 27–35.

Yount, J.C., Schermer, E.R., Felger, T.J., Miller, D.M., and Stephens, K.A., 1994, Preliminary geologic map of Fort Irwin Basin, north-central Mojave Desert: U.S. Geological Survey Open File Report 94–173, scale 1:24000, 27 p.

MANUSCRIPT ACCEPTED BY THE SOCIETY MAY 9, 2001

Geological Society of America
Memoir 195
2002

Extensional arc setting and ages of Middle Jurassic eolianites, Cowhole Mountains (eastern Mojave Desert block, California)

Cathy J. Busby
Department of Geological Sciences and Institute for Crustal Studies, University of California,
Santa Barbara, California 93106, USA
Elizabeth R. Schermer
Department of Geology, Western Washington University, Bellingham, Washington, USA
James M. Mattinson
Department of Geological Sciences and Institute for Crustal Studies, University of California,
Santa Barbara, California 93106, USA

ABSTRACT

Mesozoic strata in the Cowhole Mountains, eastern Mojave block, California, include 200–800 m of eolian quartz arenite (Aztec Sandstone) overlain by more than 575 m of silicic ignimbrites, lava flows, and minor sedimentary rocks (Cowhole volcanics). U-Pb zircon geochronologic data on a crystal-rich dacite lava flow in the Aztec Sandstone indicate that the sandstone is Middle Jurassic and is therefore age equivalent to backarc eolianites of the Temple Cap and Carmel Formations, not the Lower Jurassic Navajo Formation as previously assumed. Our U-Pb zircon data on two ignimbrites of the Cowhole volcanics indicate that they are the same age, within error, as the lava flow in the Aztec Sandstone at 170 ± 3 Ma. New structural and stratigraphic data, together with published data, indicate syndepositional normal faulting and deposition of landslide blocks throughout deposition of this section. These results are consistent with our previous volcanologic studies in Middle Jurassic rocks of southern Arizona, southeastern California, and the central Mojave block, which document ignimbrite eruptions from calderas contemporaneous with deposition of craton-derived eolian sands, in extensional or transtensional intra-arc basins.

INTRODUCTION

The Triassic–early Middle Jurassic continental arc of California, Arizona, and western Nevada has been postulated to have occupied a more-or-less-continuous graben-type depression, more than 1000 km long, similar to the setting of the modern extensional arc of Central America (Busby-Spera, 1988; Busby-Spera et al., 1990a). This graben-type depression apparently acted as a long-lived (>40 m.y.) trap for Lower and Middle Jurassic craton-derived quartz arenites (Busby-Spera, 1988; Riggs et al., 1993; Fackler-Adams et al., 1997). Observations remain too scattered to determine the degree of lateral continuity of the postulated graben-type depression, largely because late Mesozoic shortening (Fleck et al., 1994) and voluminous plutonism overprinted structural and sedimentologic features of the earlier extensional arc in many places. Furthermore, a recent paleographic reconstruction of the southern Inyo Mountains of eastern California suggests at least local uplift of the Jurassic arc (Dunne et al., 1998). Nonetheless, extensional or transtensional basins have been documented in relatively little deformed and only weakly metamorphosed domains along the length of the Jurassic arc in the Cordilleran United States

Busby, C.J., Schermer, E.R., and Mattinson, J.M., 2002, Extensional arc setting and ages of Middle Jurassic eolianites, Cowhole Mountains (eastern Mojave Desert block, California), *in* Glazner, A.F., Walker, J.D., and Bartley, J.M., eds., Geologic Evolution of the Mojave Desert and Southwestern Basin and Range: Boulder, Colorado, Geological Society of America Memoir 195, p. 79–91.

and Mexico (see previously cited references; also, Riggs and Busby-Spera, 1990; Fisher, 1990; Schermer and Busby, 1994; Wyld, 2000). South Cowhole Mountain (Fig. 1) is one of these domains.

In the late 1980s, we made a detailed map of the eastern half of the Cowhole Mountains at a scale of 1:5000, published for the first time here (Fig. 1). We restricted our field and petrographic studies to the eastern half of the range because silicic volcanic rocks datable by the U-Pb zircon method are interstratified with eolian quartz arenites there. In a 1989 abstract (Busby-Spera et al., 1989), as well as an informal guidebook article for a 1991 Penrose Conference field trip, we summarized evidence for extension during accumulation of the upper part of the section, and we reported dates indicating that the eolianites are age equivalent to the Middle Jurassic Temple Cap Sandstone or Carmel Formation, not the Lower Jurassic Navajo Sandstone. Subsequent mapping of the entire range by Wadsworth et al. (1995) supported our intra-arc extension model because they documented normal growth faults and landslide deposits in the lower part of the section. In this paper, we provide more detailed description and interpretation of the upper part of the section than given by Wadsworth et al. (1995). We describe the volcanologic and sedimentologic characteristics of the section, incorporating petrographic interpretation of ~100 thin sections. We also give map-scale and outcrop evidence, not recognized by other workers, for landsliding during normal faulting of the upper part of the section. Finally, we present and interpret our U-Pb zircon age data, which indicate a Middle Jurassic age for the section.

Although the Cowhole Mountains are only a "postage stamp" relative to the length of the Jurassic arc, the rocks there are particularly good for determining the age and paleogeographic setting of a segment of the Jurassic arc because (1) the sedimentary and volcanic strata are unusually well preserved and well exposed and (2) the numerous silicic volcanic units in the section allow us to check for geologic consistency in our U-Pb zircon age results. This check is important because U-Pb studies of continental metavolcanic rocks commonly suffer from zircon inheritance as well as Pb loss from the zircons, making their age interpretation difficult.

PREVIOUS WORK ON JURASSIC EOLIANITES IN THE EASTERN MOJAVE BLOCK

Hewett (1931) first applied the name "Aztec Sandstone" to eolian quartz arenite that overlies Triassic strata in the Spring Mountains of southwestern Nevada and correlated it with the Lower Jurassic Navajo Sandstone of the Colorado Plateau. He later extended this correlation to the Mescal Range in eastern California (Hewett, 1956), and this name and correlation have since been applied to the eolian quartz arenites in many other ranges of the Mojave block (Grose, 1959; Miller and Carr, 1978), including the Cowhole Mountains (Novitsky-Evans, 1978). Our age data presented here, however, indicate that at

least three-fourths and probably all of the Aztec Sandstone in the Cowhole Mountains is Middle Jurassic and thus younger than the Navajo Sandstone. In fact, subsequent studies of the Aztec Sandstone in the type locality, the Spring Mountains, as well as in the Mescal Range, show that age constraints remain too poor to determine whether the eolianites are Early, Middle, or Late Jurassic (Fleck et al., 1994). They could thus be correlative with the Glen Canyon Group, the San Rafael Group, or the Entrada Sandstone. There is only one well-dated Lower Jurassic eolianite in the Mojave block (Schermer et al., this volume), and other intra-arc eolianites previously assumed to be Navajo equivalents have yielded Middle Jurassic ages (e.g., southeast California, Fackler-Adams et al., 1997; southern Arizona, Riggs et al., 1993). To summarize, the name "Aztec Sandstone" has been applied to eolianites ranging from Early through Middle to possibly Late Jurassic age; thus that name no longer has any significance in terms of correlation with specific backarc eolianites of the present-day Colorado Plateau. Because so many previous workers have called the eolianites in the Cowhole Mountains "Aztec Sandstone," we continue to do so (unit Ja, Figs. 1, 2, and 3). We emphasize, however, that "Aztec Sandstone" appears to span much of the Jurassic from locality to locality in the southwest Cordilleran United States.

Dunne (1972) and Novitsky-Evans (1978) termed the section of volcanic rocks that overlies the Aztec Sandstone in the Cowhole Mountains the "Delfonte Volcanics," extending this name from the Mescal Range 25 km to the east. More recently, we dated the Delfonte Volcanics in the Mescal Range at 100.5 ± 2 Ma (Busby et al., 1994; Fleck et al., 1994). This is much younger than the preliminary age of 167 Ma we reported for the "Delfonte Volcanics" in the Cowhole Mountains (Busby-Spera et al., 1990b). For this reason, Wadsworth et al. (1995) renamed the volcanic rocks above the eolian sandstones the "Cowhole volcanics." We follow this usage here (unit Jcv, Figs. 1, 2, and 3).

Marzolf (1980) reported that volcanic rocks not only overlie the Aztec Sandstone, but are interstratified with it at two stratigraphic levels, termed the upper volcanic unit and the lower volcanic unit. Wadsworth et al. (1995) referred to these as the lower and upper volcanic members of the Aztec Sandstone. We do not follow this subdivision because we interpret the "upper volcanic unit" (or "upper volcanic member") as a sill, not a volcanic rock, as described subsequently. For this reason, we refer to the "lower volcanic unit" as "Aztec volcanics" (unit Jav, Figs. 1 and 2).

STRATIGRAPHY

Mesozoic strata in the Cowhole Mountains include up to 200–800 m of eolian quartz arenite overlain by more than 575 m of ignimbrites, lava flows, and minor sedimentary rocks (Fig. 2; Busby-Spera et al., 1990b; Wadsworth et al., 1995).

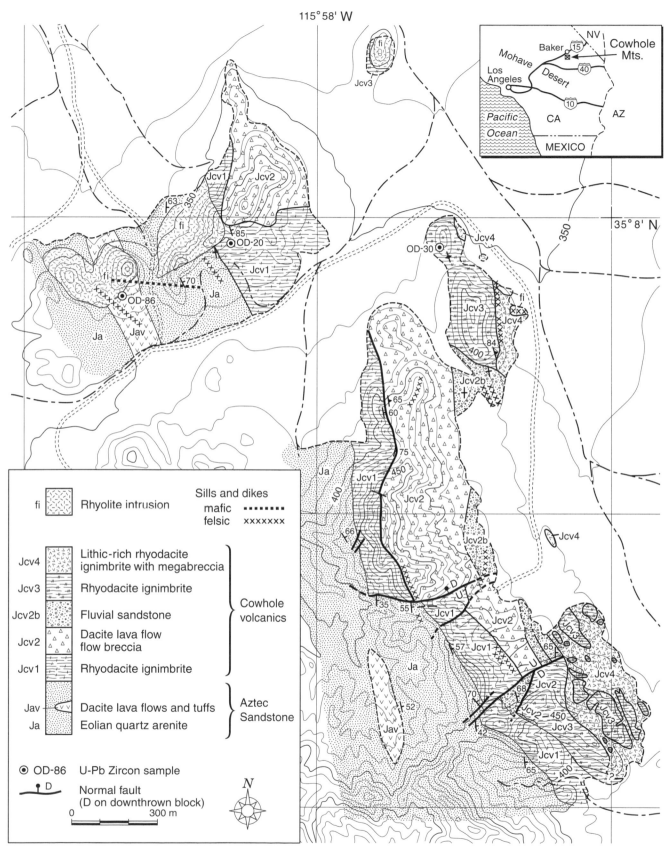

Figure 1. Geologic map of part of the Cowhole Mountains, eastern Mojave block, south of Baker, California (locality on inset). For descriptions of Aztec Sandstone and Cowhole volcanics, see Figure 2 and text. (Mapping and sampling for U-Pb zircon dating, begun by Cathy Busby in 1979 and 1985, were completed by Cathy Busby and Elizabeth Schermer in 1988.)

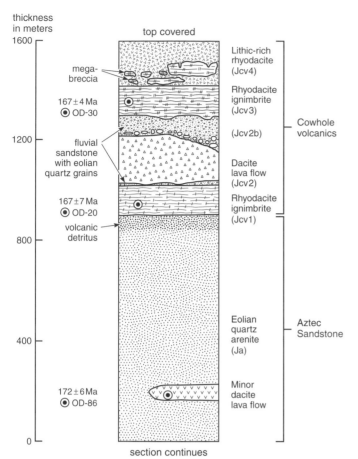

Figure 2. Composite stratigraphic column through Jurassic strata of the Cowhole Mountains. Thicknesses of most map units vary across area (see Fig. 1).

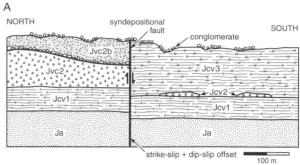

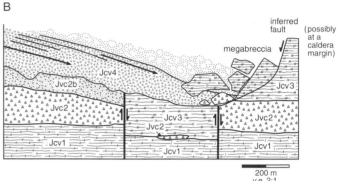

Figure 3. Cross-sectional reconstruction of syndepositional faulting and deposition of landslide megabreccias during accumulation of the Cowhole volcanics. (A) Syndepositional fault that bounds the southern margin of the uplifted block within the Aztec Sandstone and Cowhole volcanics (Fig. 1). The fault that bounds the northern margin of the uplifted block is incompletely exposed and is not portrayed here. The thickness of Cowhole volcanics unit 1 (Jcv1) does not change across the fault, although the fault clearly offsets its contact with the underlying Aztec Sandstone (Fig. 1). Changes in unit Jcv2 and Jcv2b across the fault could possibly indicate early syndepositional movements (see text). Strong evidence for syndepositional movement lies in the absence of unit Jcv3 on the upthrown block; this unit is an ignimbrite that elsewhere forms a laterally continuous sheet of even thickness (Fig. 1). We infer that uplift of this block resulted in erosional stripping of the ignimbrite (Jcv3) and deposition of a lag of boulder conglomerate composed of clasts of Jcv3 across the top of both blocks, overlapping the fault. (B) Deposition of lithic fragment–rich rhyodacite ignimbrite with megabreccia (Jcv4) across inactive syndepositional fault (left) during movement of inferred fault to the south of the present-day exposures (right). Like the underlying boulder conglomerate (Fig. 3A), the ignimbrite clearly overlies the syndepositional fault. The megabreccia wedge thickens and coarsens toward the inferred southern fault and is composed largely of clasts of the underlying two units (Jcv3 and Jcv2).

Aztec Sandstone

We agree with all previous workers in this area that the Aztec Sandstone in the Cowhole Mountains is predominantly an eolian quartz arenite (Novitsky-Evans, 1978; Marzolf, 1980; Wadsworth et al., 1995). It consists largely of stacked sets 1–10 m thick of tabular to trough cross-laminated, very well-sorted, medium-grained quartz sandstone, probably deposited on the foresets of eolian dunes. In thin section, it is a super-mature sandstone, consisting of >95% well-rounded mono-crystalline quartz grains. Along depositional contacts with some of the volcanic units, the quartz arenite is variably contaminated by volcanic lithic fragments, glass shards, and euhedral pyrogenic crystals. We refer the reader to the already-cited previous workers and others for more detailed sedimentologic descriptions of the Aztec Sandstone in the Cowhole Mountains that do not bear directly on the age and tectonic setting discussed in this paper.

Our study of the Aztec Sandstone has focused on igneous rocks within it for the purpose of (1) documenting the nature of any contemporaneous volcanism and (2) dating the Aztec Sandstone by identifying interstratified silicic volcanic rocks suitable for U-Pb zircon dating.

Aztec volcanics. We mapped two lenses of volcanic rock within the Aztec Sandstone (unit Jav); one is at the north end of the map area, interpreted as a dacite lava flow (U-Pb zircon sample locality OD-86), and the other is near the south end of the map area, interpreted as a dacite tuff (Fig. 1). An igneous body in the upper part of the Aztec Sandstone at the north end of the map area has a more controversial origin. We interpret it to be a felsic sill (Fig. 1), but Marzolf and Cole (1987) interpreted it to be a lava flow ("upper unit"), as did Wadsworth et al. (1995), who correlated it with the tuff described in this section. For that reason, we discuss the controversial igneous body in this section after describing the lava flow and the tuff.

The volcanic lens at the north end of the map area (unit Jav, Fig. 1) is interpreted as a lava flow because it is everywhere concordant with bedding in the Aztec Sandstone and has brecciated upper and lower margins, which would not be expected on the margins of sills. It is a crystal-rich lava flow, with ~40% plagioclase crystals, that is partially calcitized and epidotized. Wadsworth et al. (1995) interpreted this lava flow to be andesitic in composition (their "lower volcanic member"), but we suspect it is instead a dacite, because it yielded abundant zircon separates. Age data from this lava flow are presented subsequently.

The volcanic lens at the south end of the map area (unit Jav, Fig. 1) is a tuff that we interpret to represent a nonwelded ignimbrite (i.e., pumice-rich pyroclastic-flow deposit). It is a thick, nonstratified deposit, up to 25 m thick, composed of poorly sorted, noncompacted pumice lumps in a fine-grained matrix containing relict glass shards and lacking crystals. Its nonwelded character probably accounts for its highly altered and weathered condition relative to the thicker, more extensive welded ignimbrites of the overlying Cowhole volcanics (units Jcv1, Jcv3, Jcv4, Figs. 1 and 2). Because of this poor preservation, and because it is aphyric, we did not sample the nonwelded ignimbrite for U-Pb zircon geochronology. Wadsworth et al. (1995) correlated this volcanic lens with Marzolf and Cole's "upper unit" lava flow (which we infer is actually a sill), but that body bears phenocrysts, whereas the ignimbrite does not, so this correlation is not valid.

The igneous body that has been previously mapped as the upper volcanic unit (Marzolf and Cole, 1987) or upper volcanic member (Wadsworth et al., 1995) lies near the top of the Aztec Sandstone near its north end (to the southwest of zircon sample locality OD-20, Fig. 1). It is concordant with bedding, as a lava flow would be, but unlike most silicic lava flows, it is a perfectly tabular body with very sharp, nonbrecciated upper and lower contacts, and flow banding is best developed close to its margins. It also lacks the broken crystals or vitroclastic texture typical of tuffs, although pervasive perlitic fractures in the sill could be mistaken for vitroclastic texture. We therefore do not consider it a volcanic rock and thus did not sample it for dating of the section. The sill has large but sparse plagioclase, fewer potassium feldspar phenocrysts, and small sparse quartz phenocrysts; the rock is therefore probably a dacite. Similar greenish-tan flow-banded silicic sills and dikes cut the entire section in the Cowhole Mountains (Fig. 1).

Cowhole volcanics

We recognize four volcanic units within the Cowhole volcanics (Figs. 1 and 2). Unit 1 (Jcv1) is a rhyodacite ignimbrite

120 m thick, and unit 2 (Jcv2) is a dacite lava flow 200 m thick. Both units 1 and 2 are overlain by fluvial sandstones that contain a mixture of eolian quartz and pyroclastic debris, although the fluvial section above unit 2 is much thicker than the fluvial section above unit 1 (Fig. 2). For this reason, it is mapped separately from unit 2 and is referred to as unit 2b (Fig. 1). Unit 3 (Jcv3) is a rhyodacite ignimbrite. Unit 4 (Jcv4) is a lithic-rich rhyodacite ignimbrite, greater than 200 m, that contains a megabreccia with slabs up to 200 m thick derived from stratigraphically lower units. Its top is covered.

Unit 1 (Jcv1). The unit 1 ignimbrite is purplish red rhyodacite, with ~10% quartz, ~10% plagioclase, and ~5% potassium feldspar phenocrysts, plus sparse phenocrysts of a minor altered mafic mineral (probably hornblende). Quartz phenocrysts are large (up to 6 mm) and euhedral to embayed. The quartz and feldspar phenocrysts are commonly broken. The ignimbrite has eutaxitic texture owing to compaction of pumice. In thin section, the very well preserved matrix consists largely of sintered glass shards, indicating that the compaction fabric formed by welding in the hot state, rather than by diagenetic compaction. Volcanic lithic fragments are rare and include irregularly shaped, welded rhyolite tuff clasts. The uppermost 5–10 m of the unit 1 ignimbrite is nonwelded, with excellent preservation of nonsintered bubble-wall glass shards. Plagioclase phenocrysts are harder to recognize in the nonwelded top of the ignimbrite because they are more calcitized, probably owing to the greater permeability of the nonwelded top during diagenesis.

Fluvial sandstones overlie the nonwelded top of the unit 1 ignimbrite, but were not mapped separately because they are discontinuous and less than 2 m thick. They are thin- to medium-bedded, planar-laminated to ripple or trough cross-laminated sandstones and pebbly sandstones. The sandstones are tuffaceous, with euhedral volcanic quartz and feldspar grains and bubble-wall shards, probably derived at least in part from the underlying nonwelded top of the unit 1 ignimbrite. They contain silicic rock fragments, particularly in the coarse sand to pebble size fraction. The sandstones also contain a high proportion (25%–40%) of very well rounded, medium-sand-sized grains of monocrystalline quartz, identical to those in the Aztec Sandstone. Their presence indicates that eolian sand was still available after the eruption of unit 1 ignimbrite; the sand grains may have been supplied by active dunes or by reworking of nonlithified eolian deposits similar to those that lie beneath the unit 1 ignimbrite (Aztec Sandstone).

Unit 2 (Jcv2). Unit 2 is a dark purplish brown to dark gray dacite lava flow, with ~3% plagioclase and ~1% biotite phenocrysts, as well as rare altered mafic phenocrysts showing relict amphibole cleavage. The phenocrysts are set in a microcrystalline quartzofeldspathic mosaic with plagioclase microlites. The flow includes both coherent lava and much less common brecciated lava. The breccias occur at the base and top of the unit and have angular and closely packed clasts up to 30 cm long; these are interpreted to be autobreccias or "flow breccias." Flow alignment of phenocrysts is best developed in the coherent (nonbrecciated) interior of the dacite lava flow. At some localities, the outer 1 m of the dacite lava flow locally shows relatively poorly vesiculated pumiceous texture and thick-walled bubble shards. These features indicate local development of a vesiculated (pumiceous) carapace on the lava flow. The restriction of flow breccia and pumiceous carapace to the bottom and top of unit 2 indicates that it represents a single lava flow. The basal contact of unit 2 is conformable with unit 1 in most of the map area, but in the north, it appears to cut across the upper part of unit 1 (Fig. 1). We interpret this discordant contact to represent a paleovalley cut into unit 1 and filled by unit 2. We do not think the contact is an intrusive contact, because the lava flow retains its basal-flow breccia and pumiceous carapace along this contact.

Unit 2b (Jcv2b). The sandstones above unit 2, unlike those above unit 1, are thick enough to map separately as unit 2b (Jcv2b, Fig. 1). Unit 2b is dominated by fluvial sandstones similar to those that lie at the top of unit 1, but debris-flow deposits are locally present at the base of unit 2b.

Fluvial sandstones of unit 2b consist largely of planar-laminated and ripple cross-laminated, thin-bedded, orangish-red sandstone, interbedded with maroon siltstone. These rocks are interstratified with medium-bedded, faintly laminated, pebbly sandstone and pebble conglomerate with angular volcanic lithic fragments, in beds that are generally planar-based but locally show scoured bases.

The debris-flow deposits that locally occur at the base of the unit are thick bedded to very thick bedded and have a poorly sorted pebbly sandstone matrix of the same composition as the well-sorted fluvial pebbly sandstones and pebble conglomerates. The debris-flow deposits lack internal stratification or clast alignment, are very poorly sorted, and contain angular clasts up to 1 m in length dispersed within the pebbly sandstone matrix. Blocks within the debris-flow deposits include the following (in order of abundance): unit 1 ignimbrite (Jcv1); unit 2 lava flow (Jcv2); sedimentary intraclasts; and basalt or andesite clasts of unknown provenance, some with plagioclase and an altered mafic mineral, others aphyric and vesicular. The basal few meters of unit 2b commonly contain abundant clasts of the unit 2 dacite flow-top breccia that were reworked into the overlying debris flows.

Like the fluvial sandstones above unit 1, the unit 2b sandstones, pebbly sandstones, and debris-flow deposits contain a significant (>25%) proportion of distinctive well-rounded to "dumbbell-shaped" eolian quartz grains. The ongoing availability of eolian quartz during deposition of the Cowhole volcanics is not surprising because their age is the same as that of the Aztec volcanics, within analytical error (discussed subsequently). The eolian quartz grains are mixed with angular volcanic quartz grains in subequal proportions and with much smaller quantities of silicic volcanic lithic clasts. Sparse feldspar, mica, and mafic volcanic clasts are also present.

Wadsworth et al. (1995) named the thick fluvial section

above the unit 2 dacite lava flow (our unit 2b) the "volcaniclastic unit (Jcv3)," but we believe this name obscures the fact that well-rounded quartz sand grains make up well over 25% of these sandstones.

Unit 3 (Jcv3). Unit 3 is a gray rhyodacite ignimbrite with ~5% euhedral, embayed, and broken quartz, ~5% plagioclase, and ~5% potassium feldspar phenocrysts in a matrix of sintered glass shards (welded tuff). The total crystal content of this ignimbrite is somewhat variable (~10%–20%), but the proportions of quartz, plagioclase, and potassium feldspar remain constant, and crystal content is lower than that of unit 1 ignimbrite. Preservation of the welded shards is not as good as that of the unit 1 ignimbrite, owing to microscopic quartzofeldspathic recrystallization that may represent vapor-phase devitrification. In some areas, recrystallization has destroyed vitroclastic texture, but broken crystals are abundant throughout the unit. Pumice lapilli are sparse, suggesting a higher fragmentation index during eruption of this pyroclastic flow relative to units 1 and 4. The greater proportion of broken versus nonbroken crystals in this unit relative to the other two ignimbrite units supports this hypothesis. Fiamme are more easily recognizable on weathered outcrops than they are on fresh outcrops or in thin section and are scattered throughout the unit.

Our unit 3 rhyodacite ignimbrite was mapped by Wadsworth et al. (1995) as a rhyolite intrusion (their Jr), even though they stated that the field evidence was "not completely compelling but permissive of an intrusive nature" (p. 337). We agree with Wadsworth et al. (1995) that the pyroclastic nature of the unit is more commonly evident in thin section (in the form of relict shards and broken crystals) than it is in outcrop (in the form of eutaxitic texture and fiamme). We do not agree with their interpretation of the unit as a very shallow level, vent-related intrusion with pyroclastic textures. We prefer the simpler interpretation that it is an ignimbrite, for several reasons. The tabular shape and concordance of unit 3 would require it to be a pyroclastic sill if it is intrusive. We are not aware of any pyroclastic sills reported in the literature, although vertical ignimbrite feeder dikes with steeply dipping welding compaction have been recognized by other workers (e.g., Reedman et al., 1987; Kano et al., 1997; Miura, 1999). The compaction foliation in unit 3 is bedding parallel. Furthermore, we recognize megablocks of unit 3 ignimbrite in the unit 4 lithic-rich ignimbrite. Wadsworth et al. (1995) mapped these megablocks as rhyolite intrusions (their Jr) into our unit 4. This interpretation is not possible, because the megablocks of unit 3 ignimbrite range continuously from decameters to decimeters in size. Additionally, cobbles of unit 3 ignimbrite form a conglomerate that locally underlies the unit 4 ignimbrite (described next). These relationships indicate that unit 3 was emplaced before emplacement of unit 4, so it cannot be an intrusion.

Unit 4 (Jcv4). Unit 4 is a brick red, lithic-rich rhyodacite ignimbrite with megabreccia (Figs. 1 and 2). It is nonwelded to weakly welded and consists of nonwelded to incipiently welded bubble-wall shards, pumice shreds, and broken crystals. It contains up to 30% accidental lithic fragments, which may have helped to cool the ignimbrite below its welding temperature during emplacement. The unit 4 ignimbrite has a high crystal content similar to unit 1 (~30%), with subequal proportions of quartz, plagioclase feldspar, and potassium feldspar, and a few percent altered amphibole phenocrysts. Quartz phenocrysts are highly embayed. Lapilli-sized lithic fragments are all angular and include the following (in order of abundance): aphyric to porphyritic silicic volcanic clasts, limestone clasts, tuff clasts (with nonwelded bubble-wall shards), welded rhyolite tuff clasts, and clasts of fine-grained sandstone and siltstone.

Megablocks in the unit 4 ignimbrite are 1–200 m long and include the following (in order of abundance): unit 3 gray rhyodacite ignimbrite; unit 2 lava flow; unit 2b sedimentary rocks; and carbonate, especially toward the south end of the map area. Most megabreccia domains are dominated by very large megablocks, meters thick and tens of meters long, with lesser domains dominated by large megablocks several meters across. The largest megablocks are composed of unit 3 ignimbrite and are map scale in size (Fig. 1). Blocks of this size are found only in landslide deposits; the origin of these landslide megabreccias is discussed subsequently in a separate section.

Wadsworth et al. (1995) did not recognize the landslide blocks in the unit 4 ignimbrite, which they interpreted to be a rhyolite flow breccia with abundant lithic fragments derived from subjacent units. However, we know of no rhyolite lava flows choked with accidental fragments; furthermore, we recognize a matrix of pumice, shards, and broken crystals, indicating that unit 4 is a lithic-rich ignimbrite, not a lava flow. As noted previously, Wadsworth et al. (1995) mapped the large megablocks as intrusions, but these bodies consist of welded unit 3 ignimbrite with the orientation of pumice compaction fabrics varying from block to block, indicating that some of them tumbled. Lithic fragments become far less abundant high within the unit 4 ignimbrite (Figs. 1 and 2), and Wadsworth et al. recognized this part of the unit as an ignimbrite, dividing it off as a fifth unit; however, we consider it to be the same unit because it is in gradational contact and has identical minerals, microtextures, and field appearance (other than lower content of lithic fragments).

Rhyolite intrusions of uncertain age (fi). We discuss these under the Cowhole volcanics because they have been previously interpreted to be part of the Cowhole volcanics (Marzolf and Cole, 1987), although we reinterpret them here as shallow-level intrusions. Their alteration products are the same as those of the Cowhole volcanics (calcite plus epidote), suggesting that they may also be Jurassic, but they are not dated.

We mapped three felsic intrusions in the northern part of the map area (fi, Fig. 1): one that crosscuts the Aztec volcanics (Jav), a second that crosscuts the Aztec Sandstone (Ja) and unit 1 of the Cowhole volcanics (Jcv1), and a third that lies above unit 3 of the Cowhole volcanics (Jcv3) with a covered top (at the northeasternmost exposure on an isolated hill). These three we refer to as the lower, middle, and upper felsic intrusions,

respectively. All three felsic intrusions have sparse calcitized plagioclase phenocrysts in a felsitic groundmass (i.e., a microcrystalline mosaic of quartz and feldspar).

The middle felsic intrusion was informally referred to as "rhyolite ridge" by Marzolf and Cole (1987), who interpreted it as a lava flow filling a paleovalley in the Aztec Sandstone. We reinterpret "rhyolite ridge" as an intrusion rather than a lava flow because the body crosscuts vertically through bedding in the Aztec Sandstone and it has a pervasively well-developed flow banding that lies perfectly parallel to its vertical margins. It also lacks the flow breccias that lie along the bottoms and tops of nearly all rhyolite lava flows.

The upper felsic intrusion has not been previously mapped. We interpret this body as a sill, because its exposed lower contact and well-developed flow banding in the basal 1 m of the sill are concordant with local bedding and because it also lacks flow breccias. The sill has very well developed columnar jointing oriented perpendicular to local bedding. We speculate that the lower felsic intrusion may have been a feeder dike for this sill, although they are not connected in the cross-sectional view afforded by present-day exposures.

Summary of Cowhole volcanics. The Cowhole volcanics record the overwhelming of an eolian depositional environment (Aztec Sandstone) by proximal volcanic activity. This transition was probably gradual, as shown by the presence of silicic lava flows and ignimbrites in the upper part of the Aztec Sandstone that are similar to those of the overlying Cowhole volcanics. The abundance of eolian quartz sand grains in sedimentary units in the basal half of the Cowhole volcanics (Fig. 2) also supports the interpretation of a gradual transition from an eolian to a volcanic environment. The main evidence for proximal volcanic activity lies in the silicic lava flows of both the Aztec volcanics and the Cowhole volcanics, because nearly all silicic lava flows are too viscous to travel far from vents. The silicic lava flow in the Cowhole volcanics is much thicker than the silicic lava flow in the Aztec Sandstone, consistent with the interpretation that proximal volcanic activity (Cowhole volcanics) progressively overwhelmed eolian processes (Aztec Sandstone). U-Pb zircon dates on the Aztec volcanics and the Cowhole volcanics (presented later in this paper) support the interpretation that the two units are linked in time and basinal setting.

Three out of the four units of the Cowhole volcanics are silicic ignimbrites over 100 m thick (Jcv1, Jcv3, and Jcv4, Fig. 2). These are likely the product of highly explosive eruptions at calderas. The top of the uppermost ignimbrite is covered, so its original thickness is not known, but the lower two are not thick enough to represent intracaldera accumulations. They are therefore interpreted as welded caldera outflow deposits. The uppermost unit, with its megabreccia, could possibly represent the fill of a small exposed sector of a much bigger, largely buried caldera (discussed further later in this paper).

Several features of the Cowhole volcanics suggest deposition within a tectonically active basin. First, episodic input of large clasts from underlying units suggests that these units were quickly exposed in fault scarps. Unit 2b contains blocks derived from units 1 and 2; similarly, unit 4 contains blocks derived from units 2b and 3. Second, debris-flow deposits in unit 2b indicate local topographic relief. Third, fluvial deposits of the Cowhole volcanics are texturally and compositionally immature except for the eolian sand component; the fluvial deposits contain fewer traction structures than is typical of most such deposits, and they form aggradational sequences with little or no evidence of channelization. These characteristics suggest catastrophic sedimentation, which is typical of tectonically and volcanically active basins. In the following section, we describe two syndepositional faults within the map area, and we infer the existence of a third fault beyond the present limits of exposure.

SYNDEPOSITIONAL FAULTS AND LANDSLIDE MEGABRECCIAS

Our map shows two faults with roughly east-west trends that bound an uplifted block within the Cowhole volcanics and Aztec Sandstone (labeled with up and down symbols in Fig. 1). In this part of the paper, we provide evidence that this block was uplifted along normal faults after deposition of Cowhole volcanics unit 3 (Jcv3) and before deposition of Cowhole volcanics unit 4 (Jcv4). We discuss the southern fault boundary of the uplifted block first because the evidence for syndepositional movement on this fault is stronger. It is overlapped by unit 4 (Jcv4) of the Cowhole volcanics, so movement on it clearly predates deposition of that unit (Fig. 1). It is harder to prove that the northern fault set is syndepositional, because the relationship between it and the unit 4 ignimbrite, which presumably overlaps it, is not exposed (Fig. 1).

The subvertical fault on the southern boundary of the uplifted block separates strata of dramatically different thicknesses and lithologic characters. A cross-sectional reconstruction of this fault and the strata it cuts is presented in Figure 3A. The thickness of the unit 1 (Jcv1) ignimbrite does not change across the fault. The unit 2 (Jcv2) lava flow is considerably thinner and less continuous on the south side of the fault, relative to the north side, but silicic lava flows have very high aspect ratios with steep margins, so abrupt thinning of the lava flow cannot be used to prove syndepositional faulting. However, the sedimentary rocks above the unit 2 lava flow (unit Jcv2b) are restricted to the north side of the fault; this circumstance suggests that the fault may have had an early movement history that was down to the north, i.e., opposite in sense to its final movement (Fig. 3A). The most dramatic stratal change across the syndepositional fault is the abrupt disappearance of the unit 3 (Jcv3) ignimbrite, which is 125 m thick on the south side of the fault, but absent on the north side of the fault. Ignimbrites form sheet-like deposits that do not terminate abruptly, except against topographic barriers high enough to block the highly expanded, mobile flows that deposit them. We propose that the

unit 3 ignimbrite was originally deposited across the entire field area and then stripped off the uplifted block bounded by the southern and northern faults. The unit 3 ignimbrite reappears to the north of the uplifted block, where it is the same thickness (125 m) as it is to the south of the uplifted block.

The major fault on the northern boundary of the uplifted block dips 70°–80° to the north. It drops younger strata on its north side onto older strata on its south side and is thus mapped as a normal fault (Fig. 1). The other fault in the northern set (plus a small intervening fault) is subvertical, with minor displacement of uncertain sense. A minimum age of offset on the normal fault could be established by dating the felsic dike that crosscuts it (Fig. 1), but even if the age proved to be the same as the Cowhole volcanics, within analytical error, one could always argue that the fault is immediately postdepositional. We suggest that the reappearance of the 125-m-thick unit 3 ignimbrite in the area north of this fault provides more conclusive evidence that this fault is the same age as the syndepositional fault to the south (Fig. 1).

Erosional stripping of the entire 125 m of ignimbrite unit 3 (Jcv3) from the upthrown side of the southern fault resulted in deposition of a cobble to boulder lag deposit across the southern fault (Fig. 3A). The resulting conglomerate is composed entirely of clasts of the unit 3 welded ignimbrite. The conglomerate is too thin (only as much as 2 m thick) to map separately (Fig. 1), but it rests directly upon unit 3 ignimbrite south of the upthrown block and upon unit 2b sedimentary rocks north of the fault on the upthrown block (Fig. 3A). This stratigraphy indicates that the upthrown block was planed off by erosion prior to deposition of the unit 4 ignimbrite.

Just outside the map area, we infer the presence of a third fault having a listric geometry. Landslide blocks were shed along this inferred fault into the map area during eruption and emplacement of the unit 4 ignimbrite (Fig. 3B). Slide blocks are largest in the southernmost exposures of the unit 4 ignimbrite, and they are absent from the northern exposure of the unit 4 ignimbrite (Fig. 1), which is dominated by mesobreccias bearing clasts less than 1 m in diameter. The landslide megabreccia in the southern exposure of unit 4 has blocks up to 200 m long derived from Cowhole volcanics units 2 and 3, and at least one Paleozoic carbonate megablock at the southernmost end of the unit. We infer that the slide blocks were shed along a fault to the south beyond the limits of present-day exposures (Fig. 3B). This scarp exposed units 2 and 3, but apparently did not expose the unit 1 welded ignimbrite. The carbonate megablock in the south suggests that basement may also have been exposed, although this megablock could have been reworked from the Aztec Sandstone, which also contains carbonate megablocks that Wadsworth et al. (1995) inferred were shed from syndepositional normal faults. The Aztec Sandstone was probably not lithified enough to form slide blocks in the Cowhole volcanics at the time of their eruption.

The fact that the megabreccia is encased in ignimbrite suggests that it represents an intracaldera accumulation. If so, the present-day exposures afford a view of only a small part of the floor of a presumably much larger buried caldera. The non-welded to weakly welded nature of the ignimbrite matrix, however, could be used to argue against an origin as an intracaldera accumulation, because intracaldera ignimbrites are commonly strongly welded. If the unit 4 ignimbrite is not a caldera fill, the catastrophic landslides may have been generated by seismicity along a fault outside the field area, similar to the syndepositional fault overlapped by the megabreccia within our field area. It seems unlikely, however, that this seismicity would precisely coincide with the emplacement of an outflow ignimbrite in the area; the poor welding could be explained by rapid cooling against the floor of the caldera, aided considerably by avalanching of cold rock fragments into the ignimbrite from a caldera wall. Thus it seems more likely that unit 4 represents an intra-caldera megabreccia.

We speculate that the unit 4 caldera was sited along an extensional fault zone that we informally term "the Cowhole fault zone," using our data and data from Wadsworth et al., (1995). We tentatively reinterpret the Cowhole thrust of Novitsky-Evans (1978), which lies immediately to the west of the area mapped in Figure 1, as a normal fault, because it puts younger Paleozoic carbonates on top of older Paleozoic carbonates and attenuates strata. That fault appears to be onlapped by part of the Aztec Sandstone, but ongoing normal faulting is indicated by fanning dips in the Aztec Sandstone–Cowhole volcanics section, abrupt stratal-thickness changes within the Aztec Sandstone, and the presence of carbonate-block breccias and megabreccias at two different stratigraphic levels within the Aztec Sandstone (Wadsworth et al., 1995). Our work shows that normal faulting continued through deposition of the Cowhole volcanics.

U-PB ZIRCON GEOCHRONOLOGY

Tera-Wasserburg plots for the three dated units from the Cowhole Mountains are in Figure 4, and data are presented in Table 1. All of the units show significant inheritance of older zircons. During the handpicking process, we separated frosted, rounded zircons, which we interpret to have been "entrained" during the passage of the ash flows over the ground surface. These entrained zircons (Fig. 4B) are not necessarily representative of the age of components inherited by the magma as it passed through the crust; inherited zircons, in contrast, serve as cores within the euhedral "igneous" zircons. Thus, our age interpretations are based heavily on data from the igneous zircons (Fig. 4A). For some of the fractions, we attempted to minimize common Pb and also the effects of possible later Pb loss by using step-wise dissolution techniques (e.g., Busby-Spera et al., 1990a; Mattinson, 1994). However, many of the samples still show some scatter about the regression lines. This scatter probably results from a range in ages of inherited components and/or from our inability to "see through" all of the effects of later Pb loss in the zircons. In addition, the data points for each

sample only show a moderate spread along the regression lines and are concentrated near the lower intercepts on concordia. These factors combine to produce moderately large uncertainties in the lower-intercept ages and very large uncertainties on the upper-intercept ages.

Regressions of the data for igneous-zircon fractions give the following intercept ages: Sample OD-86 (four igneous fractions) has a lower-intercept age of 172.4 ± 6.2 Ma and an upper-intercept age of 1334 ± 308 Ma. Sample OD-20 (four igneous fractions) has a lower-intercept age of 166.5 ± 6.7 Ma and an upper-intercept age of 764 ± 306 Ma. Sample OD-30 (three igneous zircons) has a lower-intercept age of 167.4 ± 3.5 Ma and an upper-intercept age of 1275 ± 302 Ma. The regressions thus all give lower intercepts that agree within errors at ca. 170 Ma. However, the argument could be made that the stratigraphically youngest sample, OD-30 (unit 3 of the Cowhole volcanics), is ~3 m.y. younger than a reference chord defined by the two stratigraphically older samples, OD-86 and OD-20 (shown in Fig. 4A). All three fractions for sample OD-30 lie clearly to the right (young side) of the reference chord. The upper-intercept ages for all three samples are very poorly determined, in part because of the long projection to the upper intercept with concordia. Nevertheless, they clearly indicate a Proterozoic inherited component.

A second concordia diagram (Fig. 4B) is shown with the same data but with the entrained, Precambrian fractions included. The entrained zircons seem generally older than the inherited fraction in the igneous zircons, although the upper intercept of the reference chord would just overlap within errors the apparently youngest entrained zircon point. This effect is a caution against using the ages of entrained zircons as a forced upper intercept for discordant igneous zircons.

Overall, our most robust conclusion is that the Aztec volcanics and the Cowhole volcanics all crystallized over a period of a few million years at ca. 170 Ma (Fig. 4A). The volcanics inherited zircons during the formation and evolution of their magmas and also entrained detrital zircons during their eruption and flow across the surface. The inherited and entrained zircons are Proterozoic, but span a range of ages; the inherited and entrained zircons do not necessarily represent the same population of zircons.

CONCLUSIONS AND REGIONAL CORRELATIONS

Intra-arc eolianites in the Cowhole Mountains, previously correlated with backarc eolianites of the Lower Jurassic Navajo Sandstone (Marzolf, 1980, 1990), are instead age equivalent to backarc eolianites of the Middle Jurassic Temple Cap and Carmel Formations dated by Kowalis et al. (2001). They are also age equivalent to intra-arc eolianites in the Palen Mountains of southeastern California (Fackler-Adams et al., 1997), as well as intra-arc eolianites of the upper member of the Mount Wrightson Formation and the strata of Cobre Ridge in southern Arizona (Riggs et al., 1993). These Middle Jurassic eolianites were

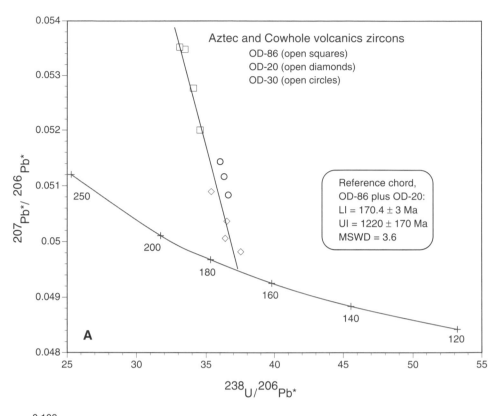

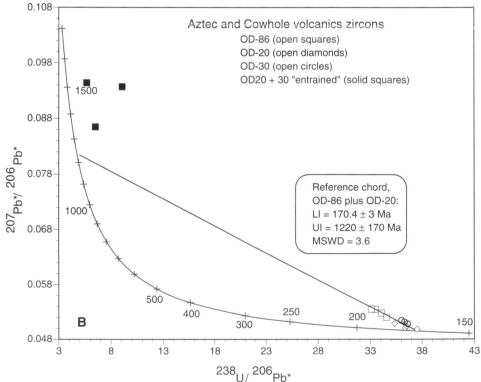

Figure 4. Tera-Wasserburg plots for U-Pb zircon data from the Aztec volcanics (OD-86) and the Cowhole volcanics (OD-20, from Cowhole volcanics unit 1, and OD-30, from Cowhole volcanics unit 3). Sample localities are presented in Figure 1 and stratigraphic relationships in Figure 2. (A) Regression of the data using igneous fractions only. (B) Concordia diagram shown with same data as Figure 4A plus inferred entrained Precambrian fractions. See text for interpretations. Abbreviations: LI—lower-intercept age, UI—upper-intercept age, MSWD—mean square of weighted deviates.

TABLE 1. ZIRCON DATA, COWHOLE MOUNTAINS

Sample†	Concentrations (ppm)			Isotopic ratios§	
	^{206}Pb*	^{238}U	^{204}Pb/^{206}Pb	^{238}U/^{206}Pb*	^{207}Pb*/^{206}Pb*
OD-86 100–151	3.858	147.5	0.000214	33.102 (191.9 ± 1.9)	0.05352 (351 ± 4)
OD-86 151–206	5.976	231.1	0.000109	33.473 (189.7 ± 1.9)	0.05348 (349 ± 2)
OD-86 206–320A	6.988	275.1	0.000074	34.087 (186.4 ± 1.9)	0.05277 (319 ± 2)
OD-86 206–320B	7.844	313.1	0.000051	34.566 (183.8 ± 1.8)	0.05201 (286 ± 2)
OD-20 100–200	10.005	408.6	0.000122	35.361 (179.7 ± 1.8)	0.05090 (236 ± 6)
OD-20 100–200	5.592	235.7	0.000541	36.496 (174.3 ± 1.7)	0.05037 (212 ± 5)
OD-20 <200	9.398	394.8	0.000128	36.377 (174.8 ± 1.7)	0.05006 (198 ± 6)
OD-20 <200	8.254	357.8	0.000355	37.523 (169.6 ± 1.7)	0.04982 (187 ± 4)
OD-20 100–200pC	13.391	140.6	0.000074	9.088 (673 ± 7)	0.09368 (1502 ± 2)
OD-30 100–200	5.488	228.3	0.000245	36.010 (176.5 ± 1.8)	0.05144 (260 ± 5)
OD-30 <200	7.535	315.9	0.000161	36.298 (175.1 ± 1.8)	0.05117 (248 ± 10)
OD-30 <200	5.626	237.9	0.000218	36.603 (173.8 ± 1.7)	0.05084 (234 ± 3)
OD-30 100–200pC	23.031	150.9	0.000047	5.670 (1047 ± 10)	0.09440 (1516 ± 2)
OD-30 <200pC	22.242	167.1	0.000069	6.504 (922 ± 9)	0.08649 (1349 ± 3)

*Radiogenic.
†"pC" designates frosted, rounded "entrained zircon fraction." Numbers refer to grain size range in micrometers.
§ ^{204}Pb/^{206}Pb ratio = measured, corrected for amount of ^{204}Pb in spike. Calculated isotopic ratios for Terra-Wasserburg concordia diagram shown with calculated ages and uncertainties shown in parentheses. We have assigned a conservative 1% error to the ^{238}U/^{206}Pb* ratios to account for any minor fractionations during the step-wise dissolution procedure. For other analytical details, see Mattinson (1994).

also previously correlated with the Lower Jurassic Navajo Sandstone (Drewes, 1971; Bilodeau and Keith, 1986; Marzolf, 1990). Other intra-arc eolianites in Arizona and California, however, are age-equivalent to the Lower Jurassic Navajo and Wingate Sandstones (see discussion in Riggs et al., 1993). Craton-derived eolian sand was therefore trapped within intra-arc rift basins for a protracted period of time (at least 40 m.y.), not just during deposition of the Lower Jurassic Navajo Sandstone. Our Middle Jurassic dates from the Cowhole Mountains provide further evidence for this regional-scale interpretation.

We have previously obtained ages on volcanic rocks from the central and southeastern Mojave block that are similar to the ages from the eastern Mojave block reported here. Outflow ignimbrites of the Cowhole volcanics (Jcv1 and Jcv3), as well as the dacite lava flow within the Aztec Sandstone, are age equivalent to two of the intracaldera ignimbrites of the lower Sidewinder Volcanic Series of the central Mojave block, described by Schermer and Busby (1994) and Schermer et al. (this volume). The ignimbrites of the Cowhole volcanics are younger than the oldest lower Sidewinder ignimbrite and older than the youngest lower Sidewinder ignimbrite (Schermer et al., this volume). The ages of the Aztec volcanics and the Cowhole volcanics in the Cowhole Mountains also overlap with the basal Dome Rock volcanic sequence in the Palen Mountains. There we dated a silicic block-and-ash-flow deposit within a volcaniclastic unit that interfingers with underlying eolian quartz arenites, at 174 ± 8 Ma (Fackler-Adams et al., 1997). Our date on the top of the Dome Rock sequence, which interfingers with the basal McCoy Mountains Formation, is younger than the Cowhole volcanics, with an age of 162 ± 3 Ma on an ignimbrite (Fackler-Adams et al., 1997).

Our structural data from the upper half of the Cowhole

Mountains section, together with the data of Wadsworth et al. (1995) from the lower half of the section, indicate extension throughout deposition of the section there. Syndepositional normal faulting and deposition of landslide megabreccias accompanied Middle Jurassic eolian sedimentation and volcanism in the Cowhole Mountains (Wadsworth et al., 1995, and this study). Our volcanologic data show that silicic welded tuffs are the predominant volcanic rock type in the Cowhole Mountains, suggesting the presence of nearby calderas, and the youngest ignimbrite may represent an intracaldera accumulation.

Our previous studies in Middle Jurassic rocks of southern Arizona, southeastern California, eastern California, and the central Mojave block document ignimbrite eruptions from calderas contemporaneous with deposition of craton-derived eolian sands within the arc, in transtensional or extensional basins (Riggs and Busby-Spera, 1991; Schermer and Busby, 1994; Fackler-Adams et al., 1997). Silicic calderas are best developed in arcs undergoing extension or transtension, be they continental (e.g., Central America; North Island, New Zealand; Sumatra) or oceanic (e.g., Izu-Bonin). Extensional or transtensional arcs are also low-standing enough to act as a depocenter for sediment derived from outside of the arc, rather than acting as a high-standing topographic barrier the way neutral or compressional arcs commonly do. We suggest that extensional or transtensional basins within the Middle Jurassic arc of Arizona and southern California acted as efficient "traps" for eolian sands derived from the North American craton.

ACKNOWLEDGMENTS

This work was begun when C. Busby was a Ph.D. student (1978–1982), supported by Princeton University's Department of Geological Sciences and a National Science Foundation (NSF) dissertation fellowship. She thanks Princeton and, in particular, John Suppe and Franklyn Van Houten for their very generous financial and intellectual support throughout her graduate career. She thanks the editor of this volume, Allen Glazner, for encouraging her to pursue studies in the Mojave Desert when she bumped into him in the field there in 1979. Continued support for this study was provided by NSF grants EAR-8519124 and EAR-8803769 (to Busby and Mattinson). We are most grateful to John Marzolf and Doug Walker for field discussions in the Cowhole Mountains. Formal reviews by George Dunne and an anonymous reviewer helped to improve the manuscript substantially.

REFERENCES CITED

Bilodeau, W.L., and Keith, S.B., 1986, Lower Jurassic Navajo-Aztec-equivalent sandstones in southern Arizona and their paleogeographic significance: American Association of Petroleum Geologists Bulletin, v. 70, p. 690–701.

Busby, C.J., Mattinson, J.M., Parris, M., and Fackler-Adams, B., 1994, Timing and nature of late Mesozoic deformational events in southeastern California: Stratigraphic and geochronologic constraints: Boulder, Colorado, Geological Society of America Abstracts with Programs, v. 26, no. 2, p. 42.

Busby-Spera, C.J., 1988, Speculative tectonic model for the early Mesozoic arc of the southwest Cordilleran United States: Geology, v. 16, p. 1121–1125.

Busby-Spera, C.J., Schermer, E.R. and Mattinson, J.M., 1989, Volcano-tectonic controls on sedimentation in an extensional continental arc: A Jurassic example from the eastern Mojave Desert, California: Socorro, New Mexico, New Mexico Bureau of Mines and Mineral Resources Bulletin 131, p. 34.

Busby-Spera, C.J., Mattinson, J.M., Riggs, N.R., and Schermer, E.R., 1990a, The Triassic-Jurassic magmatic arc in the Mojave-Sonoran deserts and the Sierran-Klamath region: Similarities and differences in paleogeographic evolution, in Harwood, D., and Miller, M.M., eds., Paleozoic and early Mesozoic paleogeographic relations, Sierra Nevada, Klamath Mountains, and related terranes: Geological Society of America Special Paper 255, p. 325–338.

Busby-Spera, C.J., Mattinson, J.M., and Schermer, E.R., 1990b, Stratigraphic and tectonic evolution of the Jurassic arc: New field and U-Pb zircon geochronological data from the Mojave Desert: Geological Society of America Abstracts with Programs, v. 22, no. 3, p. 11–12.

Drewes, H., 1971, Mesozoic stratigraphy of the Santa Rita Mountains, southeast of Tucson, Arizona: U.S. Geological Survey Professional Paper 748, 35 p.

Dunne, G.C., 1972, Geology of the Devil's Playground area, eastern Mojave Desert, California [Ph.D. thesis]: Houston, Texas, Rice University, 79 p.

Dunne, G.C., Garvey, T.P., Oborne, M., Schneidereit, D., Fritsche, A.E., and Walker, J.D., 1998, Geology of the Inyo Mountains volcanic complex: Implications for Jurassic paleogeography of the Sierran magmatic arc in eastern California: Geological Society of America Bulletin, v. 110, p. 1376–1397.

Fackler-Adams, B.N., Busby, C.J. and Mattinson, J.M., 1997, Jurassic magmatism and sedimentation in the Palen Mountains, southeastern California: Implications for regional tectonic controls on the Mesozoic magmatic arc: Geological Society of America Bulletin, v. 109, p. 1464–1484.

Fisher, G.R., 1990, Middle Jurassic syntectonic conglomerate in the Mount

Tallac roof pendant, northern Sierra Nevada, California: Geological Society of America Special Paper 255, p. 339–350.

Fleck, R.J., Mattinson, J.M., Busby, C.J., Carr, M.D., Davis, G.A., and Burchfiel, B.C., 1994, Isotopic complexities and the age of the Delfonte volcanic rocks, eastern Mescal Range, southeastern California: Stratigraphic and tectonic implications: Geological Society of America Bulletin, v. 106, p. 1254–1266.

Grose, L.T., 1959, Structure and petrology of the northeast part of the Soda Mountains, San Bernardino County, California and southwestern Arizona: Geological Society of America Bulletin, v. 70, p. 1509–1548.

Hewett, D.F., 1931, Geology and ore deposits of the Goodsprings quadrangle, Nevada: U.S. Geological Survey Professional Paper 162, 162 p.

Hewett, D.F., 1956, Geology and mineral resources of the Ivanpah quadrangle, California and Nevada: U.S. Geological Survey Professional Paper 275, 172 p.

Kano, K.J., Matsura, H., and Yamauchi, S., 1997, Miocene rhyolitic welded tuff infilling a funnel-shaped eruption conduit, Shiotani, southeast of Matsue, SW Japan: Bulletin of Volcanology, v. 59, p. 125–135.

Kowalis, B.J., Christiansen, E.H., Deino, A.L., Zhang, C., and Everett, B., 2001, The record of Middle Jurassic volcanism in the Carmel and Temple Cap Formations of southwestern Utah: Geological Society of America Bulletin, v. 113, p. 373–387.

Marzolf, J.E., 1980, The Aztec sandstone and stratigraphically related rocks in the Mojave Desert, in Fife, D.L., and Brown, G.R., eds., Geology and mineral wealth of the California desert: Santa Ana, California, South Coast Geological Society, p. 215–220.

Marzolf, J.E., 1990, Reconstruction of extensionally dismembered early Mesozoic sedimentary basins, southwestern Colorado Plateau to the eastern Mojave Desert, in Wiernicke, B.P., ed., Basin and range extensional tectonics near the latitude of Las Vegas, Nevada: Boulder, Colorado, Geological Society of America Memoir 176, p. 477–500.

Marzolf, J.E., and Cole, R.D., 1987, Relationship of the Jurassic volcanic arc to backarc stratigraphy, Cowhole Mountains, San Bernadino County, California, in Hill, M.L., ed., Cordilleran section of the Geological Society of America: Boulder, Colorado, Geological Society of America, Geology of North America, Centennial Field Guide, v. 1, p. 115–120.

Mattinson, J.M., 1994, A study of complex discordance in zircons using stepwise dissolution techniques: Contributions to Mineralogy and Petrology, v. 116, p. 117–129.

Miller, E.L., and Carr, M.D., 1978, Recognition of possible Aztec-equivalent sandstones and associated Mesozoic metasedimentary deposits within the Mesozoic magmatic arc in the southwestern Mojave Desert, in Howell, D.G., ed., Paleogeography of the western United States: Pacific Section, Society of Economic Paleontologists and Mineralogists, Pacific Coast Paleogeography Symposium, p. 283–289.

Miura, D., 1999, Arcuate pyroclastic conduits, ring faults, and coherent floor at Kumano caldera, southwest Honshu, Japan: Journal of Volcanology and Geothermal Research, v. 92, p. 271–294.

Novitsky-Evans, J.M., 1978, Geology of the Cowhole Mountains, southern California; Structural, stratigraphic and geochemical studies [Ph.D. thesis]: Houston, Texas, Rice University, 95 p.

Reedman, A.J., Park, K.H., Merriman, R.J., and Kim, S.E., 1987, Welded tuff infilling a volcanic conduit at Weolseong, Republic of Korea: Bulletin of Volcanology, v. 49, p. 541–546.

Riggs, N.R., and Busby-Spera, C.J., 1990, Evolution of a multi-vent volcanic complex within a subsiding arc graben depression: Mount Wrightson Formation, Arizona; Geological Society of America Bulletin, v. 102, p. 1114–1135.

Riggs, N.R., and Busby-Spera, C.J., 1991, Facies analysis of an ancient, dismembered, large caldera complex and implications for intra-arc subsidence: Middle Jurassic strata of Cobre Ridge, southern Arizona, U.S.A: Sedimentary Geology, v. 74, p. 39–68.

Riggs, N.R., Mattinson, J.M., and Busby, C.J., 1993, Correlation of Mesozoic eolian strata between the magmatic and the Colorado Plateau: New U-Pb geochronologic data from southern Arizona: Geological Society of America Bulletin, v. 105, p. 1231–1246.

Schermer, E.R., and Busby, C.J., 1994, Jurassic magmatism in the central Mojave Desert: Implications for arc paleogeography and preservation of continental volcanic sequences: Geological Society of America Bulletin, v. 106, p. 767–790.

Wadsworth, W.B., Ferriz, H., and Rhodes, D.D., 1995, Structural and stratigraphic development of the Middle Jurassic magmatic arc in the Cowhole Mountains, central-eastern Mojave Desert, California, *in* Miller, D.M., and Busby, C., eds., Jurassic magmatism and tectonics of the North American Cordillera: Geological Society of America Special Paper 299, p. 327–349.

Wyld, S.J., 2000, Triassic evolution of the arc and back-arc of northwest Nevada, and evidence for extensional tectonism, *in* Gehrels, G.E., ed., Paleozoic and Triassic paleogeography and tectonics of western Nevada and northern California: Geological Society of America Special Paper 347, p. 185–207.

Manuscript Accepted by the Society May 9, 2001

Geological Society of America
Memoir 195
2002

Paleogeographic and tectonic implications of Jurassic sedimentary and volcanic sequences in the central Mojave block

Elizabeth R. Schermer
Department of Geology, Western Washington University, Bellingham, Washington 98225, USA
Cathy J. Busby
James M. Mattinson
Department of Geological Sciences, University of California, Santa Barbara, California 93106, USA

ABSTRACT

Sedimentologic, stratigraphic, and geochronologic data from strata of early Mesozoic age in the central Mojave block elucidate the paleogeographic and tectonic evolution of the magmatic arc in the southern U.S. Cordillera. A sequence of calcareous siltstone, volcaniclastic conglomerate, tuff, and quartzose sandstone records the transition from shallow-marine rocks of the Fairview Valley Formation to the subaerial Sidewinder volcanic series. Quartzose sandstones occur below, within, and above the transitional sequence and indicate that texturally mature, craton-derived quartz sand gained access to the arc during the initial stages of volcanism. U-Pb data indicate that explosive volcanism began at 179.5 ± 3.0 Ma and continued until 151 ± 1.3 Ma (Lower Sidewinder volcanic series). A rhyolite dike of the Independence dike swarm (Upper Sidewinder volcanic series) that postdates normal faulting and tilting of the ignimbrites yielded a U-Pb date of 151.9 ± 5.6 Ma. The data define the age of extension and development of the angular unconformity between the Upper and Lower Sidewinder volcanic series at ca. 151 Ma.

The data suggest that at least part, and possibly all, of the Fairview Valley Formation is late Early Jurassic in age. We correlate the Fairview Valley Formation with Mesozoic metasedimentary rocks in the Rodman Mountains and Fry Mountains, and at Cave Mountain to the east. Eolian quartz arenites in these sequences suggest a coastal environment coeval with the Navajo Sandstone on the Colorado Plateau. The reinterpretation of the shallow-marine rocks as Jurassic instead of Triassic suggests a period of uplift and erosion or nondeposition extending from the Early Triassic into the Early Jurassic, followed by a return to marine conditions. Shallow-marine conditions persisted until the beginning of arc volcanism in the late Early Jurassic time. Similarities to the early Mesozoic arc of the Sierra Nevada, together with the structural evolution of the region, suggest that the change from high-standing to low-standing paleogeography reflects a large-scale tectonic control on relative sea level related to a period of intra-arc extension or transtension.

Schermer, E.R., Busby, C.J., and Mattinson, J.M., 2002, Paleogeographic and tectonic implications of Jurassic sedimentary and volcanic sequences in the central Mojave block, *in* Glazner, A.F., Walker, J.D., and Bartley, J.M., eds., Geologic Evolution of the Mojave Desert and Southwestern Basin and Range: Boulder, Colorado, Geological Society of America Memoir 195, p. 93–115.

INTRODUCTION

Understanding of the paleogeography and tectonic evolution of the early stages of the continental-margin magmatic arc in the southern U.S. Cordillera has been hampered by incomplete knowledge of the ages and depositional environments of sedimentary and volcanic rocks in the greater Mojave Desert region (e.g., Glazner et al., 1994). In the central Mojave block, well-preserved volcanic and sedimentary sequences record the initiation of arc volcanism and provide insight into the paleogeography of the early arc. In this study we present sedimentologic, stratigraphic, and U-Pb geochronologic data on the Fairview Valley Formation and the overlying Sidewinder volcanic series, a sedimentary and volcanic sequence of early Mesozoic age exposed in the Victorville area of the Mojave block (Fig. 1). Our results suggest new correlations of lower Mesozoic sequences across the Mojave block and a revised interpretation of the paleogeographic evolution of the region. Our new U-Pb ages also define the duration of explosive volcanism and set limits on the ages of intra-arc deformational events. Inasmuch as direct dating of specific structures has been difficult, we also attempt to relate the style of intra-arc sedimentation and magmatism to the tectonic setting.

GEOLOGIC SETTING

The Mesozoic magmatic arc in the Mojave Desert was built across Precambrian–Paleozoic cratonal-miogeoclinal strata that were deformed and metamorphosed in Pennsylvanian–Triassic time, possibly during strike-slip truncation of the continental margin (Burchfiel and Davis, 1972, 1981; Miller and Cameron, 1982; Stone and Stevens, 1988; Walker, 1988; Martin and Walker, 1995). Permian or Early Triassic alkalic plutonic rocks intrude deformed Paleozoic strata and record the initiation of subduction-related magmatism (Barth et al., 1990; C. Miller, 1978; Miller, 1978b; Miller et al., 1995). Shallow-marine rocks that unconformably overlie the Paleozoic rocks have been interpreted as a Lower Triassic overlap assemblage deposited across the deformed margin from the Victorville region to Cave Mountain (Fig. 1) and across undeformed rocks farther east (Walker, 1987, 1988). Facies boundaries within the overlap sequence strike northwest, indicating that the change in trend of the continental margin from northeast prior to the truncation event to northwest afterward was accomplished by Early Triassic time (Walker, 1988). The shallow-marine rocks are typically overlain by thick sequences of volcanic rocks that reflect the transition to the tectonics of the fully active magmatic arc. In several areas, including the Victorville region, Cave Mountain, and the Soda Mountains (Fig. 1), quartzite and quartz-rich sandstone occur between and are locally interfingered with the shallow-marine rocks and the volcanic rocks. The age of the quartzose sandstones has been somewhat controversial, and some exposures have been considered Triassic whereas others have been interpreted as Jurassic in age (e.g., Walker, 1987).

Jurassic and Cretaceous batholithic rocks intrude the supracrustal rocks and are widely exposed throughout the Mojave Desert (Fig. 1).

The shallow-marine Fairview Valley Formation (Bowen, 1954; Dibblee, 1960a, 1960b; Miller, 1978b, 1981) forms part of Walker's (1988) overlap assemblage in the Victorville region (Fig. 2) and was interpreted to be Early Triassic in age. Coarse conglomeratic units within the Fairview Valley Formation were interpreted by Miller (1978b, 1981) as alluvial-fan facies reflecting intra-orogenic deposition following a Permian–Triassic orogenic event. Quartzose sandstone overlies the shallow-marine rocks and the conglomerate. The contact of the Fairview Valley Formation and the quartzose sandstone with overlying volcanic rocks is parallel to bedding in the underlying strata across the region and appears to be conformable.

An important aspect of early Mesozoic arc paleogeography is reflected in the observed association of quartzose sandstones and volcanic rocks in the early Mesozoic arc. Busby-Spera (1988) noted that supermature eolian quartz arenites are commonly associated with proximal volcanic rocks throughout the southwestern Cordillera, and she interpreted the association to reflect trapping of eolianites in a low-standing arc graben-depression. The eolianites were correlated by earlier workers with the Lower Jurassic Navajo Sandstone of the Colorado Plateau and the Aztec Sandstone of the Las Vegas region (Cameron et al., 1979; Hewett, 1931, 1954; Marzolf, 1980, 1983; Miller and Carr, 1978). More recent work (Busby-Spera, 1988; Busby-Spera et al., 1990; Fackler-Adams et al., 1997; Riggs et al., 1993) has indicated that some eolianites intercalated with arc-type volcanic rocks are age-equivalent to several younger quartz arenites of the Colorado Plateau, including the Middle Jurassic Temple Cap and Page Sandstones and the upper Middle Jurassic Carmel Formation. Quartzites and quartz-rich sandstones also occur in sequences interpreted by Walker (1987, 1988) to be Early Triassic in age, but most of these occurrences are too metamorphosed to determine whether they were deposited in an eolian environment. To understand the paleogeography of coeval backarc and arc environments and to determine whether deformation events in the arc are related to those in the backarc, better understanding of the ages and depositional environments of these quartzose strata is required (e.g., Bjerrum and Dorsey, 1995; Burchfiel and Davis, 1981; Lawton, 1994).

Most of the pre-Tertiary volcanic rocks in the Mojave Desert are silicic and intermediate-composition rocks of Jurassic age. The largest exposure, the Sidewinder volcanic series (Bowen, 1954) (Figs. 1, 2, 3), consists of a >4-km-thick sequence of Jurassic rhyolitic to dacitic intracaldera ignimbrites (Lower Sidewinder volcanic series) overlain with angular unconformity by a thin sequence of rhyolite to basalt lavas (Upper Sidewinder volcanic series); (Karish et al., 1987; Schermer and Busby, 1994). Recent dating of ignimbrites and lavas in the Cowhole Mountains at 172 ± 6 to 167 ± 4 Ma defines the age of magmatism in that region as Middle Jurassic (Busby-Spera et al., 1989; Busby et al., this volume). Dating of the

A

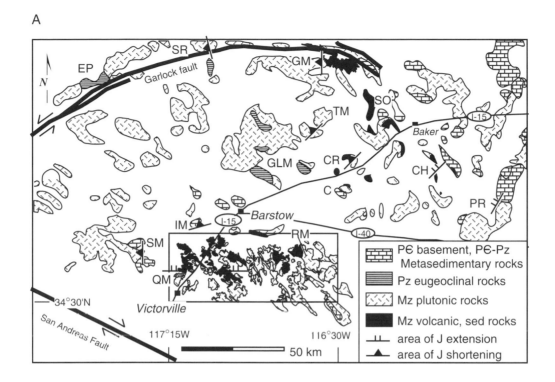

B

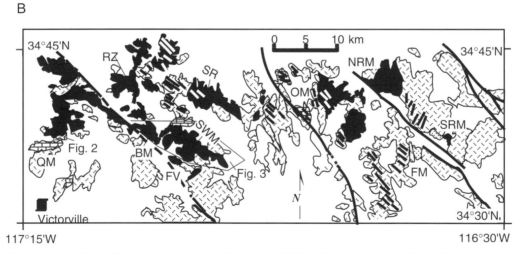

Figure 1. (A) Generalized geologic map of the western Mojave Desert, showing Mesozoic supracrustal and plutonic rocks, pre-Mesozoic strata, and localities mentioned in text. Abbreviations: C—Cave Mountain, CH—Cowhole Mountains, CR—Cronese Hills, EP—El Paso Mountains, GLM—Goldstone-Lane Mountain, GM—Granite Mountains, IM—Iron Mountain, PR—Providence Mountains, QM—Quartzite Mountain, RM—Rodman Mountains, SM—Shadow Mountains, SO—Soda Mountains, SR—Slate Range, TM—Tiefort Mountains. Box outlines study area. After Martin and Walker (1991). (B) Location map of areas containing Sidewinder volcanic series: BM—Black Mountain, FM—Fry Mountains, FV—Fairview Valley, NRM—Northern Rodman Mountains, OM—Ord Mountain, QM—Quartzite Mountains, RZ—Ritz Mountain, SR—Stoddard Ridge, SRM—Southern Rodman Mountains, SWM—Sidewinder Mountain. Short bold black and white lines indicate Independence dike swarm, light shading indicates location of Aztec Sandstone. After Karish et al. (1987).

Figure 2 (on this and next two pages). (A) Geologic map of northern Quartzite Mountain showing contact between the Fairview Valley Formation and the Sidewinder volcanic series. Bold numbers 1–4 refer to fault blocks and stratigraphic columns in B; map units are explained in C except for the following: fbr—Jurassic? hypabyssal rhyolite, Kqm—Cretaceous quartz monzonite, Pzu—undifferentiated Paleozoic rocks. Structural symbols show strike and dip direction of bedding in sedimentary units and compacted pumice foliation in ignimbrites. Inset shows generalized geology of Quartzite Mountain area; bold lines are faults, with ticks showing dip direction of normal faults. (B) Stratigraphic columns showing gradational contact between Fairview Valley Formation and Sidewinder volcanic series. Thicknesses are approximate owing to poor exposure, and except for column 1 (that section was paced), are estimated from mapped extents of units. (C) Diagram showing inferred lithofacies correlation of units in A and B. Unit descriptions are in Table 1.

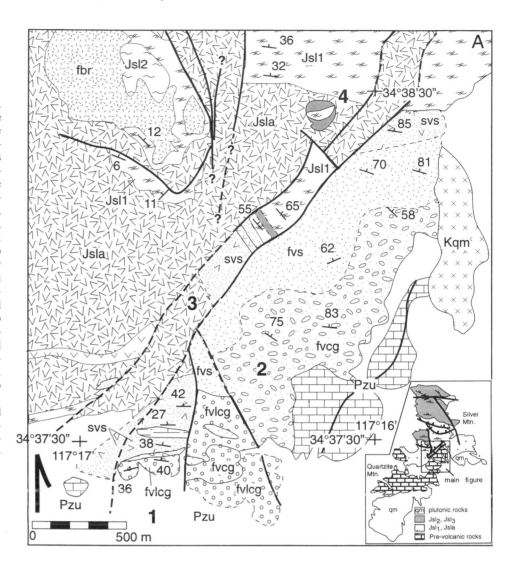

Dome Rock sequence in the Palen Mountains indicates that volcanism spanned 174 ± 8 to 155 ± 8 Ma (Fackler-Adams et al., 1997). Permian basaltic and andesitic volcanic rocks are present in eugeoclinal assemblages in the El Paso Mountains and the Goldstone–Lane Mountain region (Miller and Sutter, 1982; Carr et al., 1984).

One of the major controversies in the interpretation of the Mesozoic tectonic setting of the southwestern Cordillera has been whether the tectonic regime was contractional, neutral, or extensional during the early evolution of the magmatic arc (e.g., Burchfiel and Davis, 1981; Karish et al., 1987; Busby-Spera, 1988; Walker et al., 1990a). Contrasting interpretations have been proposed not only for different time frames but also for different segments of the arc and backarc during the same time frame. The volcanic sequences have been affected by thrusting, folding, and normal faulting in different areas (e.g., Schermer, 1993; Saleeby and Busby-Spera, 1992, and references therein); therefore, obtaining radiometric ages for the volcanic rocks helps to define the duration of volcanism and the ages of deformational events.

THE FAIRVIEW VALLEY FORMATION AND CONTACT RELATIONSHIPS WITH THE SIDEWINDER VOLCANIC SERIES

We used the maps, stratigraphic descriptions, and facies analysis of E. Miller (1978a, 1978b, 1981) and Schermer and Busby (1994) as a basis for detailed examination of the sedimentology and stratigraphy of the Fairview Valley Formation and Sidewinder volcanic series. In this section we describe the upper Fairview Valley Formation and the lowermost Sidewinder volcanic series and the nature of the contact between the two sequences at each occurrence in the central Mojave block. We have not studied the lower part of the Fairview Valley Formation in detail and have relied on descriptions and interpretations of Miller (1978a, 1978b, 1981) and Walker (1987). We interpret the data in terms of depositional environments, propose new correlations with other exposures in the eastern Mojave block and discuss the tectonic and paleogeographic implications of these interpretations. The time scale used is that of Gradstein et al. (1994), with revisions to the Permian-Triassic

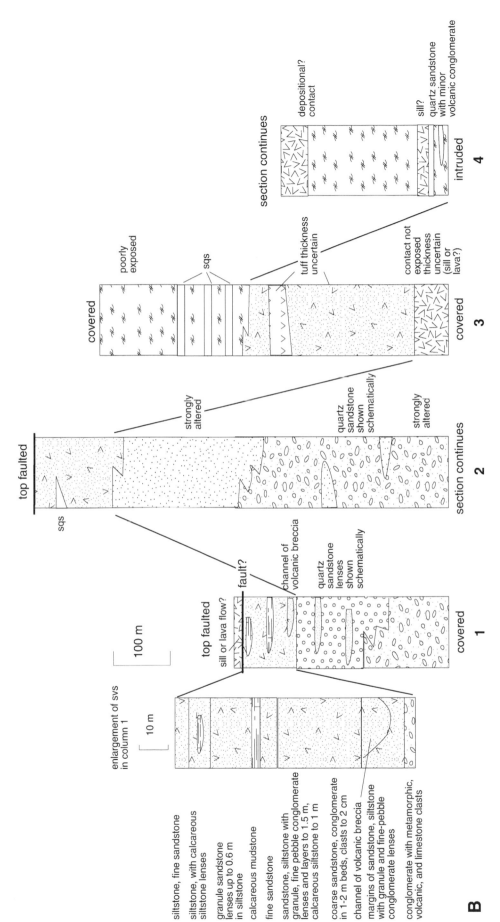

B

Figure 2. (*continued*)

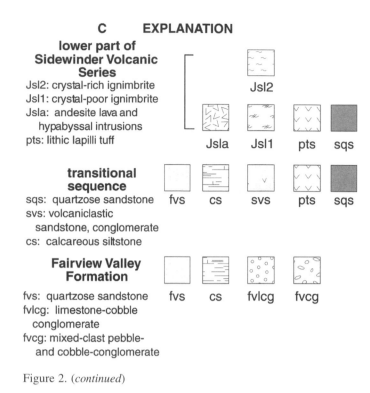

Figure 2. (*continued*)

boundary and Middle Triassic time scales as reported by Bowring et al. (1998) and Mundil et al. (1996), respectively.

Previous work

The Fairview Valley Formation was named and first described by Bowen (1954). Miller (1978a, 1978b, 1981) studied the formation in detail at several locations in the Victorville region and described a sequence of calc-silicate hornfels, silty limestone, calcareous siltstone, and conglomerate overlain by quartzite and rocks of the Sidewinder volcanic series. The contact between the Fairview Valley Formation and overlying rocks has been variably interpreted as unconformable (Miller, 1978b, 1981) or conformable (Walker, 1987).

Interpretation of the age and depositional environment of the Fairview Valley Formation has been hampered by a lack of fossils and by low-grade metamorphism and deformation. Miller (1978a, 1978b, 1981) interpreted sedimentary structures such as small-scale herringbone cross-stratification, burrows, and mudcracks to indicate either a shallow-marine or a lacustrine setting for finer-grained parts of the sequence and an alluvial-fan setting for limestone-cobble conglomerates exposed at Black Mountain and Sidewinder Mountain (Fig. 3B). Walker (1987, 1988) correlated the sequence at Black Mountain with similar, better-preserved Lower Triassic sequences in other parts of the Mojave Desert, e.g., the Soda Mountains (Fig. 1). He interpreted the presence of conodonts, in addition to the sedimentary structures indicative of shallow-water deposition,

to reflect a marginal-marine environment. One of the limestone beds sampled by Walker (1987), however, contains a mixed fauna of Permian and Triassic age, indicating that at least some of the conodonts are reworked, and thus the interpretations of marine setting and an Early Triassic age remain uncertain. A monzonite pluton, unconformably overlain by the Fairview Valley Formation at Black Mountain, has been dated by U-Pb at 243 ± 2 Ma (Miller et al., 1995); the age of this pluton also suggests that the formation must be younger than Early Triassic.

New results

At Quartzite Mountain, Black Mountain, and Sidewinder Mountain (Figs. 2, 3), we interpret the Sidewinder volcanic series to lie conformably above the Fairview Valley Formation, and we show that both units contain quartz-rich sandstones. At Quartzite Mountain, a gradational contact records the transition between the Fairview Valley Formation and the Sidewinder volcanic series (Fig. 2). The stratigraphic sequences at Black Mountain, Sidewinder Mountain, and other areas to the east (Figs. 3, 4) provide additional facies characteristics and age constraints. The Fairview Valley Formation and the Sidewinder volcanic series are variably deformed, hydrothermally altered, and contact metamorphosed. Because sedimentary structures, textures, and compositions are typically visible despite the alteration, we omit the prefix "meta-" in our descriptions herein; however, we note particular locations where alteration is so intense as to hamper sedimentologic interpretation.

Quartzite Mountain. A newly identified transitional sequence between the Fairview Valley Formation and the Sidewinder volcanic series at Quartzite Mountain reveals that the contact is gradational. Miller (1978a, 1978b, 1981), in contrast, interpreted the Fairview Valley–Sidewinder contact there as an angular unconformity. Further mapping establishes that the contact is a fault at localities where there is an angular discordance, but is depositional at other localities (Fig. 2A). The Fairview Valley Formation at Quartzite Mountain consists of ≥1000 m of conglomerate (Miller, 1978a, 1978b, 1981). The transitional sequence comprises four lithologic units: (1) volcaniclastic sandstone and conglomerate (svs), (2) lower quartzose sandstone (fvs), (3) calcareous siltstone (cs), and (4) upper quartzose sandstone (sqs) (see Fig. 2 and Table 1) (all four units were combined as unit sws1 by Schermer and Busby, 1994). Contacts between most of the units are poorly exposed, but generally parallel the bedding within each fault block.

Correlation of stratigraphy between the various fault blocks at Quartzite Mountain provides a composite link between the Fairview Valley Formation and the Sidewinder volcanic series. The map and stratigraphic columns in Figure 2 show the transition from calcareous siltstone (cs), quartzose sandstone (fvs), and conglomerate (fvcg, fvlcg) typical of the Fairview Valley Formation upward into increasing proportions of fine- to medium-grained quartzose sandstone (sqs) and interbedded volcaniclastic sandstone and conglomerate (svs), intermediate-

Late Jurassic
Upper Sidewinder
volcanic series

basalt, andesite, rhyolite lavas,
dike swarm, hypabyssal intrusions

variable thickness

rhyolite dike: **151.9 ± 5.6 Ma**

angular unconformity

Jurassic quartz monzonite

late Early to Late Jurassic
Lower Sidewinder volcanic series

Tuff of Stoddard Ridge >1750 m

(intracaldera) dacite (Jsl4) **151.1 ± 1.3 Ma**

L: 0–40%; P: 0–25%; C: 6–20%

locally underlain by rhyolite dome

Tuff of Turtle Mt. 600–800 m
(intracaldera) dacite (Jsl3) **163.1 ± 6.5 Ma**
tuff L: <1%; P: 0–15%; C: 35%
tuff breccia L: 50–80%

Local reworked tuffs, ignimbrites 0–600 m

Tuff of Sidewinder Mt. ~1400 m
(intracaldera) dacite + rhyolite (Jsl2) **164 ± 10 Ma**
L: 0–30%; P: 0–30%; C: 30%

local tuffs, sedimentary rocks, 20–200 m (lts)
Tuff of Black Mt. 500–840 m (intracaldera)
rhyolite (Jsl1) **179.5 ± 3.0 Ma**
L: 0–3%; P:1–25%; C: 0–12%
andesite lavas, thickness unknown (Jsla)
conformable, gradational contact marked
locally by intercalated sed. and volc. rocks
Fairview Valley Formation (fv)

1000 m

A

Figure 3. (A) Generalized stratigraphic column of the Sidewinder volcanic series showing units dated in this study. Compositions indicated by percentage ranges of lithic lapilli (L), pumice lapilli (P), and crystal content (C) from entire study area. (B) Simplified geologic map of Sidewinder (SWM) and Black (BM) Mountains showing location of samples dated, modified from Schermer and Busby (1994). Sample data listed in Table 2. CMG = sample from Graubard et al. (1988).

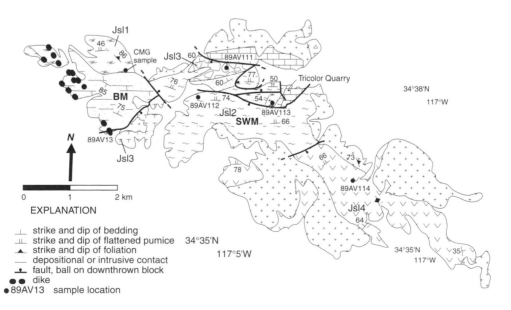

B

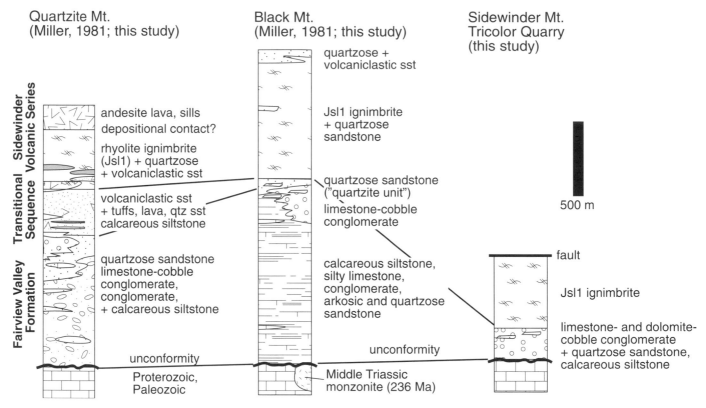

Figure 4. Stratigraphic columns showing characteristics of Fairview Valley Formation–Sidewinder volcanic series contact at Quartzite Mountain, Black Mountain, and the Tricolor Quarry area of Sidewinder Mountain.

composition tuffs (pts), and andesite lava (Jsla). Descriptions are given in Table 1. The stratigraphically lowest exposures of the Fairview Valley Formation at Quartzite Mountain are pebble and cobble conglomerates (fvcg). These conglomerates are locally interbedded with and overlain by limestone-cobble conglomerate (fvlcg); clasts in both types of conglomerate were derived from Paleozoic units (Miller, 1978b, 1981). Both types of conglomerate contain lenses of quartzose sandstone (unit fvs), and locally a thick section dominated by this sandstone overlies the conglomerate section (e.g., Fig. 2B, column 2). The quartzose sandstones and siltstones contain well-rounded monocrystalline quartz grains and little or no polycrystalline quartz or quartzite lithic fragments. Similar quartzose sandstones (unit sqs) occur stratigraphically higher, intercalated with the volcaniclastic units (Fig. 2B, column 2) and with basal lavas, tuffs, and ignimbrite (Jsl1) of the Sidewinder volcanic series (Fig. 2B, columns 3, 4). These stratigraphically higher quartzose sandstones contain fine- to medium-grained well-rounded quartz grains in addition to volcanic material. The volcaniclastic units (svs) contain porphyritic and aphyric rhyolitic to andesitic clasts in an altered, sandy to silty matrix.

Although the transitional sequence is faulted, we are able to correlate upper parts of the sequence in the southern fault blocks (Fig. 2B, columns 1, 2) with the lower parts of the sequence in the northern fault blocks (Fig. 2B, columns 3, 4). The

fault blocks that contain the basal Sidewinder volcanic series (Fig. 2B, columns 3, 4) comprise ignimbrites, tuffs, and lavas intercalated with volcaniclastic and quartzose sandstone beds whose compositions and sedimentary structures are similar to those in lower parts of the sequence where no primary volcanic rocks are present. The ignimbrites occur in thin (2–15-m-thick) layers that are weakly to moderately welded and are interpreted to be outflow sheets from a caldera located near or at Black Mountain (Schermer and Busby, 1994).

The composition of the sedimentary units from the upper part of the Fairview Valley Formation upward through the transitional sequence records a continual supply of texturally mature quartz sand in combination with other, more local, sources. The contrast in texture between the uniformly sized, well-rounded quartz grains with the wide grain-size range and angular to subangular nature of the clasts of the volcanic material suggests two distinct sources. Both quartzose sandstones (Fairview Valley unit fvs and transitional sequence unit sqs) contain a population of the texturally mature grains, suggesting that the quartz-sand source persisted during the initial stages of volcanism. Texturally mature quartz sandstones in other parts of the Mojave Desert have been interpreted to be derived from cratonal eolian sources (e.g., Miller and Carr, 1978; Busby-Spera, 1988), and we concur with this interpretation for the quartzose sandstones at Quartzite Mountain.

TABLE 1. LITHOLOGIC DESCRIPTIONS FOR ROCKS AT QUARTZITE MOUNTAIN*

Unit	Outcrop Description	Composition
Jsl2	CRYSTAL RICH IGNIMBRITE*	Rhyolite to dacite, complexly zoned. Crystals avg. 30%, include coarse K-feldspar, quartz, biotite. Lithics (silicic volcanics) rare, pumice sparse.
Jsl1	CRYSTAL POOR IGNIMBRITE*	Rhyolite; crystals avg. <10–12%; lithics 0–3% (silicic and mafic volcanics, calc-silicate rock, marble, quartzite); pumice 1–25%.
Jsla	ANDESITE LAVA AND HYPABYSSAL INTRUSIONS*	Andesite; phenocrysts avg. 30–35%, include plagioclase and pyroxene, groundmass typically recrystallized, altered.
pts[†]	LITHIC LAPILLI TUFF in part may grade laterally into Jsla	Andesite or dacite with up to 15% volcanic lithics, 20–45% crystals including plagioclase, biotite, Fe-oxides.
svs[§]	VOLCANICLASTIC SANDSTONE, CONGLOMERATE 1. Med. to cse gr. volcanic-lithic sst, siltst., rare thin tuff? or mudst. laminae 2mm thick. Thin-bedded (0.2–1 cm) with indistinct planar, rare low-angle cross strat. 2. Volcanic-lithic granule, pbl sst with clasts 0.2–1 cm; lenses 20–60 cm thick, locally to 2m. 3. Volcanic breccia, matrix-supported med-thick bedded, crudely stratified, nongraded or normally graded, rare scour/fill; angular to subangular volcanic clasts; subangular to subrounded metamorphic clasts 1–10 cm, rarely to 25 cm.	Clasts include intermed. comp. plag. porphyry, silicic porphyritic and aphyric volc. clasts, quartzite, marble, siltst, rare gneiss and granite. Metamorphic clasts generally <15% of clasts. matrix is altered, sandy to silty, composed of clay and/or white mica, fine quartz and feldspar grains, epidote, and altered biotite.
sqs[§]	QUARTZOSE SANDSTONE Fine-med gr. planar laminated, thin bedded; indistinct bedding and grain size where altered.	Fine to medium-grained well-rounded quartz grains, angular feldspar grains, and minor rounded to subrounded plutonic clasts and polycrystalline quartz. Matrix of sericite, quartz, and Fe-oxides may represent altered volcanic material.
cs[§]	CALCAREOUS SILTSTONE Parallel-laminated, beds 0.2–1 cm, intercalated with volcanic lithic sst in beds, lenses up to 60 cm.	Fine-grained quartz, epidote, calcite, white mica.
fvs	QUARTZOSE SANDSTONE Fine-med gr, planar laminated. Typically extremely altered.	Contains well-rounded quartz grains in altered matrix, quartzite lithics.
fvlcg	LIMESTONE COBBLE CONGLOMERATE Massive to crudely stratified	Limestone, dolomite clasts in silty limestone matrix.
fvcg	MIXED PEBBLE, COBBLE CONGLOMERATE Massive to crudely strat. cgl with metamorphic, rare volc and limestone clasts in altered calcerous? sst matrix. Local quartzose and metacalc sst, siltst. lenses. Typically strongly altered.	Abundant metasedimentary and gneiss clasts derived from underlying Paleozoic and Precambrian units, lesser monzonitic to granitic clasts, and minor volcanic clasts. Matrix contains carbonate, quartz, feldspar, chert, and volcanic debris (Miller, 1978a).

*Descriptions of units in other areas and detailed descriptions and point counts of all Sidewinder volcanic units are given in Schermer and Busby (1994).
[†]Included in unit lts of Schermer and Busby (1994).
[§] Included in unit sws1 of Schermer and Busby (1994).

Volcanic detritus is abundant in the transitional sequence. The volcanic lithic conglomerates in unit svs contain clasts that resemble, in phenocryst composition and abundance, the andesite lavas and shallow intrusions (Jsla) interpreted to overlie and intrude the volcaniclastic sequence and possibly interfinger with it (Fig. 2B, columns 1, 3). The conglomerates also contain abundant silicic volcanic clasts that cannot be positively identified as derived from part of the Sidewinder volcanic series, but are similar in composition and texture to porphyritic rhyolite in adjacent ranges described by Schermer and Busby (1994). Upper stratigraphic levels of the volcaniclastic unit (svs) are interlayered with primary volcanic rocks (pts, Jsl1; Fig. 2B, column 3). Metamorphic and rare limestone clasts represent <15% of the clasts in the conglomerates of unit svs and are typically more rounded than the volcanic clasts. Sandstones in the unit also contain plutonic lithic grains that appear similar to those in unit fvcg. The metamorphic and plutonic clast types are identical to those found in lower parts of the Fairview Valley Formation.

Sedimentary structures and textures are locally well preserved in the volcaniclastic part of the sequence in the west (Fig. 2B, column 1), whereas in other fault blocks (columns 2, 3), poor exposures and hydrothermal alteration hinder interpretation of the depositional environments. Matrix-supported conglomerate and coarse-sand layers locally exhibit crude stratification and normal grading. In fault block 1, a channel ≥15 m wide and ~10–15 m deep is filled with volcanic-lithic breccias and medium- to coarse-grained sandstones. These form an upward-thinning and -fining sequence of beds; the proportion of sandstone lenses (as opposed to conglomerate) increases upward, and siltstone beds up to 2 m thick fill the top of the channel. The channel appears to be faulted on its eastern margin, but is bounded on its western margin by a sequence of siltstone and fine-grained sandstone with thin granule sandstone lenses that also overlie the channel. The strata above the channel become finer grained up section as shown by increasing amounts of planar-laminated, thin-bedded calcareous siltstone and mudstone with rare low-angle cross-lamination. Possible tuff layers 1–3 mm thick are altered to sericite.

The volcaniclastic sedimentary rocks appear to have been deposited in a subaqueous environment. The predominance of fine-grained parallel-laminated deposits outside the channel-filling sequence suggests a quiet-water setting. The grading and crude stratification in the coarse-grained deposits suggest deposition from high-density turbidity currents and/or dilute debris flows; the general absence of cross-bedding and scour-and-fill structure argues against fluvial deposition. We interpret this sequence to represent gravity flows having a high concentration of sediment shed from nearby volcanic sources into a quiet-water setting that apparently records the latest stages of Fairview Valley Formation shallow-marine or lacustrine deposition.

Black Mountain. The Fairview Valley Formation at Black Mountain (Figs. 3, 4), its type locality, consists of >1200 m of conglomerate, silty limestone, and calcareous siltstone and sandstone (Bowen, 1954; Miller, 1978a, 1978b, 1981). Above the basal unconformity, marked by a conglomerate with monzonite clasts, the sequence is dominated by fine-grained calcareous rocks interpreted to have been deposited in a shallow-marine or lacustrine environment (Miller, 1978b; Walker, 1987). The sequence also contains thin conglomerate lenses in the lower part with clasts of marble, monzonite, and rare rhyolite, granite, quartzite, chert, limestone, and gneiss (Miller, 1981). A 675-m-thick conglomerate in the upper part of the formation contains cobble- to boulder-sized clasts of Paleozoic limestone and is generally unsorted, with thick to massive beds. Miller (1978a, 1978b, 1981) interpreted these characteristics to reflect an alluvial-fan setting; however, because the conglomerate interfingers westward with limestones and calc-silicates interpreted to have been deposited subaqueously, we suggest that "fan delta" is a better term for this paleo–depositional environment.

The nature of the contact between the Fairview Valley Formation and Sidewinder volcanic series at Black Mountain differs from that to the west at Quartzite Mountain. Miller (1978a, 1978b, 1981) interpreted the Fairview Valley Formation at Black Mountain to be overlain along an erosional unconformity by a distinct "quartzite unit" (Miller's term) that is conformably overlain by rocks of the Sidewinder volcanic series. Miller's interpretation of an unconformable contact between the quartzite unit and the Fairview Valley Formation was based on the observations that (1) the quartzite unit overlapped contrasting facies (conglomerate and calcareous siltstone-sandstone) in the Fairview Valley Formation (Fig. 4) and (2) the quartzite unit, composed of 50%–90% fine-sand-sized quartz grains in a matrix of calc-silicate minerals, was mineralogically distinct from arkosic sandstones in the Fairview Valley Formation.

Our new results confirm the alternative interpretation of Walker (1987) that the quartzite unit is part of the upper Fairview Valley Formation and records an increase in the supply of quartz sand to the basin. Miller (1978a, 1978b) interpreted the calc-silicate matrix as altered volcanic material, but we have found no evidence for relict volcanic crystals or other volcanic debris; we therefore reinterpret the matrix as altered calcareous siltstone, similar to calcareous siltstones that occur throughout the Fairview Valley Formation at Black Mountain. Further evidence for a gradational contact at the base of the quartzite unit includes the following: (1) The matrix of the carbonate-clast conglomerate is rich in quartz sand in at least the upper 15–20 m of the conglomerate facies. (2) Beds of quartzose sandstone averaging ~1 m thick are intercalated in the upper ~75 m of the conglomerate. (3) A similar upward increase in the abundance of quartzose sandstone relative to limestone and calcareous siltstone occurs in the sandstone-siltstone facies west of the conglomerate. (4) Limestone-clast conglomerate lenses up to 1 m thick occur within what Miller (1978a, 1981) mapped as the quartzite unit. (5) Bedding is subparallel above, within, and below the quartzite unit, as also noted by Miller (1978, 1981; Fig. 4). An interpretation of a gradational contact between the quartzite unit and the Fairview Valley Formation at Black Mountain is also consistent with the upward increase in quartzose sandstone observed in the Fairview Valley Formation at Quartzite Mountain.

At Black Mountain, quartzose sandstone also occurs interstratified with the lowest volcanic strata of the Sidewinder volcanic series, similar to the sequence at Quartzite Mountain. Miller (1978a, 1981) and Walker (1987) interpreted the Sidewinder volcanic series to conformably overlie the quartzite unit and noted the similarity of the sandstones above and below the contact, and we agree with this interpretation. Graubard et al. (1988) interpreted the contact at the base of the volcanic rocks as a fault; further mapping indicates that this fault reflects local shearing along a predominantly depositional contact. Quartzose sandstone containing a mixture of angular and well-rounded fine-sand-sized quartz grains occurs within and at the top of the first ignimbrite unit (Jsl1, Fig. 3, 4) at Black Mountain. Schermer and Busby (1994) interpreted the ignimbrite to represent one caldera-forming eruption, although distinct flow units were recognized on the basis of variations in abundance of pumice lapilli. The quartzose sandstone unit within the ignimbrite is a lens <20 m thick, has bedding subparallel to compacted pumice foliation, is intercalated with laminated (reworked?) tuffs, and shows no evidence of brecciation or disruption that would be expected if the sandstone was derived from caldera-rim landslides; thus we interpret it to have been deposited during a brief(?) hiatus in the eruption. The quartzose sandstone above the ignimbrite is ~70 m thick and occurs at a stratigraphic height of ~690 m above the base of the ignimbrite where the sandstone appears to interfinger with the top of the ignimbrite unit (Fig. 4). Sedimentary structures in the quartzose sandstone are poorly preserved, showing only local planar lamination, and therefore the depositional environment is uncertain. The rhyolite ignimbrite (Jsl1) and overlying volcanic units show no evidence for interaction with water and thus have been interpreted as subaerial deposits (Schermer and Busby, 1994), although the quartzose sandstones may have formed during fluvial or lacustrine reworking associated with pauses in volcanic activity. The compositional similarity of the rhyolite ignimbrite throughout its thickness (see Schermer and Busby, 1994) suggests that the thin sandstone within the ignimbrite represents less time than typical intereruptive intervals for small rhyolite calderas ($\sim 10^2 - 10^5$ yr; e.g., Cas and Wright, 1987); absolute-age constraints discussed subsequently suggest that the upper sandstone unit could represent anywhere from ~ 2 m.y. to 28 m.y.

Sidewinder Mountain and adjacent regions. The Fairview Valley Formation–Sidewinder volcanic series contact is sharp and planar along its ~ 400 m of exposure at Tricolor Quarry on the eastern flank of Sidewinder Mountain (Figs. 3, 4). The Fairview Valley Formation here consists of dolomite-cobble conglomerate intercalated with and overlain by lesser amounts of thin-bedded siltstone, quartzose sandstone, and calcareous siltstone (Miller, 1981). Although the conglomerate facies at Tricolor Quarry is similar to that at Black Mountain, no distinct quartzose sandstone is present above the conglomerate, and Miller (1981) interpreted the overlying volcanic rocks to be in fault contact. However, bedding in the Fairview Valley Formation and pumice compaction foliation in the overlying rhyolite ignimbrite (unit Jsl1) are parallel to each other and to the contact. The basal ~ 1 m of the rhyolite ignimbrite contains fine-grained lithic fragments of calcareous siltstone. We suggest that the concordant and unsheared appearance of the contact, together with the presence of clasts probably derived from the underlying Fairview Valley Formation, indicates that the contact is depositional.

Miller (1981) noted that the composition (carbonate-cobble conglomerate intercalated with fine-grained rocks) of the Fairview Valley Formation at Tricolor Quarry strongly resembles the upper parts of the Black Mountain section, but expressed uncertainty about its stratigraphic position. However, our reinterpretation of the Black Mountain quartzite as gradational upward from the carbonate-cobble conglomerate wedge would allow for such lateral facies variation. We infer that quartzose sandstones are more abundant in the finer-grained subaqueous basinal facies and fringing fan-delta facies at Black Mountain than would be expected in the subaerial or more proximal fan-delta facies at Tricolor Quarry.

The Fairview Valley Formation also crops out at two locations southwest of Sidewinder Mountain on the eastern margin of Fairview Valley (Fig. 1). In the more northern locality, calcareous siltstones of the Fairview Valley Formation occur as a megabreccia block within caldera-margin facies of one of the major ignimbrite units (Jsl2) of the Sidewinder volcanic series (Schermer and Busby, 1994). In the more southern locality, Fairview Valley Formation occurs in fault contact against another ignimbrite unit (Jsl4). The limited exposure of Fairview Valley Formation in these areas prevents further consideration of the facies or paleogeographic significance.

Source terranes and depositional environment of the Fairview Valley Formation

The provenance of the coarse-grained upper part of the Fairview Valley Formation and the transitional sequence includes three distinct sources: metamorphic basement rocks, arc-type volcanic rocks, and a quartz-rich terrane. Nearby Precambrian to Paleozoic basement was an important source for conglomerate clasts including calcitic and dolomitic marble, quartzite, chert, foliated granite, and gneiss (Miller, 1978b, 1981). Laterally restricted carbonate-cobble conglomerates were derived from Paleozoic limestone and dolomite as young as Early Permian (Bowen, 1954; Miller, 1978b, 1981). Intermediate-composition to silicic volcanic clasts also occur in the conglomerates, and interlayered sandstones contain both texturally mature quartz sand grains and angular (volcanic?) crystals; the matrix composition cannot be positively identified owing to alteration but appears to contain quartz and altered volcanic debris.

Volcanic detritus is abundant only near the contact between the Fairview Valley Formation and the Sidewinder volcanic series; Miller (1978a, 1978b, 1981) reported only "minor" silicic volcanic clasts at lower stratigraphic levels. The intermediate-composition volcanic clasts in the volcaniclastic conglomerates (svs) of the transitional sequence at Quartzite Mountain closely resemble the immediately adjacent andesite lavas and shallow intrusions (Jsla, Fig. 2B, column 1). Further, upper levels of the volcaniclastic unit (svs) at Quartzite Mountain are definitely interlayered with dacitic to andesitic lithic lapilli tuff and may be interlayered with andesite lavas and rhyolite ignimbrite (Fig. 2B, column 3). The angularity and abundance of the clasts and the presence of the tuffs suggest a nearby active volcanic source, and the similarity in textures and compositions to those of the lower part of the Sidewinder volcanic series suggests that these rocks or their precursors were the source of volcanic detritus in the Fairview Valley Formation. However, there are no primary volcanic rocks at the lowest stratigraphic levels of the transitional sequence, and intermediate-composition volcanic rocks of Permian age are also a possible source for the volcanic debris. Permian basaltic and andesitic volcanic rocks occur in the El Paso Mountains (Carr et al., 1984), and minor low-grade metabasaltic or andesitic rocks of inferred Permian age occur in the Goldstone–Lane Mountain area (Miller and Sutter, 1982). Metamorphic rocks (talc-chlorite schist) of uncertain protolith and age in the Shadow Mountains were inferred to be derived from Permian volcanic rocks (Martin and Walker, 1995). Although it is possible that these rocks could have formed a source terrane for the Fairview Valley Formation and the transitional sequence, we consider it unlikely because of the sparse occurrence of inferred Permian volcanic rocks south of the Garlock fault, the absence of silicic volcanic rocks in the Permian sequences, and the close similarity of the clasts to adjacent exposures of the Sidewinder volcanic series.

Sandstone and siltstone in most of the Fairview Valley Formation are arkosic (Miller, 1978a, 1981) whereas those in the upper 90–150 m of the stratigraphic section at Quartzite Mountain and Black Mountain (including Miller's quartzite unit) are more quartz rich and contain up to 90% well-rounded quartz grains. The source of the mature quartz sand may have been any one of several ergs (sand seas) that were active in the Colorado Plateau region in Early and Middle Jurassic time (discussed later in this paper), but there is no direct evidence for an eolian depositional environment. The stratigraphy of the Fairview Valley Formation, notably the increasing volcanic and quartz components upward in its section, suggests that the provenance changed over the course of its deposition, from basement sources to arc-type volcanic and cratonal eolian sources.

Our new data support the interpretation of Miller (1978a, 1978b, 1981) that the Fairview Valley Formation was primarily deposited in a shallow-marine or lacustrine environment and in local alluvial-fan (fan-delta) subenvironments. Regional correlation favors the shallow-marine interpretation (see later discussion). We reinterpret the upper part of the formation to grade, over several tens to a few hundred meters of section, into quartz-rich sandstones, volcanic lithic breccias and sandstones, and ignimbrites typical of the Jurassic arc. Thus it appears that volcanism in this part of the arc overlapped in time with marine sedimentation. However, only volcanic lithic sandstones and breccias—i.e., no primary volcanic rocks other than possible thin tuffs—are observed interlayered with the shallow-marine rocks, and the bulk of the Sidewinder volcanic series was deposited subaerially (Schermer and Busby, 1994). Thus it appears that the stratigraphy near the contact records a transition from shallow-marine and lacustrine to subaerial environments at the same time that the arc became established.

Facies differences between the various fault blocks of Fairview Valley Formation appear to record a transition from shallower facies in the east (Tricolor Quarry) to deeper facies in the west (Black Mountain and Quartzite Mountain) that was maintained until shortly after the initiation of volcanism (Fig. 4). At Tricolor Quarry, the volcanic sequence overlies carbonate-clast conglomerate of the fan-delta facies of the Fairview Valley Formation. At Black Mountain we see the transition from fan-delta conglomerates to shallow-marine(?) siltstone and sandstone over a lateral distance of ~600 m westward (Miller, 1978a, 1981); the earliest ignimbrite overlaps this facies transition and contains interlayered quartzose sandstones similar to those in the underlying Fairview Valley Formation, but does not contain evidence of submarine deposition. At Quartzite Mountain, the transition from the Fairview Valley Formation to the Sidewinder volcanic series is interpreted to record subaqueous gravity flows of volcanic debris intercalated with fine-grained well-laminated calcareous siltstones that may be shallow marine, but the primary volcanic rocks of the Sidewinder volcanic series appear to be subaerial (Schermer and Busby, 1994). Volcanic, volcaniclastic, and minor quartzose strata above the oldest ignimbrite (Jsl1) are also thicker at Quartzite

Mountain (up to 200 m) than at Black Mountain (~130 m) and Sidewinder Mountain (0 m) and overlap the edge of the caldera formed during eruption of Jsl1, thus suggesting that the westward-deepening basin persisted through the local onset of volcanism.

The lack of a significant time gap between Fairview Valley shallow-marine deposition and the initiation of arc volcanism is suggested by the presence of the volcaniclastic unit (svs) of the transitional sequence at Quartzite Mountain (Fig. 2B, columns 1, 3). The age range of the transitional sequence is unknown, and the change from Fairview Valley Formation deposition to arc volcanism could represent significant time. However, if our interpretation of the depositional environment is correct, rapid sedimentation of sediment-rich gravity flows could have produced the maximum ~300-m-thick sequence in <0.3–3 m.y., on the basis of typical sedimentation rates of 100–1000 m/m.y. in active basins (e.g., foreland and rift basins; Leeder, 1999).

Age of the Fairview Valley Formation

The age of the Fairview Valley Formation has important implications for the timing of deformation and changes in paleogeography in the Mojave Desert region. The Fairview Valley Formation unconformably overlies monzonite at Black Mountain that intrudes deformed Precambrian and Paleozoic sequences (Fig. 4; Miller 1978b, 1981), and thus the age of the Fairview Valley Formation places an upper limit on the deformation and plutonism interpreted to be associated with continental-margin truncation and the initiation of the magmatic arc (Walker, 1988). Walker (1987) considered the formation to be Early Triassic in age from the presence of conodonts as young as Early Triassic and by correlation with better-dated sequences to the east. More recent U-Pb data from the Black Mountain monzonite is interpreted to reflect crystallization at 243 ± 2 Ma (Miller et al., 1995); however, we reinterpret the age as ca. 236 Ma (see subsequent discussion). These data—together with recent revisions to the geologic time scale that place the Permian–Triassic boundary at 251 ± 0.3 Ma (Bowring et al., 1998) and the boundary between the Anisian and Ladinian Stages of the Middle Triassic at either 240.7 or 241.3 Ma (Mundil et al., 1996)—indicate that the base of the Fairview Valley Formation is late Anisian or younger. The age of the boundary between the Lower Triassic and the Middle Triassic is, however, poorly determined (Gradstein et al., 1994).

The age of the Black Mountain monzonite is of considerable importance to this study, because the age of the base of the Fairview Valley Formation is not tightly defined. We reevaluate the Miller et al. (1995) data to interpret the age as ca. 236 Ma. Miller et al. (1995) analyzed five fractions of zircon from the monzonite. Two multigrain fractions are concordant within errors, one with a $^{206}Pb*/^{238}U$ age of 236.0 ± 1.2 Ma (where the * indicates radiogenic) and a $^{207}Pb*/^{206}Pb*$ age of 236.7 ± 3 Ma, and the other with a $^{206}Pb*/^{238}U$ age of 236.1 ± 1.3 Ma and a $^{207}Pb*/^{206}Pb*$ age of 239.1 ± 3 Ma. An air-abraded, single, large (>60 mesh) zircon was discordant with a $^{206}Pb*/^{238}U$ age of 235.8 ± 1.3 and an older $^{207}Pb*/^{206}Pb*$ age of 243.4 ± 2 Ma. The other fractions are also discordant, one with a Pb/Pb age of 260 Ma. Miller et al. (1995, p. 1449) interpreted the Pb/Pb age of the single grain "as the most likely crystallization age." We find this interpretation is not supported by isotopic systematics of this sample and prefer the alternative interpretation that the two concordant fractions at ca. 236 Ma yield the most likely crystallization age of the monzonite. The slightly older Pb/Pb age of the large single grain reflects minor inheritance. With this interpretation, the base of the Fairview Valley Formation is probably Ladinian or younger.

On the basis of (1) the evidence for gradational contact between the Fairview Valley Formation and the Sidewinder volcanic series and (2) new U-Pb data presented subsequently, we conclude that at least part of the Fairview Valley Formation is late Early Jurassic in age. The basal Sidewinder ignimbrite (Jsl1, Fig. 3) at Black Mountain and Sidewinder Mountain yields similar U-Pb ages of 171 ± 9 (Graubard et al., 1988) and 179.5 ± 3.0 (this study; see subsequent section), respectively. This unit is correlated with the lowest ignimbrite at Quartzite Mountain (Fig. 4; Schermer and Busby, 1994). These data suggest that at least the upper calcareous siltstones, the cobble conglomerates, and the quartz-rich and volcanogenic sandstone-siltstone parts of the sequence are late Early or early Middle Jurassic. The apparent absence of any major breaks within the Fairview Valley Formation suggests that the entire formation may be Jurassic.

AGE OF THE SIDEWINDER VOLCANIC SERIES

Further constraints on the early evolution of the magmatic arc and its relationship to quartzose sand deposition in the central Mojave block are provided by examining the time span recorded by the Sidewinder volcanic series. Stratigraphic, volcanologic, and compositional details of the Sidewinder volcanic rocks are given in Schermer and Busby (1994) and are not repeated here, but are summarized in Figure 3A. We report here new U-Pb ages for the predominant volcanic units.

Samples ~90 kg each of the four major ignimbrite units (Jsl1–Jsl4) of the lower Sidewinder volcanic series were collected at Sidewinder Mountain. Although all ignimbrites except Jsl1 contain flow units with lithic lapilli (Fig. 3), we sampled outcrops and flow units with no visible lithic fragments. A sample of a rhyolite dike from the Upper Sidewinder volcanic series was collected near where it crosscuts a normal fault between an ignimbrite unit (Jsl3) and the Fairview Valley Formation (Fig 3). Zircons were separated from the samples by the usual methods of crushing, Wilfley table concentration, heavy-liquid and magnetic separation, and handpicking.

U-Pb zircon dating of ignimbrites presents various challenges. First, the petrogenesis of these high-silica rocks commonly involves incorporation of some preexisting crustal com-

ponents, leading to some zircon inheritance. In the simplest case, the inherited zircons are of a single age, but in more complicated cases, their ages fall in a range. Next, eruption of the ignimbrite and its energetic flow over the Earth's surface can lead to entrainment of mineral grains, including zircons, from unconsolidated sediments at the ground surface. Finally, as in all zircon dating, there is the likelihood of some postdepositional Pb loss via a range of mechanisms.

In order to minimize age uncertainties related to the factors previously discussed, we first carefully handpicked all zircon grains that showed any rounding, pitting, or frosting inferred to reflect surficial (eolian?) processes. These "entrained" zircon fractions were analyzed separately. The more euhedral, unfrosted zircons were split into a series of fractions by size, shape, etc., and regarded as "igneous" zircons. By this term, we include not only newly crystallized zircon, but also any inherited components from the source(s) of the magma. Obviously, it is difficult to totally exclude every entrained zircon as some with minimal exposure to surficial processes closely resemble the igneous zircons. This is an important point because the age or age range of the entrained zircons is not necessarily representative of the age or age range of the inherited components in the igneous zircon population.

We attempted to minimize the effects of any posteruptive Pb loss by applying step-wise dissolution techniques to the zircon analyses (e.g., Busby-Spera et al., 1990; Mattinson, 1994). Each fraction of zircon reported is actually the residue left after partial digestion of the zircons at either 80°C for 16 days or 160°C for 24 h in 50% HF plus a small amount of nitric acid. In some cases, the partial digestion represents a single step; in others, a preliminary, lower-temperature step preceded the 160°C step. A full discussion of the partial-digestion steps is beyond the scope of this paper. However, in all cases, the measured ages of the residues are older than ages of the "bulk" zircon fractions obtained by recombining the results from the residues plus the partial dissolution step(s). This result indicates that the bulk fractions had in fact lost some Pb, but suggests that much or all of the disturbed zircon material was removed by the partial dissolution step(s). After these grain-selection and analysis methods, some of the samples show reasonably well defined arrays on concordia diagrams that we interpret to yield lower intercepts indicating the age of eruption and upper intercepts reflecting the age (or a limited range in ages) of the inherited components. Other samples still show considerable scatter about the regression lines. This scatter probably results from a range in ages of inherited components (including any entrained zircons we failed to recognize and remove) and/or from our inability to remove all the effects of later Pb loss by our partial-dissolution approach.

The results for the zircon-residue analyses are presented in Table 2 and Figure 5. The oldest unit, a crystal-poor welded rhyolite ignimbrite collected at Tricolor Quarry (Fig. 3; Jsl1, sample AV113, yields a reasonably well-defined lower-intercept age of 179.4 ± 3.4 Ma, and a poorly defined upper-intercept

TABLE 2. U-Pb DATA FOR SIDEWINDER VOLCANIC SERIES

Sample	Mass (mg)	Concentration (ppm)		Isotopic ratios[†]				
		$^{206}Pb^{*}$	^{238}U	$^{208}Pb/^{206}Pb$	$^{207}Pb/^{206}Pb$	$^{204}Pb/^{206}Pb$	$^{238}U/^{206}Pb^{*}$	$^{207}Pb^{*}/^{206}Pb^{*}$
89AV111-1	0.5	4.643	167.1	0.2191 (2)	0.06246 (3)	0.000117	31.143 (203.8 ± 2.0)	0.06078 (631 ± 6)
89AV111-3	1.9	3.221	139.5	0.2572 (2)	0.05214 (2)	0.000046	37.481 (169.7 ± 1.7)	0.05147 (262 ± 2)
89AV111-5	4.1	3.023	133.2	0.2621 (2)	0.05187 (2)	0.000039	38.139 (166.8 ± 1.7)	0.05130 (254 ± 2)
89AV111-6	2.3	1.941	83.65	0.2589 (2)	0.05327 (2)	0.000145	37.327 (170.5 ± 1.7)	0.05115 (248 ± 3)
89AV112-1	5.7	5.577	237.9	0.2262 (2)	0.05218 (2)	0.000113	36.914 (219.0 ± 2.2)	0.05053 (219 ± 2)
89AV112-2	0.3	4.555	178.8	0.2294 (2)	0.05790 (2)	0.000217	33.967 (187.1 ± 1.9)	0.05474 (402 ± 2)
89AV112-3A	6.9	5.019	221.6	0.2178 (2)	0.05124 (2)	0.000015	38.212 (166.5 ± 1.7)	0.05101 (241 ± 2)
89AV112-3B	4.5	5.104	215	0.2150 (2)	0.05192 (2)	0.000039	36.469 (174.4 ± 1.7)	0.05134 (256 ± 2)
89AV112-5A	3.8	4.576	197.2	0.2145 (2)	0.05178 (2)	0.000058	37.299 (170.6 ± 1.7)	0.05093 (238 ± 2)
89AV112-5B	2.5	3.506	146.4	0.2170 (2)	0.05362 (2)	0.000171	36.153 (175.9 ± 1.8)	0.05112 (246 ± 2)
89AV113-1	4.2	3.322	120.57	0.3683 (3)	0.05777 (2)	0.000105	31.407 (202.0 ± 2.0)	0.05625 (462 ± 3)
89AV113-2A	0.2	3.445	125.7	0.3700 (3)	0.05826 (2)	0.000085	31.576 (201.0 ± 2.0)	0.05702 (492 ± 2)
89AV113-2	4.7	9.514	390.1	0.4135 (3)	0.05435 (2)	0.000301	35.486 (179.1 ± 1.8)	0.04994 (192 ± 4)
89AV113-4	2.1	7.557	296.2	0.4051 (3)	0.05405 (2)	0.000160	33.921 (187.3 ± 1.9)	0.05170 (272 ± 2)
89AV113-5	1.9	6.654	266.6	0.4134 (3)	0.05358 (2)	0.000198	34.698 (183.2 ± 1.8)	0.05069 (227 ± 2)
89AV113-6	0.2	6.231	243.7	0.5058 (4)	0.09516 (9)	0.002990	34.554 (183.9 ± 1.8)	0.05144 (260 ± 30)
89AV114-1	0.1	5.61	271.1	0.4698 (3)	0.05116 (2)	0.000122	41.916 (152.0 ± 1.5)	0.04938 (166 ± 10)
89AV114-2	0.1	5.912	286	0.4716 (3)	0.04962 (2)	0.000101	41.941 (151.9 ± 1.5)	0.04962 (177 ± 4)
89AV114-3	0.2	5.594	265.7	0.4364 (3)	0.05081 (2)	0.000040	41.142 (154.8 ± 1.5)	0.05023 (206 ± 3)
89AV114-4	0.1	5.773	252.6	0.3966 (2)	0.05721 (5)	0.000171	37.985 (167.5 ± 1.7)	0.05472 (401 ± 19)
89AV13-1	2.8	2.499	91.65	0.2648 (2)	0.06848 (2)	0.000179	31.746 (200.0 ± 2.0)	0.06591 (804 ± 3)
89AV13-3A	4.1	2.523	112.6	0.3062 (2)	0.05624 (2)	0.000126	38.625 (164.8 ± 1.6)	0.05440 (388 ± 2)
89AV13-3B	1.5	2.535	115.6	0.3142 (2)	0.05470 (2)	0.000115	39.463 (161.3 ± 1.6)	0.05302 (330 ± 4)
89AV13-4	0.9	1.629	78.31	0.3535 (2)	0.05266 (4)	0.000021	41.615 (153.1 ± 1.5)	0.04957 (175 ± 8)
89AV13-5	4.9	3.791	164	0.2980 (1)	0.05469 (2)	0.000035	37.467 (169.8 ± 1.7)	0.05418 (378 ± 2)
89AV13-8	2.4	5.293	234.3	0.3139 (1)	0.05416 (2)	0.000054	38.358 (165.9 ± 1.7)	0.05338 (345 ± 2)

*Radiogenic.

[†]$^{208}Pb/^{206}Pb$, $^{207}Pb/^{206}Pb$, and $^{204}Pb/^{206}Pb$ ratios = measured ratios, corrected for 0.125%/amu isotopic fractionation and for isotopic composition of spike. Errors on most $^{208}Pb/^{206}Pb$ and $^{207}Pb/^{206}Pb$ ratios are controlled by ±0.03%/amu uncertainty in the fractionation correction. Errors for the $^{204}Pb/^{206}Pb$ ratios are typically in the 1% range. Calculated isotopic ratios for Tera-Wasserburg concordia diagram shown with calculated ages and uncertainties on the least significant digit(s) shown in parentheses. We have assigned a conservative 1% error to the $^{238}U/^{206}Pb^{*}$ ratios to account for any minor fractionations during the step-wise dissolution procedure. For other analytical details, see Mattinson (1994).

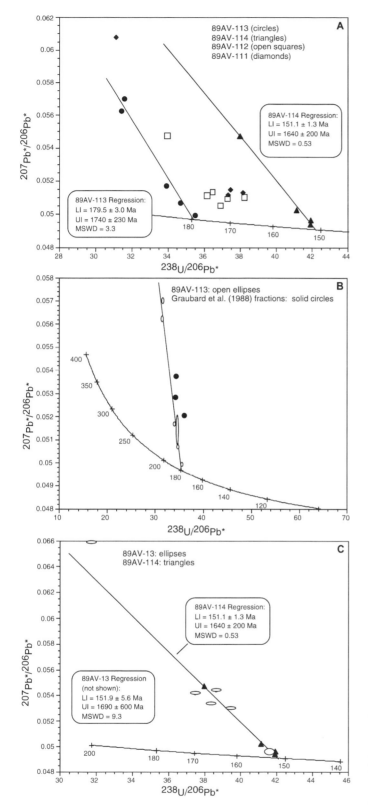

Figure 5. Tera-Wasserburg concordia plots for Sidewinder volcanic series. (A) Data for ignimbrites from the lower part of the Sidewinder volcanic series. Regressions shown for 89AV-113 (Ludwig, 1991, model 4 lower-intercept fit) and 89AV-114 (Ludwig, 1991, model 1 fit). LI—lower-intercept age, UI—upper-intercept age, MSWD—mean square of weighted deviates. (B) Data from Graubard et al. (1988), with the data and regression line for the oldest ignimbrite, 89AV-113, shown for reference. See text for discussion. Only the three igneous fractions from Graubard et al. (1988) are shown. The fourth Graubard fraction is a handpicked fraction of rounded, frosted, entrained zircons and is not necessarily representative of the inherited components in the "igneous fraction." For this reason we have not included it here. (C) Data for 89AV-13 and 89AV-114. The data and regression line for the youngest lower Sidewinder volcanic series ignimbrite (89AV-114) are shown for comparison with the more scattered 89AV-13 data. See text for further discussion.

age of 1680 ± 440 Ma, on the basis of six fractions of zircon (Fig. 5A). The ages are based on a lower-intercept fit according to model 4 of Ludwig (1991). The MSWD (mean square of weighted deviates) of 3.3 indicates moderate real scatter in the data. We interpret the lower-intercept age of 179.4 ± 3.4 as the eruption age of AV113 and as the best estimate of the age of the base of the section. Because this result is based on large, multigrain fractions rather than single-grain analyses, a reviewer has suggested that we should use our lower-intercept ages, or perhaps even the $^{207}Pb/^{206}Pb$ age of the fraction with the least inheritance, as maximum ages. Certainly the lowest Pb/Pb age of 192 ± 4 for fraction 89AV113-2 is an absolute maximum age for the sample, but this age clearly reflects a significant inherited component. The lower intercept might more properly be regarded as a *minimum* age because of the possibility of minor posteruptive Pb-loss effects that we might not have totally removed with our partial-dissolution methods. However, the overall result from six fractions indicates a rather well-behaved system, and we prefer our interpretation that 179.4 ± 3.4 Ma is the best measure of the eruptive age of the sample.

Graubard et al. (1988) reported a lower-intercept age of 171 ± 9 Ma on a sample collected from Black Mountain that we think is correlative with our sample AV113 on the basis of lithology and petrology. This age overlaps within its rather large errors with our lower-intercept age of 179.4 ± 3.4 Ma. The Graubard et al. (1988) age was based on three igneous fractions, plus one strongly rounded, frosted entrained fraction. The igneous fractions show considerable scatter and do not, by themselves, define a discordia line with reasonable errors. The reported age was obtained by using the entrained fraction to pin the upper end of the discordia line. Moreover, only one of the Graubard et al. (1988) fractions was subjected to a light "leach" procedure. The three igneous fractions are plotted in Figure 5B along with the AV113 data and the regression line for reference. The entrained fraction would plot well off scale and is not shown. The Graubard igneous fractions all plot slightly to the right of the AV113 regression line. The slightly leached fraction (the middle one) lies closest to the regression line. This result suggests that all of the Graubard fractions reflect slight Pb loss. We interpret these results as indicating that the two units are in fact correlative at ca. 179 Ma.

Stratigraphically above AV113 are two samples of dacitic ignimbrites. Sample AV112 was collected from near the top of a >1400-m-thick ignimbrite (Jsl2) that is zoned from rhyolite to dacite. The contact of this unit with Jsl1 is not well exposed anywhere in the region, and Schermer and Busby (1994) and Schermer (1993) interpreted the contact to be conformable. Re-analysis of our map data, however, suggests the possibility of up to 10°–15° of angular discordance. Sample AV111 was collected from a dacitic tuff breccia unit (Jsl3) that depositionally overlies Jsl2 (Schermer and Busby, 1994). The two units represent nearly half of the >4 km thickness of the lower part of the Sidewinder volcanic series. Schermer and Busby (1994) reported that a period of depositional reworking occurred following eruption of Jsl2, but bedding and pumice-compaction foliations above and below the top of Jsl2 are parallel. There was also a probable period of erosion following emplacement of unit Jsl3, as evidenced by the absence of sedimentary rocks and unit Jsl3 beneath several of the sections of the overlying ignimbrite (Jsl4). Although the original depositional contact above unit Jsl3 is poorly exposed or affected by intrusion or faulting, the fact that the pumice compaction foliation appears subparallel in units above and below the contact (maximum of ~5°–10° discordance) suggests minimal tectonic activity at that time.

The U-Pb data yield lower-intercept ages for AV-112 and AV-111 of 164 ± 10 Ma (six fractions, MSWD = 13) and 163.1 ± 6.5 Ma (four fractions, MSWD = 5), respectively. As can be seen in Figure 5, and also from the large MSWD values, the zircon fractions show considerable scatter, and we have not shown the regression lines in Figure 5. Nevertheless, the zircon data are consistent with the stratigraphic position of these units between the more precisely dated AV113 unit below them and the AV114 unit above them (discussed subsequently). Despite the large error on the sample from unit Jsl2, map relationships demonstrate it is no younger than Jsl3. Unit Jsl2 closely resembles deformed dacitic meta-volcanic rocks of the Hodge Volcanics at Iron Mountain to the north (Fig. 1), dated at 164 ± 2 (minimum, lower-intercept age) by Boettcher and Walker (1993). Our age data are consistent with the suggestion of Boettcher and Walker (1993) that the units are correlative.

The youngest ignimbrite (Jsl4, AV114), a dacite lithic lapilli ignimbrite, is also the thickest (>1.7 km) and the most complex, with several eruptive units separated by intervals of reworking (Schermer and Busby, 1994). The sample was collected from a pumice-rich, lithic-poor layer at Sidewinder Mountain from the upper half of unit Jsl4 but, because the base is intruded and the top is faulted, the exact stratigraphic level is uncertain. The sample is stratigraphically above at least two intervals of reworked tuff. The lower-intercept age of this sam-

ple is 151.0 ± 1.3 Ma (Fig. 5), based on four fractions of igneous zircon, and is interpreted as the eruption age of the sample.

The only sample of the Upper Sidewinder volcanic series (AV13) was obtained at Black Mountain from a rhyolite dike that crosscuts a normal fault between an ignimbrite (unit Jsl3) in the Lower Sidewinder volcanic series and the Fairview Valley Formation (Fig. 3). The northwest-trending rhyolite and basaltic dikes at Black Mountain and elsewhere in the region are correlated with the Independence dike swarm (Karish et al., 1987) and are interpreted to be the feeders for rhyolite and basalt lavas that overlie tilted ignimbrites along an angular unconformity (Schermer and Busby, 1994). Six fractions of igneous zircons from the dike sample yield a lower-intercept age of 151.9 ± 5.6 Ma that is within error of sample AV-114 (Fig. 5). The relatively large error in the lower-intercept age for AV13 results from considerable scatter in the data. The intercept age itself is strongly dependent on the one fraction that is almost concordant. Although at the sampling locality we cannot determine crosscutting relationships between the dike and the youngest ignimbrite (AV-114), relationships at Ritz Mountain to the north and at Stoddard Ridge to the northeast (Fig. 3) indicate that (1) quartz monzonite intrudes unit Jsl4 and (2) the northwest-trending dike swarm intrudes both the quartz monzonite and unit Jsl4 and thus must be younger. The age is consistent with other ages of ca. 150 ± 2 Ma determined from the Independence dike swarm in the eastern Sierra Nevada and the greater Mojave Desert region (Carl et al., 1998; Chen and Moore, 1979; James, 1989; Lahren et al., 1990).

The apparent gap in time from ca. 179 to ca. 164 Ma between the two oldest ignimbrite units (Jsl1, Jsl2) suggests the possibility of an unconformity; because of the large error on sample AV112, however, the time gap could be as short as 2 m.y. or as long as 28 m.y. Three pieces of evidence—the slight angular discordance; the existence of local deposits of fluvially reworked tuff, andesite lava, and minor quartzose sandstones up to 200 m thick between the two ignimbrite units at Black Mountain and Quartzite Mountain; and the absence of such deposits at Sidewinder Mountain (Schermer and Busby, 1994)—suggests some deposition, erosion, and perhaps some faulting, between the two caldera-forming eruptions. Quartzose sandstones identical to those in the upper Fairview Valley Formation occur at the top of the lower ignimbrite (Jsl1), but volcaniclastic sandstones farther up section contain only minor rounded quartz grains, thus suggesting a waning of the source of mature quartz sand. Thus the best estimate of age of the quartzose sandstones is ca. 180 Ma.

Our new age data provide important age constraints on a period of north-south extension in the Mojave Desert. The time span between the ca. 163 and ca. 151 Ma eruptions (which produced units Jsl3 and Jsl4, Fig. 3) is marked by a period of differential erosion, deposition, and possible minor faulting. However, the major angular unconformity in the Victorville region (~45°–60°) occurs above the upper ignimbrite (Jsl4), be-

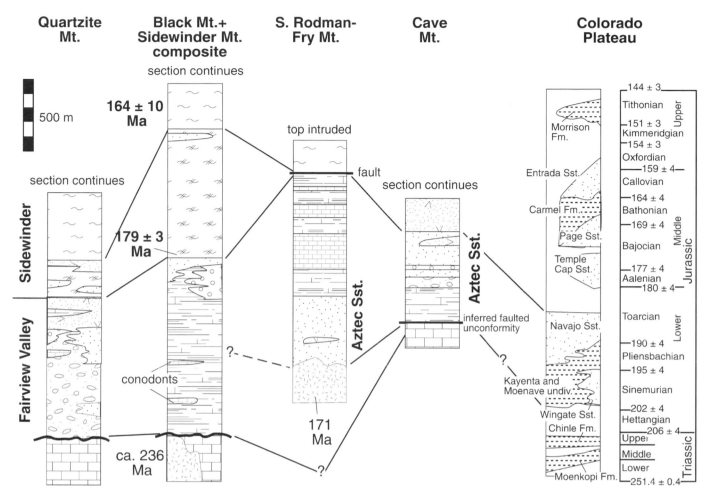

Figure 6. Correlation of lower Mesozoic sequences from the central Mojave block and Colorado Plateau, with new U-Pb dates shown in bold. Stratigraphy modified from the following: Quartzite Mountain and Sidewinder Mountain—Miller (1978a, 1978b, 1981) and Walker (1987); Rodman Mountains—Miller (1978a, 1978b, 1981), Miller and Carr (1978), and Karish et al. (1987); Cave Mountain—Miller and Carr (1978), Cameron et al. (1979), and Miller and Cameron (1982); Colorado Plateau—Blakey et al. (1988) and Peterson (1994). See Figure 1 for locations.

tween the Lower and Upper Sidewinder volcanic series. The unconformity is interpreted to be due to extension, tilting, and intrusion of quartz monzonite plutons (Schermer 1993; Schermer and Busby, 1994). Structures documented by Schermer (1993) include several large-displacement normal faults that together accomplished ~15% extension between the time of emplacement of the Lower and Upper Sidewinder volcanic series. Both Upper and Lower Sidewinder volcanic series were then folded about northwest-trending axes. The concordia intercept ages and age uncertainties (at their extremes) of the Upper Sidewinder dike (AV13) and the Lower Sidewinder ignimbrite (AV114; Fig. 6) permit a *maximum* of 6 m.y. to have elapsed between ignimbrite eruption, reworking, intrusion by quartz monzonite, tilting, uplift, erosion, and intrusion and overlap by Independence dikes and equivalent lavas. The quartz monzonite beneath the unconformity is only dated in the Fry and Ord Mountains to the east (Fig. 1B), at 166–171 Ma (Ar/ Ar hornblende; Karish et al., 1987), where a similar sequence

of events is recognized, but where the ignimbrites have not been dated. Northeast-southwest shortening, possibly associated with dextral transpression (Schermer, 1993) must have occurred after 151 Ma and prior to the emplacement of the undeformed Late Cretaceous (ca. 75 Ma; Miller and Morton, 1980) plutonic suite.

CORRELATIONS WITH OTHER PARTS OF THE ARC

Facies characteristics of the Upper Jurassic rocks in the central Mojave block suggest that this region occupied a location transitional between marine (outboard and to the north) and nonmarine (inboard and to the south) parts of the arc in Early Jurassic time. In this section we briefly describe some of the other Mojave sequences and propose new correlations between the eastern and western Mojave that suggest that a marine transgression occurred in the Mojave block during Early Jurassic time.

Southern Rodman Mountains

We correlate the Fairview Valley Formation in the Victorville region with Mesozoic volcanic and sedimentary rocks in the Rodman and Fry Mountains (Fig. 1) studied by Miller and Carr (1978) and Karish et al. (1987). In that area, eolian quartz arenite is overlain by calcareous siltstone, quartz arenite, limestone, and volcanic-cobble conglomerate interpreted to have been deposited in a lacustrine or shallow-marine environment during volcanic arc activity (Fig. 6; Miller and Carr, 1978). Rhyolite ignimbrite that occurs in fault contact with the quartz arenite is correlated with unit Jsl2 in the Victorville region (Fig. 3A; Schermer and Busby, 1994). Although no depositional contact is exposed in the Rodman Mountains, the ignimbrite contains clasts of calc-silicate and quartz arenite that may have been derived from the shallow-marine sequence, although older sources for the clasts are possible. We infer a relationship similar to that observed farther to the west at Quartzite Mountain and Black Mountain, with ignimbrite eruption following shallow-marine deposition; however, unit Jsl1 is not present in the Rodman Mountains. In agreement with Miller and Cameron (1982), we correlate the eolian quartz arenite in the Rodman Mountains with quartzose sandstone at Black Mountain (the quartzite unit of Miller, 1981); we further correlate the associated calcareous rocks with the upper part of the Fairview Valley Formation on the basis of similar lithology (in particular, interlayered volcanic-clast conglomerates), facies (shallow marine), and age relative to the Sidewinder ignimbrites (units Jsl1 and Jsl2).

Our correlation of the Rodman Mountains strata with the Fairview Valley Formation and Sidewinder Volcanic Series suggests an Early Jurassic age for the eolian quartz arenite, in agreement with Miller and Carr's (1978) correlation of the eolianites with the Aztec Sandstone in the Spring Mountains of Nevada. Both upper and lower contacts are faulted or intruded, and there are no fossils in the sequence. However, age constraints are provided by the younger (164 ± 10 Ma, Jsl2) ignimbrite and by crosscutting plutonic rocks ~5 km to the southwest dated at 170.8 ± 0.4 Ma (two Ar/Ar plateau ages on hornblende; Karish et al., 1987). Although these data could be interpreted to indicate an Early or Middle Jurassic age for the eolianites, correlation with strata on the Colorado Plateau (discussed subsequently) suggest that an Early Jurassic age is more likely.

Eastern Mojave Block

Calcareous rocks intercalated with quartz arenites and volcanic and volcaniclastic rocks in the Victorville region and areas as far east as Cave Mountain (Figs. 1, 6) provide evidence that shallow-marine conditions in the Mojave segment of the magmatic arc persisted into Middle Jurassic time in a fairly wide area. At Cave Mountain (Fig. 6), Cameron et al. (1979), Miller and Cameron (1982), and Walker (1987) described a sequence of marble, calc-silicate hornfels, metaconglomerate, and quartzite that is interpreted to overlie deformed Paleozoic(?) marble. Conglomerates below and within a thick sequence of quartzite are similar to those in the Fairview Valley Formation in that they contain clasts of marble, calc-silicate hornfels, quartzite, and volcanic rock (Fig. 6). Conglomerate above the quartzite contains volcanic clasts. Cameron et al. (1979) and Miller and Cameron (1982) correlated the quartzite in the Cave Mountain sequence with the Aztec Sandstone, but Walker (1987) correlated it with Lower Triassic sequences on the basis of similarities of composition and sedimentary structures, such as low-angle cross-stratification, that indicate shallow-water deposition. The age of the Cave Mountain sequence is unknown, and we propose that the volcanic-clast conglomerates may be equivalent to the top of the Rodman Mountains "Aztec" sequence and that the quartzite and possibly some of the marble and calc-silicate rock may correlate with Jurassic sequences farther west (Fig. 6). This interpretation is consistent with the observation that all of the dated volcanic rocks in the vicinity that would be likely sources for the conglomerates are Jurassic, not Triassic or Permian, in age. Therefore, we agree with the correlation of the Rodman Mountains and Cave Mountain sequences (Miller and Cameron, 1982), and we further suggest correlation with the Fairview Valley Formation.

Eolian quartz arenite associated with arc-type volcanic rocks occurs in the Cowhole Mountains (Fig. 1) where it has been correlated with the Aztec Sandstone (Marzolf, 1980; Novitsky-Evans, 1978). Volcanic rocks intercalated with and overlying the eolianite sequence are dated as 172 ± 6 to 167 ± 4 Ma (U-Pb, zircon; Busby-Spera et al., 1989, Busby et al., this volume) and are thus within error of and younger than the lowest dated ignimbrite in the Sidewinder Volcanic series (180 Ma), which interfingers with and overlies quartzite and quartzose sandstones. The quartz arenite in the Cowhole Mountains is more likely age equivalent to the Temple Cap or Carmel Formations (Busby et al., this volume).

PALEOGEOGRAPHIC AND TECTONIC IMPLICATIONS

Three aspects of our results are important to understanding the paleogeography of the early Mesozoic convergent margin. First, shallow-marine conditions existed in the central Mojave block during late Early to early Middle Jurassic time. The Victorville area appears to record entirely shallow-marine deposition of the quartz arenites, while areas to the east were locally above sea level and received eolian sand. Second, if all of the shallow-marine sequences from Victorville to Cave Mountain are Jurassic instead of Triassic, marine conditions were fairly widespread within the arc until as late as Middle Jurassic time. Third, the geochronologic, sedimentologic, and stratigraphic data suggest a period of uplift and erosion or nondeposition extending from the Early Triassic into the Early Jurassic. These conditions may have reflected relict highlands remaining from Permian deformation (e.g., Stone and Stevens, 1988; Walker, 1988) or some as-yet-unrecognized Triassic deformation similar to that proposed for southeastern California and Arizona (Reynolds et al., 1989). These characteristics of the paleogeography, together with the structural evolution of the region, suggest that the change from high-standing to low-standing paleogeography reflects a large-scale tectonic control on relative sea level that we interpret as the beginning of a period of intra-arc extension or transtension.

Paleoelevation of the Jurassic arc and backarc

The occurrence of craton-derived quartz sand in shallow-marine rocks of the upper Fairview Valley Formation and within the Sidewinder Volcanic series implies that the Mojave segment of the arc was low standing and possibly undergoing active subsidence during early Mesozoic time (Miller and Carr, 1978; Karish et al., 1987; Busby-Spera, 1988). Our new results and correlations also imply that this part of the arc was near sea level in late Early or early Middle Jurassic time. Despite the uncertainty in the age of the lower part of the Fairview Valley Formation, it is evident from the gradational nature of the upper contact that volcanism began prior to or shortly following the end of shallow-marine deposition. Although the Sidewinder Volcanic series were subaerially deposited (Schermer and Busby, 1994), it seems likely that the area remained low-standing at least until after the oldest (Jsl1) volcanic units were erupted because craton-derived quartz sands continued to be an important source for the early intra-arc sediments even in areas outside of calderas, such as at Quartzite Mountain (Schermer and Busby, 1994).

Sedimentologic data from the Victorville region indicate that craton-derived quartz sands gained access to this shallow-marine segment of the arc, similar to the deeper-marine and subaerial segments (Busby-Spera, 1988). We suggest correlation of the shallow-marine facies in the central Mojave block (Victorville area, Rodman Mountains, and Cave Mountain) with Lower Jurassic marine quartz arenites and volcanic rocks that are shallow-marine facies in the southern Sierra Nevada (Busby-Spera, 1984) and deep-marine facies in the northern Sierra Nevada (Fisher, 1990). Early and Middle Jurassic eolianites are also interstratified with subaerial arc-type volcanic rocks in southeastern California and Arizona (see summaries in Busby-Spera, 1988; Saleeby and Busby-Spera, 1992).

The age constraints on the quartzose sandstones suggest that the arc may provide a more complete record of Jurassic quartz arenite deposition than the backarc. Our age of 179.5 ± 3.0 Ma corresponds to the boundary between the Early and Middle Jurassic, at 180 ± 4 Ma (Gradstein et al., 1994) and permits correlation with the Aztec and Navajo Sandstones (Pliensbachian–Toarcian or Aalenian; Peterson, 1994), but not with the Temple Cap Sandstone, which is well dated at 170 ±

1 Ma (Kowallis et al., 2001). In the backarc at this time, a period of removal and/or nondeposition of the eolianites is recorded by the J1 unconformity on the Colorado Plateau (Peterson and Pipiringos, 1979). Although contacts are uncertain at Iron Mountain because of deformation, quartzite intercalated with the Hodge volcanics may be depositionally related, suggesting that quartz sand continued to gain access to the arc as late as ca. 164 Ma (Boettcher and Walker, 1993).

The conformable nature of the Fairview Valley–Sidewinder contact over ~20 km along strike and the occurrence of fine-grained sedimentary rocks along much of this length suggest relatively little tilting during this time. Nonetheless, the presence of volcanic breccias and conglomerates with Paleozoic limestone clasts suggests relief due to both volcanic and tectonic activity. The limestone-cobble conglomerates were previously interpreted as intra-orogenic deposits derived from relief created during Permian–Triassic deformation (Miller, 1978b, 1981; Walker, 1988). Alternatively, the conglomerates could record Jurassic deformation. A third possibility is that there are major problems in the Permian–Triassic time scale, and the conodonts in the Fairview Valley Formation are not reworked; in this case, deposition of the formation would have to have spanned Early Triassic through early Middle Jurassic time with no apparent breaks. This possibility would suggest the unlikely scenario of ~60 m.y. of quiet, shallow-marine deposition during a time when much tectonic activity was occurring elsewhere along the arc and in the backarc (e.g., Burchfiel et al., 1992; Saleeby and Busby-Spera, 1992, and references therein).

Mesozoic tectonics of the Mojave Desert and adjacent regions

The tectonic setting of the Mesozoic arc and backarc and the influence of deformation on paleogeography have been the subject of much controversy. Early workers considered much of the Mesozoic tectonism in the Mojave Desert to be contractional, with major thrusting occurring at several different times throughout the Triassic, Jurassic, and Cretaceous (e.g., as summarized by Burchfiel and Davis, 1981). Preservation of thick volcanic sequences and craton-derived quartz arenites has been attributed to extension (Busby-Spera, 1988) or shortening and transpression (Walker et al., 1990a, 1990b; Dunne et al., 1998), and there is evidence for both extensional and contractional structures in intra-arc, arc-flank, and backarc settings.

Evidence for Jurassic shortening. The East Sierran thrust system in the Inyo Mountains, Slate Range, and its continuation into the Mojave block (e.g., Tiefort Mountains, Cronese Hills, western Mojave block; Fig. 1) appears to be late Early to Late Jurassic in age (Dunne, 1986; Dunne et al., 1978, 1998; Dunne and Walker, 1993; Glazner et al., 1994; Walker et al., 1990a, 1990b). The best-dated Jurassic shortening in the Mojave block involves southeast-vergent ductile thrusting in the Cronese Hills, between 166 ± 3 and 155 ± 1 Ma as shown by U-Pb dating of pre- and postkinematic plutonic units (Walker et al., 1990a). Southeast-vergent shear movement in the Tiefort Mountains is bracketed between ca. 164 and 148 Ma and is interpreted to be related to the East Sierran thrust system (Schermer et al., 2001). Middle Jurassic east-vergent thrusting occurred east (i.e., inboard) of the study area, in the Clipper Mountains, at ca. 161 ± 10 Ma, (Howard et al., 1995; McCaffrey et al., 1991). Age constraints on most of the other thrusts previously inferred to be Triassic and Jurassic show that these are Permian (Last Chance thrust system; Snow, 1992) and middle Cretaceous (Keystone–Clark Mountain thrust system; Fleck and Carr, 1990; Fleck et al., 1994).

Other structures in the Mojave block inferred to be part of the East Sierran thrust system have less-certain kinematics and/or timing. At Iron Mountain, Boettcher and Walker (1993) interpreted contractional deformation to be bracketed by U-Pb dating of ca. 164 Ma prekinematic Hodge Volcanics and 151 ± 11 Ma postkinematic granite. However, structural orientations and metamorphic grade are different in pre-Mesozoic and Mesozoic rocks, suggesting that northwest-southeast shortening may instead have occurred in Paleozoic (Permian?) time. Structures in the Jurassic volcanic rocks are parallel to those inferred by Boettcher and Walker (1993) to be post–148 Ma and could instead be interpreted to be related to a Cretaceous deformational event; kinematics of those structures suggest strike-slip deformation. In the Shadow Mountains, west-vergent folding and fabrics that predate the intrusion of 148 Ma gabbro are also considered to be Jurassic, but poor age constraints also permit the interpretation of Permian deformation (Martin and Walker, 1991). Although the source of coarse debris in the lower Fairview Valley Formation could be related to the belt of Jurassic shortening, the deformation would have had to begin by Early Jurassic and/or Triassic time.

Evidence for extension. Recent work suggests that at the same time that shortening occurred across the East Sierran thrust system, adjacent areas were subject to north-south or northwest-southeast extension (Schermer, 1993). McKenna et al. (1993) inferred that east-west extension in the Panamint Mountains, north of the Garlock fault, is Jurassic (pre–Late Jurassic) in age. In the Cowhole Mountains, Wadsworth et al. (1995) documented northwest-southeast extension, and new age constraints bracket the extension to between ca. 172 and 164 Ma (Busby et al., this volume). In the Providence Mountains, Miller et al. (1994) reported pre–165 Ma east-west extension. The timing of the main phase of north-south extension in the Victorville region is interpreted herein to be ca. 151 Ma, although evidence for minor tilting between eruptions of the ignimbrites in the lower part of the Sidewinder Volcanic Series (i.e., between Jsl1 and Jsl2 and between Jsl3 and Jsl4) may suggest earlier extension.

Implications for plate-tectonic regime and paleogeography. The tectonic significance of Jurassic deformation in the Mojave Desert is controversial. In contrast to the arc-flank setting of the Inyo Mountains, deformation in the Mojave Desert was clearly in an intra-arc setting, as evidenced by the long time span and large volume of volcanic rocks and broadly coeval plutonic rocks (Miller and Busby, 1995). The mode of preservation of volcanic rocks in the Inyo Mountains—arc-flank sequences preserved in the footwalls of thrusts (Dunne and Walker, 1993; Dunne et al., 1998)—cannot apply to areas where contraction was either older or not present. Furthermore, thick volcanic sequences in the Mojave Desert are generally separated from areas of thrusting by many kilometers (Fig. 1). Calderas were the primary mode of preservation of most of the Lower Sidewinder volcanic series (Schermer and Busby, 1994). Our new data on the age of major tilting and extension (151 Ma) show that the mapped normal faults are too young to have been the cause of initial subsidence in the Victorville region. This determination does not preclude an earlier phase of extension during deposition of the Fairview Valley Formation and eruption of the earliest ignimbrite, but there are no dated Early Jurassic or Triassic structures in the region. Normal faulting and tilting of the Lower Sidewinder volcanic series shortly after eruption of the youngest ignimbrite, combined with transtension during emplacement of the Independence dike swarm and Upper Sidewinder volcanic series, probably enhanced preservation of the volcanic rocks (Schermer, 1993; Schermer and Busby 1994).

The apparent continuity and broad consistency of timing of the East Sierran thrust system has been interpreted to indicate that the arc was contractional (Walker et al., 1990a, 1990b), and some workers have argued that shortening was limited to the Middle Jurassic and entirely predates Late Jurassic extension (Miller et al., 1994; Howard et al., 1995). However, in the areas described herein, there is no systematic overprinting of extensional structures on contractional ones (or vice versa), and age constraints permit simultaneous shortening and extension (e.g., Cowhole Mountains and Cronese Hills). Analysis of the spatial and temporal relationships suggest that the two regimes may have been broadly coeval but spatially distinct in late Middle to Late Jurassic time (Schermer, 1993). Coeval north-south to northwest-southeast extension and east-west shortening within the arc have been interpreted to be due to a sinistral oblique subduction regime (Saleeby and Busby-Spera, 1992; Schermer, 1993; Schermer and Busby, 1994; Schermer et al., 2001). The emplacement of the Independence dike swarm in Late Jurassic time has also been previously recognized to be related to sinistral transtension and/or transpression (Glazner et al., 1999; Moore and Hopson, 1961). The Independence dike swarm and coeval extension in the Victorville region appear fairly limited in time (ca. 152–148 Ma); however, if the swarm spans as much as 10 m.y. (Carl et al., 1998), it would overlap the timing of east-west shortening in the Mojave, suggesting a longer period of sinistral shear. Extensional regions within this oblique-subduction regime may have been subsiding; the widespread nature of the low paleoelevation inferred here would then suggest that much of the southern part of the arc was extensional.

CONCLUSIONS

Stratigraphic, sedimentologic, and geochronologic data from the Victorville region of the Mojave Desert indicate the Fairview Valley Formation, previously considered to be Early Triassic, is at least in part Early Jurassic in age. The area may have been high and erosional from Permian until the Early Jurassic; coarse debris near the top of the Fairview Valley Formation could be related to Mesozoic rather than Permian deformation. A gradational contact between shallow-marine rocks of the Fairview Valley Formation and Sidewinder Volcanic Series indicates that shallow-marine conditions existed at the beginning of arc volcanism. Similar sequences in the Rodman Mountains and at Cave Mountain contain associated eolianites, suggesting a coastal environment. Subaerial explosive volcanic activity began at 179.5 ± 3.0 Ma and continued until 151 ± 1.3 Ma (lower Sidewinder Volcanic Series). A U-Pb date of 152 ± 6 Ma on a rhyolite dike of the Independence dike swarm (upper Sidewinder Volcanic Series) that postdates normal faulting and tilting of the ignimbrite sequence limits the age of extension in this region to ca. 151 Ma. These data suggest that the Victorville area underwent transtension- or extension-related subsidence during the Late Jurassic. We interpret the regional pattern and timing of deformation to suggest that the Mojave segment of the arc underwent approximately east-west shortening and approximately north-south extension related to sinistral oblique subduction during late Middle to Late Jurassic time.

ACKNOWLEDGMENTS

We thank Nelleena Beedle, Karen Maley, and Ben Adams for able field assistance, and the "chain gang" (Karl Otto, Jeff Johnson, Eric Schmidtke, and David Vaughan) for help with collection of the U-Pb samples. Cinda Graubard collected, processed, and helped analyze the U-Pb sample from Black Mountain. Southwest Portland Cement Company generously allowed access to the Black Mountain area. Numerous (animated) field discussions with Doug Walker and Mark Martin helped clarify our interpretations of the Fairview Valley Formation. Reviews by Mark Martin and an anonymous reviewer improved the manuscript. Elizabeth Miller provided maps and advice in the early stages of this project. We are also indebted to Tom Dibblee, Jr., for his pioneering work in the central Mojave Desert. Funding was provided by National Science Foundation grants EAR-8803769 and EAR-9018606 (to Busby-Spera and Mattinson) and EAR 9104915 (to Schermer), and a University of California President's Fellowship (to Schermer).

REFERENCES CITED

Barth, A.P., Tosdal, R.M., and Wooden, J.L., 1990, A petrologic comparison of Triassic plutonism in the San Gabriel and Mule Mountains, Southern California: Journal of Geophysical Research, v. 95, p. 20075–20096.

Bjerrum, C.J., and Dorsey, R.J., 1995, Tectonic controls on deposition of Middle Jurassic strata in a retroarc foreland basin, Utah-Idaho trough, western interior, United States: Tectonics, v. 14, p. 962–978.

Blakey, R.C., Peterson, F., and Kocurek, G., 1988, Synthesis of late Paleozoic and Mesozoic eolian deposits of the western interior of the United States: Sedimentary Geology, v. 56, p. 3–125.

Boettcher, S., and Walker, J.D., 1993, Mesozoic tectonic history of Iron Mountain, central Mojave Desert, California: Tectonics, v. 12, p. 372–386.

Bowen, O.E., Jr., 1954, Geology and mineral deposits of the Barstow Quadrangle, San Bernardino County, California: California Division of Mines Bulletin, v. 165, p. 208 p.

Bowring, S.A., Erwin, D.H., Jin, Y.G., Martin, M.W., Davidek, K., and Wang, W., 1998, U/Pb zircon geochronology and tempo of the end-Permian mass extinction: Science, v. 280, p. 1039–1045.

Burchfiel, B.C., and Davis, G.A., 1972, Structural framework and evolution of the southern part of the Cordilleran orogen, western United States: American Journal of Science, v. 272, p. 97–118.

Burchfiel, B.C., and Davis, G.A., 1981, Mojave Desert and environs, in Ernst, W.G., ed., The geotectonic development of California, Rubey Volume 1: Englewood Cliffs, New Jersey, Prentice-Hall, p. 217–252.

Burchfiel, B.C., Cowan, D.S., and Davis, G.A., 1992, Tectonic overview of the Cordilleran orogen in the western United States, in Burchfiel, B.C., et al., eds., Cordilleran Orogen: Conterminous U.S.: Boulder, Colorado, Geological Society of America, Geology of North America, v. G-3, p. 407–480.

Busby-Spera, C.J., 1984, The lower Mesozoic continental margin and marine intra-arc sedimentation at Mineral King, California, in Bachman, S., and Crouch, J., eds., Tectonics and sedimentation along the California Margin: Pacific Section, Society of Economic Paleontologists and Mineralogists, p. 135–156.

Busby-Spera, C.J., 1988, Speculative tectonic model for the Lower Mesozoic arc of the southwest Cordilleran United States: Geology, v. 16, p. 1121–1125.

Busby-Spera, C.J., Schermer, E.R., and Mattinson, J.M., 1989, Volcanotectonic controls on sedimentation in an extensional continental arc: A Jurassic example from the eastern Mojave Desert: New Mexico Bureau of Mines and Mineral Resources Bulletin, v. 131, p. 34.

Busby-Spera, C.J., Mattinson, J.M., Riggs, N.R., and Schermer, E.R., 1990, The Triassic-Jurassic magmatic arc in the Mojave-Sonoran Deserts and the Sierran-Klamath region: Similarities and differences in paleogeographic evolution, in Harwood, D.S., and Miller, M.M., eds., Paleozoic and early Mesozoic paleogeographic relations, Sierra Nevada, Klamath Mountains, and related terranes: Geological Society of America Special Paper 255, p. 325–338.

Cameron, C.S., Guth, P.L., and Burchfiel, B.C., 1979, The early Mesozoic Cave Mountain sequence: Its implications for Mesozoic tectonics: Geological Society of America Abstracts with Programs, v. 11, no. 7, p. 397.

Carl, B.S., Glazner, A.F., Bartley, J.M., Dinter, D.A., and Coleman, D.S., 1998, Independence dikes and mafic rocks of the eastern Sierra, in Behl, R.J., ed., Guidebook to Field Trip No. 4, Geological Society of America Cordilleran Section Meeting Field Trip Guidebook, California State University–Long Beach, Department of Geological Sciences, 26 p.

Carr, M.D., Christiansen, R.L., and Poole, F.G., 1984, Pre-Cenozoic geology of the El Paso Mountains, southwestern Great Basin, California: A summary, in Lintz, J., Jr., ed., Western geological excursions: Reno, Nevada, Cordilleran section, Geological Society of America Field Trip Guidebook 7, v. 4, p. 84–93.

Cas, R.V., and Wright, J.V., 1987, Volcanic successions, modern and ancient: Winchester, Massachusetts, Allen and Unwin, 528 p.

Chen, J.H., and Moore, J.G., 1979, Late Jurassic Independence dike swarm in eastern California: Geology, v. 7, p. 129–133.

Dibblee, T.W., Jr., 1960a, Preliminary geologic map of the Apple Valley quadrangle, California: U.S. Geological Survey, Mineral Investigations Field Studies Map MF-232, scale 1:62 500.

Dibblee, T.W., Jr., 1960b, Preliminary geologic map of the Victorville quadrangle, California: U.S. Geological Survey, Mineral Investigations Field Studies Map MF-229, scale 1:62 500.

Dunne, G.C., 1986, Geologic evolution of the southern Inyo Range, Darwin Plateau, and Argus and Slate Ranges, east-central California: An overview: Los Angeles, Cordilleran Section, Geological Society of America, Field Trip Guidebook, p. 3–21.

Dunne, G.C., and Walker, J.D., 1993, Age of Jurassic volcanism and tectonism, southern Owens Valley region, east-central California: Geological Society of America Bulletin, v. 105, p. 1223–1230.

Dunne, G.C., Gulliver, R.M., and Sylvester, A.G., 1978, Mesozoic evolution of rocks of the White, Inyo, Argus, and Slate Ranges, eastern California, *in* Howell, D.G., and McDougall, K.A., eds., Mesozoic paleogeography of the western United States: Pacific Section, Society of Economic Paleontologists and Mineralogists, Pacific Coast Paleogeography Symposium 2, p. 189–208.

Dunne, G.C., Garvey, T.P., Oborne, M., Schneidereit, D., Fritsche, A.E., and Walker, J.D., 1998, Geology of the Inyo Mountains volcanic complex: Implications for Jurassic paleogeography of the Sierran magmatic arc in eastern California: Geological Society of America Bulletin, v. 110, p. 1376–1397.

Fackler-Adams, B.N., Busby, C.J., and Mattinson, J.M., 1997, Jurassic magmatism and sedimentation in the Palen Mountains, southeastern California: Implications for regional tectonic controls on the Mesozoic continental arc: Geological Society of America Bulletin, v. 109, p. 1464–1484.

Fisher, G.R., 1990, Middle Jurassic syntectonic conglomerate in the Mount Tallac roof pendant, northern Sierra Nevada, California, *in* Harwood, D.S., and Miller, M.M., eds., Paleozoic and early Mesozoic paleogeographic relations; Sierra Nevada, Klamath Mountains, and related terranes: Geological Society of America Special Paper 255, p. 339–350.

Fleck, R.J., and Carr, M.D., 1990, The age of the Keystone thrust: Laser-fusion ^{40}Ar/^{39}Ar dating of foreland basin deposits, southern Spring Mountains, Nevada: Tectonics, v. 9, p. 467–476.

Fleck, R.J., Mattinson, J.M., Busby, C.J., Carr, M.D., Davis, G.A., and Burchfiel, B.C., 1994, Isotopic complexities and the age of the Delfonte volcanic rocks, eastern Mescal Range, southeastern California: Stratigraphic and tectonic implications: Geological Society of America Bulletin, v. 106, p. 1242–1253.

Glazner, A.F., Walker, J.D., Bartley, J.M., Fletcher, J.M., Martin, M.W., Schermer, E.R., Boettcher, S.S., Miller, J.S., Fillmore, R.P., and Linn, J.K., 1994, Reconstruction of the Mojave Block, *in* McGill, S.F., and Ross, T.M., eds., Geological investigations of an active margin: San Bernardino, California, Geological Society of America Cordilleran Section Guidebook, p. 3–30.

Glazner, A.F., Bartley, J.M., and Carl, B.S., 1999, Oblique opening and noncoaxial emplacement of Jurassic Independence dike swarm, California: Journal of Structural Geology, v. 21, p. 1275–1283.

Gradstein, F.M., Agterberg, F.P., Ogg, J.G., Hardenbol, J., van Veen, P., Thierry, J., and Huang, Z., 1994, A Mesozoic time scale: Journal of Geophysical Research, v. 99, p. 24 051–24 074.

Graubard, C.M., Mattinson, J.M., and Busby-Spera, C.J., 1988, Age of the lower Sidewinder Volcanics and reconstruction of the early Mesozoic arc in the Mojave Desert, California: Geological Society of America Abstracts with Programs, v. 20, no. 7, p. A274–A275.

Hewett, D.F., 1931, Geology and ore deposits of the Goodsprings Quadrangle, Nevada: U.S. Geological Survey Professional Paper 1062, 134 p.

Hewett, D.F., 1954, A fault map of the Mojave Desert region, California: California Division of Mines Bulletin 170, p. 15–18.

Howard, K.A., McCaffrey, K.J.W., Wooden, J.L., Foster, D.A., and Shaw, S.E., 1995, Jurassic thrusting of Precambrian basement over Paleozoic cover in the Clipper Mountains, southwestern California, *in* Miller, D.M., and Busby, C., eds., Jurassic magmatism and tectonics of the North American Cordillera: Geological Society of America Special Paper 299, p. 375–392.

James, E.W., 1989, Southern extension of the Independence dike swarm of eastern California: Geology, v. 17, p. 587–590.

Karish, C.R., Miller, E.L., and Sutter, J.F., 1987, Mesozoic tectonic and magmatic history of the central Mojave Desert: Arizona Geological Society Digest, v. 18, p. 15–32.

Kowallis, B.J., Christiansen, E.H., Deino, A.L., Zhang, C., and Everett, B.H., 2001, The record of Middle Jurassic volcanism in the Carmel and Temple Cap Formations of southwestern Utah: Geological Society of America Bulletin, v. 113, p. 373–387.

Lahren, M.M., Schweickert, R.A., Mattinson, J.M., and Walker, J.D., 1990, Evidence of uppermost Proterozoic to Lower Cambrian miogeoclinal rocks and the Mojave-Snow Lake fault: Snow Lake pendant, central Sierra Nevada, California: Tectonics, v. 9, p. 1585–1608.

Lawton, T., 1994, Tectonic setting of Mesozoic sedimentary basins, Rocky Mountain region, United States, *in* Caputo, M.V., et al., eds., Mesozoic systems of the Rocky Mountain Region, USA: Denver, Rocky Mountain Section, SEPM (Society for Sedimentary Geology), p. 1–25.

Leeder, M., 1999, Sedimentology and sedimentary basins: Oxford, Blackwell Science Ltd., 592 p.

Ludwig, K.R., 1991, PBDAT: A program for processing Pb-U-Th isotope data, version 1.20: U.S. Geological Survey Open-File Report 88–542.

Martin, M.W., and Walker, J.D., 1991, Upper Precambrian to Paleozoic Paleogeographic reconstruction of the Mojave Desert, California, *in* Cooper, J.D., and Stevens, C.H., eds., Paleozoic paleogeography of the western United States—II: Pacific Section, SEPM (Society for Sedimentary Geology), p. 167–192.

Martin, M.W., and Walker, J.D., 1995, Stratigraphy and paleogeographic significance of metamorphic rocks in the Shadow Mountains, western Mojave Desert, California: Geological Society of America Bulletin, v. 107, p. 354–366.

Marzolf, J.E., 1980, The Aztec Sandstone and stratigraphically related rocks in the Mojave Desert, *in* Fife, D.L., and Brown, G.R., eds., Geology and mineral wealth of the California desert: Santa Ana, California, South Coast Geological Society, p. 215–220.

Marzolf, J.E., 1983, Early Mesozoic eolian transition from cratonal margin to orogenic-volcanic arc: Utah Geological and Mineral Survey Special Studies, v. 60, p. 39–46.

Mattinson, J.M., 1994, A study of complex discordance in zircons using stepwise dissolution techniques: Contributions to Mineralogy and Petrology, v. 116, p. 117–129.

McCaffrey, K.J.W., Howard, K.A., Bailey, C.M., and Foster, D.A., 1991, Jurassic syntectonic pluton emplacement in the Clipper Mountains, eastern Mojave Desert, California: Geological Society of America Abstracts with Programs, v. 23, no. 5, p. A250.

McKenna, L.W., Stern, S.M., Whitmarsh, R., and Baer, E., 1993, Pre-Late Jurassic extension and subsequent East Sierran thrusting in the southern Cordillera of California: Geological Society of America Abstracts with Programs, v. 25, no. 6, p. A284.

Miller, C.F., 1978, An early Mesozoic alkalic magmatic belt in western North America, *in* Howell, D.G., and McDougall, K.A., eds., Mesozoic paleogeography of the western United States: Pacific Section, Society of Economic Paleontologists and Mineralogists, Pacific Coast Paleogeography Symposium 2, p. 163–174.

Miller, D.M., and Busby, C., editors, 1995, Jurassic magmatism and tectonics of the North American Cordillera: Geological Society of America Special Paper 299, 411 p.

Miller, D.M., Walker, J.D., De Witt, E., and Nakata, J.K., 1994, Mesozoic episodes of horizontal crustal extension, U.S. Cordillera: Geological Society of America Abstracts with Programs, v. 26, no. 2, p. 74.

Miller, E.L., 1981, Geology of the Victorville region, California: Geological Society of America Bulletin, v. 92, p. 160–163; 554–608.

Miller, E.L., and Cameron, C.S., 1982, Late Precambrian to Late Cretaceous evolution of the southwestern Mojave Desert, California: Geological Society of America Field Trip Guide, Trip No. 9, Anaheim Meeting, p. 21–34.

Miller, E.L., and Carr, M.D., 1978, Recognition of possible Aztec-equivalent sandstones and associated Mesozoic metasedimentary deposits within the Mesozoic magmatic arc in the southwestern Mojave Desert, *in* Howell, D.G., and McDougall, K.A., eds., Mesozoic paleogeography of the western United States: Pacific Section, Society of Economic Paleontologists and Mineralogists, Pacific Coast Paleogeography Symposium 2, p. 283–289.

Miller, E.L., and Sutter, J.F., 1982, Structural geology and ^{40}Ar/^{39}Ar geochronology of the Goldstone-Lane Mountain area, Mojave Desert, California: Geological Society of America Bulletin, v. 93, p. 1191–1207.

Miller, F.K., and Morton, D.M., 1980, Potassium-argon geochronology of the eastern Transverse Ranges and southern Mojave Desert, Southern California: U.S. Geological Survey Professional Paper 1152, 30 p.

Miller, J., Glazner, A.F., Walker, J.D., and Martin, M.W., 1995, Geochronologic and isotopic evidence for Triassic-Jurassic emplacement of the eugeoclinal allochthon in the Mojave Desert region, California: Geological Society of America Bulletin, v. 107, p. 1441–1457.

Moore, J.G., and Hopson, C.A., 1961, The Independence dike swarm in eastern California: American Journal of Science, v. 259, p. 241–259.

Mundil, R., Breck, P., Meier, M., Rieber, H., and Oberli, F., 1996, High resolution U-Pb dating of Middle Triassic volcaniclastics: Time-scale calibration and verification of tuning parameters for carbonate sedimentation: Earth and Planetary Science Letters, v. 141, p. 137–151.

Novitsky-Evans, J.M., 1978, Geology of the Cowhole Mountains, southern California: Structural, stratigraphic and geochemical studies [Ph.D. thesis]: IIouston, Texas, Rice University, 95 p.

Peterson, F., 1994, Sand dunes, sabkhas, streams, and shallow seas: Jurassic paleogeography in the southern part of the western interior basin, *in* Caputo, M.V., et al., eds., Mesozoic systems of the Rocky Mountain region, USA: Denver, Colorado, Rocky Mountain Section, SEPM (Society for Sedimentary Geology), p. 233–272.

Peterson, F., and Pipiringos, G.N., 1979, Stratigraphic relations of the Navajo Sandstone to Middle Jurassic formations, southern Utah and northern Arizona: U.S. Geological Survey Professional Paper 1035-A, 29 p.

Reynolds, S.J., Spencer, J.E., Asmerom, Y., DeWitt, E., and Laubach, S.E., 1989, Early Mesozoic uplift in west-central Arizona and southeastern California: Geology, v. 17, p. 207–211.

Riggs, N.R., Busby, C.J., and Mattinson, J.M., 1993, Correlation of Mesozoic eolian strata between the magmatic arc and the Colorado plateau: New U-Pb geochronologic data from southern Arizona: Geological Society of America Bulletin, v. 105, p. 1231–1246.

Saleeby, J.B., and Busby-Spera, C.J., 1992, Early Mesozoic tectonic evolution of the western U.S. Cordillera, *in* Burchfiel, B.C., et al., eds., The Cordilleran orogen: Conterminous U.S.: Boulder, Colorado, Geological Society of America, Geology of North America, v. G-3, p. 107–168.

Schermer, E.R., 1993, Mesozoic structural evolution of the west-central Mojave Desert, *in* Dunne, G.C., and McDougall, K.A., eds., Mesozoic paleogeography of the western United States II: Pacific Section, SEPM (Society for Sedimentary Geology), p. 307–322.

Schermer, E.R., and Busby, C.J., 1994, Jurassic magmatism in the central Mojave Desert: Implications for arc paleogeography and preservation of continental volcanic sequences: Geological Society of America Bulletin, v. 106, p. 767–790.

Schermer, E.R., Stephens, K.A., and Walker, J.D., 2001, Paleogeographic and tectonic implications of the geology of the Tiefort Mountains, northern Mojave Desert, California: Geological Society of America Bulletin, v. 113, p. 920–938.

Snow, J.K., 1992, Large-magnitude Permian shortening and continental-margin tectonics in the southern Cordillera: Geological Society of America Bulletin, v. 104, p. 80–105.

Stone, P., and Stevens, C.H., 1988, Pennsylvanian and early Permian paleogeography of east-central California: Implications for the shape of the continental margin and the timing of continental truncation: Geology, v. 16, p. 330–333.

Wadsworth, W.B., Ferriz, H., and Rhodes, D.D., 1995, Structural and stratigraphic development of the Middle Jurassic magmatic arc in the Cowhole Mountains, central-eastern Mojave Desert, California, *in* Miller, D.M., and Busby, C., eds., Jurassic magmatism and tectonics of the North American Cordillera: Geological Society of America Special Paper 299, p. 327–349.

Walker, J.D., 1987, Permian to Middle Triassic rocks of the Mojave Desert: Arizona Geological Society Digest, v. 18, p. 1–14.

Walker, J.D., 1988, Permian and Triassic rocks of the Mojave Desert and their implications for timing and mechanisms of continental truncation: Tectonics, v. 7, p. 685–709.

Walker, J.D., Martin, M.W., Bartley, J.M., and Coleman, D.S., 1990a, Timing and kinematics of deformation in the Cronese Hills, California, and implications for Mesozoic structure of the southern Cordillera: Geology, v. 18, p. 554–557.

Walker, J.D., Martin, M.W., Bartley, J.M., and Glazner, A.F., 1990b, Middle to Late Jurassic deformation belt through the Mojave Desert, California: Geological Society of America Abstracts with Programs, v. 22, no. 3, p. 91.

MANUSCRIPT ACCEPTED BY THE SOCIETY MAY 9, 2001

Geological Society of America
Memoir 195
2002

Extent and significance of the Independence dike swarm, eastern California

Brian S. Carl*
Allen F. Glazner
Department of Geological Sciences, University of North Carolina, Chapel Hill, North Carolina 27599-3315, USA,
and White Mountain Research Station, Bishop, California 93514, USA

ABSTRACT

Since it was first recognized in the late 1950s, the 148 Ma Independence dike swarm has been a valuable structural and stratigraphic marker in eastern California. The swarm extends at least 600 km from the central Sierra Nevada to the southern Mojave Desert and serves as an important geologic marker because of its regional extent and relatively short period of injection. Although the swarm is predominantly mafic, it differs from other large dike swarms in two important regards: (1) intermediate-composition and silicic dikes are common, and dikes are locally highly alkalic; and (2) dike injection was apparently predominantly vertical, not horizontal. The dikes cross many lithospheric provinces, and their compositions reflect the composition of the underlying lithosphere. Dikes strike predominantly northwest and are locally rotated up to 30–40° clockwise by late Cenozoic faulting and block rotation. In the High Sierra, dikes opened in a north-south direction, oblique to their walls in a sinistral sense. Although dikes swarms are generally linked to dike-perpendicular extension, the Independence dike swarm apparently formed by local fracturing of the carapace above the Late Jurassic Sierran batholith during rapid changes in plate motions.

INTRODUCTION

Moore and Hopson (1961) first correlated northwest-striking dikes in the eastern Sierra Nevada with similar dikes in the Alabama Hills, Owens Valley, and the Inyo Mountains of California. They named this set of dikes the Independence dike swarm after a town lying within the swarm. Smith (1962), working farther south, correlated similar dikes across the Garlock fault and suggested that all of the dikes belonged to one swarm. Later studies extended the swarm northward to its northernmost exposure in the Mount Morrison 15′ quadrangle (Rinehart and Ross, 1964) and southward to the southern Mo-

jave Desert (Davis et al., 1994), close to 600 km along strike. At present, dikes assigned to the swarm are found on more than 50 geologic maps of 15′ quadrangles (Fig. 1, A and B; Table 1).

The swarm serves as an important temporal and structural marker in eastern California. It was apparently intruded during a brief interval at ca. 148 Ma along its entire length. Such a marker is important in areas with few other markers or age data, especially in the plutonic areas of the eastern Sierra Nevada (e.g., Moore, 1963) or the Inyo Mountains where stratigraphic units are significantly older than the swarm (e.g., Dunne and Walker, 1993). The consistent northwest strike of the swarm has proved valuable in reconstructing the deformational history

---

*Present address: ExxonMobil Corporation, 222 Benmar Street, Houston, Texas 77067, USA.

Carl, B.S., and Glazner, A.F., 2002, Extent and significance of the Independence dike swarm, eastern California, *in* Glazner, A.F., Walker, J.D., and Bartley, J.M., eds., Geologic Evolution of the Mojave Desert and Southwestern Basin and Range: Boulder, Colorado, Geological Society of America Memoir 195, p. 117–130.

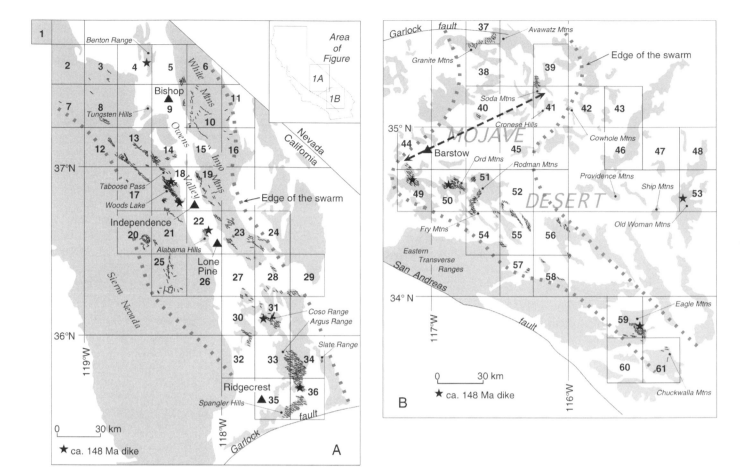

Figure 1. Areal extent and 15′ quadrangle map coverage of the Independence dike swarm in eastern California. (A) Northern Independence dike swarm, eastern Sierra Nevada and western Basin and Range. (B) Southern Independence dike swarm across the Mojave Desert. Double-headed dashed arrow in Figure 1B shows Miocene offset of dike swarm from Soda Mountains to southwest of Barstow. Shaded areas outline pre-Tertiary exposure. Dike orientations and abundances are representative and reflect mapped dikes only. Correlation with the swarm is tentative in some places. Numbered quadrangles and references are listed in Table 1.

in areas along the swarm that have undergone vertical-axis rotation and lateral displacement, such as the Mojave Desert (e.g., Smith, 1962; Schermer et al., 1996; Glazner et al., 1989; Dunne and Walker, 1993; Ron and Nur, 1996; Hopson et al., 2000).

Understanding the origin of the swarm may help to clarify an enigmatic time in California's geologic history. Studies of Late Jurassic tectonism in western North America indicate orogenic activity in the western Sierra Nevada just before and perhaps during swarm intrusion (e.g., Schweickert and Cowan, 1975), as well as rapid, dramatic changes in the direction of plate motions (e.g., Engebretson et al., 1985; May et al., 1986). Models that seek to explain plate interactions must consider their impact on the swarm's intrusion. Understanding the physical, geochemical, and structural characteristics of the swarm may help to set limits on these models.

This paper provides a comprehensive summary of the geology of the Independence dike swarm. Summary information about the physical, geochemical, and structural characteristics

of the swarm is included as well as an explanation of its importance in the broader context of the Late Jurassic tectonics of western North America. The paper also includes an updated map of the present extent of the swarm (keyed to a comprehensive reference list), tables of geochronologic, geochemical, and structural data, and a discussion of possible origins of the swarm.

AGE

Early study of the swarm suggested a Cretaceous age (Moore and Hopson, 1961), but U-Pb zircon analyses of felsic dikes in the Alabama Hills and southern Argus Range indicated an age of ca. 148 Ma for several dikes (Chen and Moore, 1979). Subsequent U-Pb analyses have confirmed this age for Independence dikes in other parts of the swarm, including dikes in the eastern Sierra Nevada, the Coso Range, and the central and

**TABLE 1. MAP COVERAGE OF THE INDEPENDENCE
DIKE SWARM**

15' Quadrangle	References
1. Tuolumne Meadows	Lahren et al. (1990)
2. Devils Postpile	Huber and Rinehart (1965)
3. Mount Morrison	Rinehart and Ross (1964)
4. Casa Diablo Mountain	Rinehart and Ross (1957)
5. White Mountain Peak	Crowder and Sheridan (1972)
6. Mount Barcroft	Krauskopf (1971)
7. Kaiser Peak*	Bateman et al. (1971)
8. Mount Abbot	Lockwood and Lydon (1975)
9. Bishop	Glazner and Coleman, mapping in 1998
10. Blanco Mountain	Nelson (1966a)
11. Soldier Pass*	McKee and Nelson (1967)
12. Blackcap Mountain	Bateman (1965)
13. Mount Goddard	Bateman and Moore (1965)
14. Big Pine	Moore and Hopson (1961)
15. Waucoba Mountain	Nelson (1966b)
16. Waucoba Spring	Nelson (1971)
17. Marion Peak	Moore and Sisson (1985)
18. Mount Pinchot	Carl (2000)
	Longiaru (1987)
	Moore (1963)
	Moore and Hopson (1961)
19. Independence	Moore and Hopson (1961)
	Ross (1965)
20. Triple Divide Peak	Moore and Sisson (1987)
21. Mount Whitney	Moore (1981)
22. Lone Pine	Chen and Moore (1979)
	Dunne (1986)
	Dunne and Walker (1993)
	Moore and Hopson (1961)
23. New York Butte	Dunne (1986)
	Dunne and Walker (1993)
	Merriam (1963)
	Moore and Hopson (1961)
24. Ubehebe Peak	McAllister (1956)
	Moore and Hopson (1961)
25. Kern Peak	Moore and Sisson (1985)
26. Olancha	du Bray and Moore (1985)
27. Keeler	Moore and Hopson (1961)
	Stinson (1977)
28. Darwin	Gay and Wright (1954)
	Hall and MacKevett (1958)
	Moore and Hopson (1961)
29. Panamint Butte	Moore and Hopson (1961)
30. Haiwee Reservoir	Whitmarsh and Walker (1997)

*Uncertain affinity with the swarm (see text).

southern Mojave Desert (Table 2). However, relatively few (<20) dikes have been dated precisely.

Dikes of other ages are present in several parts of the swarm. In the Mount Pinchot 15' quadrangle (eastern Sierra Nevada), Cretaceous mafic dikes strike parallel to Jurassic Independence dikes (Coleman et al., 2000). The Cretaceous dikes are likely related to east Sierran mafic plutonic complexes such as those exposed in Onion Valley, in the Lamarck granodiorite, and the Aberdeen mafic intrusive suite (e.g., Coleman et al., 1995; Sisson et al., 1996). Cretaceous mafic dikes have not been identified elsewhere along the swarm and may be limited to the eastern Sierra Nevada.

On the basis of field data, at least two episodes of dike intrusion occurred in the White-Inyo Mountains. Diorite dikes in the White-Inyo Mountains are truncated and metamorphosed

within the mapped aureoles of Jurassic granitic rocks, but other mafic dikes cut these granitic rocks and were metamorphosed during Late Jurassic–Cretaceous magmatism (Ernst, 1997). In the Coso Range, southern Owens Valley, a dated northwest-striking mafic dike is older than the swarm (ca. 166 Ma: R. Whitmarsh, 2000, personal communication). Multiple episodes of dike intrusion likely occurred in the southern Mojave Desert as well, where dikes in the Eagle and Chuckwalla Mountains cut plutons of both Jurassic and younger Cretaceous batholithic suites (Powell, 1981).

EXTENT OF THE SWARM

The Independence dike swarm is separated into northern and southern parts by the Garlock fault. The northern part of the swarm is relatively contiguous whereas exposures to the south are more fragmented and isolated owing to Cenozoic faulting and extension in the Mojave Desert (e.g., Smith, 1962; Glazner et al., 1989; Schermer et al., 1996). The northern part of the swarm includes dikes (from north to south) in the Sierra Nevada, Benton Range, White Mountains, Inyo Mountains, Alabama Hills, Coso, Argus and Slate Ranges, and the Spangler Hills (Fig. 1A). The southern part of the swarm includes dikes in the Mojave Desert but can be subdivided into three regions separated by prominent gaps in the swarm (Fig. 1B): (1) northeastern Mojave Desert including dikes in the Granite, Avawatz, and Soda Mountains, (2) central Mojave Desert, including dikes in the Fry, Rodman, Black, and Ord Mountains, and (3) southern Mojave Desert, in the Pinto, Eagle, and Chuckwalla Mountains.

The width of the Independence dike swarm is difficult to estimate because of its discontinuous exposure owing to intrusion by younger plutons, postemplacement deformation, and Cenozoic cover. At its narrowest near the Sierran crest (e.g., Mount Pinchot 15' quadrangle; Moore, 1963), the width is ~10 km. However, if Sierran dikes are considered together with those in the White-Inyo Mountains, then the width locally exceeds 90 km (Fig. 1).

Criteria for correlation

Criteria required to formally correlate dikes with the swarm are not well defined. Although the Independence dike swarm extends hundreds of kilometers across eastern California, few isotopic ages exist (Table 2). In previous studies, U-Pb ages of representative dikes implicitly provided the best correlation, yet dikes only a few kilometers apart were sampled (e.g., Chen and Moore, 1979) whereas large areas of the swarm remained unsampled. Also, most age data originate from felsic samples (largely because they were thought to contain more abundant zircons), but mafic dikes predominate along the swarm. In this paper, individual dikes correlated with the swarm lie on strike with other predominantly northwest-striking dikes across eastern California and are located near (within ~30 km of) a dated

TABLE 2. DATED INDEPENDENCE DIKES AND COEVAL PLUTONS AND VOLCANIC ROCKS OF EASTERN CALIFORNIA

Rock type	Location	Age* (Ma)	Reference
Independence dikes			
granite	Onion Valley	139 ± 11	Coleman et al. (2000)
felsite	S. Inyo Mountains	140 ± 8	Dunne and Walker (1993)
rhyolite	Eagle Mountains	145 (+6/−14)	James (1989)
dacite	Colton Hills	145.7 ± 3.6	Fox and Miller (1990)
felsic	Ship Mountains	~145 (K/Ar)	Gerber et al. (1995)
rhyolite	Stoddard Well	147 (+1/−2)	James (1989)
rhyolite	Benton Range	~148 (Ar/Ar)	Renne et al. (1999)
silicic	Alabama Hills	148 ± 2	Chen and Moore (1979)
silicic	Argus Range	148 ± 2	Chen and Moore (1979)
silicic	Argus Range	148 ± 2	Chen and Moore (1979)
rhyolite	Tiefort Mountains	148 ± 14	Schermer et al. (1994)
rhyolite	Woods Lake	148	Coleman et al. (2000)
microdiorite	Coso Range	148	R. Whitmarsh (2000 personal commun.)
diorite	Woods Lake	148 ± 1.4	Coleman et al. (2000)
diorite	Woods Lake	148 ± 2	Carl (2000)
rhyolite	Benton Range	148	Chen and Moore (1982)
silicic	Coso Range	148 ± 3	R. Whitmarsh (2000 personal commun.)
silicic	Cowhole Mountains	148	Carl (2000)
felsic	Cronese Mountain	152	J.D. Walker[†]
felsic	North Sierra	150 ± 3	Lahren et al. (1990)
rhyolite	Black Mountain	152 ± 3	J.M. Mattinson, E.R. Schermer, and C.J. Busby[§]
mafic	Coso Range	151 ± 3	R. Whitmarsh (2000 personal commun.)
mafic	Coso Range	166	R. Whitmarsh (2000 personal commun.)
Volcanic rocks			
rhyolite tuff	North Inyo Mountains	147	T.W. Stern and P.C. Bateman[#]
silicic tuff	Ord Mountains	148	Schermer and Busby (1994)
silicic tuff	South Slate Range	148–150	Dunne et al. (1994)
silicic tuff	South Inyo Mountains	148–150	Dunne et al. (1994)
dacite tuff	West Inyo Mountains	148 ± 2	Dunne et al. (1998)
dacite tuff	West Inyo Mountains	150 ± 2	Dunne et al. (1998)
dacite tuff	West Inyo Mountains	154 ± 7	Dunne et al. (1998)
rhyolite tuff	North Inyo Mountains	154 +3/−1	Hanson et al. (1987)
Plutons			
granite	Slate Range	~145	Walker et al. (1994)
quartz diorite	Courthouse Rock, West Sierra	146 +2/−1	Saleeby et al. (1989)
granodiorite	East Spangler Hills	147	Chen and Moore (1982)
granodiorite	Cabin Creek, White Mountains	~147	McKee and Conrad (1996)
?	Santa Cruz Mountain, West Sierra	147 +2/−1	Saleeby et al. (1989)
syenite	Chuckwalla Mountains	147 ± 4	Davis et al. (1994)
gabbro	Kennedy Meadows, East Sierra	148?	Dunne and Walker (1991)
hbl gabbro	central Mojave Desert	148	Walker et al. (1990a, 1990b)
gabbro-granite	Shadow Mountains	148	Martin (1992)
gabbro	Alvord Mountain, Mojave Desert	148	Miller and Glazner (1995)
hbl diorite	North Sierra (Sachse Monument)	148.4 ± 1.5	Lahren et al. (1990)
granite	French Spring, South Inyo Mountains	148.5 ± 1	Dunne and Walker (1993)
gabbro	Fort Irwin	148 ± 2	Miller and Sutter (1982)
granite	Butte Valley, Inyo Mountains	149	C. Wrucke**
felsic	Coso Range	149	Whitmarsh (1996)
leucotonalite	La Paloma, West Sierra	149 ± 2	Saleeby et al. (1989)
granite	Bigelow Lake, North Sierra	150	Lahren (1989)
gabbro	Tungsten Hills, East Sierra	150	Frost and Mattinson (1993)
gabbro	McMurry Meadows, East Sierra	150	Frost and Mattinson (1993)
granite	Ship Mountains, Mojave Desert	150	L.T. Silver[‡]
granite	Chuckwalla Mountains (Ar/Ar?)	150 ± 0.4	Davis et al. (1994)
?	Hornitos, West Sierra	150 +2/−1	Saleeby et al. (1989)
granite	Woods Ridge, central Sierra	151	Bateman (1992)
?	Guadalupe, West Sierra	151 ± 1	Saleeby et al. (1989)
granite	Iron Crossing, Mojave Desert	151 ± 11	Chen and Moore (1979)
granite	Cronese Mountain, Mojave Desert	152 ± 1	Walker et al. (1990a)
monzonite	Paiute, Inyo Mountains	152	Chen and Moore (1982)
granite	Colton Hills, Mojave Desert	152 ± 4	Fox and Miller (1990)
monzonite	North Spangler Hills	154	Chen and Moore (1982)
gabbro	Armstrong Canyon, East Sierra	154	Frost and Mattinson (1993)

*All analyses U/Pb zircon except where noted.
[†]Cited in Wadsworth et al. (1995).
[§]Cited in Schermer and Busby (1994).
[#]Cited in Hanson et al. (1987).
**Cited in Dunne et al. (1998).
[‡]Cited in Bishop (1964).

ca. 148 Ma dike (Fig. 1). By using these criteria, the following areas are correlated with the swarm.

Northern Independence dike swarm

The Mount Pinchot 15′ quadrangle (no. 18, Fig. 1A), eastern Sierra, contains perhaps the densest exposure of dikes in the northern Independence dike swarm. Abundant mafic dikes cut metamorphic wall rocks and Jurassic plutons across the length of the quadrangle. Sheeted dikes (up to ~40 m in total thickness) are found locally in the center of the quadrangle, near Woods Lake. Both a diorite and a rhyolite dike from the Woods Lake area have yielded ca. 148 Ma ages (Table 2).

Independence dikes cut metavolcanic wall rocks in the northern Alabama Hills, near Lone Pine, California. One of the first ca. 148 Ma ages for a dike in the swarm came from a felsic dike in this area (Chen and Moore, 1979). In the northern Alabama Hills, dikes intruded so close to one another that they locally form a sheeted-dike complex at least 100 m across (Carl et al., 1998).

Ages of ca. 148 Ma for mafic and felsic dikes support the presence of Independence dikes in the Coso Range, southern Owens Valley (R. Whitmarsh, 2000, personal communication). Numerous northwest-striking dikes mapped across the width of the range lie on strike with other 148 Ma dikes to the north and south (Duffield and Bacon, 1981; Whitmarsh and Walker, 1997; Fig. 1A). Map coverage of the swarm in the Coso area is available on detailed 1:24 000 geologic maps (Whitmarsh and Walker, 1997).

Dated ca. 148 Ma Independence dikes occur in the western and southern Inyo Mountains (e.g., Dunne et al., 1978; Dunne, 1986; Dunne and Walker, 1993; Table 2). No geochronologic data exist for dikes within the Darwin and Panamint Butte 15′ quadrangles, but dikes in these areas lie on strike with a dated dike to the north in the southern Inyo Mountains (Dunne and Walker, 1993; Fig. 1A) and are considered correlative with the swarm.

Two ca. 148 Ma dikes are present in the southern Argus Range and northern Spangler Hills east of Ridgecrest, California (Chen and Moore, 1979; Fig. 1A). Dikes in the Argus Range to the north share a similar thickness, structural trend, and petrology with the dated dikes and are also considered part of the swarm (Chen and Moore, 1979; McManus and Clemens-Knott, 1997; Carl, 2000).

Southern Independence dike swarm

Dikes in the Granite Mountains, northeastern Mojave Desert (Leach Lake 15′ quadrangle), are firmly correlated with the swarm despite a lack of geochronologic data from the region. These dikes represent the southern continuation of dikes in the Argus Range and Spangler Hills, but have been offset ~60 km sinistrally from the northern Independence dike swarm across the Garlock fault (Smith, 1962).

A silicic dike in the Tiefort Mountains area, Fort Irwin Military Reservation, northeastern Mojave Desert, yielded a 148 ± 14 Ma U-Pb age (Stephens et al., 1993), supporting the correlation of at least some dikes in this area with the swarm.

A felsic dike in the northwestern Cowhole Mountains (Old Dad 15′ quadrangle) yielded a ca. 148 Ma U-Pb age, confirming Independence dikes in that area (Fig. 1B; Table 2). Dikes in the Cowhole Mountains resemble those on Cronese Mountain that are tentatively dated at ca. 152 Ma (preliminary U-Pb data, J.D. Walker, cited in Wadsworth et al., 1995). Some andesite dikes in the Cowhole Mountains are probably younger than the swarm because they intrude fractures in landslide blocks that are likely Cenozoic (Wadsworth et al., 1995).

A prominent gap (>80 km) between the Cronese Hills and the area southwest of Barstow (Fig. 1B) occurs within the swarm between dikes in the northeastern and the central Mojave Desert. On the south side of the gap, the swarm continues in the central Mojave Desert near Black Mountain and Stoddard Ridge (Apple Valley 15′ quadrangle; Fig. 1B). Dikes in this area have yielded ca. 148 Ma ages (James, 1989; Schermer, 1993). Dikes in the Fry, Ord, and Rodman Mountains lie on strike with these dated dikes and are correlated with the swarm (Karish et al., 1987; Schermer, 1993; Schermer and Busby, 1994).

Tentatively correlated dikes

Dikes in some regions remain only tentatively correlated with the swarm owing to their relatively isolated location and lack of geochronologic data. In the central Sierra Nevada, dikes in the Mount Morrison, Kern Peak, Mount Whitney, and Triple Divide Peak 15′ quadrangles are located away from semicontinuous dike exposure near the range crest (Fig. 1A). Dikes in the Triple Divide Peak 15′ quadrangle may be both Jurassic and Cretaceous (Moore and Sisson, 1987). Independence dikes mapped in the Mount Morrison 15′ quadrangle (Rinehart and Ross, 1964) define the northern end of the Independence dike swarm. Dated ca. 148 Ma dikes are found still farther north in the Snow Lake pendant, Yosemite National Park (Lahren et al., 1990; Fig. 1A and Table 1), but these dikes likely formed hundreds of kilometers to the south in the Mojave Desert prior to Cretaceous dextral faulting along the proposed Mojave–Snow Lake fault (Lahren et al., 1990; Schweickert and Lahren, 1990).

Abundant dikes in the Benton Range east of the Sierra Nevada (Casa Diablo Mountain 15′ quadrangle) are petrologically unlike the swarm because of their overwhelmingly felsic composition (Rinehart and Ross, 1957; Moore and Hopson, 1961; Fig. 1A). Potassium-argon data from a dike in the Benton Range yielded an age (>160 Ma) older than that of the Independence dike swarm, and these dikes previously were considered part of a separate intrusive event (ca. 160 Ma: Renne and Turrin, 1987). However, more recent Ar-Ar analyses of the same dike permit correlation of these dikes with the swarm (Renne et al., 1999). In this paper, dikes in the Benton Range are tentatively correlated with the swarm pending additional age data.

Dikes in the White Mountains extend across six 15′ quadrangles and have been correlated with the swarm owing to their mafic composition and dominant northwest strike (Fig 1A; Moore and Hopson, 1961). However, none have been dated. Metamorphism, the variable geochemistry, and field relationships of mafic dikes in the White Mountains indicate that dikes of several ages are present and make correlation of any given dike with the swarm unreliable (Ernst, 1997). A few mapped mafic dikes in the eastern White Mountains strike northeast and likely are not part of the swarm (McKee and Nelson, 1967). The longest mapped Independence dike in the swarm extends >8 km across the Blanco Mountain and Waucoba Mountain 15′ quadrangles in the northern Inyo and southern White Mountains (Nelson, 1966a, 1966b). Our attempts to date this dike were unsuccessful owing to low zircon yield.

South of the Garlock fault, abundant dikes in the Soda Mountains, northeastern Mojave Desert, range from <1 to 30 m in width and up to ~3 km in length; they strike consistently northwest, ~300°–310° (Baker and Soda Lake 15′ quadrangles: Grose, 1959; Fig. 1B). The composition of these dikes varies from mafic to felsic, but diabase is generally the most abundant. Locally, dikes are so densely spaced that they compose nearly half of the exposed outcrop (Grose, 1959). These dikes compare well with Independence dikes north of the Garlock fault, but lack geochronologic data and are therefore tentatively correlated with the swarm.

Jurassic plutons in the southern Providence Mountains and Colton Hills, eastern Mojave Desert (Flynn and Colton Well 15′ quadrangles, Fig. 1B), are cut by extensive north-northwest-striking felsic to intermediate dikes (Fox and Miller, 1990). The dikes are particularly abundant, forming a sheeted-dike complex on the western side of the southern Providence Mountains (Fox and Miller, 1990). Mostly rhyodacite dikes are found in the Colton Hills. Biotite from a dacite dike in the Colton Hills yielded a ca. 146 Ma K/Ar age (Fox and Miller, 1990), and dikes in the area are tentatively correlated with the swarm.

Dikes are much less common in the Bristol and Granite Mountains area, eastern Mojave Desert (Kerens and Flynn 15′ quadrangles, Fig. 1B); dikes there consist of scattered lamprophyre and diorite. East-striking mafic dikes cut deformed, probably Jurassic, plutons in the Bristol Mountains and are themselves cut by undeformed Cretaceous plutons and mafic dikes (Howard et al., 1987). Northwest-striking rhyolite dikes also cut Mesozoic plutonic rocks but are petrologically similar and likely related to rhyolite Miocene flows within a few kilometers to the south of the dikes (Howard et al., 1987).

Northwest-striking dikes in seven 15′ quadrangles, central Mojave Desert (Barstow, Lavic, Old Woman Springs, Emerson Lake, Deadman Lake, Joshua Tree, Twentynine Palms: Fig. 1B), lie southeast of but on strike with ca. 148 Ma dikes in the Rodman Mountains and cut similar plutonic rocks (James, 1989; Schermer, 1993).

Mafic dikes in Old Woman Mountains area (Danby and Essex 15′ quadrangles; Fig. 1B), southeastern Mojave Desert, may represent the easternmost exposure of the swarm. A ca. 145 Ma U-Pb age from one dike in the Old Woman Mountains supports this assertion (Gerber et al., 1995). Dikes in this area, however, lie ~80 km east of the nearest major exposure of the swarm in the Deadman Lake 15′ quadrangle and ~80 km north of dikes in the Eagle Mountains.

Mafic and felsic dikes that possibly correlate with the swarm occur in the Mule Mountains, southeastern California (Tosdal et al., 1989). The dikes are distinguished from known Tertiary dikes because they are commonly altered. Dikes in the Mule Mountains are undated.

STRUCTURE

Independence dikes consistently strike northwest, and many dikes are correlated with the swarm by using this criterion alone (e.g., Moore, 1963). However, the northwest strike of Independence dikes is a generalization. In early published maps of the swarm (e.g., Moore and Hopson, 1961; Chen and Moore, 1979), dikes were schematically drawn parallel to the swarm's overall trend, but true dike orientations vary from this trend. Dikes north of the Garlock fault, including dikes in the Alabama Hills, Coso Range, and Spangler Hills, consistently strike west-northwest (~315°), counterclockwise to the overall ~330° trend of the swarm (Glazner et al., 1999; Figs. 1B, 2). Independence dikes may have intruded fractures oriented oblique to the swarm's trend to produce this pattern (Glazner et al., 1999). Locally in the Sierra Nevada, dikes also deviate substantially, up to 90°, from a northwest trend (e.g., Mount Goddard, Mount Whitney, Triple Divide Peak, Kern Peak 15′ quadrangles: Fig. 1A, Table 2). Many of these dikes possibly were rotated during intrusion of Cretaceous plutons (Moore and Sisson, 1987). Dikes in the Inyo Mountains predominantly strike northwest, but a few strike northeast (e.g., Smith, 1962; Nelson, 1966a).

Structural trends across the Mojave Desert

Dikes immediately south of the Garlock fault were variably rotated by Cenozoic faulting and crustal extension (e.g., Smith, 1962; Schermer et al., 1996). Dikes in the Granite Mountains, northeastern Mojave Desert, have been rotated ~50° clockwise relative to dikes in the Sierra Nevada (Smith, 1962; Ron and Nur, 1996). Our new structural data support clockwise rotation in the northeastern Mojave Desert. Orientations of mafic Independence dikes in the western Avawatz Mountains, northeastern Mojave Desert, strike predominantly ~340° (Fig. 2), close to the ~346° mean azimuth for this area determined by Ron and Nur (1996) from aerial photographs. Clockwise rotation associated with movement across the Garlock fault likely caused rotation of dikes in the Granite and Avawatz Mountains (e.g., Smith, 1962; Luyendyk et al., 1985; Schermer et al., 1996).

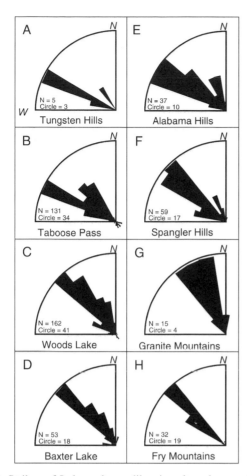

Figure 2. Strikes of Independence dikes in selected areas. Locations shown on Figure 1 except for Baxter Lakes, which is 5 km south of Woods Lake. Data collected 1994–1998 by J.M. Bartley, B.S. Carl, B. Coffey, A.F. Glazner, K. Ratajeski, and M. Woodbury.

As noted previously, a prominent gap occurs within the swarm between the northeastern Mojave Desert and the Stoddard Ridge area, central Mojave Desert, a distance of >80 km (Figs. 1B and 3). The swarm is not exposed in this area because it has likely been separated across a region of significant structural deformation in the central Mojave Desert associated with low-angle detachment faulting. Northeast-directed extension possibly exceeded 40 km (e.g., Glazner et al., 1989; Walker et al., 1990a; Martin et al., 1993; Glazner et al., 1994). The swarm continues to the south again in the Stoddard Ridge area southwest of Barstow in the west-central Mojave Desert. Dikes in the Stoddard Ridge area have a mean strike of ~312°, subparallel to presumably unrotated Independence dikes north of the Garlock fault (Ron and Nur, 1996).

Dikes in the Fry Mountains, located ~30 km to the east-southeast of Stoddard Ridge (Fig. 1B), have a mean orientation of ~310°, similar to dikes in the Stoddard Ridge area and in the Sierra Nevada (Ron and Nur, 1996), and thus do not appear to have been rotated about a vertical axis. In contrast, paleomagnetic data from the Cady, Newberry, Rodman, and Bullion

Mountains, ~30 km to the northeast, indicate significant clockwise vertical-axis rotations in that area (locally >90°: Ross et al., 1989). This difference in rotation is probably a result of deformation associated with early Miocene extension in the central Mojave Desert (Glazner et al., this volume).

On the scale of an outcrop, dike orientations commonly vary 20° or more over short distances. In some Sierran dikes, dike attitudes change as much as 60° within 1–10 m, consistent with intrusion along pre-existing, or possibly conjugate, fractures (Bartley et al., 1996; Carl et al., 1998; Glazner et al., 1999). A similar zigzag pattern is reported for dikes in the Colton Hills, eastern Mojave Desert (Fox and Miller, 1990).

Oblique fabrics

Some Independence dikes contain distinctive deformational fabrics. In the eastern Sierra Nevada, many mafic dikes contain an oblique foliation across their width (Moore and Hopson, 1961). These fabrics formed by sinistral deformation within the dikes; this deformation may be related to sinistral strike-slip motion along the latest Jurassic arc (e.g., Carl et al., 1998; Wolf and Saleeby, 1995). Similar oblique fabrics are found locally in the Coso Range (Whitmarsh et al., 1996), and we have observed them in the Spangler Hills and within mafic dikes that intrude Jurassic granodiorite in the Kern Peak quadrangle.

In addition to oblique fabric, several studies have reported dike-parallel foliations in dikes south of the Garlock fault. A "protoclastic lamination" parallel and adjacent to the dike margins of silicic dikes occurs in the Ord Mountains, west-central Mojave Desert (Karish et al., 1987). Altered mafic dikes in the Eagle Mountains contain a pervasive foliation parallel to their contacts (Powell et al., 1984). It is uncertain whether these features share a common origin with obliquely foliated Sierran dikes. Possibly they developed during local shearing between intruding viscous magma and wall rock.

PETROLOGIC STUDIES

Field and geochemical data indicate that the swarm is predominantly mafic in the northern Independence dike swarm, notably in the Sierra Nevada and White-Inyo Mountains (e.g., Moore and Hopson, 1961; Moore, 1963; Ross, 1965; Nelson, 1966a, 1966b; Ernst, 1997; Carl et al., 1998; Table 2). However, felsic and intermediate compositions are present as well (Table 2). Abundant felsic dikes, tentatively correlated with the swarm, are present in the Benton Range, northern Independence dike swarm (Renne and Turrin, 1987) but generally more intermediate and felsic compositions are located in the southern part of the swarm (Carl et al., 1997; Carl, 2000).

Only a few studies have addressed the petrogenesis of Independence dikes. Felsic and mafic Independence dikes in the northern Spangler Hills and southern Argus Range vary in

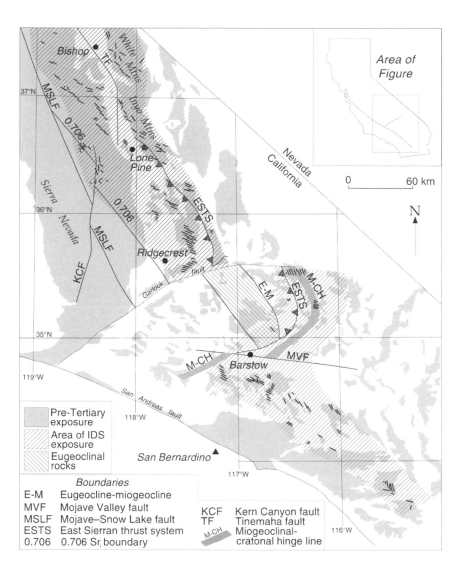

Figure 3. Generalized map of the Independence dike swarm and major geologic boundaries in eastern California: East Sierran thrust system (Dunne, 1986; Walker et al., 1990a; Dunne and Walker, 1993), Mojave-Snow Lake fault (e.g., Schweickert and Lahren, 1990), Tinemaha fault (Stevens et al., 1997), Kern Canyon fault (Busby-Spera and Saleeby, 1990), eugeoclinal-miogeoclinal facies boundary (e.g., Martin and Walker, 1992), miogeoclinal-cratonal hinge line (Martin and Walker, 1992), Mojave Valley fault (Martin et al., 1993), and the $Sr_i = 0.706$ line, which is not extended south of the Garlock fault (e.g., Kistler and Peterman, 1973; Kistler, 1990).

composition from 47% to 72 wt% SiO_2 with a gap from 58% to 67% (McManus and Clemens-Knott, 1997). These authors concluded that the compositional variability could be due to fractionation of hornblende or pyroxene and plagioclase from a mafic parent. Quartz xenocrysts with reaction rims indicate that assimilation occurred. Oxygen isotope data for the most unaltered samples support a mantle source for the mafic magma (McManus and Clemens-Knott, 1997). In a petrologic study of mafic dikes in the White-Inyo Mountains, dikes range from 46 to 61 wt% SiO_2 (Ernst, 1997). Geochemical trends in the analyses of sampled dikes suggest that the dikes formed by fractionation of pyroxene, hornblende, and plagioclase from a mafic magma.

Unusually alkalic dikes are found in the Fry Mountains of the central Mojave Desert, where comendite, trachyte, and basaltic andesite dikes occur (Karish et al., 1987). Both subalkalic and peralkalic dikes are present, some with sodic amphibole (Karish et al., 1987). These dikes are probably related to nearby volcanic flows of similar composition and age (Karish et al., 1987; Schermer, 1993).

Whole-rock Sr, Nd, and Pb isotope analyses of mafic to felsic dikes (51–69 wt% SiO_2) in the Old Woman Mountains, Kilbeck Hills, and Piute Mountains, southeastern California (Fig. 1B), suggest that these dikes are related to other Jurassic rocks in the Mojave Desert and may have formed by mixing of mantle and crustal magmas (Gerber et al., 1995).

FEATURES CUT BY THE SWARM

Isotopic studies suggest a regional correlation between lithospheric provinces in eastern California and Independence dike isotopic compositions (Coleman et al., 1992). This section briefly describes the major stratigraphic boundaries, structures, and tectonic features that could potentially influence the observed chemical heterogeneity among Independence dikes.

Isotopic boundaries

The 0.706 line, a major isotopic boundary in eastern California defined by the initial $^{87}Sr/^{86}Sr$ ratios of Mesozoic plutons (e.g., Kistler and Peterman, 1973; Kistler, 1990), lies entirely north and west of the Independence dike swarm north of the Garlock fault (Fig. 3). Classically, the 0.706 line has been defined as the limit of Precambrian basement underlying the North American continent (e.g., Kistler, 1990). Alternatively, this boundary may reflect the presence of enriched lithospheric mantle beneath the Sierra Nevada (Coleman and Glazner, 1997).

In contrast to areas north of the Garlock, the 0.706 line across the Mojave Desert is difficult to define and varies with bulk-rock composition (Glazner and O'Neil, 1989; Miller et al., 2000). Tertiary extension across the Mojave Desert complicates reconstructions and interpretations regarding underlying sources of Mesozoic and Tertiary igneous rocks (e.g., Glazner et al., 1989). Initial $^{87}Sr/^{86}Sr$ (Sr_i) ratios <0.706 are found within the area of eugeoclinal rocks in the northeastern Mojave Desert (Fig. 3), but values higher than this are found both to the east and west of this area. However, Sr_i ratios generally increase to the east. The 0.706 line defined for silicic volcanic rocks roughly aligns with the 0.706 line in the Sierra Nevada when ~65 km of left-lateral offset across the Garlock fault is restored (Miller et al., 2000).

The Independence dike swarm cuts the "Mojavia" region of province 1 of Bennett and DePaolo (1987), defined by characteristic Nd isotope compositions for Proterozoic and younger rocks in eastern California. Proterozoic rocks within this region have ε_{Nd} values of ~0 and depleted mantle model ages of 2–2.3 Ga. The eastern edge of this boundary approximately coincides with the California-Arizona border. This region is interpreted to have formed from a mixture of predominantly depleted mantle and a substantial amount of older crust. The presence of Archean crust is supported by a highly discordant U-Pb zircon age that is older than 2.7 Ga from a mafic dike in the Alabama Hills that likely contains an Archean inherited component (Chen and Moore, 1979).

Stratigraphic boundaries

The swarm intrudes the miogeoclinal-cratonal hinge line in the northeastern Mojave Desert, defined by exposures of Paleozoic sedimentary and metasedimentary rocks in the Mojave Desert that can be correlated with similar rocks in the Death Valley region (Fig. 3; Martin and Walker, 1991, 1992). Independence dikes cross the inferred trace of the eugeoclinal-miogeoclinal boundary just north of the Garlock fault in the general vicinity of the western Spangler Hills (Martin and Walker, 1992; Fig. 3). Dikes in the Granite and Avawatz Mountains lie just west of this hinge line, whereas dikes in the Soda

Mountains, Cowhole, Bristol, and Providence Mountains lie east of the hinge line. Independence dikes in the central Mojave Desert cut cratonal rocks east of the hinge line.

Tinemaha fault

Correlation of Devonian metasedimentary rocks in the Mount Morrison roof pendant (eastern Sierra) with similar deposits in the western Inyo Mountains supports the existence of the north-northwest-striking dextral Tinemaha fault separating the two regions (e.g., Stevens et al., 1997; Stevens and Greene, 1999). The Tinemaha fault is located beneath the present trace of Owens Valley (Fig. 3) and is probably Triassic in age (Stevens and Greene, 1999). Approximately 65 km of right-lateral displacement is estimated across this inferred fault, which is crossed by the Independence dike swarm near Independence, California (Fig. 1A).

East Sierran thrust system

A northwest-trending belt of thrust faults places Paleozoic strata and Jurassic plutons over Mesozoic rocks along the East Sierran thrust system, eastern California. This belt extends from as far north as the Snow Lake pendant, Yosemite National Park, southward to the Alabama Hills, across the Inyo Mountains, Argus Range, and Slate Range and into the Mojave Desert (e.g., Dunne and Walker, 1993; Stevens et al., 1997). Independence dikes cut faults in the East Sierran thrust system but are also folded and form boudins in the southern Inyo Mountains (e.g., Dunne, 1986; Dunne and Walker, 1993). Deformation along this thrust system began in the Late Triassic and possibly extended to the middle Cretaceous (Stevens et al., 1997).

STRUCTURES THAT OFFSET THE SWARM

Mojave–Snow Lake fault

Independence dikes are found in the Snow Lake roof pendant, Yosemite National Park (Lahren et al., 1990), north of more extensive dike exposures in the eastern Sierra Nevada. Although located well to the north of more abundant dike exposure in the central Sierra Nevada, U-Pb age data confirm correlation of Snow Lake dikes with the swarm (Table 1). These dikes may have originally intruded rocks in the Mojave Desert and were later translated >400 km northward to their present position in the northern Sierra Nevada along the postulated Cretaceous dextral Mojave-Snow Lake fault (Lahren et al., 1990; Schweickert and Lahren, 1990; Fig. 3). Coincidentally, translation along the Mojave-Snow Lake fault places dikes in the Snow Lake pendant directly on strike with the northernmost exposure of the swarm east of this proposed fault.

Owens Valley fault

Cenozoic right-lateral movement is associated with the Owens Valley fault (e.g., Beanland and Clark, 1994) and is probably responsible for slight clockwise rotation and offset of Independence dikes in the northern Alabama Hills (Richardson, 1972). It is unlikely that major (i.e., many kilometers of) strike-slip displacement occurred across the fault, because the dike swarm shows no apparent offset across Owens Valley (Moore and Hopson, 1961). However, such displacement might not be readily recognized because the Independence dike swarm is oriented at a low angle to the fault.

Garlock fault

Smith (1962) first estimated ~60 km of sinistral displacement across the Garlock fault (Fig. 3) by correlating dikes in the southern Argus Range with others in the Granite Mountains, northeastern Mojave Desert. Movement across the Garlock fault resulted in 20°–80° clockwise rotation of dikes in the Granite Mountains (e.g., Smith, 1962; Schermer et al., 1996). Mylonitization associated with deeper levels of movement may have deformed Independence dikes at the eastern end of the fault (Burks, 1987).

Mojave Valley fault

A proposed cryptic fault across the central Mojave Desert (Fig. 3) may explain >80 km of dextral separation of several prominent paleogeographic features in the northern Mojave Desert, including the western edge of the Independence dike swarm (Walker et al., 1990a; Martin et al., 1993; Fig. 3). Miocene detachment faulting in the central Mojave Desert may be kinematically linked to deformation of similar age in the Colorado River extensional corridor along this cryptic fault, but the underlying connecting structures are not well understood (Bartley and Glazner, 1991; Martin et al., 1993).

Left-lateral faults, eastern Transverse Ranges

Several east-striking sinistral faults offset dikes in the eastern Transverse Ranges, southern Mojave Desert. These faults include the Pinto Mountain and Blue Cut faults (Hope, 1966; Powell, 1981; Powell et al., 1984). Cumulatively, these faults are responsible for >40 km of sinistral displacement across the range and the Independence dike swarm as well (Powell et al., 1984).

ORIGIN OF THE SWARM

Previous studies have interpreted the Independence dike swarm to have formed in response to (1) extension perpendicular to the swarm (e.g., Chen and Moore, 1979, 1982; Karish et al., 1987; James, 1989; Schermer, 1993; Schermer and

Busby, 1994; Davis et al., 1994), (2) tectonic activity associated with the Nevadan orogeny (e.g., Page and Engebretson, 1984), (3) expanding plutons associated with the Jurassic arc (Hopson, 1988), or (4) sinistral shear along the latest Jurassic arc (Wolf and Saleeby, 1995; Carl et al., 1998; Glazner et al., 1999).

Intrusion of the Independence dike swarm overlapped the waning stages of the Nevadan orogeny (e.g., Moore and Hopson, 1961; Chen and Moore, 1982; James, 1989), that was responsible for intense deformation in the Sierra Nevada (e.g., Tobisch et al., 1987; Harper et al., 1994). The near-coincidence of these two events suggests a causal relationship between them. However, recent studies indicate that Nevadan deformation and metamorphism are largely limited to the western Sierra (e.g., Tobisch et al., 1987) and spanned a broader interval of >20 m.y. (ca. 155–130 Ma: e.g., Wright and Fahan, 1988; Harper et al., 1994). Recognition of the Nevadan orogeny as a protracted event thus undermines the inference of a causal connection between it and intrusion of the Independence dike swarm.

Dike intrusion in the eastern Sierra Nevada may have closely overlapped deformation along mylonitic shear zones (Carl et al., 1995, 1998). These relationships can be explained by dike intrusion and deformation above a subduction zone dominated by sinistral shear. Sinistral transpression and/or transtension may be responsible for mylonitic shear zones and deformed dikes in the western Sierra Nevada (Wolf and Saleeby, 1995). Paleomagnetic data and paleogeographic reconstructions of plate-motion studies support a western North American margin dominated by sinistral shear in the latest Jurassic (e.g., Engebretson et al., 1985; May et al., 1986; May and Butler, 1989). Possibly, the Independence dike swarm intruded in response to rapid changes in plate motion at that time. However, recent studies of deformation in the east Sierra indicate that sinistral transpression may have lasted until 95 Ma (Kelley and Engebretson, 1994). The tectonic origin of the swarm thus remains uncertain.

CONCLUSIONS

1. The Independence dike swarm extends ~600 km from the eastern Sierra Nevada to the southern Mojave Desert. According to our criteria, dikes correlated with the swarm lie on strike with other predominantly northwest-striking dikes across eastern California and are located within ~30 km of a dated ca. 148 Ma dike. Tentatively correlated dikes lie farther from dated dikes, are located away from the main trend of the swarm, and/or are petrologically unusual compared to the well-correlated dikes.

2. Although predominantly mafic, the Independence dike swarm is not bimodal and includes many intermediate compositions as well.

3. The Independence dike swarm transects major stratigraphic, structural, and isotopic boundaries in eastern California. The regional extent of the swarm can potentially be used

to test proposed geochemical differences in lithospheric sources within provinces defined by these boundaries.

4. New structural data indicate ~30°–40° clockwise vertical-axis rotation of Independence dikes in the Granite Mountains, northeastern Mojave Desert, and minimally rotated dikes in the Fry Mountains, west-central Mojave Desert.

5. Although many dike swarms have been linked to extension, the Independence dike swarm may have formed in response to rapid changes in latest Jurassic plate movements accommodating sinistral shear.

ACKNOWLEDGMENTS

Supported by National Science Foundation grant EAR-9526803 (to Glazner). Forrest Hopson and John Bartley provided excellent reviews. We thank John Bartley, David Dinter, Max Woodbury, Brian Coffey, Kent Ratajeski, Scott Hetzler, and Cecil Patrick for field assistance and other help. Carl received support from the Geological Society of America, the White Mountain Research Station (University of California), and the Martin Fund (University of North Carolina).

REFERENCES CITED

Bartley, J.M., and Glazner, A.F., 1991, En echelon Miocene rifting in the southwestern United States and model for vertical-axis rotation in continental extension: Geology, v. 19, p. 1165–1168.

Bartley, J.M., Carl, B.S., and Glazner, A.F., 1996, Injection of dikes along faults: Geological Society of America Abstracts with Programs, v. 28, no. 5, p. 47.

Bateman, P.C., 1965, Geologic map of the Blackcap Mountain quadrangle, Fresno County, California: U.S. Geological Survey Geologic Quadrangle Map GQ-428, scale 1:62 500.

Bateman, P.C., 1992, Plutonism in the central part of the Sierra Nevada batholith: U.S. Geological Survey Professional Paper 1483, 186 p.

Bateman, P.C., and Moore, J.G., 1965, Geologic map of the Mount Goddard quadrangle, Fresno and Inyo Counties, California: U.S. Geological Survey Geologic Quadrangle Map GQ-429, scale 1:62 500.

Bateman, P.C., Lockwood, J.P., and Lydon, P.A., 1971, Geologic map of the Kaiser Peak quadrangle, central Sierra Nevada, California: U.S. Geological Survey Map GQ-894, scale 1:62 500.

Beanland, S., and Clark, M., 1994, The Owens Valley fault zone, eastern California, and surface faulting associated with the 1872 earthquake: U.S. Geological Survey Bulletin B 1982, 29 p.

Bennett, V.C., and DePaolo, D., 1987, Proterozoic crustal history of the western United States as determined by neodymium isotopic mapping: Geological Society of America Bulletin, v. 99, p. 674–685.

Bishop, G.C., 1964, Needles sheet, geologic map of California: California Division of Mines and Geology, scale 1:250 000.

Bowen, O.E., 1954, Geology and mineral deposits of the Barstow quadrangle, San Bernardino County, California: California Division of Mines Bulletin, v. 165, 208 p.

Burks, R.J., 1987, Occurrence of mylonites within the Garlock fault zone, Quail Mountains, southeastern California: Geological Society of America Abstracts with Programs, v. 19, no. 6, p. 363.

Busby-Spera, C.J., and Saleeby, J.B., 1990, Intra-arc strike-slip fault exposed at batholithic levels in the southern Sierra Nevada, California: Geology, v. 18, p. 255–259.

Byers, F.M., 1960, Geology of the Alvord Mountain quadrangle, San Bernardino County, California: U.S. Geological Survey Bulletin 1089-A, 71 p.

Carl, B.S., 2000, Structure, intrusion, and tectonic origin of the Independence dike swarm, eastern California [Ph.D. thesis]: Chapel Hill, University of North Carolina, 269 p.

Carl, B.S., Bartley, J.M., and Glazner, A.F., 1995, Structural geology of Independence dikes, eastern Sierra Nevada, California: Geological Society of America Abstracts with Programs, v. 27, no. 5, p. 9.

Carl, B.S., Glazner, A.F., and Bartley, J.M., 1997, Composite Independence dikes: Geological Society of America Abstracts with Programs, v. 29, no. 6, p. 391.

Carl, B.S., Glazner, A.F., Bartley, J.M., Dinter, D.A., and Coleman, D.S., 1998, Independence dikes and mafic rocks of the eastern Sierra, *in* Behl, R., ed., Geological Society of America Cordilleran Section 1998 Field Trip Guidebook: Long Beach, California State University at Long Beach, p. 4.1–4.26.

Chen, J.H., and Moore, J.G., 1979, Late Jurassic Independence dike swarm in eastern California: Geology, v. 7, p. 129–133.

Chen, J.H., and Moore, J.G., 1982, Uranium-lead isotopic ages from the Sierra Nevada batholith, California: Journal of Geophysical Research, v. 87, p. 4761–4784.

Coleman, D.S., and Glazner, A.F., 1997, The Sierra Crest magmatic event: Rapid formation of juvenile crust during the Late Cretaceous in California: International Geology Review, v. 39, p. 768–787.

Coleman, D.S., Glazner, A.F., Miller, J.S., and Frost, T.P., 1992, Along-strike isotopic variations in mafic rocks and Independence dikes from the Sierra-Mojave batholith [abs.]: Eos (Transactions, American Geophysical Union), v. 73, p. 658–659.

Coleman, D.S., Glazner, A.F., Miller, J.S., Bradford, K.J., Frost, T.P., Joye, J.L., and Bachl, C.A., 1995, Exposure of a Late Cretaceous layered mafic-felsic magma system in the central Sierra Nevada batholith, California: Contributions to Mineralogy and Petrology, v. 120, p. 129–136.

Coleman, D.S., Carl, B.S., Glazner, A.F., and Bartley, J.M., 2000, Cretaceous dikes within the Jurassic Independence dike swarm in eastern California: Geological Society of America Bulletin, v. 112, p. 504–511.

Crowder, D.F., and Sheridan M.F., 1972, Geologic map of the White Mountain Peak quadrangle, Mono County, California: U.S. Geological Survey Map GQ-1012, scale 1:62 500.

Davis, M.J., Farber, D.L., Wooden, J.L., and Anderson, J.L., 1994, Conflicting tectonics? Contraction and extension at middle and upper crustal levels along the Cordilleran Late Jurassic arc, southeastern California: Geology, v. 22, p. 247–250.

Dibblee, T.W., Jr., 1960a, Preliminary geologic map of the Apple Valley quadrangle, California: U.S. Geological Survey Miscellaneous Field Studies Map MF-232, scale 1:62 500.

Dibblee, T.W., Jr., 1960b, Preliminary geologic map of the Barstow quadrangle, San Bernardino County, California: U.S. Geological Survey Miscellaneous Field Studies Map MF-233, scale 1:62 500.

Dibblee, T.W., Jr., 1964a, Geologic map of the Ord Mountains quadrangle, San Bernardino County, California: U.S. Geological Survey Miscellaneous Geologic Investigations Map I-427, scale 1:62 500.

Dibblee, T.W., Jr., 1964b, Geological map of the Rodman Mountains quadrangle, San Bernardino County, California: U.S. Geological Survey Miscellaneous Geologic Investigations Map I-430, scale 1:62 500.

Dibblee, T.W., Jr., 1966a, Geologic map of the Cady Mountains quadrangle, San Bernardino County, California: U.S. Geological Survey Miscellaneous Investigations Map I-467, scale 1:62 500.

Dibblee, T.W., Jr., 1966b, Geologic map of the Lavic quadrangle, San Bernardino County, California: U.S. Geological Survey Miscellaneous Investigations Map I-472, scale 1:62 500.

Dibblee, T.W., Jr., 1967a, Geologic map of the Deadman Lake quadrangle, San Bernardino County, California: U.S. Geological Survey Miscellaneous Geologic Investigations Map I-488, scale 1:62 500.

Dibblee, T.W., Jr., 1967b, Geologic map of the Emerson Lake quadrangle, San Bernardino County, California: U.S. Geological Survey Miscellaneous Geologic Investigations Map I-490, scale 1:62 500.

Dibblee, T.W., Jr., 1967c, Geologic map of the Joshua Tree quadrangle, San Bernardino County, California: U.S. Geological Survey Miscellaneous Geologic Investigations Map I-516, scale 1:62 500.

Dibblee, T.W., Jr., 1967d, Geologic map of the Old Woman Springs quadrangle, U.S. Geological Survey Geologic Miscellaneous Investigations Map I-518, scale 1:62 500.

Dibblee, T.W., Jr., 1968, Geologic map of the Twentynine Palms quadrangle, San Bernardino and Riverside Counties, California: U.S. Geological Survey Miscellaneous Geologic Investigations Map I-561, scale 1:62 500.

du Bray, E.A., and Moore, J.G., 1985, Geologic map of the Olancha quadrangle, southern Sierra Nevada, California: U.S. Geological Survey Miscellaneous Field Studies Map MF-1734, scale 1:62 500.

Duffield, W.A., and Bacon, C.R., 1981, Geologic map of the Coso volcanic field and adjacent areas, Inyo County, U.S. Geological Survey Miscellaneous Investigations Map I-1200, scale 1:62 500.

Dunne, G.C., 1977, Geology and structural evolution of the Old Dad Mountain, Mojave Desert, California: Geological Society of America Bulletin, v. 88, p. 737–748.

Dunne, G., 1986, Mesozoic evolution of the southern Inyo Range, Darwin Plateau, and Argus and Slate Ranges, *in* Dunne, G., ed., Mesozoic and Cenozoic structural evolution of selected areas, east-central California: Geological Society of America, Cordilleran Section Fieldtrip Guidebook, p. 22–43.

Dunne, G.C., and Walker, J.D., 1991, New age constraints on Jurassic volcanism, southern Owens Valley area, east-central California: Geological Society of America Abstracts with Programs, v. 23, no. 5, p. 248–249.

Dunne, G.C., and Walker, J.D., 1993, Age of Jurassic volcanism and tectonism, southern Owens Valley region, east-central California: Geological Society of America Bulletin, v. 105, p. 1223–1230.

Dunne, G.C., Gulliver, R.M., Sylvester, A.G., 1978, Mesozoic evolution of rocks of the White, Argus, and Slate ranges, eastern California, *in* Howell, D.G., and McDougall, K.A., eds., Mesozoic paleogeography of the western United States: Pacific Section, Society of Economic Paleontologists and Mineralogists, p. 189–207.

Dunne, G.C., Walker, J.D., Stern, S.M., and Linn, J.K., 1994, New U-Pb age constraints on Late Jurassic magmatism and contractile deformation in east-central California: Geological Society of America Abstracts with Programs, v. 26, no. 7, p. A386.

Dunne, G.C., Garvey, T.P., Osborne, M., Schneidereit, D., Fritsche, A.E., and Walker, J.D., 1998, Geology of the Inyo Mountains volcanic complex: Implications for Jurassic paleogeography of the Sierran magmatic arc in eastern California: Geological Society of America Bulletin, v. 110, p. 1376–1397.

Engebretson, D.C., Cox, A., and Gordon, R.G., 1985, Relative motions between oceanic and continental plates in the Pacific basin: Geological Society of America Special Paper 206, 59 p.

Ernst, W.G., 1997, Metamorphism of mafic dikes from the central White-Inyo Range, eastern California: Contributions to Mineralogy and Petrology, v. 128, p. 30–44.

Fox, L.K., and Miller, D.M., 1990, Jurassic granitoids and related rocks of the southern Bristol Mountains and Colton Hills, Mojave Desert, California: Geological Society of America Memoir 174, p. 111–132.

Frost, T.P., and Mattinson, J.M., 1993, Age and tectonic implications of mid-Mesozoic calc-alkalic hornblende-rich mafic plutonic rocks of the eastern Sierra Nevada, California: Isochron-West, no. 59, p. 11–16.

Gay, T.E., and Wright, L.A., 1954, Geology of the Talc City area, Inyo County, *in* Jahns, R.H., ed., Geology of southern California: California Division of Mines Bulletin 170, Map Sheet 12.

Gerber, M.E., Miller, C.F., and Wooden, J.L., 1995, Plutonism at the interior margin of the Jurassic magmatic arc, Mojave Desert, California, *in* Miller, D.M., and Busby, C., eds., Jurassic magmatism and tectonics of the North America Cordillera: Geological Society of America Special Paper 299, p. 351–374.

Glazner, A.F., and O'Neil, J., 1989, Crustal structure of the Mojave Desert,

California: Inferences from Sr and O isotope studies of Miocene volcanic rocks: Journal of Geophysical Research, v. 94, p. 7861–7870.

Glazner, A.F., Bartley, J.M., and Carl, B.S., 1999, Oblique opening and non-coaxial emplacement of the Jurassic Independence dike swarm: Journal of Structural Geology, v. 21, p. 1275–1283.

Glazner, A.F., Bartley, J.M., and Walker, J.D., 1989, Magnitude and significance of Miocene crustal extension in the central Mojave Desert, California: Geology, v. 17, p. 50–54.

Glazner, A.F., Walker, J.D., Bartley, J.M., Fletcher, J.M., Martin, M.W., Schermer, E.R., Boettcher, S.S., Miller, J.S., Fillmore, R.P., and Linn, J.K., 1994, Reconstruction of the Mojave block (guidebook and roadlog), *in* McGill, S.F., and Ross, T.M., eds., Geological investigations of an active margin: Geological Society of America Cordilleran Section Guidebook, Redlands, California, San Bernardino County Museum Association, p. 3–30.

Goldfarb, R.J., Miller, D.M., Simpson, R.W., Hoover, D.B., Moyle, P.R., Olson, J.E., and Gaps, R.S., 1988, Mineral resources of the Providence Mountains Wilderness study area, San Bernardino County, California: U.S. Geological Survey Bulletin 1712-D, p. 1–70.

Grose, L.T., 1959, Structure and petrology of the northeast part of the Soda Mountains, San Bernardino County, California: Geological Society of America Bulletin, v. 70, p. 1509–1547.

Hall, W.E., and MacKevett, E.M., 1958, Economic geology of the Darwin quadrangle, Inyo County, California: California Division of Mines Special Report 51, 73 p.

Hanson, R.B., Saleeby, J.B., and Fates, D.G., 1987, Age and tectonic setting of Mesozoic metavolcanic and metasedimentary rocks, northern White Mountains, California: Geology, v. 15, p. 1074–1078.

Harper, G.D., Saleeby, J.S., and Heizler, M., 1994, Formation and emplacement of the Josephine ophiolite and the Nevadan Orogeny in the Klamath Mountains, California-Oregon: U/Pb zircon and $^{40}Ar/^{39}Ar$ geochronology: Journal of Geophysical Research, v. 99, p. 4293–4321.

Hope, R.A., 1966, Geology and structural setting of the Eastern Transverse Ranges, Southern California [Ph.D. thesis]: Los Angeles, University of California, 201 p.

Hopson, C.A., 1988, Independence dike swarm: Origin and tectonic significance [abs.]: Eos (Transactions, American Geophysical Union), v. 69, p. 1479.

Hopson, R.F., Hillhouse, J.W., and Howard, K.A., 2000, Rotation of the Late Jurassic Independence dike swarm, southern California: Geological Society of America Abstracts with Programs, v. 32, no. 7, p. A173.

Howard, K.A., Kilburn, J.E., Simpson, R.W., Fitzgibbon, T.T., Detra, D.D., Raines, G.L., and Sabine, C., 1987, Mineral resources of the Bristol/Granite Mountains wilderness study area, San Bernardino County, California: U.S. Geological Survey Bulletin 1712-C.

Huber, N.K., and Rinehart, C.D., 1965, Geologic map of the Devils Postpile quadrangle, Sierra Nevada, California: U.S. Geological Survey Geologic Quadrangle Map GQ-437, scale 1:62 500.

James, E.W., 1989, Southern extension of the Independence dike swarm of eastern California: Geology, v. 17, p. 587–590.

Karish, C.R., Miller, E.R., and Sutter, J.F., 1987, Mesozoic tectonic and magmatic history of the central Mojave Desert: Arizona Geological Digest, v. 18, p. 15–32.

Kelley, K.P., and Engebretson, D.C., 1994, Updated relative motions and terrane trajectories for North America and oceanic plates: Cretaceous to present: Geological Society of America Abstracts with Programs, v. 26, no. 7, p. 459.

Kistler, R.W., 1990, Two different lithosphere types in the Sierra Nevada, California, *in* Anderson, J.L., ed., The nature and origin of Cordilleran magmatism: Geological Society of America Memoir 174, p. 271–281.

Kistler, R.W., and Peterman, Z.E., 1973, Variations in Sr, Rb, K, Na, and initial $^{87}Sr/^{86}Sr$ in Mesozoic granitic rocks and intruded wall rocks in central California: Geological Society of America Bulletin, v. 84, p. 3489–3512.

Krauskopf, K.B., 1971, Geologic map of the Mount Barcroft quadrangle, California-Nevada: U.S. Geological Survey Map GQ-960, scale 1:62 500.

Lahren, M.M., 1989, Tectonic studies of the Sierra Nevada: Structure and stratigraphy of miogeoclinal rocks in Snow Lake pendant, Yosemite-Emigrant Wilderness, and TIMS analysis of the northern Sierra terrane [Ph.D. thesis]: University of Nevada, Reno, 326 p.

Lahren, M.M., Schweickert, R.A., Mattinson, J.M., and Walker, J.D., 1990, Evidence of uppermost Proterozoic to Lower Cambrian miogeoclinal rocks and the Mojave-Snow Lake fault: Snow Lake pendant, central Sierra Nevada, California: Tectonics, v. 9, p. 1585–1608.

Lockwood, J.P., and Lydon, P.A., 1975, Geologic map of the Mt. Abbot Quadrangle, central Sierra Nevada, California: U.S. Geological Survey Geologic Quadrangle Map GQ-1155, scale 1:62 500.

Longiaru, S.J., 1987, Tectonic evolution of the Oak Creek volcanic roof pendant, eastern California [Ph.D. thesis]: University of California, Los Angeles, 205 p.

Luyendyk, B.P., Kamerling, M.J., Terres, R.R., and Hornafius, J.S., 1985, Simple shear of southern California during Neogene time suggested by paleomagnetic declinations: Journal of Geophysical Research, v. 90, p. 12 454–12 466.

Martin, M.W., 1992, Stratigraphic and structural evolution of the Shadow Mountains, western Mojave Desert, California: Implications for the tectonic development of the central and western Mojave Desert [Ph.D. thesis]: University of Kansas, Lawrence, 196 p.

Martin, M.W., and Walker, J.D., 1991, Upper-Precambrian-Paleozoic paleogeographic reconstruction of the Mojave Desert, California, *in* Cooper, J.D., and Stevens, C.H., eds., Paleozoic paleogeography of the western United States—II: Pacific Section, SEPM (Society for Sedimentary Geology), v. 67, p. 167–192.

Martin, M.W., and Walker, J.D., 1992, Extending the western North American Proterozoic and Paleozoic continental crust through the Mojave Desert: Geology, v. 20, p. 753–756.

Martin, M.W., Glazner, A.F., Walker, J.D., and Schermer, E.R., 1993, Evidence for right-lateral transfer faulting accommodating en echelon Miocene extension, Mojave Desert, California: Geology, v. 21, p. 355–358.

May, S.R., and Butler, R.F., 1989, North American Jurassic apparent polar wander: Implications for plate motion, paleogeography, and Cordilleran tectonics: Journal of Geophysical Research, v. 91, p. 11 519–11 544.

May, S.R., Beck, M.E., Jr., and Butler, R.F., 1986, North American apparent polar wander, plate motion, and left-oblique convergence: Late Jurassic-Early Cretaceous orogenic consequences: Tectonics, v. 8, p. 443–451.

McAllister, J.F., 1956, Geology of the Ubehebe Peak quadrangle, California: U.S. Geological Survey Geologic Quadrangle Map GQ-95, scale 1:62 500.

McKee, E.H., and Conrad, J.E., 1996, A tale of 10 plutons, revisited: Age of granitic rocks in the White Mountains, California and Nevada: Geological Society of America Bulletin, v. 108, p. 1515–1527.

McKee, E.H., and Nelson, C.A., 1967, Geologic map of the Soldier Pass quadrangle, California and Nevada: U.S. Geological Survey Geologic Quadrangle Map GQ-654, scale 1:62 500.

McManus, S.G., and Clemens-Knott, D., 1997, Geochemical and oxygen isotope constraints on the petrogenesis of the Independence dike swarm, San Bernardino Co., California, *in* Girty, G.H., et al., eds., Geology of the western Cordillera: Perspectives from undergraduate research: Pacific Section, SEPM (Society for Sedimentary Geology), v. 82, p. 91–102.

Merriam, C.W., 1963, Geology of the Cerro Gordo mining district, Inyo County, California: U.S. Geological Survey Professional Paper 408, 83 p.

Miller, E.L., and Sutter, J.F., 1982, Structural geology and ^{40}Ar-^{39}Ar geochronology of the Goldstone-Lane Mountain area, Mojave Desert, California: Geological Society of America Bulletin, v. 93, p. 1191–1207.

Miller, J.S., and Glazner, A.F., 1995, Jurassic plutonism and crustal evolution in the central Mojave Desert, California: Contributions to Mineralogy and Petrology, v. 118, p. 379–395.

Miller, J.S., Glazner, A.F., Farmer, G.L., Suayah, I.B., and Keith, L.B., 2000, Middle Tertiary magmatism across the Mojave Desert and southeastern

California: A Sr, Nd, and Pb isotopic study of mantle domains and crustal structure: Geological Society of America Bulletin, v. 112, p. 1264–1279.

Moore, J.G., 1963, Geology of the Mount Pinchot quadrangle, southern Sierra Nevada, California: U.S. Geological Survey Bulletin 1138, 152 p.

Moore, J.G., 1981, Geologic map of the Mount Whitney quadrangle, Inyo and Tulare Counties, California: U.S. Geological Survey Geologic Quadrangle Map GQ-1545, scale 1:62 500.

Moore, J.G., and Hopson, C.A., 1961, The Independence dike swarm in eastern California: American Journal of Science, v. 259, p. 241–259.

Moore, J.G., and Sisson, T.W., 1985, Geologic map of the Kern Peak quadrangle, Tulare County, California: U.S. Geological Survey Geologic Quadrangle Map GQ-1584, scale 1:62 500.

Moore, J.G., and Sisson, T.W., 1987, Geologic map of the Triple Divide Peak quadrangle, Tulare County, California: U.S. Geological Survey Geologic Quadrangle Map GQ-1636, scale 1:62 500.

Nelson, C.A., 1966a, Geologic map of the Blanco Mountain quadrangle, Inyo and Mono Counties, California: U.S. Geological Survey Geologic Quadrangle Map GQ-529, scale 1:62 500.

Nelson, C.A., 1966b, Geologic map of the Waucoba Mountain quadrangle, Inyo County, California: U.S. Geological Survey Geologic Quadrangle Map GQ-528, scale 1:62 500.

Nelson, C.A., 1971, Geologic map of the Waucoba Spring quadrangle, Inyo County, California: U.S. Geological Survey Geologic Quadrangle Map GQ-921, scale 1:62 500.

Page, B.M., and Engebretson, D.C., 1984, Correlation between the geologic record and computed plate motions for central California: Tectonics, v. 3, p. 133–155.

Powell, R.E., 1981, Geology of the crystalline basement complex, Eastern Transverse ranges, southern California: Constraints on regional tectonic interpretation [Ph.D. thesis]: California Institute of Technology, Pasadena, 205 p.

Powell, R.E., Whittington, C.L., Grauch, V.J.S., and McColly, R.A., 1984, Mineral resources potential of the Eagle Mountains wilderness study area (CDCA-334), Riverside County, California: U.S. Geological Survey Open File Report 84–631, 25 p.

Renne, P.R., and Turrin, B.D., 1987, Constraints on timing of deformation in the Benton range, southeastern California, and implications to Nevadan orogenesis: Geology, v. 15, p. 1031–1034.

Renne, P.R., Mudd, S., Gatdula, J., and Carmichael, I., 1999, Age of the Benton Range dikes revisited: Geological Society of America Abstracts with Programs, v. 31, no. 6, p. 87.

Richardson, L., 1972, Left-lateral, east-trending faults in the Alabama Hills: California Geology, v. 25, p. 62–64.

Rinehart, C.D., and Ross, D.C., 1957, Geology of the Casa Diablo Mountain quadrangle, California: U.S. Geological Survey Geologic Quadrangle Map GQ-99.

Rinehart, C.D., and Ross, D.C., 1964, Geology and mineral deposits of the Mount Morrison quadrangle, Sierra Nevada, California: U.S. Geological Survey Professional Paper 385, 106 p.

Ron, H., and Nur, A., 1996, Vertical axis rotation in the Mojave: Evidence from the Independence dike swarm: Geology, v. 24, p. 973–976.

Ross, D.C., 1965, Geology of the Independence quadrangle, Inyo County, California: U.S. Geological Survey Bulletin 1181-O, 64 p.

Ross, T.M., Luyendyk, B.P., and Haston, R.B., 1989, Paleomagnetic evidence for Neogene clockwise rotations in the central Mojave Desert, California: Geology, v. 17, p. 470–473.

Saleeby, J.B., Geary, E.E., Paterson, S.R., and Tobisch, O.T., 1989, Isotopic systematics of Pb/U (zircon) and ^{40}Ar/^{39}Ar (biotite-hornblende) from rocks of the central Foothills terrane, Sierra Nevada, California: Geological Society of America Bulletin, v. 101, p. 1481–1492.

Schermer, E.R., 1993, Mesozoic structural evolution of the west-central Mojave Desert, *in* Dunne, G., and McDougall, K.A., eds., Mesozoic paleogeography of the western United States II: Pacific Section, SEPM (Society for Sedimentary Geology), p. 307–322.

Schermer, E.R., and Busby, C.J., 1994, Jurassic magmatism in the central Mojave Desert: Implications for arc paleogeography and preservation of continental volcanic sequences: Geological Society of America Bulletin, v. 106, p. 767–790.

Schermer, E.R., Luyendyk, B.P., and Cisowski, S., 1996, Late Cenozoic structure and tectonics of the northern Mojave Desert: Tectonics, v. 15, p. 905–932.

Schermer, E.R., Stephens, K.A., Walker, J.D., Busby, C.J., and Mattinson, J.M., 1994, Jurassic and Cretaceous magmatism and tectonism in the Mojave Desert, California: Geological Society of America Abstracts with Programs, v. 26, no. 2, p. 89.

Schweickert, R.A., and Cowan, D.S., 1975, Early Mesozoic tectonic evolution of the western Sierra Nevada, California: Geological Society of America Bulletin, v. 86, p. 1329–1336.

Schweickert, R.A., and Lahren, M.M., 1990, Speculative reconstruction of the Mojave-Snow Lake fault: Implications for Paleozoic and Mesozoic orogenesis in the western United States: Tectonics, v. 9, p. 1609–1629.

Sisson, T.W., Grove, T.L., and Coleman, D.S., 1996, Hornblende gabbro sill complex at Onion Valley, California, and a mixing origin for the Sierra Nevada batholith: Contributions to Mineralogy and Petrology, v. 126, p. 81–108.

Smith, G.I., 1962, Large left-lateral displacement on Garlock fault, California, as measured from offset dike swarm: American Association of Petroleum Geologists Bulletin, v. 46, p. 85–104.

Stephens, K.A., 1994, Mesozoic tectonic evolution of the Tiefort Mountains, NE Mojave Desert, California [M.S. thesis]: Bellingham, Washington, Western Washington University, 130 p.

Stephens, K.A., Schermer, E.R., and Walker, J.D., 1993, Mesozoic intra-arc tectonics in the northeast Mojave Desert, California: Geological Society of America Abstracts with Programs, v. 25, no. 5, p. 150.

Stevens, C.H., and Greene, D.C., 1999, Stratigraphy, depositional history, and tectonic evolution of Paleozoic continental-margin rocks in roof pendants of the eastern Sierra Nevada, California: Geological Society of America Bulletin, v. 111, p. 919–933.

Stevens, C.H., Stone, P., Dunne, G.C., Greene, D.C., Walker, J.D., and Swanson, B.J., 1997, Paleozoic and Mesozoic evolution of east-central California: International Geology Review, v. 39, p. 788–829.

Stinson, M.C., 1977, Geology of the Keeler 15′ quadrangle, Inyo County, California: California Division of Mines and Geology Map Sheet 38.

Stone, P., Dunne, G.C., Stevens, C.H., and Gulliver, R.M., 1989, Geologic map of Paleozoic and Mesozoic rocks in parts of the Darwin and adjacent quadrangles, Inyo County, California: U.S. Geological Survey Miscellaneous Investigations Series Map I-1932, scale 1:62 500.

Tobisch, O.T., Paterson, S.R., Longiaru, S., and Bhattacharya, T., 1987, Extent of the Nevadan Orogeny, central Sierra Nevada, California: Geology, v. 15, p. 132–135.

Tosdal, R.M., Haxel, G.B., and Wright, J.E., 1989, Jurassic geology of the Sonoran Desert region, southern Arizona, southeastern California, and northernmost Sonora: Construction of a continental-margin magmatic arc, *in* Jenny, J.P., and Reynolds, S.J., eds., Geologic evolution of Arizona: Tucson, Arizona Geological Digest, v. 17, p. 397–434.

Wadsworth, W.B., Horacio, F., and Rhodes, D.D., 1995, Structural and stratigraphic development of the Middle Jurassic magmatic arc in the Cowhole Mountains, central-eastern Mojave Desert, *in* Miller, D.M., and Busby, C., eds., Jurassic magmatism and tectonics of the North America Cordillera: Geological Society of America Special Paper 299, p. 327–349.

Walker, J.D., Bartley, J.M., and Glazner, A.F., 1990a, Large-magnitude extension in the central Mojave Desert: Implications for Paleozoic to Tertiary paleogeography and tectonics: Journal of Geophysical Research, v. 95, p. 557–569.

Walker, J.D., Martin, M.W., Bartley, J.M., and Coleman, D.S., 1990b, Timing and kinematics of deformation in the Cronese Hills, California, and implications for Mesozoic structure of the south-western Cordillera: Geology, v. 18, p. 554–557.

Walker, J.D., Martin, M.W., Stern, S.M., and Linn, J.K., 1994, Structural development of the southern Slate range, east-central California: Geological Society of America Abstracts with Programs, v. 26, no. 2, p. 101.

Whitmarsh, R.S., 1996, A geologic map of the Coso Range, with supplemental U-Pb geochronology and Ar-Ar thermochronology: Geological Society of America Abstracts with Programs, v. 28, no. 5, p. 124.

Whitmarsh, R., and Walker, J.D., 1997, Geological maps of the Coso Range, California: Geological Maps on the Web, University of Kansas, Lawrence, URL: http://geomaps.geo.ukans.edu/.

Whitmarsh, R.S., Walker, J.D., and Monastero, F.C., 1996, Mesozoic and Cenozoic structural framework of the Coso Range and adjacent areas of eastern California: Geological Society of America Abstracts with Programs, v. 28, no. 5, p. 124.

Wolf, M.B., and Saleeby, J.B., 1995, Late Jurassic dike swarms in the southwestern Sierra Nevada foothills terrane, California: Implications for the Nevadan Orogeny and North American plate motion, *in* Miller, D.M., and Busby, C., eds., Jurassic magmatism and tectonics of the North American Cordillera: Geological Society of America Special Paper 299, p. 203–228.

Wright, J.E., and Fahan, M.R., 1988, An expanded view of Jurassic orogenesis in the western United States Cordillera: Middle Jurassic (pre-Nevadan) regional metamorphism and thrust faulting within an active arc environment, Klamath Mountains, California: Geological Society of America Bulletin, v. 100, p. 859–876.

MANUSCRIPT ACCEPTED BY THE SOCIETY MAY 9, 2001

Geological Society of America
Memoir 195
2002

Cretaceous arc tectonism in the Mojave block: Profound crustal modification that controlled subsequent tectonic regimes

John M. Fletcher*
CICESE (Centro de Investigación Científica y de Educación Superior de Ensenada),
Km107 Carratera Tijuana-Ensenada, Baja California, México, CP 22860
Jonathan S. Miller*
Department of Geology, San Jose State University, San Jose, California 95192-0102, USA
Mark W. Martin*
Massachusetts Institute of Technology, Department of Earth, Atmospheric, and Planetary
Sciences Building 54-1124, Cambridge, Massachusetts 02139-4307, USA
Stefan S. Boettcher*
Exxon Production Research Company, P.O. Box 2189, Houston, Texas 77027, USA
Allen F. Glazner*
University of North Carolina, Department of Geology, CB3315 Mitchell Hall,
Chapel Hill, North Carolina 27599-3315, USA
John M. Bartley*
University of Utah, Department of Geology and Geophysics, 717WBB,
Salt Lake City, Utah 84112-1183, USA

ABSTRACT

The products of Late Cretaceous intra-arc tectonism in the Mojave block (the north-central part of the greater Mojave Desert region) are recorded in a belt that extends 75 km southeastward from the central part of the Garlock fault. Deformation in the belt is characterized by three generations of folding that occurred during prograde metamorphism to near the transition from the amphibolite facies to the granulite facies. In the vicinity of Fremont Peak and The Buttes, extensive partial melting and migmatization occurred synchronously with formation of subvertical gneissic foliation (S1) and mesoscopic crenulation cleavage (S2). Mesoscopic fabrics are folded into a pair of range-scale folds (F3) that have a similar fold geometry. The macroscopic F3 folds plunge steeply southeast, have near-vertical axial surfaces that strike east, and likely formed in response to regional north-south contraction. No mesoscopic fabrics were found to be unequivocally associated with the F3 folds that are inferred to have formed by penetrative flow of a rheologically homogeneous rock mass during peak metamorphic conditions.

At Fremont Peak, a suite of intermediate to felsic plutons was emplaced synchronously with Cretaceous deformation. A large granodiorite pluton contains the S1

---

*E-mails: Fletcher, jfletche@cicese.mx; Miller, jsmiller@email.sjsu.edu;
Martin, mwmartin@shell.com; Boettcher, ssboett@epr.exxon.com; Glazner,
afg@unc.edu; Bartley, jbartley@bingham.mines.utah.edu

Fletcher, J.M., Miller, J.S., Martin, M.W., Boettcher, S.S., Glazner, A.F., and Bartley, J.M., 2002, Cretaceous arc tectonism in the Mojave block: Profound crustal modification that controlled subsequent tectonic regimes, in Glazner, A.F., Walker, J.D., and Bartley, J.M., eds., Geologic Evolution of the Mojave Desert and Southwestern Basin and Range: Boulder, Colorado, Geological Society of America Memoir 195, p. 131–149.

foliation and has a crystallization U-Pb age of 91.5 Ma. A leucogranite intrusion that has a U-Pb monazite age of 84–86 Ma is strongly transposed into parallelism with the S1 foliation, but is largely unfoliated, suggesting that it crystallized post-tectonically and was present as a melt during all three generations of deformation. The duration between emplacement and crystallization of the leucogranite is not well constrained, but may be more than 6.5 m.y. In The Buttes, U-Pb monazite dates from leucosome indicate that syntectonic migmatite formation occurred at 93–95 Ma.

The belt of high-grade deformation and plutonism in the Mojave block correlates with the middle to eastern part of the Cretaceous batholith in the Sierra Nevada, consistent with 65–85 km of sinistral displacement across the Garlock fault. A Miocene detachment fault of the Central Mojave extensional belt (which includes the Central Mojave metamorphic core complex) does not cut the belt of Cretaceous tectonism, but instead merges into parallelism with it over a strike length of 40 km. The distribution of Miocene mylonites in the footwall of the detachment is restricted to rocks that record the Cretaceous arc tectonism, which suggests that crustal weaknesses generated in the Cretaceous may have controlled the magnitude and character of subsequent Miocene extension.

INTRODUCTION

A Cretaceous batholith is found along nearly the entire length of western North America making it the dominant tectonic element of the western Cordillera. It is arguable that no other Phanerozoic tectonic event in North America generated as much new continental crust as the emplacement of the Cretaceous batholith. For example, Barton et al. (1988) showed that over 50% of the exposed rocks in eastern California are Mesozoic granitic rocks and Coleman and Glazner (1997) demonstrated that, at least locally, these intrusive rocks are largely juvenile additions from the mantle. Additionally, the quartzo-feldspathic batholith significantly changed the thermal and mechanical structure of the crust and had a profound effect on later tectonic events as we show below.

In California and Baja California, the Cretaceous batholith is exposed principally in two elevated granitic massifs of the Sierra Nevada and Peninsular Ranges (Fig. 1). Most of our knowledge of variations of the architecture, geochemistry, and geochronology of the batholith come from detailed studies in these ranges where it is preserved as relatively coherent crustal blocks. However, at the latitudes of the Mojave Desert, the batholith is transected and strongly dismembered by faults of the Pacific-North America plate boundary (Fig. 1).

This study documents the existence a belt of high-grade metamorphism, tectonism and plutonism in the Mojave block, which is geographically in the north-central part of the greater Mojave Desert region. We correlate this belt with highly deformed gneissic rocks found throughout the core of the magmatic arc of the Sierra Nevada. The correlation is made on the basis of structural style, metamorphic grade, and timing of deformation. We show that arc-related tectonism produced a characteristic suite of gniessic foliations and mesoscopic cleavages related to multiple generations of range-scale folds with sub-

vertical axial planes. Syntectonic metamorphism reached the uppermost amphibolite to granulite facies, and deformation was accompanied by extensive migmitization of prebatholithic rocks. Our geochronologic data indicate that the main pulses of plutonism and deformation occurred between ca. 105 Ma and 85 Ma, and we infer that elevated temperatures persisted through most of the Cretaceous. Our data provide an important test for the proposed existence of a major extensional phase immediately following the emplacement of the magmatic arc and indicate that superimposed Miocene crustal extension was strongly affected by crustal weaknesses generated in the Cretaceous.

MOJAVE BLOCK

The Mojave block lies within the zone of modern deformation produced by shearing between the Pacific and North American plates. The block is bounded to the north by the sinistral Garlock fault and to the south by the dextral San Andreas fault and, consequently is being extruded to the east. The block is also internally cut by northwest-striking dextral faults spaced 10–30 km apart that typically record less than 10 km of finite offset (e.g., Garfunkel, 1974; Bartley et al., 1990; Bartley et al., 1992). Prior to the onset of wrench faulting, crustal extension dominated tectonism in the Mojave block (Glazner et al., 1989; Fletcher et al., 1995). A northeast-directed detachment fault system developed between 23 and 18 Ma (Walker et al., 1995). This system extends nearly 50 km along strike and constitutes a classic cordilleran metamorphic core complex with extensive footwall mylonitization and syntectonic plutonism (Fletcher et al., 1995, Fig. 2). Both of these major Cenozoic tectonic regimes are superimposed on heterogeneous continental crust that was produced during a long period of plate-margin tectonics including: (1) Proterozoic rifting followed by passive margin

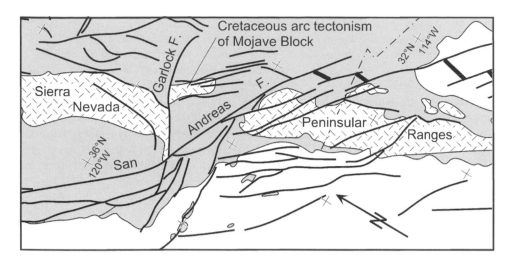

Figure 1. Tectonic map showing distribution of the Cretaceous batholith exposures (dash pattern) and major faults of the Pacific-North America plate boundary. The products of Cretaceous arc tectonism in the Mojave block (the north-central part of the greater Mojave region) are found between the Garlock and San Andreas faults.

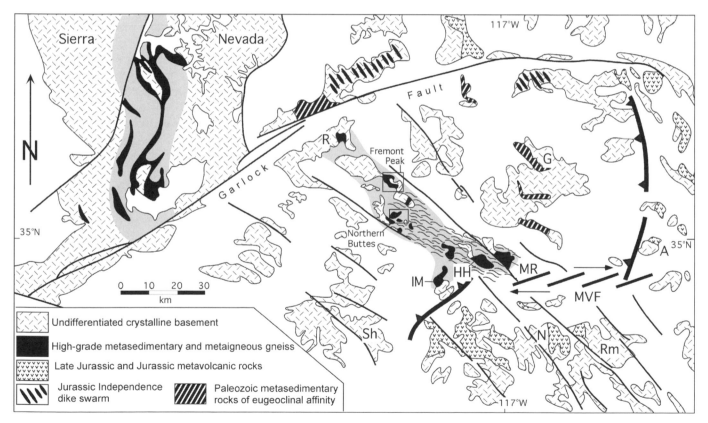

Figure 2. Schematic geologic map of the Mojave block showing the distribution of pre-Tertiary crystalline basement. Belts of Cretaceous high-grade metamorphism and tectonism on either side of the Garlock fault are shown in gray. The Fremont Peak and northern part of The Buttes study areas are outlined with rectangles. Wavy line pattern denotes the Central Mojave metamorphic core complex, which overlaps with belt of Cretaceous tectonism. Jurassic thrust belt denoted by the heavy barbed line is cut by the central Mojave extensional belt (after Martin and Walker, 1991; Martin et al., 1993). Mojave Valley fault (MVF) is a dextral transfer zone proposed by Martin et al. (1993) that links Miocene extension in the Mojave block with that in the Colorado River trough. Geographic features abbreviated as follows: A—Alvord Mountain, G—Goldstone, IM—Iron Mountain, HH—Hinkley Hills, MR—Mitchel Range, N—Newberry Mountains, R—Rand Mountains, RM—Rodman Mountains, Sh—Shadow Mountains.

sedimentation, (2) Permian tectonism that resulted in west-vergent contraction and/or sinistral truncation of the continental margin by north-striking faults, and (3) several pulses of magmatic arc tectonism developed throughout the Mesozoic.

The abundance of Mesozoic granitic rocks throughout the Mojave block suggests that arc tectonism was one of the dominant processes of the formation of modern continental crust in the region. The onset of arc magmatism in the Mojave block is represented by plutons that range in age from 245–220 Ma (Barth et al., 1990; Miller et al., 1995). However, deformation associated with the emplacement of these early plutons cannot be demonstrated (Glazner et al., 1994). The next major pulse of arc activity occurred in the Middle to Late Jurassic (179–148 Ma) and was marked by eruption of the Sidewinder volcanic series, emplacement of hornblende gabbro and peraluminous granite plutons, and emplacement of the Independence dike swarm (Fig. 2). Schermer et al. (this volume) suggested that the Sidewinder volcanic series was erupted between 179 and 151 Ma in an extensional back-arc setting. However, some of the volcanic and associated sedimentary rocks were incorporated into a regional contractional belt and metamorphosed at greenschist facies conditions by 155 Ma (Boettcher and Walker, 1993; Walker et al., this volume, Chapter 1; Martin et. al., this volume). This Jurassic thrust belt can be traced from the Garlock fault for 75 km due south where it is cut and displaced 60–70 km to the west by a dextral accommodation zone related to Miocene detachment faulting (Martin et al., 1993, Fig. 2).

Although Cretaceous arc magmatism is widespread and voluminous throughout the Cordillera, its disposition in the Mojave block has only recently been recognized (Miller et al., 1996). In the Fremont Peak and northern part of The Buttes areas, we have discovered a metamorphic and plutonic complex that likely represents the lower- to middle-crustal roots of the Cretaceous magmatic arc (Fig. 2). We infer that this tectonism can be correlated as a belt that extends from the Rand Mountains, south of the Garlock fault, to at least as far south as Iron Mountain (Fig. 2). Unlike the Jurassic thrust belt, the belt of Cretaceous arc tectonism is not displaced by the belt of Miocene extension. Instead the belt of Cretaceous tectonism roughly coincides with the core-complex segment of the Miocene extensional belt. The significance of this tectonic superposition and details of the correlations are discussed below.

LITHOLOGY OF ARC PLUTONISM

Fremont Peak

Pre-Cretaceous igneous and metamorphic rocks. The Fremont Peak region is dominated by a diverse suite of plutonic and metaplutonic units that represent all of the major pulses of Permian to Cretaceous arc magmatism in the Mojave block. Preintrusive metasedimentary rocks are extremely rare; only two thin screens (10 m thick) of calareous quartzite elongated parallel to a gneissic foliation have been observed. One of the most extensive rock units in the Fremont Peak area is a coarse-grained orthogneiss derived from hornblende-biotite diorite (Fig. 3). This orthogneiss is commonly strongly foliated and cut by several deformational fabrics and we infer that it is one of the oldest metaplutonic phases. Miller et al., (1995) found the zircon systematics of the orthogneiss to be complicated, but inferred that its protolith is likely to be part of the Permian-Triassic intrusive suite that made up the first pulse of arc magmatism in the Mojave block. The metadiorite gneiss may be part of a regionally extensive intrusive suite and is tentatively correlated with similar mafic igneous complexes in The Buttes, Hinkley Hills and Mitchel Range (e.g., Fletcher et al., 1995, Fig. 2).

A distinctive pegmatitic to coarse-grained hornblende gabbro is found throughout the Fremont Peak region. The gabbro occurs as small irregular intrusions that range from 5 to 500 meters in width and typically contains 70%–100% hornblende that forms subhedral oikocrysts up to 3 cm in diameter. The gabbro is generally unfoliated but locally shows a strong layering. The lack of high-grade deformational fabrics in this unit is likely related to the rheologic competency of the gabbro relative to other rock units and is not considered to be indicative of the timing of emplacement relative to deformation. This unit resembles well-dated Upper Jurassic gabbros and diorites found in areas near Fremont Peak and throughout the Mojave block, including the Shadow Mountains, Iron Mountain, Goldstone, and Alvord Mountain (Fig. 2) (Boettcher and Walker, 1993; Martin and Walker, 1995, Miller and Walker, this volume).

Cretaceous migmatites. In this region, strongly banded migmatites are commonly associated with the dioritic orthogneiss. Leucosome horizons are compositionally heterogeneous and range from biotite- and hornblende-bearing granitic rocks to aplitic granite devoid of ferromagnesian minerals. Melanosome horizons are composed predominantly of biotite + plagioclase ± K feldspar ± quartz. Scarcity of aluminous phases such as aluminosilicate polymorph, garnet, and white mica in either the leucosome or melanosome assemblages indicates that the migmatites were derived from a metaluminous protolith. The most likely candidate is the older dioritic orthogneiss, which is observed as rafts within the migmatite complex. Leucosome-melanosome boundaries vary from diffuse to sharp, and leucosome commonly is found as thin (1–2 cm) layers that can be traced to the limits of outcrops. However, it also occurs as discrete lozenge-shaped bodies 2–5 cm in length (Fig. 4A). The distribution of leucosome layers appears to have been strongly controlled by preexisting planar anisotropies. Some layers make abrupt (90°) changes in course at the intersections of crosscutting sets of foliations (Fig. 4, B and C). Leucosome horizons are generally not deformed, and thus we interpret the leucosomes to have crystallized late in the deformational history as did other larger Cretaceous plutons in the area. These textural relationships, along with the compositional diversity of the leucosomes, suggest that the migmatites formed by hybrid

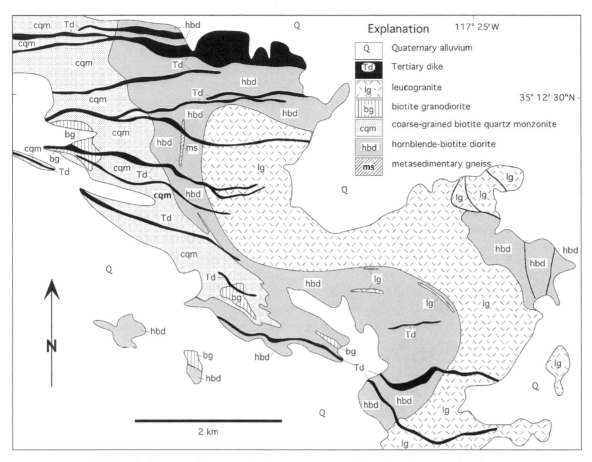

Figure 3. Simplified geologic map of Fremont Peak showing distribution of main rock units. Geologic compilation based on mapping at a scale of 1:9000.

processes of in situ partial melting, of a meta-igneous protolith, and by injection of externally derived magma.

Cretaceous plutonic suite. A diverse suite of Cretaceous plutons intrudes the older meta-igneous rocks. We interpret the Cretaceous plutons to have been emplaced during a major pulse of tectonism that produced three generations of deformational fabrics and macroscopic folds. In general, the synkinematic suite of plutons is less strongly foliated and shows none of the banding or melt segregation that is common in the older orthogneiss and migmatite. The Cretaceous plutonic suite at Fremont Peak comprises three main intrusive bodies: (1) biotite granodiorite; (2) coarse-grained biotite quartz monzonite; and (3) garnet leucogranite. Pegmatite dikes, some with coarse muscovite and garnet, crop out locally and are related to the quartz monzonite and/or leucogranite.

The biotite granodiorite is the smallest volume unit within the Cretaceous suite. This unit is predominantly medium grained and equigranular with 1–3 mm flecks of biotite and minor hornblende. Potassium feldspar phenocrysts occur locally but are rare. The unit is present as relatively small masses or screens within the biotite quartz monzonite but also has extensively intruded the orthogneiss as discussed subsequently. In

the south-central part of the range (Fig. 3), the biotite granodiorite has extensively injected the older hornblende-biotite orthogneiss and locally forms a migmatitic injection gneiss. Rafts of orthogneiss paleosome in the injection migmatite, as well as more schlieren-like or nebulitic migmatite, are present in this area and indicate extensive igneous remobilization of the orthogneiss during emplacement of the biotite granodiorite. Small pockets (10–20 cm) and larger sheets (1–2 m thick) of leucocratic biotite granite with concordant hornblende and biotite selvages have foliations that are concordant with the foliation in the orthogneiss and may represent either small-scale in situ melting of the orthogneiss prior to or during injection by the younger granodiorite. The biotite granodiorite has a weak foliation defined mainly by biotite oriented subparallel to the main foliation (S1) in the older hornblende-biotite orthogneiss. Preliminary microstructural work suggests that this fabric developed with little apparent sub-solidus recrystallization. A second deformational fabric (S2) is also present in these units but is less well developed than in the older melanocratic orthogneiss that forms the host rock of the intrusion.

Conventional U-Pb geochronology was performed on seven zircon fractions from this sample; five were large unabraded

A

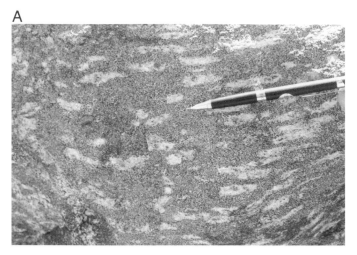

B

C

Figure 4. Outcrop photos of migmatite textural relationships. (A) Leucosome found as isolated pockets with diffuse boundaries. (B) Outcrop photo of granitoid dikelets. Ptygmatically folded layers lie parallel to S1 and straight layers lie parallel to S2. (C) Close-up of interaction between granitoid dikelets and deformational fabrics. Dikelets lie parallel to folded S1 layering, but abruptly change course at intersection with S2 cleavage. Dikelets lack internal deformational fabrics.

multigrain fractions, and two were abraded, single-grain fractions (Table 1; Fig. 5A). The two single crystal fractions, z1(1) and z2(1), are concordant at 246.6 Ma and 91.5 Ma, respectively. The remaining multigrain fractions (z1–z5) are variably discordant and have $^{207}Pb/^{206}Pb$ dates that range from 131 to 193 Ma. These discordant fractions and the z1(1) single grain fraction, are interpreted either to contain significant inheritance or to be xenocrystic. A linear regression (MSWD [mean square of weighted deviates] = 0.01) through the concordant z2(1) analysis and the analyses of the three analyses with the least amount of inheritance (z3–z5) yields a lower- and an upper-intercept of 91 ± 8 Ma and 181 ± 21 Ma, respectively (Fig. 5A). The lower intercept age is interpreted to represent the crystallization age of this sample; however, the error about this age, we believe is unrealistically high. We interpret the age of this intrusive phase to be best represented by the age of the concordant analysis, which is 91.5 ± 0.5 Ma.

In the south-central part of the range (Fig. 3), the biotite granodiorite extensively injects the older hornblende-biotite orthogneiss and locally forms a migmatitic injection gneiss. Rafts of orthogneiss paleosome in the injection migmatite, as well as more schlieren-like or nebulitic migmatite, are present in this area and indicate that the orthogneiss was extensively remobilized during emplacement of the biotite granodiorite. Small pockets (10–20 cm) and larger sheets (1–2 m thick) of leucocratic biotite granite with concordant hornblende and biotite selvages have foliations that are concordant with the foliation in the orthogneiss and may represent either small-scale in situ melting of the orthogneiss prior to or during injection by the younger granodiorite.

The second Cretaceous phase is a biotite quartz monzonite, which is considerably coarser-grained than the biotite granodiorite. The quartz monzonite is plagioclase prophyritic; biotite is typically present as phenocrysts up to several millimeters across and makes up 5%–10% of the modal abundance. Xenoliths of older hornblende-biotite orthogneiss occur near the orthogneiss contact. Near these xenoliths, the color index of the quartz monzonite increases, presumably because of mechanical disaggregation and perhaps partial assimilation of the orthogneiss. The quartz monzonite also contains xenoliths of the biotite granodiorite and dikes of the quartz monzonite cut the larger outcrops of the biotite granodiorite. The age of this unit is unknown but it must be younger than the biotite granodiorite, which is 91.5 ± 0.5 Ma (see earlier description of U-Pb dating). Like the biotite granodiorite, the quartz monzanite contains the S1 and S2 foliations, but both are more weakly developed in the pluton compared to the same fabrics its immediate host rock.

A leucocratic granite that crops out at the highest point in the range (Fremont Peak) forms the third principal unit of the Cretaceous plutonic suite. This granite typically contains only 2%–3% biotite, but locally it contains up to 5% muscovite and sparse (<1%) 1–5mm size garnet. The Fremont Peak leucogranite is part of the belt of Cretaceous garnet ± muscovite

TABLE 1. ANALYTICAL DATA FOR ZIRCON AND MONAZITE FROM FREMONT PEAK AND THE BUTTES

Sample fractions	Mass* (mg)	Concentration U (ppm)	Pb (ppm)	$\frac{205Pb†}{204Pb}$	$\frac{208Pb§}{206Pb}$	$\frac{206Pb\#}{238U}$	Err. (%)	$\frac{207Pb\#}{235U}$	Err. (%)	$\frac{207Pb\#}{206Pb}$	Err. (%)	Age (Ma) $\frac{206Pb}{238U}$	$\frac{207Pb}{235U}$	$\frac{207Pb}{206Pb}$	corr. coef.	$\frac{Th}{U}$
FP-926																
z1(1)	0.0210	705	27	2911	0.090	0.03899	0.11	0.2749	0.15	0.05113	0.09	246.6	246.6	246.6	0.77	n.a.
z2	0.4030	410	9	13987	0.096	0.02208	0.05	0.1520	0.07	0.04995	0.04	140.8	143.7	192.5	0.78	n.a.
z1	0.3140	485	10	12210	0.099	0.02072	0.05	0.1425	0.07	0.04986	0.04	132.2	135.2	188.3	0.76	n.a.
z4	2.3600	171	3	488	0.179	0.01933	0.51	0.1301	0.59	0.04881	0.26	123.4	124.2	138.5	0.90	n.a.
z5	1.3450	352	6	462	0.182	0.01864	0.51	0.1252	0.57	0.04872	0.23	119.1	119.8	134.1	0.92	n.a.
z3	1.4400	312	6	476	0.183	0.01827	0.84	0.1226	0.88	0.04865	0.25	116.7	117.4	130.9	0.96	n.a.
z2(1)	0.0166	512	9	304	0.078	0.01430	0.23	0.0943	0.45	0.04785	0.37	91.5	91.5	91.6	0.58	n.a.
FP-gg																
z2(1)	0.0046	396	14	415	0.092	0.03229	0.44	0.2243	0.60	0.05038	0.40	204.9	205.5	212.8	0.75	0.28
z1(1)	0.0049	976	22	1737	0.064	0.02327	0.26	0.1598	0.30	0.04982	0.15	148.3	150.5	186.6	0.87	0.20
z3(2)	0.0039	1432	26	492	0.119	0.01658	0.29	0.1098	0.53	0.04804	0.42	106.0	105.8	101.5	0.61	0.37
z2	0.0740	3088	43	21948	0.072	0.01453	0.05	0.0964	0.07	0.04810	0.04	93.0	93.4	104.4	0.75	0.20
z3	0.1410	3669	51	19806	0.074	0.01445	0.05	0.0958	0.07	0.04810	0.04	92.5	92.9	104.2	0.80	0.21
z4	0.1990	4895	68	14368	0.076	0.01428	0.06	0.0947	0.07	0.04810	0.04	91.4	91.9	104.3	0.81	0.21
m1	0.0510	3718	373	4044	7.280	0.01392	0.07	0.0886	0.09	0.04617	0.05	89.1	86.2	6.7	0.81	n.a.
m2	0.2220	3941	404	5209	7.506	0.01384	0.10	0.0880	0.11	0.04609	0.05	88.6	85.6	2.1	0.89	n.a.
m1(1)	0.0037	5944	558	2391	6.686	0.01397	0.10	0.0879	0.13	0.04563	0.09	89.4	85.5	−22.0	0.77	n.a.
m4(1)	0.0014	7903	715	806	6.431	0.01384	0.18	0.0874	0.24	0.04581	0.16	88.6	85.1	−12.5	0.75	n.a.
m3(1)	0.0027	5366	548	1858	7.463	0.01381	0.17	0.0872	0.50	0.04578	0.46	88.4	84.9	−13.9	0.44	n.a.
m2(1)	0.0018	4767	491	1083	7.498	0.01386	0.23	0.0871	0.33	0.04556	0.23	88.7	84.8	−25.8	0.72	n.a.
z1	0.2390	4980	63	14448	0.080	0.01300	0.15	0.0862	0.16	0.04810	0.06	83.3	84.0	104.3	0.93	0.20
m5(1)	0.0024	8482	787	986	6.708	0.01371	0.11	0.0860	0.18	0.04551	0.14	87.8	83.8	−28.2	0.64	n.a.
B-57																
z1(aa)	4.195	419	6	16596	0.083	0.01547	0.48	0.10525	0.48	0.04934	0.07	99.0	101.6	163.9	0.99	n.a.
z4	2.033	406	6	8376	0.080	0.01507	0.46	0.10126	0.47	0.04873	0.08	96.4	97.9	134.7	0.98	n.a.
m2	2.264	1610	198	1749	8.106	0.01530	3.79	0.10081	3.82	0.04782	0.50	97.9	97.5	90.6	0.99	n.a.
z3	1.258	502	7	9743	0.072	0.01469	0.46	0.09840	0.47	0.04857	0.09	94.0	95.3	127.1	0.98	n.a.
m1(1)	0.003	1352	140	458	6.907	0.01479	0.46	0.09789	0.76	0.04799	0.58	94.7	94.8	98.8	0.65	n.a.
m4	0.555	1820	200	4249	7.451	0.01483	0.91	0.09776	0.95	0.04782	0.26	94.9	94.7	90.3	0.96	n.a.
z2	1.085	539	7	32301	0.063	0.01445	0.46	0.09730	0.47	0.04884	0.08	92.5	94.3	140.3	0.99	n.a.
m3	1.054	1917	202	2879	7.198	0.01465	1.78	0.09603	1.78	0.04754	0.15	93.8	93.1	76.5	0.99	n.a.
m2(1)	0.006	788	109	402	9.862	0.01448	0.41	0.09592	0.50	0.04805	0.28	92.7	93.0	101.6	0.83	n.a.
m3(1)	0.003	3280	288	563	5.838	0.01447	0.21	0.09547	0.46	0.04783	0.39	92.6	92.6	91.1	0.53	n.a.
m1	4.043	1625	181	1554	7.808	0.01432	4.54	0.09446	4.55	0.04783	0.30	91.7	91.7	90.9	0.99	n.a.
m4(1)	0.003	2748	356	515	9.419	0.01413	0.24	0.09343	0.44	0.04796	0.35	90.5	90.7	97.2	0.60	n.a.

Note: Zircon and monazite analyses were performed at the University of Kansas (KU), University of North Carolina (UNC), and Massachusetts Institute of Technology (MIT). Zircon (z) and monazite (m) fractions designated with (1) are single crystal analyses and were performed at MIT. The remaining analyses are large, multigrain samples; samples FP-926 and FP-gg were analyzed at UNC, and B-57 was analyzed at KU. The zircons analyzed at UNC were not air abraded, whereas those analyzed at KU and MIT were air abraded; (aa) signifies a longer duration of air abrasion (see text for explanation). Mass-fractionation correction of 0.10% ± 0.5% to KU and UNC analyses and 15%/amu ± 0.04%/amu (atomic mass unit) was applied to single-collector Daly analyses at MIT. Total procedural blank for Pb ranged from 20 to 50 pg and <1.0 pg for U at KU and UNC and from 1 to 3pg (Pb) and <0.5pg (U) at MIT. Age calculations are based on the decay constants of Steiger and Jäger (1977). Common-Pb corrections were calculated by using the model of Stacey and Kramers (1975) and the interpreted age of the sample. Corr. coef. = correlation coefficient. Err. = error.
*Sample masses were determined on Cann balance and are known to within 10%. Samples at MIT were estimated by using a video monitor and are known to within 40%.
†Measured ratio corrected for spike and fractionation only.
§Radiogenic Pb.
#Corrected for fractionation, spike, blank, and initial common Pb.

granitic rocks that crop out sporadically in the western Mojave block (Miller et al., 1996). The leucogranite intrudes the orthogneiss but is also folded into a subvertical antiform-synform fold pair that defines the macroscopic structure of the Fremont Peak area (Fig. 3). Most of the pluton shows no tectonic fabric; however, in the immediate vicinity of its margin, the leucogranite locally displays a gneissic foliation parallel to that in the host rock. The western contact is concordant with the oldest (S1) gneissic foliation of the host rock, whereas the eastern contact is discordant, but the leucogranite here is also cut by the S1 gneissic foliation. Thus the pluton is strongly folded and contains some of the earliest deformational fabrics, but its final crystallization coincided with the end of Cretaceous tectonism in the Fremont Peak region.

Seven fractions each of monazite and zircon from this sample were dated by conventional U-Pb geochronology. The monazite analyses consist of two large multigrain fractions and five single crystal fractions (Table 1; Fig. 5B). The single-grain monazite fractions consisted of yellow, inclusion free, euhedral crystals, whereas the multigrain fractions comprised both clear

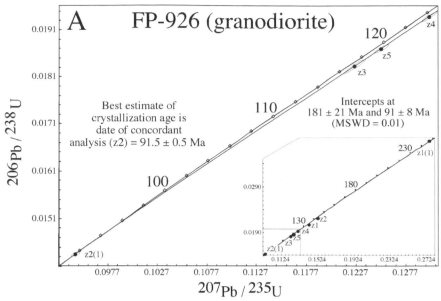

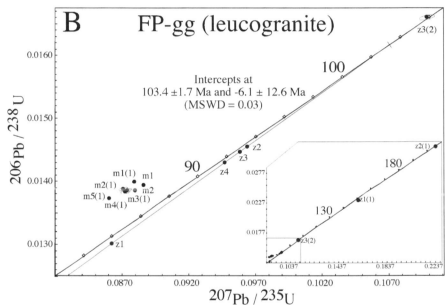

Figure 5. U-Pb concordia plots for Cretaceous plutonic rocks in the Mojave block. Analytical data for zircon and monazite given in Table 1. (A) Fremont Peak biotite granodiorite. (B) Fremont Peak garnet leucogranite. (C) Migmatitic leucosome of The Buttes.

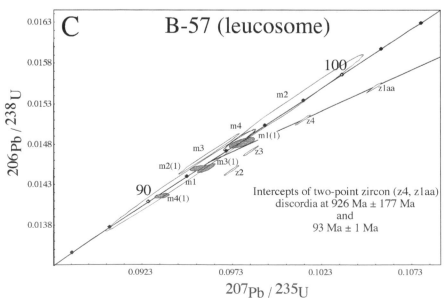

and turbid euhedral to anhedral crystals. The resulting analyses are all reversely discordant and have $^{207}Pb/^{235}U$ dates that range from 83.8 to 86.2 Ma. Reverse discordance is common for monazite (e.g., Parrish, 1990) and with such reversely discordant behavior the $^{207}Pb/^{235}U$ date provides the best estimate of the crystallization age for the reversely discordant monazites (Parrish, 1990).

Of the seven zircons fractions analyzed, four were large multigrain fractions that were not air abraded and contained euhedral and dominantly turbid zircons, one fraction contained two air abraded, euhedral, clear and inclusion free crystals, and two fractions consisted of air abraded, euhedral, clear and inclusion free single crystals. The two single-grain analyses are discordant and have $^{207}Pb/^{206}Pb$ dates of 187 and 213 Ma (Table 1; Fig. 5B) and are interpreted to be inherited. The fraction containing two crystals yielded a concordant analysis at 106 Ma. The remaining multigrain analyses are discordant and have identical $^{207}Pb/^{206}Pb$ dates; the weighted mean of these four $^{207}Pb/^{206}Pb$ dates is 104.3 ± 0.6 Ma. A linear regression through these four analyses yields an upper intercept of 103.4 ± 1.7 Ma (MSWD = 0.03) and a lower intercept indistinguishable from zero suggesting that their discordance can be explained by present day Pb loss.

The large age discordance between the monazite and zircon U-Pb data raises questions about the age of the leucogranite. Direct cross-cutting relationships between the biotite granodiorite or monzonite and the leucogranite were not observed and therefore do not help to restrict the interpretation of the U-Pb data from this sample. Many, if not most peraluminous leucogranites contain inherited zircons derived from the crustal source region from which their melts originated (e.g., Watson and Harrison, 1983; Harrison et al., 1987). Zircons that do precipitate from peraluminous melts tend to be more enriched in uranium and are prone to Pb loss due to radiation damage of the crystal structure because of their high U contents. It is for these reasons that monazite is the mineral of choice when dating leucogranites by the U-Pb method. Petrography from the leucogranite indicates that the monazite resides within the major mineral phases and not at grain boundaries, ruling out the possibility that the monazite ages represent a later postcrystallization metamorphic event possibly associated with fluid movement through the rock (e.g., Hawkins and Bowring, 1997). Therefore, we conclude that the monazite data represent the crystallization age of this intrusion at about 84–86 Ma.

Multiple interpretations of the zircon data from the leucogranite are possible. Inspection of the U concentrations from this sample (Table 1) show that the four multigrain fractions that contain turbid zircons have high U concentrations (which correlate with their degree of Pb loss) as compared to the concordant double crystal fraction and the two single grain analyses. In addition the Th/U ratio for the multigrain fractions (Table 1) are the same (0.20–0.21) but distinct from that of the concordant double-crystal analysis (0.37). These chemical differences suggest that a component of the zircons from each of

the four multigrain fractions did not crystallize from the same magma as did the two zircons crystals that are concordant at 106 Ma. We tentatively conclude that the two zircons from the concordant fraction are xenocrystic from the melt region from which the leucogranite magma originated and that the magma crystallization age is 103.4 ± 1.7 Ma or younger. Although the zircons that makeup the multigrain fractions may have precipitated from the leucogranite magma at 103 Ma, this possibility would require that the leucogranite magma did not fully crystallize until 84–86 Ma when the monazite crystallized. Another possibility is that the statistically significant regression of the multigrain fractions is a false discordia an represents both inheritance and Pb loss, rather than simply present day Pb loss. It is clear that inherited zircons reside in this rock so inheritance most likely plays some role in the multigrain U-Pb systematics. Depending on the degree of and age of inheritance associated with the zircon it is possible that the zircon precipitated closer to the age 84–86 Ma given by the monazite data. However, without more detailed conventional or SHRIMP (sensitive high-resolution ion microprobe) U-Pb geochronology determining the timing of zircon crystallization in this rock cannot be satisfactorily addressed at this time.

Undeformed pegmatitic dikes related to the biotite quartz monzonite and the garnet leucogranite cut all solid state and magmatic fabrics. At least one thin dike with coarse muscovite and garnet appears to emanate from the garnet leucogranite pluton and we infer it to represent the final stages of magmatism related to cooling and crystallization of the garnet leucogranite, which occurred at ~85 Ma (Fig. 3). Although the late-stage dikes are undeformed, their subvertical north-striking orientation is kinematically consistent with inferred configuration of strain axes associated with the final phases of folding (discussed subsequently). Therefore, we consider these dikes to be the youngest synkinematic intrusions in the area. Similar relationships are seen at Iron Mountain, where a ductilely deformed peraluminous granite is cut by undeformed muscovite-garnet dikes that are dated at 83 Ma and thought to have been derived from the granite (Boettcher and Walker, 1993).

Other intrusive phases. West-northwest striking Miocene dikes are common throughout the Fremont Peak area (Fig. 3). The swarm is bimodal in composition, with rhyolitic to dacitic dikes and subordinate basaltic dikes. The felsic dikes range from aphanitic to porphyritic, with up to 30% feldspar and biotite phenocrysts. Dikes of all different textural and compositional classes show mutual cross cutting relationships, which suggest they were emplaced in the same episode. Walker et al. (1995) reported that zircons from the dikes have complex U-Pb systematics but yielded a minimum age of 23 Ma. These dikes are part of a regionally extensive swarm found throughout the footwall of the brittle-ductile detachment that defines the core-complex segment of the central Mojave extensional belt (Fletcher et al., 1995). Greenschist-facies mylonite zones that crosscut the dikes are rare, but many of the porphyritic dikes contain a lineated mylonitic foliation oriented parallel to the dike margins. These margin-parallel fabrics are interpreted to be related to either dike emplacement or to local shearing associated with the Miocene detachment system, which likely resided at structurally higher levels above the present exposure. Nonetheless, the Miocene dikes provide an important frame of reference as they are subparallel to dikes throughout the Mojave block that range from Jurassic to Miocene (Glazner et al., this volume). Dikes at Fremont Peak strike ~20° more toward the west than some of the other dike swarms, perhaps owing to drag along the Garlock fault. These relationships suggest that Cretaceous structures of Fremont Peak likely has not been significantly affected my Cenozoic vertical-axis rotation.

The Buttes

Pre-Cretaceous igneous and metamorphic rocks. In contrast to the predominantly meta-igneous units of Fremont Peak, pre-Cretaceous rocks in The Buttes region consist mostly of strongly folded metasedimentary rocks that are made up principally of calcareous psammite (amphibolitic carbonaceous quartzite) and arkosic quartzite. Marker units within the metasedimentary sequence include black para-amphibolite, white calcitic marble, bluish-gray siliceous marble, tan dolomitic marble and greenish to purplish gray quartzite (Fig. 6). The tan dolomitic marble commonly contains variable amounts of hornblende and grades into para-amphibolite and amphibolitic quartzite as bulk composition decreases in carbonate and increases in silica and aluminum. The abundance of marble in the sequence suggests that it may represent Proterozoic to lower Paleozoic strata of miogeoclinal affinity. We tentatively correlate the dolomitic marble with the Noonday Dolomite and the peltic schist, quartzite, and calcite marble sequence with the Johnnie Formation.

The dominant pre-Cretaceous metaplutonic phase in The Buttes area is a mafic complex of diorite with subordinate hornblende gabbro (Fig. 6). This mafic igneous complex contains a variably developed magmatic to submagmatic foliation. This phase is widespread to the east in the Mitchel Range and Hinkley Hills (e.g., Fletcher et al., 1995) and may be correlative with the dioritic orthogneiss of Fremont Peak (Fig. 2).

Cretaceous migmatites and intrusives. The Proterozoic-lower Paleozoic metasedimentary sequence of The Buttes also contains migmatitic gneiss, but these rocks are not as widespread as in the Fremont Peak complex. Melanosome horizons are rich in biotite and also contain garnet + aluminum silicate + K feldspar ± quartz ± white mica. Leucosome horizons are composed of biotite- and garnet-bearing granite. The outer margins of K-feldspar grains within the leucosome are commonly replaced by myrmekite. Biotite grains within the leucosome show a strong preferred crystallographic fabric with basal cleavages oriented parallel to the gneissic foliation. However, quartz and feldspar show very little sign of dynamic recrystallization or other forms of solid-state deformation. In general feldspar is anhedral to subhedral with straight twin sets that could have formed during primary crystallization. Boundaries between the leucosome and melanosome are typically diffuse at the grain-scale. The fact that the migmatitic gneiss is restricted to rocks of semipelitic bulk compositions suggests that it formed by in situ partial melting and not by injection of magma along foliation surfaces. We infer that the in-situ melting and segregation of the leucosome occurred during deformation, but that final crystallization postdated formation of the gneissic foliation.

Zircon and monazite were dated by the U-Pb method from a sample of the leucosome. Four zircon analyses consisting of handpicked optically core-free, euhedral zircon were air abraded for 12 h, and a split from one of these fractions (z1aa) was then air abraded for another 16 hours (Table 1, Fig. 5C). Because of their euhedral morphology and lack of physical evidence for mechanical abrasion, these zircons are interpreted to be zircons that grew during high-grade metamorphism that lead to formation of the leucosome. The four analyses are discordant and plot near concordia at 105–95 Ma. Of the pair of splits from the same fraction that were air abraded for different durations, the strongly abraded split shifted toward an older $^{207}Pb/^{206}Pb$ date along a two-point isochron that has a lower intercept age of 93 Ma (Fig. 5C). The systematics of the four zircon analyses suggest that these metamorphic zircon contain an older inherited component probably consisting of cores of detrital zircon from the melted metapelite and that more recent Pb loss also plays a role in their discordance.

Eight monazite analyses were performed. Four of these were large multigrain fractions and four were single grain fractions. The multigrain analyses scatter along concordia between 100-90 Ma, whereas the single grain analyses scatter along concordia between 95–90 Ma. We are uncertain whether the monazite grew during prograde metamorphism that gave rise to the gniessic fabric and ultimately the leucosome melt or on the retrograde cooling path. Omitting the two multigrain monazite analyses with errors in the Pb/U ratios in excess of 3% and the one single grain analysis that is normally discordant near 90 Ma, the remaining monazite analyses cluster at $^{207}Pb/^{235}U$ dates of 95 Ma (2 analyses) and 93 Ma (3 analyses). These systematics suggest that monazite had grown by ca. 95 Ma and that closure to diffusive Pb loss (~725C; Parrish, 1990) was over by ca. 93 Ma. We interpret these analyses as indicating that monazite grew during the metamorphic event that gave rise to the leucosome at 95–93 Ma. This conclusion is consistent with the lower intercept of the two-point zircon discordia suggesting strong partial resetting of the detrital zircons and new metamorphic zircon growth from the metasedimentary host rock that melted. Other muscovite-bearing pegmatitic dikes cut the foliation and have subplanar wall-rock contacts. These dikes commonly are bluish gray and likely related to the latest synkinematic pegmatitic dikes at Fremont Peak and Iron Mountain. Dikes from Iron Mountain yield U-Pb ages of 83 Ma (Boettcher and Walker, 1993).

Other intrusive phases. The youngest intrusive rocks in

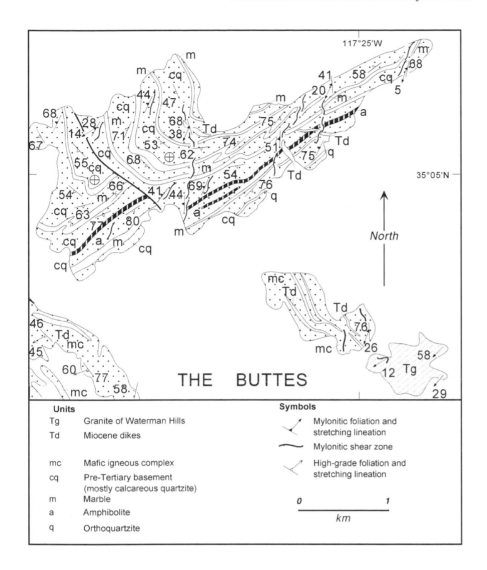

Figure 6. Schematic geologic map of The Buttes showing distribution of rock units and relationships between Cretaceous gneissic layering and Miocene mylonitic fabrics.

The Buttes include a Miocene granite and porphyryitic dikes that were emplaced synkinematically throughout the core-complex segment of the central Mojave extensional belt (Fletcher et al., 1995; Walker et al., 1995, Fig. 6). Greenschist-facies mylonites are common and Fletcher et al. (1995) inferred that rocks in The Buttes lie near the base of penetrative shearing of the brittle-ductile shear zone. Undeformed dikes in the region strike west-northwest, similar to those found in Fremont Peak. However, macroscopic folds of gneissic layering are thought to be the product of shear associated with Miocene mylonitization (Fletcher et al., 1995). Therefore, the orientation of Cretaceous fabrics locally may have been significantly modified by younger tectonic events.

DEFORMATIONAL STYLES OF ARC TECTONISM

Fremont Peak

Gneissic foliation (S1). Gneissic rocks of Fremont Peak record multiple generations of folds and deformational fabrics that re-

cord a complex history of tectonism associated with varied strain fields. Two distinct deformational fabrics are typically observed in outcrop. The oldest deformational fabric (S1) is a penetrative foliation that commonly lies parallel to transposed compositional layering. With only a few exceptions, the S1 fabric contains no stretching lineation, which indicates that it formed in a flattening strain regime. The style of the S1 foliation varies with rock type. In migmatitic rocks, the S1 fabric can be defined by strong banding that formed as a result of metamorphic and magmatic segregation. Typically, the banded gneissic fabric is much more strongly developed within the older suite of metaplutonic rocks, whereas the S1 foliation in each of the synkinematic Cretaceous igneous phases is defined mainly by penetrative preferred orientations of grain shapes with little mineralogic segregation. We interpret the differences in deformational style of the S1 foliation to reflect differences in the lithologically controlled responses of rocks to deformation as well as the timing of emplacement and crystallization of a given rock during the progressive deformation. Although the different styles of the S1 foliation are typically subparallel, local obliquities occur. In one case, the foliation within the migmatitic gneiss complex wraps around xenoliths of hornblende-biotite orthogneiss, which themselves contain an obliquely oriented internal foliation (Fig. 7A). Such complexities suggest the possibility that the deformational fabric in the older metaplutonic rocks originated during an earlier tectonic event and experienced subsequent transposition in the Cretaceous.

Mesoscopic crenulation cleavage (S2). The S1 gneissic foliation is commonly cut by a mesoscopic cleavage which we designate S2. The S2 cleavage shows all of the distinctive morphology of crenulation cleavages developed in micaceous rocks. However, in the Fremont Peak gneisses, the scale of the S2 cleavage is significantly greater than the scale typically associated with crenulation cleavages. The S2 cleavage locally occur as sets of congruent mesoscopic folds of the gneissic foliation with wavelengths on the order of 10 cm (Fig. 7B). More commonly though, it is found as a disjunctive cleavage that divides outcrops into domains analogous to microlithon and cleavage domains of crenulation cleavages (e.g., Gray, 1979; Powell, 1979; Bell and Rubenach, 1980). That is, the folded S1 gneissic foliation is preserved only in lenticular rock volumes between anastomosing S2 cleavage surfaces. Cleavage domains are typically 1–3 cm thick and are spaced on the order of 10 cm apart (Fig. 7C). Therefore, in order to be consistent with the scale of observation, we use the terms "cleavage" and "mesolithon" domains to describe the two components or domains of the disjunctive S2 cleavage.

In the mesolithon domains, the S1 gneissic layering typically becomes deflected and ultimately truncated as it is traced toward the S2 cleavage domains, although locally it is relatively planar. The deflected S1 foliation commonly shows a consistent sense of drag observed on either side of the cleavage domain, which indicates noncoaxial shear occurred across S2. In such cases, shear displacement commonly resulted in both layer-parallel extension and contraction of the S1 gneissic foliation, and shear sense was not consistent throughout the Fremont Peak area. Another common geometry of the disjunctive mesoscopic cleavage is represented by a more strongly folded S1 foliation within the mesolithon domain. However, more than a single antiformal or synformal fold closure is rarely observed in any one mesolithon domain. Instead the S1 foliation is deflected about rootless fold hinges and cannot be continuously traced across cleavage domains. Curiously, cleavage domains can juxtapose rootless mesofolds with the same sense of closure, such as two antiforms with no synform between them. These cleavage geometries indicate that the rock volume was affected by strongly heterogeneous contraction partitioned into the cleavage domains.

Although there are many geometric similarities between the S2 fabric and microscopic crenulation cleavages, several important distinctions can be inferred about the processes that formed them. The most obvious difference between crenulation cleavages developed in micaceous rocks and those found in the migmatitic gneisses of Fremont Peak is the difference in scale

Figure 7. Outcrop photos of deformational fabrics of Fremont Peak. (A) Foliation of migmatitic gneiss complex wraps around xenoliths of hornblende-biotite orthogneiss, which themselves contain an obliquely oriented internal foliation (emphasized by orientation of pencil). (B) S2 cleavage defined by axial surfaces of congruent mesocopic folds of S1 gneissic layering. (C) Disjunctive form of S2 cleavage.

of the phenomena, which commonly exceeds one or two orders of magnitude. We infer that the scale of overprinting cleavages must reflect the scale of the rheologic anisotropy of the folded layering. That is, microscopic crenulation cleavages likely form when the rheologic layering is on the scale of individual mica grains, whereas mesoscopic cleavages are favored when the anisotropy is controlled by larger-scale gneissic layering. As for the microscopic disjunctive cleavages, we infer that the intense cleavage-domain contraction was accomplished by shearing and volume loss. Under such high-grade metamorphic conditions, volume loss would have most likely occurred by the extraction of in situ melt rather than through aqueous processes. As mentioned earlier, thin layers and stringers of granitoid leucosome are commonly observed along the cleavage domains. If it is assumed that this granitoid melt was the most mobile phase of the rock mass, its presence in cleavage domains seems to contradict the interpretation that volume loss and contraction are focused in the cleavage domains. By analogy, volume loss in microscopic disjunctive cleavages is manifested by the concentration of the most *immobile* mineral phases along cleavage domains. However, this apparent contradiction exists in many migmatite complexes, which are characterized by thin melt horizons that lie parallel to the gneissic foliation and thus perpendicular to the inferred maximum shortening direction that produced it. To explain the contradiction, Hand and Dirks (1992) proposed that differential stress likely plays a subordinate role to tensile strength in controlling the orientation of melt horizons in migmatites. That is, under such high-grade conditions, rocks are not likely to support differential stress over geologically significant time periods. Owing to the very low effective viscosity and yield strength of quartzo-feldspathic rocks at uppermost-amphibolite-facies to granulite-facies conditions, contractional strain would be induced by the application of very low-magnitude differential stress. However, the tensile strength of the rock should be strongly anisotropic and much weaker perpendicular to the rheologic anisotopy of gneissic foliation (Hand and Dirks, 1992). The presence of melt would elevate fluid pressure and would be expected to produce tensile failure and opening perpendicular to the foliation. We infer that a similar mechanism is likely to explain the presence of melt along the disjunctive cleavage domains in Fremont Peak. Moreover, it is possible that alternating periods of tensile opening and superimposed contraction may lead to a pumping mechanism that would have a profound effect on the transport of melt through the crust.

Macroscopic structure (F2 and F3 folds). The macroscopic structural geometry of the range is characterized by an antiform-synform fold pair that has a wavelength of 6 km and spans the entire exposure of the gneiss complex (Fig. 8). The folds are defined largely by an igneous contact between the Cretaceous leucogranite and the older dioritic orthogneiss, but it can be demonstrated that all mesoscopic deformational fabrics are also refolded by these range-scale folds, which we interpret to represent a third generation (F3) of folding. The F3

fold pair has an amplitude of 4 km and a tight to isoclinal form. Analysis of the fold morphology is limited because of the lack of complete exposure of folded layers at the macroscopic scale. However, down-plunge projections show that the shape of the antiformal and synformal closures are nearly identical, which is consistent with a similar fold morphology and would indicate little rheological contrast between the orthogneiss and leucogranite (e.g., Ramsay and Huber, 1987).

At the range scale, inferred strike lines of the S1 foliation broadly follow the shape of the folded leucogranite-orthogneiss contact (Fig. 8). As a result of this macroscopic folding, poles to the S1 foliation define a great circle distribution that has a maximum cluster associated with foliations from the fold limbs, which strike east and dip steeply to the south (Fig. 9A). The macroscopic F3 fold axis, as defined by the minimum eigen vector of the S1 orientation matrix, plunges 56° toward 178°. Macroscopic distribution of the S2 cleavage shows that it is not axial planar to the range-scale folds of Fremont Peak, but is itself folded in a similar manner as the gneissic layering and the leucogranite contact (Fig. 8). Stereograms of poles to S2 show slightly more scatter, but define essentially the same pattern as poles to S1 (Fig. 9B). The inferred macroscopic F3 fold axis, as determined by the minimum eigen vector of the S2 orientation tensor, plunges 65° toward 159°, which is only 12°

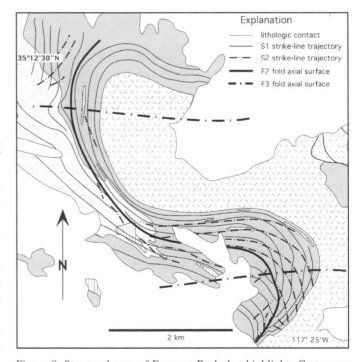

Figure 8. Structural map of Fremont Peak that highlights Cretaceous structures and fabrics and ignores Miocene dikes. Inferred strike lines of the gneissic foliation (S1) and mesoscopic crenulation cleavage (S2) are projected trajectories that lie tangent to the strike of the fabrics. Trace of axial surface of macroscopic F2 fold inferred from reversal in symmetry between S1 and S2. Trace of the axial surface of macroscopic F3 folds inferred from macroscopic geometry. Rock units have same pattern scheme as in Figure 3.

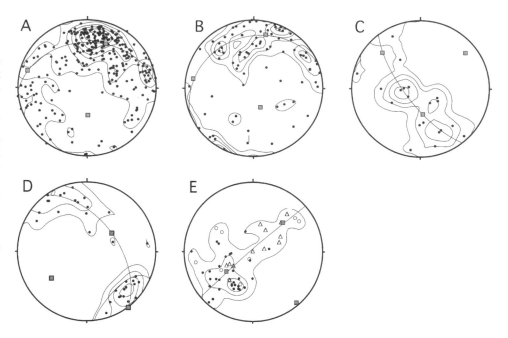

Figure 9. Stereograms of mesoscopic deformational fabrics from Fremont Peak and The Buttes. Squares are eigen vectors of linear data. (A) Poles to S1 gneissic foliation from Fremont Peak, 282 data, contoured at 0.5, 1.5, 2.5, 3.5, 4. (B) Poles to S2 mesoscopic cleavage from Fremont Peak, 82 data, contoured at 1, 2, 3, 4. (C) Lineations from Fremont Peak, 20 data, contoured at 1, 2, 3. (D) Poles to gneissic foliation from the northern part of The Buttes, 33 data, contoured at 1, 3, 5. (E) Fold hinge lines from the northern part of The Buttes33 data (12 Z folds—triangles, 9 S folds—open circles, 12 other folds—closed circles), contoured at 1, 3, 5.

oblique to the fold axis estimated from the S1 data. Mesoscopic folds and S1–S2 intersection lineations are highly scattered, but the maximum eigen vector plunges 59° toward 173°, which is subparallel to F3 fold axes defined by the distribution of S1 and S2 layering (Fig. 9C). Therefore, we interpret both F2 and F3 fold generations to be coaxial.

The S2 cleavage is nearly parallel to the gneissic foliation on the well-exposed east-striking limb that is common to both folds. However, a reversal in symmetry of the S1–S2 intersection geometry allows the inference of the axial surface of a macroscopic F2 fold that closes to the southeast (Fig. 8). As strike lines are traced to the east the angle between S1 and S2 increases to about 30°, indicating the approaching proximity of an antiformal fold closure that plunges steeply to the south. However, it is notable that both fabrics are systematically folded through the obvious range-scale fold (Fig. 8). In the southern extreme of Fremont Peak, S2 shows a more variable orientation with northeast-, north-, and northwest-striking sets. Angles between S1 and S2 are commonly greater than 45° and range up to 90°. In this complexzone it is not possible to draw smoothly varying S2 strike-line trajectories between different field stations. However, the strike lines of S1 foliation permit the inference of an antiformal closure, which defines the expected F2 fold (Fig. 8).

The Buttes

The characterization of Cretaceous deformational fabrics in The Buttes is severely limited by poor exposure and strong overprint of early Miocene mylonitization. The dominant mesoscopic fabric is a gneissic foliation that generally does not contain an obvious stretching lineation. Prismatic metamorphic

minerals such as sillimanite commonly lie parallel to the foliation but show no preferential alignment within it. The gneissic fabric is strongly folded at all scales. However, the large macroscopic folds are likely to be the product of Tertiary mylonitization (Fletcher et al., 1995).

A structural analysis of Cretaceous folding is best performed on the northeast-striking limb of the macroscopic fold in the northern part of The Buttes area, which is least affected by Miocene mylonitization (Fig. 6). Most of the mesoscopic folds and small map-scale folds in this region are tight to isoclinal with axial surfaces parallel to the local orientation of the gneissic foliation. The fold axes define a great circle girdle that strikes northeast, parallel to the gneissic foliation, but also show a strong cluster that plunges moderately to the southwest (Fig. 9, D and E). The orientation of this cluster may define the principal extension axis of the fold-related deformation, or the orientation could define the intersection between an earlier planar fabric and the present gneissic foliation. The symmetry of mesoscopic folds does not show a clean Hansen-type separation on either side of the cluster (e.g., Marshak and Mitra, 1988), but Z folds generally dominate a 135° sector of the girdle, which may indicate west-side-up and dextral shear across the northeast-striking gneissic foliation (Fig. 9E). However, the original orientation of these fabrics may have been significantly modified by younger tectonism.

DISCUSSION

Tectonic versus emplacement-related deformation

Multiple generations of fabrics in the Fremont Peak region indicate a complex history of deformation related to changing strain fields that were likely produced by a combination of varying regional tectonism and pluton emplacement. The strong parallelism of igneous contacts with the macroscopically folded gneissic fabrics indicates that macroscopic folding affected all rocks in the gneissic package including both those that acquired a high-grade solid-state fabric and those that did not. The contacts of the leucogranite are generally concordant with the S1 gneissic fabric and, in places along its margin, the leucogranite contains the S1 foliation. Throughout the batholith of the Sierra Nevada and Peninsular Ranges, it is common to observe concordant wall-rock foliations developed concentrically around the contacts of large plutons (e.g., Gastil et al., 1975). Although these deformation aureoles are commonly interpreted to be related to emplacement and/or expansion of magma chambers, in the Fremont Peak area, we have documented at least two generations of folding that overprint the S1 gneissic foliation. These relationships suggest that the leucogranite was present as a crystal mush in the deforming rock package throughout all three generations of folding and thus that a significant part of the deformational history post-dated emplacement of the leucogranite magma, which is the youngest arc-related intrusion in the area. The S1 deformational fabric was not observed to diminish in intensity with distance away from the margin of the leucogranite pluton, which would be expected if the fabric formed primarily in response to emplacement of the granite. Additionally, it is important to reiterate that the leucogranite contact and concordant S1 foliation define a regional antiform-synform pair and that this fold geometry would not likely form by the expansion of the magma chamber, which is a leading mechanism for developing a concordant wall rock foliation by emplacement-related processes. In summary, the S1 foliation formed during or after emplacement of the leucogarnite magma and it is difficult to evaluate the relative importance of regional-versus emplacement-related processes for the formation of the penetrative gneissic layering. However, we are more confident that at least the last two folding events (F2 and F3) reflect regional tectonism and not local emplacement-related perturbations. The geometry of the F3 range-scale folds indicates that the strain field associated with the last generation of folding was characterized by north-south contraction. The other two principal strain axes likely lie within the axial surface of the range-scale folds, which is subvertical and strikes east. We infer that deformation was extensional along both of these two principal strain axes, which is consistent with the preponderance of flattening fabrics observed at the mesoscopic scale. Pegmatitic dikes related to final crystallization of the leucogranite are typically subvertical with north strikes. This geometry is consistent with the inferred strain field and suggests that the principal axis of extension was oriented east-west. As discussed previously, the orientation of Miocene dikes does not require post Cretaceous rotations of the Fremont Peak area, which permits the interpretation that the strain field inferred from the F3 folds has not been significantly altered by younger tectonism. Therefore, the north-south contraction and east-west extension may have

been produced by right lateral wrenching across the north-northwest–trending arc.

Deformational processes and syntectonic thermal evolution

The lack of mesoscopic fabrics associated with the range-scale F3 folds may have important implications for the metamorphic and deformational processes that formed them. If F3 deformation was partitioned at the mesoscopic scale, the deformation must have occurred by reactivation of preexisting fabrics (S1 or S2). Because both fabrics are now systematically folded about F3 axes, the inferred reactivation should have been dominated by flexural slip kinematics (yielding opposite senses of shear on opposing limbs of F3 folds). However, it is equally plausible that the F3 folds formed by penetrative flow of the rock mass and left no mesoscopic signature. This process might be expected if metamorphic grade was sufficiently high to reduce the yield strength and effective viscosity of all rock types to minimal values. Specifically, we propose that high temperatures could produce not only an extremely weak rock mass but also a rheologically homogeneous one, which would permit penetrative flow without the formation of a mesoscopic deformational fabric.

The proposed development of high temperatures and rheologic homogenization during Cretaceous tectonism in the Fremont Peak region is consistent with inferred peak metamorphic temperatures (~850 °C) in The Buttes (Fletcher et al., 1991; Henry and Dokka, 1992). In addition, cross-cutting relationships indicate that the leucogranite was present as a melt throughout all three generations of folding. However, more importantly, the similar fold geometry of the macroscopic F3 folds indicates little or no rheologic contrast between the leucogranite magma and solid dioritic orthogneiss.

Evolution of the Cretaceous arc in the central Mojave

New geochronology and field relationships helps set limits on interpretations of the geodynamic evolution of the roots of the Cretaceous batholith in the Mojave block. Due to the very high-grade conditions of tectonism it has been necessary to re-evaluate criteria used to establish relative timing between plutonism metamorphism and deformation. Traditionally, it is acceptable to expect that plutons are emplaced very close to their liquidus temperatures and crystallize on time scales that are orders of magnitude shorter than the duration of the orogenic event (e.g., Paterson and Tobisch, 1992). However, with ambient temperatures reaching ~850 °C, it is possible for granitoid magmas to exist for much more extended periods in the semi-molten state. Moreover, it would be expected that crystallization will be controlled more by bulk composition of the magma than by relative timing of emplacement when ambient temperatures exceed the wet granite solidus. In the case of the Fremont Peak area, each Cretaceous pluton records all three generations of folding, however, the complete crystallization of the more felsic phases like the leucocratic granite postdated the last phase of folding. This finding suggests that measurable diachroneity may exist between emplacement and crystallization of the granitoid plutons in the high-grade roots of magmatic arcs.

Although no direct cross-cutting relationships exist between the two dated Cretaceous plutons at Fremont Peak the relative timing of crystallization is straightforward on the basis of field relationships. The biotite granodiorite contains a penetrative, albeit weak, S1 foliation, and the leucogranite only locally contains the fabric. Therefore, we interpret that the granodiorite achieved solid state during the formation of the first-generation gneissic foliation, whereas, the vast majority of the leucogranite did not achieve solid state until after the cessation of all three phases of Cretaceous tectonism. This sequence is corroborated by the U-Pb geochronology and we infer that the concordant zircon from the granodiorite dates its crystallization at 91.5 ± 0.5 Ma and the reversely discordant monazite of the leucogranite dates its crystallization at ca. 85 Ma.

Although the leucogranite crystallized post-tectonically it is strongly folded with the gneissic package into the macroscopic F3 folds and locally contains both generations of earlier mesoscopic fabrics. Therefore, it must have existed in the semi-molten state throughout most if not all of the history of Cretaceous tectonism in the Fremont Peak area. The U-Pb data by themselves do not define the time interval between emplacement and crystallization the leucogranite because the leucogranite zircon data have multiple interpretations. If the concordant zircon fraction that yielded a 106 Ma age is xenocrystic to the leucogranite, there is no minimum limit on the emplacement-crystallization time interval. Alternatively, if the concordant zircon crystallized early from the leucogranite magma, the pluton may have existed in a semimolten state for ~21 m.y. This is an extremely long period for a magma to exist, but we do not consider it outside of the realm of possibilities given that this gneiss terrane likely experienced temperatures of ~850 °C (Fletcher et al., 1991; Henry and Dokka, 1992) and the terrane formed in the roots of the Cretaceous batholith, the plutons of which was emplaced over a period of 40 m.y.

The combination of field relationships and geochronology add more insight to answer the question of how long the leucogranite existed as a magma during Cretaceous tectonism. In the southwestern Fremont peak area where the two plutons are present, the leucogranite is fully transposed into parallelism with the S1 gneissic fabric and the granodiorite is not. This difference generally would indicate that the leucogranite was subject to a longer part of the deformation history related to the formation of the S1 fabric. It is possible that strain near the leucogranite was more intense than strain near the granodiorite or that the granodiorite was intruded at a higher angle to the S1 foliation. However, the former is not likely because the two plutons lie very close to each other and no significant gradient in fabric intensity was observed in the host rocks that separate them. We do not favor the latter possibility because in the extreme eastern part of the study area the leucogranite margin is

discordant and does not seem to have been controlled by a preexisting host rock anisotropy. Therefore, we tentatively propose that the leucogranite was emplaced before but crystallized after the granodiorite. This scenario places a minimum of 6.5 m.y. on the emplacement and crystallization time interval of the leucogranite, which also is a long duration, but perhaps not unrealistic within the context of the Cretaceous batholith of western North America. Alternatively, if the leucogranite was emplaced after the granodiorite, nearly the entire history of Cretaceous tectonism at Fremont peak is bracketed between 91.5 and 85 Ma.

Monazite and zircon dates of 93–95 Ma from migmatitic leucosome in The Buttes are consistent with The Fremont Peak data, suggesting that high-grade metamorphic conditions existed over a relatively large area. Pegmatitic dikes that represent the final stages of crystallization of the leucogranite at Fremont peak cut all ductile fabrics and were likely emplaced at conditions well below peak metamorphic grade. Similar dikes at Iron Mountain yield U-Pb age of 83 Ma (Boettcher and Walker, 1993, Boettcher et al., this volume). Although the pegmatitic dikes post-date all the major phases of ductile deformation, their emplacement orientation is consistent with the inferred stain field of the third and last phase of folding at Fremont Peak.

Regional correlations of Cretaceous arc tectonism

Cretaceous arc tectonism in the Fremont Peak and The Buttes areas is characterized by a distinctive association of rock types and deformational fabrics that can be correlated throughout the Mojave block and beyond. The uppermost-amphibolite-facies to granulite-facies Cretaceous metamorphism is significantly higher grade than the lower greenschist facies metamorphism associated with most well documented Jurassic tectonism (e.g., Walker et al., 1990; Boettcher and Walker, 1993). Although it is possible that high-grade metamorphism was associated with Jurassic or other pre-Cretaceous orogenic events, such an occurrence has not yet been documented in the Mojave block. Only in the Shadow Mountains does Jurassic metamorphism approach middle- to upper-amphibolite facies (Martin et al., this volume, Fig. 2). Thus, metamorphic grade in the uppermost amphibolite facies may be a defining characteristic of Cretaceous arc-related tectonism in the Mojave block. As observed in both The Buttes and Fremont Peak areas, the development of a penetrative subvertical gneissic foliation and extensive in situ migmitization of rocks with appropriate bulk compositions are other characteristic features of Cretaceous tectonism. Throughout the Mojave block, rocks with these distinctive characteristics crop out in the Johannesburg gneiss of the Rand Mountains, Fremont Peak, The Buttes, Hinkley Hills, Mitchel Range, and Iron Mountain (Fig. 2). We propose that together these exposures form a belt of Cretaceous deformation that can be traced 75 km to the southeast of the Garlock fault.

To the north, the Cretaceous batholith of the Sierra Nevada shows a strong temporal zonation and plutons become younger to the east (Chen and Moore, 1982). The ages of syntectonic plutons in the Fremont Peak and The Buttes region are consistent with those from the middle to eastern portions of more complete exposures of the Cretaceous batholith in the Sierra Nevada and Peninsular Ranges. In addition, two-mica granite plutons commonly are found as a belt along the extreme eastern margin of the batholith (Miller and Bradfish, 1980; Miller et al., 1996). The belt of Cretaceous tectonism is likely correlative with a series of gneissic screens that occur throughout the middle of the Cretaceous batholith of the Sierra Nevada (Fig. 2). These gneissic rocks have a subvertical foliation with a locally developed mesoscopic crenulation cleavage and syntectonic metamorphism approaching the lower granulite facies (Saleeby et al., 1987; Pickett and Saleeby, 1993). This correlation is consistent with the accepted offset on the Garlock fault of approximately 65 km (Smith, 1962).

It is difficult to make direct correlations between Cretaceous tectonism in the Mojave block and the batholith of the Peninsular Ranges to the south (Fig. 1). However, the Cretaceous mylonite zone exposed at Iron Mountain may be correlative with the eastern Peninsular Ranges mylonite zone, which lies just east of the axis of the batholith (e.g. Sharp, 1979; Grove, 1994; Thomson and Girty, 1994).

Cretaceous tectonism and Miocene extension

As mentioned earlier, the Miocene central Mojave extensional belt does not cut the belt of high-grade Cretaceous tectonism at a high angle. Instead, the two belts merge over a strike length of ~40 km, and throughout this segment, the Cretaceous high-grade gneisses are exposed in the footwall of the detachment fault of the Central Mojave metamorphic core complex. It is interesting that the marked segmentation of the Central Mojave extensional belt occurs between the Mitchel Range and the Newberry Mountains, which coincides exactly with the eastern limit of possible Cretaceous high-grade basement (Fig. 2). The northwestern segment is a classic Cordilleran metamorphic core complex in which greenschist-facies mylonites and Miocene synkinematic intrusions overprint high-grade gneisses and intrusions of the Cretaceous arc. In contrast, throughout the Newberry and Rodman Mountains to the southeast, no Miocene mylonites or synkinematic intrusions have been observed (Fig. 1) (e.g., Glazner et al., 1989; Glazner et al., this volume). Only brittle faults, many of which are related to postextensional dextral shearing, are found, indicating that the amount of early Miocene extension is radically reduced and/ or nonexistent in the Newberry and Rodman Mountains (Fig. 1) (e.g., Glazner et al., 1989; Fletcher et al., 1995; Glazner et al., this volume). In this region, the pre-Tertiary basement is composed mainly of Jurassic volcanic rocks and older intrusions of low metamorphic grade that were not affected by Cretaceous tectonism.

High-grade Cretaceous tectonism and large-magnitude mid-Tertiary extension are commonly spatially associated throughout the Cordillera of the western United States, a fact that has led many workers to propose a genetic relationship between the two tectonic events (e.g., Coney and Harms, 1984). The strong eastward bend in the belt of metamorphic core complexes in the Colorado River Trough coincides well with a nearly 90° oroclinal bend in the belt of late Cretaceous deep-seated ductile thrusting and plutonism that lies immediately to the west (e.g., Fletcher and Karlstrom, 1990). However, such a strong spatial coincidence between a radical change in style and magnitude of Cenozoic extension and the limit of a Mesozoic contractional belt is unique to the Mojave block. It could be argued that the surface distribution of Cretaceous high-grade deformation is controlled by the distribution of early Miocene tectonic unroofing and that the high-grade belt may exist at lower crustal levels throughout much of the rest of the Mojave block, including the Newberry and Rodman Mountains. If true, it would be highly unlikely that such intense tectonism would have affected only the lower crust and not the upper crust. Deformation in the lower crust could be transferred laterally to other parts of the upper crust, but the extensive plutonism and paths of magmatic ascent would not likely be laterally offset. Therefore, the upper crustal expression of Cretaceous tectonism should exist either in the Newberry and Rodman Mountains or in the region to the northeast, which would lie along strike of the Cretaceous belt after restoration of 50 km of displacement across the Miocene brittle-ductile detachment. Alternatively, the spatial coincidence of the two deformational belts may suggest that Miocene extension was localized by crustal weaknesses generated during Cretaceous tectonism, such as development of overthickened crust with a high gravitational potential energy. In this case, the lack of Miocene extension in the Newberry and Rodman Mountains could be related to the lack of significant Cretaceous tectonism that would have preconditioned the crust for large-magnitude extension.

CONCLUSIONS

In the north-Mojave block (the north-central part of the greater Mojave region), and extensive suite of Cretaceous granitic plutons was emplaced at mid-crustal levels during a major pulse of regional deformation and high-grade metamorphism. The plutons are typically intermediate to felsic in composition and yield U-Pb zircon and monazite ages of 92–85 Ma, which we interpret to date their syntectonic and posttectonic crystallization. However, some plutons like the Fremont Peak leucogranite are interpreted to have been emplaced during the earliest stages of deformation and to have crystallized in the latest stages, and we infer that significant diachroneity of order as high as 10 m.y. may exist between emplacement and crystallization of felsic plutons in high-grade gneiss terranes. More geochronology is needed to define the onset of Cretaceous tectonism and the time interval between emplacement and crystallization of the Fremont Peak leucogranite. High-grade, syntectonic leucosomes associated with migmatite development in The Buttes formed at 95–93 Ma (U-Pb monazite).

Synplutonic deformation is characterized by at least three generations of folding that produced a subvertical gneissic foliation and steeply plunging folds. Although the last two generations of folding are coaxial, mesoscopic strain partitioning associated with each generation is distinctly different. F2 folding is characterized by a regionally developed crenulation cleavage that reflects profound strain partitioning at the mesoscopic scale. In contrast, no mesoscopic fabrics can be definitively correlated to F3 folds and we infer that these folds formed by penetrative flow at the mesoscopic scale. This change in character of strain partitioning would require a rheological homogenization of the rock mass, which could have occurred during an increase in temperature. Therefore we infer that all three generations of folding occurred during prograde metamorphism, which is consistent with the extensive migmatization that accompanied the folding.

This distinctive style of high-grade Cretaceous tectonism occurs as a belt that extends 75 km to the southeast from the Garlock fault. We correlate this belt with the middle to eastern parts of the Cretaceous batholith. For approximately 40 km along the southern extreme of the belt, high-grade Cretaceous structures or fabrics are strongly overprinted by a brittle-ductile detachment fault that accommodated up to 50 km of horizontal extension in the Miocene. It is interesting that the style and magnitude of Miocene extension underwent a radical change where the basement was not affected by high-grade Cretaceous tectonism.

ACKNOWLEDGMENTS

This study was supported by National Science Foundation grants EAR-8816944 and EAR-8916838 to Bartley, EAR-8917291 and EAR-8917300 to Glazner, and internal grants provided by CICESE. The manuscript was significantly revised based on comments by Carl Jacobson and Calvin Miller. Drew Coleman and Ismail Suayah helped with field mapping. Discussions with Ron Vernon, Michael Brown and Kenneth Hickey greatly improved the paper. Fletcher thanks Ramón Mendoza-Borunda, José Mojarro, Luis Gradilla and Lisa Skerl from CICESE for technical support provided during data compilation and preparation of this manuscript.

REFERENCES CITED

Barth, A.P., Tosdal, R.M., and Wooden, J.L., 1990, A petrologic comparison of Triassic plutonism in the San Gabriel and Mule Mountains, southern California: Journal of Geophysical Research, v. 95, p. 20075–20096.
Bartley, J.M., Glazner, A.F., Fletcher, J.M., Martin, M.W., and Walker, J.D., 1992, Amount and nature of dextral offset on Neogene faults near Barstow, California: Eos (Transactions, American Geophysical Union), v. 73, p. 363.
Bartley, J.M., Glazner, A.F., and Schermer, E.R., 1990, North-south contraction of the Mojave block and strike-slip tectonics in southern California: Science, v. 248, p. 1398–1401.
Barton, M.D., Battles, D.A., Bebout, G.E., Capo, R.C., Christensen, J.N., Davis, S.R., Hanson, R.B., Michelsen, C.J., and Trim, H.E., 1988, Mesozoic contact metamorphism in the western United States, in Ernst, W.G., ed., Metamorphism and crustal evolution of the western United States, Rubey Volume 7: Englewood Cliffs, New Jersey, Prentice Hall, p. 110–178.
Bell, T.H., and Rubenach, M.J., 1980, Crenulation cleavage development-evidence for progressive bulk inhomogeneous shortening from "millipede" microstructures in the Robertson River Metamorphics: Tectonophysics, v. 68, p. T9–T15.
Boettcher, S.S., and Walker, J.D., 1993, Geologic evolution of Iron Mountain, central Mojave Desert, California: Tectonics, v. 12, no. 2, p. 372–386.
Chen, J.H., and Moore, J.G., 1982, Uranium-lead isotopic ages from the Sierra Nevada batholith, California: Journal of Geophysical Research, v. 87, p. 4761–4784.
Coleman, D.S., and Glazner, A.F., 1997, The Sierra crest magmatic event: Rapid formation of juvenile crust during the Late Cretaceous in California: International Geology Review, v. 39, p. 768–787.
Coney, P.J., and Harms, T.A., 1984, Cordilleran metamorphic core complexes: Cenozoic extensional relics of Mesozoic compression: Geology, v. 12, p. 550–554.
Fletcher, J.M., Bartley, J.M., Martin, M.W., Glazner, A.F., and Walker, J.D., 1995, Large-magnitude continental extension: An example from the central Mojave metamorphic core complex: Geological Society of America Bulletin, v. 107, p. 1468–1483.
Fletcher, J.M., and Karlstrom, K.E., 1990, Late Cretaceous ductile deformation, metamorphism and plutonism in the Piute Mountains, eastern Mojave Desert: Journal of Geophysical Research, v. 95, p. 487–500.
Fletcher, J.M., Martin, M., and Bendixen, J., 1991, Mid-Tertiary mylonitization and deep-seated Mesozoic contraction in The Buttes: Geologic Society of America Abstracts with Programs, v. 23, p. A25.
Garfunkel, Z., 1974, Model for the late Cenozoic tectonic history of the Mojave Desert, California, and for its relation to adjacent regions: Geological Society of America Bulletin, v. 85, p. 1931–1944.
Gastil, R.G., Phillips, R.P., and Allison, E.C., 1975, Reconnaissance geology of the State of Baja California: Boulder, Colorado, Geological Society of America Memoir 140, 169 p.
Glazner, A.F., Walker, J.D., and Bartley, J.M., 1989, Magnitude and significance of Miocene crustal extension in the central Mojave Desert, California: Geology, v. 17, p. 50–53.
Glazner, A.F., Walker, J.D., Bartley, J.M., Fletcher, J.M., Schermer, E.R., Martin, M.W., Boettcher, S.S., Miller, J.S., Linn, J.K., and Fillmore, R.P., 1994, Reconstruction of the Mojave Block, in McGill, S.F., and Ross, T.M., eds., Geologic Investigations of an Active Margin, Geological Society of America Cordilleran Section Guidebook: Redlands, California, San Bernardino County Museum Association, p. 3–30.
Gray, D.R., 1979, Microstructure of crenulation cleavages: An indicator of cleavage origin: American Journal of Science, v. 279, p. 97–128.
Grove, M., 1994, Contrasting denudation histories within the east-central Peninsular Ranges Batholith (33°N), Geological Society of America Guidebook for the 1994 Cordilleran Meeting: San Bernadino, California, p. 235–240.
Hand, M., and Dirks, P.H.G.M., 1992, The influence of deformation on the formation of axial planar leucosomes and the segregation of small melt bodies within the migmatitic Napperby Gneiss, central Australia: Journal of Structural Geology, v. 14, no. 5, p. 591–604.
Harrison, T.M., Aleinikoff, J.N., and Compston, W., 1987, Observations and controls on the occurrence of inherited zircon in Concord-type granitoids, New Hampshire: Geochimica et Cosmochimica Acta, v. 51, p. 2549–2558.
Hawkins, D.P., and Bowring, S.A., 1997, U-Pb systematics of monazite and xenotime: Case studies from the Paleoproterozoic of the Grand Canyon, Arizona: Contributions to Mineralogy and Petrology, v. 127, p. 87–103.

Henry, D.J., and Dokka, R.K., 1992, Metamorphic evolution of exhumed middle to lower crustal rocks in the Mojave Extensional Belt, southern California, USA: Journal of Metamorphic Geology, v. 10, p. 347–364.

Marshak, S., and Mitra, G., 1988, Basic methods of structural geology: Englewood Cliffs, New Jersey, Prentice Hall, 445 p.

Martin, M.W., Glazner, A.F., Walker, J.D., and Schermer, E.R., 1993, Evidence for right lateral transfer faulting accommodating en echelon Miocene extension, Mojave Desert, California: Geology, v. 21, p. 355–358.

Martin, M.W., and Walker, J.D., 1995, Stratigraphy and paleogeographic significance of metamorphic rocks in the Shadow Mountains, western Mojave Desert, California: Geological Society of America Bulletin, v. 107, p. 354–366.

Martin, M.W., and Walker, J.D., 1991, Upper Precambrian-Paleozoic paleogeographic reconstruction of the Mojave Desert, California, *in* Cooper, J.D., and Stevens, C.H., eds., Paleozoic paleogeography of the western United States—II: Society of Economic Paleontologists and Mineralogists, Pacific Section, p. 167–192.

Miller, C.F., and Bradfish, L.J., 1980, An inner Cordilleran belt of muscovite-bearing plutons: Geology, v. 8, p. 412–416.

Miller, J.S., Glazner, A.F., and Crowe, D.E., 1996, Muscovite-garnet granites in the Mojave Desert: Relation to crustal structure of the Cretaceous arc: Geology, v. 24, p. 335–338.

Miller, J.S., Walker, J.D., Glazner, A.F., and Martin, M.W., 1995, Geochronologic and isotopic evidence for the Triassic-Jurassic emplacement of the eugeoclinal allochthon in the Mojave Desert region, California: Geological Society of America Bulletin, v. 107, p. 1441–1457.

Parrish, R.R., 1990, U-Pb dating of monazite and its application to geological problems: Canadian Journal of Earth Sciences, v. 27, p. 1435–1450.

Paterson, S.R., and Tobisch, O.T., 1992, Rates of processes in magmatic arcs: implications for the timing and nature of pluton emplacement and wall rock deformation: Journal of Structural Geology, v. 14, no. 3, p. 291–300.

Pickett, D.A., and Saleeby, J.B., 1993, Thermobarometric constraints on the depth and conditions of plutonism and metamorphism at deep levels of the Sierra Nevada batholith, Tehachapi Mountains, California: Journal of Geophysical Research, v. 98, p. 609–629.

Powell, C.M., 1979, A morphological classification of rock cleavage: Tectonophysics, v. 58, p. 21–34.

Ramsay, J.G., and Huber, M.I., 1987, Techniques of modern structural geology; Volume 2: Folds and fractures: London, Academic Press, 700 p.

Saleeby, J.A., Sams, D.B., and Kistler, R.W., 1987, U-Pb zircon, strontium and oxygen isotopic and geochronological study of the southernmost Sierra Nevada Batholith, California: Journal of Geophysical Research, v. 92, p. 10443–10466.

Sharp, R.V., 1979, Some characteristics of the eastern Peninsular Ranges mylonite zone, *in* Speed, R., et al., Proceedings of Conference VIII: Analysis of Actual Fault Zones in Bedrock, U.S. Geological Survey Open-File Report 79-1239, p. 258–267.

Smith, G.I., 1962, Large lateral displacement on the Garlock fault, California, as measured from an offset dike swarm: American Association of Petroleum Geologists Bulletin, v. 46, p. 85–104.

Stacey, J.S., and Kramers, J.D., 1975, Approximation of terrestrial lead isotope evolution by a two-stage model: Earth and Planetary Science Letters, v. 26, p. 207–221.

Steiger, R.H., and Jäger, E., 1977, Subcommission on geochronology: Convention on the use of decay constants in geo- and cosmochronology: Earth and Planetary Science Letters, v. 36, p. 359–362.

Thomson, C.N., and Girty, G.H., 1994, Early Cretaceous intra-arc ductile strain in Triassic Jurassic and Cretaceous continental margin arc rocks, Peninsular Ranges, California: Tectonics, v. 13, p. 1108–1119.

Walker, J.D., Fletcher, J.M., Fillmore, R.P., Martin, M.W., Taylor, W.J., Glazner, A.F., and Bartley, J.M., 1995, Connection between igneous activity and extension in the central Mojave metamorphic core complex, California: Journal of Geophysical Research, v. 100, p. 10477–10494.

Walker, J.D., Martin, M.W., Bartley, J.M., and Coleman, D.S., 1990, Timing and kinematics of deformation in the Cronese Hills, California, and implications for Mesozoic structure of the southwestern Cordillera: Geology, v. 18, p. 554–557.

Watson, E.B., and Harrison, T.M., 1983, Zircon saturation revisited: Temperature and composition effects in a variety of crustal magma types: Earth and Planetary Science Letters, v. 64, p. 295–304.

MANUSCRIPT ACCEPTED BY THE SOCIETY MAY 9, 2001

Geological Society of America
Memoir 195
2002

Stratigraphy and geochemistry of volcanic rocks in the Lava Mountains, California: Implications for the Miocene development of the Garlock fault

Eugene I. Smith
Alexander Sánchez
Deborah L. Keenan
Department of Geoscience, University of Nevada, Las Vegas, Nevada 89154-4010, USA
Francis C. Monastero
Geothermal Program Office, Naval Air Weapons Station, China Lake, California 93555-6001, USA

ABSTRACT

Volcanism in the Lava Mountains occurred between 11.7 and 5.8 Ma and was contemporaneous with sinistral motion on the Garlock fault. Volcanic rocks, equivalent in age and chemistry to those in the Lava Mountains, crop out 40 km to the southwest in the El Paso Mountains across the Garlock fault. Three chemical groups of volcanic rocks erupted in the Lava Mountains over a period of 5 m.y. These are (1) andesite of Summit Diggings, Almond Mountain volcanic section, and Lava Mountains Andesite, (2) basalt of Teagle Wash, and (3) tuffs in the northeastern Lava Mountains and dacite in the Summit Range. Volcanic rocks of each group have distinctive chemical signatures useful for correlation of units across the Garlock fault. Our work demonstrated that tuffs in the Almond Mountain volcanic section may be equivalent to a tuff in member 5 of the Miocene Dove Spring Formation, El Paso Mountains. The basalt of Teagle Wash probably correlates with basalt flows in member 4, and tuffs in the northeast Lava Mountains may be equivalent to tuff of member 2. Correlation of these units across the Garlock fault implies that the Lava Mountains were situated south of the El Paso Mountains between 10.3 and 11.6 Ma and that 32–40 km of offset occurred on the Garlock fault in ~10.4 m.y., resulting in a displacement rate of 3.1 to 3.8 mm/yr. Projecting this rate to the total offset of 64 km on the Garlock suggests that left-lateral slip began at ca. 16.4 Ma.

INTRODUCTION

The Lava Mountains lie just south of the active Garlock fault, a major continental strike-slip fault that separates the southwestern Basin and Range to the north from the Mojave block to the south. The fault extends 250 km from the San Andreas fault to the Avawatz Mountains just south of Death Valley (Fig. 1). Total sinistral displacement on the Garlock fault is ~64 km (Smith, 1962; Smith and Ketner, 1970; Davis and Burchfiel, 1973; Monastero et al., 1997). Estimates of the initiation of faulting vary from 10 to 9 Ma (Burbank and Whistler, 1987; Loomis and Burbank, 1988) to after 17 Ma (Monastero et al., 1997). Faulting continued to the present with a minimum of 18 km of displacement occurring across the central Garlock fault since the Pleistocene (Carter, 1980). Volcanism in the Lava Mountains began at ca. 11.7 Ma, ended at 6.4 Ma, and is unique

Smith, E.I., Sánchez, A., Keenan, D.L., and Monastero, F.C., 2002, Stratigraphy and geochemistry of volcanic rocks in the Lava Mountains, California: Implications for the Miocene development of the Garlock fault, *in* Glazner, A.F., Walker, J.D., and Bartley, J.M., eds., Geologic Evolution of the Mojave Desert and Southwestern Basin and Range: Boulder, Colorado, Geological Society of America Memoir 195, p. 151–160.

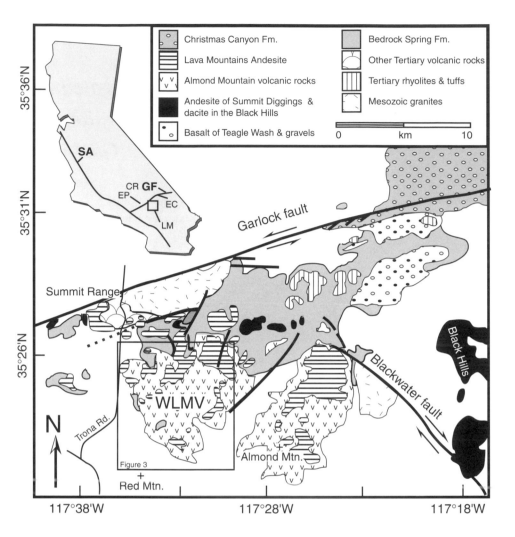

Figure 1. Geologic map of the Lava Mountains and neighboring Summit Range and Black Hills modified from Smith (1964), Dibblee (1967), and Keenan (2000). WLMV—Western Lava Mountains Volcano. Inset map of California shows the following locations: GF—Garlock fault, SA—San Andreas fault, LM—Lava Mountains, EC—Eagle Crags volcanic field, EP—El Paso Mountains, and CR—Coso Range. Box indicates area covered by Figure 3.

in that it represents a period of major volcanic activity astride the Garlock fault that occurred during lateral displacement. The Lava Mountains, originally described by Smith (1964) and Dibblee (1967), were remapped in part to clarify stratigraphic relationships, to determine the petrogenesis of the volcanic rocks, and to calculate offset on the Garlock fault. Smith (1964) established the basic stratigraphic framework for the Lava Mountains and generally located source areas for the Almond Mountain volcanic section and the Lava Mountains Andesite in both the western and eastern Lava Mountains.

The close proximity of volcanic centers in the Lava Mountains to the Garlock fault and the potential for locating units that either flowed or were transported across the fault provide the opportunity to more fully understand the development of the Garlock fault during Tertiary time. Units coeval and geochemically identical to those in the Lava Mountains occur north of the Garlock fault in the El Paso Mountains in the Miocene Dove Spring Formation (Loomis and Burbank, 1988). Furthermore, lithologies characteristic of the El Paso Mountains occur as conglomerate clasts in the eastern Lava Mountains (Carter, 1982, 1987, 1994).

This paper presents the results of new stratigraphic, geochronologic, and geochemical investigations of the Miocene volcanic rocks of the Lava and El Paso Mountains and relies on earlier studies by Smith (1964) and Carter (1980, 1982, 1987, 1994). The principal objective is the correlation of volcanic units between the Lava and El Paso Mountains across the Garlock fault with the purpose of estimating slip rate on the fault. Field studies described a volcanic center in the western Lava Mountains, the source of a significant volume of andesite and dacite lava and pyroclastic material.

VOLCANIC STRATIGRAPHY

On the basis of detailed and reconnaissance mapping, Smith (1964) developed a stratigraphy for the Lava Mountains composed of six volcanic units and basin-fill gravels and sandstones. Although he lacked isotopic dates, volcanic units were assigned ages varying from pre–middle Pliocene to Quaternary on the basis of paleontological and stratigraphic observations. Our work based on geochemistry, geochronology, and field studies required the revision of this stratigraphy and demonstrated that volcanic activity in the Lava Mountains occurred in three episodes spanning about 5 m.y. in the middle Miocene to late Miocene (Fig. 2).

Rocks of the first episode were mapped by Smith (1964) as volcanic units older than the Bedrock Spring Formation. These units are shown herein to range in age from 11.7 to 10.7 Ma, are lithologically diverse, and include (1) dacite (11.7 Ma; Table 1) with large (2 cm) phenocrysts of plagioclase, herein

termed "the dacite of Summit Range"; (2) dacite containing quartz, hornblende, biotite, and plagioclase dated at 10.73 Ma (Table 1); and (3) volcaniclastic rocks. A vent area for dacite is marked by a volcanic dome in the Summit Range (Fig. 3). Also included in episode 1 are pyroclastic flows mapped by Smith (1964) in the northeastern part of the Lava Mountains as "other upper Pliocene (?) volcanics (Tt)." The age of this unit is unclear. Smith (1964) indicated that it may overlie the Bed-

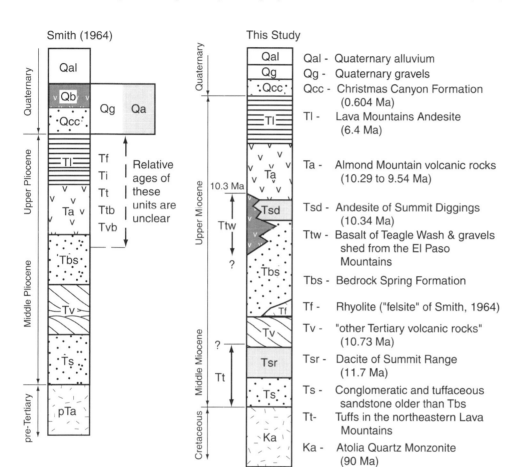

Figure 2. Comparison of the volcanic stratigraphy of Smith (1964) with the revised stratigraphy of this paper. Note that Qb and Qa in Smith's (1964) stratigraphy are equivalent to Ttw and Tsd, respectively, in the revised stratigraphy. Qb—Quaternary basalt; Ti—Tertiary intrusives; pTa—Atolia Quartz Monzonite; Ttb—Tertiary tuff breccia; Tvb—Tertiary volcanic breccia.

TABLE 1. DATES BY ⁴⁰Ar/³⁹Ar INCREMENTAL-HEATING TECHNIQUE OF SAMPLES FROM THE LAVA MOUNTAINS

Sample	Unit	Date (Ma)	Uncertainty (2σ) (± m.y.)	Date type	MSWD	Mineral
LM96-2	Tsd	10.34	0.69	plateau (inc. 3–9)		hornblende
LM96-2	Tsd	7.81	0.14	plateau (inc. 5–9)		biotite
LM96-15	Tv	10.73	0.10	plateau (inc. 7–11)		biotite
LM96-16	Ta	9.54	1.14	plateau (inc. 10–11)		hornblende
LM96-16	Ta	7.82	0.21	plateau (inc. 7–9)		biotite
LM96-17	Tat	10.29	0.78	plateau (inc. 10–11)		hornblende
LM96-17	Tat	8.73	1.58	isochron (inc. 3–11)	1.73	hornblende
LM1132	Tl	6.4	0.1	isochron (inc. 3–9)	0.9	biotite
GFZ-85	Tsr	11.7	0.2	isochron (inc. 4–10)	2.0	sanidine

Note: ⁴⁰Ar/³⁹Ar dates by the Cambridge Laboratory for Argon Isotopic Research (CLAIR), Massachusetts Institute of Technology. Tsd—dacite of Summit Diggings, Tv—other Tertiary volcanic rocks, Ta—Almond Mountain andesite, Tat—Almond Mountain tuff, Tl—Lava Mountains andesite, Tsr—dacite of Summit Range. Inc. = Increments of the Ar spectrum used to calculate either the isochron or plateau age. MSWD = mean square of weighted deviates for isochron dates.

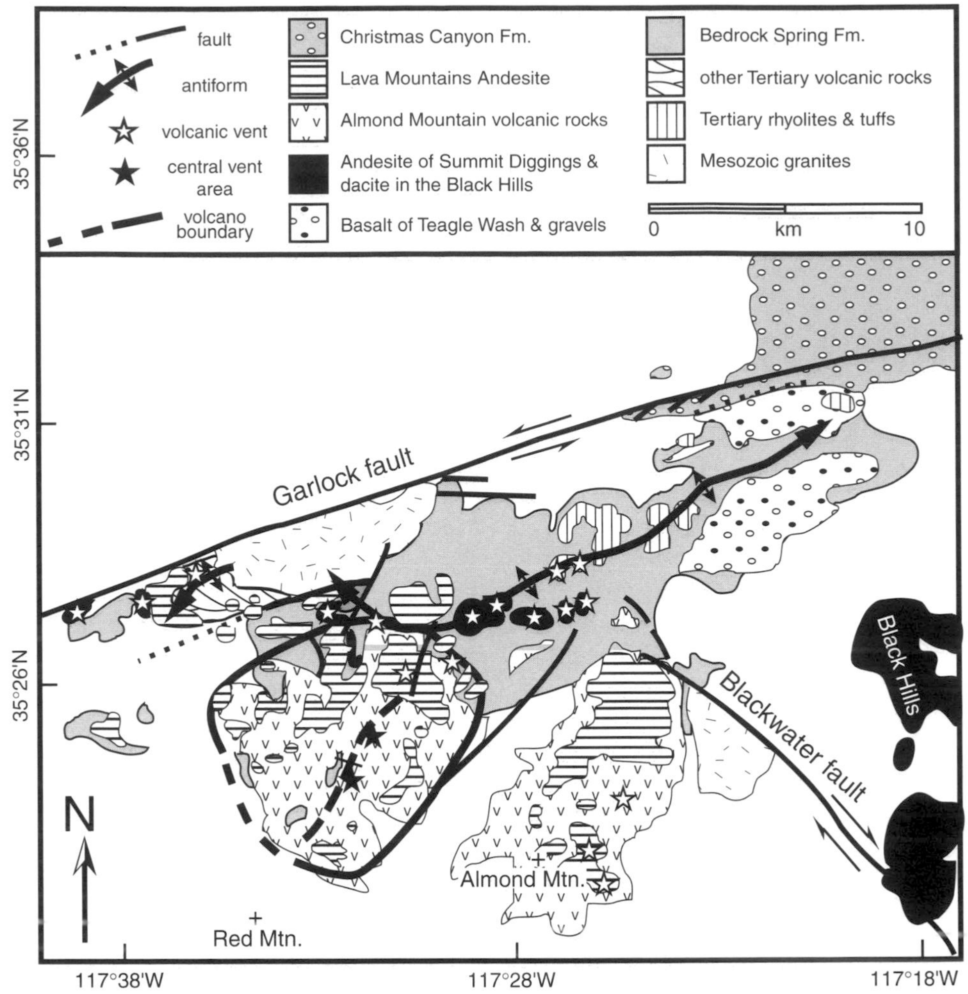

Figure 3. Geologic map showing the locations of volcanic centers and major fold axes in the Lava Mountains and adjacent areas. Geology modified from Smith (1964), Dibblee (1967), and Keenan (2000). Note that many of the vent areas lie on the axes or flanks of major folds. The area of the western Lava Mountains volcano includes the central-vent area and moat composed of inward-dipping block-and-ash and debris-flow deposits, and pyroclastic and lava flows. The domes of the central-vent area intruded tilted, topographically and structurally high beds of Bedrock Spring Formation.

rock Spring Formation, but field relationships are obscure. Geochemical similarities between these pyroclastic units and tuffs of member 2 of the Dove Spring Formation (15.1 to 11.8 Ma; Loomis and Burbank, 1988) support assignment of the flows to episode 1. These pyroclastic units either erupted from nearby domes of rhyolite (mapped as felsite [Tf] by Smith, 1964) or from an unidentified source to the south of the Lava Mountains.

Rocks of the second episode (10.4 to 9.54 Ma; Table 1) are volumetrically the most important and are separated from volcanic rocks of the first episode by the sandstones of the Bedrock Spring Formation (Fig. 2). The following units were produced during the second episode: (1) volcanic rocks in the uppermost part of the Bedrock Spring Formation, (2) the Almond Mountain volcanic section, (3) "Quaternary" andesite (Smith, 1964) herein termed "the andesite of Summit Diggings," and (4) the "Quaternary" basalt (Smith, 1964) herein termed "the basalt of Teagle Wash."

The Almond Mountain volcanic section erupted from the 9-km-diameter western Lava Mountains volcano. This volcanic center was originally recognized by Smith (1964) and briefly described by Carter (1994), but detailed mapping, volcanology,

and geochemistry were done by Keenan (2000) (LAVAMT on CD-ROM accompanying this volume). The western Lava Mountains volcano (Fig. 3) was active between 10.29 Ma and ca. 9.54 Ma. Coalescing andesite and dacite domes and subvolcanic intrusive rocks make up the central vent area. Domes are surrounded by a thick section of inward-dipping andesite breccia, flows, and lapilli tuff. The dacite breccia contains block-and-ash, rock-avalanche, sandstone and conglomerate, and debris-flow deposits that represent explosive and passive destruction of volcanic domes in the central-vent area. Breccia commonly contains bombs and blocks of andesite up to 3 m in size.

Placing the andesite of Summit Diggings, the basalt of Teagle Wash, and volcanic rocks of the Bedrock Spring Formation into the same time frame as the Almond Mountain volcanic section represents a major revision of Smith's (1964) stratigraphy. Detailed justification for assigning these units to the second episode of volcanism follow.

Smith (1964, p. 44) based the Quaternary age of the andesite of Summit Diggings on one contact where "andesite rests on the upper part of a surface that was elsewhere covered by older gravels of early Quaternary age." A new $^{40}Ar/^{39}Ar$ date of 10.34 Ma (Table 1) brings this field-based interpretation into question and places the andesite of Summit Diggings stratigraphically below the Almond Mountain volcanic section. New field observations also support this age assignment. A dome and several flows of the andesite of Summit Diggings intrude and overlie the Bedrock Spring Formation. Resting on the flows are the lapilli tuff and breccia of the Almond Mountain volcanic section and flows of Lava Mountains Andesite (Fig. 2).

Assignment of the basalt of Teagle Wash to this episode is based mainly on field relationships. Smith (1964) assigned a Quaternary age to the basalt because he mapped it lying on and intruding the conglomerate facies of the Quaternary Christmas Canyon Formation. We do not question the age assignment of the Christmas Canyon Formation, which appears to be firmly based on fossil evidence and a 602 ka $^{40}Ar/^{39}Ar$ date from an interbedded tuff (Gansecki et al., 1998). However, we question the assignment of the conglomerate beneath the basalt to this formation. The conglomerate described by Carter (1982, 1987, 1994) contains clasts of spotted Mesquite Schist, carbonate clasts of the Paleocene Goler Formation, weakly lineated hornblende quartz diorite, and vesicular basalt that is chemically identical to basalt flows in member 4 of the Dove Spring Formation (see Geochemistry and Implications section). These clasts only could have been derived from the El Paso Mountains north of the Garlock fault (Carter 1982, 1987, 1994). The conglomerate probably represents part of a fanglomerate sheet that extended from drainages in the El Paso Mountains south into the Lava Mountains and then was cut and displaced by movement along the Garlock fault (Carter, 1982). If we assume that the conglomerate belongs to the Christmas Canyon Formation and is Quaternary in age as mapped by Smith (1964), at least 30 km of displacement must have occurred along the Garlock fault in ~620 k.y. This interpretation results in a displacement rate as high as 5 cm/yr, a value that is one order of magnitude higher than the estimated average long-term slip rate of 7 mm/yr (Carter, 1987, 1994). A slip rate of 5 cm/yr is unreasonable for the Garlock fault; we suggest, therefore, that the conglomerate and overlying basalt are Tertiary in age. Furthermore, this age assignment is strengthened by the geochemical correlation of 11.6 to 10.4 Ma basalt in the Dove Spring Formation with both the basalt boulders in the conglomerate and the basalt of Teagle Wash (see Geochemistry and Implications section).

Volcanic units in the uppermost part of the Bedrock Spring Formation contain block-and-ash deposits and pyroclastic flows. The block-and-ash deposits resemble those of the Almond Mountain section in that they contain lithologically identical clasts. Clasts are similar in three important ways. First, they commonly show radial fractures and fine-grained mantles that contain micro–columnar joints, features that indicate eruption while still hot. Clasts similar to these are otherwise only found in breccias of the Almond Mountain volcanic section. Second, clasts are mineralogically identical to Almond Mountain dacite in that they contain phenocrysts of plagioclase, horn-

blende, and biotite. Finally, they are chemically identical to clasts within block-and-ash deposits of the Almond Mountain section (Table DR1).[1] From these observations, we suggest that the volcanic units within the Bedrock Spring Formation represent the initial stages of Almond Mountain activity.

After a hiatus of 2–3 m.y., activity continued with the eruption of the Lava Mountains Andesite (6.4–5.8 Ma, Table 1) forming the volcanic rocks of the third episode.

Lava Mountains Andesite crops out about the central-vent area of the western Lava Mountains volcano and in the eastern Lava Mountains and is mineralogically and chemically similar to volcanic rocks formed during the two preceding episodes. Although the Lava Mountains Andesite covers considerable area and is topographically prominent (Fig. 3), it is usually composed of one to three flows that rarely exceed 100 m in thickness.

In summary, volcanism in the Lava Mountains occurred in three episodes. The first episode was separated from the second by deposition of the Bedrock Spring Formation and ~500 k.y. of time. The period between episode 2 and 3 was no longer than 3 m.y. The period of quiescence may have been shorter considering that the younger date for the Almond Mountain volcanic section is from a bomb in the upper-middle part of the section.

GEOCHEMISTRY, GEOCHRONOLOGY, AND STRATIGRAPHY: IMPLICATIONS FOR MIOCENE DEVELOPMENT OF THE GARLOCK FAULT

Geochemical fingerprinting of volcanic rocks is useful for correlation of units between separate localities. Of specific interest is the correlation of volcanic rocks between the Lava and El Paso Mountains to provide markers that can be used to estimate the slip rate on the Garlock fault. Our geochemical database includes 71 new samples from the Lava and El Paso Mountains. All samples were analyzed for major oxides and trace elements by X-ray fluorescence spectrometry on fused disks at the Rock Chemistry Laboratory, University of Nevada, Las Vegas. Concentrations of rare earth elements (REEs) and other selected trace elements were determined for 69 samples at the GeoAnalytical Laboratory at Washington State University by ICP-MS (inductively coupled plasma–mass spectrometry). The Isotope Geochemistry Laboratory at the University of Kansas provided radiogenic isotopic analyses (Sm/Nd, Rb/Sr, and Pb systems) of 41 samples. The Cambridge Laboratory for Argon Isotopic Research (CLAIR), Massachusetts Institute of Technology, dated six samples by using the $^{40}Ar/^{39}Ar$ incremental-release technique (Tables 1, DR1, and DR2 [see footnote 1]).

---

[1]GSA Data Repository item 2002099, Table DR1, Major Element Oxide, Trace, and Rare Earth Element Analyses, and Table DR2, Sr, Nd, and Pb Isotope Ratio and Trace Element Analyses, is available on request from Documents Secretary, GSA, P.O. Box 9140, Boulder, CO 80301-9140, USA, editing@geosociety. org, or at www.geosociety.org/pubs/ft2002.htm.

On the basis of these new geochemical and geochronologic data and the stratigraphic studies described in the preceding section, we argue that during late Miocene time, the El Paso Mountains lay just to the north of the Lava Mountains across the Garlock fault. Four lines of evidence support this contention: (1) chemical correlation of the basalt of Teagle Wash with basalt in member 4 of the Dove Spring Formation in the El Paso Mountains, (2) chemical correlation of basalt boulders in a conglomerate beneath the basalt of Teagle Wash to both the basalt of Teagle Wash and to basalt in member 4 of the Dove Spring Formation, (3) chemical correlation of tuff in the Almond Mountain section with tuff of member 5 of the Dove Spring Formation, and (4) correlation of clasts in a conglomerate beneath the basalt of Teagle Wash to sources in the El Paso Mountains.

Volcanic rocks in the Lava Mountains are age equivalent to the volcanic section in the upper part of the Dove Spring Formation, El Paso Mountains. The Dove Spring Formation, divided into six members, consists of a section of conglomerate, sandstone, mudrock, chert, tuff, and basalt (Loomis and Burbank, 1988). Although occurring throughout the section, volcanic units are most prevalent in members 2, 4, and 5 (Fig. 4).

Tuffs in member 2 thin to the north and form prominent cliffs in Red Rock Canyon in the western El Paso Mountains. These tuffs may correlate with rhyolitic tuffs (mapped by Smith [1964] as Tt) in the northeastern Lava Mountains (Fig. 4). Member 2 tuff and Tt share low Ba, P, Ti, and Zr contents, high Rb, Th, and U contents, and negative Eu anomalies compared to Almond Mountain tuff (Fig. 5). Tt differs from member 2 tuff in having higher REE abundances. Tuffs in member 2 are too old (fission-track ages of 15.1-11.8 Ma in Loomis and Burbank, 1988) to correlate with tuffs of the Almond Mountain volcanic section.

Basalt in member 4 occurs as two flows (Tdb2 and Tdb3 of Loomis and Burbank, 1988), is fine grained, and vesicular and contains phenocrysts of olivine and plagioclase. Loomis and Burbank (1988) bracketed the age of these flows to between 10.4 and 11.8 Ma by dating tuffs higher and lower in the section (Fig. 4). A new $^{40}Ar/^{39}Ar$ date of 11.6 Ma on member 4 basalt (unit Tdb2 of Loomis and Burbank, 1988) falls into this age range. Major and trace element abundances and isotopic ratios for member 4 flows are similar to the basalt of Teagle Wash in the Lava Mountains. REEs share a common smooth pattern with 60 to 70 times chondrite enrichment in La and about 10 times chondrite enrichment in Lu (Fig. 6). Samples from the two member 4 flows were analyzed in different laboratories, perhaps explaining the small differences in chemistry between them. Isotopic ratios are also remarkably similar; $^{206}Pb/^{204}Pb$ varies between 19.2 and 19.3 and $^{887}Sr/^{86}Sr$ is 0.7054 $\pm$ 0.0001. On the basis of these similarities in major and trace element chemistry and isotopic ratios, we suggest that the member 4 basalt in the El Paso Mountains correlates with the basalt of Teagle Wash in the Lava Mountains (Fig. 4).

The source of the fine-grained, vesicular basalt boulders in Quaternary deposits in the Lava Mountains and in the conglomerate beneath the basalt of Teagle Wash is controversial. Smith (1964, 1991) suggested that they originated to the southeast in the Black Hills, and Carter (1980, 1982) thought they might represent Black Mountain basalt from the northern El Paso Mountains (Fig. 7). Geochemical data clearly indicate that neither one of these possibilities is tenable. Dark colored volcanic rock in the Black Hills, thought to be basalt by Smith (1964, 1991), is fine- to medium-grained, flow-banded hornblende dacite with 63.4 to 64.8 wt% SiO_2 and 1.71 to 2.55 wt% MgO; thus it is too felsic to correlate with the basalt boulders in the Lava Mountains. Black Mountain basalt from the El Paso Mountains is too low in SiO_2 (48.3 to 49.1 wt%) and too high in Al_2O_3 (15.5 to 17 wt%) to correlate with the basalt of Teagle Wash (51 wt% and 14.5 wt%, respectively). The chemistry of a basalt boulder in the conglomerate beneath the basalt of Teagle Wash is, however, nearly a perfect match for basalt in member 4 of the Dove Spring Formation (Fig. 8). The basalt boulders, therefore, are Tertiary in age and were derived from basalt flows in member 4 of the Dove Spring Formation in the El Paso Mountains. Many of these boulders were transported to the north during the Quaternary and deposited in the Christmas Canyon Formation. If this history is correct, then the basalt boulders were twice reworked; first transported to the south in Tertiary time and then transported to the north during the Quaternary. These observations reconcile apparent differences between the interpretation of Smith (1964) that the Christmas Canyon Formation and overlying basalt are Quaternary in age and our suggestion that although the Christmas Canyon Formation is Quaternary, the basalt and underlying conglomerate are Tertiary in age.

A thin tuff (10 m thick) in the lower part of member 5 in the Dove Spring Formation (Fig. 4) was dated at 10.4 $\pm$ 1.6 Ma (fission-track date, Loomis and Burbank, 1988). In the Lava Mountains, the basal ash flow of the Almond Mountain section is 10.29 $\pm$ 0.8 Ma and a lapilli tuff in the lower middle part of the same section is between 10.29 and 9.54 Ma. Both tuffs are potentially candidates for correlation with the member 5 tuff in the Dove Spring Formation, El Paso Mountains. REE plots show that the member 5 tuff is similar in composition to both the basal and lapilli tuffs in the Almond Mountain section (Fig. 9), although member 5 tuff has higher heavy-REE abundances than the Almond Mountain tuffs. On the basis of these observations, we suggest that the member 5 tuff is the distal equivalent of tuffs in the Almond Mountain volcanic section (Fig. 4).

Correlations based on lithology, age, and geochemistry suggest that the El Paso Mountains lay just to the north of the Lava Mountains between ca. 11.6 and 10.3 Ma. Although these were adjacent areas, sedimentary units were transported to the south from the El Paso Mountains into the Bedrock Spring basin (the future site of the Lava Mountains), and volcanic units from the Lava Mountains traveled to the north into the El Paso Mountains. In the past 10.4 m.y. the El Paso Mountains moved

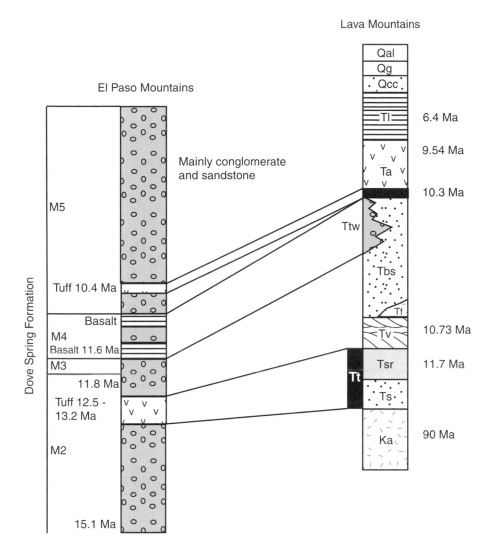

Figure 4. Comparison of the stratigraphic section in the El Paso Mountains (modified from Loomis and Burbank, 1988) with the section in the Lava Mountains. Note that the stratigraphic sections are not to scale. Correlations of tuff and basalt units proposed in this paper are shown by tie lines between sections. See Fig. 2 for definitions of abbreviations.

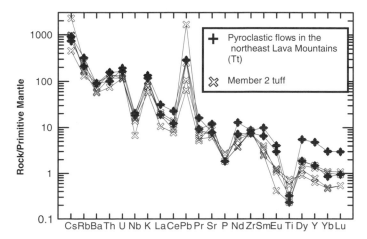

Figure 5. Trace element diagram emphasizing that the pyroclastic flows in the northeastern Lava Mountains (Tt) probably correlate with member 2 tuff in the El Paso Mountains. Elements are normalized to primitive mantle of Sun and McDonough (1989).

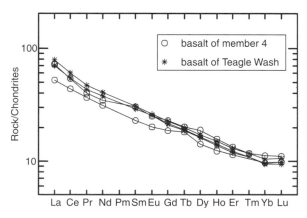

Figure 6. REE plot normalized to chondritic abundances showing the geochemical similarities between samples of the basalt of Teagle Wash in the Lava Mountains and samples of the basalt of member 4 of the Dove Spring Formation in the El Paso Mountains. REEs are normalized to the chondritic abundances of Sun and McDonough (1989).

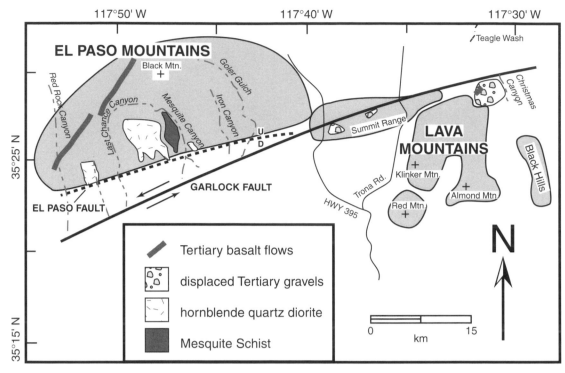

Figure 7. Location map of the central Garlock fault area.

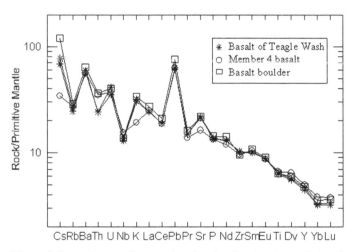

Figure 8. Trace element diagram showing that the chemistry of a basalt boulder in the conglomerate beneath the basalt of Teagle Wash (Lava Mountains) is similar to both the basalt of member 4 (Dove Spring Formation, El Paso Mountains) and the basalt of Teagle Wash, Lava Mountains. Elements are normalized to primitive mantle of Sun and McDonough (1989).

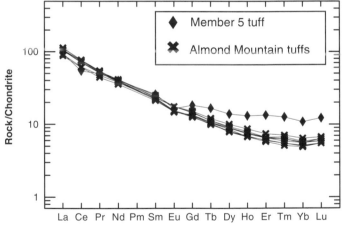

Figure 9. REE plot showing that tuff of member 5 of the Dove Spring Formation (El Paso Mountains) is chemically similar to and probably correlates with tuffs of the Almond Mountain volcanic section (Lava Mountains). Member 5 tuffs (El Paso Mountains), however, have higher heavy-REE abundances than Almond Mountains tuffs.

32 to 40 km to the west along the Garlock fault. This distance and time translate into a displacement rate of ~3.1–3.8 mm/yr. The calculated rate is less than the average Holocene rate of 6–8 mm/yr (McGill and Sieh, 1993) and the Pleistocene rate of 7 mm/yr (Carter, 1987). It is very similar, however, to the rate inferred from the work of Monastero et al. (1997) who assumed

64 km of offset in ~17 m.y., resulting in an average displacement rate of 3.5 mm/yr.

From the preceding information, we suggest the following history for the central Garlock fault (Fig. 10).

Rhyolite tuff erupted from sources to the south of the Lava Mountains or from domes in the eastern Lava Mountains and

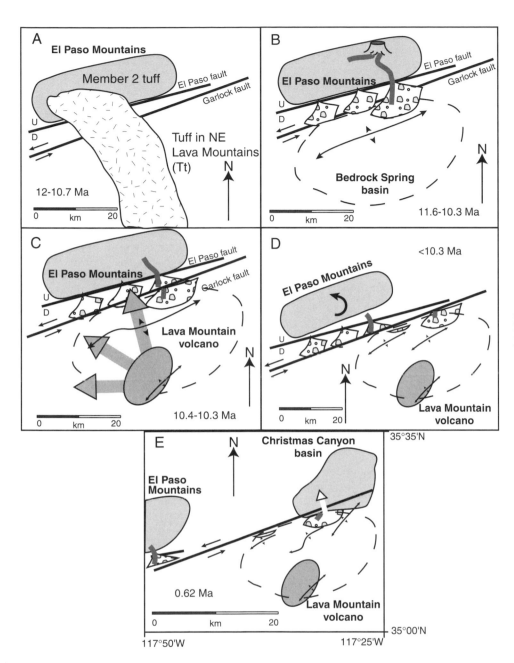

Figure 10. Five-step model for the evolution of the central Garlock fault. See text for details.

flowed to the north across the Garlock fault into the El Paso Mountains (Fig. 10A). This tuff forms the tuffs in the northeastern Lava Mountains and the member 2 tuff in the El Paso Mountains.

Fanglomerate fans from the El Paso Mountains extended across the trace of the Garlock fault into the Bedrock Spring basin (Fig. 10B). These fans contain clasts and slide blocks of Mesozoic basement rock and boulders of basalt from member 4 of the Dove Spring Formation. Member 4 basalt flows erupted from sources in the El Paso Mountains and flowed to the south through channels cut into the fan. Inclusion of the basalt boulders in the fanglomerate fan and the overlying basalt requires that the fan formed during the eruption of the member 4 basalt

(11.6 to 10.4 Ma). Distinctive clast types, especially hornblende quartz diorite, indicate that the fan may have originated at the mouth of Mesquite Canyon in the El Paso Mountains (Figs. 7, 10B). Similar conclusions were reached by Carter (1982, 1987, 1994).

At ca. 10.3 Ma, pyroclastic flows from the western Lava Mountains crossed the trace of the Garlock fault and are now exposed in the western El Paso Mountains in member 5 of the Dove Spring Formation. This correlation requires that the Lava Mountains and El Paso Mountains were in close proximity at 10.3 Ma (Fig. 10C).

Sinistral motion on the Garlock fault after 10.3 Ma resulted in the separation of the Lava and El Paso Mountains, counterclockwise rotation of the El Paso Mountains (Loomis and Burbank, 1988), and folding in the Lava Mountains (Smith, 1964). The latter two events may have occurred simultaneously (Fig. 10D).

In Quaternary time, the sediment transport direction reversed, and sandstone accumulated north of the Garlock fault in the Christmas Canyon basin. At ca. 602 ka, ash from eruptions of the Yellowstone caldera accumulated in the upper part of the Christmas Canyon Formation (Gansecki et al., 1998). Topographically high gravels including member 4 basalt clasts were shed to the north and deposited on the sandstone facies of the Christmas Canyon Formation. These gravels produced the conglomerate facies described by Smith (1964) (Fig. 10E).

CONCLUSIONS

Volcanism in the Lava Mountains occurred between 11.7 and 5.8 Ma and was contemporaneous with sinistral motion on the Garlock fault (after 17 Ma to the present).

Three chemical groups of volcanic rocks erupted in the Lava Mountains in three episodes over a period of 5 m.y. These are (1) a main group consisting of the andesite of Summit Diggings, Almond Mountain tuff, and Lava Mountains Andesite, (2) the basalt of Teagle Wash, and (3) tuffs in the northeastern Lava Mountains and dacite in the Summit Range. Volcanic rocks of each group have distinctive chemical signatures useful for correlation of units across the Garlock fault. Tuffs in the Almond Mountain volcanic section may be equivalent to a thin tuff in member 5 of the Dove Spring Formation, El Paso Mountains. Basalt of Teagle Wash probably correlates with basalt flows in member 4, and tuffs in the northeast Lava Mountains may be equivalent to the tuff of member 2. Correlation of these units across the Garlock fault implies that the Lava Mountains were situated just south of the El Paso Mountains between 11.6 and 10.3 Ma and that 32 to 40 km of offset occurred on the Garlock fault in ~10.4 m.y., resulting in a displacement rate of 3.2 to 3.8 mm/yr. Projecting this rate to the total offset of 64 km on the Garlock suggests that left-lateral slip began at about 16.4 Ma. This value agrees with Monastero et al. (1997) and is very close to the time of onset of extension in the Death Valley area (15.7–15.1 Ma) (Davis and Burchfiel, 1973).

ACKNOWLEDGMENTS

We thank the U.S. Navy's Geothermal Program Office for providing the funding for this project. Jonathan Miller, Peter Weigand, and Allen Glazner provided excellent reviews that substantially improved the paper. We especially thank Monica C. Camin and Easte M. Warnick for their help in preparing and analyzing samples in the University of Nevada, Las Vegas, Rock Chemistry Laboratory.

REFERENCES CITED

Burbank, D.W., and Whistler, D.P., 1987, Temporally constrained tectonic relations derived from magnetostratigraphic data: Implications for the initiation of the Garlock fault, California: Geology, v. 15, p. 1172–1175.

Carter, B.A., 1980, Quaternary displacement on the Garlock fault, California, *in* Fife, D.L., and Brown, A.R., eds., Geology and mineral wealth of the California desert: Santa Ana, California, South Coast Geological Society Guidebook, Santa Ana, South Coast Geological Society, Dibblee Volume, p. 457–466.

Carter, B.A., 1982, Neogene displacement on the Garlock fault, California: Eos (Transactions, American Geophysical Union), v. 63, p. 1124.

Carter, B.A., 1987, Quaternary fault-line features of the central Garlock fault, Kern County, California: Geological Society of America Centennial Field Guide, Cordilleran Section, p. 133–135.

Carter, B.A., 1994, Neogene offsets and displacement rates, central Garlock fault, California, *in* McGill, S.F., and Ross, T.M., eds., Geological investigations of an active margin: San Bernardino, California, Geological Society of America Cordilleran Section Guidebook, p. 348–356.

Davis, G.A., and Burchfiel, B.C., 1973, Garlock fault: An intracontinental transform structure, southern California: Geological Society of America Bulletin, v. 84, p. 1407–1422.

Dibblee, T.W., Jr., 1967, Areal geology of the western Mojave Desert, California: U.S. Geological Survey Professional Paper 522, 153 p.

Gansecki, C.A., Mahood, G.A., and McWilliams, M., 1998, New ages for the climactic eruptions at Yellowstone: Single crystal ^{40}Ar/^{39}Ar dating identifies contamination: Geology, v. 26, p. 343–346.

Keenan, D.L., 2000, The geology and geochemistry of volcanic rocks in the Lava Mountains, California: Implications for Miocene development of the Garlock fault [M.S. thesis]: Las Vegas, University of Nevada, 81 p.

Loomis, D.P., and Burbank, D.W., 1988, The stratigraphic evolution of the El Paso basin, southern California: Implication for the Miocene development of the Garlock fault and uplift of the Sierra Nevada: Geological Society of America Bulletin, v. 100, p. 12–28.

McGill, S., and Sieh, K., 1993, Holocene slip rate of the central Garlock fault in southeastern Searles Valley, California: Journal of Geophysical Research, v. 98, p. 14217–14231.

Monastero, F.C., Sabin, A.E., and Walker, J.D., 1997, Evidence for post-early Miocene initiation movement on the Garlock fault from offset of the Cudahy Camp Formation, east-central California: Geology, v. 25, p. 247–250.

Smith, G.I., 1962, Large lateral displacement on the Garlock fault, California, as measured from offset dike swarm: American Association of Petroleum Geologists Bulletin, v. 46, p. 85–104.

Smith, G.I., 1964, Geology and volcanic petrology of the Lava Mountains, San Bernardino County, California: U.S. Geologic Survey Professional Paper 457, 97 p.

Smith, G.I., 1991, Anomalous folds associated with the east-central part of the Garlock fault, southeast California: Geological Society of America Bulletin, v. 103, p. 615–624.

Smith, G.I., and Ketner, K.B., 1970, Lateral displacement on the Garlock fault, southeastern California, suggested by offset sections of similar metasedimentary rocks: U.S. Geologic Survey Professional Paper 700-D, p. D1–D9.

Sun, S., and McDonough, W.F., 1989, Chemical and isotopic systematics of oceanic basalts: Implications for mantle composition and processes, *in* Saunders, A.D., and Norry, M.J., eds., Magmatism in the ocean basins: Geological Society [London] Special Publication 41, p. 313–314.

MANUSCRIPT ACCEPTED BY THE SOCIETY MAY 9, 2001

Geological Society of America
Memoir 195
2002

Late Cenozoic crustal contraction in the Kramer Hills, west-central Mojave Desert, California

Jonathan K. Linn*
J. Douglas Walker
Department of Geology, University of Kansas, Lawrence, Kansas 66045, USA
John M. Bartley
Department of Geology and Geophysics, University of Utah, Salt Lake City, Utah, 84112-0111, USA

ABSTRACT

Folding and faulting of Miocene Tropico Group rocks in the Kramer Hills, west-central Mojave Desert, is interpreted to record crustal contraction. North-trending folds and spatially associated north-striking faults with probable small reverse displacements are interpreted to record east-west contraction. North-south contraction that probably is somewhat younger resulted in widespread east-northeast–trending, close-to-isoclinal folds that are associated with faults that are interpreted mainly to dip to the south and accommodate north-verging reverse slip. Bed-length calculations indicate at least 2.5 km (30%) of shortening during east-west contraction and at least 4.8 km (50%) of shortening during north-verging contraction. Both deformation episodes affect the 21.3 Ma Red Buttes Quartz Basalt, and some deformation may affect Pleistocene(?) fanglomerate deposits. Late Cenozoic crustal shortening recorded in the Kramer Hills is interpreted to reflect the contractional component of regional dextral transpression of the Mojave block.

INTRODUCTION

Most geologic studies of the Mojave Desert region have interpreted Cenozoic rocks and structures in terms of crustal extension (Dokka and Glazner, 1982; Dokka, 1983, 1986; Glazner et al., 1989; Walker et al., 1990) or strike-slip faulting related to the transform boundary between the North American and Pacific plates (Dibblee, 1961; Garfunkel, 1974; Dokka and Travis, 1990; Schermer et al., 1996). However, interpretations of the tectonic history of the western part of the greater Mojave Desert region diverge widely. Dokka (1989) interpreted much

of the Mojave Desert west of Barstow to have been highly extended in the early Miocene to form what he termed the Edwards terrane. He interpreted deformed Miocene strata in the Kramer Hills to form southwest-tilted fault blocks bounded by northeast-dipping normal faults that merge downward into a regional extensional detachment (Plate 3c of Dokka, 1989). Dokka interpreted the regional detachment to be exposed near The Buttes (Dokka and Woodburne, 1986). In contrast, Walker et al. (1990) interpreted the same contact near The Buttes to be an intrusive or faulted intrusive contact rather than a major extensional detachment. Bartley et al. (1990) interpreted stratal

*E-mail: Jon_Linn@emainc.com
Present address: Eagan, McAllister Assoc., Inc., P.O. Box 986, Lexington Park, Maryland 20653, USA.

Linn, J.K., Walker, J.D., and Bartley, J.M., 2002, Late Cenozoic crustal contraction in the Kramer Hills, west-central Mojave Desert, California, *in* Glazner, A.F., Walker, J.D., and Bartley, J.M., eds., Geologic Evolution of the Mojave Desert and Southwestern Basin and Range: Boulder, Colorado, Geological Society of America Memoir 195, p. 161–172.

tilts in the Kramer Hills and other nearby ranges to reflect contractional folding caused by late Cenozoic dextral transpression of the Mojave block. They concluded that convincing evidence for major Cenozoic crustal extension in the western Mojave Desert is lacking, and they further suggested that late Cenozoic basins that have commonly been interpreted as extensional pull-aparts may actually be bounded by reverse faults (also see Glazner and Bartley, 1994; Glazner et al., 2000).

The Kramer Hills are located within domain I of the strike-slip fault-block reconstruction of the Mojave region presented by Dokka and Travis (1990). Those authors interpreted the domain to include a small number of strike-slip faults that they inferred probably to be inactive and to accommodate only small displacements. Dibblee (1960a) mapped four northwest-striking faults to the west and southwest of the Kramer Hills that are poorly exposed and largely concealed by Quaternary alluvium. Only the Blake Ranch fault, ~10 km southwest of the Kramer Hills, shows conclusive evidence of right-lateral displacement, and the most laterally continuous of the faults, the Spring fault, probably possesses less than 75 m of separation (Dibblee, 1960a).

This paper describes detailed geologic mapping of the Kramer Hills. On the basis of the mapping results, we address the tectonic significance of the Cenozoic faults and stratal tilts, and we place the study area into the overall tectonic framework of the Mojave block.

GEOLOGY OF THE KRAMER HILLS

The Kramer Hills are a low-lying range underlain by four rock assemblages (Figs. 1 and 2; see also map in KRAMER on CD ROM): metamorphic rocks of probable pre-Mesozoic age, Mesozoic plutonic rocks, Miocene sedimentary and volcanic rocks assigned to the Tropico Group (Bowen, 1954; Dibblee, 1958a, 1960a, 1960b, 1967), and Quaternary fanglomerate and alluvium. Our mapping focused on the Tropico Group, the stratigraphy and sedimentology of which were previously described by Dibblee (1958a, 1960a, 1960b). Fillmore et al. (1994) placed the Tropico Group into an early Miocene regional stratigraphic framework for the Mojave Desert.

The Tropico Group is dominated by lacustrine sedimentary rocks including arkose, shale, limestone, and dolostone, with intercalated basalt flows (Dibblee, 1958a, 1958b, 1958c, 1960a, 1960b, 1967). Mafic lava flows in the middle part of the Tropico Group are referred to as the Red Buttes Quartz Basalt in the Kramer Hills and as the Saddleback Basalt in the Saddleback Mountain and Castle Buttes areas (see Fig. 1 for locations); these rocks yielded K-Ar dates of 21.3 ± 0.5 Ma (Dokka and Baksi, 1989) and 19.8 ± 0.7 Ma (Armstrong and Higgins, 1973), respectively. The relatively thin and fine-grained Tropico Group records deposition in a shallow, tectonically stable early Miocene basin (Fillmore et al., 1994).

Lower Tropico Group strata are the most widely exposed Miocene rocks in the Kramer Hills. Exposures are best in the southern part of the area where seven informal units were mapped (Figs. 2, 3). Overlying the lower Tropico Group is the Red Buttes Quartz Basalt, which is the dominant ridge former in the central and southern Kramer Hills. Stratigraphic relationships of the lower Tropico Group and Red Buttes Quartz Basalt vary significantly across the area (Fig. 3). Overlying the Red Buttes Quartz Basalt are sedimentary strata of the upper Tropico Group, but exposures of this part of the section are sparse, poor, and largely rather uninformative. Several isolated ridges in the Kramer Hills are underlain by an unnamed dacite that probably is also Miocene in age. However, its relationship to the Tropico Group is unknown because the contact between the two is everywhere concealed.

KRAMER HILLS STRUCTURES

The Kramer Hills as a whole define an anticline that is cored by basement and flanked by highly deformed Tropico Group strata. Structures that deform the Tropico Group include poorly exposed faults and both map-scale and mesoscopic folds. The faults generally strike either north or east-northeast. The folds generally are closely associated with the faults and can be grouped into three categories by orientation and interlimb angle: (1) east-northeast–trending, close-to-isoclinal folds, (2) south-plunging, close-to-tight folds, and (3) north-trending, tight folds. Whereas east-northeast–trending structures appear throughout the study area, north-trending structures mainly were found in the central Kramer Hills and locally in the southern part of the range. The absence of north-trending structures in the northern Kramer Hills may largely result from poor exposure.

North-striking faults

North-striking faults mainly were recognized in the central Kramer Hills (Fig. 2A, areas 3 and 4). Six faults were mapped in the vicinity that have approximately north-trending traces. No actual fault surface is exposed, but the traces are clearly defined by offsets of resistant beds in the Tropico Group. Neither the sense nor amount of slip across the faults could be determined conclusively owing to limited exposure.

The northern two faults in area 3 sinistrally separate a limestone unit in the lower Tropico Group by ~10 m. Another north-striking fault that may be the southern continuation of these faults sinistrally separates lower Tropico Group strata by ~300 m. A southward continuation of the same zone of faults is suggested by the sinistral offset between the strike ridges of the Red Buttes Quartz Basalt in areas 1 and 2 (Fig. 2B), but any such fault or fault zone is entirely concealed by alluvium (see dashed contact in Fig. 2B). The consistent sinistral separation across all of these faults suggests either sinistral slip or east-side-down dip slip that would be reverse if the faults dip to the west and normal if they dip east.

In area 4, a north-northeast–striking fault separates mod-

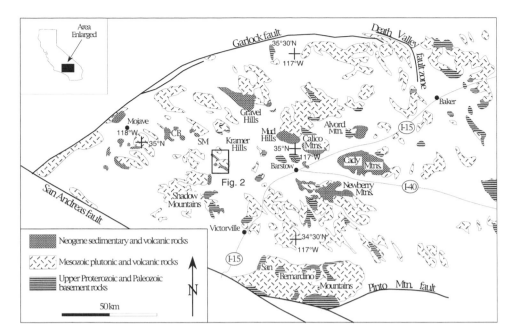

Figure 1. Simplified geologic and location map of the west-central Mojave Desert. Location of Figure 2 is shown by the box around the Kramer Hills. CB—Castle Butte; SM—Saddleback Mountain.

erately west-dipping lower Tropico Group strata on its west from roughly equivalent strata on the east that are folded into a north-plunging, overturned syncline (Fig. 2). The fault is concealed by alluvium but is required by the obvious structural discordance. Immediately to the west of this fault, two poorly exposed, north-northwest–striking faults dextrally separate lower Tropico Group beds by small distances.

East- to northeast-striking faults

Faults with traces that trend east to northeast were mapped throughout the Kramer Hills. In the southern Kramer Hills, an east-northeast-striking fault, oriented at a low angle to the strike of bedding, places the middle limestone unit (Mltlm) adjacent to a younger limestone unit (Mltls) and places the basal tuff unit (Mlttu) against the sandstone unit (Mltss) (Fig. 2B, northwest corner of area 1). The fault continues for at least 1 km along strike and has less than 100 m of stratigraphic separation. The fault trace is difficult to locate precisely but must trend east-northeast on the basis of outcrop patterns of the rocks that it displaces (Fig. 2B). Westward, it probably bends to a west or northwest strike, subparallel to the basalt ridge to its south. Eastward, the fault trace trends east-northeast under the alluvium. North-side-up dip separation requires the fault to accommodate reverse slip if north dipping and normal slip if south dipping.

In the central Kramer Hills, an east-northeast-striking fault places basement rocks against the lower Tropico Group (Fig. 2, southern part of area 4). The fault has ~1 km of dextral separation across a mapped trace length of nearly 2 km. Dibblee (1960a, 1960b, 1967) inferred the fault to continue 4 km northeastward to bound a ridge of dacite. The relatively large sepa-

ration across the fault makes a trace at least this long likely. The fault surface is unexposed, but deflection of the fault trace across topography indicates that the fault dips steeply southward. Therefore, the fault probably accommodated reverse or dextral slip. To the north of and subparallel to this fault are two additional faults that were recognized from smaller amounts of dextral separation of both lower and upper Tropico Group rock units.

Two east-northeast–striking faults were mapped in the northern Kramer Hills (Fig. 2A, area 5). The fault with larger separation places the basal tuff unit, lower limestone unit, and overlying basalt against dolostone. The stratigraphic position of the dolostone north of the fault is uncertain, but it must be younger than the basalt overlying the lower limestone unit south of the fault. The fault cannot be traced to the northeast beyond the contact between basement and Miocene rocks, and the western continuation of the fault cannot be traced beyond exposures of the lower Tropico Group. The stratigraphic relationships of the rocks adjacent to the fault permit the fault to be a south-dipping reverse fault, a north-dipping normal fault, or a right-lateral strike-slip fault. Because the stratigraphy is poorly known in this area, the separation across the fault is unknown. Another north-northeast–striking fault cuts interbedded carbonate and shale exposed in a prospect pit ~500 m north of the fault just described. Less than 1 m of separation is evident. The fault nonetheless is important because it is the only well-exposed fault in the Kramer Hills and because it displays a clear reverse sense of separation. The fault dips ~60° to the south, and several smaller faults with similar sense of separation splay off of it to the north. Because of these relationships, we interpret this fault to have some component of reverse slip.

Finally, a broadly east-striking fault may be present in the

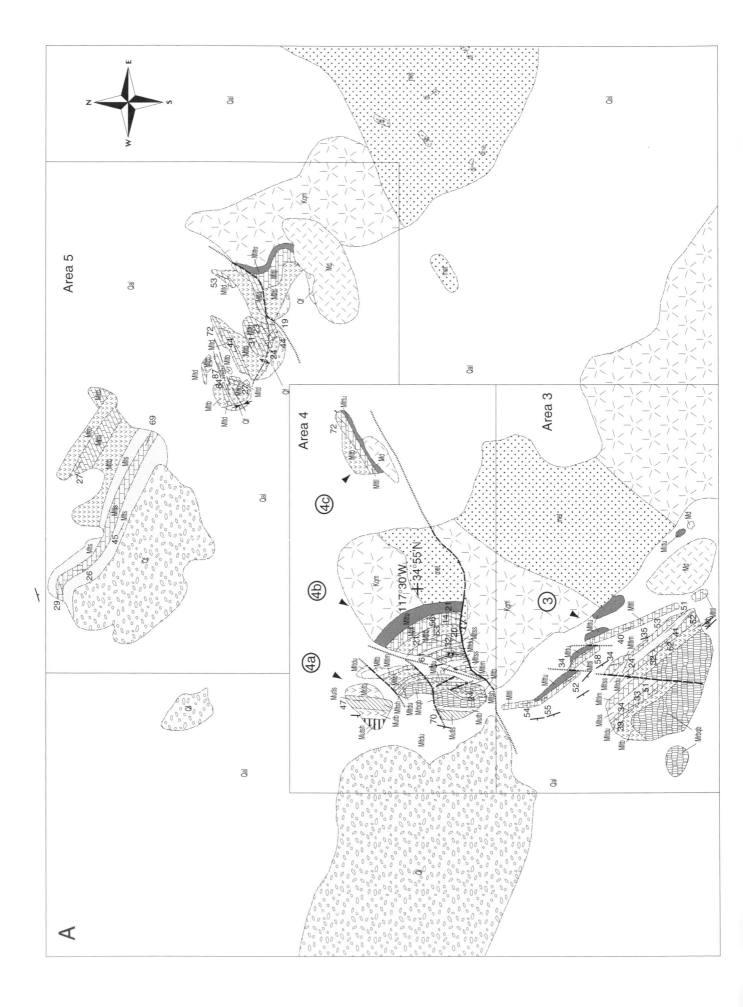

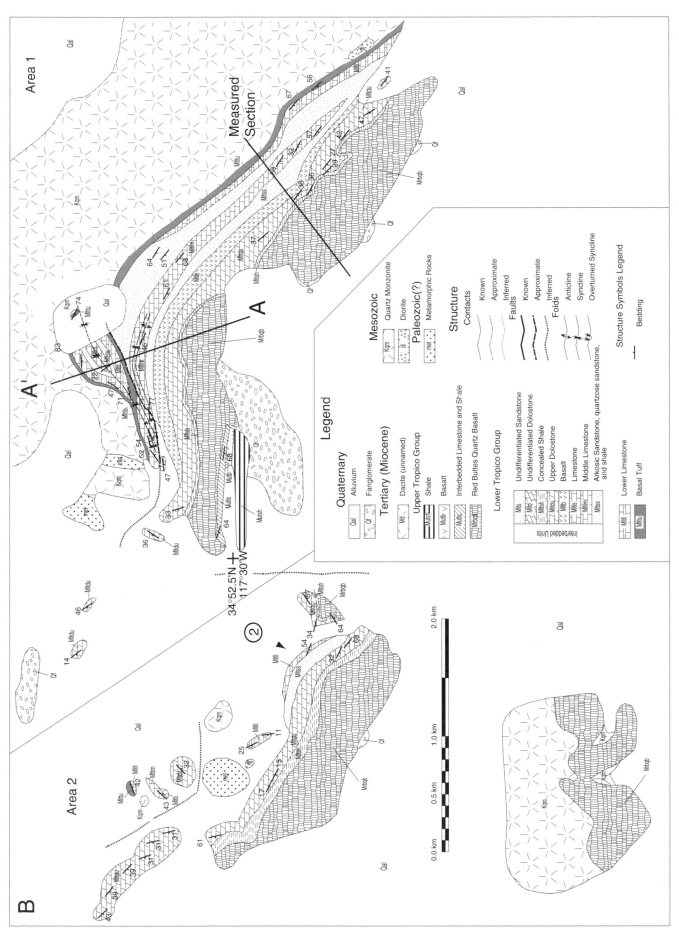

Figure 2. Geologic map of the Kramer Hills: (A) northern Kramer Hills, (B) southern Kramer Hills. Note location of measured section on B. Circled numbers indicate locations of stratigraphic columns illustrated in Figure 3. Parts A and B join directly at their bottom and top, respectively.

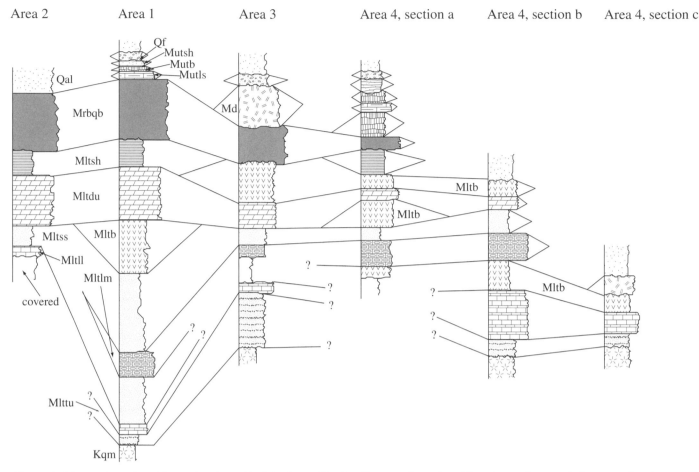

Figure 3. Measured stratigraphic section (area 1) of the lower Tropico Group and stratigraphic columns for correlative strata in other areas (see Fig. 2 for locations and for explanation of unit ornaments). Except for the measured section, thicknesses were estimated from dips and outcrop widths of rock units. Contacts in the upper Tropico Group are assumed to be conformable but are unexposed.

central part of area 2 (Fig. 2B) because a structure probably is required between basement outcrops to the south and southwest-dipping exposures of the upper dolostone on the north. Exposures in this area, however, are extremely poor; therefore, the nature and precise orientation of any such structure are unknown.

East-northeast–trending, close-to-isoclinal folds

East-northeast–trending, close-to-isoclinal folds are present throughout the Kramer Hills. Folds of this set are typically found adjacent to east-northeast–striking faults. In the southern part of the study area, tight to isoclinal folds are exposed in the lower Tropico Group north of the east-northeast–striking fault and in the middle limestone unit to the south of the fault (Fig. 2, northwestern area 1). North of the fault, an anticline and syncline fold the basal tuff, lower limestone, and sandstone units. The folds verge north, are closed to tight, and plunge to the southwest (Fig. 4A). The axial planes strike subparallel to the east-northeast–striking fault. The anticline abuts the fault

and is much tighter than the syncline; however, the relationship of the fold pair to the fault cannot be determined conclusively. Exposures of the folds are much poorer both to the northeast and southwest of this area

South of the fault, tight to isoclinal folds in the middle limestone unit are exposed in several prospect pits. Folds are most common in shale and thinly bedded limestone. In shale-rich intervals, coaxially refolded isoclinal folds are abundant whereas in carbonate-rich intervals, the folds are typically tight (Fig. 5). The folds verge to the south, and their hinge lines generally plunge gently to the east (Fig. 4B). A large excavation ~250 m east of the prospect pits exposes a syncline-anticline pair in the middle limestone unit. Because this interval of the middle limestone is composed predominantly of competent carbonate strata, the folds are close-to-tight rather than isoclinal. The folds are parallel and verge to the south, and their hinge lines plunge gently to the northwest. Although the prospect pit provides the only exposure of folded strata of middle limestone in this area, the folds probably extend from the east-northeast–striking fault through the prospect pit and southwest of the pit

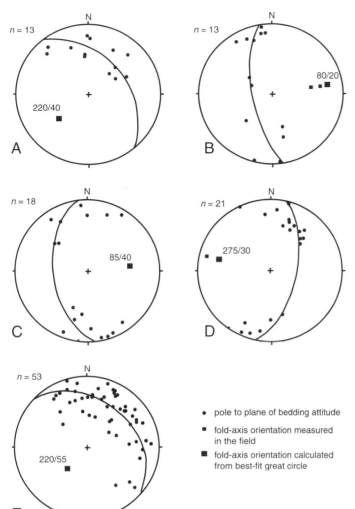

- pole to plane of bedding attitude
- ■ fold-axis orientation measured in the field
- ■ fold-axis orientation calculated from best-fit great circle

Figure 4. Equal-area plots of bedding and fold axes. (A) Area 1, north of east-northeast–striking fault. (B) Northern part of area 1, south of fault. (C) Area 2. (D) Area 5, north of east-northeast–striking fault. (E) Area 5, south of east-northeast–striking fault.

Figure 5. Outcrop photographs of folded strata in the Kramer Hills. (A) Folded carbonate-rich beds. (B) Coaxially refolded folds in shale-rich interval. Note quarter for scale.

an unknown distance. The isolated exposures of limestone may reflect intrafolial folds of competent beds within the incompetent shale-rich sequence.

An isoclinally folded shale-rich interval in the upper part of the lower Tropico Group is exposed in a prospect pit in the southeastern Kramer Hills. Fold orientations vary (Fig. 4C), and most folds are coaxially refolded. Where more-competent carbonate beds are present, folds are intrafolial in character. Axial planes typically strike east and range in dip from steeply north to steeply south. Folds in the upper dolostone are exposed only in the prospect pit, and therefore the lateral extent of folding in this area is uncertain.

A mesoscopic anticline-syncline pair that trends roughly east is exposed in the northern Kramer Hills (Fig. 2A, southeastern area 5). An east-northeast–striking fault cuts the anticline. North of the fault, a prospect pit exposes a smaller north-

verging, close anticline that is interpreted to be related to the map-scale fold (Fig. 4D). The northern limb of the anticline dips steeply to the northeast, and the southern limb dips 50°–60° to the southwest. Two distinct yellow-colored dolostone beds permit the anticline to be traced laterally in both directions from the prospect pit ~100 m to where the beds disappear beneath alluvium. The trace of the fold's hinge surface is sub-parallel to the east-northeast–striking fault. A syncline presumably related to the faulted anticline is poorly exposed to its north.

The lower limestone unit south of the east-northeast–striking fault contains many mesoscopic isoclinal and intrafolial folds (Fig. 4E). The folds generally can be recognized by following resistant carbonate beds, but several isoclinally folded shale-rich intervals also are exposed. The hinges of the folds were rarely located but, where exposed, the hinge lines plunge gently to the east, and axial surfaces appear to be vertical.

South-plunging, close-to-tight folds

Map-scale south-plunging folds are preserved in the quartz basalt and lower Tropico Group in the southern Kramer Hills. In the southeastern Kramer Hills, a south-plunging, close syncline affects the generally southwest-dipping strata of the Tropico Group. A comparable but much tighter fold also is present to the west. Evidence for folds in this orientation elsewhere in the Kramer Hills is lacking.

North-trending tight fold

The only north-plunging fold in the area is the previously mentioned east-verging overturned syncline in the central Kramer Hills (Fig. 2, area 4). The core of the fold consists of fragmented, poorly exposed basalt. Facing indicators suggest that the east limb of the syncline, which dips on average ~40° to the west, is upright, consistent with a stratigraphic contact with underlying basement rocks. The west limb of the syncline dips ~70° to the west and probably consists of overturned beds of the Tropico Group. Unfortunately, no facing indicators were found to confirm this interpretation. However, overall stratigraphic relationships favor the presence of a fold. The sequence basalt, middle limestone, micaceous sandstone, upper dolostone, and basalt in the eastern limb of the syncline is repeated in reverse order westward. This mirror-image sequence of units is most readily explained by a syncline. Also, if there were no fold repetition, then the 12 distinct units in the lower Tropico Group recognized here would greatly exceed the number of lower Tropico Group units found anywhere else in the Kramer (no more than seven; Fig. 3). On the basis of measured bedding attitudes, the fold axis plunges shallowly to the north.

STRUCTURAL INTERPRETATION

Senses of slip across faults in the Kramer Hills are difficult to determine owing to poor exposure. However, the map patterns and spatially associated folds permit some reasonable inferences.

The fault in area 4 with the largest dextral separation also dips to the south, and its separation suggests either reverse or right-lateral slip. East-northeast–striking strike-slip faults in the Mojave block are consistently left lateral (e.g., Carter et al., 1987; Schermer et al., 1996). Although it is conceivable that the fault formed as a northwest-striking dextral fault and was later reoriented by vertical-axis rotation, two lines of evidence argue against this interpretation. First, paleomagnetic data (Golombek and Brown, 1988) from Miocene basalts in this vicinity suggest 50° of clockwise vertical-axis rotation. It is not clear that this paleomagnetic result should be applied to this particular fault in the Kramer Hills but, if such a rotation were restored, the fault would have originated with a north-northeast strike that is no better match for the regional pattern of Neogene strike-slip faults. Second, large vertical-axis block rotations in the Mojave Desert appear mainly to be found in the areas dominated by east-striking left-slip faults. Vertical-axis block rotations appear generally to be small or negligible in areas like the western Mojave Desert that mainly expose northwest-striking right-slip faults (e.g., Schermer et al., 1996; Miller and Yount, this volume). Hence, we interpret this to be primarily a reverse-slip fault.

Other similarly oriented faults in the Kramer Hills also are interpreted to accommodate mainly reverse slip because of their close spatial association to contractional folds. In area 1, tight to isoclinal folds adjacent to the east-northeast–striking fault verge away from the fault on both sides, i.e., to the south on the south side of the fault and to the north on its north side. The locations of the folds, orientations of their axes, and the pattern of fold vergence all suggest that the folds developed during displacement across the fault. The fault therefore is interpreted to be a reverse fault that dips to the north and that may be antithetic to an inferred south-dipping reverse fault located at or near the contact between Miocene and basement rocks (Fig. 6). The outcrop geometry broadly resembles a positive flower structure (e.g., Harding, 1976); therefore, it is possible that this structure is transpressive rather than purely contractional. The sense of obliquity of the folds to the fault suggests a component of left slip across the fault, consistent with the kinematics of similarly oriented faults elsewhere in the Mojave Desert (e.g., Schermer et al., 1996; Miller and Yount, this volume).

Interpretations of the north-trending structures are yet more uncertain. North-striking faults have smaller separations, rarely can be traced for more than a few hundred meters, and were not observed in clear crosscutting relationships with other structures. However, because all of the mapped north-striking faults are located broadly on strike with one another, the faults are interpreted to belong to a single fault zone.

We interpret the north-striking fault zone to have accommodated broadly east-west contraction for two reasons. First, the sense of separation across the faults changes from uniformly sinistral in area 3 to mainly dextral in area 4. The change correlates with location relative to the range-scale basement-cored anticline: sinistral separations are found where Tropico Group strata dip off of the range toward the southwest, and dextral separations exist where these strata dip off of the range overall toward west and northwest. The pattern of separation senses therefore favors overall west-side-up dip slip rather than strike slip. Second, much as east-northeast–trending folds are linked to the north-northeast–striking faults, the north-plunging, overturned syncline in area 4 is located adjacent and subparallel to the zones of north-striking faults. We interpret the east-verging

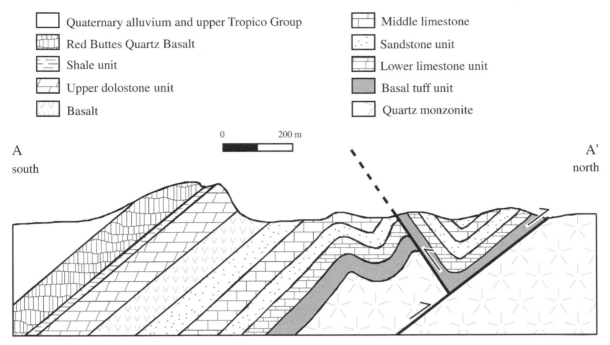

Figure 6. Interpretive geologic cross section of the northern part of area 1, illustrating the inferred fault geometry including the mapped north-dipping reverse fault and its connection to an inferred south-dipping reverse fault. Location of cross section shown in Figure 2. Vertical exaggeration ~2.

overturned syncline in area 4 to be related to slip across the north-striking fault zone that cuts its western limb. If so, then the orientation and vergence of the fold suggest that the fault zone dips to the west and accommodated reverse slip.

The overturned syncline is truncated at a high angle by an east-northeast–striking fault. The intersection between this fault and the north-northeast–striking fault concealed to the west is unexposed. However, if the overturned syncline formed along the adjacent north-striking fault zone, then the east-northeast–striking fault appears to be younger than the north-striking faults.

This timing relationship might seem inconsistent with the fact that the zone of north-striking faults appears relatively unaffected by the east-northeast–striking faults that project into it. However, if the east-northeast–striking faults accommodated mainly reverse slip as suggested, and if the north-striking faults are steep as suggested by their relatively straight traces, then slip vectors across east-northeast–striking faults were oriented at a low angle to north-striking fault planes. Therefore, slip across the east-northeast–striking faults may not have greatly affected the traces of north-striking faults.

The significance of the fault in area 2 is difficult to determine because the location of its western continuation is unknown. However, based on the locations and attitudes of adjacent Tropico Group outcrops, the fault is interpreted to bend to the northwest and juxtapose northeast-striking Tropico Group strata overlying basement quartz monzonite with northwest-striking upper dolostone on the south (Fig. 2). The north-

east-striking strata may be the west limb of a poorly exposed syncline whose eastern limb is represented only by small outcrops of the northwest-striking upper dolostone unit in the northwestern part of area 1 (Fig. 2). The northeast-striking strata in area 2 correlate better with the strata in area 1 than the strata south of the fault in area 2. Basalt and the middle limestone units are exposed in a prospect pit north of the fault in area 2: no basalt is present in the section of Tropico Group strata south of the fault. On the basis of these stratigraphic relationships and the fault's general trend, this fault, if the interpretation is correct, appears to be kinematically related to other east-northeast–trending faults in the Kramer Hills.

Fault exposures are sufficiently poor that, on the basis of only our observations of faults, we could not exclude the possibility of significant early Miocene crustal extension in the area (Dokka, 1989). However, several observations lead us to doubt that the hypothesis is tenable. The tilted rocks do not form the southwest-dipping homoclinal repetitions that might be expected in such an extensional system and that were illustrated by Dokka (1989). Instead, tilted Miocene strata form the limbs of contractional folds. None of the mapped faults strikes to the northwest, and, although some map relationships permit normal slip, none particularly favors such an interpretation. Normal slip across the faults would leave unexplained their close spatial association with tight upright folds. Finally, the Tropico Group is broadly age correlative with the synextensional Pickhandle Formation of the central part of the Mojave Desert region but drastically differs from it (Fillmore et al., 1994). The Pickhandle Formation is composed of thick pyroclastic debris flows and coarse detrital deposits that include megabreccia sheets, whereas the Tropico Group is characterized by carbonate and fine-grained fluviolacustrine clastic strata that indicate relative tectonic quiescence in the western part of the Mojave Desert region when the Central Mojave metamorphic core complex was being formed (also see Glazner et al., this volume).

Structural evolution

Two episodes of Miocene–Holocene crustal contraction may be recorded in the Kramer Hills. On the basis of the inferred crosscutting relationships in area 4, the older event caused east-west contraction that is recorded in north-trending structures. Although overprinting relationships were not observed in areas 1 and 2 between map-scale south-plunging folds and east-northeast–trending structures, on the basis of orientation, the south-plunging folds are interpreted also to reflect the episode of east-west shortening.

East-west contraction apparently was followed by broadly north-south shortening. All east-northeast–trending structures in the Kramer Hills are interpreted to reflect the same period of north-south shortening, although present exposures do not indicate whether the structures actually all formed synchronously. Another permissible alternative is that all of the structures formed in a single strain field. The orientations of the faults may have been mainly governed by preexisting fractures in the basement complex. Because the folds are largely localized along the faults, their locations and orientations may have been governed more by the faults than by the regional strain field. Under such circumstances, crosscutting relationships may indicate more about the inherited basement fracture geometry than about age relationships.

The amount of shortening recorded by structures in the Kramer Hills is difficult to determine owing to poor exposure. However, the east-northeast–trending structures appear to record a greater amount of contraction than the north-trending structures. Bed-length restoration across the east-northeast–trending structures indicates a minimum of 4.8 km (50%) shortening in a north-south direction (for example, Fig. 6; see Linn, 1992, for further details). Figure 6 is based on an assumed fault dip of 60° and the minimum dip slip required to account for the observed separations across mapped faults. Bed-length restoration across the south-plunging folds in areas 1 and 2 indicates a minimum of 2.5 km (30%) shortening in an east-west direction. A similar amount of shortening presumably is recorded by the north-northeast–striking fault zone and overturned syncline in area 4, but there are insufficient data to make an independent estimate in that area.

Timing of deformation

The age of crustal shortening in the Kramer Hills is poorly known because the only Tropico Group rock that has been dated is the 21.3 ± 0.5 Ma Red Buttes Quartz Basalt (Dokka and Baksi, 1989). However, the quartz basalt and overlying upper Tropico Group strata appear to have been affected by all episodes of contraction. The character of the Tropico Group itself also suggests that the deformation is entirely younger than its deposition. The extent to which younger fanglomerate or alluvium is deformed is uncertain. Quaternary(?) fanglomerate in some areas of the Kramer Hills dips as much as 25° (Dibblee, 1960a), which suggests that some deformation occurred since its deposition. Dibblee (1960a) also interpreted Quaternary fanglomerate west of the Kramer Hills to be cut by an east-striking fault. Overall, most deformation probably occurred after deposition of the upper Tropico Group and before deposition of the Quaternary fanglomerate, but minor deformation younger than fanglomerate deposition is apparent.

TECTONIC SETTING

Deformation in the Kramer Hills has been interpreted to record either extension or contraction. Dokka (1989) interpreted tilting in the Kramer Hills to reflect tilting of normal-fault—bounded blocks within an extensional detachment terrane (his Edwards terrane) that encompasses most of the western Mojave Desert. However, stratal tilts in the Kramer Hills appear to be largely, if not exclusively, a result of folding rather than tilting of fault-bounded blocks. Although evidence relating to fault geometries and kinematics is disappointingly sparse, that sparse evidence tends to favor contraction over extension across the mapped faults. Combined with the contrast between the Tropico Group and coeval, synextensional Pickhandle Formation (Fillmore et al., 1994), we interpret the structure of the Kramer Hills largely to reflect contractional or transpressional deformation.

Contractional deformation elsewhere in the Mojave Desert is overprinted on early Miocene crustal extension (e.g., Bartley et al., 1990; Glazner et al., 2000) and is interpreted to be related to the right-slip fault regime that has dominated Mojave tectonics since the middle Miocene (e.g., Dibblee, 1961; Garfunkel, 1974; Dokka, 1983; Glazner et al., this volume). Some of the contractional structures are found at leftward (restraining) bends or stepovers along right-slip faults. However, for the contractional structures in the Kramer Hills to have formed at such a restraining bend or stepover, the net slip across the related strike-slip fault must equal or exceed the amount of shortening. If the contraction estimates reported previously are accurate, then the Kramer Hills would have to be located at a restraining bend in a strike-slip fault with several kilometers of late Cenozoic right slip. Although such a major strike-slip fault is not excluded at this location by present knowledge of the regional geology, we are unaware of direct evidence for it.

The alternative is that structures in the Kramer Hills record horizontal contraction that is not directly linked to a strike-slip fault. Such contractional structures are common in obliquely convergent tectonic regimes because vertical faults can accommodate only the strike-slip component of the displacement vector. The contractional component must be accommodated elsewhere by other structures. Partitioning of convergent and lateral components of motion is typical of obliquely convergent tectonic systems (e.g., Jarrard, 1986; Namson and Davis, 1988; Jackson, 1992; Ave Lallemant, 1997). Therefore, late Cenozoic contractional structures in the Mojave Desert region that, as in the Kramer Hills, do not appear to be associated with restraining bends along major strike-slip faults may reflect the contractional component of a regionally transpressive displacement field, similar to the hypothesis put forward by Bartley et al. (1990).

CONCLUSIONS

The structure of the Kramer Hills is characterized by upright to inclined, close-to-isoclinal folds of Miocene stratified rocks along two general trends, north and east-northeast. The folds are spatially associated with, and oriented subparallel to, faults that are poorly exposed although clearly identifiable via map patterns. Direct evidence for either the dips or the kinematics of the faults is very sparse. However, the faults are interpreted to be contractional on the basis of (1) their close spatial association with obviously contractional folds and (2) patterns of stratal separation and fault dip that are at worst consistent with, and at best supportive of, reverse movement. The results corroborate an earlier suggestion (Bartley et al., 1990) that tilting of Miocene strata in the western part of the Mojave Desert region primarily reflects contractional folding rather than tilting of normal-fault–bounded blocks. The contractional deformation probably is related to ongoing regional dextral shear of the Mojave block, as a result either of localized shortening at a restraining bend in a strike-slip fault or of partitioning of the contractional component of regional transpression away from vertical faults that accommodate the lateral component. The lack of evidence for a major strike-slip fault passing through or near the Kramer Hills leads us to favor partitioned regional transpression.

ACKNOWLEDGMENTS

Field work in the Kramer Hills was supported by a field scholarship from the Kansas Geology Associates Fund and National Science Foundation grant EAR-8916802. Constructive reviews by Tim Ross and Wanda Taylor led to substantial improvements in presentation.

REFERENCES CITED

Armstrong, R.L., and Higgins, R.E., 1973, K-Ar Dating of the beginning of Tertiary volcanism in the Mojave Desert, California: Geological Society of America Bulletin, v. 84, p. 1095–1100.

Ave Lallemant, H.G., 1997, Transpression, displacement partitioning, and exhumation in the eastern Caribbean/South American plate boundary zone: Tectonics, v. 16, p. 272–289.

Bartley, J.M., Glazner, A.F., and Schermer, E.R., 1990, North-south contraction of the Mojave block and strike-slip tectonics in southern California: Science, v. 248, p. 1398–1401.

Bowen, O.E., 1954, Geology and mineral deposits of the Barstow quadrangle, San Bernardino County, California: California Division of Mines Bulletin, v. 165, p. 1–85.

Carter, J.N., Luyendyk, B.P., and Terres, R.R., 1986, Neogene clockwise rotation of the eastern Transverse Ranges, California, suggested by paleomagnetic vectors: Geological Society of America Bulletin, v. 98, p. 199–206.

Dibblee, T.W., Jr., 1958a, Geologic map of the Boron Quadrangle, Kern and San Bernardino Counties, California: United States Geological Survey Mineral Investigations Field Studies Map MF-204.

Dibblee, T.W., Jr., 1958b, Tertiary stratigraphic units of western Mojave Desert, California: American Association of Petroleum Geologists Bulletin, v. 42, p. 135–144.

Dibblee, T.W., Jr., 1958c, Geologic map of the Castle Butte Quadrangle, Kern County, California: United States Geological Survey Mineral Investigations Field Studies Map MF-170.

Dibblee, T.W., Jr., 1960a, Geology of the Rogers Lake and Kramer Quadrangles California: United States Geological Survey Bulletin, v. 1089-B, 137 p.

Dibblee, T.W., Jr., 1960b, Geologic map of the Hawes Quadrangle, San Bernardino County, California: United States Geological Survey Mineral Investigations Field Studies Map MF-226.

Dibblee, T.W., Jr., 1961, Evidence of strike-slip movement on northwest-trending faults in the Mojave Desert, California: United States Geological Survey Professional Paper 424-B, p. B197–B199.

Dibblee, T.W., Jr., 1967, Areal geology of the western Mojave Desert, California: United States Geological Survey Professional Paper, v. 522, 153 p.

Dokka, R.K., 1983, Displacements on late Cenozoic strike-slip faults of the central Mojave Desert, California: Geology, v. 11, p. 305–308.

Dokka, R.K., 1986, Patterns and modes of early Miocene crustal extension, central Mojave block, California, in Mayer, L., ed., Continental extension processes: Geological Society of America Special Paper 208, p. 75–95.

Dokka, R.K., 1989, The Mojave extensional belt of southern California: Tectonics, v. 8, p. 363–390.

Dokka, R.K., and Baksi, A.K., 1989, Age and significance of the Red Buttes Andesite, Kramer Hills, Mojave Desert, California, in Reynolds, R.E., ed., The west-central Mojave Desert: Quaternary studies between Kramer and Afton Canyon: San Bernardino County Museum Association, Redlands, California, p. 51.

Dokka, R.K., and Glazner, A.F., 1982, Aspects of Early Miocene extension of the central Mojave Desert, in Geological excursions in the California Desert, compiled by Cooper, J., Cordilleran Section, Geological Society of America Field Trip Guidebook, Anaheim, California, p. 31–46.

Dokka, R.K., and Travis, J.T., 1990, Late Cenozoic strike-slip faulting in the Mojave Desert, California: Tectonics, v. 9, p. 311–340.

Dokka, R.K., and Woodburne, M.O., 1986, Mid-Tertiary extensional tectonics and sedimentation, central Mojave Desert, California: L.S.U. Publications in Geology and Geophysics, Tectonics and Sedimentation, v. 1, 55 p.

Fillmore, R.P., Walker, J.D., Bartley, J.M., and Glazner, A.F., 1994, Development of three genetically related basins associated with detachment-style faulting: Predicted characteristics and an example from the central Mojave Desert, California: Geology, v. 22, p. 1087–1090.

Garfunkel, Z., 1974, Model for the late Cenozoic tectonic history of the Mojave Desert, California, and for its relation to adjacent areas: Geological Society of America Bulletin, v. 85, p. 1931–1944.

Glazner, A.F., Bartley, J.M., and Walker, J.D., 1989, Magnitude and significance of Miocene crustal extension in the central Mojave Desert, California: Geology, v. 17, p. 50–53.

Glazner, A.F., and Bartley, J.M., 1994, Eruption of alkali basalts during crustal shortening in southern California: Tectonics, v. 13, p. 493–498.

Glazner, A.F., Bartley, J.M., and Sanner, W.J., 2000, Nature of the southern boundary of the central Mojave Tertiary Province, Rodman Mountains, California: Geological Society of America Bulletin, v. 112, p. 34–44.

Golombek, M.P., and Brown, L.L., 1988, Clockwise rotation of the western Mojave Desert: Geology, v. 16, p. 126–130.

Harding, T.P., 1976, Tectonic significance and hydrocarbon trapping consequences of sequential folding synchronous with San Andreas faulting, San Joaquin Valley, California: American Association of Petroleum Geologists Bulletin, v. 60, p. 356–378.

Jackson, J.A., 1992, Partitioning of strike-slip and convergent motion between Eurasia and Arabia in eastern Turkey and the Caucausus: Journal of Geophysical Research, v. 97, p. 12471–12479.

Jarrard, R.D., 1986, Terrane motion by strike-slip faulting of fore-arc slivers: Geology, v. 14, p. 780–783.

Linn, J.K., 1992, Kinematics of late Cenozoic deformation, The Kramer Hills, southern California [M.S. thesis]: Lawrence, Kansas, University of Kansas, 94 p.

Namson, J.S., and Davis, T.L., 1988, Structural transect of the Western Transverse Ranges, California: Implications for lithospheric kinematics and seismic risk evaluation: Geology, v. 16, p. 675–679.

Schermer, E.R., Luyendyk, B.P., and Cisowski, S., 1996, Late Cenozoic structure and tectonics of the northern Mojave Desert: Tectonics, v. 15, p. 905–932.

Walker, J.D., Bartley, J.M., and Glazner, A.F., 1990, Large-magnitude Miocene extension in the Central Mojave Desert: Implications for Paleozoic to Tertiary paleogeography and tectonics: Journal of Geophysical Research, v. 95, p. 557–569.

MANUSCRIPT ACCEPTED BY THE SOCIETY MAY 9, 2001

Geological Society of America
Memoir 195
2002

Late Cenozoic tectonic evolution of the north-central Mojave Desert inferred from fault history and physiographic evolution of the Fort Irwin area, California

David M. Miller*

U.S. Geological Survey, 345 Middlefield Road, MS 975, Menlo Park, California 94025, USA

James C. Yount

U.S. Geological Survey, Box 25046, Denver Federal Center, Denver, Colorado 80225, USA

ABSTRACT

Part of the displacement between the Pacific and North American plates is accommodated by strike-slip fault systems east of the San Andreas fault in the central Mojave Desert, about which relatively little is known. The Fort Irwin area, covering the northeast part of this strike-slip realm, contains faults in two domains, one characterized by northwest- and the other by east-striking faults. The area also exposes Pliocene deposits that provide details about fault behavior. We studied fault histories, the nature of junctions between the two domains, and internal deformation within the blocks themselves to provide new constraints for models of fault evolution.

Strain within many of the blocks bounded by the principal strike-slip faults is manifested as strike-slip faults, thrust faults and folds, and normal faults. Cumulative displacement on these internal faults may be as great as 50% of displacement on block-bounding faults, providing an explanation for discrepancies in vertical-axis rotations determined paleomagnetically and in smaller rotations modeled by strike-slip faulting because internal strain accommodates greater rotations. Internal strain is not uniform within blocks near boundaries between the two fault-orientation domains, and characteristics of the main north-south boundary change dramatically along its length.

The principal strike-slip faults bounding blocks in the northwest-striking fault domain dip steeply both to the southwest and northeast and show little oblique slip, whereas faults of the east-striking fault domain show significant oblique slip. The principal strike-slip faults in the latter domain generally dip south, show a generally large component of thrust slip, and coincide with topographic steps up to the south.

A ca. 5 Ma basalt flow and 3.4 Ma ash bed provide chronology for Pliocene reversal of topography. The basalt appears to have flowed west, whereas subsequent Pliocene alluvial fans carried sediment east. After the fans were deposited ca. 3.4 Ma, they were deformed and cut by faults, as the Coyote Lake basin block dropped and the Alvord Mountain block rose. This change in block elevation was roughly coincident with the development of much of the modern physiography of the central Mojave Desert.

*E-mail: dmiller@usgs.gov

Miller, D.M., and Yount, J.C., 2002, Late Cenozoic tectonic evolution of the north-central Mojave Desert inferred from fault history and physiographic evolution of the Fort Irwin area, California, *in* Glazner, A.F., Walker, J.D., and Bartley, J.M., eds., Geologic Evolution of the Mojave Desert and Southwestern Basin and Range: Boulder, Colorado, Geological Society of America Memoir 195, p. 173–197.

INTRODUCTION

Although most of the slip along the North American–Pacific plate boundary takes place across the San Andreas fault, part is accommodated by strike-slip faults west of the San Andreas and part by faults to the east, in the western and central greater Mojave Desert region (Atwater, 1970). Syntheses by Dibblee (1961) and Dokka and Travis (1990a, 1990b) provide a framework for modeling the behavior of faults in the Mojave Desert region, but the time-space evolution of these faults is incompletely known. For instance, needing elucidation are the histories of fault slip, vertical-axis rotations of smaller-scale fault blocks, and rotations and behaviors of these blocks and their bounding faults with respect to major tectonic boundaries such as the San Andreas and Garlock faults. Although the area of active strike-slip faults within the Mojave Desert region that appears to transfer slip to the Death Valley fault zone was termed the "Eastern California shear zone" (Dokka and Travis, 1990a), we will use the more general phrase "Mojave strike-slip province" to represent the entire area east of the San Andreas fault that is typified by late Cenozoic strike-slip faults (Fig. 1). This usage includes faults of the western Mojave Desert (Dibblee, 1961; Ponti and Burke, 1980; Miller and Bedford, 2000), which have the same strike, sense of offset, and age as those in the Eastern California shear zone (as defined by Dokka

and Travis, 1990a) in that they strike northwest and cut Pleistocene to Miocene deposits. In addition to kinematic models for dextral faulting in the Mojave strike-slip province (Garfunkel, 1974; Dokka and Travis, 1990a; Ron et al., 1984; Schermer et al., 1996), geodetic data provide evidence for 8 to 10 mm of dextral shear across the province annually (Sauber et al., 1986, 1994), which indicates that past strain corresponds with present stress fields. Schelle and Grunthal (1996) summarized geophysical data that led to conclusions that brittle behavior of the upper crust extends to ~10 km depth and that maximum principal stress in the brittle crust is oriented ~010°. Recent analysis of earthquake focal mechanisms indicates that the maximum principal stress is oriented ~020° (Hardebeck and Hauksson, 1999). Unruh et al. (1996) modeled the crustal response to the Landers earthquake and arrived at the conclusion that, across a broad zone of the Mojave strike-slip province, the upper brittle crust is coupled to an underlying ductile crust.

The Mojave strike-slip province is characterized by dextral northwest-striking faults (Dibblee, 1961) that bound blocks ~10 to 20 km wide and 50 km long (Fig. 1). In the southern and northeastern extremes of the province, two domains characterized by sinistral east-striking faults (the ESF domains) depart from the remainder (the dextral northwest-striking fault [NWSF] domain) of the province (Carter et al., 1987; Schermer et al., 1996). We term each of the boundaries between the ESF

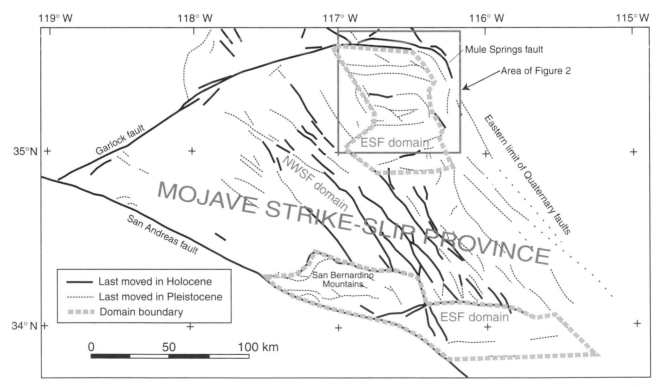

Figure 1. Location of the Fort Irwin area (box, enlarged in Fig. 2) in the north-central Mojave Desert, in the northeastern part of the Mojave strike-slip province. Significant faults bounding relatively undeformed blocks are distinguished by the recency of last movement along them. Data from Jennings (1994) with modifications from mapping for this paper. East-striking fault (ESF) domains and northwest-striking fault (NWSF) domain are shown.

and NWSF domains a *domain boundary*; in most places the domain boundary is a collection of faults. Paleomagnetic studies of vertical-axis block rotations have documented little or no rotation of deposits of late early and middle Miocene age in the blocks in the NWSF domain but large (~60°) clockwise rotations of those deposits in blocks in the ESF domain (Luyendyk et al., 1980; Wells and Hillhouse, 1989; Luyendyk, 1991; Valentine et al., 1993; Ross, 1995; Schermer et al., 1996).

Several hypotheses have been put forward for how strain is accommodated within the Mojave strike-slip province, how the bounding faults have behaved through time, and the origins of the contrasting orientations of faults in the ESF and NWSF domains. Most hypotheses are model-based and rely on the mapped faults of Dibblee (1961) and other early workers. Garfunkel (1974) initially recognized the broad distribution of parallel strike-slip faults as resembling card-deck shear; he suggested that homogeneous simple shear of the region produced fault slip and rotation of the internal fault blocks through time but that the external fault systems (San Andreas and Garlock faults) bounding the western Mojave Desert remained fixed. His model called for overall east-west extension and north-south shortening of the Mojave between the Garlock and San Andreas faults. Paleomagnetic studies (e.g., Wells and Hillhouse, 1989; Valentine et al., 1993) showed that blocks in the NWSF domain had not undergone the predicted vertical-axis rotations, however; this result required that the major tectonic boundaries (i.e., the Garlock fault) of the Mojave strike-slip province rotated with time or that small-scale blocks did not behave rigidly. Dokka and Travis (1990a, 1990b) improved understanding of the area by pointing out that early faults in the east are now inactive and the active faults in the center of the Mojave strike-slip province describe a zone of shear that they termed the "Eastern California shear zone." They created a model that predicted that blocks of what we call the ESF domains rotated clockwise, forming dilational holes at domain boundaries as the province extended east-west. Bartley et al. (1990) pointed out that, in addition to the north-south shortening accommodated by strike-slip faults, a component of shortening within the small-scale blocks created folds and thrusts. They cautioned that internal strain within blocks may significantly weaken the appropriateness of models used to up to that time, and they interpreted the dilational holes of Dokka and Travis as depressions caused by thrust loading. Schermer et al. (1996) studied the ESF domain in the northeast part of the Mojave strike-slip province in detail, providing much new data on slip timing and magnitude for several faults. They documented left slip in this domain and hypothesized that as the blocks rotated clockwise, their ends deformed into long, curving tails, producing few or no dilational holes as a result of vertical-axis rotations. They also identified an incongruity between paleomagnetically determined vertical-axis rotations of ~60° and vertical-axis rotations of ~25° that can be accommodated by fault slip for simple block-rotation models; they suggested that the discrepancy is largely accounted for by the locations of paleomagnetic

determinations in extra-rotated "tails" of blocks. Many workers have implicitly or explicitly assumed rigid-block behavior for rock lying between strike-slip faults, but documentation that internal strain is limited within blocks is sparse.

This paper summarizes the results of detailed field investigations of bedrock and surficial deposits of Fort Irwin National Training Center, in the north-central Mojave Desert (Yount et al., 1994; Miller et al., 1994; mapping by Miller and Yount in 1995). Our work builds on studies by Schermer et al. (1996), Valentine et al. (1993), and Ford et al. (1992) and on the framework mapping of Byers (1960), Jennings et al. (1962), and Miller and Sutter (1982). We report new information about the faults that bound blocks, internal faulting within blocks, and distinctive Pliocene deposits that, when taken in combination, compel new models for strike-slip faulting in this part of the Mojave Desert strike-slip province.

GEOLOGIC SETTING

The Fort Irwin area encompasses the northeast part of the Mojave strike-slip province (Fig. 1), including its bounding faults (the Garlock and Mule Springs faults), much of the ESF domain in the northeastern Mojave strike-slip province, and a boundary between the ESF and NWSF domains. This region is underlain primarily by Mesozoic granitoids and minor metamorphic rocks, on which thick piles of Miocene (ca. 21 to 12 Ma) volcanic rocks are locally present (Spencer, 1990; Luyendyk et al., 1993; Schermer et al., 1996). Over much of the area, the volcanic rocks filled in earlier topographic lows, which had topographic relief as great as 100 m, and created new constructional volcanic topography of the same magnitude. West of the Avawatz Mountains, volcanic rocks contributed to thick extensional-basin fill.

The present geomorphology of the Fort Irwin area consists of linear mountain ranges, of both northwest and east trends, and intervening alluvial basins that generally contain thin (<200 m) accumulations of alluvial sediment (Fig. 2). Basins and mountains in general climb from a low at Coyote Lake (520 m) in the southwest to highs near Goldstone (1100 m) and the Avawatz Mountains (1875 m). In some places, the geomorphology is influenced by youthful faulting and uplift; in other places, features such as pediments and domes indicate a more stable and mature geomorphology. Although the most seismically active part of the Mojave strike-slip province lies west and south of Fort Irwin, scattered seismicity extends to the Mule Springs fault.

Within the Fort Irwin area, most faults strike east (i.e., this area is mainly in the ESF—east-striking-fault—domain), but part of the area shows northwest-striking faults (i.e., it lies in the NWSF—northwest-striking-fault—domain). Schermer et al. (1996) described evidence for 2–6 km of left slip across each main east-striking fault and 3–4 km of right slip across the East Goldstone Lake fault (Fig. 3), and they demonstrated that faulting took place after the 11 Ma volcanism. The northern and

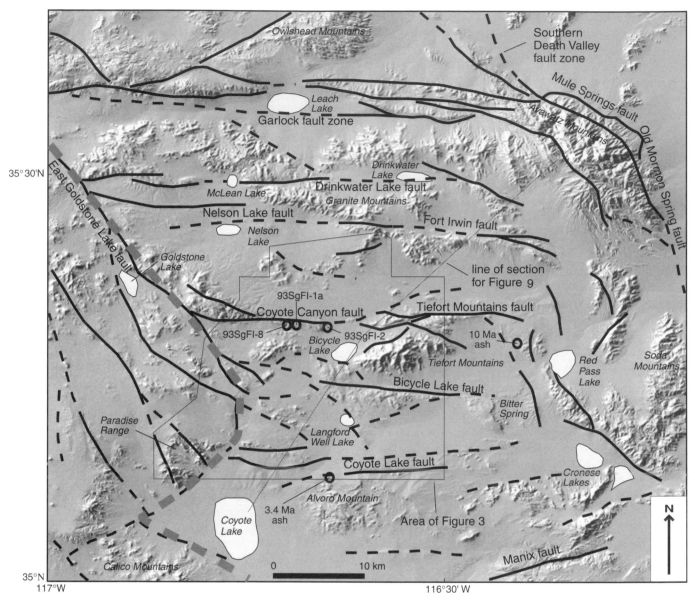

Figure 2. Shaded-relief map of the Fort Irwin area, showing principal faults, mountains, and playas. Location of Figure 3 is indicated, as is the profile line for Figure 10. Locations for dated samples (Table 2) and tephrochronology identifications are also shown.

eastern boundaries of the Fort Irwin area are represented by the sinistral Garlock and the dextral-thrust Mule Springs faults (Fig. 2).

The age constraints for initiation and termination of movement across faults in the Fort Irwin area are sparse. Some faults appear to have displaced 17 Ma and 5.6 Ma volcanic rocks by similar amounts (Schermer et al., 1996). The last movement along most of the faults we have studied in the Fort Irwin area was during the late Quaternary. The precise age of last movement is not firmly known in many cases. However, the general lack of fresh scarps, combined with the character of soil development in deposits that overlap the most recently faulted materials, suggests that many of the faults within the Fort Irwin

area last ruptured between 100 000 and 10 000 yr ago (Miller et al., 1994). However, the Garlock and Coyote Canyon faults show evidence of movement during the past 10 000 yr (Miller et al., 1994), and the Manix fault has had historic rupture.

GEOCHRONOLOGY

Determining accurate ages for map units is necessary for bracketing ages and rates of fault slip and other deformation. Spencer (1990), Fillmore (1993), Sobieraj (1994), and Schermer et al. (1996) provided evidence for early Miocene ages for most volcanic rocks in the area. The youngest rocks in this sequence typically are ca. 16 Ma, but a few flows as young

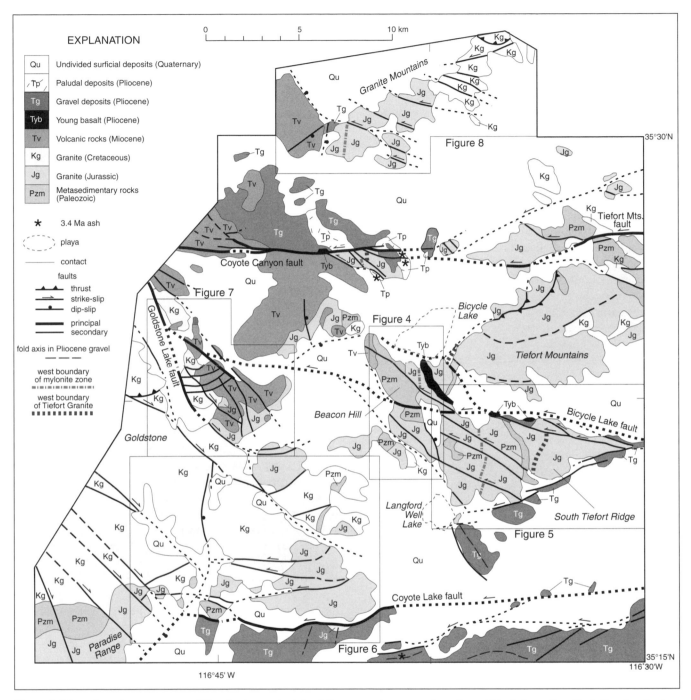

Figure 3. Map of southwestern part of Fort Irwin emphasizing Miocene and younger deposits and block-bounding (dark lines) and minor (light lines) faults. Note steeply dipping marker planes (dashed lines) that illustrate total offset along east-striking faults. Boxes indicate locations of detailed maps. Map based on Schermer et al. (1996), Yount et al. (1994), and McCulloh (1960).

as 12 to 10 Ma are documented in the upper part of the Avawatz basin and nearby basins. We used the K/Ar method to date one basalt flow low in the sequence at Coyote Canyon at 14.5 ± 0.4 Ma (Table 1, sample 93SgFI-8). This result is younger than the 21 to 16 Ma ages for basalts in similar stratigraphic settings nearby (Schermer et al., 1996), and we therefore are uncertain

of its reliability. Ash in the upper part of a basin lying southeast of the Tiefort Mountains we identified by tephrochronology as 10 Ma ash from Snake River Plain hotspot eruptions (A. Sarna-Wojcicki, 1995, written communication), indicating that some of these basins accumulated detritus into the middle Miocene.

A much younger basalt, separated from the early Miocene

TABLE 1. K-AR DATA FOR BASALT AND ASH FROM COYOTE CANYON AREA

Sample no.	Latitude	Longitude	Material	K₂O (wt %)	⁴⁰Ar* (%)	Age (Ma)	Error
93SgFI-1a	35°19′07″N	116°41′21″W	basalt	0.399	15	3.7	0.3
				0.399ξ	9ξ	3.1ξ	0.2ξ
93SgFI-2	35°19′06″N	116°38′34″W	biotite	8.450	13	3.4	0.2
93SgFI-8	35°17′02″N	116°41′03″W	basalt	1.218	65	14.7	0.4
				1.218ξ	70ξ	14.3ξ	0.4ξ

Note: Decay constants from Steiger and Jager (1977). Analytical work by John K. Nakata.
ξ Second analysis of whole-rock powder from same sample.
*Radiogenic.

volcanic sequence by alluvial gravel, was assigned Ar-Ar ages of 5.57 ± 0.26 and 5.5 ± 0.2 Ma by Schermer et al. (1996) for samples at Bicycle Lake and Bitter Spring, respectively. We have used the conventional K/Ar method to date chemically and petrographically similar basalt farther west at the Coyote Canyon area (Table 1, sample 93SgFI-1a) at 3.4 ± 0.5 Ma. Whereas there is a remote possibility that we dated a different basalt than that dated by Schermer et al. (1996), we consider the chemical and morphologic similarity to be convincing. We therefore interpret the age differences to reflect the two different methods. Until full analytical data are published for the two Ar-Ar ages, it is difficult to assess which result is more reliable. Our conventional K/Ar age is based on very low radiogenic Ar. Until the age is better resolved, we will refer to this basalt as "Pliocene basalt" to differentiate it from basalts in the early and middle Miocene volcanic sequence.

A white fine-grained ash containing biotite, quartz, and feldspar lies in alluvial gravel and paludal sediment above the Pliocene basalt. Biotite in the ash yielded a conventional K/Ar date of 3.4 ± 0.2 Ma (Table 1, sample 93SgFI-2). This ash and samples from other exposures of this ash were correlated by chemical similarity of major elements in glass shards (A. Sarna-Wojcicki, 1995, written communication) to ash in Fish Lake Valley, Nevada, that lies stratigraphically between two ashes also dated as 3.4 Ma. We therefore consider the ash to be firmly dated at 3.4 Ma.

Quaternary gravel sequences are widespread and were assigned relative ages on the basis of soil development and morphologic evolution (Yount et al., 1994), following other studies of Mojave Desert soils and geomorphology (e.g., Ponti and Burke, 1980; McFadden and Weldon, 1987; Reheis et al., 1989). By these criteria, the deposits can be distinguished as approximately middle Pleistocene, late Pleistocene, and Holocene.

NONRIGID BEHAVIOR OF BLOCKS

Nonrigid behavior of blocks bounded by intermediate-scale faults that have accumulated several kilometers of separation is indicated by folds and by strike-slip, thrust, and normal faults within the blocks. Structures such as these indicate that internal strain is present in all blocks (Fig. 3), but the degree of internal strain varies. Because exposures of rock in blocks

also varies considerably, ambiguity about internal strain persists. In this section, we describe examples of strain within blocks in several settings.

Beacon Hill block

Near the westernmost exposures of the Bicycle Lake fault zone, a prominent hill south of Bicycle Lake is deeply dissected (Fig. 4), exposing granitoid and metamorphic rocks. Immediately east of this location, the Bicycle Lake fault zone is interpreted to bifurcate (Byers, 1960; Schermer et al., 1996), with strands lying south of Bicycle Lake and cutting through the central part of Beacon Hill (Fig. 3).

Faults that cut Beacon Hill, and probably some that border the southwest front of Beacon Hill, are mappable eastward toward the Bicycle Lake fault system proper, where ~4.7 km of offset across this southern strand is known (Schermer et al., 1996). Faults within Beacon Hill consist of a central strike-slip fault that passes the length of the hill, several nearly north-striking faults along the east side, a zone of frontal faults along the southwest side of the hill, two thrust faults, and a northeast-striking fault that cuts Pliocene basalt (Fig. 4).

The central strike-slip fault is marked by a breccia and gouge zone between 4 and 10 m wide that strikes between 330° and 310°. The zone contains discrete fault planes that generally dip southwest between 53° and 85°, but also a few planes that dip northeast between 40° and 80°. Striae within the zone are rare; only two nearly horizontal examples of striae were observed (Fig. 4). At its west end, nearly horizontal flows of early Miocene basalt are offset down ~10 m to the north by the fault. Near its east end, the fault is cut by a north-striking reverse fault (fault 3), east of which an apparent continuation of the central strike-slip fault continues eastward to merge with the southern strand of the Bicycle Lake fault zone. Local examples of separation sense are given by striae and offset strata such as the basal Pleistocene deposits. These examples range from nearly pure strike slip to dextral reverse and reverse. The dextral-reverse example is on a northeast-dipping plane that probably does not represent the principal fault zone. If contributions from other faults within the Beacon Hill block are ignored and the mapped steep contact between plutons and metasedimentary rocks is considered to be an adequate marker for horizontal separation, the central fault has accumulated 0.8 km

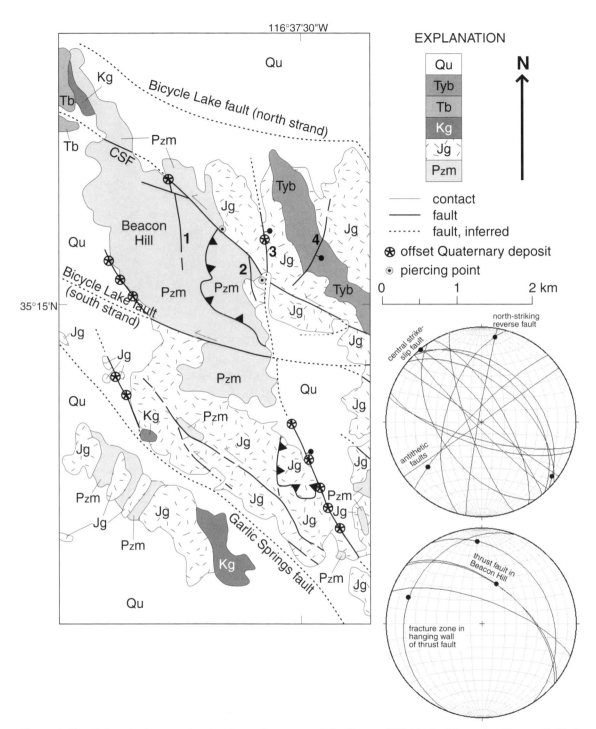

Figure 4. Detailed geologic map showing internal structure of the Beacon Hill block. Map units: Qu—undivided surficial deposits (Quaternary), Tyb—young basalt (Pliocene), Tb—basalt (Miocene), Kg—granite (Cretaceous), Jg—granitoids and mafic rocks (Jurassic), Pzm—marble and schist (Paleozoic). CSF—central strike-slip fault; north-striking reverse faults are labeled 1 to 4 (see text). Bar and ball symbol indicates fault with ball on downthrown side; teeth indicate the hanging wall of thrust fault. Stereonet plots illustrate fault-plane measurements.

of sinistral slip (Fig. 4). A similar magnitude and sense for separation across the fault is indicated by a lack of correspondence between numerous pegmatite dikes cutting metamorphic rocks south of the fault and no dikes north of the fault.

Four north-striking, steeply-dipping faults within the Beacon Hill block appear to be reverse faults, numbered 1 to 4 from west to east (Fig. 4). Fault 1 forms a straight trace across steep topography, indicating a steep dip, but no direct measurements of structures in fault materials were possible. It is truncated by the central strike-slip fault in Beacon Hill and offset sinistrally by a strand of the central strike-slip fault. Fault 2 is a short north-striking fault 0.4 km west of fault 3. In one exposure, it strikes 318° and dips 47°NE. It is overlapped by middle Pleistocene alluvium in its central sector. A lack of correspondence of bedrock units across it indicates at least tens of meters of separation. Fault 3 strikes north and terminates several faults to the west. It separates the mountainous part of Beacon Hill on the west and a linear valley and lower areas covered by Pliocene basalt on the east. One fault plane has a strike of 015° and dip of 58°west; striae in the plane plunge gently north (Fig. 4). Judging from effects on topography, the fault is probably reverse sinistral oblique. It is overlapped by late Pleistocene alluvium but cuts middle Pleistocene alluvium. An apparent continuation of fault 3 extends 3 km south of the Bicycle Lake fault zone. That fault dips west, and nearly horizontal drag folds developed within middle Pleistocene alluvium indicate reverse slip. East of fault 3, a north-northeast–striking fault (fault 4, Fig. 4) cutting Pliocene basalt displays ~6 m of down-to-the-southeast separation of the basalt.

West of Beacon Hill and the hills to the south lies the enigmatic Garlic Springs fault, which bears evidence for older fault movement compared to many other faults at Fort Irwin. The Garlic Springs fault contains moderate- to high-temperature hydrothermal minerals and pseudotachylites, which indicate that part of the breccia developed under significantly higher pressure and temperature than other fault breccias, which lack those features. The fault cuts no Quaternary deposits, although a possible splay northeast of the fault does cut Pleistocene materials. Mesozoic fabrics and trends of wall-rock septa in plutons differ across the fault, indicating that the fault represents a fundamental boundary, but separation across the fault is not known (Schermer et al., 1996). The lack of evidence for late Cenozoic activity on the Garlic Springs fault leads us to conclude that it may not have a role in the late Cenozoic fault evolution of the area.

Two low-angle faults that dip 20°–55°E we interpret as thrust faults (shown in Fig. 4 with thrust-fault symbols) on the basis of their orientations in this block that has undergone internal sinistral slip. Each is marked by a 5–10-m-thick zone of breccia and gouge. Striae measured on fractures near the breccia zone and on fracture planes within the gouge are quite variable and indicate strike slip to dip slip; they are of uncertain significance. Both thrust faults are truncated by Quaternary north-

striking, steeply dipping reverse faults and northwest-striking, strike-slip faults.

The topography of Beacon Hill provides clues for dip-slip components of faulting. The Bicycle Lake fault strand at the north margin of the hill is not exposed, but presumably has an up-on-the-south component to account for the juxtaposition of a steep mountain front and a playa. The strand of the Bicycle Lake fault system fronting the hill on its southwest dips northeast and, by reasoning analogous to the northern strand, also has a component of vertical separation. This fault system cuts middle Pleistocene alluvium in several places, and fault traces are overlapped by late Pleistocene alluvium. The Garlic Springs fault is a complex zone that shows features of inheritance from older faulting (Miller et al., 1994), but one splay cuts Pleistocene sediment and is of uncertain significance for latest Cenozoic tectonism. Two basalt flows and a small remnant erosion surface at the crest of the northern part of Beacon Hill are not noticeably deformed. The western flow is early Miocene in age and dips gently south. The eastern flow is Pliocene and nearly horizontal.

Sinistral faults within the Beacon Hill block accommodate >0.8 km of slip, and reverse faults accommodate more internal strain. In comparison with the total sinistral slip along the southern Bicycle Lake fault system of >4.7 km, this strain is >15% and therefore an important part of the strain budget. The internal faults of the block may have formed as a result of migration of the Bicycle Lake fault, for instance during the development of a stepover (e.g., Westaway, 1995) in the Bicycle Lake fault system. However, the internal faults are nearly identical south and north of the current trace of the Bicycle Lake fault. We favor the interpretation that the internal structures formed as the block rotated between intermediate-scale fault zones while accommodating far-field stress.

South Tiefort Ridge block

South and east of Beacon Hill is a nearly 10-km-long east-trending ridge that we informally term "South Tiefort Ridge." South Tiefort Ridge occupies the central part of the block bounded by the Bicycle Lake and Coyote Lake faults. The Bicycle Lake fault bounds the ridge on the north (Byers, 1960), north of which is a narrow Quaternary basin (Fig. 5). Much of the ridge is underlain by Jurassic plutonic rocks, which are heterogeneous in the west and form a homogeneous felsic body (Tiefort Granite, Jt) in the east. The Bicycle Lake fault offsets exposures of possibly once-contiguous parts of the Pliocene basaltic lava flow by 3–8 km, and a band of steeply dipping marble (unit PZm) is offset by more than 4.7 km (Byers, 1960; Schermer et al., 1996). The west edge of the Tiefort Granite apparently is offset more than 6 km to a position west of the westernmost exposures of rock in the Tiefort Mountains (see Fig. 3). South Tiefort Ridge is bounded to the south by another fault zone that cuts pre-Quaternary gravel of uncertain age and forms small scarps in middle and late Pleistocene alluvial ma-

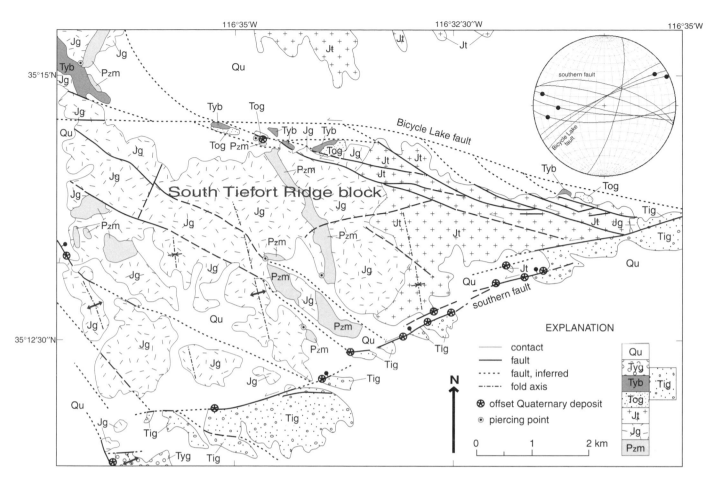

Figure 5. Detailed geologic map showing internal structure of South Tiefort Ridge block. Map units as in Figure 4, with additional units as follows: Tyg—younger gravel (Pliocene), Tig—intermediate-age gravel (Pliocene and late Miocene), Tog—older gravel (late Miocene), Jt—Tiefort Granite (Jurassic). Note that the strikes of most measured faults plotted on stereonet are 30°–40° different from the overall strike of the Bicycle Lake and southern faults. Main trace of Bicycle Lake fault is not exposed, so most measurements are of R shears near the main trace. Many measured faults that make up southern fault are en echelon small faults that strike ~270°.

terials. The fault displaces the gravel up on the south but otherwise does not offset markers. Exposed fault planes dip steeply north and south and strike en echelon to the overall zone, at 265°–290° (Fig. 5). Three examples of fault striae plunge 10°–35°W. The kinematics of the south fault are therefore sinistral with a small up-to-the-south component. The gravel cut by the southern fault is similar geomorphically to deformed Pliocene gravel elsewhere, but clasts in it have a source from the Tiefort Mountains, unlike Pliocene gravel exposed farther south in Fort Irwin. Along the Bicycle Lake fault, similar gravel underlies the Pliocene basalt, indicating that the older gravel unit (Tog) is probably older than the widespread Pliocene gravel (Tyg) farther south in Fort Irwin.

Within the South Tiefort block, three northwest-striking faults lie along linear troughs. The two northern faults together apparently offset the Paleozoic marble band by ~260 m in a dextral sense. Only one of these internal faults has an exposed fault plane; it strikes 315° and dips steeply southwest. The faults are parallel to, and in one case nearly continuous with,

northwest-striking sinistral faults in Beacon Hill. Therefore, we question whether the faults are dextral in South Tiefort Ridge. The map relationships at South Tiefort Ridge are complicated by the wider and repeated sections of Paleozoic strata southward in the ridge, which are the result of complex intrusive relationships. We interpret the map relationships as due to complex interactions between intrusive margins and faults, possibly with vertical components of fault slip having large effects on the map pattern. At any rate, the northwest-striking faults appear to have several hundred meters of separation, but the direction of slip on them is uncertain.

Several faults traverse the northern 1 km of rock in South Tiefort Ridge, adjacent to the inferred trace of the Bicycle Lake fault, as noted by Schermer et al. (1996). Within this zone, rocks are highly disrupted by numerous small faults, broad bands of breccia, and wisps of gouge, forming on the whole a broad zone of intense brittle deformation. Measured fault striae in this zone are horizontal to subhorizontal, and fault planes dip moderately to steeply both north and south. The southernmost fault strand of the broad, northern zone offsets the intrusive margin of the Tiefort Granite 400 m in a sinistral sense.

Byers (1960) mapped north-trending upright folds with wavelengths of ~3 km across South Tiefort Ridge. The folds are expressed in foliations in Jurassic plutonic rocks. Similar orientations of folds, with comparable wavelengths and amplitudes, are observed in Pliocene gravel (Fig. 3), suggesting that the folds in plutonic rocks of South Tiefort Ridge may also be Pliocene and younger (Byers, 1960; Schermer et al., 1996).

Much of the strain internal to the South Tiefort Ridge block is near the Bicycle Lake fault; faults traversing the center of the block probably total less than 0.5 km of separation. If the southern fault underwent long-term slip parallel to its ~20°W-plunging striae, the 50-m-high scarp in gravel indicates a minimum of 250 m of sinistral separation. After accounting for greater erosion rates in the unconsolidated materials than in rocks, separation is possibly as much as 1 km. This fault therefore represents a significant tectonic element within the block between the Coyote Lake and Bicycle Lake faults (Fig. 3 shows location).

North of Coyote Lake fault

North of the Coyote Lake fault (Fig. 6), a broad pediment dome cut into granite is disrupted by topographic steps at east-striking faults. The faults terminate to the west at a poorly defined transition from the ESF domain to the NWSF domain (Fig. 6), west of which is undisrupted pediment. To the east in Langford Well basin, the faults are not exposed. The pediment formed in early Quaternary or late Pliocene time, on the basis of middle Pleistocene sediments deposited on it, and apparently did not exist at the time that Pliocene alluvial sediments were shed from the Goldstone area to areas east and southeast of the dome. However, it should be noted that this youthful age is at odds with several other pediments in the Mojave Desert, which owe their origin to Miocene or older erosion (Oberlander, 1974; Miller, 1995). The pediments provide marker surfaces for studies of vertical offset across faults.

The Coyote Lake fault was identified by McCulloh (1960), who inferred that the fault bends to the southwest along the steep front of the Paradise Range (see Figs. 2 and 3) on the basis of topography and gravity data showing a sharp step in depth to basement. However, we have mapped an apparent continuation of the east-striking segment of the fault (west of Jack Spring, Fig. 6) into the Paradise Range, where the fault swings to the southwest and forms a wide zone of breccia and gouge and disrupts middle Pleistocene sediments. This apparent splay of the Coyote Lake fault may represent an abandoned early trace of the fault. Small-slip dextral faults cut granitoids and Paleozoic metasedimentary rocks in the Paradise Range, apparently terminating at the inferred Coyote Lake fault. The east-striking part of the Coyote Lake fault truncates Pliocene and Quaternary deposits, generally producing a north-facing scarp in Pliocene gravel that is 10 to 50 m high. Pliocene gravel is

deformed into open folds with axes trending ~020°, vertical axial planes, and limb dips of ~20°.

The family of east-striking faults north of the Coyote Lake fault includes the north Noble Dome fault (Fig. 6) of Miller et al. (1994), which strikes 085° and bends to the northeast near its eastern end. The western half is expressed by an alignment of north-facing mountain fronts that indicate up-to-the-south separation greater than 40 m. The eastern segment is defined by breccia and gouge within granite and shows ~110 m of sinistral separation of a distinctive vertical gabbro dike. Elsewhere along that dike, smaller faults accomplish an additional 90 m of sinistral separation (Fig. 6). Most fracture surfaces within the fault zone are not lineated, but striae measured on fractures that are close to parallel with the overall zone (085°, 70°N) at one locality are within 23° of horizontal and plunge both east and west (Fig. 6).

Faults similar to the north Noble Dome fault lie to the south, forming gently undulating map patterns. Each of these faults is characterized by a topographic step up to the south and each cuts Pleistocene sediment. The south Noble Dome fault shows 10 m of sinistral offset of dikes. At one locality, the fault plane is vertical with striae plunging downdip (Fig. 6).

Faults at Jack Spring represent a joining of the south Noble Dome fault and related faults with the east-striking family of faults associated with the Coyote Lake fault. The faults at Jack Spring strike from 070° to 100°, dip from vertical to 75°S, and form zones of breccia and gouge as wide as 50 m. One fault offsets late Pleistocene alluvial-fan deposits down 1.5 m to the north.

A north-striking normal fault apparently terminates the east-striking faults such as the north Noble Dome fault. Granitoid plutons are identical across the normal fault, suggesting small offset. On both sides of the fault, coarse-grained porphyritic biotite granite grades south to coarse-grained equigranular biotite granite, which in turn grades south to medium-grained biotite-rich granite. The gradations in rock types do not provide markers for measuring offset but do affirm the lack of separation greater than a few hundred meters along the north-striking fault. The fault is characterized by gouge and intense fracturing, and in two places cuts late Pleistocene deposits. Fractures strike from 350° to 006°, dip east (Fig. 6), and are associated with a down-to-the-east topographic step as great as 10 m. Striae on fractures plunge moderately south, and steps in slickenside surfaces suggest oblique slip: normal with a dextral component. The normal fault terminates to the north at a splay of the northwest-striking dextral Goldstone Lake fault (Fig. 6), which separates muscovite-bearing granite on the north from biotite granite on the south. The Goldstone Lake fault may continue southeast 10 km along a prominent wash of that orientation, locally separating Cretaceous and Jurassic granitoids. However, no definitive exposures of the proposed fault have been found to test this hypothesis.

Southwest and west of the north-striking normal fault, zones of small-offset faults lie in pediment exposures at the

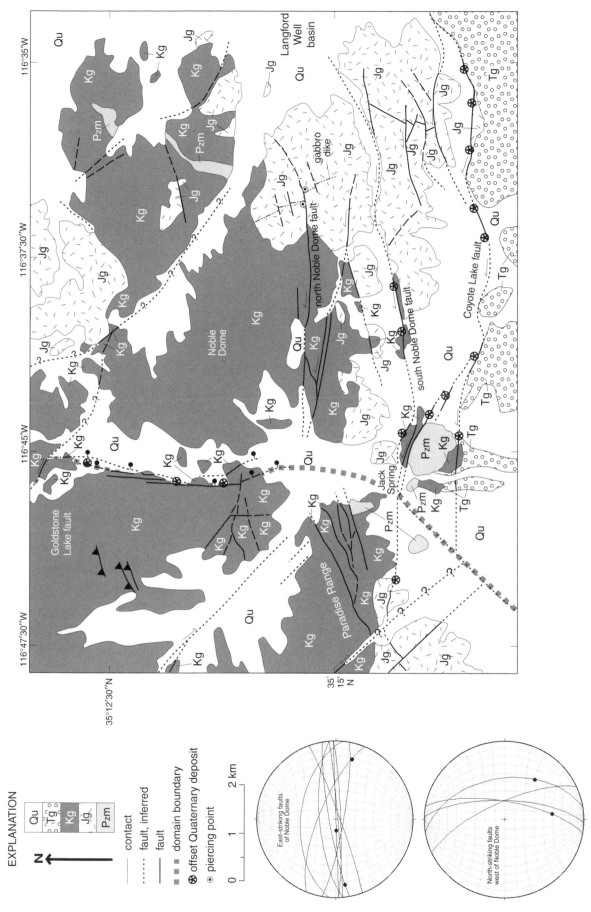

EXPLANATION

Qu
Tg
Kg
Jg
Pzm

— contact
---- fault, inferred
—— fault
▪▪▪ domain boundary
⊗ offset Quaternary deposit
⊙ piercing point

N

0   1   2 km

East-striking faults of Noble Dome

North-striking faults west of Noble Dome

Figure 6. Detailed geologic map showing structures north of the Coyote Lake fault. Map units as in Figures 4 and 5, plus Tg—Pliocene gravel. Bar and ball symbol indicates fault with ball on downthrown side.

northeast end of the Paradise Range and 2 km north. Faults in the Paradise Range strike ~065° and dip moderately to steeply north (65°–85°). One fault offsets a dike ~30 m in apparent sinistral separation. Northwest-striking faults farther west in the Paradise Range, and to the northwest, are poorly exposed but appear to be dextral on the basis of tens of meters of separation of granitoid contacts. These faults are defined by breccia and gouge zones collinear with subdued swales and linear washes. Faults north of the Paradise Range occur in east- and north-striking sets. One east-striking fault cuts the north-striking normal fault just described, displacing it in a sinistral sense a few tens of meters. This array of small faults appears to accomplish the sinistral and normal separations exhibited by larger faults to the east and north. Few faults lie in the pediment directly west of the north-striking normal fault.

The group of east-striking faults cutting the pediment and Quaternary deposits of the Noble Dome area has a demonstrated minimum cumulative sinistral offset of 120 m measured on two of the six faults and another 90 m on smaller faults; total offset may be several hundred meters more. The faults terminate at a north-striking normal fault of Quaternary age, west of which the pediment and Quaternary deposits are not cut by the sparse northwest-striking faults.

Goldstone Lake Fault terminus

The Goldstone Lake fault branches into several strands as it approaches its terminus to the southeast (Fig. 3). Through this region of branching faults, the Goldstone Lake fault separates a terrane of granite overlain by volcanic rocks on the northeast from a broad expanse of generally unfaulted granite forming pediments on the southwest. Between the branching strands of the fault system, numerous smaller faults cut the granite and its overlying Miocene volcanic sequence (Fig. 7). In this area, the Bicycle Lake fault of the ESF domain is inferred to meet the northern strand of the Goldstone Lake fault system because the Bicycle Lake fault must extend west from mapped exposures at Beacon Hill and the volcanic sequences north of the Goldstone Lake fault system are offset in a sinistral sense by an unexposed fault in the intervening valley. South of the Goldstone Lake fault strands, the north-striking fault (Fig. 6) connects southward with the Coyote Lake fault. We next describe the five significant strands of the Goldstone Lake fault system and intervening structures from northeast to southwest.

The northeastern strand of the Goldstone Lake fault system (Fig. 7, fault 1) cuts early Miocene basalt and middle and late Pleistocene alluvium, dropping the alluvium down on the southwest. The fault appears to terminate in a splay of small-slip faults that curve to the south. The adjacent strand of the fault system (fault 2) behaves similarly, with more pronounced splaying and curving of fault segments near its termination. Fault 2 drops basalt down to the west by 20–40 m. The curving splay of faults displays several scarps, with latest Pleistocene alluvium inset against, and/or faulted against, middle Pleisto-

cene alluvium, and possible offset of Holocene alluvium. Eastward 3 km from the splays of fault 2, Miocene strata describe a broad syncline whose axis plunges gently northward (Schermer et al., 1996). Southwest of fault 2, seven east- to east-northeast–striking faults can be mapped on the basis of (1) offsets of the nonconformity at the base of early Miocene basalt and (2) coextensive breccia and gouge zones in granite (Fig. 7). Most of the faults show down-to-the-south offset of the nonconformity. The east-striking faults cut, and are also cut by, a northwest-striking fault (fault 3, Fig. 7) in a complex pattern. Where fault 3 cuts the east-striking faults, it offsets them in a dextral sense as much as 150 m. Fault 3 appears to die out to the southeast in the flow-dome mass of rhyolite near the tips of faults 1 and 2 and merges to the northwest with fault 4.

In the area between faults 2 and 4, sedimentation patterns have changed several times. Gravel older than middle Pleistocene (and perhaps older than latest Pliocene) in age carries abundant clasts of rhyolite derived from the southeast. The gravel is cut by canyons directed down gradient to the east and northeast, in which granite clasts derived from plutons to the southwest were deposited in middle and late Pleistocene time (as shown by soil development). One of these east-directed canyons is underfit, its head along fault 4 apparently having been uplifted until sediment bypassed the system. This abandonment of the canyon took place during the middle and early late Pleistocene because late Pleistocene geomorphic surfaces blanket the floor of the underfit valley.

Fault 4 bounds alluvium and pediment cut into granite on the southwest and hills composed of granite on the northeast, suggesting that a down-to-the-southwest component is involved in the movement along the fault. Both sinistral (Miller et al., 1994) and dextral (Schermer et al., 1996) offsets are possible on the basis of map interpretations. Schermer et al. (1996) noted kinematic indicators on this fault pointing to dextral horizontal slip and inferred 3–4 km of dextral offset on the basis of projecting contacts between Jurassic and Cretaceous granites. We have not found reliable markers for slip magnitude.

Fault 5 is poorly exposed as a zone of intense fracturing in pediment materials and is identified on the basis of linear contrast between outcrops of muscovite-bearing granite and biotite granite. The fault appears to bifurcate to the northwest, where a thrust fault crosses between the two segments and sharply uplifts the mountain to the northwest. The thrust dips 67°N and is oblique dextral, with striae in splays plunging gently to the northwest (Fig. 7). The two types of granite are juxtaposed across fault 5 with ~6 km in apparent dextral offset. The fault has such subdued expression and poorly developed breccia that we suspect that it represents much less than the apparent 6 km separation across a nearly planar intrusive contact. Alternatively, the fault may have had substantial early slip but little slip during the time of development of the present geomorphic expression.

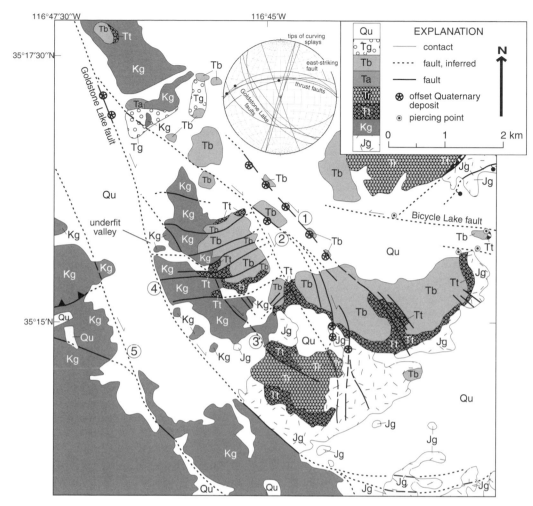

Figure 7. Detailed geologic map showing structures along the terminus of the Goldstone Lake East fault. Map units as in Figures 4 and 5, with additional Miocene volcanic units (from bottom to top): Tt—tuff, Tr—rhyolite flows, Ta—andesite, Tg—Pliocene or Miocene gravel. Bar and ball symbol indicates fault with ball on downthrown side. Faults numbered 1–5 are discussed in text.

Granite Mountains block

Several roughly east-striking faults are exposed in the low hills of the southern Granite Mountains (Fig. 8), which lie near the center of the block lying north of the Coyote Canyon–Tiefort Mountains fault (Fig. 3). Four poorly exposed faults cutting Jurassic granitoids accomplish ~500 m cumulative sinistral separation of a vertical screen of quartzite. To the northeast, faults cutting Cretaceous granitoids are well exposed, forming zones of gouge and breccia 5 to 20 m wide. One fault cuts Pleistocene deposits. Fault planes dip south between 65° and 85°, except for the west-northwest-striking thrust fault in the northeast corner of the area (Fig. 8). Striae in the fault zones range from horizontal to gently plunging (to a maximum of 37°) to the west. The faults are therefore reverse sinistral. The thrust fault in the northeast corner of the area dips ~45° northward and contains striae trending between 000° and 006°. At one location, the thrust fault bifurcates; there, it cuts a distinctive

vertical dike with ~30 m reverse-sinistral separation across the two zones, which is compatible with striae observed elsewhere on the fault.

Faults bounding and within the dacite block (Fig. 8) appear to have youthful down-to-the-east and -north components of movement, judging from the high topography of the block. The faults are mostly buried under talus and colluvium, however. The fault along the east flank of the dacite block cuts middle Pleistocene deposits and warps late Pleistocene deposits.

Faults in the Granite Mountains appear to have been sites of sinistral slip with a minor reverse component. If slip across the northern five or six faults is comparable to that across the four southern faults, which offset a quartzite marker ~0.5 km, then ~1 km of sinistral slip takes place across this 6-km-wide area. More study is needed to determine whether this slip is distributed through the whole block or just in the area mapped, but the internal displacement appears to be greater than 15% of the ~4 km slip along each bounding fault.

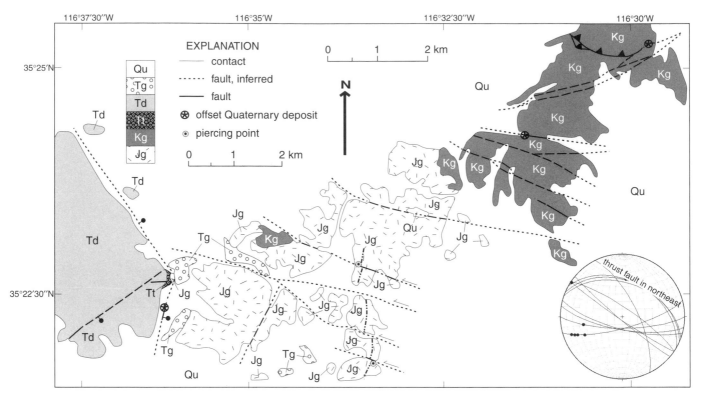

Figure 8. Detailed geologic map showing structures along the southern Granite Mountains. Map units as in Figures 4 and 7 plus Td—dacite flow dome. Marker unit is thin, steeply dipping band of quartzite. Bar and ball symbol indicates fault with ball on downthrown side.

Synthesis

The detailed geologic maps presented in the preceding section document concentrations of strike-slip, thrust, and normal faults within blocks between intermediate-scale faults spanning much of the distance between the Coyote Lake and Nelson Lake faults (see Fig. 2). The detailed slip history of faults bounding these blocks—"external faults"—versus those within the blocks—"internal faults"—is not known, and the details of the importance of internal faults in accommodating strain within the Mojave strike-slip province remain undetermined. However, we consider the internal and external faults to be coeval, as they share many general characteristics: (1) The external faults appear to offset early Miocene volcanic rocks and Mesozoic rocks by equal amounts (Sobieraj, 1994; Schermer et al., 1996), indicating that they are mostly middle Miocene and younger. (2) Internal faults similarly consistently cut the early Miocene volcanic rocks. (3) Both external and internal faults contain abundant gouge and breccia that lack low- or moderate-temperature hydrothermal minerals. (4) Some locations, such as north and east of Coyote Ridge and south of South Tiefort Ridge—where Pliocene deposits of basalt and gravel are widespread—are cut both by external and internal faults. (5) North-trending folds affecting Mesozoic and older rocks in South Tiefort Ridge are geometrically similar to those affecting Pliocene gravel to the south (Byers, 1960). (6) An empirical correlation

exists between faults marked by thick gouge zones and Quaternary age of last movement, as indicated by ruptured Quaternary surficial deposits. (7) Lastly, many internal faults cut Pleistocene deposits, as do external faults. We conclude that most external and internal faults are middle Miocene to Quaternary in age, but ages of inception remain loosely bracketed between ca. 15 Ma and 5 Ma. For the following synthesis, we maintained conservative criteria for the age of faulting, eliminating any faults likely to have a history older than latest Miocene such as the Garlic Springs fault (Miller et al., 1994) and the chlorite breccia zones in granite southeast of Goldstone.

Figure 9 presents a qualitative summary of the distribution of strain in rocks and sediment in the map area of Figure 3. Strain was assigned to high, intermediate, and low values by using spacing of faults and folds, moderated by the presence of distributed breccia, gouge, and other evidence of disruption of the rocks not associated with mappable faults. The strain map shows significant strain within blocks, particularly in high-strain zones near external faults that range from 1 to 3 km wide. A lack of such a high-strain zone adjacent to much of the Coyote Lake fault might be spurious because most exposures are in Pliocene gravel, in which identification of faults is difficult. The area near Jack Spring where Mesozoic and older rocks are adjacent to the Coyote Lake fault does show close-spaced faulting classified as high internal strain. These high strain zones adjacent to external faults validate the observation by Schermer

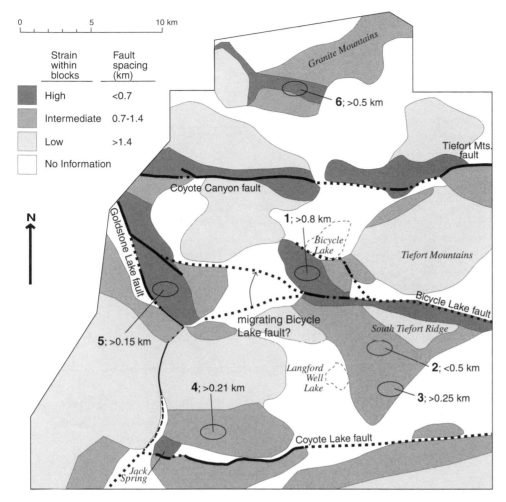

Figure 9. Map showing strain within blocks; area same as Figure 3. Qualitative units are based on minimum fault slip (locations keyed to Table 2 and offset indicated), fault spacing and length, folds, and pervasive shearing. Categories for internal strain are based primarily on spacing of throughgoing faults, as described in the legend. High strain near significant block-bounding faults, described by Schermer et al. (1996), is confirmed, and generally higher internal strain is seen in blocks of the east-striking-fault domain as compared to blocks of the northwest-striking-fault domain.

et al. (1996) that the external faults are typically nests of fault splays or anastomosing faults forming distinct high-strain fault zones. The strain map also depicts (1) high- and intermediate-strain zones near the terminus of each of the Goldstone Lake and Bicycle Lake faults and (2) intermediate strain in much of the region between the Bicycle Lake and Coyote Lake faults. These patterns may be due to, respectively, migrating loci of faults with time and significant internal strains needed to accommodate shape changes within the blocks, as we outline in a later section.

High and moderate strains in the southern Granite Mountains are within an unusually wide block—i.e., 30 km as compared to the more common 5–10-km-wide block (Schermer et al., 1996)—and may indicate a significant fault system within the block. As described previously, the aggregate slip across faults within this area alone is greater than 15% of the slip across the bounding faults. The strain map pattern suggests that this faulting may be related to an internal fault system and thus is not distributed through the whole block.

Areas that expose materials of a wide age range can reveal displacement rate histories. High and intermediate internal strains present in Pliocene deposits near Coyote Canyon and

along the Coyote Lake fault occur in areas also showing significant deformation of Quaternary surfaces (Miller et al., 1994). In these areas, faulting has continued for at least the past 3 m.y. In contrast, the terminus of the Goldstone Lake fault system is more readily interpreted as strain migrating northeast with time. Fault strands to the southwest do not disrupt Quaternary materials, whereas those to the northeast may deform Holocene materials. The Bicycle Lake fault system may have undergone a shift northward corresponding with that of the Goldstone Lake fault, which could partly explain the wide distribution of intermediate- and high-strain rocks along the west half of that fault system.

Estimates of cumulative displacement on faults within blocks of the ESF domain are greater than 13% of that given by Schermer et al. (1996) for external faults (Table 2). Therefore, intrablock displacement is an important factor for successful modeling of faults. If this displacement is extrapolated to areas internal to the blocks and covered by valley fill, the total internal displacement could be as great as 40% to 50% of the external displacement. Schermer et al. (1996) noted that simple block-rotation models using observed fault-displacement data underpredicted the paleomagnetically determined

TABLE 2. FAULT-SLIP DATA FOR TECTONIC BLOCKS OF FORT IRWIN AREA

Location (Fig. 9)	Internal fault	Slip (km)	External fault	Slip (km)
1	Central fault	>0.8	Bicycle Lake	>4.7
2	Internal faults	<0.5	Bicycle Lake	>4.7
3	South fault	>0.25	Bicycle Lake	>4.7
4	Noble Dome	>0.21	Coyote Lake	unknown
5	Northwest faults	>0.15	Goldstone Lake	3 to 4
6	Granite Mountains	>0.53	Coyote Canyon	4

Note: Data for all external faults, from Schermer et al. (1996); data for internal faults, this paper.

vertical-axis rotations by about a factor of two. Including internal displacement will improve the fit of that model.

With this areally limited strain analysis, we are not able to confidently contrast strain in blocks in the two domains (i.e., ESF and NWSF) and near and far from the domain boundary. The limited data hint at lower internal strain in blocks in the NWSF domain. Further study is needed to compare and contrast fault behaviors of the two domains.

BEHAVIOR OF BLOCK-BOUNDING FAULTS

The most significant faults of the Fort Irwin area were identified by Dibblee (1961), Byers (1960), and Jennings et al. (1962). Schermer et al. (1996) described geologic relationships along the faults that provide kinematics, estimates of offsets, and orientations for some faults. These data are integrated with our observations in the following section.

Faults in the ESF domain

Most block-bounding faults in the ESF domain dip south, show a component of thrust separation, and are associated with topographic steps up to the south. An exception is the Drinkwater Lake fault (Fig. 2), which dips to the north. South dips are 50°–85°, measured in six locations on four faults systems: Coyote Lake fault, Bicycle Lake fault, Coyote Canyon–Tiefort Mountains fault, and Nelson Lake-Fort Irwin fault. Studies by Schermer et al. (1996) ascribe between 4 and 6 km of sinistral displacement to each of these faults, and ~2 km of sinistral displacement to the Drinkwater Lake fault. Separation across the Coyote Lake fault is unknown. Schermer et al. (1996) also documented components of vertical separation on many faults and east-trending folds. These relationships suggest that a regional reverse component of fault slip is expressed on most faults in the ESF domain. Not only do faults lie at topographic steps, but topography systematically climbs northeastward toward the Avawatz Mountains (Fig. 10). The topography suggests that reverse components of fault slip increase toward the Avawatz Mountains.

Faults in the NWSF domain

Several faults in the NWSF domain cut across pediments without deflecting the surface. Faults strike northwest and dip steeply both southwest and northeast. These data indicate that faults in the NWSF domain, within the area of Figure 2, have little dip-slip component. Despite the general lack of topography associated with faults, in places where faults converge (such as those in Fig. 7), significant topography may result (Dokka, 1992). Elsewhere in the Mojave strike-slip province, northwest-striking dextral faults typically show strong control on topography, with many mountains aligned along the faults. These relationships suggest that dip slip may be more common in parts of the NWSF domain distant from Fort Irwin.

Faults at the domain boundary

The boundary between the ESF and NWSF domains changes character dramatically along strike. Its northern part coincides with the dextral Goldstone Lake fault, which displays a consistent topographic step up to the northeast. At the southeast terminus of the Goldstone Lake fault, the domain boundary bends sharply to the southwest, where a small-slip normal fault appears to mark the boundary between the domains of east- and northwest-striking faults. That normal fault probably connects to the northeast-striking Paradise Range frontal fault, which is the western segment of the Coyote Lake fault. That segment of the Coyote Lake fault was inferred by McCulloh (1960) to have significant normal offset across it. Thus, the domain boundary varies from a low to moderately high ridge along the northwest-trending part, to a steep escarpment down to the southeast along the northeast-trending segment. Faults of the ESF domain bend northwest as they merge with faults of the NWSF domain along the northwest-trending segment of the domain boundary. The sinistral faults acquire a pronounced thrust component at these locations, which also are marked by high topography. In contrast, faults of the ESF domain must join the south segment of the domain boundary in a broad low area occupied by Coyote Lake (Fig. 2). Here, the Paradise Range in the NWSF domain forms a topographic high.

LATE CENOZOIC PHYSIOGRAPHIC EVOLUTION

Volcanic and sedimentary rocks deposited from the Miocene to the present provide information on the changing physiography of the area over ~21 m.y. Schermer et al. (1996) showed that deposits of early and middle Miocene age in the

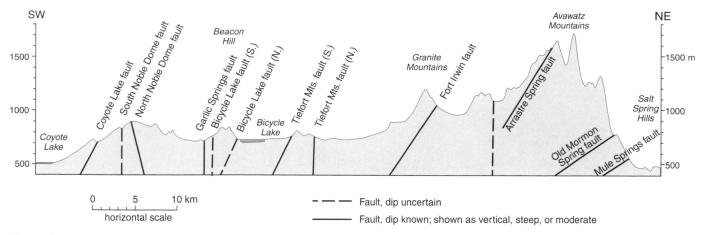

Figure 10. Topographic profile from Coyote Lake across the Avawatz Mountains to Salt Spring Hills, illustrating rise of elevation to the Avawatz Mountains and topographic steps associated with faults in the east-striking-fault domain. Fault dips and sense of dip-slip component shown where known; dashed faults are of uncertain orientation. See Figure 2 for location of profile.

area predated inception of strike-slip faulting because deposits younger than 11 Ma are offset as much as older units (see also Sobieraj, 1994). We focus the following description of evolving paleogeography on the post-10 Ma time period associated with strike-slip faulting in the Mojave strike-slip province. Although deposits younger than 10 Ma are generally difficult to date in the Mojave Desert region owing to a paucity of volcanic rocks of this age, at Fort Irwin the presence of a Pliocene basalt flow and 3.4 Ma ash in sediments provides age control for "snap-shots" of physiography.

Late Miocene physiography

Most volcanic activity occurred during the early Miocene (Schermer et al., 1996), with the development of large edifices and complexes of volcanic strata that are especially notable in the northwest part of the area (Fig. 11A). In the east and south, volcanic rocks lie in thick sedimentary sequences that received detritus from several sources (Spencer, 1990; Fillmore, 1993). In the southwest, basins largely early and middle Miocene in age were formed by detachment faulting (Fillmore, 1993; Glazner et al., 1994). By ca. 10 Ma, nearly all volcanic activity had ceased, but a few alluvial basins in the east (Fig. 11A) may have received their last sediments from sources to the north and northeast (Sobieraj, 1994) and south (Spencer, 1990). Basins at the east end of the Garlock fault received thick sequences of sediment derived from the east (Brady, 1984) after 10 Ma and possibly as late as the Pliocene. Thin alluvial sections above volcanic rocks in several places across the region probably record deposition during the time period from 10 to 6 Ma, but all are undated. South of the Tiefort Mountains, thick coarse alluvial deposits that were derived from a northern source in the vicinity of the current Tiefort Mountains formed steep, stubby fans older than 5 Ma and probably reflect uplift in the Tiefort area. The volcanic province north and northeast of Goldstone probably persisted as a complex of topographically high edi-

fices through the Miocene, providing sediment to alluvial systems to the northeast.

Early Pliocene (6 to 4 Ma) physiography

Fragments of basalt flows dated at ca. 5 Ma provide indications of early Pliocene physiography. The large complex of basalt flows near Bitter Spring is probably close to its source (Schermer et al., 1996). Fragments of chemically similar flows, some of which are also dated at ca. 5 Ma, extend west-northwest as far as Coyote Canyon, currently ~25 km in distance. Many fragments occur along the Bicycle Lake fault and are much more widely spaced than can be explained by offset along the fault (determined from several older markers) (Schermer et al., 1996). As a result, we infer that the flows traveled westward down a valley that formed along the fault system (Fig. 11B). The presence of a linear valley along the Bicycle Lake fault strongly suggests that the fault was active at ca. 5 Ma and controlled topography. If correct, these inferences require that Bitter Spring was higher than points to the west, such as the future Coyote Canyon area, and that the Bicycle Lake fault had destroyed the earlier fan system shed southward from the paleo-Tiefort Mountains.

To the east, the Avawatz Mountains were undergoing uplift by thrust faulting along the northeast side during the early Pliocene, with a corresponding southwest tilt of Miocene strata in sedimentary basins on the southwest side (Spencer, 1990). Folds in the upper part of the Miocene Avawatz Formation trend 270°–285° and were ascribed by Spencer to the tilting of the Avawatz Mountains. However, such tilting would not induce very large strain; the folds may instead be due to north-south shortening as tectonic blocks in the ESF domain rotated and the entire area underwent north-south shortening.

By ca. 4 Ma, all block-bounding faults in the ESF domain were active, because many of them significantly displace younger Pliocene deposits as described in this paper.

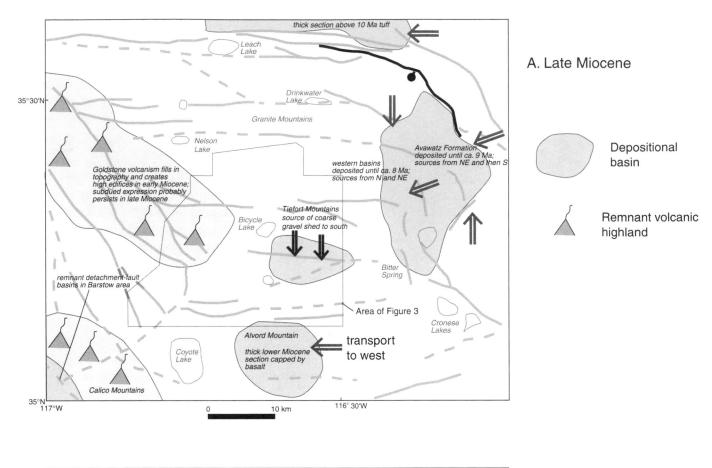

A. Late Miocene

thick section above 10 Ma tuff

Leach Lake

35°30'N

Drinkwater Lake

Granite Mountains

Nelson Lake

Avawatz Formation deposited until ca. 9 Ma; sources from NE and then S

Goldstone volcanism fills in topography and creates high edifices in early Miocene; subdued expression probably persists in late Miocene

western basins deposited until ca. 8 Ma; sources from N and NE

Bicycle Lake

Tiefort Mountains source of coarse gravel shed to south

remnant detachment-fault basins in Barstow area

Bitter Spring

Area of Figure 3

Cronese Lakes

Coyote Lake

Alvord Mountain

transport to west

thick lower Miocene section capped by basalt

Calico Mountains

35°N
117°W

0   10 km

116° 30'W

Depositional basin

Remnant volcanic highland

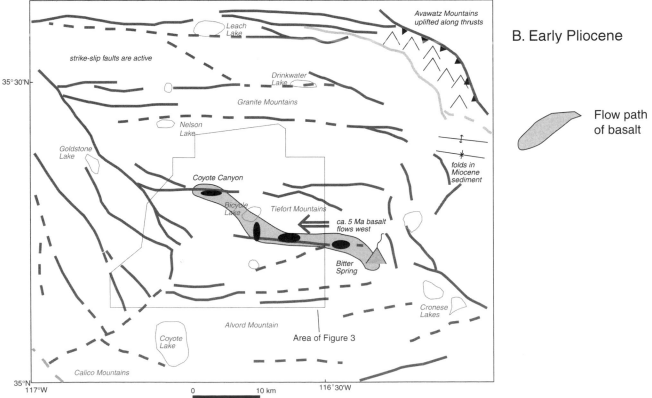

B. Early Pliocene

Avawatz Mountains uplifted along thrusts

Leach Lake

strike-slip faults are active

Drinkwater Lake

35°30'N

Granite Mountains

Nelson Lake

Goldstone Lake

folds in Miocene sediment

Coyote Canyon

Bicycle Lake

Tiefort Mountains

ca. 5 Ma basalt flows west

Bitter Spring

Cronese Lakes

Coyote Lake

Alvord Mountain

Area of Figure 3

Calico Mountains

35°N
117°W

0   10 km

116°30'W

Flow path of basalt

Figure 11 (on this and facing page). Geologic and physiographic maps of upper Miocene, Pliocene, and Quaternary deposits for southern Fort Irwin area shown on map of modern geography for reference. Reference units are 5.6 Ma basalt and deposits containing 3.4 Ma ash. (A) Late Miocene. (B) Early Pliocene (6–4 Ma). (C) Late Pliocene (4–2 Ma). (D) Holocene. Faults in black are known or inferred to be active; faults in gray are inactive. Double arrows indicate sediment-transport directions.

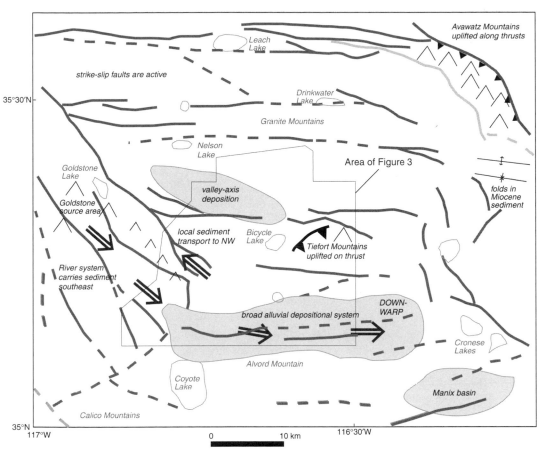

C. late Pliocene

Avawatz Mountains uplifted along thrusts

Leach Lake

strike-slip faults are active

35°30'N

Drinkwater Lake

Granite Mountains

Depositional province

Nelson Lake

Area of Figure 3

Goldstone Lake

valley-axis deposition

folds in Miocene sediment

Goldstone source area

local sediment transport to NW

Bicycle Lake

Tiefort Mountains uplifted on thrust

River system carries sediment southeast

broad alluvial depositional system

DOWN-WARP

Cronese Lakes

Coyote Lake

Alvord Mountain

Manix basin

Calico Mountains

35°N
117°W   116°30'W

0   10 km

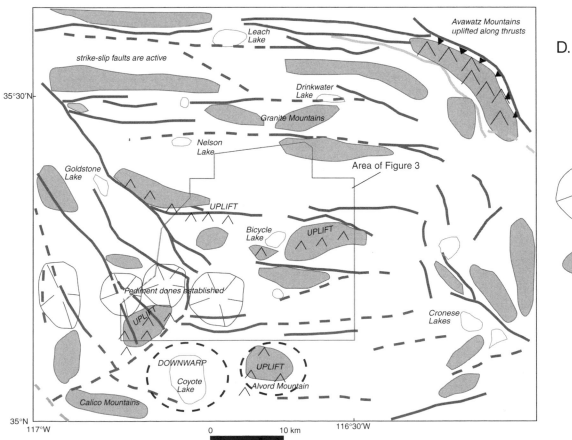

D. Quaternary

Avawatz Mountains uplifted along thrusts

Leach Lake

strike-slip faults are active

35°30'N

Drinkwater Lake

Granite Mountains

Nelson Lake

Area of Figure 3

Goldstone Lake

UPLIFT

Pediment dome

Bicycle Lake

UPLIFT

Mountains

Pediment domes established

UPLIFT

DOWNWARP

Cronese Lakes

Coyote Lake

UPLIFT

Alvord Mountain

Calico Mountains

35°N
117°W   116°30'W

0   10 km

Late Pliocene (4 to 2 Ma) physiography

Two deposits are dated by the presence of an interbedded ash at ca. 3.4 Ma. Similar and more widespread deposits are correlated with these middle Pliocene deposits to describe the physiography of this time. Along the north and east sides of Coyote Ridge, alluvial-fan deposits overlying the Pliocene basalt grade upward from medial- to distal-fan deposits and then to fine-grained valley-bottom deposits with nearly 10 m of associated fine-grained paludal deposits in places. Within the paludal deposits lies the 3.4 Ma ash. Underlying alluvium contains clasts of granitoids and volcanic rocks that lack distinctive sources, but the area was probably topographically low and received sediment from sources that were nearby. Paludal deposits represent valley-bottom groundwater discharge, perhaps partly caused by groundwater disruption by the Coyote Canyon fault. The paludal deposits are gradationally overlain by distal alluvial-fan sand and gravel, probably late Pliocene in age.

The 3.4 Ma ash also is present within a widespread alluvial sequence stretching along the Coyote Lake fault (Fig. 11C) that bears a distinctive clast assemblage. This alluvial depositional system continued eastward at least to Bitter Spring. Clasts such as striped red-and-green calc-silicate rock, thin-bedded quartzite, and granitoids that include muscovite-bearing dikes indicate a source from the Goldstone area (Carr et al., 1992). Paleocurrent indicators such as imbricate clasts and cross-beds confirm the east-southeast current directions. Deposits consistently contain angular boulders of rock types present nearby and smaller well-rounded clasts of the rock types present at Goldstone. We interpret these relationships as a trunk stream or long, broad alluvial fan that carried sediment down a long gradient some 55 km from Goldstone to Bitter Spring, with local mountains along the stream providing proximal alluvial-fan debris. South of Langford Well Lake, the alluvial sequence contains granitoid boulders derived from a few kilometers west or northwest that are 3 to 4 m in diameter. Thus, by middle Pliocene time, Bitter Spring was a low area receiving far-traveled alluvial deposits, in contrast to its earlier high position from which basalt flowed west-northwest. The Coyote Canyon area was near a basin axis, but was separated from the Goldstone source area.

The Avawatz Mountains continued to be uplifted by thrust faults along the northeast side, tilting sediment to the southwest, during the late Pliocene. The Tiefort Mountains probably began to rise along thrust faults on the northwest side during the late Pliocene because several thrust faults predate middle Pleistocene alluvium derived from the west face of the Tiefort Mountains.

Near the south edge of the area (Fig. 11C), the Manix basin formed before ca. 2.4 Ma (Nagy and Murray, 1996). The basin received playa and encroaching alluvial-fan deposits until ca. 500 ka. Although the inception of the local basin is not directly dated, it probably formed shortly before 2.4 Ma because small terminal basins probably do not persist for long periods of time.

Quaternary physiography

The present physiography departs significantly from that of the Pliocene. Sheets of Pliocene alluvial gravel are folded, faulted, and warped in most exposures. Most noteworthy is downwarping of the gravel toward Coyote Lake and upwarping of the gravel along the north and northeast margins of Alvord Mountain (Fig. 11D). Where downwarped toward Coyote Lake, the sediment was transported east-southeast, not southward down the current gradient, requiring that the Coyote Lake low area did not exist during the middle Pliocene. Currently, detritus from the Goldstone area sheds into the Coyote Lake basin. Suggestions that the Coyote Lake area is low due to thrust loading (Bartley et al., 1990) are not supported by detailed investigations that indicate that escarpments next to the playa are not tectonic in origin (Albert, 1998). Where upwarped along the margin of Alvord Mountain, the gravel is generally concordant on deformed Miocene volcanic sequences (Fillmore, 1993), indicating that some of the folding and uplift of the Alvord Mountain area was latest Pliocene in age. A similar conclusion of latest Miocene to Pliocene uplift and unroofing of the Alvord Mountain area was reached by J.S. Miller and J.D. Walker (this volume) on the basis of fission-track studies.

Widespread folds and faults in the Pliocene alluvial gravels attest to considerable deformation of the area during the past 3 m.y. Pliocene paludal deposits near Coyote Canyon, deposited in a low valley-bottom setting, are now perched on the crest of a ridge as a result of displacement across the Coyote Canyon fault. Pediment domes southeast of Goldstone and north of the widespread Pliocene alluvial gravel apparently formed after the Pliocene gravel was deposited, because the gravel must have been carried across the area of the present pediment to its depositional site. This pediment is therefore unusually young for the Mojave Desert region.

Several fault blocks in the ESF domain display a distinctive topographic signature. Their southwest and northeast corners form small- to moderate-size mountains where their bounding faults curve into northwest strikes. An example is the block bracketed by the Nelson Lake-Fort Irwin faults and the Coyote Canyon-Tiefort Mountains faults. We concur with Schermer et al. (1996) that this topography indicates local contraction of the blocks as they rotated. The contraction indicates that block rotation and its attendant east-west elongation was not totally accommodated by east-west extension of the Mojave Desert region. Corroboration of this implication comes from playa basins, which do not appear to be dilational holes in the crust, as modeled by Dokka (1992), because they do not have large negative gravity signatures and they are rimmed in some cases by contractional structures (e.g., Figs. 3, 4, 5).

The Avawatz Mountains continued to rise during the Quaternary as a result of thrusting along their northeast side, achieving a minimum of 1000 m of uplift relative to deposits of late Miocene age along the north side (Brady, 1984). The Tiefort

Mountains continued to rise along thrust faults on the northwest side, some of which cut middle Pleistocene materials.

Near the south edge of the area (Fig. 11D), the Manix basin received encroaching alluvial-fan deposits until ca. 500 ka, when a facies change to lake deposits resulted from the introduction of a regional drainage system, the Mojave River (Nagy and Murray, 1996).

Physiographic evolution elsewhere in the Mojave strike-slip province

The inferences for late Pliocene and early Pleistocene topographic evolution in the northeast part of the Mojave strike-slip province are corroborated by histories determined farther south The San Bernardino Mountains underwent uplift at ca. 2 Ma, and further uplift and tilting at ca. 1.0 Ma (Meisling and Weldon, 1989; Spotila et al., 1998). Uplift apparently continued adjacent to the San Bernardino Mountains, as indicated by a northwestward-propagating uplift along the northeast side of the San Andreas fault (Kenney and Weldon, 1999). This uplift apparently is being accommodated by late Pleistocene and Holocene faults. The uplift of the San Bernardino Mountains contributed to the development of the Mojave River by creating a high-precipitation landmass that drained into the desert. Studies of the early evolution of the Mojave River by Cox and Tinsley (1999) demonstrated that the deposits carried by the river prograded northward across the desert from ca. 2.0 to ca. 1.0 Ma, eventually integrating several formerly isolated basins such as Harper Lake, Coyote Lake, and the Manix basin. The period from ca. 2 to 1 Ma apparently saw rapidly changing physiography in several parts of the central and western Mojave Desert. We suspect that most physiography in this part of the desert is due to latest Pliocene and Quaternary tectonics.

STRIKE-SLIP FAULT EVOLUTION

North-south contraction of the greater Mojave Desert region has been modeled conceptually as distributed shear along strike-slip faults, which produces rotations of the blocks and faults. Most models have invoked overall pure shear of the Mojave region. The models vary in geometric simplicity, boundary conditions, and sequence of fault movement. As noted by Bartley et al. (1990) and Schermer et al. (1996), internal deformation of blocks remains unevaluated in these models and can significantly alter the results. Our studies indicate that some blocks contain aggregate displacements that are 10% to 25%, and possibly as much as 50%, of the slip along the block-bounding faults.

We have reconstructed the post-10 Ma evolution of the Fort Irwin area by using the actual geometries of faults, slip documented by Schermer et al. (1996) and in this paper, and strain between the block-bounding faults as estimated in this paper (Fig. 12). We assume that fault blocks of the NWSF domain

are little deformed internally and have undergone no post-early Miocene vertical-axis rotations, as documented by paleomagnetic studies (e.g., Ross et al., 1989). We assume that east-domain fault blocks underwent 40° of clockwise vertical-axis rotation associated with fault slip. This value is less than the ~60° suggested by paleomagnetic studies but consistent with the ~25° modeled by Schermer et al. (1996) on the basis of slip on external faults, plus a block shear accommodated by internal strain. We take the maximum stress as horizontal and 020° and the minimum stress as horizontal and 110°.

We assume that the close match of geology where the Goldstone Lake and Bicycle Lake faults meet indicates minimal net slip in that reach of the boundary between the ESF and NWSF domains, and we designate that location as a pivot point. It is actually a complexly deforming corner as the two faults migrate in space, but much of the area contains little-deformed rock expressed in pediment domes (Fig. 9). We reconstruct north-south shortening by simple translations of rigid blocks, and we adjust markers to account for internal strain within blocks by imposing a simple shear on each block in the ESF domain. We assume that modern topography provides a qualitative measure of vertical deformation during the past 1 to 2 m.y.; that is, rates of topographic change by erosion and sedimentation of volcanic and granitoid rocks are much slower than the vertical strain rate associated with faulting. We also assume approximately rigid behavior of the greater Avawatz Mountains block and its fixed location, although many other possibilities exist. The reconstruction does not require any particular behavior of this block and does not force any assumptions about proto-southern Death Valley fault zone locations.

The reconstruction produces a net northward translation of the Goldstone area with respect to the Avawatz area of ~25 km, as a result of rotation of blocks in the ESF domain accommodated by slip along the boundaries of the blocks and by simple shear within them. The reconstruction predicts vertical-axis rotations of several features in addition to the blocks of the ESF domain. Slip across faults of the NWSF domain causes the Garlock fault to rotate clockwise with time. Slip across and vertical-axis rotation of ESF-domain faults causes the eastern Garlock fault boundary to rotate clockwise and move south with time, creating a bend in the fault as has been previously suggested by others. Overall, the ESF domain stays about the same width east-west, but shortens and translates north-south. Contraction at corners of rotating blocks accommodates most of the change of shape within the domain.

The domain boundary is fixed at the pivot point, so fault slip varies north and south from that position. In the north, faults of the two domains merge by east-striking faults bending to the northwest in contractional zones of high topography. In the south, a large normal or normal-oblique fault is required (but not exposed) at the base of the Paradise Range. This part of the domain boundary must undergo a small clockwise rotation as slip accumulates across the faults of the NWSF domain. The original orientation—north-northeast—of the Paradise Range

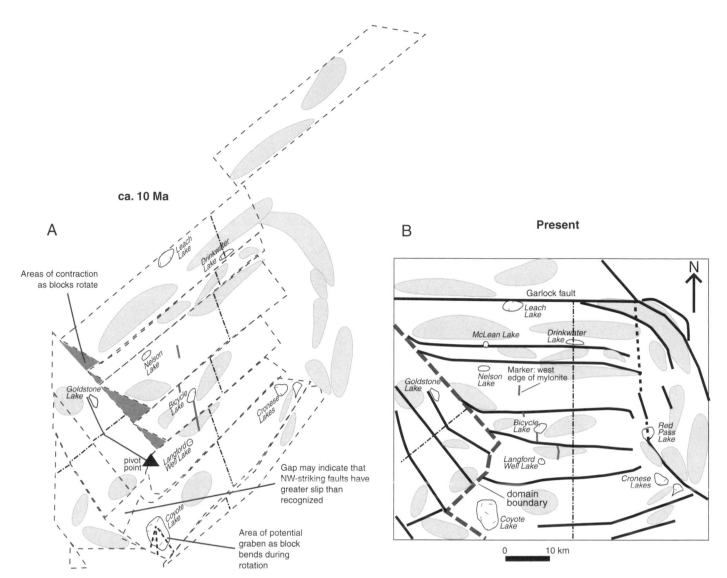

Figure 12. Cartoon of (A) possible configuration of faults at ~10 Ma inception of north-south contraction in northeastern part of Mojave strike-slip province and (B) present configuration. Note boundary between domains of differently oriented (east-striking and northwest-striking) faults. That boundary and external boundaries such as the Garlock fault are required to undergo vertical-axis rotations as a result of strike-slip faulting within this part of the Mojave strike-slip province. Overlaps of edges of fault blocks as a result of slip and block rotation coincide with loci of present mountains (gray areas), and potential openings as blocks bend coincide with loci of present low areas. Note that because of an assumed coupled pivot point (marked by a solid triangle in the left cartoon), based on nearly continuous geology across the domain boundary, the faults along domain boundaries (such as the Goldstone Lake fault) accumulate slip progressively away from this point. Fit would be improved if greater separations were invoked for faults in the domain of northwest-striking faults; misfit west of Coyote Lake could be greatly reduced. Note small separation required for Coyote Lake fault in its east-striking segment.

segment of the boundary between the NWSF and ESF domains in the reconstruction is appropriate for initial normal slip, changing to oblique slip as the domain boundary and faults rotate. The block bounded by the Coyote Lake and Manix faults is reconstructed with the least misfits by requiring it to bend as fault slip and block rotation accumulate. The bend in the block may cause the downwarp of Coyote Lake basin and the upwarp of the Alvord Mountain area.

The simple reconstruction indicates that strike-slip faulting in this part of the Mojave strike-slip province can be accomplished with little east-west elongation and considerable north-south shortening. The boundaries of the province—the Garlock and San Andreas faults—undergo rotations as the area changes shape. The simple reconstruction does not address the behavior of northwest-striking faults south of the Manix and Cady faults. If the reconstruction is valid, those faults must have been the sites of increasing slip from west to east to accommodate the rotation of blocks in the ESF domain. The reconstruction can be tested by study of these faults and also by reconciling with the model of Richard (1993) for faults farther to the south.

CONCLUSIONS

Much internal strain is documented within fault-bounded blocks in the northeastern part of the Mojave strike-slip province, especially near the boundary between NWSF and ESF domains. In comparison to the NWSF domain, the apparent association of more internal strain in blocks of the ESF domain needs further study. The higher internal strain helps to account for disparate results from paleomagnetic studies and rigid-block simple-shear models. The internal strain apparently results from (1) proximity to block-bounding fault zones, where splays are as far as 3 km from the primary fault, (2) complex strain near stepovers, (3) complex strain near a primary bend in the domain boundary, where blocks apparently pivot about the bend, and (4) internal strain as blocks rotate during sinistral faulting.

The boundary between ESF and NWSF domains displays many styles of accommodation. Along the northern segment of the domain boundary, which is the Goldstone Lake fault, east-striking faults bend to the northwest and merge with the Goldstone Lake fault. High topography associated with this segment suggests proximal contraction. We interpret the contraction to result from indentation of a corner of a block as it rotates and is compressed against the nonrotating boundary. A pivot point in the center of the domain boundary appears to be fixed because geologic features are virtually continuous across the faults. As a consequence, fault slip increases in both directions away from the pivot point along the domain boundary as ESF-domain blocks rotate about vertical axes. South of the pivot point, the boundary is made up of normal faults, including the large fault along the southeast front of the Paradise Range. As dextral faults in the NWSF domain moved, the domain boundary adjacent to the Paradise Range rotated clockwise; as a consequence, it probably changed from normal to oblique-sinistral slip with time.

Pliocene and younger time saw sharp changes in topography. The Coyote Lake basin downwarped and the Alvord Mountain area uplifted after ca. 3 Ma, probably from rotational misfits south of the pivot point in the domain boundary that caused the block to bend. Fission-track data for Alvord Mountain indicate final cooling of rocks in the late Miocene or Pliocene (Miller and Walker, this volume), an event that fits well with the evidence for Pliocene uplift of the mountain based on sedimentologic data from this study.

Topographic steps up from the Coyote Lake fault to the Garlock fault and the Avawatz Mountains, in combination with data that most east-striking faults dip south and have reverse-slip components, suggest that overall roughly north-south compression has been accommodated by thrust movement across those faults. The east-striking faults no longer adequately accommodated strain by strike slip and thus must have a significant thrust component of slip. Deformation associated with this thrusting is younger than 3 Ma near the Coyote Lake fault and probably of similar timing elsewhere.

Much physiography in this part of the greater Mojave Desert region is younger than 3 Ma. A few areas, such as the Goldstone mining district and the Avawatz Mountains, have been persistent high areas since the beginning of the Pliocene. Other parts of the western Mojave Desert developed modern physiography after ca. 2 Ma, raising the possibility that much of the physiography of the central and western Mojave Desert is latest Pliocene and Quaternary in age.

ACKNOWLEDGMENTS

We have benefited from discussions with Liz Schermer, Doug Walker, Brett Cox, Laura Albert, and Roy Dokka about various aspects of the geology of southern Fort Irwin and its regional setting, and we thank them for sharing ideas and data. Laboratory and field work by Dennis Sorg, Charlie Meyer, and El-mira Wan greatly helped with K/Ar analyses and tephrochronology. John Nakata and Andrei Sarna-Wojcicki graciously provided K/Ar data and tephrochronology results, respectively. Rene Quinones, Directorate of Public Works, Fort Irwin, provided partial funding and logistics support, without which this work could not have been accomplished. We appreciate thorough reviews by John Hillhouse, Angela Jayko, Tim Ross, Elizabeth Schermer, and John Bartley, which led to considerable improvement of an earlier draft of this paper.

REFERENCES CITED

Albert, L.J., 1998, Geomorphology and genesis of the northern Coyote Basin escarpment, Coyote Lake, San Bernardino County, California [M.S. thesis]: California State University, Los Angeles, 76 p.

Atwater, T., 1970, Implications of plate tectonics for Cenozoic tectonic evolution of western North America: Geological Society of America Bulletin, v. 81, p. 3513–3536.

Bartley, J.M., Glazner, A.F., and Schermer, E.R., 1990, North-south contraction of the Mojave block and strike-slip tectonics in southern California: Science, v. 248, p. 1398–1401.

Brady, R.H., III, 1984, Neogene stratigraphy of the Avawatz Mountains between the Garlock and Death Valley fault zones, southern Death Valley, California: Implications as to late Cenozoic tectonism: Sedimentary Geology, v. 38, p. 127–157.

Byers, F.M., 1960, Geology of the Alvord Mountain quadrangle, San Bernardino County, California: U.S. Geological Survey Bulletin 1089-A, 71 p.

Carr, M.D., Harris, A.G., Poole, F.G., and Fleck, R.J., 1992, Stratigraphy and structure of Paleozoic outer continental-margin rocks in Pilot Knob Valley, north-central Mojave Desert, California: U.S. Geological Survey Bulletin 2015, 33 p.

Carter, J.N., Luyendyk, B.P., and Terres, R.R., 1987, Neogene clockwise rotation of the eastern Transverse Ranges, California, suggested by paleomagnetic vectors: Geological Society of America Bulletin, v. 98, p. 199–206.

Cox, B.F., and Tinsley, J.C., III, 1999, Origin of the late Pliocene and Pleistocene Mojave River between Cajon Pass and Barstow, California, *in* Reynolds, R.E., and Reynolds, J., eds., Tracks along the Mojave: San Bernardino County Museum Quarterly, v. 46, no. 3, p. 49–54.

Dibblee, T.W., Jr., 1961, Evidence of strike-slip movement on northwest-trending faults in the western Mojave Desert, California: U.S. Geological Survey Professional Paper 424-B, p. B197–B199.

Dokka, R.K., 1992, The eastern California shear zone and its role in the creation of young extensional zones in the Mojave Desert region, *in* Craig, S.D., ed., Structure, tectonics, and mineralization of the Walker Lane: Geological Society of Nevada, p. 161–186.

Dokka, R.K., and Travis, C.J., 1990a, Role of the eastern California shear zone in accommodating Pacific-North American plate motion: Geophysical Research Letters, v. 17, p. 1323–1326.

Dokka, R.K., and Travis, C.J., 1990b, Late Cenozoic strike-slip faulting in the Mojave Desert, California: Tectonics, v. 9, p. 311–340.

Fillmore, J.P., 1993, Sedimentation and extensional basin evolution in a Miocene metamorphic core complex setting, Alvord Mountain, central Mojave Desert, California, USA: Sedimentology, v. 40, p. 721–742.

Ford, J.P., MacConnell, D.F., and Dokka, R.K., 1992, Neogene faulting in the Goldstone-Fort Irwin area, California: A progress report, *in* Richard, S.M., ed., Deformation associated with the Neogene eastern California shear zone, southeastern California and southwestern Arizona: San Bernardino County Museum Special Publication 92–1, p. 32.

Garfunkel, Z., 1974, Model for the late Cenozoic tectonic history of the Mojave Desert, California, and its relation to adjacent areas: Geological Society of America Bulletin, v. 85, p. 1931–1944.

Glazner, A.F., Walker, J.D., Bartley, J.M., Fletcher, J.M., Martin, M.W., Schermer, E.R., Boettcher, S.S., Miller, J.S., Fillmore, R.P., and Linn, J.K., 1994, Reconstruction of the Mojave block, *in* McGill, S.F., and Ross, T.M., eds., Geological investigations of an active margin: Redlands, California, San Bernardino County Museum Association, p. 3–30.

Hardebeck, J.L., and Hauksson, E., 1999, Roles of fluids in faulting inferred from stress field signatures: Science, v. 285, p. 236–239.

Jennings, C.W., 1994, Fault activity map of California and adjacent areas: California Division of Mines and Geology Geologic Data Map No. 6, scale 1:750000.

Jennings, C.W., Burnett, J.L., and Troxel, B.W., 1962, Geologic map of California: Trona sheet: California Division of Mines and Geology, scale 1:250000.

Kenney, M.D., and Weldon, R.J., 1999, Timing and magnitude of mid to late Quaternary uplift of the western San Bernardino and northeastern San Gabriel Mountains, southern California, *in* Reynolds, R.E., and Reynolds, J., eds., Tracks along the Mojave: San Bernardino County Museum Quarterly, v. 46, no. 3, p. 33–46.

Luyendyk, B.P., 1991, A model for Neogene rotations, transtension and transpression in southern California: Geological Society of America Bulletin, v. 103, p. 1528–1536.

Luyendyk, B.P., Kamerling, M.J., and Terres, R.R., 1980, Geometric model for Neogene crustal rotations in southern California: Geological Society of America Bulletin, v. 91, p. 211–217.

Luyendyk, B.P., Schermer, E.R., and Cisowski, S., 1993, Post-Early Miocene clockwise rotation in the northeast Mojave Desert, California [abs.]: Eos (Transactions, American Geophysical Union), v. 74, p. 207.

McCulloh, T.H., 1960, Geologic map of the Lane Mountain quadrangle, California: U.S. Geological Survey Open File Report, scale 1:62500.

McFadden, L.D., and Weldon, R.J., II, 1987, Rates and processes of soil development on Quaternary terraces in Cajon Pass, California: Geological Society of America Bulletin, v. 98, p. 280–293.

Meisling, K.E., and Weldon, R.J., 1989, Late Cenozoic tectonics of the northwestern San Bernardino Mountains, southern California: Geological Society of America Bulletin, v. 101, p. 106–128.

Miller, D.M., 1995, Characteristics, age, and tectonic implications of the Mid Hills pediment, *in* Reynolds, R.E., and Reynolds, J., eds., Ancient sur-

faces of the east Mojave Desert: San Bernardino County Museum Association Quarterly, v. 42, no. 3, p. 69–74.

Miller, D.M., and Bedford, D.R., 2000, Geologic map database of the El Mirage Lake area, San Bernardino and Los Angeles Counties, California: U.S. Geological Survey Open-File Report 00-222.

Miller, D.M., Yount, J.C., Schermer, E.R., and Felger, T.J., 1994, Preliminary assessment of the recency of faulting at southwestern Fort Irwin, north-central Mojave Desert, California: San Bernardino County Museum Association Special Publication 94-1, p. 41–52.

Miller, E.L., and Sutter, J.S., 1982, Structural geology and $^{40}Ar/^{39}Ar$ geochronology of the Goldstone-Lane Mountain area, Mojave Desert, California: Geological Society of America Bulletin, v. 93, p. 1191–1207.

Nagy, E.A., and Murray, B., 1996, Plio-Pleistocene deposits adjacent to the Manix fault: Implications for the history of the Mojave River and Transverse Ranges uplift: Sedimentary Geology, v. 103, p. 9–21.

Oberlander, T.M., 1974, Landscape inheritance and the pediment problem in the Mojave Desert of southern California: American Journal of Science, v. 274, p. 849–875.

Ponti, D.J., and Burke, D.B., 1980, Map showing Quaternary geology of the eastern Antelope Valley and vicinity, California: U.S. Geological Survey Open-File Report 80–1064, scale 1:62500.

Reheis, M.C., Harden, J.W., McFadden, L.D., and Shroba, R.R., 1989, Development rates of late Quaternary soils, Silver Lake Playa, California: Soil Science Society of America Journal, v. 53, p. 1127–1140.

Richard, S.M., 1993, Palinspastic reconstruction of southeastern California and southwestern Arizona for the middle Miocene: Tectonics, v. 12, p. 830–854.

Ron, H., Freund, R., Garfunkel, Z., and Nur, A., 1984, Block rotation by strike-slip faulting: Structural and paleomagnetic evidence: Journal of Geophysical Research, v. 89, p. 6256–6270.

Ross, T.M., 1995, North-south directed extension, timing of extension, and vertical-axis rotation of the southwest Cady Mountains, Mojave Desert, California: Geological Society of America Bulletin, v. 107, p. 793–811.

Ross, T.M., Luyendyk, B.P., and Haston, R.B., 1989, Paleomagnetic evidence for Neogene tectonic rotations in the central Mojave Desert, California: Geology, v. 17, p. 470–473.

Sauber, J., Thatcher, W., and Solomon, S., 1986, Geodetic measurement of deformation in the central Mojave Desert, California: Journal of Geophysical Research, v. 91, p. 12683–12694.

Sauber, J., Thatcher, W., Solomon, S., and Lisowski, M., 1994, Geodetic slip rate for the eastern California shear zone and the recurrence time of Mojave Desert earthquakes: Nature, v. 367, p. 264–266.

Schelle, H., and Grunthal, G., 1996, Modeling of Neogene crustal block rotation: Case study of southeastern California: Tectonics, v. 15, p. 700–710.

Schermer, E.R., Luyendyk, B.P., and Cisowski, S., 1996, Late Cenozoic structure and tectonics of the northern Mojave Desert: Tectonics, v. 15, p. 905–932.

Sobieraj, J.A., 1994, Sedimentology and tectonics of Tertiary fan deposits, Fort Irwin, northern Mojave Desert [M.S. thesis]: Bellingham, Western Washington University, 111 p.

Spencer, J.E., 1990, Late Cenozoic extensional and compressional tectonism in the southern and western Avawatz Mountains, southeastern California, *in* Wernicke, B.P., ed., Basin and range extensional tectonics near the latitude of Las Vegas, Nevada: Geological Society of America Memoir 176, p. 317–333.

Spotila, J.A., Farley, K.A., and Sieh, K., 1998, Uplift and erosion of the San Bernardino Mountains associated with transpression along the San Andreas fault, California, as constrained by radiogenic helium thermochronology: Tectonics, v. 17, p. 360–378.

Steiger, R.H., and Jäger, E., 1977, Subcommission on geochronology: Convention on the use of decay constants in geo- and cosmochronology: Earth and Planetary Science Letters, v. 36, p. 359–362.

Unruh, J.R., Twiss, R.J., and Hauksson, E., 1996, Seismogenic deformation field in the Mojave block and implications for tectonics of the eastern

California shear zone: Journal of Geophysical Research, v. 101, p. 8335–8361.

Valentine, M.J., Brown, L.L., and Golombek, M.P., 1993, Cenozoic crustal rotations in the Mojave Desert from paleomagnetic studies around Barstow, California: Tectonics, v. 12, p. 666–677.

Wells, R.E., and Hillhouse, J.W., 1989, Paleomagnetism and tectonic rotation of the lower Miocene Peach Springs Tuff: Colorado Plateau, Arizona, to Barstow, California: Geological Society of America Bulletin, v. 101, p. 846–863.

Westaway, R., 1995, Deformation around stepovers in strike-slip fault zones: Journal of Structural Geology, v. 17, p. 831–846.

Yount, J.C., Schermer, E.R., Felger, T.J., Miller, D.M., and Stephens, K.A., 1994, Preliminary geologic map of Fort Irwin Basin, north-central Mojave Desert, California: U.S. Geological Survey Open-File Report 94–173, scale 1:24000, 27 p.

MANUSCRIPT ACCEPTED BY THE SOCIETY MAY 9, 2001

Geological Society of America
Memoir 195
2002

Neogene evolution of the Indian Wells Valley, east-central California

Francis C. Monastero
Geothermal Program Office, Naval Air Weapons Station, China Lake, California 93555, USA
J. Douglas Walker
Department of Geology, University of Kansas, Lawrence, Kansas 66045, USA
Allan M. Katzenstein
Geothermal Program Office, Naval Air Weapons Station, China Lake, California 93555, USA
Andrew E. Sabin
*Innovative Technical Solutions, Inc., 2730 Shadelands Drive, Suite 100,
Walnut Creek, California 94598, USA*

ABSTRACT

The Indian Wells Valley located in east-central California has been an active sedimentary basin off and on throughout Tertiary time. During the Paleogene, the Indian Wells Valley was part of the Goler basin, and in the Miocene, the valley received volcaniclastic and terrigenous sediment correlated with rocks of the Ricardo Group. In the Pliocene, the Indian Wells Valley became the locus of deposition in a half graben formed by low-angle normal faulting along the eastern front of the Sierra Nevada.

Two significant structural and tectonic changes are recorded in the stratigraphy of the Indian Wells Valley: one at the close of the Miocene and the second at the end of the Pliocene. The late Miocene transition occurred sometime between 7 and 5 Ma and resulted in the uplift of the nearby Sierra Nevada and the formation of a half graben. Transition from a regime of east-west extension to one dominated by transtensional dextral faulting occurred in the late Pliocene, marking a change in regional stress, the cause of which is, as yet, undocumented. Dextral strike-slip faulting dominates the modern structural setting and controls the sparse sedimentation in the valley. This pattern of extension followed by transtension appears to be part of a progression that began in Death Valley ca. 16 Ma and moved westward. Today the Indian Wells Valley accommodates a component of integrated transtensional shear and is part of the evolving margin between the North American and Pacific plates.

INTRODUCTION

The Basin and Range province has been the focus of studies on continental extension since 1975 (e.g., Wernicke, 1992). One of the most intensely studied parts of this region is the central Basin and Range, which encompasses much of the area from the Colorado Plateau to the Sierra Nevada at the latitude

of Las Vegas (Fig. 1). Because of the excellent exposure and numerous geologic studies here, the timing and magnitude of Tertiary extension in this area is fairly well understood (Wernicke et al., 1988; Serpa and Pavlis, 1996). One important area that remains poorly known and not well integrated into the regional picture for the central Basin and Range province is the Indian Wells Valley, located at the southwesternmost corner of

Monastero, F.C., Walker, J.D., Katzenstein, A.M., and Sabin, A.E., 2002, Neogene evolution of the Indian Wells Valley, east-central California, *in* Glazner, A.F., Walker, J.D., and Bartley, J.M., eds., Geologic Evolution of the Mojave Desert and Southwestern Basin and Range: Boulder, Colorado, Geological Society of America Memoir 195, p. 199–228.

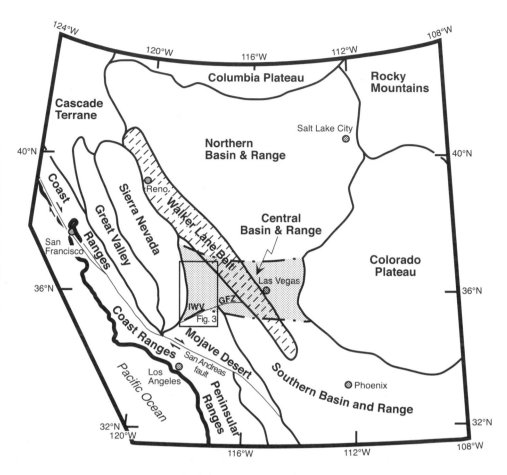

Figure 1. Map of the western United States showing the major tectono-physiographic provinces. The central Basin and Range designation acknowledges the uniqueness of the highly extended area around, and to the west of, Las Vegas. The Walker Lane belt is closely tied to physiographic and structural features; for a summary discussion of the Walker Lane belt, see Stewart (1983). The area covered by Figure 3, and the location of Indian Wells Valley (IWV) and the Garlock fault zone (GFZ), are shown in the box. Adapted from Wernicke (1992).

the central Basin and Range (see Fig. 1). Understanding the evolution of the Indian Wells Valley is important because of its location in the broad zone of transtensional shear in eastern California. The valley is bounded on the south by the Garlock fault, long recognized for its key role in the accommodation of differential extension between the Basin and Range and the relatively unextended Mojave Desert region (Davis and Burchfiel, 1973). Unraveling the geologic history of the Indian Wells Valley provides valuable information about the Cenozoic evolution of the Pacific–North American plate boundary and the partitioning of strain along the eastern front of the Sierra Nevada (Wesnousky and Jones, 1994).

Modern seismicity is abundant in the Indian Wells Valley; an average of 5000 events occur there annually. Between August 1995 and January 1996 there were three earthquakes of >5.0 magnitude. First motion for these events is consistent with the differential movement between the Pacific and North American plates. Epicenters define a north-northwest–trending belt of seismicity through the area. Nur et al. (1993) speculated that the 1992 Landers earthquake sequence, and related earlier dextral events in the Mojave Desert, represented the latest evidence of an eastward shift in the plate boundary. The seismic activity in the Indian Wells Valley fits well with this model.

This paper presents many new data and interpretations for

the structure, stratigraphy, and tectonic setting for the Indian Wells Valley and surrounding areas throughout the Neogene. We first review the geologic and tectonic setting of the central Basin and Range, and then we present results of geophysical and geological work we have conducted over the past several years. We conclude with an integrated model of the evolution of the Indian Wells Valley from Miocene to the present and speculate on the future of the basin in the context of continued large-scale extension and transtension in the southwestern Basin and Range.

BACKGROUND

The southwestern part of the central Basin and Range is a triangle-shaped area bounded on the west by the Sierra Nevada batholith, on the south by the Garlock fault, and on the east by the Walker Lane belt (Fig. 2). Greensfelder et al. (1980) recognized the uniqueness of this area as shown in the obvious topographic features, which they attributed to a greater extensional strain rate than affected surrounding areas. They referred to it as the Owens Valley block although that is a misnomer because it covers a wider area than just the Owens Valley. In this paper we refer to it as the "Owens Valley–Death Valley extended terrane" because the term both encompasses the most widely recognized geographic landmarks found there and describes the most salient tectonic feature. It should be emphasized, however, that the area described includes the Indian Wells, Panamint, Owens, Saline, and Death Valleys and the intervening mountain ranges.

The Owens Valley–Death Valley extended terrane exhibits unique topographic features that set it apart from the rest of the Basin and Range. Figure 2 shows that topographic elements in this area are irregularly spaced, and there is a distinct north-northwest to northwest orientation to the ranges. Basins and ranges are wider by a factor of two than their counterparts to the east and north, and relief is much greater. Although the average elevation within the northern Basin and Range is higher, both the highest (4418 m) and the lowest (−70.7 m) points in the contiguous 48 states are found within the southwestern area. These two points are separated from one another by only 120 km, attesting to the dynamic nature of the forces currently acting on the area.

Regional structural and tectonic setting of the Owens Valley–Death Valley extended terrane

For the most part, present-day deformation within the Owens Valley–Death Valley extended terrane is dominated by right-lateral shearing. Extension began in Death Valley itself at ca. 16 Ma and continued until ca. 6 Ma. Much of the extension was accommodated by dextral strike-slip movement on the Death Valley fault zone (McKenna and Hodges, 1990) with total offset estimated at 120 km (Wernicke et al., 1982). Dextral displacement across the Walker Lane began at ca. 15 Ma (Hardyman and Oldow, 1991) and has accommodated a minimum of 48–60 km of right-lateral displacement. Strike-slip movement has been documented on faults bounding both the Panamint Valley and the Saline Valley (Fig. 3, Hodges et al., 1989), and dextral displacement along the Owens Valley fault zone was dramatically expressed in the 1872 earthquake when that single event resulted in more than 10 m of offset (Beanland and Clark, 1994).

One of the most significant strike-slip faults in the region is the Garlock fault (Davis and Burchfiel, 1973) that forms the southern boundary of the Owens Valley–Death Valley extended terrane. Movement on the Garlock fault began after 17.5 Ma (Monastero et al., 1997) and continues today (McGill and Sieh, 1993). More than 64 km of left-lateral movement has been accommodated along this 250-km-long structure.

Nitchman et al. (1990) recognized the significance of the

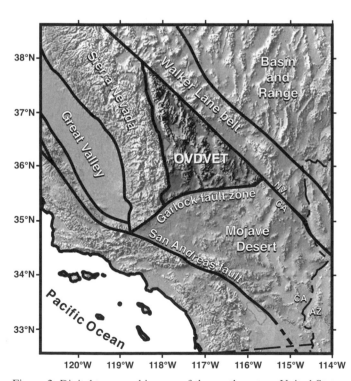

Figure 2. Digital topographic map of the southwestern United States. The Walker Lane belt separates the "traditional" Basin and Range from the Sierra Nevada, Mojave Desert region, and other features to the west approximately along the northwest-trending Nevada-California border. The Owens Valley–Death Valley extended terrane (OVDVET) is characterized by physiographic elements that are distinctly different from either the Basin and Range itself or any of the areas to the west.

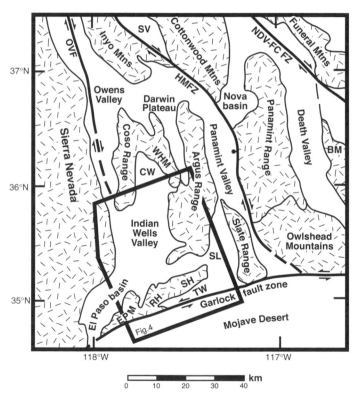

Figure 3. Map of the study area and the surrounding geographic features. BM—Black Mountains, CW—Coso Wash, EPM—El Paso Mountains, HMFZ—Hunter Mountain fault zone, NDV-FC FZ—Northern Death Valley–Furnace Creek fault zone, OVF—Owens Valley fault, RH—Rademacher Hills, SH—Spangler Hills, SV—Saline Valley, SL—Searles Lake, TW—Teagle Wash, WHM—Wild Horse Mesa. The area covered by Figure 4 is shown by the box.

Owens Valley–Death Valley extended terrane in the tectonic framework of the region by proposing that it was an accommodation zone that reconciled deformation in the Walker Lane belt with northwest-directed movement of the Sierra Nevada batholith. This concept of accommodation has been supported by the work of other investigators (e.g., Wernicke et al., 1982; Stewart, 1983; Hodges et al., 1989; McKenna and Hodges, 1990; and Walker and Glazner, 1999) and will be further tested in this paper.

Wernicke and Snow (1998) proposed that in middle Oligocene time, the Sierra Nevada lay ~320 km closer to the Colorado Plateau than at present. Snow and Wernicke (2000) presented a detailed kinematic model of intraplate deformation across the central Basin and Range showing that most of the Neogene deformation occurred in the Owens Valley–Death Valley extended terrane and the Lake Mead terrane to the east. This area of intraplate deformation has been called the eastern California shear zone by Dokka and Travis (1990), who proposed that between 10% and 15% of the total Pacific–North American plate-boundary deformation was accommodated by right-lateral shearing in a broad zone extending from the Mojave Desert eastward into Nevada. Although it is clear that this dextral shearing is distributed over the central and northeast Mojave Desert eastward to the Death Valley fault zone, it is not clear how it is accommodated at the Garlock fault nor how shear is transferred northward into the Owens Valley–Death Valley extended terrane.

Westward progression of extension in the Owens Valley–Death Valley extended terrane is also well documented (Wernicke, 1992) with onset occurring in Death Valley itself at ca. 16 Ma (Fitzgerald et al., 1991; Gans and Bohrson, 1998). By ca. 6-5 Ma, extension had begun to wane in southern Death Valley (Davis et al., 1993), and the locus had shifted westward to Panamint Valley and the northern Argus Range (Fig. 3, Hodges et al., 1989; Schweig, 1989; Bacon et al., 1982). Deformation in Panamint Valley was accommodated along a low-angle normal fault that makes up the western slope of the Panamint Range (Fig. 3, Conrad et al., 1994). Strata in the Nova basin, located at the north end of the Panamint Range, were deposited as a result of this extension. Schweig (1989) documented the onset of extension west of the Darwin Plateau at 6.0 Ma, and Bacon et al. (1982) proposed that extension was initiated in the Panamint and Owens Valleys by 6-4 Ma. By ca. 4 Ma, tectonism was focused in the Coso and Saline Ranges (Schweig, 1989). Transtension began in the Saline and Panamint Valleys after 3.7 Ma (Zhang et al., 1991; Conrad et al., 1994; Hodges et al., 1989) with onset of right-oblique displacement along the Hunter Mountain fault (Burchfiel et al., 1987) and vertical movement on the east face of the Inyo Mountains.

Farther west, Bachman (1978) suggested that the eastern Sierran escarpment began to form between 3.4 and 2.3 Ma on the basis of stratigraphic correlation of lacustrine sediments in the central Owens Valley. Step faulting of the Wild Horse Mesa area of the Coso Range, reflecting the onset of major extension

of Coso Wash, began between 3 and 2 Ma (Duffield and Bacon, 1980; Duffield et al., 1981; Whitmarsh et al., 1996). This extension coincided with a hiatus in volcanism that separates Pliocene calc-alkalic (mostly intermediate) volcanism from later bimodal volcanism that began at ca. 2.0 Ma (Duffield and Bacon, 1980). On the basis of the foregoing, the locus of extension was in the Indian Wells Valley and the Owens Valley during the late Pliocene and into the Holocene. Regional stresses during this time were accommodated by a series of faults reaching from the Garlock fault on the south to Bishop in the north and eastward to the Walker Lane belt. The pattern of distributed strain in this area is complex and is the subject of other, neotectonic studies (e.g., Reheis and Sawyer, 1997; Humphreys and Weldon, 1994).

The Indian Wells Valley

The focus of this paper is on the development of the Indian Wells Valley, which is situated at the southeastern terminus of the Sierra Nevada. It is located directly north of the Garlock fault at the extreme southwest corner of the Owens Valley–Death Valley extended terrane (see Fig. 3). The valley is nearly as wide (30 km) as it is long (35 km), making it anomalous for the central Basin and Range. Adjacent to the Indian Wells Valley and extending along the southern front of the Sierra Nevada is a small northeast-southwest-oriented valley, referred to locally as the El Paso basin.

The Indian Wells Valley is bounded by the Sierra Nevada on the west, the Argus Range on the east, the Coso Range on the north, and the relatively low-relief Spangler and Rademacher Hills on the south. For the most part, these higher-elevation areas are composed of Mesozoic plutonic basement rocks typical of the Sierra Nevada. The Coso Range has an areally restricted, but significant volcanic cover consisting of basaltic and rhyolitic flows and associated pyroclastic rocks. Basalt flows extend south from the Coso Range into the northwestern part of the valley.

Modern drainage from ranges surrounding the Indian Wells Valley is internal; there are no perennial streams feeding the valley. For the most part, the surface of the valley is covered with recent alluvium of either lacustrine (playa) or fluvial origin (Fig. 4) with minor eolian deposits. Sedimentation is dominated by alluvial fans emanating from canyons of the Sierra Nevada on the west and the Argus Range on the east. Two small playas occupy the southeast part of the valley, and there are small inliers of older alluvial material that protrude through the modern sedimentary cover on the northern, northwestern, and eastern sides of the valley.

Previous geologic studies of the valley have primarily focused on understanding the hydrologic conditions that control groundwater availability and recharge (e.g., Berenbrock and Martin, 1991; Berenbrock and Schroeder, 1994; Kunkel and Chase, 1969; Moyle, 1963). The only combined geological

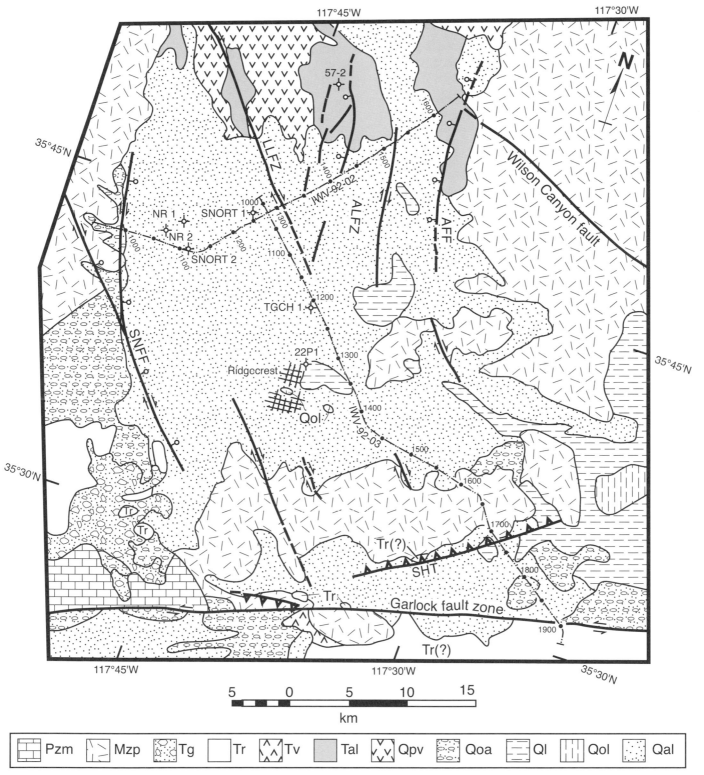

Figure 4. General geologic map of the Indian Wells Valley and surrounding areas. Heavier lines represent faults, dashed where approximate. Dash and double-dot lines are locations of seismic reflection lines discussed in the text and shown in Plates 2, 3, and 4; numbers represent every hundredth shot point. ALFZ—Airport Lake fault zone, AFF—Argus frontal fault, LLFZ—Little Lake fault zone, SHT—Spangler Hills thrust, SNFF—Sierra Nevada frontal fault. Geologic units (oldest to youngest; some are unpatterned on the map): Pzm—Paleozoic metamorphic rocks, Mzp—Mesozoic plutonic rocks (undifferentiated), Tg—Paleocene–lower Eocene Goler Formation, Tr—Ricardo Group consisting of lower Miocene Cudahy Camp Formation and middle to upper Miocene Dove Spring Formation, Tv—Miocene Lava Mountains volcanic rocks, Tal—Pliocene White Hills sequence, Qpv—Pliocene-Pleistocene volcanic rocks of the Coso Range, Qoa—older alluvium for which there are no conclusive data to permit assignment to a specific formation, Qol—older lacustrine rocks for which there are no conclusive data to permit assignment to a specific formation, Qal—Quaternary alluvium, Ql—Quaternary lacustrine deposits. Basic geology from Jenkins (1963) with some areas remapped by Monastero.

and geophysical study of the Indian Wells Valley was conducted by von Huene (1960), who examined the structural geology of the basin by using gravity data and a limited amount of refraction seismic data. Zbur (1963) acquired seismic refraction data over seven lines in the Indian Wells Valley that provided valuable constraints for the subsurface geology of the valley. However, these data have three limitations. First, the lines are not all interconnected; second, not all of the profiles were shot in both directions; and, finally, two of the profiles were quite short. Roquemore (1981) and Roquemore and Zellmer (1987) mapped surface features associated with neotectonic activity along two major fault zones in the Indian Wells Valley: the Little Lake and Airport Lake fault zones. Both have been active since 1980 and accounted for a significant percentage of the total seismicity recorded in California in 1995 and 1996.

Monastero and Katzenstein (1995), and Monastero et al. (1995) discussed geophysical, petrophysical, and geological data supporting the hypothesis that there has been substantial extension and crustal thinning in the Indian Wells Valley. The work presented in this paper expands on those previous efforts and provides a more definitive interpretation for timing of tectonic and sedimentary events related to the formation of the valley.

Local stratigraphy. The documented stratigraphy for the area in and around the Indian Wells Valley includes deposits ranging in age from Paleocene to Holocene (Fig. 5). The El Paso Mountains rise nearly 1600 m above the southwest corner of the valley floor and are the site of the most significant outcrops of Paleogene and Neogene rocks. The core of this range consists of Paleozoic metasedimentary and metaigneous rocks and Mesozoic plutonic rocks, which are overlain by Cenozoic sedimentary and volcanic rocks of the Goler Formation and the Ricardo Group. The total measured section for these rocks is ~4000 m (Loomis, 1984; Cox, 1982; Cox and Diggles, 1986).

The Goler Formation was first described in detail by Cox (1982) and ranges in age from Paleocene to early Eocene (Cox and Diggles, 1986). It rests disconformably on highly eroded, irregular, and weathered plutonic basement and, for the most part, consists of nonmarine conglomerate, sandstone, siltstone, and shale, with characteristic reddish-brown to dark brown color. Rocks were deposited in an east-west elongate basin whose axis was more or less coincident with the present location of the Garlock fault (Cox and Diggles, 1986). Coarser facies consist of alluvial-fan- and alluvial-plain-type deposits that formed on a southward-sloping piedmont adjacent to a mountainous area to the north (Cox and Diggles, 1986). The principal environment of deposition was an internally draining alluvial basin with marginal fans and broad outwash plains covered at times by meandering braided streams.

The Ricardo Group consists of two formations: the lower to middle Miocene Cudahy Camp Formation and the middle to upper Miocene Dove Spring Formation. These rocks were deposited in the El Paso basin (Loomis, 1984; Loomis and Burbank, 1988) and crop out today in the El Paso Mountains, al-

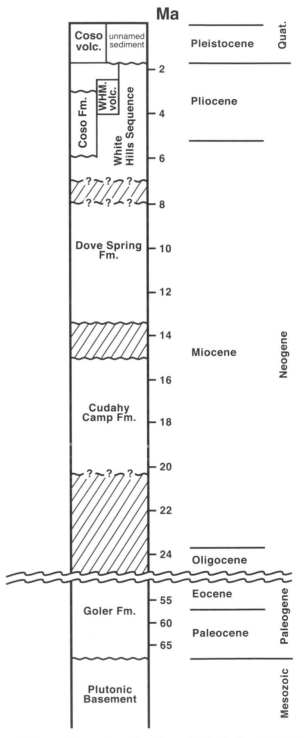

Figure 5. Composite stratigraphic column for the Indian Wells Valley area. WHM refers to the Wild Horse Mesa calc-alkalic volcanic suite. The Coso volcanic rocks are the bimodal suite that constitutes the youngest volcanic rocks in the Coso Range. Age ranges for the Goler Formation are from Cox (1982); for the Cudahy Camp and Dove Spring, they are from Loomis and Burbank (1988) and Whistler and Burbank (1992). Note the change in the time scale between the Eocene and Oligocene.

though remnants of the Cudahy Camp Formation are exposed in Teagle Wash south of the Indian Wells Valley (Figs. 3 and 4).

The Cudahy Camp Formation ranges in age from 20 to 15 Ma (Loomis and Burbank, 1988). It consists primarily of volcanic tuffs, lava flows, and epiclastic rocks that were deposited in an east-trending basin whose axis, like that of the Goler basin, approximated the present location of the Garlock fault. Monastero et al. (1997) showed that the source of these rocks was a volcanic field that was situated south of the El Paso basin in early Miocene time. These authors showed that the full 64 km of offset on the Garlock fault must be restored in order to properly juxtapose correlative rocks in the volcanic field with those of the Cudahy Camp Formation and that there was no evidence at 17 Ma of the existence of the Garlock fault.

In the middle Miocene (ca. 16 Ma) there was a major change in regional tectonics with the advent of significant northwest-directed crustal extension (Wernicke and Snow, 1998). If the Garlock fault is an intercontinental transform as suggested by Davis and Burchfiel (1973), then movement on the fault had to have commenced at that time. This movement may have been the cause of a hiatus in deposition from 15.1 to 13.6 Ma in the El Paso basin that is reflected in an angular unconformity between the Cudahy Camp Formation and the overlying Dove Spring Formation (Loomis, 1984). The Dove Spring Formation was deposited from early Miocene to Pliocene (?) (Loomis and Burbank, 1988; Whistler and Burbank, 1992) in a basin that first subsided, then was simultaneously rotated and translated, and finally was tilted and uplifted.

Deposition in the lower part of the Dove Spring section was dominated by alluvial-fan and alluvial-plain sediments that were derived from the south and southeast (Loomis and Burbank, 1988). Several tuffs and basalt flows that have been radiometrically dated by us as well as others (Cox and Diggles, 1986; Whistler and Burbank, 1992) occur in the section. The upper parts of member 4 and member 5 of the Dove Spring Formation reflect a shift of depositional style and provenance to fluvial-lacustrine with a source area to the north and possibly northeast (Loomis, 1984; Loomis and Burbank, 1988). Younger units of the Dove Spring Formation have a high proportion of angular and subangular alkali feldspar and quartz grains, indicating a nearby granitic source, probably a rejuvenated Sierra Nevada. Biostratigraphy and radiometric dating of tuffs by Whistler and Burbank (1992) established an age of ca. 7 Ma for the youngest Dove Spring Formation rocks (member 6). The top of the Dove Spring Formation is an angular unconformity; the Dove Spring is capped by a Holocene nonmarine sedimentary unit that has yielded mammal bones with radiocarbon ages between 19 000 and 16 000 yr (D. Whistler, 1999, personal commun.).

Pliocene rocks of the Indian Wells Valley are limited to the White Hills sequence. These rocks were described by Kunkel and Chase (1969), who did a detailed measured section through the upper part of the unit. They determined that the rocks were lacustrine in origin from the occurrence of freshwater diatoms,

very fine grained clastic sediments, and thin ostracod-bearing limestone beds. They observed that the White Hills sequence was older than the unnamed Pleistocene and Holocene volcanic rocks that flow south from the Coso Range to partially cover the outcrops in the northwest corner of the valley.

Kunkel and Chase (1969) also described outcrops in the northwest corner of the Indian Wells Valley that they referred to as Quaternary older alluvium (Tal; Fig. 4). These outcrops are undeformed to moderately deformed lenticular deposits of semi-indurated silt, sand, gravel, and boulders. They have an open framework structure, are poorly sorted, and are matrix supported with angular to subangular clasts derived from nearby plutonic and metamorphic sources (Fig. 6). There is no evidence of volcanic clasts in the outcrops. The total exposure is more than 240 m thick, but the maximum thickness is unknown. These deposits project eastward ~1 km to a position beneath the same basalt flows that cover the White Hills sequence. Outcrops beneath the basalt flows measure up to 50 m in thickness. Because of the stratigraphic position relative to the basalt flows, it is likely that these alluvial deposits are a facies of the White Hills sequence and are grouped as such.

GEOPHYSICAL AND GEOLOGICAL DATA

The rocks just described project into the subsurface of the Indian Wells Valley with a limited number of outcrops on the periphery of the valley. We have used a combination of geological and geophysical techniques to image these rocks and to relate those images to specific formations. Two principal types of data are presented in this study: reflection seismic data collected in 1992 and geophysical and lithologic logs from four deep exploration holes drilled on, or in close proximity to, the seismic lines. Other sources of data are regional gravity measurements augmented by finer-scale surveys to verify local features, surface geologic mapping, and seismicity data.

The reflection seismic data referenced in this study were acquired by using the parameters listed in Table 1. The survey design was based on the objective of imaging the Moho, so the far offsets were nearly 9200 m, and the sweep range was gauged for optimal penetration to the desired maximum record length of 8 s two-way traveltime (TWTT). The data are two-dimensional and are subject to all of the pitfalls associated with processing and interpreting such data, e.g., noise from out of the plane of the section, multiples, etc. They are, however, high-quality 180-fold data with a good signal-to-noise ratio.

Reflection seismic data were processed in two separate ways to achieve different objectives (Table 2). Initial processing focused on clearly imaging the basement contact, gross structural features, mid-crustal reflectors, and the top of the Moho, if possible. In the first round of processing, the final band pass was a 12–48 Hz time-invariant filter that was selected to preserve and enhance deep reflectors. By using this low-frequency band pass, we were able to more clearly image the basement contact, but sacrificed shallow detail in the predominantly sed-

Figure 6. Outcrop of the debris-flow facies (Tal) of the White Hills sequence in the northwest Indian Wells Valley along Highway 395. These rest nonconformably on Sierran basement and are representative of the very coarse clastic deposits found in the bottom of SNORT 2. Note the open framework, poor sorting, and matrix support of clasts. Hammer (center) is 28 cm long.

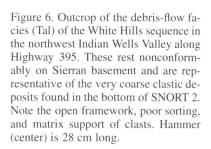

TABLE 1. FIELD DATA ACQUISITION PARAMETERS FOR INDIAN WELLS VALLEY REFLECTION SEISMIC DATA

Shot By	Halliburton Geophysical Services, Party 1776
Date Shot	October 1992
Recorder/Format	MDS-18/SEG-D
No. Channels	362
Field Filter	7.5/12–125/90 Hz
Geophone Array	24 phones/158 feet, in-line
Energy Source	Vibroseis
Source Array	4 Vibes, in-line, move-up over 161 feet
Sweep Freq/Type	12–72 Hertz, linear
No. Sweeps/Length	10 sweeps/10 seconds
Field Sample Rate	2 milliseconds
Data Length	8 seconds
Shot Point Interval	165 feet
Group Interval	165 feet
Spread Geometry	30,112.5–412.5–X–412.5–30,112.5

imentary section. The second round of processing was designed to better image shallow stratigraphic features. Long-offset data were muted to eliminate normal-moveout stretch effects, two rounds of residual statics analysis were performed, a shot-domain dip moveout was applied, and the final band-pass filter was time varying (see Table 2). These processing steps resulted in preservation of a significant amount of shallow stratigraphic detail that is the underpinning of our interpretation.

The basic gravity data set was assembled from government, university, state, and local sources. We acquired additional data by using a Scintrex model CG-3M gravimeter that provides repeatability to ± 1 µgal. These new data were especially helpful in addressing specific questions associated with interpretation of seismic line IWV-92-02.

Since 1993, four exploratory holes have been drilled in the Indian Wells Valley (see Fig. 4 for locations) by the Geothermal

Program Office (GPO) of the U.S. Navy for the purpose of gaining information about the subsurface geology of the valley and to test the potential for exploitable geothermal resources. The holes are designated SNORT (Supersonic Naval Ordnance Research Track) 1, which was drilled to 2437 m; SNORT 2, drilled to 3050 m; TGCH 1, drilled to 749 m; and White Hills 57-2, which reached 914 m. SNORT 1, SNORT 2, and TGCH 1 all penetrated plutonic basement rocks; White Hills 57-2 bottomed in older lacustrine sedimentary rocks.

Resistivity, self-potential, gamma, sonic, and Formation MicroScanner (FMS) geophysical logs were acquired for each hole. Continuous coring of the entire length of TGCH 1, and coring of selected intervals of the other three holes, provided valuable material for detailed stratigraphic and geochemical analysis and geochronology. Nearly 1200 m of FMS images from SNORT 2 were interpreted, resulting in identification of more than 2000 separate interfaces in the interval from 658 to 1865 m (Fig. 7). Approximately ninety percent (90%) of these were judged to be bedding features, and the rest were fractures or faults.

STRUCTURE AND STRATIGRAPHY OF THE INDIAN WELLS VALLEY BASIN

The Indian Wells Valley is filled with sedimentary rocks that are equivalent to all of the formations found in nearby surface outcrops. Seismic reflectors have great lateral continuity and relatively high amplitude, indicating relatively uniform depositional conditions over large areas (Plates 2, 3, and 4). The average depth to basement in the central Indian Wells Valley, as measured from the seismic data and the drill holes, is

TABLE 2. PROCESSING PARAMETERS FOR INDIAN WELLS VALLEY REFLECTION SEISMIC DATA

Low frequency processing

Zero-Phase Correlation
Minimum Phase Conversion
Data Initialization—Generation of Spatial Attributes
Mute
True Amplitude Recovery
Correction for Spherical Divergence and Inelastic Attenuation
Time Variant Deconvolution
Time Variant Equalization
Velocity Analysis
Surface Consistent Statics
Velocity Analysis
NMO Correction
Mute
CDP Stack
Wave Equation Migration
Time Invariant Filter (12–48 Hz)
Time Variant Trace Equalization

High frequency reprocessing

Geometry File Generation
Correction for Spherical Divergence and Inelastic Attenuation
Spectral Whitening
Source Record Predictive Deconvolution
Time Variant Equalization
Common Depth Point Gather
Velocity Analysis
Residual Statics Analysis
Velocity Analysis
Residual Statics Analysis
Application of Weathering Statics
Shot Domain Dip Moveout
Removal of NMO Correction
DMO Velocity Analysis
Application of Datum Statics
Space Variant First Arrival Mute
Common Depth Point Stack
Finite Difference Migration
Space and Time Variant Bandpass Filter (12–70 Hz/12–50 Hz)
Time Variant Equalization

2 km although it is likely as deep as 3 km or more in the northwest corner on the basis of gravity anomalies (Black et al., this volume). The sedimentary section thins to a depositional basin boundary toward the south, but is terminated on the northeast end of line IWV-92-02 by a fault on which there is at least 300 m of vertical offset (see Plate 2). Modern transtensional faulting, evident in flower structures seen in the seismic data, overprints the entire stratigraphic section.

Throughout this paper, reference will be made to four key horizons in the reflection seismic sections that have been used in interpretation of the data. From oldest to youngest, they are as follows: A—top of crystalline basement, B—top of older, more lithified rocks including the Goler Formation and the Ricardo Group, C—middle Pliocene basalt, and D—base of a clay layer in Pleistocene (?) sediments. Other local reflectors that highlight important features germane to the interpretation are shown on Plates 2 and 3, but do not have time-stratigraphic

significance, e.g., clinoform reflectors. In Figure 8, we use a sonic log from SNORT 1 to correlate time in the reflection sections with depth in the stratigraphic section.

IWV-92-02 (Fig. 4 and Plate 2) is the principal seismic line used for describing the structure and stratigraphy of the Indian Wells Valley. The section originates within the Sierra Nevada, extends eastward 7 km where it turns northeast, traversing the width of the valley, and terminates near the western front of the Argus Range. Total length of the line is ~35 km. We use the higher-resolution version of this line because it more clearly depicts key stratigraphic features. The lower-resolution version was used to verify basement picks and to crosscheck fault locations. Key horizons on IWV-92-02 have been tied to IWV-92-03 (Fig. 4 and Plate 3), which extends southward across the valley and provides information on the stratigraphy of the southern margin of the basin.

Gravity data and Indian Wells Valley basin structure

Gravity data indicate that there is a very large (15 mgal), slightly north-south–elongated Bouguer gravity low that occupies the west-central part of the Indian Wells Valley (Fig. 9). This low is bounded by steep (~3 mgal/km) gradients on three sides, and the reflection seismic data indicate that it correlates with a ~3-km-thick sedimentary section. On the south, it opens gradually at a rate of ~1.5 mgal/km into a broad north-north-east–trending trough that merges to the southwest with the El Paso basin. The presence of the Sierra Nevada frontal fault on the west of this low undoubtedly enhances that gradient on that side. The reasons for the steep gradients on the north and east margins are not as obvious but also appear to be fault controlled. The fault located at SP (shotpoint[s]) 1328–1350 on IWV-92-02 (Plate 2) and SP 1057–1086 on IWV-92-03 (Plate 3) has ~400–425 m of down-to-the-west normal offset and appears to contribute to the gravity gradient on the east side of this low.

We conducted a gravity survey directly over seismic line IWV-92-02 as a means of independently verifying the reflection seismic interpretation and to shed further light on the nature of the eastern boundary of the gravity low. These data were modeled to approximate the stratigraphy and structure of the basin (Fig. 10) as defined by the interpretation of the seismic section and the lithologic data from drill holes. Gravity station spacing was 161 m, resulting in 210 data points along the 33.8 km line. Sedimentary units were assigned average density values based on results from drill-hole data and assumptions about correlation with units exposed in surface outcrops. Depths to the tops of units are calculated from root-mean-squared stacking velocities and from formation velocities derived from borehole sonic logs. Locations of faults are taken from the interpreted reflection seismic line. The mafic basement rock shown in the gravity model is necessary to make the calculated gravity measurements best fit the observed data. On the basis of outcrops of

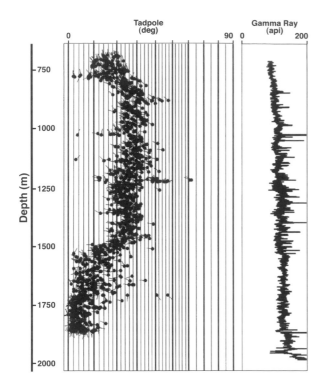

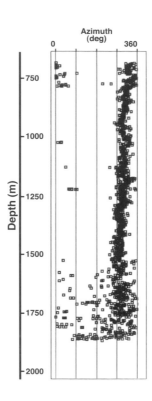

Figure 7. Results of interpretation of Formation MicroScanner images of the SNORT 2 hole. Images are based on electrical resistivity. The plots show the orientation of sedimentary bedding in the interval 683 m to 1856 m, which is the top of the plutonic basement. There are 1380 separate images that have been picked in this interval. The left-hand plot consists of bedding tadpoles with dip represented by the tail and strike by position on the horizontal axis. The curve in the center plot is the natural gamma-ray log. The right-hand plot shows bedding azimuth versus depth. Note the systematic rotation of bedding with depth. The lower part of the section has dips in the 0°–15°; range, and with decreasing depth, the dips increase to 20°–35° and then go back to the 10°–20° range. Azimuths are consistently in the 270°–290° range, but there is a distinctive rotation of dip azimuth to the north with decreasing depth. This type of feature is characteristic of bedding orientation in a growth-fault setting (Hatcher, 1990).

Mesozoic basement in the Sierra Nevada and the Argus Range that consist of plutonic rocks ranging in composition from leucogranite to gabbro, it is reasonable for a mafic rock body to exist in the subsurface of the valley. For instance, the basement core from SNORT 1 is an altered hornblende diorite. The collocation of a strong positive anomaly in our aeromagnetic data (AEROMAG on the CD-ROM accompanying this volume) also supports the assertion that there is a more mafic body buried there. For purposes of modeling, we have assigned a density of 2.9 g/cm^3 to this body, which is reasonable for a hornblende diorite. Gravity models are in excellent agreement with the observed gravity values (green circles in Fig. 10) along IWV-92-02, and the percentage error of calculated versus observed values is less than 1%. Despite the fact that gravity solutions are nonunique, we think that this modeling lends substantial strength to our interpretation of the structure and stratigraphy of the basin.

Sierran basement

Basement in the Indian Wells Valley consists of plutonic rocks of Cretaceous and Jurassic age. Basement was encountered in SNORT 1, SNORT 2, and TGCH 1 where propylitically

altered plutonic rocks were penetrated at depths of 2208, 1856, and 702 m, respectively (Fig. 11). An easily discernible 18–20 Hz doublet reflector characterizes the top of basement on the seismic sections, marking a velocity contrast between the overlying sedimentary rocks (3000–3700 m/s) and the underlying plutonic basement (~4900 m/s). The basement throughout the Indian Wells Valley has a highly irregular surface, as evidenced on the seismic sections, with a maximum of 1500 m relief.

Sierra Nevada frontal fault. Evidence of the Sierra Nevada frontal fault that resulted in the relief on the eastern Sierran escarpment is found on IWV-92-02 (Plate 2). East-dipping reflectors at SP 990 (300–400 ms) and SP 1054–1080 (1600–1800 ms) have been interpreted as splays of the frontal fault. These reflectors project to the surface at the eastern front of the Sierra Nevada and at a prominent northwest-trending lineament within the Sierra basement rocks (western end of IWV-92-02, Plate 2). The average dip of these features is 25° to the east, although they become more steeply dipping near the surface. Where the reflectors project to the surface within the Sierra Nevada, there is a lineament that separates competent, relatively unweathered granitic basement on the west from less competent, highly fractured basement on the east (Fig. 12). Kunkel and Chase (1969) and Jenkins (1963) mapped faults within the southern Sierra Nevada that are subparallel to the eastern front

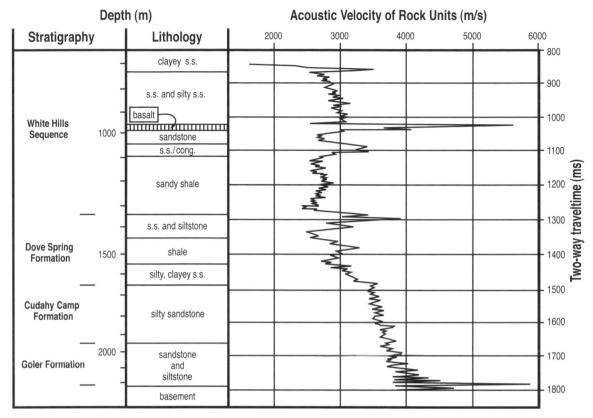

Figure 8. Acoustic velocity profile derived from sonic log of SNORT 1 showing correlation with stratigraphic intervals derived from lithologic log. The steady increase in velocity beginning at ~1550 m and continuing to ~1658 m marks the top of the Ricardo Group rocks. The relatively high velocities of the rocks from that point to the bottom of the log indicate a significant amount of lithification. Horizons A-D correspond to reflection seismic sections; s.s.—sandstone.

of the range coinciding with this lineament. Soil cover on the east side of this lineament makes it difficult to ascertain the precise geologic relationships at this location. However, to the north of IWV-92-02, we found that monolithic megabreccia blocks measuring tens to hundreds of meters on a side are exposed on the east side of the lineament. These blocks consist of locally derived Sierran basement and are interpreted as fault-proximal breccia blocks related to the Sierra Nevada frontal fault (see, for instance, Miller and John, 1999).

When traced along strike to the south, the lineament emerges from the Sierra Nevada and turns to the south-southeast where it joins with the Sierra Nevada frontal fault and continues beneath the sedimentary cover of the Indian Wells Valley (Fig. 4). The presence of the Sierra Nevada frontal fault buried in the southwestern part of the valley was first proposed by Zbur (1963) on the basis of his refraction survey. Later, Kunkel and Chase (1969) inferred a fault in the same location to explain a steep groundwater gradient in local wells. This latter assertion has been substantiated by recent measurements of the groundwater surface that show a >150 m difference over a distance of 8 km along the location of this buried fault (Indian Wells Valley Water District, 1996, personal commun.). This fault is also the northeast boundary for outcrops of older sedi-

mentary rocks of the Goler, Cudahy Camp, and Dove Spring Formations found in the El Paso Mountains.

Older rocks in the Indian Wells Valley

From the similarity of lithology, degree of induration, and acoustic velocity of rocks in SNORT 1 and the El Paso basin, we infer that horizon B marks the top of a section of sedimentary rocks equivalent to parts of the Goler, Cudahy Camp, and Dove Spring Formations. This horizon—interpreted to be time varying because of differences in depositional conditions and subsequent erosion of parts of the section—occurs over much of the Indian Wells Valley. The basis for selecting horizon B for interpretation was lateral continuity and evidence of an angular unconformity seen in pinching out of reflectors against the bottom of the horizon (e.g., SP 1240–1280, IWV-92-02). This horizon has a strong coefficient of reflectivity in conjunction with a 1400 m/s velocity increase (see Fig. 8), which usually is the result of an increase in lithification and/or change in rock type. To date, no outcrops of Miocene or older rocks have been identified in the Indian Wells Valley.

Goler formation. Evidence of the Goler Formation occurs in both SNORT 1 and TGCH 1, but not in SNORT 2 (Fig. 11).

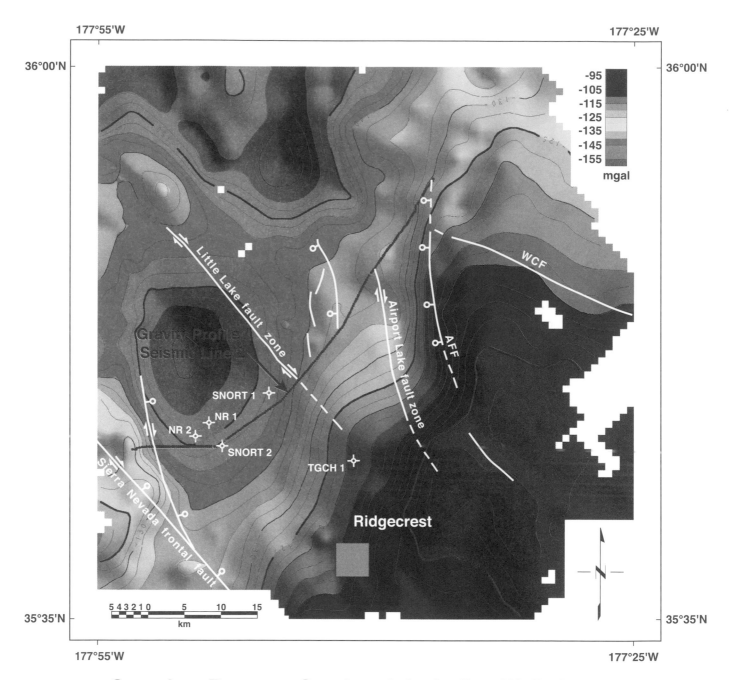

Complete Bouguer Gravity of the Indian Wells Valley

Countour Interval: 2.5 mgal
Reduction Density: 2.67 g/cm³

Figure 9. Gravity map compiled from more than 20 000 individual measurements made in and around the Indian Wells Valley. Location of the gravity profile for seismic line IWV-92-02 (see Fig. 15) is shown in red. The large gravity low in the northwest part of the Indian Wells Valley corresponds to the deepest part of the sedimentary basin.

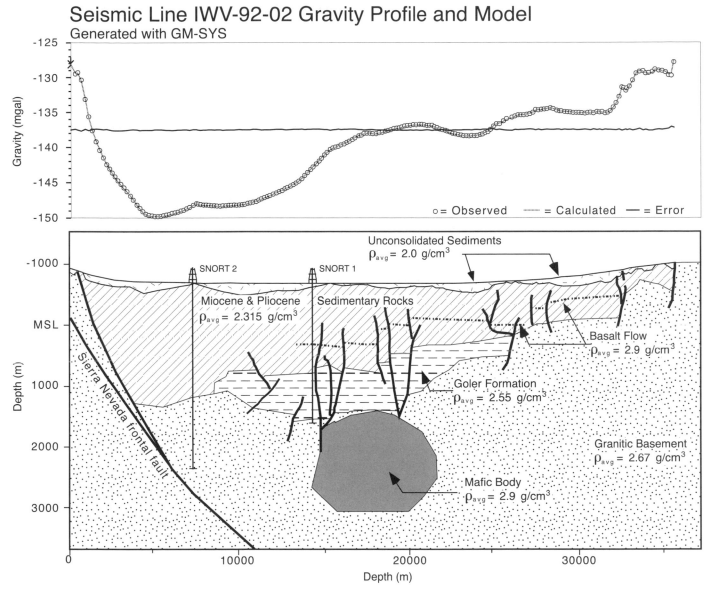

Seismic Line IWV-92-02 Gravity Profile and Model
Generated with GM-SYS

o = Observed   .... = Calculated   —— = Error

Figure 10. This gravity profile coincides with the location of seismic line IWV-92-02. Modeling was done with GM-SYS software. Densities were derived from samples taken in cores from TGCH 1, SNORT 1, and SNORT 2 and are, in some cases, average densities for thicker sequences. Locations of faults and approximate thickness of sedimentary sections were taken from the interpreted reflection seismic profile. Circles in the upper part of the figure represent actual gravity measurements; the solid line running through the circles is the resulting gravity profile derived from the model (bottom cross section).

On the basis of degree of induration and the fact that the rocks are almost exclusively red beds, the lower 227 m (1981–2208 m) of the sedimentary section in SNORT 1 is assigned to the Goler Formation. Most of the rocks in this interval are sandstone with small and varying amounts of admixed silt. They are red and reddish brown, and shape of the constituent grains is more angular to subangular than those in the units immediately above. Silica cement is prominent, and there are persistent trace occurrences of epidote, calcite, chlorite, pyrite, and plagioclase; black lithic fragments occur in the lower part of the section. There is a steady increase in acoustic velocity from 3350 m/s

at the top of the interval to 3810 m/s at the bottom. These types of acoustic velocities are characteristic of well-indurated sedimentary rocks, an observation that agrees with a reduced drilling rate of penetration in the interval. The stratigraphic section between basement and horizon B varies in thickness with distance northeastward along IWV-92-02 owing to basement relief, distance from source, erosion, and strike-slip displacement.

The lower 100 m of core from TGCH 1 consists of red to red-brown conglomerates with angular to subangular plutonic, metamorphic, and occasional volcanic clasts in a matrix of

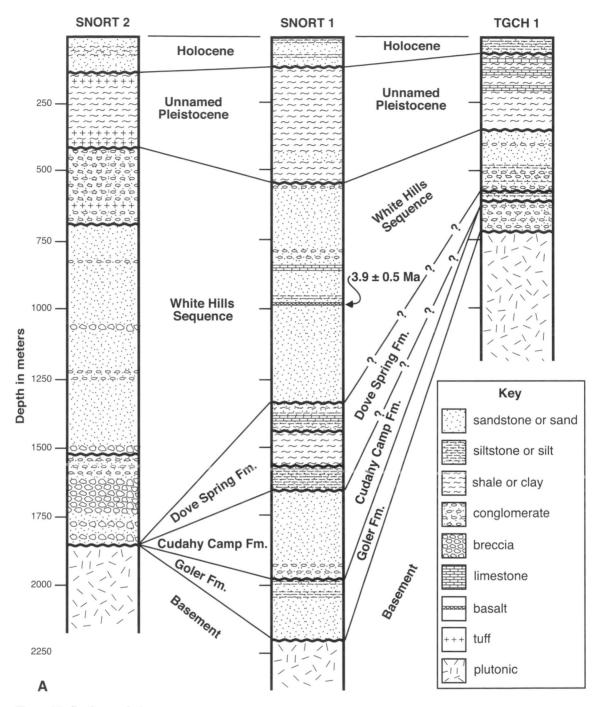

Figure 11. Caption on facing page.

A

sand- and silt-sized grains. These match outcrops of the Goler Formation in the El Paso Mountains (B. Cox, 1993, personal commun.). In his refraction study of the Indian Wells Valley, Zbur (1963) assigned the stratigraphic unit just above basement to the Ricardo Group because the average formation velocity was in the range of 2774 to 2938 m/s, which he thought was too slow for the better indurated Goler. Core samples from TGCH 1, which is coincident with one of Zbur's profiles, lead us to conclude that the unit just above plutonic basement is a facies of member 4 of the Goler Formation (Cox, 1982). Additional evidence of Goler rocks in the Indian Wells Valley was reported by Berenbrock and Martin (1991), who described 140 m of lithified continental deposits overlying plutonic basement in well 25/40-22P1 located 5 km south of TGCH 1 (Fig. 4). On

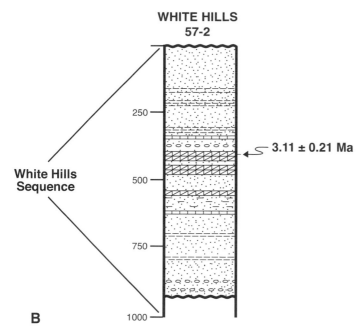

**WHITE HILLS
57-2**

White Hills
Sequence

3.11 ± 0.21 Ma

250

500

750

1000

B

Figure 11. (A) Stratigraphic columns for SNORT 1, SNORT 2, and TGCH 1. Symbols are for both unconsolidated sediments and consolidated sedimentary rocks, i.e., sandstone and sand. The unconsolidated sediments generally occur above the Dove Spring–White Hills contact. The basalt at 1000 m in SNORT 1 is the 3.9 ± 0.5 Ma flow that is horizon C on the seismic sections (Plates 2–4). (B) Stratigraphic column for White Hills 57-2. The hole was spudded in the White Hills sequence and was terminated at 914 m in the same unit. The 3.11 ± 0.21 Ma basalt is located at 418 m.

Figure 12. Photograph of southern Sierra Nevada ~2 km west of the end of seismic line IWV-92-02, showing relationship between exposed basement in the background and soil-covered megabreccia blocks in the foreground.

the basis of lithologic descriptions, and close proximity of these continental deposits to TGCH 1, we infer that they are probably correlative with Goler and/or Cudahy Camp Formation rocks.

It is noteworthy that in SNORT 2 there are no occurrences of red or reddish-brown rocks, nor any well-lithified rocks at all, that could be correlated with rocks of either the Goler or Cudahy Camp Formations. In fact, other than the basement itself and basement clasts in the breccia layers there was little competent rock encountered in the hole during drilling. This circumstance indicates that older rocks were either never deposited in this location or they were eroded subsequent to deposition.

Ricardo Group. Evidence of Ricardo Group rocks in the subsurface of the Indian Wells Valley is found in SNORT 1 and TGCH 1. These rocks appear to be distal facies of both the Cudahy Camp Formation and the Dove Spring Formation that crop out in the El Paso Mountains southwest of the valley.

Petrology, color, and texture of rocks in the interval 1341–1981 m in SNORT 1 likely make them distal facies of the Cudahy Camp and Dove Springs Formations although there is no datable material in this section to verify this interpretation. We place the boundary between the two formations at a depth of 1658 m where there is a break in acoustic formation velocity in SNORT 1 that correlates favorably with the greater degree of lithification seen in outcrops of the Cudahy Camp Formation (compared to the Dove Spring Formation) in the El Paso basin. From a lithologic point of view, the rocks are fine-grained sandstone, siltstone, and shale throughout most of the section with an abundance of lithic fragments and scattered volcanic detritus. There is no evidence of a granitic source that is common in latest Dove Spring rocks. The sedimentary section beneath horizon B thins in a southeastward direction along IWV-92-03 (Plate 3 and Fig. 4). Core from TGCH 1 (Fig. 11) shows that there is an absence of section between well-lithified red beds at the bottom of the hole, which we assign to the Goler Formation, and overlying poorly lithified rocks that appear to be Dove Spring. This stratigraphic feature leads us to the conclusion that thinning of the section between horizons A and B is due to the disappearance of the Cudahy Camp from the section.

Between 1658 and 1981 m in SNORT 1, most of the rocks are poorly to well-sorted, fine- to medium-grained sandstone, with subangular to round, often frosted, grains. The average formation velocity is ~3810 m/s. There is an increase in lithification and calcite cement in this interval as well as a pronounced increase in iron oxide stain, mica, pyrite, chlorite, and epidote when compared to the next higher interval. This mineral suite is representative of detritus from altered and unaltered plutonic rocks found in the nearby mountain ranges. From 1570 to 1658 m, sand proportion increases, but for the most part there is little change in either the mineral contents or the physical properties of the intervals. There is a uniform 575 m/s upward decrease in acoustic velocity in this interval, which probably reflects decreasing lithification. The interval 1448 m to 1570 m consists predominantly of shale and siltstone that are mostly green, gray, and less commonly, tan with varying amounts of silt, locally abundant calcite cement, and traces of pyrite and chlorite. From 1341 to 1448 m in SNORT 1, the section consists of a thick sandstone and silty sandstone sequence with local occurrences of limestone throughout (Fig. 11). Drill cuttings show that sand grains are subrounded to subangular quartz with trace amounts of biotite. Grains are typically well sorted and clear to frosted; they range in color from pink to tan to red and red-brown. These rocks compare favorably with units of the Cudahy Camp and Dove Spring Formations described by Loomis (1984).

East of SP 1340 on IWV-92-02, the stratigraphic section between horizons A and B thins, suggesting approach to the depositional margin of the basin. However, at SP 1485, the section abruptly terminates against a high-angle fault, thus preventing that determination. The fact that horizon B is relatively flat in this part of the seismic section indicates that there was no significant syntectonic basin growth on the northeast side of the Indian Wells Valley during this period. Furthermore, the well-developed internal reflectivity in this section suggests that the rocks are likely fluvial or lacustrine, as opposed to alluvial-fan- or delta-type deposits. The shallow depression centered on SP 1400 at 880 ms depth appears to be a broad fluvial channel. This feature, in combination with the absence of clinoform reflector sequences, supports the interpretation of an alluvial-plain depositional environment in the eastern Indian Wells Valley at this time.

Subsurface Miocene rocks in the Teagle Wash. Additional evidence for subsurface occurrence of rocks of the Cudahy Camp and Dove Spring Formations is found on the southeast end of seismic line IWV-92-03 (Fig. 4 and Plate 3). Coring in Searles Lake, 10 km to the northeast of this line, found 915 m of Pliocene and younger sedimentary rocks resting on quartz monzonite basement (Smith et al., 1983). There was no indication of Miocene rocks in that section. Data from the seismic line, however, show evidence of a sedimentary section that is more than 4000 m thick. There are at least two angular unconformities, at 550 ms and 700 ms depth (SP 1820), separating rocks with relatively high interval velocities (3300 to 3500 m/s) in the lower part of the seismic section (700 to 2000 ms) from those with lower interval velocities (1980 to 2440 m/s) in the 550–700 ms part of the section. Loomis (1984) described angular unconformities between the two formations and at the top of the Dove Spring Formation in the El Paso basin. These unconformities, in combination with outcrops of Cudahy Camp rocks a few kilometers southwest of the seismic line in the Teagle Wash, lead us to conclude that this previously unrecognized buried section is correlative to the Cudahy Camp and Dove Spring Formations. It is reasonable, therefore, to assign the lower unconformity (700 ms at SP 1820) to the top of the Goler and the upper one (550 ms at SP 1820) to the top of the Cudahy Camp Formation on the basis of the fact that interval velocities in the lower part of the section are consistent with well-indurated Goler rocks, whereas those in the upper interval are similar to Dove Spring Formation rocks found in SNORT 1.

White Hills sequence

The stratigraphic unit between horizons B and D is assigned to the White Hills sequence. The age of this sequence is established on the basis of a whole-rock $^{40}Ar/^{39}Ar$ date of 3.11 ± 0.21 Ma on a basalt encountered at 418 m in White Hills test hole 57-2 (Fig. 4; Figure DR1[1]). An attempt to date a deeper flow found at 469 m was unsuccessful. We also successfully recovered a 3.9 ± 0.5 Ma date on a basalt flow found at 1000 m in SNORT 1 (Fig. 11; Figure DR2 [see footnote 1]) that we have designated horizon C. Correlation of the SNORT 1 basalt flow sequence with the seismic section was accomplished by comparing the acoustic velocity profile (Fig. 8) developed from a sonic log with the lithology log and seismic line IWV-92-02. The depth of the basalt sequence in SNORT 1 corresponds to a large spike in the reflection coefficient and an increase in acoustic velocity of nearly 2500 m/s. By virtue of the similarity in ages of horizon C and the basalt flow within the White Hills section, we are able to correlate the stratigraphic section from horizon D to horizon B on seismic line IWV-92-02 with the rock outcrops in the White Hills anticline. This correlation is the foundation for the subsequent comprehensive discussion of the half-graben depositional setting in the Indian Wells Valley during the Pliocene.

Beneath the basalt flows in White Hills 57-2 there is a 445-m-thick section of sandstone with some limestone, siltstone, and claystone. For the most part, sand grains are rounded to subangular quartz with minor occurrences of feldspar and locally common fragments of basalt. They range in color from gray to yellow orange and are moderately well sorted. In all, the rocks appear to be have been deposited in a shallow-lake environment or on alluvial plains.

Western subsurface facies. Besides the lacustrine rocks described by Kunkel and Chase (1969), we define several other facies that are age equivalent to the White Hills sequence. The following discussion focuses on a combination of the nature of seismic reflectors and lithology from drill holes to describe five facies of the White Hills sequence found within the subsurface of the Indian Wells Valley: debris flow and avalanche, alluvial fan, fan delta, lacustrine, and alluvial plain or sheet flood. These facies are associated with the Sierra Nevada frontal fault, and their depositional characteristics appear to be tied to the structure.

Evidence of synsedimentary deposition associated with movement on the low-angle Sierra Nevada frontal fault is seen on the west end of IWV-92-02 between SP 1045 and 1120 (700 to 1400 ms) where reflectors at the bottom of the interval dip

---

[1]GSA Data Repository item 2002104, Figure DR1 and Figure DR2, is available on request from Documents Secretary, GSA, P.O. Box 9140, Boulder, CO 80301-9140, USA, editing@geosociety. org, or at www.geosociety.org/pubs/ft2002.htm.

to the west, and those at the top of the interval dip eastward. This type of dip reversal is characteristic of growth-fault-type deposition associated with low-angle normal faults (Christensen, 1983). Reflectors are absent or have limited lateral continuity in the seismic section immediately above horizon A (SP 990 to 1120, IWV-92-02). However, reflectors increase in both strength and continuity with distance from the Sierran front and at shallower depths. When this pattern is correlated with rock units found in SNORT 2, we find that reflectors correlate with crudely bedded, coarse breccia admixed with sand and pebbles (Fig. 13A), which dominates the stratigraphic section from horizon A to 1527 m depth (see Fig. 11). Breccias in the lower part of the section are more massive, have larger, angular clasts (i.e., up to 70 cm in diameter), are less well sorted, and are more common than they are in the upper part of the section. There are also numerous examples of scoured surfaces in the FMS images (Fig. 13C). Lithologically these correlate with older alluvium (Kunkel and Chase, 1969) that crops out in the northwest corner of the valley. Megabreccia deposits lie in fault contact with the Sierran basement on the west (Fig. 12), and they are separated from landslide deposits (Fig. 14) by down-to-the-east normal faults. Landslide deposits grade eastward into debris flows that are covered by the Quaternary basalt flows

mentioned earlier. Megabreccia blocks range up to 50–60 m in diameter and are completely engulfed by pulverized, poorly sorted debris and slump-type deposits.

The combination of seismic reflection characteristics, data from the drill hole, and outcrops leads us to conclude that the stratigraphic sequence in the western part of the Indian Wells Valley represents the landslide, slump, and debris-flow facies characteristic of syntectonic deposition proximal to a low-angle normal fault in a half-graben setting (Leeder and Gawthorpe, 1987; Crowell, 1982). The pattern of seismic reflectors on the west end of IWV-92-02 can be interpreted as follows. Slump blocks closest to the normal faults have few internal reflectors because they are the same lithology as the underlying bedrock and there is no internal structure that results in acoustic impedance contrast. Overlying the acoustically transparent slump blocks is a sequence of laterally limited reflectors that pinch out in an eastward direction (SP 1000 to SP 1045). On the basis of the length of the reflectors and their location relative to the sediment source to the west, they probably represent debris flows. These offlap the Sierran basement (see, e.g., 580 ms beneath SP 1017) and are truncated abruptly on their upper surfaces. Weak internal reflectivity is the result of stacking of debris flows and crude layering caused by hydrodynamic effects

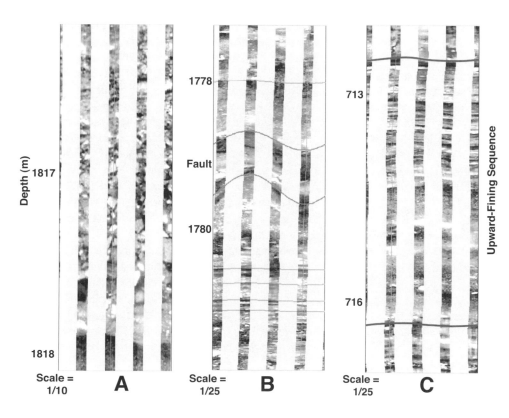

Figure 13. Formation MicroScanner (FMS) images from the SNORT 2 hole. Lighter tones indicate greater electrical resistivity of the material being imaged. Note that the scale of A is 1:10 whereas B and C are 1:25. (A) Breccia of the type shown here is common throughout the lower part of the SNORT 2 hole. Such breccia units become less commonplace with decreasing depth. These are interpreted as landslide-dominated alluvial fans related to early movement on the Sierra Nevada frontal fault. (B) High-angle fault surface located at a depth of 1779 to 1780 m. The fault appears as a high-amplitude sigmoidal curve because each of four sensor pads is 90° away from the one next to it and thus any dipping surface will appear as a sigmoid. This fault dips ~55°–60° to the west and correlates with one of the antithetic faults interpreted on the seismic section. (C) This upward-fining sequence from just below 716 m to just above 713 m is typical of what is seen throughout the upper part of SNORT 2. The sequences consist of laminated sandy, silty, and clayey material that exhibits cross-bedding and cut-and-fill structures. These are interpreted as facies (proximal, medial, and distal) of fan deltas and are related to the axial drainage system that fed into the Indian Wells Valley from the north. There are scoured surfaces at 712.8 and 714.3 m.

Figure 14. Large block of plutonic basement rock fully involved in the landslide debris. These types of clasts are common in the landslide deposits found in the northwest part of the Indian Wells Valley and are indicative of proximity to the Sierra Nevada frontal fault.

within the flows. The zone of poor reflectivity directly above the basement extends eastward to SP 1135 and correlates with massive debris-flow and avalanche-type deposits found in the lower part of SNORT 2. Reflectivity increases in the upper part of the section until there is a continuous sequence of reflective beds from the surface to basement east of SP 1135.

This lateral and vertical pattern of reflectivity is consistent with a progressive time shift in depositional style from a fault-proximal- to an alluvial-fan-type environment and is supported by data from SNORT 2. The stratigraphic interval 1524–686 m consists primarily of sand and gravel units with local, interspersed breccia (Fig. 11). This clast-supported material is composed of angular to subangular granitic detritus including feldspar, quartz, and biotite grains and lithic clasts of granite and metamorphic rocks in a very fine grained clay-rich and locally oxidized matrix. The poorly sorted, ungraded character is commonly observed throughout the sedimentary interval of SNORT 2 and is the product of alluvial-fan-dominated depositional processes with a local plutonic source. There is abundant evidence of cut-and-fill structures and cross-bedding in the FMS images from this interval, and there are upward-fining sequences (Fig. 13B) that range in thickness from a few meters to as much as 10 m. These sequences usually have scoured lower contacts that are immediately overlain by pebble conglomerate grading upward into finer-grained, typically cross-bedded, sandstone and siltstone. We interpret these features as progradational alluvial-fan-type deposits (Leeder and Gawthorpe, 1987; Kerr, 1984) whose source was in the Sierra Nevada.

In the stratigraphic interval 686-411 m, the rocks become much finer-grained with almost no evidence of breccia. There are local pebble conglomerates, cross-beds, and cut-and-fill structures, although they are much less abundant than in the interval below. We interpret these strata as the product of sed-

imentation in a lower-energy, fluvial-dominated alluvial-fan depositional environment. Because horizon C projects westward from SNORT 1 into the middle of this reflective sequence, we interpret these rocks to represent the fault-proximal basin-margin facies of the Pliocene White Hills sequence.

Central subsurface sequence. Reflectors associated with the White Hills sequence in the central part of the Indian Wells Valley are a mixture of strong, laterally continuous features interspersed with ones that are alternately strong and weak. This pattern is usually indicative of sand-shale sequences characteristic of fluvial or lacustrine depositional environments (Sangree and Widmier, 1977). The laterally continuous reflectors generally represent more-or-less synchronous events such as erosion surfaces or tuffs. The lithology in SNORT 1 (Fig. 11) shows that the lower part of the sequence (1341-1005 m) from bottom to top consists mostly of claystone, sandy claystone, and sandstone. The sand grains are poorly to well-sorted, subangular to subrounded, clear to frosted white quartz with varying amounts of hematite stain and scattered mica. The 3.9 Ma basalt flows that occur at 1005-975 m are overlain by a 416-m-thick section of claystone, silty sandstone, and sandstone with local, thin limestone beds. For the most part, the characteristics of the sand grains are little different from those in the lower sedimentary section. The top of the section is marked by horizon D.

These lithologies, grain features, and vertical variability are consistent with deposition in lacustrine and fluvial environments. The amount of rounding and frosting of sand grains combined with the nearly monomineralic character of the intervals indicates a substantial amount of fluvial and eolian transport. Varying amounts of clay and intermittent layers of limestone record lower-energy environmental conditions when there was little sediment flux into the basin.

The fact that the thickness of the White Hills sequence from the top of horizon C to horizon D does not vary more than a few milliseconds between SP 1330 and SP 1290 on IWV-92-02 indicates a relatively stable sedimentary basin during that time. The small variation is probably as much the result of resolution of the seismic record as it is a real phenomenon. Reflectors within that interval consistently dip to the northeast except in the immediate vicinity of SP 1330 where they are flexed downward toward the southwest. This flexure may be due to postdepositional compaction or possibly to fault drag. The fact that horizon C is offset vertically along that fault indicates that movement occurred after 3.9 Ma. Horizon D is only slightly warped, however, indicating that most of the movement on that fault must have occurred before the beginning of the Pleistocene (?) (see later discussion).

Eastern facies. A change in the depositional conditions associated with the White Hills sequence in the eastern Indian Wells Valley is manifested in the difference in reflection character above and below horizon C. Pre-3.9 Ma deposition appears to have been controlled by basin subsidence whereas post-3.9 Ma conditions were dominated by westward progradation of alluvial fans and/or fan deltas. The earlier phase of deposition resulted in a local wedge of sedimentary rocks that thins toward the basin. Reflectors at 800 ms appear to define an angular unconformity at SP 1480. A small basin beneath that horizon appears to have been dropped downward, resulting in an eastward dip of internal reflectors. Subsequent deposition resulted in overlapping of rocks to the west. This unit also was downdropped prior to emplacement of horizon C, followed by onset of the deposition of the alluvial fans and fan deltas.

Duffield et al. (1981) described alluvial fans cropping out on the western margin of the Argus Range, which they divided into younger (Qya) and older (Qoa) units primarily on the basis of their state of dissection. We found that there are also distinct clast differences in the two types of fans. The older fans have a predominance of rounded to subrounded volcanic clasts, and the younger fans have mostly plutonic and very few volcanic clasts. The presumed sources for the volcanic clasts are Pliocene basalt flows that occur in the Argus Range directly east of the older fans. We attribute this change in clast type to erosion of the flows and subsequent exposure of underlying plutonic rocks. The fans were later uplifted by post-Pliocene faulting of the Argus Range, and a younger set of alluvial fans developed on the top. The older fans are likely age equivalent to the White Hills sedimentary sequence seen on the eastern end of IWV-92-02.

Between SP 1370 and SP 1420 at 500–700 ms there are at least two stacked sets of distinctive westward-prograding, fluvial-dominated fans or fan deltas (Leeder and Gawthorpe, 1987; Ballance, 1984; and Kerr, 1984) in the White Hills depositional basin. These grade westward into the lacustrine and fluvial deposits of the central basin. East of SP 1420, reflectors in this stratigraphic interval are both laterally continuous and broken features consistent with an alluvial-plain depositional environment where braided streams dominated, but occasional

total submergence and/or sheet flooding was possible. Syntectonic sedimentation associated with faulting is suggested by the increase in thickness of the White Hills sequence evidenced by the sag in horizon D from SP 1314 to SP 1344. The short reflectors between 500 and 600 ms from SP 1325 to SP 1337 dip toward the sag and are possibly foreset beds associated with small-fan construction into the depositional basin adjacent to an active fault.

Southeastern extent. The White Hills sequence thins to the south along IWV-92-03 (Plate 3) until horizon D appears to pinch out at SP 1260. Analysis of microfossils from TGCH 1 indicates that the section from 377 to 567 m is a Pliocene lacustrine suite deposited in a highly alkaline lake environment (R. Forester, 1999, personal commun.). This interval is significantly thinner (~190 m) than in the northern part of the valley, but its stratigraphic position on the seismic section appears to make it correlative with the White Hills sequence. If it is assumed that this correlation is correct, the lacustrine depositional basin during the time of White Hills deposition extended at least 20 km in a north-south direction.

Evidence of a lacustrine sequence that is possibly age equivalent to the White Hills sequence is also found in well 22P1 (Fig. 4). According to Kunkel and Chase (1969), this well penetrated a thin veneer of fine sand, then went through a 151-m-thick section of lacustrine deposits primarily consisting of clay, calcareous clay, and fine silt with minor amounts of fine gravel, some sand, and scattered fossils. The next 123-m-thick section consisted of an alternating sequence of unindurated sand, silt, and clay with one gravel zone that Kunkel and Chase (1969) characterized as older alluvium. The lower interval best correlates with the White Hills sequence, whereas the upper interval correlates with the unnamed Pleistocene rocks discussed next.

There are several locations in the southern Indian Wells Valley where older lacustrine deposits (Kunkel and Chase, 1969) crop out (Tal, Fig. 4). These consist of poorly to well-indurated fine sands, silts, and clays with locally dense limestone layers. Small pebbles (<2 cm in diameter) of granite, vesicular basalt, and diorite are present in areally limited beds of conglomerate. Microfossils are scarce in surface outcrops, but where present, indicate the same type of depositional environment indicated by the White Hills rocks. Local occurrences of conglomerate are likely due to sheet-flood deposition from low-lying basement outcrops to the south. It is noteworthy that these lacustrine beds are exposed as broad, low-relief (<2 m high) warps on an otherwise flat valley floor and they occur only in the southern part of the valley.

Pleistocene–Holocene features of the Indian Wells Valley

During the Pleistocene and into the Holocene, the Indian Wells Valley appears to have been an intermontane basin. Besides clastic input, lava flowed southward from the Coso Range into the valley. It is during this period of time that there was a major transition in structural style from low-angle normal faulting along the Sierran front to throughgoing, north-northwest–oriented dextral faulting in the Indian Wells Valley itself.

Determination of the precise point in the sedimentary section that marks the transition from Pliocene to Pleistocene in the Indian Wells Valley is not possible on the basis of available data. However, we think that a reasonable estimate can be inferred from lithology and sedimentation-rate data from the drill holes in the valley. The thickness of the sedimentary section above horizon D, which we believe marks the Pliocene–Pleistocene boundary, on IWV-92-02 (Plate 2) reaches a maximum of ~600 m at SP 1320 and thins to a basin margin at the ends of both seismic lines. In SNORT 1, SNORT 2, NR 1, and NR 2 (see Fig. 4 for location) there is a clay layer that ranges in thickness from 450 m in the central part of the valley to ~100 m on the east side of the valley. In SNORT 2, the section from 411 m upward to ~135 m (i.e., 276 m thick) consists of a blue-green to dark gray clay that is also found in the nearby NR 1 (450 m thick) and NR 2 (311 m thick) wells. This same layer is ~450 m thick in SNORT 1 and thins to ~100 m in TGCH 1. The bottom of the interval is defined by a marked upward decrease in electrical resistivity coinciding with a change from sand below to clay above. This lithologic transition gives rise to the strong, laterally pervasive seismic reflector that we refer to as horizon D.

On the basis of work done in nearby basins, we infer that the base of this clay layer is very close to the Pliocene–Pleistocene boundary at 1.8 Ma. Thick clay layers in the subsurface of Owens Valley and Searles Lake (Fig. 3) have been attributed to large lakes (Smith et al., 1983, 1997) that formed during pluvial (interstadial) periods of the Pleistocene. Using radiocarbon-dating methods, Bischoff et al. (1997) determined an average sedimentation rate of 3×10^{-2} cm/yr for lacustrine clays and 80 cm/yr for coarser sediments in a 322-m-long Pleistocene–Holocene core from the Owens Valley. By using these average sediment-accumulation rates, we find that the 450-m-thick clay in SNORT 1 and NR 1 represents ~1.5 m.y. of deposition and the 125 m of sand and silty-sand overlying the clay in SNORT 1 represents an additional ~138 k.y. The combination of the two being 1.64 m.y. justifies a reasonable estimate for the base of the clay layer being very near the Pliocene–Pleistocene boundary.

Lithologic information from water wells drilled in the Indian Wells Valley reflects the fact that the valley was an internally draining basin throughout most of the Pleistocene and Holocene. Smith and Pratt (1957) analyzed core material from China Lake playa that consisted of fine sand, clay, and some freshwater limestone and evaporite. They correlated these deposits with similar material from Searles Lake (Fig. 3) and discussed the Indian Wells Valley in the context of an interconnected Pleistocene lake system that originated in ancient Lake Lahontan. We accept this interpretation, and we apply their chronology to the valley rocks.

Smith et al. (1983) dated old lake deposits from nearby Searles Lake (Fig. 1) by using paleomagnetic stratigraphy from

a 930 m core. They concluded that the core spanned the late Pliocene and the entire Pleistocene, forming an almost continuous depositional record of pluvial lake sedimentation. The following summary of depositional conditions is taken from Smith et al. (1983). Prior to 3.2 Ma, sedimentation in Searles Valley consisted of prograding alluvial fans from the ancient Argus Range on the west. At ca. 3.2 Ma there was a change in sedimentation pattern to a deep, freshwater lacustrine environment. This pattern lasted until near the beginning of the Pleistocene (2.0 Ma) when circulation in the lake became more restricted, and the lake environment became more saline. These conditions persisted throughout the Pleistocene except for a period of 250 k.y. beginning at 1.25 Ma when the lake reverted to a more freshwater condition. From ca. 1.0 Ma until 0.6 Ma, Searles Valley was the site of a moderately saline lake in which clays and saline layers were alternately deposited with interspersed air-fall tuffs. At 0.6 Ma there was yet another change in depositional environment resulting in Searles Lake becoming a dry salt flat for the next ~300 k.y. The final episode recorded in the Searles Lake core lasted from 0.3 Ma until ca. 0.13 Ma during which time there was deposition of large thicknesses of evaporites precipitated from a highly saline lake. This condition is consistent with a climate in which there was a lot of rainfall during certain times of the year and a significant amount of evaporation at other times. Fluvial and alluvial processes dominated the basin margins forming alluvial fans, fan deltas, and sheet-flood plains.

A resurgence of volcanism in the Pleistocene resulted in basaltic rocks being erupted in the Coso Range as part of a bimodal suite of flows and tuffs. Duffield and Bacon (1980) mapped four separate flows, ranging in age from 0.49 ± 0.11 Ma to 0.14 ± 0.09 Ma that originate in the southern Coso Range and extend into the northwest corner of the Indian Wells Valley. Prior to eruption of the Coso Pleistocene basalts, the Owens River flowed south into the valley (Duffield and Smith, 1978). On the basis of geophysical profiles, Duffield and Smith (1978) postulated that the flows changed the course of the ancient Owens River by forcing it westward into a narrow channel in the extreme northwest corner of the valley where it flowed until the mid-1900s.

Lithology of cores and drill cuttings from Indian Wells Valley holes records an environment that is consistent with the findings from Searles Lake (Smith et al., 1983). Sedimentation in the central part of the valley during this time was either in lakes or playas with some likely deltaic input from the ancient Owens River that emptied into the northwest part of the valley (Duffield and Smith, 1978). We presume there was a relatively consistent inflow to the valley, normal rates of evaporation, and a more or less continuous overflow from the lake in the Indian Wells Valley to Searles Lake because there is only limited evidence of evaporites in any of the Indian Wells Valley holes during this period. On the basis of the interpreted environment of deposition, the occurrence of air-fall tuffs, and the similarities in lithology, we correlate the clay-rich interval in the Indian

Wells Lake drill holes with the lake deposits from Searles Lake (Smith et al., 1983) that were emplaced throughout the Pleistocene.

Overlying the entire basin sequence is a relatively thin (0–30 m) layer of modern alluvial-fan, lacustrine, and playa deposits with scattered patches of eolian sand. At the present time, deposition in the Indian Wells Valley is limited to alluvial-fan progradation on the extreme western and eastern margins of the basin, and aerially limited sheet-flood deposition during heavy rainfall periods. There are several small playas in the modern valley, mainly in the eastern and southern parts.

Structural features. Right-lateral faults cut through the entire Indian Wells Valley stratigraphic section in three narrow north- to northwest-trending zones. From west to east, these are the Little Lake fault zone, the Airport Lake fault zone, and the Argus frontal fault zone (Fig. 4), all of which are currently active. In the seismic sections, they form typical flower structures with fault traces cutting through to the surface for the Little Lake (SP 1250–1295) and the Airport Lake (SP 1496) faults.

DISCUSSION

The Cenozoic history of the Indian Wells Valley is recorded stratigraphically only for the Paleocene–early Eocene and Miocene–Holocene intervals. The former interval is represented by the Goler Formation; the latter, by a sequence of rocks that includes the Ricardo Group (Cudahy Camp and Dove Spring Formations), the White Hills sequence, and unnamed Pleistocene–Holocene rocks. We briefly describe the Paleogene history of the valley, followed by a more comprehensive discussion of its Neogene history.

Paleogene history of the Indian Wells Valley

The earliest record of deposition in the Indian Wells Valley is contained in the Goler Formation. We have identified rocks that are equivalent in age to the Goler in the lower parts of TGCH 1 and SNORT 1 on the basis of clast composition, degree of lithification, and physical characteristics. These rocks are principally coarse-grained, reddish-brown to dark brown conglomerates with local red to reddish-brown sandstone layers. Locating the top of the Goler in the Indian Wells Valley seismic profiles is somewhat more problematic. We have chosen a significant increase in acoustic formation velocity coupled with lithologic characteristics as the most significant criteria in making that call. Cox (1982) found that the Goler–Cudahy Camp unconformity is as much as 35°, which should make it easily recognizable on the seismic sections; however, the interface between the Cudahy Camp and the Dove Spring Formations is also an angular unconformity so this criterion alone is insufficient.

Cox (1982) noted that the Goler Formation rests nonconformably on a highly irregular, eroded, and weathered basement, which appears to be the case in the Indian Wells Valley as seen in the seismic sections. The depositional edge of the Goler basin can be distinguished only on the southeast end of line IWV-92-03 (Plate 3) where it rises very near the surface; elsewhere, the margin is faulted. Given that there are only four points available to estimate the extent of the basin and owing to structural complications discussed in subsequent sections of this paper, it is difficult to make a definitive statement about the extent of the basin during Goler time. However, on the basis of data already reviewed, we conclude that the Goler basin existed during the Paleocene at the present location of the Indian Wells Valley, was more or less elongate in an east-west direction, and was the site of alluvial-fan and sheet-flood deposition.

During the remainder of the Paleogene, general uplift and erosion occurred in the Mojave Desert region and the southwestern part of the Basin and Range, as evidenced by the fact that there are no documented occurrences of rocks of middle Eocene–early Miocene age. The cause of this regional uplift has been attributed to a worldwide adjustment in plate motions and a change from convergence to divergence along the Farallon and North American plates. This change was accompanied by a buoyancy effect resulting from subduction of young, hot lithosphere beneath western North America (Ward, 1991; Crowell, 1982; Glazner and Loomis, 1984). Active marine and nearshore nonmarine deposition proceeded during this interval in the southern San Joaquin basin (Goodman and Malin, 1992), but there is no evidence of deposition in the area of the Indian Wells Valley.

Neogene record of the Indian Wells Valley

The Miocene saw renewed deposition in the Indian Wells Valley and the adjacent El Paso basin. Rocks of the Ricardo Group attest to the fact that the area was once again a negative topographic feature receiving sediments. Throughout the next 20 m.y., the valley was for the most part a depocenter that recorded passive-basin sedimentation during the early to middle Miocene, low-angle normal faulting and uplift of the Sierra Nevada in the latest Miocene and Pliocene, and transtensional faulting from the latest Pliocene to the present.

Miocene time. Throughout the Miocene, the Indian Wells Valley was a depositional basin for Cudahy Camp and Dove Spring Formation rocks. Rocks in the lower parts of SNORT 1 and TGCH 1 appear to be distal facies of units of both formations. It does not appear that there is a complete section of either formation buried in the Indian Wells Valley, which leads to one of two conclusions. Either the valley was at the most distal edge of the depositional basins during that time, or the rocks were deposited and subsequently eroded. In Teagle Wash, located 20 km south of the Indian Wells Valley (see Fig. 4), there are outcrops of a distinctive andesite breccia (Trab of Loomis, 1984), tuffs, and basalt flows that we have correlated with units of the Cudahy Camp Formation. Although these exposures are not areally extensive, they are clearly in place, attesting to the fact that the Cudahy Camp depositional basin extended at least that far. These outcrops and the ~3000-m-thick buried section seen on the south end of line IWV-92-03 (Plate 4), which we interpret to consist of rocks of the Goler, Cudahy Camp, and Dove Spring Formations, lead us to conclude that in Miocene time, the depositional basin extended 25 km east of present outcrops in the El Paso Mountains (Fig. 15A). However, because the Miocene section in the Teagle Wash (IWV-92-03) had a source in the Eagle Crags (Monastero et al., 1997), the Indian Wells Valley must have been located northeast of the volcanic edifice. This position suggests that the valley was at the margin of the basin and the thickness of the rocks was never very great. The absence of members of the Cudahy Camp and Dove Spring Formations in the drill holes and seismic sections could then be explained simply on the basis of variation of the northern margin of the depositional basin.

During the middle to late Miocene, the Indian Wells Valley was also the locus of sedimentation at the distal margin of the Dove Spring Formation basin (Fig. 15B). The setting was predominantly lacustrine with occasional fan deltas and marginal flood-plain and sheet-flood environments. Again, because the basin was distal to the source, which was primarily the ancient Lava Mountains, the stratigraphic record for this interval is discontinuous in the Indian Wells Valley.

Abrupt termination of more than 3000 m of Goler, Cudahy Camp, and Dove Spring Formation rocks at the northeast end of the El Paso Mountains must be reconciled. It seems unlikely that the basins for all three of these formations simply stopped receiving deposits without any evidence of basin-margin features in the outcrops. It is much more likely that the section is terminated by faulting, resulting in the older rocks being dropped down and subsequently buried by younger sediments. We infer that this faulting occurred in the latest Miocene or early Pliocene in conjunction with low-angle faulting along the Sierra Nevada frontal fault (as discussed in the next section).

Latest Miocene–Pliocene low-angle faulting. At the end of the Miocene and throughout the Pliocene Epoch, the Indian Wells Valley was the locus of faulting along the Sierra Nevada frontal fault with related clastic deposition in a half graben. Coarse debris was shed into the basin along the rugged western margin, alluvial fans prograded westward from the Argus Range, and lacustrine, outwash plain, and fluvio-deltaic sedimentation dominated deposition in the central part of the valley (Fig. 15C). Volcanic rocks periodically extended into the basin from the north and northeast and are preserved in subsurface basalt flows as far south as SNORT 1.

Onset of faulting on the Sierra Nevada frontal fault is estimated to be post-7 Ma on the basis of the Dove Spring Formation stratigraphy. The top of that formation is an unconformity that is both erosional and angular. By using fossil faunas and radiometric dating of tuffs, Whistler and Burbank (1992) determined that the youngest unit in the Dove Spring Formation was deposited at 7 Ma. Therefore, it must be assumed that the

Figure 15. Schematic reconstructions of the paleogeography of the Indian Wells Valley (IWV) and the surrounding areas. For the most part, the position of the Indian Wells Valley basin relative to the El Paso basin (EPB) north of the Garlock fault and the position of the Lava Mountains (LM) relative to Eagle Crags volcanic field (ECVF) south of the Garlock fault remain the same in all reconstructions. However, relative positions of features north and south of the Garlock fault change with time owing to sinistral translation that commenced in the 16–15 Ma time frame. The relative positions of Indian Wells Valley basin and the El Paso basin separate in an east-west direction during the latest Miocene and Pliocene because of extension on the low-angle Sierra Nevada frontal fault (SNFF). Sources of information for the Cudahy Camp and Dove Spring rocks in the El Paso basin come from Loomis and Burbank (1988). (A) During the early Miocene, the Garlock fault did not exist, and the source of detritus for the Indian Wells Valley basin and El Paso basin was the Eagle Crags volcanic field. (B) In the middle to late Miocene there had been ~30–35 km of sinistral movement on the Garlock fault (Smith et al., this volume), and the Indian Wells Valley basin and El Paso basin were receiving lower Dove Spring Formation sediments and tuffs from the ancestral Lava Mountains. (C) By latest Miocene and throughout the Pliocene, the Sierra Nevada batholith (SNB) was uplifted and oblique-normal slip occurred along the Sierra Nevada frontal fault. The source of detritus for the western Indian Wells Valley basin was the newly elevated Sierra Nevada batholith. The El Paso basin was receiving detritus from the waning Lava Mountains, and alluvial fans were prograding basinward along the southern margin of the Sierra Nevada batholith and the western margin of the Argus Range. For a block diagram along the A-B line of section, see Figure 17. (D) Throughout Pleistocene and Holocene time, uplift of the Sierra had ceased, and although there was continued progradation of alluvial fans from the Sierra Nevada, the main source of sediment for the Indian Wells Valley basin was sheet-flood runoff from the south and a fluvial system from the north. Uplift along reverse faults in the southern part of the basin was due to local compression arising from restraint of the dextrally faulted blocks in the Indian Wells Valley (see text for further discussion). AFF—Argus frontal fault, ALF—Airport Lake fault zone, AR—Argus Range, CR—Coso Range, Little Lake fault—LLF.

Dove Spring Formation was uplifted and tilted sometime thereafter.

Loomis and Burbank (1988) found that between 8 and 7 Ma, the source area for the Dove Spring Formation shifted to the north from the south and southeast, and detritus from Sierra Nevada plutonic rocks began to dominate the section. It appears then, that the Sierra Nevada was already being uplifted in the latest Miocene. On the basis of stream-gradient changes on the west side of the Sierra Nevada, Unruh (1991) suggested that at ca. 5 Ma, the range was uplifted and tilted westward. Lueddecke et al. (1998) determined that westward tilting of the Sierra Nevada and simultaneous opening of the Owens Valley occurred between 6 and 3 Ma. This coincides with deposition of the fluviolacustrine Coso Formation that filled a narrow, internally draining basin between the Coso Range and the Sierra Nevada (Kamola and Walker, 1999). Additional evidence of a sweeping tectonic change at this time is provided by Schweig (1989) and Bacon et al. (1982), who documented the onset of extension in

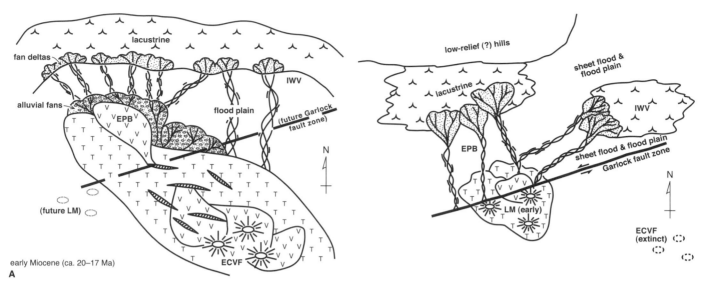

lacustrine

fan deltas

alluvial fans

EPB

flood plain

IWV

(future Garlock fault zone)

N

(future LM)

ECVF

early Miocene (ca. 20–17 Ma)

A

low-relief (?) hills

lacustrine

sheet flood & flood plain

IWV

EPB

sheet flood & flood plain

Garlock fault zone

LM (early)

N

ECVF (extinct)

middle to late Miocene (ca. 15–7 Ma)

B

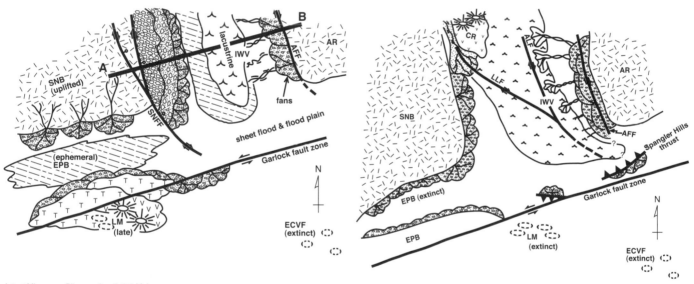

B

SNB (uplifted)

lacustrine

IWV

AFF

AR

A

SNFF

fans

(ephemeral) EPB

sheet flood & flood plain

Garlock fault zone

LM (late)

N

ECVF (extinct)

latest Miocene – Pliocene (ca. 7–3.5 Ma)

C

CR

SNB

LLF

IWV

AR

AFF

Spangler Hills thrust

EPB (extinct)

Garlock fault zone

EPB

LM (extinct)

N

ECVF (extinct)

Pleistocene – Holocene (ca. 2–0.02 Ma)

D

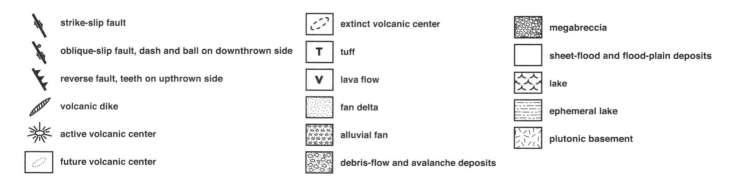

strike-slip fault	extinct volcanic center	megabreccia
oblique-slip fault, dash and ball on downthrown side	**T** tuff	sheet-flood and flood-plain deposits
reverse fault, teeth on upthrown side	**V** lava flow	lake
volcanic dike	fan delta	ephemeral lake
active volcanic center	alluvial fan	plutonic basement
future volcanic center	debris-flow and avalanche deposits	

this area between 6 and 4 Ma. The coincidence of these events leads us to conclude that uplift of the Sierra Nevada began in the latest Miocene or earliest Pliocene, between 7 and 5 Ma, and was accommodated by normal faulting along the eastern front of the Sierra Nevada.

Why the Sierra Nevada was uplifted during latest Miocene–early Pliocene time is uncertain. However, on the basis of analysis of mafic and ultramafic xenoliths, Ducea and Saleeby (1998) proposed that somewhere between 8 and 4 Ma there was delamination of an eclogitic keel from the southeastern Sierra Nevada. This process could have resulted in uplift of the range because of either isostatic rebound from loss of the dense keel or thermal forces resulting from addition of lighter, hotter asthenospheric mantle on the underside. Kay and Kay (1993) showed that such delamination is usually accompanied by rapid uplift, stress change, and changes in magmatism—conditions that were prominent in the southern Sierra Nevada–Indian Wells Valley region in the late Miocene–early Pliocene. The proposed timing of delamination under the southern Sierra Nevada by Ducea and Saleeby (1998) is permissive as a driving mechanism for movement on the Sierra Nevada frontal fault. Calc-alkalic volcanism that began at ca. 5 Ma in the Wild Horse Mesa area and was essentially over by 3.5 Ma may be related to a second period of delamination (Manley et al., 2000) or may be part of the same event.

Although normal displacement on the Sierra Nevada frontal fault is easily demonstrated in the relief of the Sierra Nevada, a component of lateral movement may also be present. Analysis of FMS logs from SNORT 2 shows a counterclockwise rotation of bedding azimuths with increasing depth (Fig. 7) that can be achieved if there is simultaneous down-to-the-east, right-oblique normal movement and east-west extension on the Sierra Nevada frontal fault. Note that in this case, rotation of the bedding planes is related to local fault drag and does not imply rotation of the entire Indian Wells Valley. East-west extension can be achieved if the axis of maximum tension is oriented as shown in Figure 16. On the basis of a geologic reconstruction, Wernicke and Snow (1998) found that the direction of extension in the southwestern Basin and Range changed from east-west to northwest-southeast between 10 and 8 Ma. This is older than our estimate of earliest onset of extension at 7.5 Ma, but is permissive, given the uncertainties in the two methods.

Over the next 3.5–4 m.y., movement on the Sierra Nevada frontal fault resulted in a classic half-graben depositional setting (see Fig. 17) as described by Leeder and Gawthorpe (1987). Rocks that are proximal to the Sierra Nevada frontal fault consist of megabreccia and coarse, poorly sorted avalanche and debris-flow deposits, all of which are represented in outcrop in the northwestern Indian Wells Valley as well as being found in the subsurface in SNORT 2. Syntectonic sedimentation along the Sierra Nevada frontal fault resulted in a thick wedge of eastward-prograding coarse clastic units that give way to sheet-flood deposits, alluvial fans, and ultimately to fluvial, deltaic, and lacustrine deposits in the central part of the valley. At the

same time, alluvial fans and fluvial-deltaic deposits were prograding westward into the valley from the Argus Range, resulting in formation of fan and fan-delta complexes (Fig. 15C). The whole of these deposits constitutes facies of the Pliocene White Hills sequence.

We have estimated the amount of extension in the Indian Wells Valley during this half-graben phase on the basis of where horizon B terminates against the basement on IWV-92-02 (Plate 2). First, we assume that the basin edge, represented by the pinch-out of horizon B against a basement high at SP 1157, was at or near the eroded surface of the Sierra Nevada in the past. The southern Sierra Nevada has a plateau at an altitude of ~2300 m. We presume that this plateau is an eroded surface that was either a low, positive feature or a slightly negative feature throughout the Miocene. When the subsurface contact between the basement and the low-angle fault is restored updip to the west such that it is at the 2300 m altitude, the amount of horizontal extension that is accommodated by the low-angle fault is on the order of 10 km. This amount represents ~40% of the total width of the modern Indian Wells Valley.

Although there is some uncertainty regarding when movement on the Sierra Nevada frontal fault ceased, we will argue subsequently that it was at ca. 3.5 Ma, which means that the duration of low-angle normal displacement was a maximum of 3.5 m.y. If correct, then the rate of extension during the early and middle Pliocene was 3.1 mm/yr. Smith et al. (this volume) have shown that since 10 Ma there has been ~30 km of sinistral displacement on the Garlock fault, a rate of 3 mm/yr. Assuming that all of this displacement is parallel to the trace of the Garlock fault, the predicted amount of east-west extension along the Sierra Nevada frontal fault would be 3.1 mm/yr with a north-northwest component of displacement of ~0.8 mm/yr (see Fig. 18). The total amount of extension accommodated by the Sierra Nevada frontal fault during this period would then be ~11 km, and the amount of north-northwestward translation would be ~2.8 km. Given the uncertainties in these rate calculations, the westward component agrees remarkably well with our calculated offset on the Sierra Nevada frontal fault. The dextral offset on the frontal fault that we have documented may represent accommodation of the north-northwest–directed translation, although we cannot document that with our data.

Pleistocene–Holocene dextral faulting

The final stage in the Neogene evolution of the Indian Wells Valley is dominated by dextral shearing evidenced by right-lateral offset in surface features (Roquemore, 1981; Roquemore and Zellmer, 1987), the large number of modern seismic events, and development of flower structures in the Little Lake, Airport Lake, and Argus Frontal fault zones. The throughgoing shear zone is oriented in a north-northwest direction consistent with modern geodetic measurements of relative crustal velocity in the area (e.g., Bennett et al., 1997).

Indian Wells Valley

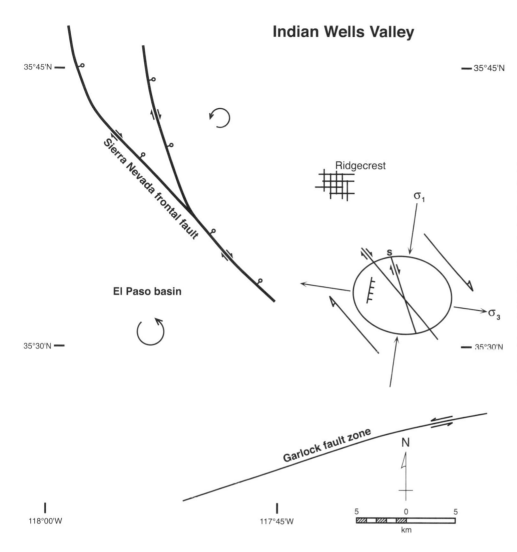

Figure 16. Simple kinematic model to explain the tectonic regime of the Indian Wells Valley during the latest Miocene–early Pliocene interval (ca. 7–3.5 Ma). All of the structures can be explained by a single stress field in which σ_1 is oriented northeast-southwest and σ_3 is oriented northwest-southeast. Simultaneous rotation of the El Paso basin block and east-dipping low-angle normal faulting can be achieved if the western component of extension is greater than the northern one. Fault symbols as in Figure 15. S—synthetic strike-slip fault orientation. Hachured lines inside strain ellipse denote idcal preferred orientation of normal faults.

During the past 2 m.y., the Indian Wells Valley has been the site of a sedimentary basin in which lacustrine deposition dominated (Fig. 15D). Alluvial fans built out from the eastern and western margins, and at varying times, depending on whether it was a glacial or an interglacial period, a delta developed where the ancient Owens River debouched into the northwest part of the valley (Duffield and Smith, 1978).

It is unclear when the transition to north-northwest–directed dextral faulting took place, but we conclude that it likely occurred after 3.5 Ma and before 2 Ma. Whitmarsh et al. (1996) have reported the occurrence of a faulted 3.5 Ma basalt at the southwest side of Coso Wash (Fig. 3) that matches in age with basalts from the east side of the wash (Tbp of Duffield and Bacon, 1980). At least one strand of the modern right-lateral fault passes through the Coso Wash. So, when drilling that we conducted between the two outcrops revealed no basalt of that same age, we assumed that the Coso Wash opened sometime after 3.5 Ma. This interpretation coincides with the findings of Zhang et al. (1991), Conrad et al. (1994), and Hodges et al.

(1989), who determined that right-oblique transtensional deformation in the Saline and Panamint Valleys began after 3.7 Ma. On the basis of the fact that there is ~1000 m of section in the half graben above the 3.9 Ma basalt (horizon C) in SNORT 1, we think that the transition was substantially later than that time. At ca. 2 Ma, step faulting was initiated on the Wild Horse Mesa (Duffield and Bacon, 1980), perhaps indicating the onset of transtension. From 2.5 Ma until 1.0 Ma there was little volcanism in the Indian Wells Valley area. Two lava flows and associated pyroclastic rocks were extruded between 2.0 and 1.75 Ma (Duffield and Bacon, 1980), but these were extremely small in volume and separated areally by more than 20 km. At 1 Ma there was an outbreak of bimodal volcanism in the Coso Range; since then, basalt flows and pyroclastic rocks were emplaced in the northern Indian Wells Valley, and rhyolite domes began forming in the Coso Range itself.

There is no report in the literature of a region-wide tectonic event that took place at this time that would explain the coincidence of these events. In reconstructing the Neogene exten-

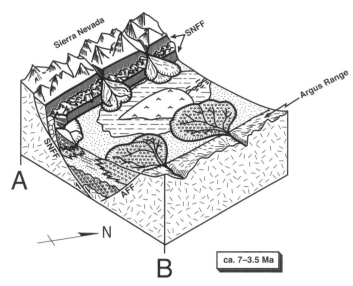

Figure 17. Block diagram of the paleogeography of the Indian Wells Valley during the latest Miocene and Pliocene; patterns as in Figure 15, and location shown in Figure 15C. Uplift has commenced on the Sierra Nevada frontal fault (SNFF), resulting in the formation of megabreccia blocks, avalanche deposits, and coarse-debris flows. Alluvial fans originate from the Argus Range along the antithetic Argus frontal fault (AFF). The axis of the basin is dominated by sheet flooding from the south, fluvial deposition from the northwest, and lacustrine sedimentation.

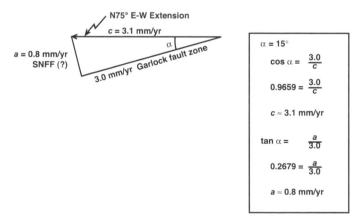

Figure 18. An average of 3.0 mm/yr of westward-directed left-lateral displacement on the Garlock fault produces 3.1 mm/yr of movement along a west-striking vector and a 0.8 mm/yr northward component. If such movement on the Sierra Nevada frontal fault for a period of 3.5 m.y. is assumed, 11 km of west-northwest–directed extension and 2.8 km of north-northwest–directed displacement would be produced. The 11 km value is in good agreement with our calculated displacement on the Sierra Nevada frontal fault (SNFF). The 2.8 km of north-northwest–directed displacement may have been accommodated by dextral movement on that fault as well although we cannot substantiate this possibility with our data.

sion direction in the Owens Valley–Death Valley extended terrane from geologic data, Wernicke and Snow (1998) showed a clockwise shift in the extension vector in the Owens Valley at ca. 2 Ma, although there is no discussion of the probable cause of that change.

Horizon D on IWV-92-02 (Plate 3) appears to represent a stratigraphic break that is manifested by progradation of reflectors over this horizon from the west and northeast where the younger unit forms a cap on the fan-delta reflectors. The section above horizon D is thicker in the middle of the valley, which may be related to downwarping and syntectonic sedimentation associated with the strike-slip faulting. We interpret the fact that this horizon represents the base of a clay layer in SNORT 2, SNORT 1, and nearby wells as evidence of a tectonic event that influenced the entire basin. As already noted, the relatively thick (300–450 m) and areally extensive clay layer indicates deposition in a deep, quiescent lake environment. This setting could be the result of a broad downwarping of the valley, analogous to that proposed by Smith et al. (1983) for Searles Lake, or could simply represent a major pluvial or interstadial period.

A consequence of dextral shearing through the Indian Wells Valley is localized compression in the southern end of the basin. Figure 19 shows the orientation of the major modern right-lateral faults that traverse the valley as well as associated structures to the south. The strain ellipse shows that orientation of the dextral faults is consistent with an extension direction of approximately N60°W, but orientations of folds and reverse faults in the southern part of the valley do not fit this stress field. This mismatch can be explained if the Garlock fault represents a significant structural barrier whose present orientation is not favorably aligned with the modern regional stress field. Therefore, dextral translation along the north-northwest–trending faults results in strain accumulation at the southern end of the valley. Several noteworthy examples of north-south shortening are found in the southern valley that cannot be related to sinistral strike-slip on the Garlock fault. In Teagle Wash there are anomalous northeast-trending folds that straddle the Garlock fault and are being actively folded (Smith, 1991). Smith (1991) recognized that the orientation of these folds was kinematically inconsistent with fault-induced folding resulting from sinistral movement on the Garlock fault, but was consistent with north-northwest–directed compression. Seismic reflectors on the southeast end of IWV-92-03 (SP 1810; Plate 4) show evidence of a reverse fault with ~800 m of throw. The absence of any remnants of the Goler, Cudahy Camp, or Dove Spring Formations in the Rademacher and Spangler Hills south of the Indian Wells Valley, but their presence in the valley and Teagle Wash, indicates that they have been uplifted and eroded. Finally, within the valley itself, outcrops of older lacustrine deposits (Qol, Fig. 4) are restricted to the southern end of the basin where they form broad, low upwarps on an otherwise flat valley floor. We suggest that all of these are the result of more or less north-south contraction related to modern right-lateral shear through the valley.

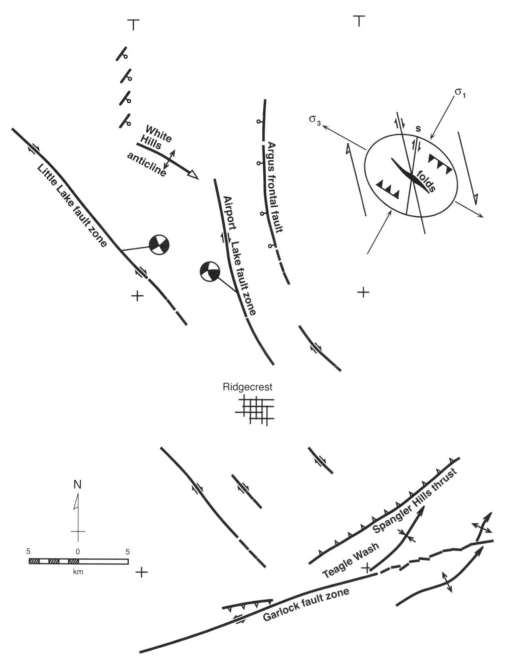

Figure 19. Orientation of modern, active structures in the Indian Wells Valley. These are forming in response to a stress field in which σ_1 (maximum stress) is oriented northeast-southwest with σ_3 (minimum stress) oriented northwest-southeast. The Airport Lake fault zone, the Argus frontal fault, and the Little Lake fault zone have all supported historical seismicity ranging from magnitude 3.0 to as high as magnitude 5.8 events. Focal mechanisms are representative of composite movement on the Airport Lake and the Little Lake fault zones. Structures shown in this plot are the result of the throughgoing right-lateral fault system, including these two fault zones and others that are unnamed, that originates near the present trace of the Garlock fault and extends into the Coso Range. The stress-strain determination is consistent with independent geodetic measurements of crustal velocity data for this area (Monastero et al., 2000). Fault symbols as in Figure 15.

Because of the absence of significant accumulations of modern sediment, the Indian Wells Valley does not appear to be downwarping rapidly at the present time. However, as noted previously, horizon D on IWV-92-02 does bow downward in the area of active strike-slip faulting (Plate 2, SP 1250–1350). Without major bends or stepovers in the plane of the faults, one could logically expect that deposition, if there was any, would be localized along the active zone of deformation. There are some relatively inconsequential deposits of alluvial-fan material that have extended over the valley floor from the surrounding ranges, but these appear to be confined to the extreme outer margins of the basin. Similarly, there are a few scattered eolian and playa deposits throughout the valley, but they are thin and patchy in their distribution.

SUMMARY AND CONCLUSIONS

The Indian Wells Valley is situated in a key location with regard to unraveling the history of the northeastern Mojave Desert and the southwestern Basin and Range. It is bounded on the south by the Garlock fault, the major accommodation structure in the development of the southwestern Basin and Range (Davis and Burchfiel, 1973), and on the west by the Sierra Nevada. Geologic information from the Indian Wells Valley documents processes that have been active over the past 65–70 m.y. at the margin of two major physiographic and tectonic provinces in the southwestern United States.

The Indian Wells Valley has been the locus of deposition during four intervals: the Paleocene–early Eocene, the Miocene, the Pliocene–Pleistocene, and the Holocene. Our data indicate that deposition was virtually all nonmarine in basins that were limited to dimensions on the order of tens of kilometers. Alluvial-fan, alluvial-plain, fluvial, and lacustrine environments dominate the stratigraphy in the Indian Wells Valley; volcanic rocks provide a relatively small, but geologically significant, percentage of the total section.

At least three major periods of deformation are recorded in the Indian Wells Valley. The first change from northeast-directed extension to west-northwest–directed extension in the Death Valley area (Fitzgerald et al., 1991; Gans and Bohrson, 1998) at ca. 16 Ma resulted in the onset of sinistral movement on the Garlock fault. This event is recorded as an angular unconformity between the Cudahy Camp and Dove Spring Formations that represents a hiatus of ~1.5 m.y. Beginning at ca. 13.5 Ma, and over the succeeding 6 m.y. period, the Indian Wells Valley was at the margin of a passive intermontane basin that received deposits now forming the distal facies of the Dove Spring Formation. The absence of parts of the Miocene stratigraphic section in the Indian Wells Valley indicates that it may also have been an intermittent topographic high where there was no sedimentation or that it was undergoing erosion.

Between 7 Ma and 5 Ma there was a significant pulse of uplift of the Sierra Nevada that was accommodated by low-angle normal faulting along the Sierra Nevada frontal fault and formation of a classic half graben in the Indian Wells Valley. This second phase of deformation may have been due to delamination of the lower crust or lithospheric mantle beneath the southern Sierra Nevada (Ducea and Saleeby, 1998). The western margin of the Indian Wells Valley was deformed at this time in conjunction with rotation and westward translation of the adjacent El Paso basin (Burbank and Whistler, 1987; Loomis and Burbank, 1988).

Finally, sometime after 3.5 Ma, but before 2 Ma, there was a regional shift in deformation to northwest-directed extension that resulted in cessation of movement on the Sierra Nevada frontal fault and initiation of simple right-lateral or right-oblique strike-slip faulting on a north-northwest–oriented system located in the central Indian Wells Valley. Sedimentation patterns changed from being basin-wide to highly localized, relatively low energy deposition in close proximity to the faults, i.e., marginal alluvial fans with central alluvial plains and restricted playas. Modern deformation of the valley is the result of this dominantly dextral faulting.

As the Pacific–North American plate boundary continues to evolve, it is likely the Indian Wells Valley will undergo further dynamic responses in sedimentation patterns. If the trends of the past 16 m.y. continue, the locus of extensional deformation will shift westward, and the Indian Wells Valley basin,

like Death Valley and Panamint Valley before, will eventually become a passive record of a small segment of this dynamic plate boundary. For the time being, however, it is one of the most tectonically active sites in the southwestern United States and the world.

ACKNOWLEDGMENTS

We thank Dick Forester of the U.S. Geological Survey, Denver, Colorado, for paleoecologic calls on the lacustrine microfossils from the White Hills and Kip Hodges of the Massachusetts Institute of Technology for performing the $^{40}Ar/^{39}Ar$ dating. The manuscript has been a monument to perseverance. It is the result of more than 10 years of field work, data interpretation, and integration. These types of synthesis papers happen because geoscientists willingly share ideas and data. Valuable insights were gained from discussions with Doug Burbank, Bob Couch, Brett Cox, Dana Loomis, and Dave Whistler, to name a few. Extensive and thoughtful written comments from Steve Richard, Bob Bohannon, Jeff Unruh, and Allen Glazner greatly improved the manuscript. We also thank Steve Bjornstad for support with preparation of figures, and Kelly Ambrecht and Bill Stephenson for their special TLC with finalizing the plates and the figures.

REFERENCES CITED

Bachman, S.B., 1978, Pliocene-Pleistocene break-up of the Sierra Nevada-White/Inyo Mountains block and formation of Owens Valley, California: Geology, v. 6, p. 461–463.

Bacon, C.R., Giovannetti, D.M., Duffield, W.A., Dalrymple, G.B., and Drake, R.E., 1982, Age of the Coso formation, Inyo County, California: U.S. Geological Survey Bulletin 1527, p. 1–18.

Ballance, P.F., 1984, Sheet-flow-dominated gravel fans of the non-marine middle Cenozoic Simmler formation, central California: Sedimentary Geology, v. 38, p. 337–359.

Beanland, S., and Clark, M.M., 1994, The Owens Valley fault zone, eastern California, and surface faulting associated with the 1872 earthquake: U.S. Geological Survey Bulletin 1982, 29 p.

Bennett, R.A., Wernicke, B.P., Davis, J.L., Elosegui, P., Snow, J.K., Abolins, M.J., House, M.A., Stirewalt, G.L., and Ferrill, D.A., 1997, Global positioning system constraints on fault slip rates in the Death Valley region, California and Nevada: Geophysical Research Letters, v. 24, p. 3073–3076.

Berenbrock, C., and Martin, P., 1991, The ground-water flow system in Indian Wells Valley, Kern, Inyo, and San Bernardino Counties, California: U.S. Geological Survey Water-Resources Investigations Report 89–4191, 81 p.

Berenbrock, C., and Schroeder, R.A., 1994, Ground-water flow and quality, and geochemical processes in Indian Wells Valley, Kern, Inyo, and San Bernardino Counties, California, 1987–1988: U.S. Geological Survey Water-Resources Investigations Report 93–4003, 59 p.

Bischoff, J.L., Stafford, T.W., Jr., and Rubin, M., 1997, A time-depth scale for Owens Lake sediments of core OL-92: Radiocarbon dates and constant mass-accumulation rate, in Smith, G.I., and Bischoff, J.L., eds., An 800,000-year paleoclimate record from Core OL-92, Owens Lake, southeast California: Geological Society of America Special Paper 317, p. 91–98.

Burbank, D.W., and Whistler, D.P., 1987, Temporally constrained tectonic rotations derived from magnetostratigraphic data: Implications for the initiation of the Garlock fault, California: Geology, v. 15, p. 1172–1175.

Burchfiel, B.C., Hodges, K.V., and Royden, L.H., 1987, Geology of Panamint Valley–Saline Valley pull-apart system, California: Palinspastic evidence for low-angle geometry of a Neogene range-bounding fault: Journal of Geophysical Research, v. 92(B10), p. 10422–10426.

Christensen, A.F., 1983, An example of a major syndepositional listric fault, *in* Bally, A.W., ed., Seismic expression of structural styles, Volume II—Tectonics of extensional provinces: American Association of Petroleum Geologists Studies in Geology Series #15, p. 2.3.1-36 to 2.3.1-42.

Conrad, J.E., McKee, E.H., and Blakely, R.J., 1994, Tectonic setting of late Cenozoic volcanism in the Saline and Last Chance Ranges, eastern California: Geological Society of America Abstracts with Programs, v. 26, no. 2, p. A46.

Cox, B.F., 1982, Stratigraphy, sedimentology, and structure of the Goler formation (Paleocene), El Paso Mountains, California: Implications for Paleogene tectonism on the Garlock fault [Ph.D. thesis]: Riverside, University of California, 248 p.

Cox, B.F., and Diggles, M.F., 1986, Geologic map of the El Paso Mountains wilderness study area, Kern County, California: U.S. Geological Survey Miscellaneous Field Studies Map MF-1827, scale 1:24000.

Crowell, J.C., 1982, The tectonics of Ridge Basin, southern California, *in* Crowell, J.C., and Link, M.H., eds., Geologic history of the Ridge Basin, southern California: Pacific Section, Society of Economic Paleontologists and Mineralogists, p. 25–42.

Davis, G.A., and Burchfiel, B.C., 1973, Garlock fault: An intercontinental transform structure, southern California: Geological Society of America Bulletin, v. 84, p. 1407–1422.

Davis, G.A., Fowler, T.K., Bishop, K.M., Brudos, T.C., Friedmann, S.J., Burbank, D.W., Parke, M.A., and Burchfiel, B.C., 1993, Pluton pinning of an active Miocene detachment fault system, eastern Mojave Desert, California: Geology, v. 21, p. 627–630.

Dokka, R.K., and Travis, C.J., 1990, Late Cenozoic strike-slip faulting in the Mojave Desert, California: Tectonics, v. 9, p. 311–340.

Ducea, M., and Saleeby, J., 1998, A case for delamination of the deep batholithic crust beneath the Sierra Nevada, California, *in* Ernst, W.G., and Nelson, C.A., eds., Integrated earth and environmental evolution of the southwestern United States, Clarence A. Hall, Jr., Volume: Columbia, Maryland, Bellwether Publishing, p. 273–288.

Duffield, W.A., and Bacon, C.R., 1980, Late Cenozoic volcanism, geochronology, and structure of the Coso Range, Inyo County, California: Journal of Geophysical Research, v. 85, p. 2381–2404.

Duffield, W.A., and Smith, G.I., 1978, Pleistocene history of volcanism and the Owens River near Little Lake, California: U.S. Geological Survey Journal of Research, v. 6, p. 395–408.

Duffield, W.A., Bacon, C.R., and Dalrymple, G.B., 1981, Geologic map of the Coso volcanic field and adjacent areas, Inyo County, California: U.S. Geological Survey Miscellaneous Field Investigation Map I-1200, scale 1:50000.

Fitzgerald, P.G., Fryxell, J.E., and Wernicke, B.P., 1991, Miocene crustal extension and uplift in southeastern Nevada: Constraints from fission-track analysis: Geology, v. 19, p. 1013–1016.

Gans, P.B., and Bohrson, W.A., 1998, Suppression of volcanism during rapid extension in the Basin and Range province, United States: Science, v. 279, p. 66–69.

Glazner, A.F., and Loomis, D.P., 1984, Effect of subduction of the Mendocino fracture zone on Tertiary sedimentation in southern California: Sedimentary Geology, v. 38, p. 287–303.

Goodman, E.D., and Malin, P.E., 1992, Evolution of the southern San Joaquin Basin and mid-Tertiary "transitional" tectonics, central California: Tectonics, v. 11, p. 479–498.

Greensfelder, R.W., Kintzer, F.C., and Somerville, M.R., 1980, Seismotectonic regionalization of the Great Basin, and comparison of moment rates computed from Holocene strain and historic seismicity: Summary: Geological

Society of America Bulletin, v. 91, Part 1, p. 518–523.

Hardyman, R.F., and Oldow, J.S., 1991, Tertiary tectonic framework and Cenozoic history of the central Walker Lane, Nevada, *in* Raines, G.L., ed., Geology and ore deposits of the Great Basin: Reno, Geological Society of Nevada, p. 279–302.

Hatcher, R.D., 1990, Structural geology: Principles, concepts, and problems: Columbus, Ohio, Merrill Publishing Company, 531 p.

Hodges, K.V., McKenna, L.W., Stock, J., Knapp, J., Page, L., Sternlof, K., Silverberg, D., Wust, G., and Walker, J.D., 1989, Evolution of extensional basins and Basin and Range topography west of Death Valley, California: Tectonics, v. 8, p. 453–467.

Humphreys, E.D., and Weldon, R.J., II, 1994, Deformation across the western United States: A local estimate of Pacific-North America transform deformation: Journal of Geophysical Research, v. 99, p. 19975–20010.

Jenkins, O.P., 1963, Geologic map of California, Trona sheet: Department of Conservation, California Division of Mines and Geology, scale 1:250000.

Kamola, D.L., and Walker, J.D., 1999, Sedimentation and tectonics study of the Mio-Pliocene Coso Formation, Coso Range, California: Geological Society of America Abstracts with Programs, v. 31, no. 7, p. A-426.

Kay, R.W., and Kay, S.M., 1993, Delamination and delamination magmatism: Tectonophysics, v. 219, p. 177–189.

Kerr, D.R., 1984, Early Neogene continental sedimentation in the Vallecito and Fish Creek Mountains, western Salton Trough, California: Sedimentary Geology, v. 38, p. 217–246.

Kunkel, F., and Chase, G.H., 1969, Geology and ground water in Indian Wells Valley, California: U.S. Geological Survey Water Resources Division, Open-File Report, 84 p.

Leeder, M.R., and Gawthorpe, R.L., 1987, Sedimentary models for extensional tilt-block/half-graben basins, *in* Coward, M.P., et al., eds., Continental extensional tectonics: Geological Society [London] Special Publication 28, p. 139–152.

Loomis, D.P., 1984, Miocene stratigraphic and tectonic evolution of the El Paso Basin, California [M.S. thesis]: Chapel Hill, University of North Carolina, 172 p.

Loomis, D.P., and Burbank, D.W., 1988, The stratigraphic evolution of the El Paso Basin, southern California: Implications for Miocene development of the Garlock fault and uplift of the Sierra Nevada: Geological Society of America Bulletin, v. 100, p. 12–28.

Lueddecke, S.B., Pinter, N., and Gans, P., 1998, Plio-Pleistocene ash falls, sedimentation, and range-front faulting along the White-Inyo Mountains front, California: Journal of Geology, v. 106, p. 511–522.

Manley, C.R., Glazner, A.F., and Farmer, G.L., 2000, Timing of volcanism in the Sierra Nevada of California: Evidence for Pliocene delamination of the batholithic root?: Geology, v. 28, p. 811–814.

McGill, S., and Sieh, K., 1993, Holocene slip rate on the central Garlock fault in southeastern Searles Valley, California: Journal of Geophysical Research, v. 98, p. 14217–14231.

McKenna, L.W., and Hodges, K.V., 1990, Constraints on the kinematics and timing of late Miocene-recent extension between the Panamint and Black Mountains, southeastern California, *in* Wernicke, B.P., ed., Basin and Range extensional tectonics near the latitude of Las Vegas, Nevada: Geological Society of America Memoir 176, p. 363–376.

Miller, J.M.G., and John, B.E., 1999, Sedimentation patterns support seismogenic low-angle normal faulting, southeastern California and western Arizona: Geological Society of America Bulletin, v. 111, p. 1350–1370.

Monastero, F.C., and Katzenstein, A.M., 1995, Multicomponent geophysical analysis in drilling target definition in an extended terrane: Proceedings, World Geothermal Congress, Florence, Italy, p. 787–791.

Monastero, F.C., Thorn, D., and Sabin, A.E., 1995, An evaluation of extension in the Indian Wells Valley, San Bernardino County, California, using geologic, geophysical, and downhole, Formation MicroScanner (FMS) data: San Francisco, California, Pacific Section, SEPM (Society for Sedimentary Geology), May 3–5, 1995.

Monastero, F.C., Sabin, A.E., and Walker, J.D., 1997, Evidence for post-early

Miocene initiation of movement on the Garlock fault from offset of the Cudahy Camp formation, east-central California: Geology, v. 25, p. 247–250.

Monastero, F.C., Walker, J.D., and Glazner, A.F., 2000, Microplates of the Pacific-North America boundary: Geological Society of America Abstracts with Programs, v. 32, no. 7, p. A156.

Moyle, W.R., Jr., 1963, Data on water wells in Indian Wells Valley area, Inyo, Kern, and San Bernardino Counties, California: State of California, Department of Water Resources Bulletin No. 91-9, 243 p.

Nitchman, S.P., Caskey, S.J., and Sawyer, T.L., 1990, Change in Great Basin tectonics at 3 to 4 Ma: A hypothesis: Geological Society of America Abstracts with Programs, v. 22, p. 72.

Nur, A., Ron, H., and Beroza, G., 1993, Landers-Mojave earthquake line: A new fault system?: GSA Today, v. 3, p. 254–258.

Reheis, M.C., and Sawyer, T.L., 1997, Late Cenozoic history and slip rates of the Fish Lake Valley, Emigrant Peak, and Deep Springs fault zones, Nevada and California: Geological Society of America Bulletin, v. 109, p. 280–299.

Roquemore, G.R., 1981, Active faults and associated tectonic stress in the Coso Range, California: Naval Weapons Center Technical Publication TP 6270, 101 p.

Roquemore, G.R., and Zellmer, J.T., 1987, Naval Weapons Center active fault map series: Naval Weapons Center Technical Publication TP 6828, 17 p.

Sangree, J.B., and Widmier, J.M., 1977, Seismic stratigraphy and global changes of sea level, Part 9: Seismic interpretation of clastic depositional facies, *in* Payton, C.E., ed., Seismic stratigraphy: Applications to hydrocarbon exploration: American Association of Petroleum Geologists Memoir 26, p. 165–184.

Schweig, E.S., III, 1989, Basin-range tectonics in the Darwin Plateau, southwestern Great Basin, California: Geological Society of America Bulletin, v. 101, p. 652–662.

Serpa, L., and Pavlis, T.L., 1996, Three-dimensional model of the Cenozoic history of the Death Valley region, southeastern California: Tectonics, v. 15, p. 1113–1128.

Smith, G.I., 1991, Anomalous folds associated with the east-central part of the Garlock fault, southeast California: Geological Society of America Bulletin, v. 103, p. 615–624.

Smith, G.I., and Pratt, W.P., 1957, Core logs from Owens, China, Searles, and Panamint Basins, California: U.S. Geological Survey Bulletin 1045-A, 62 p.

Smith, G.I., Barczak, V.J., Moulton, G.F., and Liddicoat, J.C., 1983, Core KM-3, a surface-to-bedrock record of late Cenozoic sedimentation in Searles Valley, California: U.S. Geological Survey Professional Paper 1256, 24 p.

Smith, G.I., Bischoff, J.L., and Bradbury, J.P., 1997, Synthesis of the paleoclimate record from Owens Lake core OL-92, *in* Smith, G.I., and Bischoff, J.L., eds., An 800 000-year paleoclimate record from Core OL-92, Owens Lake, southeast California: Geological Society of America Special Paper 317, p. 143–160.

Snow, J.K., and Wernicke, B.P., 2000, Cenozoic tectonism in the central Basin and Range: Magnitude, rate, and distribution of upper crustal strain: American Journal of Science, v. 300, no. 9, p. 659–719.

Stewart, J.H., 1983, Extensional tectonics in the Death Valley area, California: Transport of the Panamint Range structural block 80 km northward: Geology, v. 11, p. 153–157.

Unruh, J.R., 1991, The uplift of the Sierra Nevada and implications for late Cenozoic epeirogeny in the western Cordillera: Geological Society of America Bulletin, v. 103, p. 1395–1404.

von Huene, R.E., 1960, Structural geology and gravimetry of Indian Wells Valley, southeastern California [Ph.D. thesis]: Los Angeles, University of California, 138 p.

Walker, J.D., and Glazner, A.F., 1999, Tectonic development of the California deserts: Geological Society of America Special Paper 338, p. 375–380.

Ward, P.L., 1991, On plate tectonics and the geologic evolution of southwestern North America: Journal of Geophysical Research, v. 96, p. 12 479–12 496.

Wernicke, B.P., 1992, Cenozoic extensional tectonics of the U.S. Cordillera, *in* Burchfiel, B.C., et al., eds., The Cordilleran orogen: Conterminous U.S.: Boulder, Colorado, Geological Society of America, Geology of North America, v. G-3, p. 553–581.

Wernicke, B.P., and Snow, J.K., 1998, Cenozoic tectonism in the central Basin and Range: Motion of the Sierran-Great Valley block: International Geology Review, v. 40, p. 403–410.

Wernicke, B.P., Spencer, J.E., Burchfiel, B.C., and Guth, P.L., 1982, Magnitude of crustal extension in the southern Great Basin: Geology, v. 10, p. 489–502.

Wernicke, B.P., Axen, G.J., and Snow, J.K., 1988, Basin and Range extensional tectonics at the latitude of Las Vegas, Nevada: Geological Society of America Bulletin, v. 100, p. 1738–1757.

Wesnousky, S.G., and Jones, C.H., 1994, Oblique slip, slip partitioning, spatial and temporal changes in the regional stress field, and the relative strength of active faults in the Basin and Range, western United States: Geology, v. 22, p. 1031–1034.

Whistler, D.P., and Burbank, D.W., 1992, Miocene biostratigraphy and biochronology of the Dove Spring formation, Mojave Desert, California, and characterization of the Clarendonian mammal age (late Miocene) in California: Geological Society of America Bulletin, v. 104, p. 644–658.

Whitmarsh, R.S., Walker, J.D., and Monastero, F.D., 1996, Mesozoic and Cenozoic structural framework of the Coso Range and adjacent areas of eastern California: Geological Society of America Abstracts with Programs, v. 28, no. 5, p. A124.

Zbur, R.T., 1963, A geophysical investigation of Indian Wells Valley, California: U.S. Naval Ordnance Test Station Technical Report 2795, 98 p.

Zhang, P., Ellis, M., Slemmons, D.B., and Mao, F., 1991, Right-lateral displacements and the Holocene slip rate associated with prehistoric earthquakes along the southern Panamint Valley Fault Zone: Implications for southern Basin and Range tectonics and coastal California deformation: Journal of Geophysical Research, v. 95, p. 4857–4872.

MANUSCRIPT ACCEPTED BY THE SOCIETY MAY 9, 2001

Geological Society of America
Memoir 195
2002

Three-dimensional gravity modeling and crustal-density variations, Panamint Range to the eastern Sierra Nevada, southeastern California

Ross A. Black
J. Douglas Walker
Department of Geology, University of Kansas, Lawrence, Kansas 66045, USA
Gregory S. Baker
Department of Geology, State University of New York at Buffalo, Buffalo, New York, 14260, USA

ABSTRACT

The transition area between the Basin and Range, Sierra Nevada, and Mojave Desert is a region of active tectonics and bimodal volcanism. This study addresses the possible connection between upper-crustal geology and rock density, and the style of volcanism in the area. To better understand possible interactions between crustal density and volcanic processes, we constructed a three-dimensional gravity model for the Indian Wells Valley and surrounding ranges in southern California. This model was based on published gravity data and limited seismic reflection and well information. We used a three-dimensional, gridded, Fourier-domain forward-modeling approach (with limits set by available geological and geophysical data) to construct a density model for the upper 10 km of crust in the study area.

Results from gravity modeling lead to two conclusions. First, the isostatic residual gravity anomalies within the area have a predominantly northwest trend, parallel to one of the dominant regional structural trends, which include numerous faults and the Jurassic Independence dike swarm. One of the major density-contrast boundaries along this trend appears to cross the entire study area, separating low-density crust in the Sierra Nevada, Coso, and Argus Ranges from higher-density crust to the south. Second, mean upper-crustal density may play a role in determining the nature of eruptive lavas in the area of the Coso volcanic field and perhaps throughout the region. Specifically, basaltic lavas tend to erupt in areas of higher upper-crustal density whereas rhyolitic lavas are confined to areas of lower density. This finding may indicate that the lower the upper-crustal density, the more likely it is that basaltic magmas reach neutral buoyancy and pond within the crust, generating the silicic magmas associated with rhyolitic domes found within the Coso volcanic field.

INTRODUCTION

The transition area between the Basin and Range, Sierra Nevada, and Mojave Desert tectonic provinces (Fig. 1) is receiving new attention because of interest in the controls on

tectonic processes, earthquake hazards, and natural resources unique to this area. The area, bounded to the west by the Sierra Nevada, to the east by Death Valley, and to the south by the Garlock fault (Fig. 1), is an area of topographic transition. It is also the tectonic transition between the highly extended Death

Black, R.A., Walker, J.D., and Baker, G.S., 2002, Three-dimensional gravity modeling and crustal-density variations, Panamint Range to the eastern Sierra Nevada, southeastern California, *in* Glazner, A.F., Walker, J.D., and Bartley, J.M., eds., Geologic Evolution of the Mojave Desert and Southwestern Basin and Range: Boulder, Colorado, Geological Society of America Memoir 195, p. 229–241.

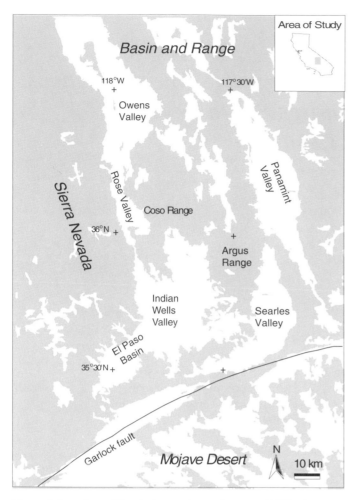

Figure 1. Location of the study area in southeastern California.

Valley corridor to the east and the actively uplifting Sierran block to the west.

Understanding the seismic velocity and density structure within the crust and upper mantle is critical to understanding tectonics and volcanism within the area. Although the central part of the area was closed to geoscientists for many years owing to munitions-testing activities, the margins of this transition area have been the subject of several regional geophysical studies since 1980. Many of the regional studies were based on large-scale active seismic experiments and associated gravity modeling (Thompson et al., 1989). Early experiments included large refraction efforts (Eaton, 1963) and several reflection experiments, such as those undertaken as part of the COCORP program (Cheadle et al., 1986; Klemperer et al., 1986; Allmendinger et al., 1987; Serpa et al., 1988). More recently, particular attention has been paid to the role played by the lithospheric mantle in controlling the regional tectonics of both the Sierran block and the Basin and Range (Fliedner et al., 1996; Ducea and Saleeby, 1996; Ruppert et al., 1998).

This paper reports the results of a regional, three-dimensional, crustal-gravity modeling study of a part of this transition

area centered over Indian Wells Valley of southeastern California (Fig. 1). This region is an area of active tectonism and magmatism superimposed on a preexisting passive margin with a long history of older arc magmatism (Stevens et al., 1997). Active tectonic features of interest exposed at the surface within the area include the Coso volcanic field, the Garlock fault, the Sierra Nevada bounding fault, and a series of right-lateral faults trending mainly northwest throughout the area (Fig. 2). The Coso area produces large quantities of geothermal energy from a reservoir directly related to Quaternary rhyolitic volcanic activity (Duffield and Bacon, 1981). Recent earthquake activity is associated with both the Coso area, mainly as microseismic activity (i.e., Wu and Lees, 1999), and the Indian Wells Valley area, as macroseismic activity apparently migrating to the north along the north-northwest-trending fault systems (Bhattacharyya et al., 1999).

In this study, specific emphasis was placed on developing a model of the distribution of basement lithology and crustal density based mainly on gravity data along with digitized surface geology, seismic reflection information, and limited deepwell data. Such models have important ramifications for the interpretation of the modern bimodal volcanic and geothermal systems and related natural hazards and economic resources. The density of the crust, for example, may be a factor in the interaction of mantle-derived melts with the crustal column (Glazner and Ussler, 1989) and in the structural behavior of plutonic rocks during emplacement (Glazner and Miller, 1997.)

A generalized basement-depth model was developed by using the surface contact between bedrock and alluvium as a zero-depth contour and subsurface basement depths from two deep drill holes within the Indian Wells Valley. Basement reflections interpreted from available seismic lines were tied to the deep-well basement depths through a simple velocity model and then used with the basement-alluvium surface contacts to generate the starting basement surface.

This approximation to the basement surface was then "sliced" and used to partition a three-dimensional cell model into "basement" and "basin-sediment" volumes. The three-dimensional cell model was then used as the basis for iterative forward gravity modeling.

STRATIGRAPHIC UNIT DEFINITIONS

Geologic units are categorized into density-related units during gravity modeling. The major categories used to construct the gravity model in this study include basement rocks, basin fill, Paleozoic sedimentary rocks, Quaternary volcanic rocks, and other volumetrically less important units. We next present a short discussion of the stratigraphic units included in each of these categories. The locations of the various units are shown in Figure 2. Details of the stratigraphy in the area are presented in Monastero et al. (this volume).

For the purposes of this study, *Sierran basement* is defined as plutonic rocks formed mainly during Jurassic-Cretaceous

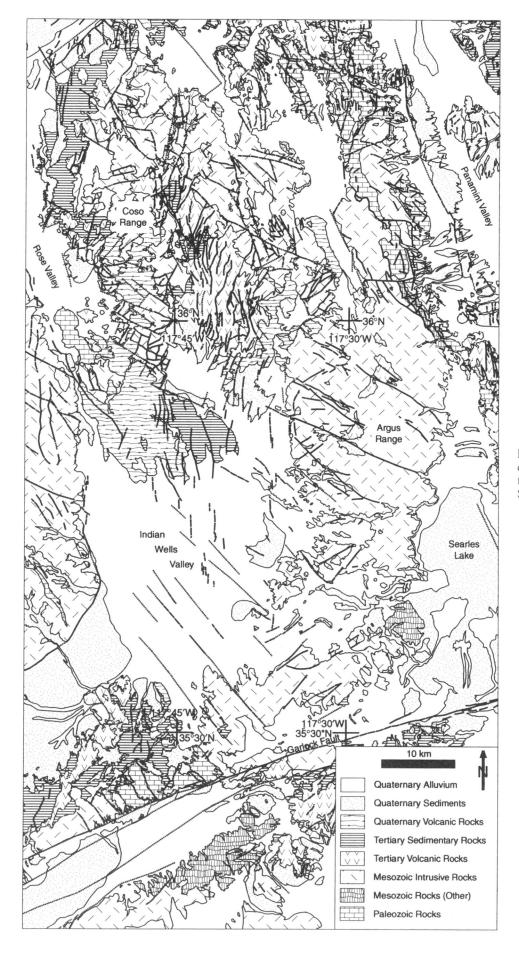

Figure 2. Geologic map of the study area centered on Indian Wells Valley. Modified from Jennings et al. (1962) and Stritz and Stinson (1974).

☐	Quaternary Alluvium
☐	Quaternary Sediments
☐	Quaternary Volcanic Rocks
☰	Tertiary Sedimentary Rocks
∨∨	Tertiary Volcanic Rocks
╲	Mesozoic Intrusive Rocks
▦	Mesozoic Rocks (Other)
▤	Paleozoic Rocks

arc-related plutonic activity as well as associated metamorphic screens. Older plutonic rocks occur within the southwestern part of the study area, but are of volumetrically minor importance. Granodiorite dominates plutonic rock exposures. However, arc-related plutons range from leucogranite to gabbro in composition. Thus, the range of density contrasts within the basement rocks is relatively large.

The term *basin fill*, as used in this study, refers to sedimentary deposits and relatively minor volcanic deposits ranging in age from Paleogene to Quaternary. Tertiary units include the Paleogene Goler Formation and the Neogene Ricardo Group and sedimentary rocks of the White Hills. The Coso Formation in the northern part of the study area may be age equivalent to the lower or middle White Hills sequence. The Ricardo Group consists of the Cudahy Camp and Dove Springs Formations. These are dominantly nonmarine clastic deposits with minor basalt flows and felsic tephra units. The degree of lithification varies, but, except for the basalts, they are generally poorly lithified. For example, deep-well SNORT-2 (Fig. 3) encountered no lithified sedimentary units above Sierran basement (Monastero et al., this volume). The Quaternary sedimentary deposits are undifferentiated and generally unlithified. The basin-fill deposits are thus low in average density and have a large negative density contrast relative to the standard Bouguer correction density of 2670 kg/m^3

Paleozoic miogeoclinal and eugeoclinal sedimentary rocks occur in the northern Argus Range and the El Paso Mountains. These occur as isolated thrust sheets and cover a relatively small part of the study area.

THE DATA SET AND PREPROCESSING

The gravity data set used in this study was assembled by the California Division of Mines and Geology (CDMG) in 1984 and is available from the National Geophysical Data Center (NGDC, 1994). Other data compilations available for this area included the 1994 Society of Exploration Geophysicists compilation and the 1993 Defense Mapping Agency compilation. Although the CDMG compilation is the oldest of the data sets available for the area and has the fewest measurements, the CDMG data set included not only standard Bouguer corrections, but also terrain corrections (Dobrin and Savit, 1988; Hammer, 1939) and isostatic corrections (Jachens et al., 1989; Simpson et al., 1986) for each raw data point. It is usually necessary to apply both of these corrections when working in high-relief areas such as this tectonic transition zone (Blakely, 1995). These measurements represent the anomaly due to rocks of the Earth's crust, with the effects of the average gravitational pull of the Earth, the variation of gravitational pull with latitude, and the variations due to elevation, terrain, and mantle topography removed.

The terrain corrections applied to the CDMG data included both outer- and inner-ring corrections (Hammer, 1939). The isostatic corrections were based on the most commonly used

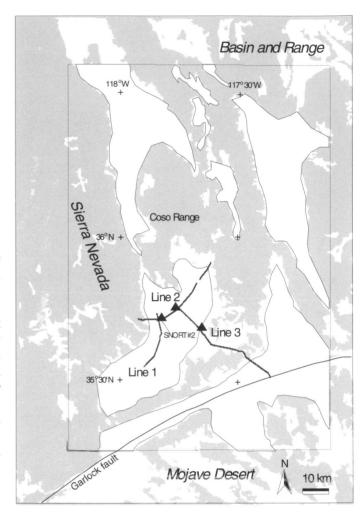

Figure 3. Location of the control data used to set limits on the initial model configuration. Approximate contact locations between alluvium and bedrock outcrops enclose white polygonal areas, modeled as basin fill. Because the basin fill (alluvium) was much less than 0.2 km thick in some areas, the final model polygons did not extend to the bedrock-alluvium contacts in some areas. Information from the deep wells (triangles) and seismic reflection data (thicker black lines) were used where available to set basin depths. The rectangle outlines the actual area of the gridded model shown in later figures.

isostatic model in the western United States, the Airy-Heiskanen model (Simpson et al., 1986; Oliver, 1986; Jachens et al., 1989; Saltus and Jachens, 1995), which assumes that terrain is compensated through undulations of the crust-mantle interface. Following the original U.S. Geological Survey work with isostatic anomalies in California (Roberts et al., 1981; Oliver, 1986), the CDMG gravity data set utilized a 25 km isostatic compensation depth, a crustal density of 2670 kg/m^3, and a density contrast of -400 kg/m^3 with the surrounding mantle. The implications of these assumptions, especially the Airy-Heiskanen assumption, are included in later discussions.

The distribution of the individual data points is shown in Figure 4. The data were gridded by using a simple inverse-distance weighting scheme with the same coordinate system used in the Indian Wells Valley database containing the surface geology, other geophysical data, and well-location information for the study area. The data could thus be compared to all available information for the area, and the various data sets could be used to spatially guide the gravity modeling. The grid totaled 300 rows by 200 columns. It covered an area of ~150 × 100 km, from south of the Garlock fault to Owens Valley in the north, and from several kilometers into the eastern part of the Sierra Nevada to the edge of the Panamint Range on the east.

FORWARD MODELING

Our main goal was to develop an accurate, three-dimensional, cell-based procedure to calculate the gravity anomaly

due to relatively large regional models by using information from a regional GIS (geographic information system) database in the calculations. All forward potential field models are by nature nonunique. Even with the limited constraints available for this area, an infinite number of different models may be constructed for any given area, and any single model is an individual interpretation. The logic used in making some of the major interpretations needed to construct the model is discussed within the modeling results section.

Modeling procedure

The three-dimensional model consisted of a series of layers. During the first iteration, the model was kept as simple as possible. Layers were added, and the density-contrast distribution within individual layers was updated where needed to reduce errors between the observed and calculated anomaly with each iteration. The main control on the number of layers and layer thickness was the component of the gravity anomaly associated with the basin deposits. Each of the basins in the model area apparently has a unique maximum depth (Fig. 5).

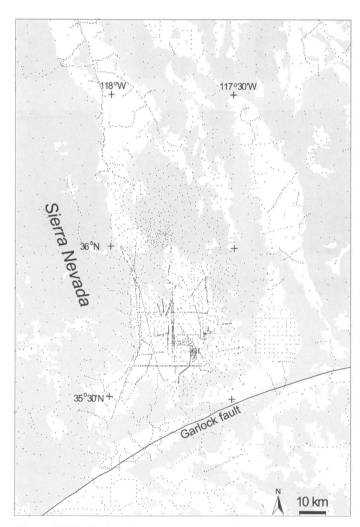

Figure 4. Distribution of gravity data points from the data set used in this study. The data were originally distributed by the California Division of Mines and Geology and were issued on the 1994 National Geophysical Data Center Gravity CD-ROM (National Geophysical Data Center, 1994). The data include complete Bouguer anomaly information and isostatic residual anomaly information. The isostatic residual anomaly was used in this study.

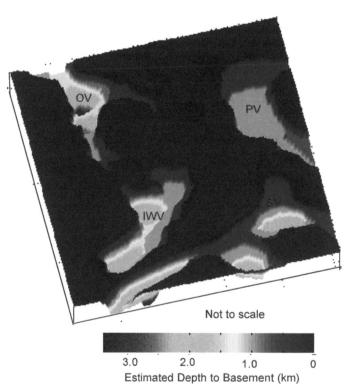

Figure 5. Perspective view of approximate depth to basement in areas modeled as basin fill. OV—Owens Valley, IWV—Indian Wells Valley, PV—Panamint Valley, and SV—Searles Valley. The geometry of the Indian Wells Valley is defined by subsurface information, and the geometries of the other basins were estimated from the gravity data during the modeling process. Note that the Owens Valley and the Indian Wells Valley estimates indicate two deep depocenters in each valley. This perspective view is not plotted to scale, except for the depth scale (indicated by colors).

The layer thicknesses of the upper layers were adjusted in modeling each apparent basin depth. For example, in the Indian Wells Valley, where the basin geometry was fairly well known, it was necessary to add an extra layer to simulate the gradual dip of the basement along the eastern margin of the basin. The layers also had to be compatible with the depth versus density model used within the basins, and the layer thicknesses were varied in multiples of 0.2 km, the minimum layer thickness in the density-depth model.

A total of nine layers, each representing a unique depth range, was eventually developed. Computationally, there was no reason to limit the layers to a narrow range of thicknesses, so the final layers varied from 0.2 to 6.4 km in thickness.

Initially the model layers were developed as a series of polygonal outlines representing different subsurface bodies. Basement density contrasts and basin-fill density contrasts were initially estimated by separate procedures discussed next. The polygonal geometries and density contrasts were then allowed to vary with each iteration, unless defined by surface or sub-surface data. Spatially limited geologic features such as small intrusions, volcanic flows, and shallow basins were added to the model if they spatially correlated with an observed gravity anomaly.

The polygons were sketched and edited within a GIS system and assigned individual density contrasts. A layer of grid-cell density contrasts was then interpolated within each polygon layer by using a point-in-polygon algorithm. The individual grid layers were then concatenated to form the multilayer, three-dimensional density-contrast grid. The three-dimensional grid model was then run through a frequency-domain forward gravity calculation algorithm (Blakely, 1995). This procedure was applied in an iterative manner until the model density contrasts yielded a calculated anomaly field within a maximum of 5 mgal of the observed anomaly field.

Basement density contrasts

The basement rocks (Fig. 2) were allowed to vary in density contrast laterally and with depth for each modeling iteration. The basement density contrasts for the first iteration of modeling, however, were simply estimated directly from the observed gravity value distribution. In areas of basement outcrop, it was initially assumed that the observed anomaly was caused by a slab of homogeneous lithology extending from the surface to the base of the model. Thus, the "infinite horizontal slab" formula (Dobrin and Savit, 1988) could be used to estimate the contrast in areas of outcropping basement. These estimates were averaged over several grid cells to smooth the initial estimates.

Basement density contrasts were then interpolated beneath the basins from the surrounding outcrop areas by using an inverse-distance weighting scheme and a large search radius. This approach tended to yield basement density-contrast estimates that were averaged over large areas, separating the base-

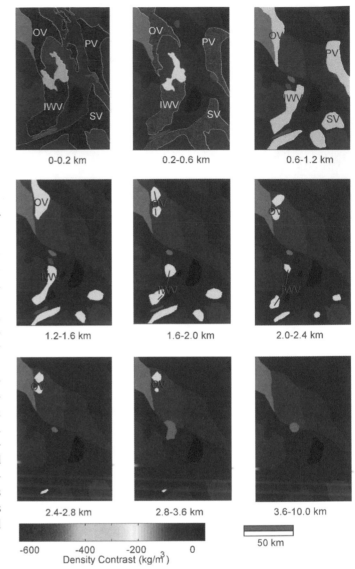

Figure 6. Nine-layer model from the last iteration of the forward modeling. This model resulted in the calculated field shown in Figure 7B. The large negative density contrasts reflect Neogene basin fill. Refer to the text for details on the basement rocks, basin fill, and volcanic rocks. Locations: OV—Owens Valley, PV—Panamint Valley, IWV—Indian Wells Valley, SV—Searles Valley.

ment into large, fairly homogeneous blocks (Fig. 6). Although the modeled basement densities were allowed to vary laterally, most of these variations correlate with surface features. There was also little need to vary the density contrast with depth from iteration to iteration.

Test calculations for intrusions several kilometers in diameter, with density contrasts of -120 kg/m^3 (density $\sim$2550 kg/m^3, at the very minimum density for broadly granitic rocks), indicated that a thickness of $\sim$10 km was adequate to explain the anomalously low density contrasts observed. In addition, the limited literature indicates that most of the laterally anomalous mass contribution across the Sierran batholith appears to occur in the upper 10 km of the crust. Oliver (1986) performed a combination of forward modeling and regression analysis on 2000 density measurements taken within the batholith, correlating surface density contrast with apparent depth extent of anomalous causative bodies. The results indicated that exposed, laterally continuous intrusive bodies of the Sierran batholith must extend to a batholith-wide average of ~10 km in depth to match the observed surface densities and gravity anomalies (Oliver, 1986). Rocks below this depth apparently contribute only a small part of the anomalous field observed at the surface because of depth considerations, rheological behavior, or other complicating factors. The calculations were thus based on a model thickness of 10 km.

Basin-fill density contrasts

Basin-fill (Fig. 2) density contrasts were estimated by using a function developed by Jachens and Moring (1990) from borehole data from many extensional basins of the Basin and Range (Table 1). This function assumes that the sediments increase systematically in density with depth, but are laterally homogeneous. Use of this function constitutes one of the major assumptions of this study.

The subsurface geometry of the Indian Wells Valley is fairly well known (Monastero et al., this volume), and this information was used in the modeling procedure (Fig. 5). The other basins in the study area were not so well known, and thus we had to rely on a combination of the Jachens and Moring (1990) function and the estimate of basement density contrast already discussed to assign basin depths for the modeling outside of the Indian Wells Valley. These depths were determined by trial and error during the model iterations (Fig. 5).

Within the Indian Wells Valley, the basin geometry could actually be used as a check on the basement density-contrast estimate. The basin and basement anomaly estimates turned out to be fairly compatible, with slight differences that are discussed in the results section. Three deep wells have been drilled in the valley, and two of these wells penetrate basement near the intersections of three seismic reflection lines in the main part of the valley area (Fig. 3). The location of the wells and the location of the main proprietary seismic lines are shown in Figure 3. The final model basement-alluvium contacts are also shown generally following range boundaries. Where they do

TABLE 1. DEPTH VERSUS DENSITY FUNCTIONS FOR BASIN FILL AND VOLCANIC SEQUENCES

Depth Range (km)	Sedimentary Density Contrast (kg/m³)	Volcanic Density Contrast (kg/m³)
0–0.2	−650	−450
0.2–0.6	−550	−250
0.6–1.2	−350	−250
>1.2	−250	−150

Note: Modified from Jachens and Moring, 1990. Modifications described in text.

not coincide with the range boundaries in Figure 3, the basement fill is significantly thinner than the final 0.2-km-thick upper grid layer of the model. The shape of the valley fill was initially interpolated from the actual basement-alluvium boundaries on the geologic map, but was allowed to be iteratively modified during modeling where it was not directly restricted by the wells, seismic, or outcrop information.

Several stacking velocity functions, along with the Dix equation (Dobrin and Savit, 1988), were used to estimate basement depth from the seismic time picks. The stacking velocity function was developed from functions developed in reprocessing of Indian Wells Valley seismic line 3. Although there is a significant velocity gradient within the basin, the different functions yielded basement-depth estimates similar to those found by using a simple conversion factor of 2.6–2.8 km/s (two-way velocity). The seismic lines simply indicated that the Indian Wells Valley basin is deepest in the west, along the Sierra Nevada frontal fault is relatively uniform in depth at its center, and gently shallows to the basement outcrop area to the east. From south to north, the combined El Paso basin–Indian Wells Valley area (see Fig. 1 for location) seems to have both a northern and southern depocenter, with a slight saddle in a mid-basinal position. This result is consistent with the location of gravity anomaly lows observed in the gridded isostatic residual gravity data (Fig. 7).

Other density contrasts

Jachens and Moring (1990) also developed a density-depth function for Cenozoic volcanic deposits based mainly on surface measurements. Their density-depth relation applies to a wide range of volcanic deposit types. Application of this function to our study area produced overly negative density-contrast estimates. We assumed a slightly more conservative, modified version of their function (Table 1). We simply assumed that the upper 200 m of a large volcanic pile would consist of a mixture of fractured, vesicular flows, tuffs, and perhaps pumice with a density contrast as low as −450 kg/m³ Owing to compaction, deeper layers were assumed to have density contrasts ranging from −150 to −250 kg/m³. This function worked adequately in areas dominated by rhyolitic volcanic rocks, but produced overly negative gravity estimates in areas of exposed basalt flows.

Density contrasts for other rock types, such as the Paleozoic sedimentary rocks associated with the East Sierran thrust system, were estimated directly from local gravity values. Positive isostatic residual anomalies (Saltus and Jachens, 1995) are sometimes observed in areas of the Basin and Range, such as the Funeral Mountains, underlain by thick sections of metamorphosed Paleozoic rocks. However, such units are areally limited here and, along with small intrusions, were assumed to be surface phenomena and propagated to depth only after the first iteration showed it to be necessary. Density contrasts for features like small "bull's-eye" highs and lows not associated

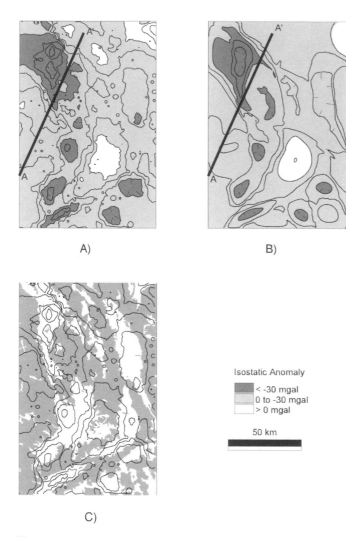

Figure 7. (A) Observed isostatic residual anomaly gridded at 500 m intervals. Note that gravity lows are shaded the darkest. Contour interval = 10 mgal. (B) Calculated output from the nine-layer model shown in Figure 6. Note the location of cross section A-A', which will be discussed further in the caption for Figure 8. (C) Contours from observed data overlain on the location map from Figure 1.

with any identifiable exposed surface feature were added to the model usually at the highest crustal level possible.

FORWARD MODELING RESULTS

The results of the forward modeling are shown in map view in Figures 5, 6, and 7. Figure 5 shows the final depth to basement used in the modeling. Figure 7 shows the calculated gravity output from the sum of the layer responses and a comparison of the observed and calculated anomaly fields. Figure 6 shows the density grids developed for individual layers of cells within the model.

The model response (Fig. 7) is similar, but generally smoother, in overall appearance compared to the observed gravity data. The major features of both the observed and modeled

anomaly fields include large gravity lows associated with the sedimentary basins and the main volcanic area, and both highs and lows associated with exposed areas of Sierran basement.

Basins

There are four areas within the model where the basins are the dominant contributor to the gravity signature: the Indian Wells Valley–El Paso basin area, the Owens Valley–Rose Valley area, the Panamint Valley area, and the valleys south of the Garlock fault, running from the Fremont Valley in the west to the Searles Valley in the east.

By far the largest negative anomalies in the entire study area occur within the Owens Valley area. A fairly broad low reaching below −40 mgal covers most of the region, but there are a pair of isolated lows reaching approximately −60 mgal (Fig. 7). This is ~10 mgal lower than any other basin within the model area. Even with relatively low density basement in the Owens Valley area accounted for, the data indicate that the two small depressions must be well over 3 km in depth. In the final iteration presented here, the base of the deepest layer in which sediments appear is 3.6 km. This depth estimate is somewhat deeper than that estimated by Kane and Pakiser (1961) from their analysis of gravity and seismic refraction data. They concluded that depths to what they referred to as the "bedrock floor" vary from ~1 km to ~3 km along the valley axis. If their analysis is accurate, then either the basin density-contrast function is predicting somewhat greater basement depths, or the basement density-contrast estimates could even be a bit lower in the layers below the valley.

The Indian Wells Valley depth control also indicates that the Jachens and Moring (1990) density function may slightly overpredict depth estimates. As a practical matter, the depth slicing was kept fairly coarse for these models, and thus basement-depth estimates in the Indian Wells Valley are not as accurate as we initially hoped, but the final model-depth estimates are within one model-layer thickness of their starting value.

Within the Indian Wells Valley, sediments extend to 2.4 km (Fig. 6). The deepest basement-penetrating well in the valley hit basement in this area at ~2.3 km. The calculated gravity values on the northern end of the basin are mostly within 2 mgal of the observed values, but some calculated values in other areas where there is depth control appear to be several milligals too high. The seismic lines do not quite reach the center of the isolated gravity low in the northern part of the valley. The low indicates that north of seismic line 2, the basin is somewhat deeper than the 2.4 km base of the modeled basin sediments. The gravity data also indicate that the southern part of the basin could be as deep or slightly deeper than the north end.

The area south of the Garlock fault is represented in Figure 6 as having a large area covered by alluvium and sedimentary basin deposits. Most of this cover is quite thin with scattered basement outcrops. However, three smaller areas contain much deeper basin deposits. The basin within the Fremont Valley in the southwestern part of the study area appears from the gravity data to be nearly as deep as the Owens Valley basins. The observed gravity values in the two basins to the east are similar to the Indian Wells Valley data and are probably also somewhat more than 2 km in depth (Fig. 6).

The basin associated with the Panamint Valley is apparently much shallower that the others so far discussed. The basin deposits disappear from the model below ~1.2 km in depth. In addition, the small basins within the ranges and plateaus between the Panamint and Owens Valleys are mainly very thin veneers of sediment, and their importance in the overall gravity field has probably been overestimated.

It appears that the density-contrast function, although very useful, may slightly underestimate the negative density contrast of the basin sedimentary deposits over the entire area of study. The function was developed to reflect the density contrast in an "average" Basin and Range-style basin. Those basins average only ~0.6 km in depth and, generally, do not have the batholithic basement source for most of the sediment filling the basins. We may also simply be underestimating the negative density contrast of the basement in this area, although negative contrasts of greater than -120 kg/m^3 are difficult to justify in a batholithic setting for reasons discussed next.

Basement features

The corrections applied to the gravity data normalize the densities to an average of 2670 kg/m^3. Thus we should be able to estimate the density contrast for granitic basement in the study area. In a standard table based on older work (Dobrin and Savit, 1988), granites are listed as having a range of density from 2520 kg/m^3 to 2810 kg/m^3, whereas a newer compilation of physical properties by Carmichael (1989) lists the grain density of orthoclase as 2570 kg/m^3 and the density of granite to have a mean of 2660 kg/m^3 and a 2σ range of 2540 to 2780 kg/m^3. Although these numbers show that the exact choice of a minimum density is somewhat arbitrary, we chose a minimum allowable density of 2550 kg/m^3, just within the 2σ interval. This value corresponds to a minimum allowable apparent density contrast of -120 kg/m^3 for basement rocks in this study.

The basement rocks of the study area can be broken down by density contrast into four general categories for discussion purposes. These categories are granitic rocks with nearly zero apparent density contrast (or rocks ~2670 kg/m^3 in density), rocks with positive apparent density contrast representing more mafic lithologies and mixed-unit lithologies (Whitmarsh, personal commun. 2001), granitic rocks with a slightly negative apparent density contrast (about -40 to -80 kg/m^3), and finally rocks with strong negative contrasts of -100 to -120 kg/m^3. This latter group probably represents units of leucogranitic lithology.

The apparent density contrast of the rocks cropping out in the Sierra Nevada proper vary considerably from about zero to

a minimum of -120 kg/m^3 in the northern end of the study area, (Fig. 6). In this part of the range, we modeled no large masses with positive density contrasts. The apparent contrasts in the range fall into five bands. From north to south, the contrasts associated with these bands (Fig. 6) are -120, 0, -70, -40, and 0 kg/m^3, respectively.

East of the Sierra Nevada, especially at several kilometers depth, rocks with density contrasts near zero apparently dominate. Almost the entire northern end of the study area consists of these rocks at depths of several kilometers and below.

South of the Garlock fault, most of the exposed basement rocks apparently have negative density contrasts. The western and eastern areas of low-density mass have contrasts of -50 kg/m^3 and -80 kg/m^3, respectively. Conversely, south of the Garlock fault, virtually all of the basement under the basins appears to be denser, having a density contrast near zero. Again, this result may be due to local effects of the basin density function.

Within the area of the Indian Wells Valley, the basement rocks appear to also have contrasts near zero, except in two small areas where the contrast is positive. These are probably areas where upthrown basement blocks represent local highs.

East and northeast of the Indian Wells Valley in the Argus Range, a large area of exposed basement occurs with a positive density contrast. Because of the method used to construct the model, this area was represented as a single unit with sharp boundaries. From the appearance of the observed anomaly data, however, the boundary may be more gradational. The area surrounding the Argus Range also has relatively high basement densities. The density contrasts in the Panamint Range are also apparently positive.

One of the most striking features of the entire model is the apparently continuous band of basement rocks with negative density contrasts running southeastward from the northern part of the Sierras in the study area, across the Coso Range, into the Argus and Slate Ranges. The density contrasts become less negative to the southeast and seem to occur in a rather block-like manner (although this too could be an artifact of the modeling procedure). The contrast has a value of -120 kg/m^3 in the Sierran block, -80 kg/m^3 in the Coso block, and about -50 kg/m^3 in the eastern part of the area. Overall, however, the feature seems to represent a fairly continuous band of relatively low density basement that cuts across all of the basins and ranges of the model area.

Across the entire southern boundary of this feature there is a consistent rise in apparent density contrast of ~100 kg/m^3. Where the apparent density contrast in the low-density belt is -120 kg/m^3, the density south of the boundary is zero, and where the contrast in the belt is -50 kg/m^3, the contrast south of the boundary rises to $+50$ kg/m^3.

This large basement density-contrast boundary can be clearly seen in cross section (Fig. 8). Along cross section A-A' (Fig. 8), the boundary is obviously the primary feature in the section, even though this is in an area where the lateral contrast

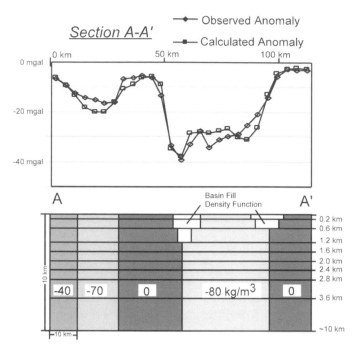

Figure 8. Comparison of the observed and calculated gravity anomaly along cross section A-A' (location shown in Fig. 7). This section crosses the boundary between the denser crust in the middle of the model and the band of lower-density crust shown on Figures 6 and 9. Note that although the boundaries between crustal blocks are nearly vertical on this particular cross section (and are plotted schematically as vertical), the density boundaries, in general, are not vertical in other areas of the three-dimensional volume.

variation is only 80 kg/m³. Note that along this cross section, the boundary is near vertical. On other cross sections, it is more irregular.

There are several small, very low density intrusive features included in the model, placed there to explain some short-wavelength feature in the field. Some are only included in one or two thin layers. There are two features that are of some significance to the overall interpretation of the model, however. There are two small, low-density bodies in the area of the El Paso Mountains, along the Garlock fault. One of these bodies is probably an intrusion, and the other low-density area is over a section of older sedimentary rocks. At depth, the second low-density area was modeled as a single body of −100 kg/m³ to a depth of 2 km. The area along the Garlock fault was difficult to model, has more error than most areas of the model, and is highly simplified. There are probably multiple low-density bodies in this area that more detailed field surveys and modeling might resolve.

The most interesting of the small, low-density intrusions occur at the north end of the Indian Wells Valley, at the boundary between the valley and the volcanic field. One low-density body was modeled as occurring at depths of ∼0.6 km to 1.6 km, but the bull's-eye anomaly associated with the other body is so high in negative amplitude that the body was modeled as

extending from ∼0.6 km to the base of the model (Fig. 6). A negative anomaly of this amplitude (Fig. 7) could be caused by a deep basin buried by the volcanic rocks, a crustal-scale feature, or a localized high in the mantle. An upper-mantle anomaly would probably be broader in wavelength and would probably be removed by the isostatic correction. A basin probably would have been detected by drilling in the Coso volcanic field. Thus, the anomaly is probably a basement feature, such as a low-density intrusion or a melt zone. At any rate, the data available for this study are not detailed enough to determine the source of this apparent anomaly. Detailed microgravity and microseismic investigations are currently being undertaken in this area in association with geothermal exploration and ongoing tectonic studies (Monastero et al., this volume). These studies will provide much more information for interpretations at the scale of this apparent anomaly.

DISCUSSION

Implications of the isostatic model

Several different isostatic models are available for use in isostatic gravity and residual calculations. The models all assume that negatively compensating masses occur immediately beneath high topography (Dobrin and Savit, 1988). In mountainous areas, it is commonly assumed that the compensating mass is directly below the average Moho depth in the surrounding area, either occurring as an extended lower-crustal root or an upper-mantle density low.

Recent studies indicate that this model may not be the appropriate one for some areas (Fliedner et al., 1996). Deep seismic studies in an area immediately north of the study area (Fliedner et al., 1996) indicate that, although there may be crustal thickening beneath the western Sierras, in the eastern Sierras, compensation probably occurs within the upper mantle. Results of mantle-xenolith studies in the same area appear to be consistent with this interpretation (Ducea and Saleeby, 1996).

In utilizing the isostatic model, only two parameters control the calculations: the crust-mantle density contrast and the compensation depth. The compensation depth is simply the depth to Moho where the surface elevation is equal to sea level. The density contrast and compensation depth are usually assumed to be 350 to 400 kg/m³ and 25 or 30 km (in the western United States), respectively (Roberts et al., 1981; Simpson et al., 1986; Oliver, 1986; Jachens et al., 1989; Saltus and Jachens, 1995). The associated crustal density is the standard constant 2670 kg/m³. Although there is no real standard for this compensation depth, more recent efforts have used an Airy-Heiskanen model with a 30 km compensation depth (Simpson et al., 1986; Jachens et al., 1989; Saltus and Jachens, 1995).

Simpson et al. (1986) emphasized that the correction was not very sensitive to the compensation model. The 25 km correction was also used by Oliver (1986) in his comparative work between actual surface density measurements and isostatic residual anomalies over Sierran rocks.

Regional tectonic implications

There appear to be three major features that stand out in the density-contrast model (Fig. 6). Two of these are partially controlled by two major tectonic boundaries. These are the eastern boundary of the Sierra Nevada and the Garlock fault. The other major feature is the northwest-trending density low that extends across the Sierran front and crosses several of the basins and ranges in the area (Fig. 9).

Much of the basement exposed throughout the Indian Wells Valley area also has a structural, lithologic, or tectonic anisotropy imposed on it. On the scale of tens of meters to kilometers, there are faults and dike swarms that define a northwest-

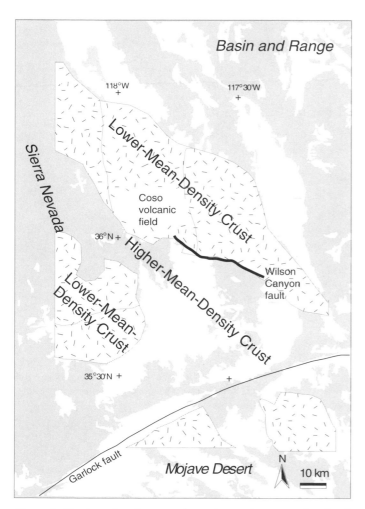

Figure 9. The boundary between the major northwest-trending band of lower-mean-density crust and the denser crust to the south occurs very close to the Wilson Canyon fault and other hypothesized features (such as a mantle chemistry boundary). The location of rhyolitic magmatism associated with the Coso volcanic field appears to be isolated within the lower-density block.

southeast anisotropy in the basement (Whitmarsh, 2001, personal commun.). There also appears, from the density distribution, to be such an anisotropy in the basement at a scale of tens of kilometers.

The southern boundary of the main low-density band cutting through the study area appears to run along the Wilson Canyon fault. Also occurring along this boundary is the small isolated gravity low in the eastern margin of the Coso Range that can be explained by a deep intrusion or melt zone, or an anomaly in the upper mantle not accounted for in the Airy corrections performed on the data. This anomaly occurs at the apparent intersection of this density boundary and the Sierran front and is associated with the occurrence of the bimodal volcanism in the area. The density boundary thus represents a local area of magmatic communication between the Earth's surface and the mantle.

Although obviously not a tectonic boundary of as much regional importance as the Sierran front or the Garlock fault, it appears, from the density-contrast model developed here, that the southern margin of the low-density crustal band may also be a crustal-block boundary at a more local scale.

CONCLUSIONS

In our modeling work, an effort was made to utilize published procedures in order to compare results with other investigations. We used the isostatic regional field (Simpson et al., 1986) as the regional correction, and a density-depth profile for basin deposits (Jachens and Moring, 1990).

At this point, it is difficult to know whether the Airy root model is still the appropriate isostatic model for use in this type of study. A sensitivity analysis needs to be run on the different types of models to see if there are significant differences in the regional field predicted for this specific area. These differences should, of course, be long in wavelength. Such an analysis, in combination with the emerging findings of the Sierran Crustal Dynamics Group (Fliedner et al., 1996; Ruppert et al., 1998) and other similar projects, may point to the use of an alternative model. The use of the basin density versus depth function was a great help as a standard in this study. The results of the forward modeling shown here indicate that this function either slightly overestimates basin depth (i.e., Owens Valley) or slightly underestimates the negative anomaly for an area where basin depth is known (i.e., the Indian Wells Valley). Part of this problem could also be the blocky nature of the model. Despite these concerns, our model fits our constraints well in most areas. However, in future work in the region, it is recommended that this function be appropriately modified, especially for more localized projects.

In this study, use of this function probably did not really affect the general results of the basement-density interpretation because much of the significant variation was interpreted to occur in areas of basement outcrop. From the combined gravity modeling, it is apparent that the study area consists of several distinct blocks with different average densities (Figs. 8, 9). The boundaries between these blocks can either be sharp or transitional, but most are fairly sharp and apparently represent crustal-scale features.

The Sierran block consists of bands of alternating lower- and higher-density granitic bodies along the western edge of the study area. The boundary between the Sierran block and the areas undergoing Basin and Range-style extension changes in character along strike. The gravity data were modeled with a fairly sharp density boundary along the Sierran front. However, because of the nonuniqueness of the modeling and because of the gradational transition due to the presence of the basin, the data would probably allow the density boundary to be placed farther east, below the Indian Wells Valley.

North of the Indian Wells Valley is the northwest-trending area of basement rocks with apparent density contrasts ranging from -50 to -120 kg/m^3. Across the southern boundary of this zone, there is a consistent rise in apparent density of ~ 100 kg/m^3. This may be enough of a density contrast to explain why the rhyolitic volcanic rocks are spatially associated with this boundary. If the hypothesis of Glazner and Ussler (1989) is correct, then areas of relatively lower crustal density favor the formation and eruption of rhyolitic magmas because of buoyancy considerations (Fig. 10). The intersection of this low-density zone with the Sierran front is then an optimal area for rhyolitic magma generation and may have played some role in controlling the location of the Coso volcanic field.

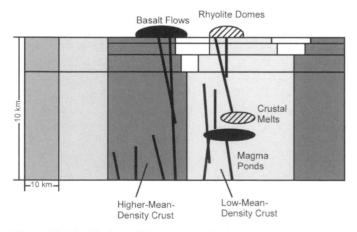

Figure 10. Model of possible scenario for the isolation of the Coso rhyolites within the lower-density crustal block. Mantle-derived mafic magmas have more positive buoyancy within the denser block and are more likely to break the surface, whereas magmas in the lower-density block will have a greater tendency to pond within the middle to upper crust and thus generate rhyolitic magmas. The geothermal resources associated with the Coso area are directly related to the location of the rhyolitic centers.

ACKNOWLEDGMENTS

This project was undertaken with the financial support of the Geothermal Program Office of the Navy (GPO), China Lake, California. We thank Frank Monastero and Allan Katzenstein of the GPO and Allen Glazner of University of North Carolina for helpful discussions concerning the geology and geophysics of the area. Detailed reviews by Richard Blakely and Allan Katzenstein greatly improved the manuscript. We would also like to thank Jon Linn and Chris Schmeissner for use of their computing expertise.

REFERENCES CITED

Allmendinger, R.W., Hauge, T.A., Hauser, E.C., Potter, C.J., Klemperer, S.L., Nelson, K.D., Knuepfer, P.L.K., and Oliver, J., 1987, Overview of the COCORP 40° transect, western United States; the fabric of an orogenic belt: Geological Society of America Bulletin, v. 98, p. 308–319.

Bhattacharyya, J., Gross, S., Lees, J.M., and Hasting, M., 1999, Recent earthquake sequences at Coso; Evidence for conjugate faulting and stress loading near a geothermal field: Seismological Society of America Bulletin, v. 89; no. 3, p. 785–795.

Blakely, R.J., 1995, Potential theory in gravity and magnetic applications: Cambridge, Cambridge University Press, 441 p.

Carmichael, R.S., 1989, Practical handbook of physical properties of rocks and minerals: Boca Raton, Florida, CRC Press, Inc., 741 p.

Cheadle, M.J., Czuchra, B.L, Byrne, T., Ando, C.J., Oliver, J.E., Brown, L.D., Kaufman, S., Malin, P.E., and Phinney, R.A., 1986, The deep crustal structure of the Mojave Desert, California, from COCORP seismic reflection data: Tectonics, v. 5, p. 293–330.

Dobrin, M.B., and Savit, C.H., 1988, Introduction to geophysical prospecting, 4th ed.: New York, McGraw-Hill Book Company, 867 p.

Ducea, M.N., and Saleeby, J.B., 1996, Buoyancy sources for a large, unrooted mountain range, the Sierra Nevada, California: Evidence from xenolith thermobarometry: Journal of Geophysical Research, v. 101, p. 8229–8244.

Duffield, W.A., and Bacon, C.R., 1981, Geologic map of the Coso volcanic field and adjacent areas, Inyo County, California: U.S. Geological Survey Miscellaneous Investigation Series Map I-1200, 1 sheet, scale 1:50000.

Eaton, J.P., 1963, Crustal structure from San Francisco, California, to Eureka, Nevada, from seismic-refraction measurements: Journal of Geophysical Research, v. 68. p. 5789–5806.

Fliedner, M.M., Ruppert, S.D., Malin, P.E., Park.S-K., Jiracek, G.R., Phinney, R.A., Saleeby, J.B., Wernicke, B.P., Clayton, R.W., Keller, G.R., Miller, K.C., Jones, C.H., Luetgert, J.H., Mooney, W.D., Oliver, H.L., Klemperer, S.L., and Thompson, G.A.,1996, Three-dimensional crustal structure of the southern Sierra Nevada from seismic fan profiles and gravity modeling: Geology, v. 24, p. 367–370.

Glazner, A.F., and Miller, D.M., 1997, Late-stage sinking of plutons: Geology, v. 25, p. 1099–1102.

Glazner, A.F., and Ussler, W.U., III, 1989, Crustal extension, crustal density, and the evolution of Cenozoic magmatism in the Basin and Range of the western United States: Journal of Geophysical Research, v. 94, p. 7952–7960.

Hammer, S., 1939, Terrain corrections for gravimeter stations: Geophysics, v. 4, p. 184–194.

Jachens, R.C., and Moring, B.C., 1990, Maps of the thickness of Cenozoic deposits and the isostatic residual gravity over basement for Nevada: U.S. Geological Survey Open-File Report 90-404, 15 p.

Jachens, R.C., Simpson, R.W., Blakely, R.J., and Saltus, R.W., 1989, Isostatic residual gravity and crustal geology of the United States, *in* Pakiser, L.C., and Mooney, W.D., eds., Geophysical framework of the continental United States: Geological Society of America Memoir 172, p. 405–424.

Jennings, C.W., Burnett, J.L., and Troxel, B.W., 1962, Geologic map of California, Trona Sheet: California Division of Mines and Geology, scale 1:250 000.

Kane, M.F., and Pakiser, L.C., 1961, Geophysical study of subsurface structure in southern Owens Valley, California: Geophysics, v. 26, p. 12–26.

Klemperer, S.L., Hauge, T.A., Hauser, E.C., Oliver, J.E., and Potter, C.J., 1986, The Moho in the norhern Basin and Range province, Nevada, along the COCORP 40°N seismic reflection transect: Geological Society of America Bulletin, v. 97, p. 603–618.

National Geophysical Data Center, 1994, Gravity, 1994 edition CD-ROM users manual: National Geophysical Data Center and National Ocean Service, 37 p.

Oliver, H.W., 1986, Specific gravity vs. gravity—central Sierra Nevada, California, Eos (Transactions, American Geophysical Union), v. 67, p. 1212.

Roberts, C.W., Jachens, R.C., and Oliver, H.W., 1981, Preliminary isostatic residual gravity maps of California: U.S. Geological Survey Open File Report 81–573, scale 1:750 000.

Ruppert, S., Fliedner, M.M., and Zandt, G., 1998, Thin crust and active upper mantle beneath the southern Sierra Nevada in the western United States: Tectonophysics, v. 286, p. 237–252.

Saltus, R.W., and Jachens, R.C., 1995, Gravity and basin-depth maps of the Basin and Range province, western United States: U.S. Geological Survey Map GP-1012, scale 1:2 500 000.

Serpa, L., de-Voogd, B., Wright, L., Willemin, J., Oliver, J., Hauser, E., and Troxel, B.W., 1988, Structure of the Death Valley pull-apart basin and vicinity from COCORP profiles in the southern Great Basin: Geological Society of America Bulletin, v. 100, p. 1437–1450.

Simpson, R.W., Jachens, R.C., Blakely, R.J., and Saltus, R.W., 1986, A new isostatic residual gravity map of the conterminous United States with a discussion on the significance of isostatic residual anomalies: Journal of Geophysical Research, v. 91, p. 8348–8372.

Stevens, C.H., Stone, P., Dunne, G.C., Greene, D.C., Walker, J.D., and Swanson, B.J., 1997, Paleozoic and Mesozoic evolution of east-central California: International Geology Review, v. 39, p. 788–829.

Stritz, R., and Stinson, M.C., 1974, Geologic map of California, Death Valley sheet: California Division of Mines and Geology, scale 1:250 000.

Thompson, G.A., Catchings, R.D., Goodwin, E.B., Holbrook, S., Jarchow, C.M., Mann, C.E., McCarthy, J., and Okaya, D.A., 1989, Geophysics of the western Basin and Range province, *in* Pakiser, L.C., and Mooney, W.D., eds., Geophysical framework of the continental United States: Geological Society of America Memoir 172, p. 177–205.

Wu, H., and Lees, J.M., 1999, Three-dimensional P- and S-wave velocity structures of the Coso geothermal area, California, from microseismic traveltime data: Journal of Geophysical Research, v. 104; p. 13 217–13 233.

MANUSCRIPT ACCEPTED BY THE SOCIETY MAY 9, 2001

Geological Society of America
Memoir 195
2002

Seismicity and seismic stress in the Coso Range, Coso geothermal field, and Indian Wells Valley region, southeast-central California

Joydeep Bhattacharyya
Center for Monitoring Research, 1300 N. 17th Street, Suite 1450, Arlington, VA 22209, USA
Jonathan M. Lees
Department of Geological Sciences, University of North Carolina–Chapel Hill, Chapel Hill, North Carolina 27599, USA

ABSTRACT

The temporal and spatial distribution of seismicity in the Coso Range, the Coso geothermal field, and the Indian Wells Valley region of southeast-central California are discussed in this paper. An analysis of fault-related seismicity in the region led us to conclude that the Little Lake fault and the Airport Lake fault are the most significant seismogenic zones. The faulting pattern clearly demarcates the region as a transition between the San Andreas-type strike-slip regime to the west and the Basin and Range extension regime to the east. We present the spatial and temporal variations in seismicity immediately following significant earthquakes in nearby regions from 1983 to 1999 with special emphasis on larger earthquakes (M ≥ 5) in 1995–1998. The Ridgecrest earthquakes of 1995 show a complicated faulting pattern as the rupture changed from normal slip to right slip at depth. The interrelationships between the Coso Range earthquakes of 1996 and 1998 are presented as a set of conjugate events. Analysis of earthquake source mechanisms shows evidence for lateral variations in the faulting pattern in southeast-central California. Earthquake focal mechanisms are used to estimate local stress orientation within the Coso geothermal field. We have identified a boundary between a transpressional regime and a transtensional regime inside the field that correlates with observed spatial variations of heat flow and seismic attenuation, velocity, and anisotropy.

INTRODUCTION

The Coso Range, the Coso geothermal field, and the Indian Wells Valley region—one of the most seismically active regions of California—lies in southeast-central California. The region lies at the southwesternmost corner of the central Basin and Range geologic province of western United States (Fig. 1). The locations of the earthquakes, the spatial and temporal patterns of seismicity, and the earthquake source mechanisms are important tools for modeling the tectonics of this area. In this study, we use a large data set of earthquakes recorded between 1960 and 1999 to characterize the seismotectonics of the Coso

Range, the Coso geothermal field, and the Indian Wells Valley. Tectonically, the Coso Range region is located at the transition from the extensional Basin and Range province to the strike-slip San Andreas fault system (Roquemore, 1980). North- to north-northeast–striking normal faults are dominant in the Coso Range (Duffield et al., 1980). Faulting is extensive in this region and includes two nearly perpendicular sets of normal faults that strike north-northeast and west-northwest (Roquemore, 1980).

The most seismically active region in our study area is the volcanic-geothermal field near Coso. The Coso geothermal field is situated in granitic Mesozoic basement rocks below silicic domes (Duffield and Bacon, 1981; Duffield et al., 1980). Pre-

Bhattacharyya, J., and Lees, J.M., 2002, Seismicity and seismic stress in the Coso Range, Coso geothermal field, and Indian Wells Valley region, southeast-central California, *in* Glazner, A.F., Walker, J.D., and Bartley, J.M., eds., Geologic Evolution of the Mojave Desert and Southwestern Basin and Range: Boulder, Colorado, Geological Society of America Memoir 195, p. 243–257.

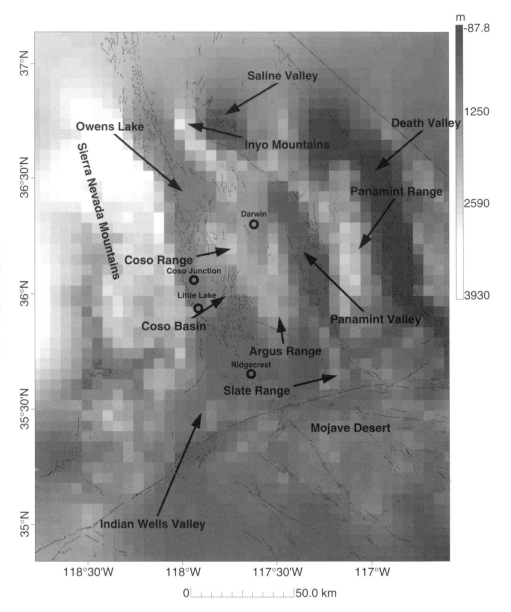

Figure 1. Map of the Coso Range, Indian Wells Valley, and adjacent regions of southeast-central California. We show the topography of this region (in meters) along with the surface mapped faults (black lines), as given by Jennings (1994). The mountain ranges, valleys, and the towns of Darwin, Little Lake, and Ridgecrest are also indicated in this map.

vious seismic studies of the Coso Range region using teleseismic traveltime residuals identified a low-velocity body in the mid-crust (below 5 km) southeast of the geothermal field (Reasenberg et al., 1980), which correlates with a high-attenuation anomaly (Sanders et al., 1988; Wu and Lees, 1996; Young and Ward, 1980). A silicic magma body, ~5 km in diameter and 1 km thick, probably partially molten, is predicted to lie at depths of >8 km under the Coso geothermal field (Bacon et al., 1980).

In this paper, we first identify the primary mapped faults in the study region and discuss the seismicity. We then describe the source mechanism and aftershock patterns of relatively large earthquakes that occurred in the region from 1995 to 1999. This description is followed by an analysis of spatial and temporal variations of present-day seismicity. Analysis of the source mechanisms of the earthquakes in this region allowed

us to map spatial variations of faulting pattern and also to investigate stress loading inside the Coso geothermal field due to large nearby earthquakes. The earthquake data sets used in the study were obtained from the microearthquake (MEQ) network located inside the Coso geothermal field (Alvarez, 1992), the Southern California Earthquake Center (SCEC), and the Northern California Earthquake Center (NCEC).

SEISMOTECTONIC SETTING

The seismotectonics of the Indian Wells Valley and the Coso Range primarily reflect the complex interaction of strike-slip faulting (San Andreas type) and extensional faulting (Basin and Range type). Fault-related seismicity is diminished inside the geothermal complex in the Coso volcanic field. Before analyzing the seismicity within the Coso Range and the Indian Wells Valley, we first describe the nature and geometry of the significant faults in the region.

Indian Wells Valley

Tectonic and volcanic activity during the past 3 m.y. shaped much of the geomorphic and geologic character of the Indian Wells Valley. The region has been affected by several major faults such as the Garlock fault, the Sierra Nevada frontal fault system, and the Panamint Valley fault, which delineate the southern, western, and eastern boundaries of this region, respectively (Fig. 2). The Death Valley–Furnace Creek fault system is ~160 km east of this region. In addition to these faults, the Indian Wells Valley contains a number of north-striking

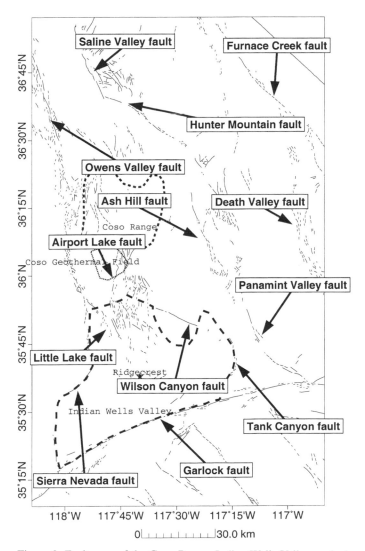

Figure 2. Fault map of the Coso Range, Indian Wells Valley, and adjacent regions (after Jennings, 1994). We have highlighted the significant faults of the region. The M = 8.0 Owens Valley earthquake was located at the intersection of the Little Lake fault and the Sierra Nevada fault.

faults (e.g., Little Lake fault, Airport Lake fault, Ash Hill fault); these consist of small fault segments mostly less than 10 km long (Fig. 2). The segments primarily trend north to northwest with a smaller number striking northeast. The faults merge in the north with the Sierra Nevada frontal fault near the rupture zone of the 1872 Owens Valley earthquake (Whitney, 1872). Southward, the segments form a broad zone of faulting truncated by the Garlock fault.

The Little Lake and the Airport Lake fault zones are the major active faults in the Indian Wells Valley (Fig. 2; Roquemore and Zellmer, 1983a). The Little Lake fault and Airport Lake fault were both formed by the regional tectonic stress field of the western Basin and Range province, i.e., right-slip shear and east-west extension. The pattern of faulting, though, differs between the Little Lake fault and the Airport Lake fault. The Little Lake fault shows predominantly right slip with a slight normal-slip component toward the central and the southern parts. On the other hand, the Airport Lake fault accommodates predominantly normal slip (Roquemore and Zellmer, 1983b).

The Little Lake fault strikes southeast from the Sierra Nevada fault diagonally across the Indian Wells Valley (Figs. 1 and 2) and is truncated at the Garlock fault. Slip rate along this fault is estimated at ~1.5 mm/yr (Roquemore, 1988; Simon McCluskey, 1988, personal commun.). Near the intersection with the Sierra Nevada fault, the Little Lake fault has a dextral slip rate of ~0.6 mm/yr (Roquemore, 1981). Farther south along the Little Lake fault, the dominant motion becomes right-normal oblique. The right-slip component led Zellmer (1988) to suggest that the Little Lake fault may accommodate a major part of the right-slip motion of the Sierra Nevada fault in the Indian Wells Valley area.

The Airport Lake fault strikes north through the Indian Wells Valley and Coso Range. Southward, where the Airport Lake fault extends into the Indian Wells Valley, the fault zone consists of highly fragmented fault segments (Hart et al., 1989; Jennings, 1994). The Little Lake fault and the Airport Lake fault intersect in the Indian Wells Valley north of Ridgecrest (Fig. 2) in a zone characterized by high levels of seismicity and changes in the surface expression of the faults. This zone has been the focus of several studies (Hauksson et al., 1995; Roquemore and Zellmer, 1983b). Seismic tomographic studies of this zone by Sanders et al. (1988) indicated that it is underlain by a volume having very strong S-wave attenuation at a depth of ~3.0 km. Comparison with surface deformation and seismicity patterns suggests a recent intrusion of a dike (Roquemore, 1987). From a study of surface geologic features, Roquemore and Zellmer (1983a, 1983b) suggested that regional extension associated with the Airport Lake fault is transferred to the Little Lake fault as right-slip displacement within this zone of intersection.

Coso Range

The Coso Range lies at the transition between right-slip deformation across the San Andreas fault system and the extensional regime of the Basin and Range. Recent folding and faulting show evidence of the characteristics of each of these provinces (Roquemore, 1980). Alternatively, the ring and arcuate faults in the Coso Range area have been explained in terms of caldera subsidence (Duffield, 1975). A recent study suggests that right-lateral shear is important to the fault structure of the Coso Range (Whitmarsh and Walker, 1996). Current strain accumulation in the Coso Range is modeled by north-striking right-lateral oblique-slip extensional faults (Roquemore et al., 1996). Present-day tectonic movements are expressed by widespread microearthquakes in the region (Walter and Weaver, 1980) though surface expressions of active faults are generally not observed (Roquemore and Simila, 1994).

Eastern California shear zone

The Coso Range, the Coso geothermal field, and the Indian Wells Valley lie within the Eastern California shear zone (Dokka and Travis, 1990a; Jones and Helmberger, 1998; Savage et al., 1990). The Eastern California shear zone extends ~500 km north-northwest from the San Andreas fault, through the Mojave Desert region, and beyond into Owens Valley and Death Valley. The Eastern California shear zone transfers a part of the relative motion between the North American and Pacific plates away from the San Andreas fault to the western Great Basin province (Dokka and Travis, 1990b). Individual faults within the region have slip rates of less than 1.0 mm/yr (Dokka, 1983). However, the total shear-displacement rate across the region from geologic and geodetic data is ~8.0 mm/yr (Dokka and Travis, 1990b; Savage et al., 1990). The Eastern California shear zone mainly consists of northwest-striking right-slip faults. The main earthquakes in the Eastern California shear zone include the 1992 M = 7.2 Landers earthquake and the 1872 M = 8.0 Owens Valley earthquake; they lie outside the region analyzed in this paper.

CHARACTERISTIC SEISMICITY

The Coso Range and Indian Wells Valley have a long history of earthquake swarms related to both tectonic and geothermal activity. Most of the earthquakes in the area are relatively small, i.e., M < 3.0. Large earthquakes (M > 4.9), although rare, have been recorded approximately every 20 years in this region until 1995—i.e., in 1938, 1961, 1982, and 1995 (Hauksson et al., 1995). The 1938 (M = 5.0; 9/17/38), 1961 (M = 5.2; 10/19/61), and 1982 sequences were on the Little Lake fault (Roquemore et al., 1996). The 1995 event occurred within the Airport Lake fault. This recurrence pattern may have been terminated by the occurrence of four M ≥ 5.0 earthquakes in this region between 1995 and 1998 (Bhattacharyya et al., 1999; Hauksson et al., 1995; Roquemore et al., 1996).

We divided the Coso Range–Indian Wells Valley region into several subregions (Fig. 3), for reasons described subsequently. The Coso Range is demarcated on the basis of the

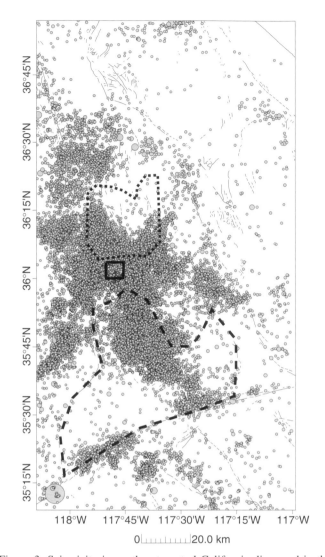

Figure 3. Seismicity in southeast-central California discussed in this paper. The seismicity of the Indian Wells Valley, the Coso Range, and the Coso geothermal field are discussed separately in the text. These regions are indicated by polygons. The faults given by Jennings (1994) are also shown.

definition of Duffield et al. (1980) except that we removed the geothermal field from the delineated area. Following Lees (this volume), we defined the Coso geothermal field area as a box between lat 36.001°N and 36.059°N and between long 117.753°W and 117.834°W. The distinction between the Coso Range and the Coso geothermal field is made because of the difference in the earthquake sources that affect these regions. The seismicity in the Coso Range is due to rupture along mapped faults (Roquemore, 1987), but earthquakes in the Coso geothermal field are also due to the injection and production of geothermal fluids (Malin, 1994) and geothermal activity (Feng and Lees, 1998; Roquemore, 1987; Walter and Weaver, 1980). The boundaries of the Indian Wells Valley are based on those of Duffield et al. (1980).

Coso Range

Seismicity in the Coso Range (Fig. 3) primarily consists of microearthquakes (Combs, 1980; Feng and Lees, 1998; Malin, 1994). Prior to 1996, recorded earthquakes with magnitudes greater than 5.0 have occurred only on the periphery of the Coso Range. Among the largest of these earthquakes was the 1946 Walker Pass earthquake (M = 6.3). However, earthquake sequences with main-shock magnitudes greater than 5.0 occurred in the Coso Range in 1996 and 1998 (Bhattacharyya et al., 1999). We discuss these earthquakes subsequently in this paper.

Most of the earthquakes inside the Coso Range have been located toward the southern end of the region (Fig. 3). A detailed analysis of the spatial distribution of earthquakes indicates several sequences. From 1981 to 1984, most of the seismicity was concentrated toward the southwestern end of the Coso Range. The same region was reactivated in 1988 following the 10/13/88 M5.4 Nevada earthquake. In Figure 4, we plot the variation of seismicity and earthquake magnitudes with time. We show the cumulative distribution of earthquake size as given by 10^M where M is the SCEC-provided magnitude of the earthquake (Fig. 4A). We use this measure as a rough estimate of seismic moment release. We observe that the monotonically increasing curve has several rapid increases ("jumps") immediately after the occurrence of large nearby earthquakes. In 1992, an increase of seismicity in the Coso Range was probably caused by seismic triggering due to the Landers event (6/28/92), which had a magnitude of M = 7.5 (Roquemore and Simila, 1994). Following the Eureka Valley earthquake of 5/27/93 (M = 6.1), there was a significant increase in seismicity in the Coso Range (Fig. 4). This seismicity was mostly located in the south-central part of the range (Fig. 3). The Coso Range earthquakes of 1996 and 1998 caused a distinct increase in seismicity in the region, as shown in Figure 4. The increased seismicity was mostly concentrated on the eastern side of the range. An interesting feature of the seismicity "jumps" is that the 1996 event caused a larger increase in seismicity, probably due to a larger source size. We observe a small increase in seismicity corresponding to the occurrence of the M = 6.4 Chalfant Valley earthquake on 7/21/86. The b-value (the slope of log(N) versus magnitude M, where N = number of earthquakes with magnitude M or less) of earthquakes within the Coso Range is 2.4.

Indian Wells Valley

There are very few large earthquakes in the Indian Wells Valley. Before 1995, the largest recorded earthquake to occur in the Indian Wells Valley itself was the M = 5.2 event in 1982 (Hauksson et al., 1995; Roquemore and Zellmer, 1983a). Prior to this event, several earthquake swarms were observed beginning during April 1981. Earthquakes with magnitudes between 4 and 5 initiated swarms (i.e., the swarms are possibly aftershocks) that lasted for more than 1 yr. The swarms were located along the intersection of the Little Lake and Airport Lake fault zones. With each successive sequence, the total number and maximum magnitude of earthquakes in each swarm increased as they migrated southward (Hauksson et al., 1995; Roquemore and Zellmer, 1983a). The 1982 event caused a large swarm in the central part of the valley.

Figure 5 shows the distribution of the magnitudes of the earthquakes in the Indian Wells Valley as a function of time. We observe that there are two "jumps" in seismicity in this region coinciding with significant regional events. The epicenters of the earthquake triggered by the Landers event trend north-northwest across the south-central part of the valley. Seismic activity following the Ridgecrest events was located close to the main-shock zone, which lies just north of the town of Ridgecrest. We do not see any evidence for increase in seismic activity in the Indian Wells Valley due to the Coso Range events of 1996 and 1998. The b-value for earthquakes within the Indian Wells Valley is 2.1 (Fig. 5C).

The Sierra Nevada fault marks the western edge of both the Coso Range and the Indian Wells Valley (Fig. 2). The southern end of the Sierra Nevada fault undergoes a bend between lat 35.25°N and lat 35.75°N; the seismicity drops drastically immediately south of this bend. From north to south, we observe a distinct increase in seismicity peaking in the region where the Sierra Nevada fault meets the Little Lake fault. In the northern part of the Sierra Nevada fault, we observe that seismicity is uniform with depth though a distinct decrease in seismicity can be seen in a 10-km-long region beginning just south of the town of Little Lake. The decrease in seismicity probably indicates a fundamental tectonic boundary south of the intersection of the Sierra Nevada fault with the Little Lake fault. The Little Lake fault is the most seismically active fault in the Indian Wells Valley region. Seismicity along this fault extends to 20 km depth. As seen in Figure 3, the intersection of the Little Lake fault and the Airport Lake fault is a region of intense seismicity, and relatively large earthquakes have been observed here (Hauksson et al., 1995). South of this region, i.e., between the junction of the Little Lake fault with the Airport Lake fault and the Garlock fault, we observe a noticeable drop in seismicity (Fig. 5). This drop in seismicity within a region that has a high seismicity rate may indicate a region of seismic quiescence and needs further analysis. Along the Airport Lake fault, seismicity is found to be uniform from the surface to a depth of 10 km.

The Coso geothermal field

Seismicity in the Coso geothermal field is controlled by the motion of geothermal fluids and the release of local tectonic stress (Feng and Lees, 1998; Fialko and Simons, 2000; Malin and Erskine, 1990; Walter and Weaver, 1980). The distribution and pattern of seismicity inside the field is described in detail in Feng and Lees (1998). We present the longer-term trends (1983–1999) in seismicity and the effect of nearby large earth-

Figure 4. Seismicity distribution and recurrence rate in the Coso Range. (A) Cumulative magnitude vs. time for 1983–1999. We calculate the magnitude as 10^M, where M is the magnitude of an earthquake as reported by Southern California Earthquake Center. We use this measure as a proxy for moment release during each earthquake. The large earthquakes of the region, i.e., Rose Valley (2/19/92), Joshua Tree (4/22/92), Landers (6/28/92), Eureka Valley (5/27/93), $M = 5.4$ at Ridgecrest (8/17/95), $M = 5.8$ at Ridgecrest (9/20/95), Coso1 (11/27/96), and Coso2 (3/6/98), are indicated. We observe evidence for seismic triggering of the Landers, Eureka Valley, and the Coso1 earthquakes. (B) Distribution of earthquake magnitudes vs. time in the Coso Range. The increases in cumulative magnitudes in 1985 and 1988 are due to occurrence of $M > 4.0$ earthquakes in this region but cannot be associated with any significant ($M \geq 5$) nearby earthquake. (C) Temporal distribution of earthquake magnitudes. We show the linear fit for the b-value calculation for this region. The b-value is calculated by using earthquakes with magnitudes ≥ 1.0 because the linear trend is not consistent below this magnitude, probably because of catalogue incompleteness at lower magnitudes. The b-value is slightly higher than what we observed at Indian Wells Valley.

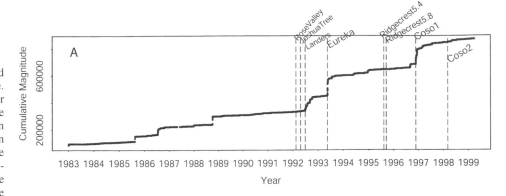

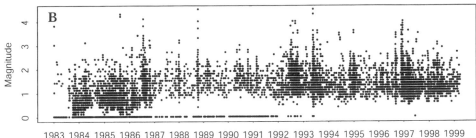

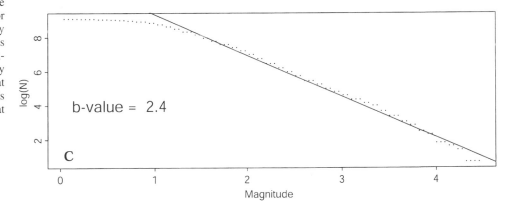

quakes. Seismicity inside the central geothermal area occurs in tight clusters inside a cylindrical region (Feng and Lees, 1998; Simila and Roquemore, 1987). Present-day daily average seismicity within the Coso geothermal field (Fig. 3) is ~22 events for earthquakes with the magnitude range $M = -2.0$ to 5.3 (as recorded by the MEQ network) (Bhattacharyya et al., 1999). Figure 6 shows the distribution of magnitude and cumulative magnitude inside the Coso geothermal field. In the cumulative distribution, the most prominent "jumps" follow the Ridgecrest events and the Coso Range events. We find that the increase in seismicity following the 1998 Coso Range earthquake is significantly larger than that following the 1996 Coso Range event. Main shocks for both of these events have nearly similar mag-

nitudes and lie approximately the same distance from the Coso geothermal field (Bhattacharyya et al., 1999). We suggest that the difference in associated seismicity is caused by the differences in source mechanism and thus in the stress-release pattern between the earthquakes. The smaller "jumps" in 1989 and 1999 are due to the occurrence of $M = 3.0$ events inside the geothermal field. It is interesting to note that an increase in cumulative seismicity in 1995 occurred before the Ridgecrest earthquakes.

Seismicity inside the Coso geothermal field shows several differences compared to that in the Coso Range and the Indian Wells Valley. Jumps in seismicity related to the occurrence of large regional events are much smaller in the Coso geothermal

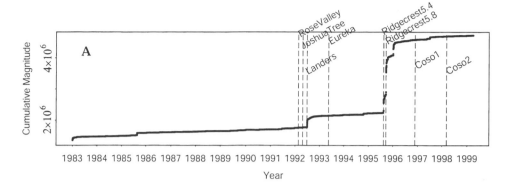

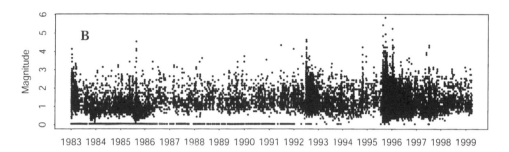

Figure 5. Seismicity distribution and recurrence rate in the Indian Wells Valley region. We observed a sharp increase in seismic moment release in the Indian Wells Valley following the Landers and the Ridgecrest events, indicating earthquake triggering following these earthquakes. The sharp increases in moment release in 1985, 1992, and 1995 are due to the occurrence of large earthquakes (M ≥ 4.0).

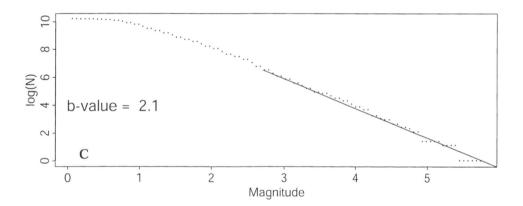

field. The geothermal field generally is affected only by the nearby events, i.e., those near Ridgecrest and Coso, and not by the much larger, more distant, Landers earthquake. Lees (1998) found that the b-value in the field was not a constant function of magnitude. This result may be due to a physical effect in the geothermal field or a function of incompleteness of the catalogue; we cannot say for sure at this time. In the center of the distribution, where the catalogue is most reliable, the b-value was estimated to be 3.1, significantly higher than either the Indian Wells Valley or the Coso Range. Kisslinger and Jones (1991) and Creamer (1994) have shown that high temporal decay of earthquakes can be explained by high temperatures in seismogenic zones because rapid relaxation of residual stress due to heat flow is expected (Mogi, 1967). We postulate that

observed high b-values in the field are primarily due to the presence of geothermal fluids and much higher heat flow compared to the surrounding regions (Combs and Rotstein, 1976).

RECENT LARGE EARTHQUAKES IN THE COSO RANGE–INDIAN WELLS VALLEY REGION

Between 1996 and 1999, some of the largest earthquakes in California hit the Coso Range and the Indian Wells Valley, each with magnitudes M ≥ 5.0. Although earthquakes in the Indian Wells Valley have similar source mechanisms (Hauksson et al., 1995), there is a fundamental change in the faulting for the Coso Range earthquakes, as described in this section (Bhattacharyya et al., 1999).

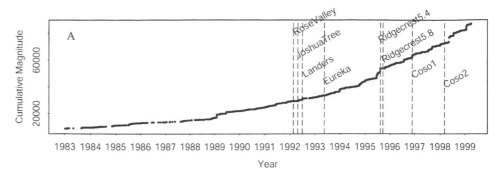

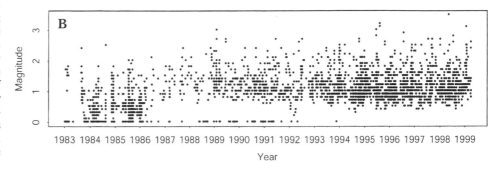

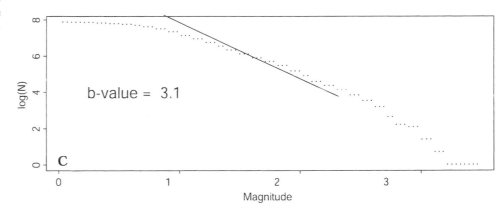

Figure 6. Seismicity distribution and recurrence rate inside the Coso geothermal field. Significant increases in seismic moment release occurred following the Ridgecrest and the Coso Range events. The small increase in 1989 coincides with the occurrence of relatively large earthquakes (M ~ 3.0) inside the geothermal field. The temporal decay of earthquakes does not follow the linear pattern as expected by the Gutenberg-Richter theory, thereby giving b-values that vary with earthquake magnitude. We use the central (linear) part of the distribution (between M = 1 and M = 2.5) to obtain a b-value that is significantly higher than those obtained for the Coso Range or the Indian Wells Valley.

Ridgecrest earthquakes of 1995

In 1995, two large earthquakes occurred in the Indian Wells Valley near the town of Ridgecrest Fig. 7; (Hauksson et al., 1995). The first event (M = 5.4) occurred on August 17, 1995, along an active segment of the Airport Lake fault. This earthquake caused discontinuous surface cracking for ~1 km along the fault and was centered 18 km north of the town of Ridgecrest (Roquemore et al., 1996). The M = 5.8 earthquake of September 20, 1995, possibly reruptured the same fault and had a maximum of 10 mm vertical and 8 mm right-slip displacement (Roquemore et al., 1996). This event was centered 2 km southeast of the August 17 earthquake. The aftershocks were located along three separate fault planes, and the focal mechanisms changed from normal slip to right slip at depth (Hauksson et al., 1995; Roquemore et al., 1996). The Ridgecrest earth-

quake of August 17 was followed by more than 2500 aftershocks over a period of five weeks, and 1900 aftershocks were recorded in the first two weeks following the September 20 event (Hauksson et al., 1995). The aftershocks migrated spatially; the seismic activity increased outward from the epicentral region in the northeast and southeast directions. The earthquake decay rates were consistent between both aftershock sequences with a b-value of ~1.1.

The Coso Range earthquakes

Two recent earthquake sequences near the Coso geothermal field show clear evidence of faulting along conjugate planes (Fig. 7). Bhattacharyya et al. (1999) presented an analysis of aftershocks following the November 27, 1996, main shock and compared them to the March 6, 1998, event. The 1998 main

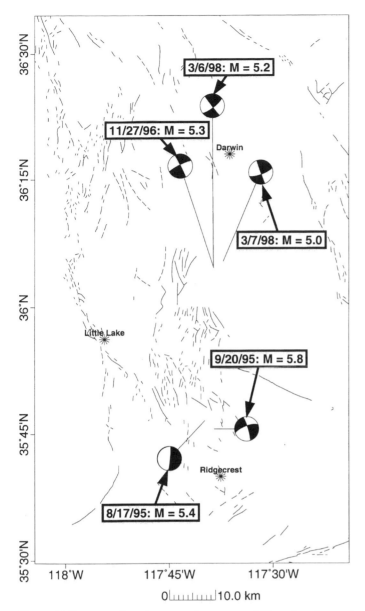

Figure 7. Large earthquakes near the towns of Coso Junction and Ridgecrest for 1995–1998. All of these earthquakes have a magnitude greater than 5.0. The source mechanisms were obtained from the Southern California Earthquake Center.

sequence was not followed by any significant (i.e., $M_L > 4.0$) aftershocks, but the 1998 sequence had four events of this magnitude.

A joint analysis of the fault-plane solutions of the main shocks and relocated aftershocks suggests that the two sequences ruptured along conjugate faults. Bhattacharyya et al. (1999) reported that, according to the conjugate-fault model, the 1996 main shock increased the shear stress acting across the fault that caused the 1998 events by ~0.15 MPa.

STRESS LOADING

The 1998 Coso Range earthquakes are used here to investigate stress loading in adjacent regions by using data from the three-component, short-period, high-dynamic-range borehole seismometers of the MEQ network.

Stress loading in the Coso geothermal field

To estimate the stress loading, we applied a stress step analysis defined as the change in static stress at the location of the earthquake produced by a different, nearby event (Bhattacharyya et al., 1999). The stress step is used to compute the change in failure stress in a region close to the main shock. The change in failure stress, a tensor field, is then compared to changes in seismicity, such that the change in aftershock locations is contrasted to the background seismicity. The MEQ data, where the recording seismic network remained the same before and after the main shock, give us a homogeneous recording that is especially suited for the stress analysis. We did not use events from other California catalogues because the MEQ stations are closer to the earthquakes (compared to, for instance, the stations of the Southern California Earthquake Network) and are therefore better for the detection, magnitude estimation, and location of microearthquakes required for a complete aftershock catalogue.

Bhattacharyya et al. (1999) estimated an average stress step of about +100 Pa inside the Coso geothermal field due to the $M > 4.5$ earthquakes of 1998, suggesting stress loading of the geothermal field. The Coso Range earthquakes were followed by a significant "jump" in seismicity inside the Coso geothermal field that was probably caused by this stress loading.

Results of stress loading

In this section, we describe three separate swarms inside the Coso geothermal field that occurred within a few months of the 1998 Coso Range main shock and probably were caused by the prestressing of the geothermal field. The main shocks for these sequences were events with $M \geq 3.0$. Injection and production of geothermal fluids has been continuous in the field for more than a decade. Although a significant number of earthquakes inside the field are due to geothermal-related activity, the recent events are the largest ones observed inside the Coso

shock ruptured with a local magnitude $M_L = 5.2$ and was located ~17 mi (~27 km) east-northeast of Little Lake, according to the SCEC. The main shock of the 1996 sequence had a local magnitude of 5.3. There were no observed surface ruptures associated with either of these earthquake sequences (Frank Monastero, 1998, personal commun.). Although the 1998 and 1996 main shocks were located less than 900 m apart and had nearly the same M_L values, they differed significantly in their temporal and spatial behavior. The 1996 sequence b-value was 1.1, whereas that for the 1998 sequence was 0.85, a number close to the average southern California value. Moreover, the 1996 geothermal field. Therefore, a connection between the nearby events and the earthquake swarms inside the field can be expected.

The largest event within the Coso geothermal field was the M = 3.5 earthquake of 5/10/98 (Fig. 8). The event was located at 2.1 km depth according to data recorded at the MEQ network. The aftershock sequence included nearly 200 earthquakes with magnitudes between $M_L = -2.6$ and 0.2. Preliminary analysis of the earthquake locations using P- and S-wave traveltimes clearly shows two distinct spatial populations. Earthquakes in one cluster align along an injection well, well 1, and are thought to be caused by fluid flow (Fig. 8). A second population forms a subhorizontal cluster that might be located along a structural feature such as a fault; however, it does not have any surface expression on geologic maps (e.g., Whitmarsh, 1998). Source mechanisms of the aftershocks do not show a clear spatial pattern although they may be complicated by the interaction of fluid overpressure with a subterranean zone of weakness. Events in the second population propagated toward an adjacent production well, well 2, where the seismicity stops. This abrupt cessation of seismicity may be due to a release of overpressure at well 2. However, we do not have access to relevant well-log data (e.g., well-head pressure, lithology, etc.) that would allow us to explore this possibility. A subsequent swarm occurred in this region on July 16, 1998, giving rise to a series of earthquakes located along a potential weak zone, suggesting a reactivation of the same fault (Fig. 8). The second sequence was initiated by two earthquakes with M = 3.1 and 2.7, located at the junction of the fault and well 2. Compared to the first sequence, the number of aftershocks in this sequence is significantly fewer (= 17), and they have larger magnitudes ranging between M = -0.1 to 0.6.

The largest swarm of seismic activity inside the Coso geothermal field started on 12/29/98 (Fig. 9). This swarm was characterized by several relatively large (M ≥ 2.5) events and was initiated by an M = 3.4 main shock. Twelve more events, with magnitudes M ≥ 2.5, occurred during this sequence. The largest event of this swarm had a magnitude of 3.5. This region of the

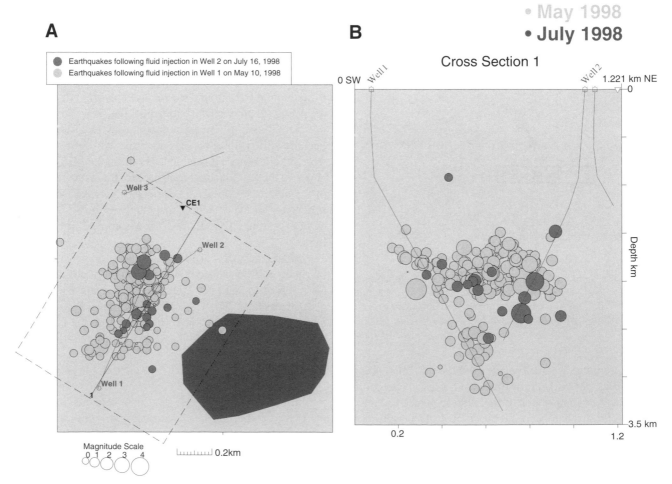

Figure 8. Locations of two earthquake swarms occurring inside the Coso geothermal field following a stress loading of the field due to the M = 5.2 event of 3/6/98; (A) map view and (B) cross section located along the solid line in A. We show the injection and production wells close to the swarms. Seismic station CE1 belongs to the microearthquake network located inside the geothermal field. We can see that the seismicity lies along the wells and along a hypothesized subhorizontal fault at a depth of ~2.0 km.

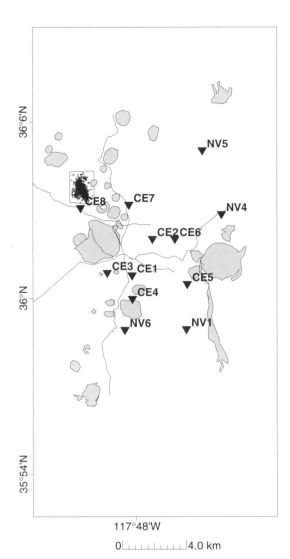

Figure 9. The earthquake swarm of December 1998–January 1999, located in the northwest corner of the Coso geothermal field. The rhyolite domes and the lava flows are indicated by the shaded regions. The locations of the seismic stations in the microearthquake (MEQ) network are shown by CE and NV labels. The earthquakes in the swarm were located by using seismic waveforms recorded at the MEQ stations and a crustal model appropriate for the Coso geothermal field (Wu and Lees, 1999).

Coso geothermal field is the center of recent fumarolic activity, and the increased seismic activity may be due to increased movement of steam and geothermal fluids, although a quantitative analysis requires additional data (e.g., well logs, geodetic measurements, etc.).

ANALYSIS OF EARTHQUAKE SOURCE MECHANISM

The combination of source mechanisms and seismicity can be used to estimate the tectonic stress release of a region. A complete discussion of this topic should include geodetic mea-surements and is therefore beyond the scope of this paper. We discuss two specific topics: (1) spatial distribution of earthquake source mechanisms and (2) orientation of principal stress axis inside the Coso geothermal field.

Distribution of earthquake source mechanisms

Focal mechanisms in the Coso Range–Indian Wells Valley region are heterogeneously distributed, forming clusters of normal, strike-slip, normal-oblique-strike-slip, and oblique-normal fault styles. We have used focal mechanisms estimated by the program FPFIT (Reasenberg and Oppenheimer, 1985) applied to databases at SCEC and NCEC. Over 9000 events are shown in Figure 10. Because so many events are plotted on top of each other, we plot ternary diagrams (Frohlich, 1992) summarizing focal styles (Fig. 11). The ternary plots provide a means to quickly assess the spatial distribution of focal mechanisms when "beach-ball" plots are too congested. The entire target region is partitioned on a 10 × 10 grid, and all events within a block are summarized within a ternary plot. We reference the grid by designating the lower left-hand corner (1,1), and block numbers increase to the east and north. The overall sense of faulting in the Coso Range–Indian Wells Valley region ranges from normal to strike slip, in general agreement with Basin and Range extension and Pacific–North American plate boundary motion. Along the Garlock fault, strike-slip and oblique-normal patterns dominate (e.g., block 3,3). South of the Garlock fault, strike-slip mechanisms are most common (blocks 4,2 and 5,2). In the eastern part of the Ridgecrest event zone (blocks 4,6 and 4,7), normal and strike-slip faults are predominant, with virtually no reverse faulting evident. To the west (blocks 5,6 and 5,7), we see considerable reverse faulting for the earthquakes in this region. The Coso geothermal field is highlighted in Figure 11. Four blocks summarize the geothermal-field activity in this view. Note the increased presence of reverse faulting in the northwest corner of the geothermal field (block 3,9) as compared to the focal mechanisms in the other geothermal-field blocks (3,8; 4,8; and 4,9).

Stress orientation inside the Coso geothermal field

The geothermal field contains three major sets of faults thought to localize subsurface hydrothermal fluid circulation (Bishop and Bird, 1987; Roquemore, 1984). The first set consists of dextral strike-slip faults striking west-northwest that are well developed to the south and northwest of the Coso geothermal field (Fig. 1) (Duffield et al., 1980; Roquemore, 1984). The second set includes normal faults striking north to northeast and is well developed throughout the geothermal field. The third set comprises northeast sinistral strike-slip faults striking northeastward from the geothermal field (see Roquemore, 1984). The distribution of stress in the geothermal field was investigated by Feng and Lees (1998) who found a correlation in time and space of microseismicity with geothermal fluid

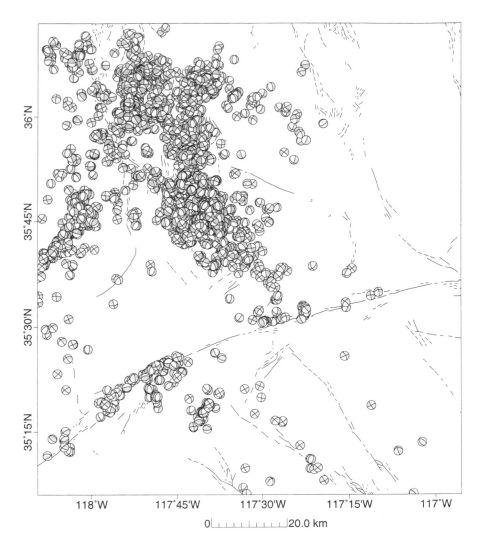

Figure 10. Focal mechanisms of earthquakes in the Coso Range and Indian Wells Valley of southeast-central California, obtained from Southern California Earthquake Center.

injection and circulation at the Coso geothermal field. High-seismicity zones were found to indicate zones of high preexisting fracture density that may be the primary fluid-flow paths within the geothermal system. Stress patterns calculated from focal mechanisms showed a sharp transition from transpressional regimes in surrounding areas to transtensional regimes in the central area of the geothermal field. The stress transition defines the boundary between significantly different stress regimes within the field, primarily observed as a rotation of the maximum principal direction of stress. This boundary correlates with observed spatial variations of heat flow (Combs, 1980), seismic attenuation (Wu and Lees, 1996), P- and S-wave velocity (Wu and Lees, 1999), seismic anisotropy (Lees and Wu, 1999), and geochemical analyses. We conclude that stress regimes potentially represent separate blocks that differ geologically from north to south and are indicated by variations of stress orientation. Fialko and Simons (2000) interpreted the data to reflect contraction due to cooling.

SUMMARY

In this paper, we report on the spatial and temporal distribution and source mechanisms of earthquakes occurring in the Coso Range–Indian Wells Valley region. We identify zones of significant seismic activity, investigate their relationship to mapped faults, and quantify the lateral variation of stress changes and faulting patterns. The important structural controls for this region are as follows:

1. The Coso Range–Indian Wells Valley region, which belongs in the Eastern California shear zone, marks a transition between the strike-slip tectonics of San Andreas fault and the extensional tectonics of the Basin and Range province. The regional deformation direction is north-northwest–trending right-lateral shear.

2. The Little Lake fault and the Airport Lake fault are the most significant active faults in the Indian Wells Valley. Several inactive faults are also present. Seismicity in the Coso Range area is mostly located in the Coso geothermal field.

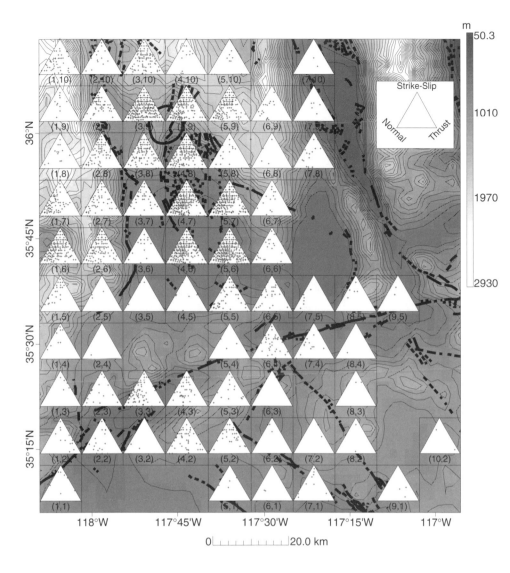

Figure 11. Ternary diagrams (Frohlich, 1992) for southeast-central California summarizing focal styles in different subregions. In each ternary diagram, strike-slip faults are plotted at the top apex, normal faults on the bottom left, and thrust faults on the bottom right. For reference, topographic relief is contoured and an outline of the Coso geothermal field is shown by a bold circle at 36°N, 117°47′W. Contour interval is 100 m.

3. Seismicity in the Indian Wells Valley is mostly characterized by swarms of earthquakes. Earthquakes in the Coso Range area are related to tectonic motion and geothermal activity.

4. We observe significant increase in seismicity in the Indian Wells Valley due to the 1992 Landers event and the 1995 Ridgecrest earthquakes. The increase in seismicity is much smaller in the geothermal field, possibly because of the elevated temperatures in the seismogenic zone.

5. The faults of the Coso Range–Indian Wells Valley region generally accommodate normal to strike slip, reflecting the transition between extensional and strike-slip tectonics. Lateral variations of source mechanisms were used to map stress changes inside the Coso geothermal field. The central geothermal area belongs to a transtensional regime and is surrounded by a region under transpression.

6. The Coso Range earthquake of 1998 caused stress loading inside the geothermal field. Some of the largest earthquakes inside the geothermal field occurred within months of this event, although the events cannot be clearly related without further corroborative data, e.g., well logs.

ACKNOWLEDGMENTS

We thank the Navy Geothermal Program for funding this project (award #N68936-94-R-0139) and providing the MEQ data. Discussions with Glenn Roquemore, Doug Walker, Simon McCluskey, and Gerry Simila have improved this manuscript. We acknowledge the Southern California Earthquake Center Data Center (SCECDC), Southern California Seismic Network, the Northern California Earthquake Data Center (NCEDC), the Northern California Seismic Network, and the Seismological Laboratory at the University of California, Berkeley, for providing us with the seismic catalogue and phase and source-mechanism data. We appreciate the help from Katrin Hafner at SCEC in retrieving these data sets.

REFERENCES CITED

Alvarez, M.G., 1992, The seismotectonics of the southern Coso Range observed with a new borehole seismograph network [M.S. thesis]: Durham, North Carolina, Duke University.

Bacon, C.R., Duffield, W.A., and Nakamura, K., 1980, Distribution of quaternary rhyolite domes of the Coso range, California: Implications for extent of the geothermal anomaly: Journal of Geophysical Research, v. 85, p. 2425–2433.

Bhattacharyya, J., Grosse, S., Lees, J.M., and Hasting, M., 1999, Recent earthquake sequences at Coso: Evidence for conjugate faulting and stress loading near a geothermal field: Bulletin of the Seismological Society of America, v. 89, p. 785–795.

Bishop, B.P., and Bird, D.K., 1987, Variation in sericite compositions from fracture zones within the Coso hot springs geothermal system: Geochemica et Cosmochemica Acta, v. 51, p. 1245–1256.

Combs, J., 1980, Heat flow in the Coso geothermal area, Inyo County, California: Journal of Geophysical Research, v. 85, p. 2411–2424.

Combs, J., and Rotstein, Y., 1976, Microearthquake studies at the Coso Geothermal Area, China Lake, California [abs.]: Proceedings of the 2nd United Nations Symposium on the Development and Use of Geothermal Resources, p. 909–916.

Creamer, F.H., 1994, The relation between temperature and earthquake aftershock decay for aftershock sequences near Japan [Ph.D. thesis]: Boulder, Colorado, University of Colorado.

Dokka, R.K., 1983, Displacements on late Cenozoic strike-slip faults of the central Mojave Desert, California: Geology, v. 11, p. 305–308.

Dokka, R.K., and Travis, C.J., 1990a, The eastern California shear zone and its role in the tectonic evolution of the Pacific-North American transform boundary: Geological Society of America Abstracts with Programs, v. 22, no. 3, p. 19.

Dokka, R.K., and Travis, C.J., 1990b, Role of the eastern California shear zone in accommodating Pacific-North American plate motion: Geophysical Research Letters, v. 17, p. 1323–1326.

Duffield, W.A., 1975, Late Cenozoic ring faulting and volcanism in the Coso Range area of California: Geology, v. 3, p. 335–338.

Duffield, W.A., and Bacon, C.R., 1981, Geologic map of the Coso volcanic field and adjacent areas, Inyo County, California: US Geological Survey Map, scale 1:62 500.

Duffield, W.A., Bacon, C.R., and Dalrymple, G.B., 1980, Late Cenozoic volcanism, geochronolgy, and structure of the Coso Range, Inyo County, California: Journal of Geophysical Research, v. 85, p. 2381–2404.

Feng, Q., and Lees, J.M., 1998, Microseismicity, stress, and fracture within the Coso geothermal field, California: Tectonophysics, v. 289, p. 221–238.

Fialko, Y.A., and Simons, M., 2000, Deformation and seismicity in the Coso geothermal area, Inyo County, California: Observations and modeling using satellite radar interferometry: Journal of Geophysical Research, v. 105, p. 21 781–21 794.

Frohlich, C., 1992, Triangle diagrams: Ternary graphs to display similarity and diversity of earthquake focal mechanisms: Physics of the Earth and Planetary Interiors, v. 75, p. 193–198.

Hart, E.W., Bryant, W.A., Wills, C.J., Treiman, J.A., Kahle, J.E., 1989, Fault evaluation program, 1987–1988, southwestern Basin and Range region and supplemental areas: Open File Report 89-16, California Division of Mines and Geology, p. 31.

Hauksson, E., Hutton, K., Kanamori, H., Jones, L., Mori, J., Hough, S., and Roquemore, G., 1995, Preliminary report on the 1995 Ridgecrest earthquake sequence in eastern California: Seismological Research Letters, v. 66, p. 54–60.

Jennings, C.W., 1994, Fault activity map of California and adjacent areas with location and ages of recent volcanic eruptions: California Division of Mines and Geology, California Geologic Data Map Series, Map No. 6.

Jones, L.E., and Helmberger, D.V., 1998, Earthquake source parameters and fault kinematics in the eastern California shear zone: Bulletin of the Seismological Society of America, v. 88, p. 1337–1352.

Kisslinger, C., and Jones, L.M., 1991, Properties of aftershock sequences in southern California: Journal of Geophysical Research, v. 96, p. 11 947–11 958.

Lees, J.M., 1998, Multiplet analysis at Coso geothermal: Bulletin of the Seismological Society of America, v. 88, p. 1127–1143.

Lees, J.M., and Wu, H., 1999, P-wave anisotropy, stress, and crack distribution at Coso Geothermal Field, California: Journal of Geophysical Research, v. 104, p. 17 955–17 973.

Malin, P., 1994, The seismology of extensional hydrothermal system: Geothermal Resources Council, v. 18, p. 17–22.

Malin, P.E., and Erskine, M.C., 1990, Coincident P and SH reflections from basement rocks at Coso geothermal field: American Association of Petroleum Geologists Bulletin, v. 74, p. 711.

Mogi, K., 1967, Earthquakes and fractures: Tectonophysics, v. 5, p. 35–55.

Reasenberg, P., Ellsworth, W., and Walter, A., 1980, Teleseismic evidence for a low-velocity body under the Coso geothermal area: Journal of Geophysical Research, v. 85, p. 2471–2483.

Reasenberg, P., and Oppenheimer, D.H., 1985, FPFIT, FPPLOT and FPPAGE; Fortran computer programs for calculating and displaying earthquake fault-plane solutions: U.S. Geological Survey Open File Report 109.

Roquemore, G., 1980, Structure, tectonics, and stress field of the Coso Range, Inyo County, California: Journal of Geophysical Research, v. 85, p. 2434–2440.

Roquemore, G., 1988, Revised estimates of slip-rate on the Little Lake Fault, California: Geological Society of America Abstracts with Programs, v. 20, no. 3, p. 225.

Roquemore, G., Simila, G.W., and Mori, J., 1996, The 1995 Ridgecrest earthquake sequence: New clues to the neotectonic development of the Indian Wells Valley and the Coso Range, eastern California: Geological Society of America Abstracts with Programs, v. 28, no. 5, p. 106.

Roquemore, G., and Zellmer, J., 1983a, Ground cracking associated with the 1982 Magnitude 5.2 Indian Wells Valley earthquake: California Geology, v. 36, p. 197–200.

Roquemore, G., and Zellmer, J., 1983b, Tectonics, seismicity, and volcanism at the Naval Weapons Center: Naval Research Reviews, v. 35, p. 3–9.

Roquemore, G.R., 1981, A hypothesis to explain anomalous structures in the western Basin and Range Province: U.S. Geological Survey Open File Report 81-0503.

Roquemore, G.R., 1984, Ground magnetic survey in the Coso Range, California: Journal of Geophysical Research, v. 89, p. 3309–3314.

Roquemore, G.R., 1987, The microseismicity of the shallow geothermal reservoir in the Coso Range, California: Seismological Research Letters, v. 58, p. 29.

Roquemore, G.R., and Simila, G.W., 1994, Aftershocks from the 28 June 1992 Landers earthquake, northern Mojave Desert to the Coso volcanic field, California: Bulletin of the Seismological Society of America, v. 84, p. 854–862.

Sanders, C., Ho, L.P., Rinn, D., and Kanamori, H., 1988, Anomalous shear wave attenuation in the shallow crust beneath the Coso volcanic region, California: Journal of Geophyical Research, v. 93, p. 3321–3338.

Savage, J.C., Lisowski, M., and Prescott, W.H., 1990, An apparent shear zone trending north-northwest across the Mojave Desert into Owens Valley, eastern California: Geophysical Research Letters, v. 17, p. 2113–2116.

Simila, G.W., and Roquemore, G.R., 1987, Earthquake history of the Owens Valley region, *in* Gath, E.M., Gregory, J.L., Sheehan, J.R., Baldwin, E.J., and Hardy, J.K., eds., Geology and mineral wealth of the Owens Valley region, California: Annual Field Trip Guidebook, South Coast Geological Society, p. 145–156.

Walter, A.W., and Weaver, C.S., 1980, Seismicity of the Coso Range, California: Journal of Geophysical Research, v. 85, p. 2441–2458.

Whitmarsh, R., 1998, Structural development of the Coso Range and adjacent areas of eastern California [Ph.D. thesis]: Lawrence, Kansas, University of Kansas.

Whitmarsh, R.W., and Walker, J.D., 1996, Structural domains within the Coso Range of east-central California: A case for right-oblique extension: Geological Society of America Abstracts with Programs, v. 28, no. 7, p. 116.

Whitney, J.D., 1872, The Owens Valley earthquake: Overland Monthly, p. 130–140.

Wu, H., and Lees, J.M., 1996, Attenuation structure of the Coso geothermal area, California, from pulse width data of P-wave: Bulletin of the Seismological Society of America, v. 86, p. 1574–1590.

Wu, H., and Lees, J.M., 1999, Three-dimensional *P* and *S* wave velocity struc-

tures of the Coso geothermal area, California, from microseismic traveltime data: Journal of Geophysical Research, v. 104, p. 13217–13233.

Young, C.Y., and Ward, R. W., 1980, Three-dimensional Q^{-1} model of the Coso Hot Springs known geothermal resource area: Journal of Geophysical Research, v. 85, p. 2459–2470.

Zellmer, J.T., 1988, Engineering and environmental geology of the Indian Wells Valley area, southeastern California: Association of Engineering Geologists, v. 25, p. 437–457.

MANUSCRIPT ACCEPTED BY THE SOCIETY MAY 9, 2001

Geological Society of America
Memoir 195
2002

Three-dimensional anatomy of a geothermal field, Coso, southeast-central California

Jonathan M. Lees

Department of Geological Sciences, University of North Carolina, Chapel Hill, North Carolina, 27599, USA

ABSTRACT

This paper reviews geophysical and seismological imaging in the Coso geothermal field, located in southeast-central California. The Coso geothermal production area covers ~6 × 10 km². Although regional seismicity is addressed, as it sheds light on the magma, or heat, sources in the field, the primary focus of this paper is on the main production area. Three-dimensional inversions for P- and S-wave velocity variations, distribution of attenuation, and anisotropy are presented side-by-side so that anomalies can be compared spatially in a direct manner. Velocity inversions for P and S waves are combined for direct determination of Poisson's ratio and indirect estimation of variations of porosity in the field. Anomalies southeast of Sugarloaf Mountain are prominent on nearly all analyses. The anomalies coincide with high levels of seismicity and with stress anomalies as determined from earthquake focal mechanism analysis and seismic anisotropy distribution. The anomalies also correlate with high heat flow in the field and the termination of geothermal production to the south. I speculate that an intrusion is present in this region that causes significant perturbation of stress in the field.

THE GEOPHYSICAL IMPORTANCE OF COSO

The importance of Coso, from a geophysical perspective, stems from the fact that it is an evolving geothermal field in its initial stages of economic development rather than in maturity. Furthermore, it is situated on the western edge of the Basin and Range province and along what has been suggested is the newly forming tectonic boundary between the Pacific and North American plates (Nur et al., 1993). As such, the active Coso geothermal field provides a living laboratory for investigating the interaction of fluids, magmatic material, and heat in the Earth.

The installation of a borehole seismic network in the region of the Coso geothermal field in the early 1990s provided a means to collect high-quality microearthquake data while monitoring activity in the field (Fig. 1). Because there is active production of geothermal energy at Coso, there are also high levels of low-magnitude seismic activity recorded daily by the seismic array. The seismic stations at Coso consist of 4 Hz, three-component geophones cemented in boreholes ranging from 30 to 70 m depth, recording at 480 samples/s. By recording away from the surface, signal-to-noise ratios are very high, and events as small as magnitude -1 to -2 are routinely recorded. This provides a high-quality data set that can be used to study structure in the field as well as the dynamics of the evolving field. In this paper, I address structural aspects of the geothermal setting by reviewing and compiling results reported in a series of papers directed at imaging seismological properties in the field (Bhattacharyya et al., 1999; Feng and Lees, 1998; Hough et al., 1999; Lees, 1998; Lees and Wu, 1999, 2000; Wu and Lees, 1996, 1999b).

Arrival times of seismic waves from earthquakes are the simplest and most precise measurements that can be made on seismic records. Location of earthquakes depends on the ability to determine traveltimes of events, which in turn requires knowledge of the seismic velocity structure in the intervening

Lees, J.M., 2002, Three-dimensional anatomy of a geothermal field, Coso, southeast-central California, *in* Glazner, A.F., Walker, J.D., and Bartley, J.M., eds., Geologic Evolution of the Mojave Desert and Southwestern Basin and Range: Boulder, Colorado, Geological Society of America Memoir 195, p. 259–276.

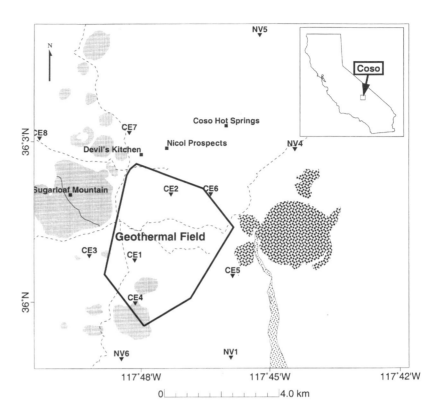

Figure 1. Mapview of the geothermal field region at Coso, California. Inset shows location of Coso in California. Circular shaded features are Quaternary rhyolitic domes. Large dotted regions are thick, Tertiary andesitic flows, and the small dotted zone is a Quaternary basalt flow. Lines show roads in the geothermal field, outlined by a bold line. Triangle symbols are seismic stations renamed from Table 1 of (Wu and Lees 1999b).

media. Generally, earthquakes are located with one-dimensional layered models. It is well known, however, that the Coso geothermal field is three-dimensional. To improve understanding of structural details in the field, a model is sought that explains the data better than the one-dimensional view and that provides information on the three-dimensional variation of seismic properties in the Earth.

Detailed discussions of the methodology used in the studies presented in this paper can be found in a series of papers that outline the tomographic techniques (Lees, 1992; Lees and Crosson, 1989; Lees and Shalev, 1992). Earthquakes are located initially with a one-dimensional layered model, derived by using the method of joint inversion for location and model parameters along with geologic constraints and external data, such as reflection data recorded in the region (E. Shalev, 1996, personal communication). In addition to the one-dimensional models, a station correction (constant time shift for each station) is incorporated in the analysis to account for near-station structure or varying station elevations (Wu and Lees, 1999b). To some extent, use of a station corrections helps compensate for inaccuracy of the one-dimensional approximation of the real Earth. Earthquake locations determined with the one-dimensional models show considerable heterogeneity, with significant clustering in those parts of the field where seismicity levels are elevated (Walter and Weaver, 1980; Feng and Lees, 1998).

Once the one-dimensional models and initial locations are established, three-dimensional analyses can be accomplished.

It is now common practice to refer to three-dimensional seismic inversion analysis for the determination of varying physical properties as "tomography." This approach is borrowed from the medical sciences, and the methods of CAT (computerized axial tomography) scanning have been adapted to seismic analysis. In actuality, there are significant differences between seismic tomography and medical imaging. In seismology, the relationship between the traveltime and the velocity of the medium can be written simply as

$$\Delta T = \int_r [1/V(s)] \, ds, \tag{1}$$

where ΔT is the traveltime, V is the velocity as a function of the position s along the raypath, and the path integral is taken along the raypath, indicated by r. The "inversion" is an attempt to extract the velocity given the traveltime data. In equation 1, I have explicitly included the dependence of the velocity on the raypath to emphasize that seismic traveltime tomography is inherently nonlinear because the paths of the rays from the earthquake source to the receivers depend on the model parameters that are being sought. Traditional medical CAT scanning, furthermore, is accomplished by inverting slices of the target region and building three-dimensional models by stacking series of two-dimensional models (the word *tomography* means "slice picture"). In seismology, three-dimensional structures are typically determined via full three-dimensional inversion, and later they are sliced for visualization purposes. At Coso, ongoing seismic studies include tomographic analysis of attenuation, velocity, and anisotropy. In each of these studies, different aspects of the data are considered and must be treated according to different assumptions. These are outlined here before discussion of specific results for each inversion. The tomography results summarized in this paper were derived from data recorded by the Navy Geothermal Program and Duke University (Peter Malin) from mid-1993 to early 1995. The network includes 16 borehole stations located in the vicinity of the geothermal field (Fig. 1). Depths to the sensors in the borehole stations are typically less than 70 m.

Ultimately, one goal for seismologists is to delineate all relevant three-dimensional seismic properties of this geothermal region. Although global seismologists have been moderately successful at simulating synthetic seismograms at low frequency, the equivalent effort for high frequency at small scales is still practically impossible. This fact is, in part, due to lack of knowledge of three-dimensional variations of properties at the necessary small scales. Tools are currently being developed for examining wave propagation in complex media at high frequency (Wu and Lees, 1992a, 1992b, 1997). High-quality data sets like those available for the Coso geothermal field will prove to be invaluable for future theoretical investigations of seismic waveform propagation.

LOCAL AND REGIONAL SEISMICITY

The Coso area is one of the most active seismic regions of southern California, clearly shown in a density plot of earthquakes in the area (Fig. 2; Walter and Weaver, 1980). According to 1980–1994 earthquake catalogues from the California Institute of Technology (Caltech), recorded earthquake counts in the Coso area are comparable to the most active regions of southern

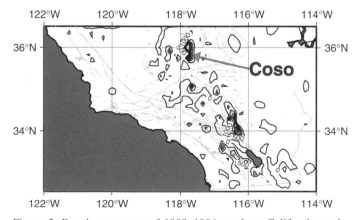

Figure 2. Density contours of 1980–1994 southern California earthquakes with magnitudes greater than zero. Catalogues were extracted from the California Institute of Technology database. The Coso–Ridgecrest area is one of the most actively seismic regions in southern California.

California, including along the San Andreas fault. Seismicity in the Coso geothermal field area has been described in detail by Walter and Weaver (1980), Roquemore and Simila (1994), Alvarez (1992), and Feng and Lees (1998) and from a more regional perspective by Bhattacharyya and Lees (this volume). Several larger events in the region highlight the importance of monitoring seismicity at Coso: the $M_b = 4.0$ event in Rose Valley (Alvarez, 1992), the Ridgecrest events (Hauksson et al., 1995), and more recently the two Coso events (1996 local magnitude $M_L = 5.3$ and 1998 $M_L = 2$) located immediately outside the geothermal field proper (Bhattacharyya et al., 1999). These events are most likely a response to local tectonic stresses associated with Basin and Range extension and North American–Pacific plate margins. For the Coso geothermal field, the most notable observation is the relatively shallow (less than 5–6 km) seismicity below the field itself. Deep earthquakes (down to 12 km depth) surround the Coso geothermal field, primarily in the form of clusters associated with larger ($M_L > 4$) events.

By using ~40 000 events from the Caltech–U.S. Geological Survey (USGS) seismic network in southern California (1988–1998), I have mapped the depth extent of seismicity in the vicinity of Coso. (Hypocenters located from the borehole array at Coso were not used here because they are nearly all shallow. By using only events from one data source, catalogue uniformity is preserved.) Contours of seismicity cutoffs (i.e., the maximum depth of seismicity) span a region 10–12 km east-west and 8 km north-south, bounded to the west by the geothermal field and extending eastward several kilometers (see contours in Fig. 3). The fact that the seismicity contours in the vicinity of the field become shallower is presumably associated with reduction in brittle behavior of the rocks due to the emplacement of magma and/or elevated heat flow (Walter and Weaver, 1980).

A region of particularly intense activity is seen in the southwestern part of the field, close to the southeast side of Sugarloaf Mountain. As is shown subsequently, this zone coincides with the location of anomalous attenuation, velocity, and anisotropy in the field. Although the regional shallowing of seismicity may represent a large anomaly that has heated over time, the concentrated seismicity in the southwest part of the field may represent a shallow intrusion affecting the brittle crust. The high heat flow observed in this corner of the field (Combs, 1980) further suggests that this is the locus of a concentrated anomaly.

It is interesting that Feng and Lees (1998) noted that the distribution of seismicity within the geothermal field showed no considerable change in seismicity rates associated with the 1992 Landers event, in contradiction to the finding of Roquemore and Simila (1994). The discrepancy lies in how the events are selected. Feng and Lees considered the geothermal field to be the area enclosed with the bold line in Figure 1, thus excluding the Ridgecrest events and their aftershocks. Expansion of the region southward would include areas that were affected after the Landers rupture.

Figure 3. Map of regional seismicity from the Caltech-USGS southern California seismic array. Contours show the maximum depth of seismicity in the Coso area based on regional seismicity. Contour interval is 400 m; the labels 5.2 and 7.2 refer to depth in kilometers. The geothermal area and region of the tomographic analyses (Fig. 1) are outlined by dashed line. Geographic features are the same as in Figure 1 with the addition of Red Hill, a volcanic cone located along Highway (HW) 398. A large cluster of shallow events is located southeast of Sugarloaf Mountain (large rhyolite dome) where numerous anomalies are observed on the tomographic analyses. Clusters outside of the geothermal field include the Rose Valley sequence west of Sugarloaf and the 1996–1998 sequences described in Bhattacharyya et al. (1999).

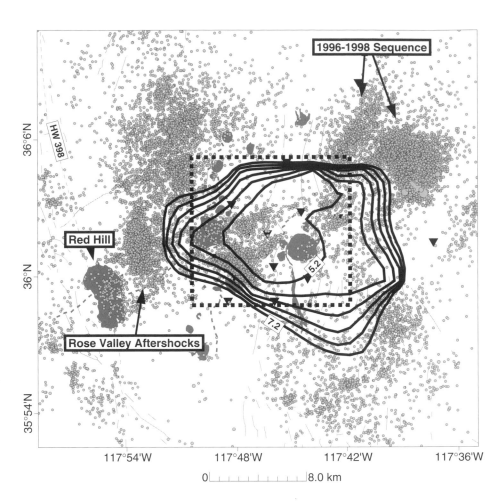

PREVIOUS GEOPHYSICAL ANALYSIS AT COSO

Three-dimensional analysis of the Coso region began in the late 1970s and early 1980s. Three-dimensional teleseismic inversions (Reasenberg et al., 1980; Walck and Clayton, 1987), gravity modeling, electric field methods (Jackson and O'Donnell, 1980), and seismicity studies (Walter and Weaver, 1980) were used to reconnoiter in a region not heavily studied previously. This initial body of work was later expanded on by efforts to characterize V_p/V_s ratios in the Coso–Indian Wells Valley region (Walck, 1988) and attenuation structure of the same region (Ho-Liu et al., 1988; Sanders et al., 1988). The main goal of these studies was to delineate the heat sources of the field: what was expected was a lowering of velocity in regions where rocks are particularly hot, especially where a large fraction of melt may be present. Another expectation was a considerable reduction of shear-wave amplitude where significant percentages of melt exist. Although these studies suggest that the heat source at Coso is fairly shallow, and there appears to be a signal-reducing velocity anomaly in conjunction with wave-amplitude attenuation, the results had relatively crude resolution (tens of kilometers), and the quality of the data was poor compared to the borehole data discussed in this paper.

Subsequent high-resolution studies in the geothermal field itself, discussed in detail in the next section, reveal complex structures associated with geothermal fluid flow and intrusion of magma.

HIGH-RESOLUTION SEISMIC VELOCITY INVERSION

Tomographic analysis for velocity anomalies begins by locating earthquakes (sources), usually with one-dimensional models. Raypaths from sources to receivers are calculated, and the target region is divided, or parameterized, into small cells. For each raypath, a weighting function is determined that estimates the influence the data for that ray have on the cells in the model that the ray traverses. For block models, this procedure amounts to estimating the penetration length of each cell the ray intersects. The traveltime residuals, i.e., the difference between the predicted traveltime and the observed traveltime, are then projected along the raypath along the cells according to the weighting function. In the computer, this process can be expressed as a large, sparse matrix inversion. Because the raypaths and the earthquake locations depend on the velocity models, the inversion is nonlinear, and the solution is achieved by iteration of linearized inversions that converge to the final solution. The size of the matrices can often be quite large (50 000 model parameters), and model resolution and error bars are usually estimated via computational approximations and simulations.

In the Coso geothermal region, high-precision P- and S-wave traveltimes from 2104 microearthquakes with focal depths of <6 km were used in a nonlinear inversion to derive high-resolution three-dimensional compressional- and shear-velocity structures (Wu and Lees, 1999b) (Figs. 4 and 5). The block size used in the inversions was 0.2 km horizontally and 0.5 km vertically. The microearthquake data allowed for imaging of the top 4–5 km. Spatial resolution was estimated in well-resolved regions to be 0.35 km for V_p and 0.5 km for V_s analyses. Model uncertainties were determined by using the "jackknife" approach, a method involving statistical subsampling of the data to assess the influence that noisy data has on the results (Lees and Crosson, 1989). Average errors in V_p and V_s perturbations were 0.4% and 0.8%, respectively.

The full inversion results are presented as horizontal and vertical cross sections through the three-dimensional models. Low-velocity zones for both P and S waves were identified at geothermal-production depths (1–3 km). A large low V_p (−6%) zone was found 2–2.5 km beneath the triangular region bounded by stations CE1-CE3-CE4 where high attenuation was also found. A high V_p zone was seen under Coso Hot Spring with a slightly contrasting low V_s zone (Figs. 6 and 7), characteristic of fluid saturation. In general, the overall distribution of V_p and V_s perturbations do not correlate directly. An isolated high V_s (+9%) feature, ~2 km in diameter, was delineated between stations CE2 and CE6, extending from the surface to the deeper parts of the model. This feature is surrounded by a circular, low-V_s belt with a width of ~1 km. This belt was interpreted as a cracked, high-porosity reservoir and/or conduit for geothermal fluid. In the CE1-CE3-CE4 region, contrary to low V_p, a broad high-V_s zone was observed at geothermal-production depths, from 1 to 2.5 km.

POISSON'S RATIO AND POROSITY

Perturbations of velocity is one way to view the three-dimensional variation of properties in the target region, but it is often useful to consider alternative combinations of the acoustic parameters that may be sensitive to different physical properties. As a follow-on to the description of Coso velocity perturbations and their respective relationship to lithologic and hydrothermal distributions in the field, perturbations of the V_p/V_s ratio and the $\Pi = V_p \times V_s$ product can be used to determine Poisson's ratio and porosity (Lees and Wu, 2000). Poisson's ratio is the ratio of the fractional lateral contraction to the fractional longitudinal extension and depends on lithology and fluid saturation. Poisson's ratio σ is related to $r = V_p/V_s$ by

$$\sigma = (r^2 - 2)/[2(r^2 - 1)], \qquad (2)$$

and thus r is a proxy for Poisson's ratio. Porosity, on the other hand, is more difficult to estimate because there is no a simple analytical relationship between porosity and velocity. Lees and Wu (2000) used studies of the relationship of porosity and Π in sedimentary rocks (Pickett, 1963; Tatham, 1982) to estimate the distribution of porosity at Coso. Although for sedimentary rocks, porosity is introduced by pore spaces inherent in the fabric, at Coso, on the other hand, cracks and fractures are assumed to be analogous to the pore structures of the sediment, thus providing an analogous mechanism for spatial variations of Π to be related to porosity changes. The velocity combinations thus help delineate zones of intense heat, fracture accumulation, and fluid saturation. I summarize the results in Figures 8, 9, 10, and 11, although detailed descriptions of V_p/V_s and Π inversions and interpretations can be found in Lees and Wu (2000).

The average Poisson's ratio at Coso was estimated to be 0.224, lower than the crustal average of 0.25. Two major features with low Poisson's ratio and low porosity were identified at geothermal-production depths (1–3 km) near stations CE2-CE6 and CE1-CE3-CE4 (Figs. 8 and 9). These two low-σ, lower-porosity features are separated by a northwest-trending, arcuate band having a high Poisson's ratio and high porosity. The diameter of this circular structure is 0.8–1.2 km. Because of the correlation to the low-Π anomalies (Figs. 10 and 11), it is interpreted as a potentially highly porous feature suspected to be fluid saturated (obviously correlated to the Vs tomography results in Figs. 5 and 6). My interpretation of this feature is that it most likely represents a conduit or reservoir of geothermal fluids. The east-west and north-south arms of the arc correlate well with observed mainstream fluid-flow directions and are probably primary avenues through which hot water is transported from the heat center around stations CE1-CE3-CE4 (Lees and Wu, 2000; Leslie, 1991). The vertical, low-σ and high-Π channel beneath the triangular region defined by CE1-CE3-CE4 corresponds to a high-attenuation feature found in the attenuation inversion described next. On the basis of the tomographic analyses, I interpret this feature as the hot, unfractured core of the last major magmatic intrusion in the Coso geothermal field.

P-WAVE ATTENUATION

Although simple traveltimes provide the basis for velocity analysis, the amplitudes and the frequency content of seismic waves contain rich information on the absorption of seismic energy in the intervening media. Seismic velocity tends to be a relatively insensitive estimator of temperature variations in rocks. Attenuation, on the other hand, is a relatively sensitive indicator of rock temperature. Usually physicists measure the "quality factor" of materials, i.e., the efficiency of the material to pass energy at a particular frequency. The quality factor, Q, is defined as the ratio of stored to dissipated energy in material as seismic waves propagate through. Attenuation is then defined

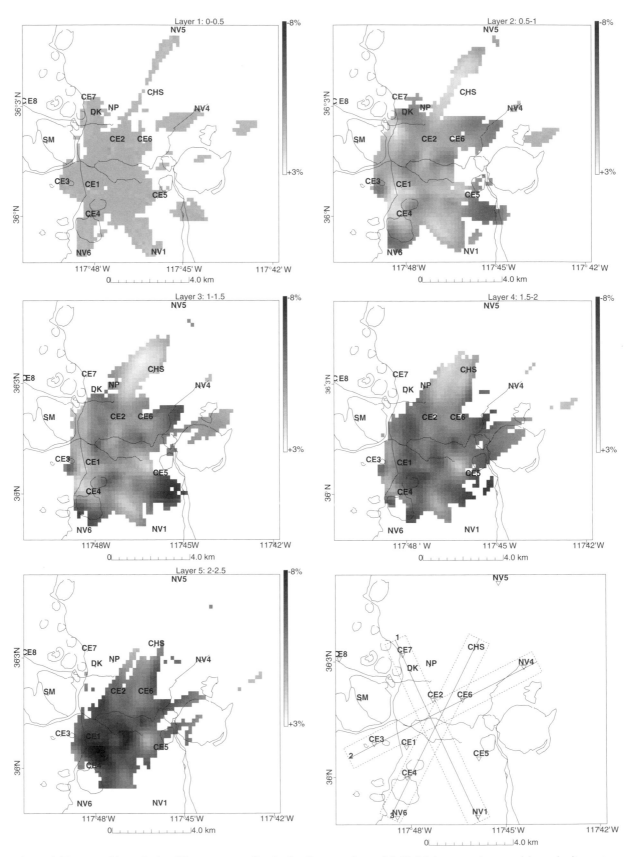

Figure 4. Tomographic analysis of P-wave anomalies in the Coso geothermal field. Light areas show positive velocity perturbations representing higher-velocity zones. Dark areas have relatively lower velocity. Blocks that are not sampled are blanked out (white). Map features and stations are plotted for geographic reference (see Fig. 1). Map orientations of cross sections 1, 2, and 3 (numbered) are presented in lower right map for reference in subsequent cross-section figures. Layers are numbered, and the depth in kilometers that they represent is shown at the top of each map.

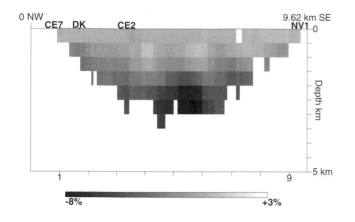

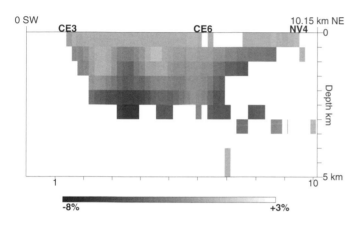

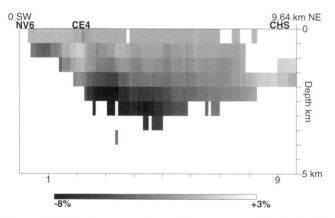

Figure 5. Vertical cross sections of P-wave anomalies in the Coso geothermal field. Locations of cross sections are presented in Figure 4, lower right.

as the reciprocal of Q and thus represents a measure of the absorption or loss of energy in the seismic waves as they pass through intervening material. Q values range typically from 10 to 100 in laboratory measurements on sandstones and 100–1000 in igneous and metamorphic rock measurements (Johnston et al., 1979). These measurements, naturally, are performed on

simple samples and do not take into account large-scale structures, fractures, and mixtures.

Attenuation usually comes in two guises: intrinsic and scattering. Intrinsic attenuation relates to losses associated with heat and friction. Scattering attenuation is due to losses from waves diffracted throughout the medium as they propagate from source to receiver. For the Coso geothermal field, it was shown that intrinsic absorption, as opposed to scattering, appears to be the dominant attenuation factor, at least in the upper 4 km (Wu and Lees, 1996). This result implies that three-dimensional Q variations may be interpreted as being related to intrinsic physical properties of the rocks such as lithology, temperature, and porosity.

In a study of Q distribution at Coso, Wu and Lees (1996) used P-wave pulse widths to estimate the three-dimensional distribution of attenuation in the geothermal field (Figs. 12 and 13) They used pulse width broadening to estimate loss of energy in seismic P-wave arrivals that can be shown to be linearly related to Q^{-1} if microseismic sources are assumed to be impulsive or nearly so (Wu and Lees, 1996). The equations for deriving (inverting for) a three-dimensional quality-factor distribution are nearly identical to the formulas used to derive three-dimensional velocity in equation 1. Once the velocity is determined, three-dimensional raypaths are calculated in the three-dimensional model, and the quality factor is linearly related to the attenuation of seismic waves along each path.

The average Q in the Coso geothermal area was estimated to be ~49. A broad region of low Q (30–37) was identified at 0.5–1.2 km depth below Devil's Kitchen, Nicol Prospects, and Coso Hot Springs. Another larger and deeper (2.5–3.6 km) low-Q feature was observed 2–3 km southeast of Devil's Kitchen and Nicol Prospects. This feature was interpreted as the main origin of Coso's hydrothermal energy and may be related to a suspected rising magma accumulation although the vertical extent of the presumed magma body is not defined by the current data set. Southwest of Devil's Kitchen and Nicol Prospects, a vertical, low-Q channel ~1 km in width and connecting the deeper to the shallower regions of low Q was identified and may be a conduit supplying geothermal energy to the surface at Coso Hot Springs.

An independent study of Q can be accomplished by examining the distortion of the frequency spectrum of the P or S wave trains. In this approach, the source spectrum has specific characteristics that must be either assumed or derived, and deviations in the observed spectrum are attributed to attenuation of the waves during transmission (Hough, 1997; Lees and Lindley, 1994). At Coso it has been observed that numerous earthquakes are very similar in waveform, forming clusters of events called multiplets (Lees, 1998). The high-resolution locations from these multiplet earthquake clusters were used to estimate Q via frequency-spectrum methods. The results agreed with pulse-broadening results already described that put a low-Q anomaly ~1 km in the region of high heat flow in Coso (Hough

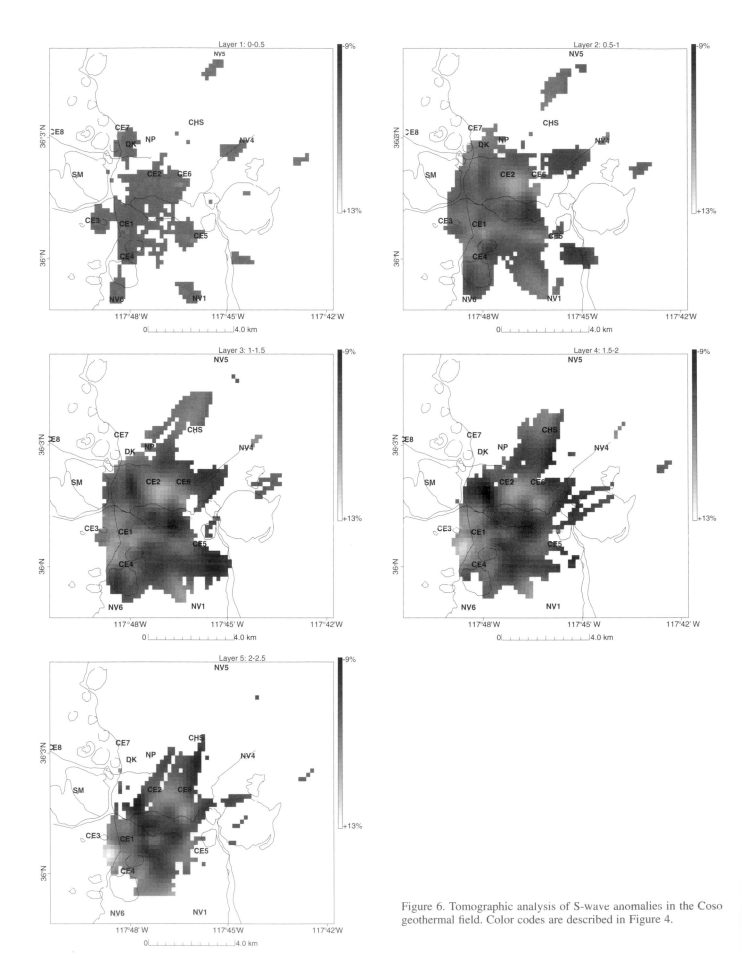

Figure 6. Tomographic analysis of S-wave anomalies in the Coso geothermal field. Color codes are described in Figure 4.

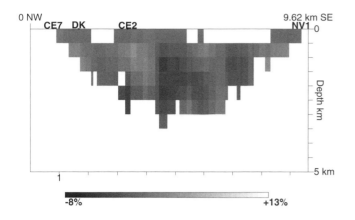

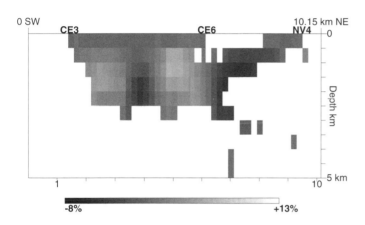

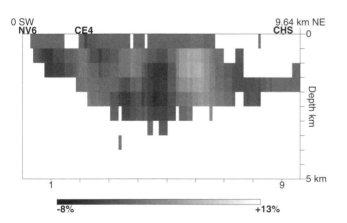

Figure 7. Vertical cross sections of S-wave anomalies in the Coso geothermal field. Locations of cross sections are presented in Figure 4, lower right.

et al., 1999). Unfortunately, very few data were available for this analysis, and thus resolution was poor.

P-WAVE ANISTROPY

Since 1980, seismic anisotropy has been studied extensively in the Earth's crust and upper mantle. The effects of anisotropy on seismic waves are complex compared with the isotropic inhomogeneities (Anderson, 1989; Babuska and Cara, 1991) and therefore should be studied in any investigation of three-dimensional variations of seismic parameters. In geothermal fields, velocity anisotropy was previously observed and associated with fracture zones (Leary and Henyey, 1985; Lou and Rial, 1997). Both internal rock fabric and external physical conditions give rise to velocity anisotropy. Possible origins include preferred crystal orientation, lithologic layering, crack alignment, deviatoric stress field, and fluid flow (Schön, 1996). For the Coso region, I suspect that all these effects influence observed anisotropy to some extent. The preponderance of significant fractures in the geothermal field suggests that fractures, cracks, and ambient stresses are the dominant factors at Coso. A material containing an aligned system of cracks is effectively anisotropic for elastic waves, whereas materials containing randomly oriented microcracks exhibit bulk isotropy (Crampin, 1984; Hudson, 1981, 1994). Application of a deviatoric stress can preferentially open and close cracks, however, depending on their orientation with respect to the principal stress directions (Nur, 1971). The resultant nonuniform crack orientation distribution can introduce elastic anisotropy into an otherwise isotropic material (Nur and Simmons, 1969). Measurements of velocity anisotropy have been used to derive the density distribution of crack orientation, which can be used in turn to predict permeability anisotropy for fluid flow (Gibson and Toksoz, 1990). Researchers modeling geothermal-field evolution would like to have access to this information that will ultimately provide constraints on forward modeling of fluid flow in the crust.

Most researchers have concentrated on anisotropy associated with shear waves traveling through media. These waves are differentially polarized after passing through the anisotropic region, and information relating the level and direction of anisotropy can be determined from analysis of two separated shear waves. This kind of analysis was applied at Coso by Lou and Rial (1997), and three-dimensional variations of shear-wave splitting were determined and used to estimate crack density. The data available for such a study, though, are limited for tomographic analysis because the data must lie within a specific cone beneath the station in order to record the shear-wave splitting, thus limiting the three-dimensional resolution of the analysis. Tomographic inversions generally require large data sets with extensive crossing ray paths to achieve good reduction of noise and proper reconstruction of anomalous bodies. To this end, a new method was developed for investigating three-dimensional variations of P-wave anisotropy (Lees and Wu, 1999; Wu and Lees, 1999a). The much larger data set of P-wave arrivals versus S-wave arrivals at Coso make this an attractive alternative to the shear-wave splitting approach.

Solving for P-wave anisotropy involves solving for six parameters in each sampled block of the target model. The anisotropy is represented as a velocity ellipsoid, or a 3 × 3 symmetric matrix. The anisotropy ellipsoid is thus fully described by three velocity vectors in the fast, intermediate, and slow

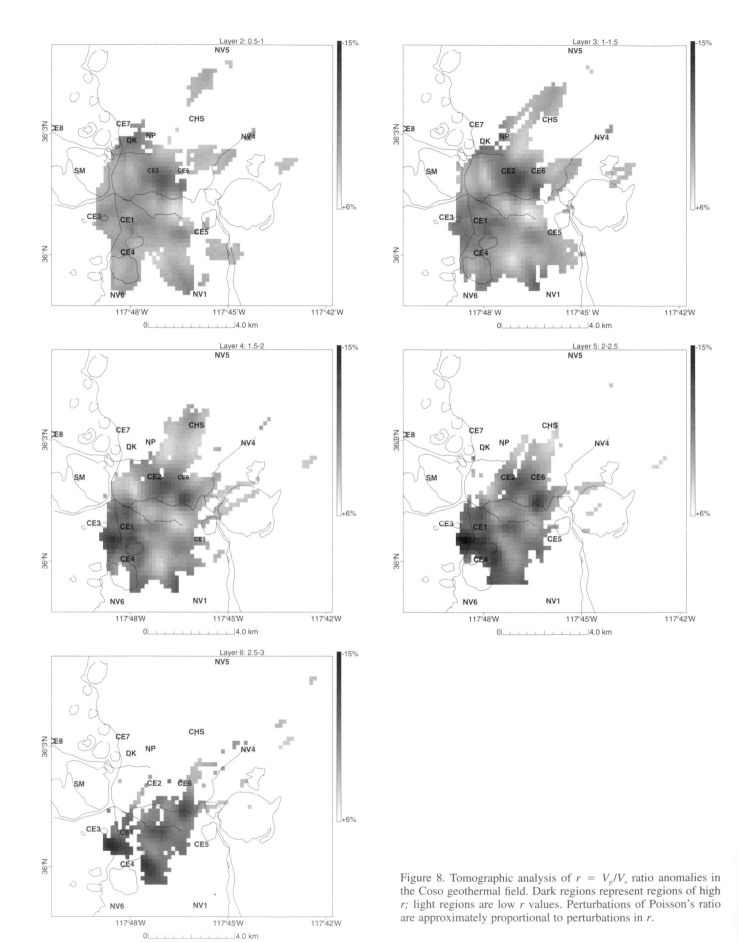

Figure 8. Tomographic analysis of $r = V_p/V_s$ ratio anomalies in the Coso geothermal field. Dark regions represent regions of high r; light regions are low r values. Perturbations of Poisson's ratio are approximately proportional to perturbations in r.

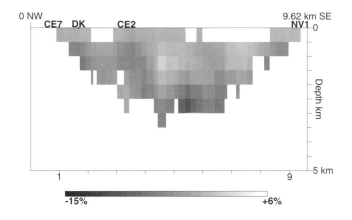

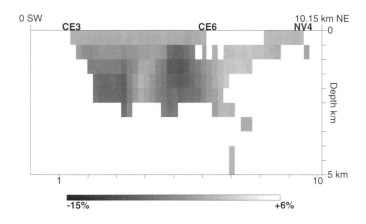

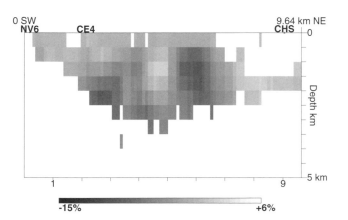

Figure 9. Vertical cross sections of $r = V_p/V_s$ ratio anomalies in the Coso geothermal field. Locations of cross sections are presented in Figure 4, lower right.

directions. To simplify the visualization and interpretation of this set of parameters, the quantity a_f, or the "anisotropy factor," is introduced as the difference between fast and slow velocities divided by the average velocities in a block. The velocities are the eigenvalues of the anisotropy matrices for each block. I present here the three-dimensional distribution of a_f in the Coso

geothermal field. Maps of the directions can be found in Lees and Wu (1999).

The overall anisotropy at the Coso geothermal field is north-south fast in the western part and east-west fast in the eastern part (Lees and Wu, 1999). A large-amplitude (8%) anisotropy anomaly was observed at depth east of stations CE1-CE4 (Figs. 14 and 15). An irregular, east-trending anisotropic transition band of 1–2 km width is identified at depth between CE5 and CE6. A dome-shaped structure is found below the triangular area bounded by CE1-CE3-CE4. The stress distribution and crack densities were estimated from the P-wave anisotropy results. Gross features of the anisotropy distributions (e.g., a significant anomaly located below the southwestern part of the field) correlate well with variations of stress inferred from earthquake focal mechanism studies. Feng and Lees (1998) found that the southwest cluster had an anomalously low vertical stress component, as compared to clusters of events north and east. Furthermore, deviatoric stress distribution was found to correlate closely with the high seismicity observed in the southwest part of the geothermal field.

I cannot say for sure, at this time, what the source of the anisotropy is at Coso. I expect that, in a geothermal setting, crack distribution rather than deviatoric stress will be the major contributor to anisotropy variations. For example, if it is assumed that 20% of the velocity anisotropy is attributable to the contemporary stress field, a total differential stress distribution of ~3 MPa is found for the geothermal field on average and nearly twice as much (~6 MPa) in the CE1-CE3-CE4 region. The largest concentration of stress was seen at the suspected intrusion or upwelling center CE1-CE3-CE4, consistent with a proposed magmatic intrusion model for this region based on seismic attenuation (Wu and Lees, 1996). Focal mechanisms and their spatial distribution further support partitioning of stress throughout the geothermal field and emphasize the unusual stress orientation in this part of the field (Feng and Lees, 1998).

Contrary to widely held assumptions, it can be shown that only the residual, unbalanced crack-density distribution produces velocity anisotropy (Wu and Lees, 1999a). Thus, only the deviatoric part of crack density can be determined from the velocity anisotropy, which, in turn, determines the anisotropic part of the permeability orientation. The estimated residual crack densities for the Coso region agree with a previous S-wave splitting study (Lou and Rial, 1997), ranging from 0.0078 to 0.041. By using the median crack density from the P-wave and the S-wave results, Lees and Wu (1999) showed that the average aspect ratio for cracks in the field should be ~1:38. Given an average crack aspect ratio and an estimated crack density, the residual permeability distribution can be estimated by assuming a simple planar fluid-flow model through flat cracks (Gibson and Toksoz, 1990). On the basis of these assumptions, Coso geothermal field permeability can be shown to be roughly proportional to velocity anisotropy (Figs. 14 and 15) (Lees and Wu, 1999). At this point I do not have enough

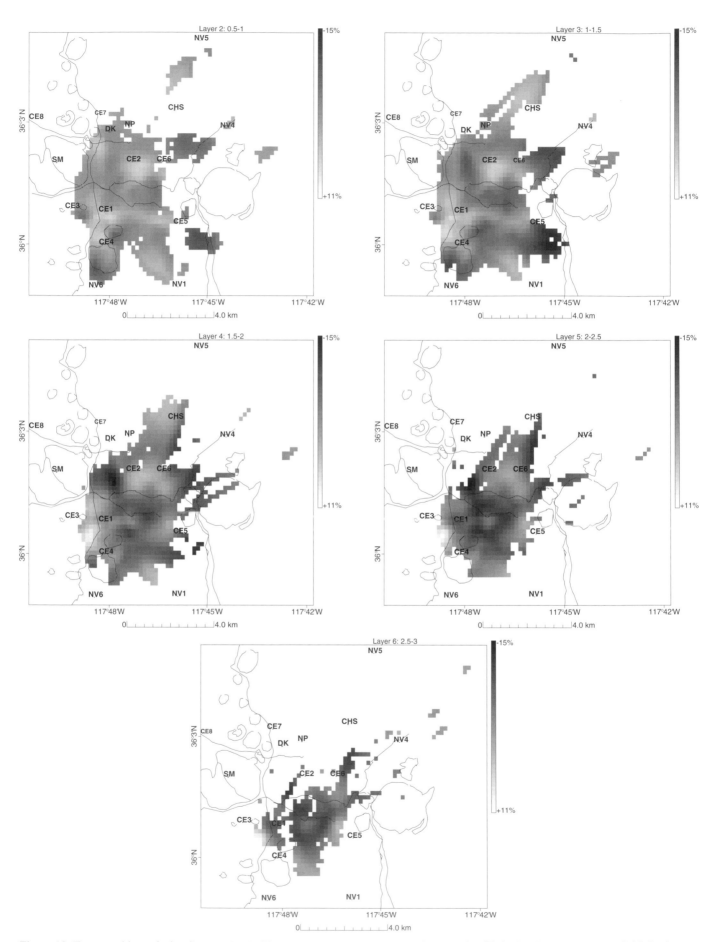

Figure 10. Tomographic analysis of anomalies in $\Pi = V_p \times V_s$ product (a proxy for porosity, Π) in the Coso geothermal field. Dark areas are high Π; light are low Π. High Π is interpreted to indicate low porosity, and low Π is high porosity.

detailed information to verify these predictions. However, they stand as testable hypotheses that can be explored as further studies of the field unfold.

DISCUSSION

The microearthquake data set acquired by the Navy Geothermal Program is one of the most detailed and high-quality data sets for investigating structure in a geothermal setting. Borehole seismic installations, station-density coverage, and high seismicity levels insure a robust database to permit detailed, reliable analysis of structural and dynamical processes in the field as injection and production continue.

There are several significant anomalous features in the Coso region that should be investigated more intensely, e.g., the small triangular area defined by stations CE3-CE4-CE1 deserves greater attention because it correlates well with high heat-flow gradients measured at the surface in the late 1970s (Combs, 1980). Velocity, attenuation, anisotropy, and stress anomalies were each found in the southwestern part of the field and suggest that this area is a focal point for heat flux in the field. I speculate that this narrow zone represents an intrusion of some sort below the active geothermal region. Perhaps it is the peak of an intrusion of magmatic material that extends more broadly at depth to the east, as suggested by the shallow seismicity cutoff that extends in that direction. Furthermore, reflections south of station CE4 suggest that there is a considerable contrast of material properties (elastic impedance) across a subsurface boundary to the south (Lees, 1997). Studies of stress distribution in the field (Feng and Lees, 1998) suggest that there is zonation, or stress partitioning, indicating barriers within the field, perhaps channeling fluid migration.

The overall tomographic inversions for attenuation and anisotropy are not as well correlated as inversions for V_p, V_s, Poisson's ratio, and velocity product, Π. This problem may be partially attributed to the fact that the data quality available for simple velocity analysis is considerably less noisy than the amplitude data used for attenuation studies or the traveltime residuals used to determine P-wave anisotropy. On the other hand, the physical parameters considered may be sampling other aspects of the material traversed and rendering simple geographic correlation fruitless. For example, although attenuation of seismic waves may be very sensitive to temperature, V_p may be more affected by lithologic variations, and anisotropy may be a response to either stress variations or crack density. Anisotropy observed in shear waves may have a different source than that observed for compressional waves. This possibility makes interpretation difficult and open to challenge. My approach here has been to consider several factors and consider external geophysical information where available.

A considerable effort has been invested in imaging details of the Coso geothermal field, including developing new methodology for analyzing three-dimensional variations of seismic properties and their geologic significance. The upper 4–5 km

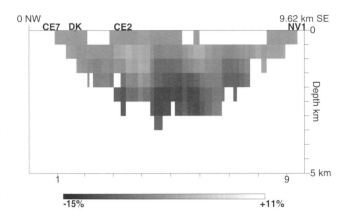

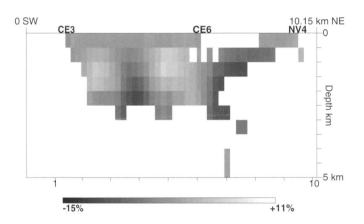

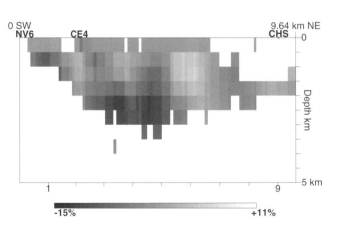

Figure 11. Vertical cross sections of anomalies in $\Pi = V_p \times V_s$ product in the Coso geothermal field. Locations of cross sections are presented in Figure 4, lower right.

in the field show significant three-dimensional variations in seismic velocity, attenuation, and anisotropy that appear to be related to natural geothermal activity as well as to commercial production in the field. It is clearly evident that significant heat sources and, perhaps, fluid flow in or below the field constitute the ultimate underlying causes of the anomalous features de-

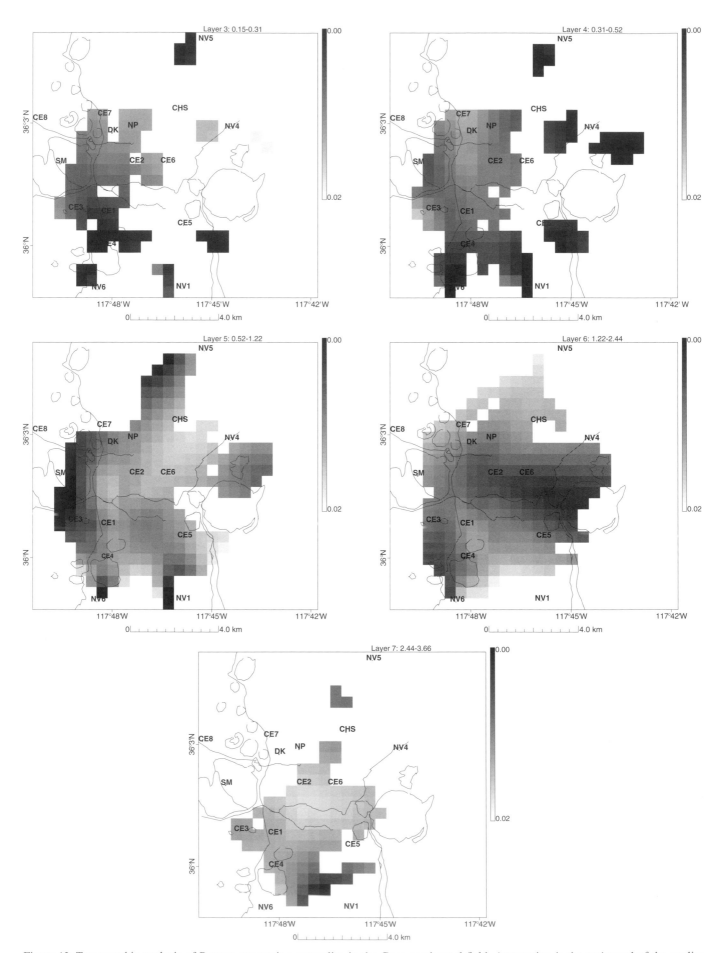

Figure 12. Tomographic analysis of P-wave attenuation anomalies in the Coso geothermal field. Attenuation is the reciprocal of the quality factor Q. Light regions have high Q (small $1/Q$, i.e., lower attenuation), and dark zones have low Q (large $1/Q$, i.e., higher attenuation).

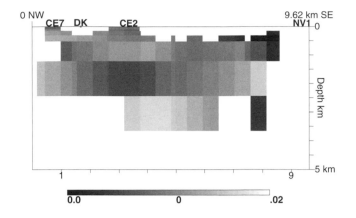

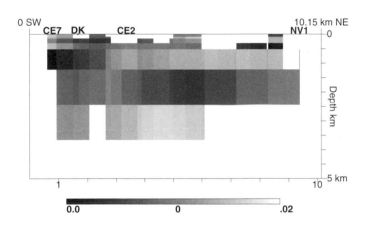

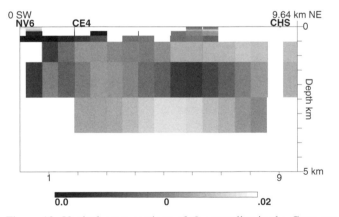

Figure 13. Vertical cross sections of Q anomalies in the Coso geothermal field. Locations of cross sections are presented in Figure 4, lower right.

scribed here. Because of the shallow seismicity, this data set, as yet, sheds little light on the shape and extent of the underlying magma body, or the deeper heat and magma sources for the Coso geothermal field. The imaging methodologies described here, however, can readily be applied to the more re-

gional data set; for example, expanding the network and considering regional waveform phases may help in delineating the magma source. In the meantime, detailed lithologic, permeability, porosity, acoustic, and other geophysical borehole logs will allow testing of assertions and interpretations made regarding the seismic inversions outlined here. These will furthermore allow better characterization of future inversions and better monitoring of temporal variations of geophysical properties as the geothermal field evolves.

ACKNOWLEDGMENTS

I thank the Navy Geothermal Program for funding this project (award #N68936-94-R-0139) and providing data. I further acknowledge California Energy Co. Inc. and Peter Malin (Duke University) for data and valuable comments.

REFERENCES CITED

Alvarez, M.G., 1992, The seismotectonics of the southern Coso Range observed with a new borehole scismograph network [M.S. thesis]: Durham, North Carolina, Duke University.

Anderson, D.L., 1989, Theory of the earth: Boston, Blackwell Scientific, 366 p.

Babuska, V., and Cara, M., 1991, Seismic anisotropy in the Earth: Modern approaches in geophysics: Dordrecht, Kluwer Academic, 217 p.

Bhattacharyya, J., Grosse, S., Lees, J.M., and Hasting, M., 1999, Recent earthquake sequences at Coso: Evidence for conjugate faulting and stress loading near a geothermal field: Bulletin of the Seismological Society of America, v. 89, p. 785–795.

Combs, J., 1980, Heat flow in the Coso geothermal area, Inyo County, California: Journal of Geophysical Research, v. 85, p. 2411–2424.

Crampin, S., 1984, Effective elastic constants for wave propagation through cracked solids: Geophysical Journal of the Royal Astronomical Society, v. 76, p. 135–145.

Feng, Q., and Lees, J.M., 1998, Microseismicity, stress, and fracture within the Coso geothermal field, California: Tectonophysics, v. 289, p. 221–238.

Gibson, R.L., Jr., and Toksoz, M.N., 1990, Permeability estimation from velocity anisotropy in fractured rock: Journal of Geophysical Research, v. 95, p. 15 643–15 655.

Hauksson, E., Hutton, K., Kanamori, H., Jones, L., Mori, J., Hough, S., and Roquemore, G., 1995, Preliminary report on the 1995 Ridgecrest earthquake sequence in eastern California: Seismological Research Letters, v. 66, p. 54–60.

Ho-Liu, P., Kanamori, H., and Clayton, R.W., 1988, Applications of attenuation tomography to Imperial Valley and Coso–Indian Wells region, southern California: Journal of Geophysical Research, v. 93, p. 10 501–10 520.

Hough, S.E., 1997, Empirical Green's function analysis: Taking the next step: Journal of Geophysical Research, v. 102, p. 5369–5384.

Hough, S.E., Lees, J.M., and Monastero, F., 1999, Attenuation and source properties at the Coso geothermal area, California: Bulletin of the Seismological Society of America, v. 89, p. 1606–1619.

Hudson, J.A., 1981, Wave speeds and attenuation of elastic waves in material containing cracks: Geophysical Journal of the Royal Astronomical Society, v. 64, p. 133–150.

Hudson, J.A., 1994, Overall properties of anisotropic materials containing cracks: Geophysical Journal International, v. 116, p. 279–282.

Jackson, D.B., and O'Donnell, J.E., 1980, Reconnaissance electrical surveys in the Coso Range, California: Journal of Geophysical Research, v. 85, p. 2502–2516.

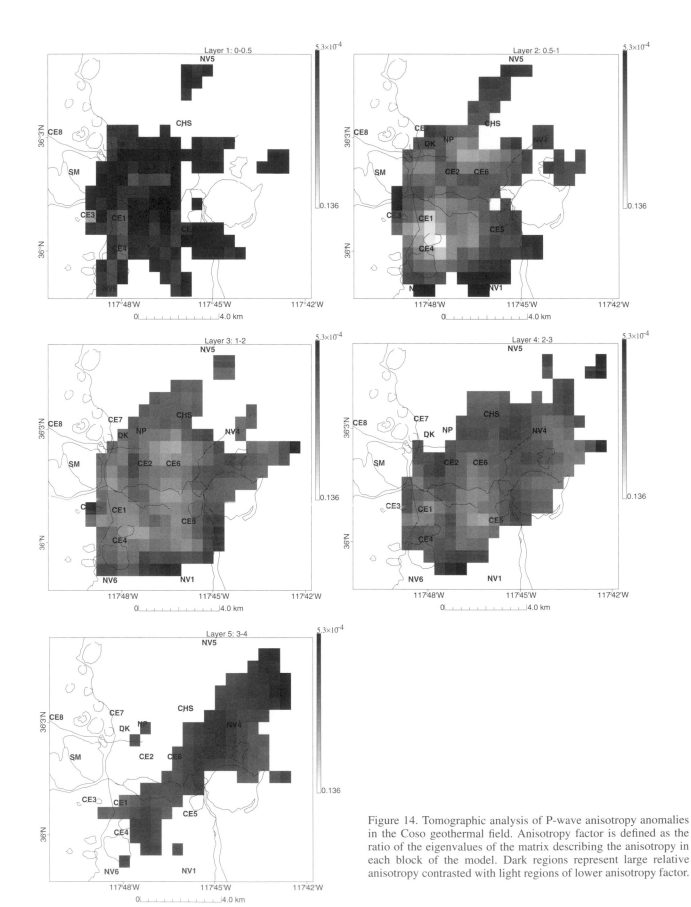

Figure 14. Tomographic analysis of P-wave anisotropy anomalies in the Coso geothermal field. Anisotropy factor is defined as the ratio of the eigenvalues of the matrix describing the anisotropy in each block of the model. Dark regions represent large relative anisotropy contrasted with light regions of lower anisotropy factor.

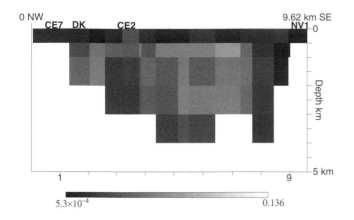

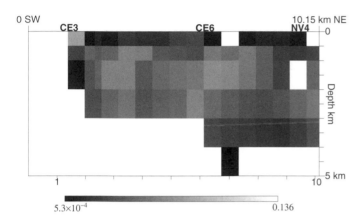

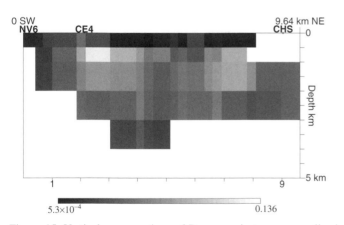

Figure 15. Vertical cross sections of P-wave anisotropy anomalies in the Coso geothermal field. Locations of cross sections are presented in Figure 4, lower right.

Johnston, D.H., Toksoz, M.N., and Timur, A., 1979, Attenuation of seismic waves in dry and saturated rocks: 2. Mechanisms: Geophysics, v. 44, p. 691–711.

Leary, P.C., and Henyey, T.L., 1985, Anisotropy and fracture zones about a geothermal well from P-wave velocity profiles: Geophysics, v. 50, p. 25–36.

Lees, J.M., 1992, The magma system of Mount St. Helens: Non-linear high resolution P-wave tomography: Journal of Volcanology and Geothermal Research, v. 53, p. 103–116.

Lees, J.M., 1997, Scattering from a vertical geothermal barrier at Coso, California: Seismological Research Letters, v. 68, p. 318–319.

Lees, J.M., 1998, Multiplet analysis at Coso geothermal: Bulletin of the Seismological Society of America, v. 88, p. 1127–1143.

Lees, J.M., and Crosson, R.S., 1989, Tomographic inversion for three-dimensional velocity structure at Mount St. Helens using earthquake data: Journal of Geophysical Research, v. 94, p. 5716–5728.

Lees, J.M., and Lindley, G.T., 1994, Three-dimensional attenuation tomography at Loma Prieta: Inverting t* for Q: Journal of Geophysical Research, v. 99, p. 6843–6863.

Lees, J.M., and Shalev, E., 1992, On the stability of P-wave tomography at Loma Prieta: A comparison of parameterizations, linear and non-linear inversions: Bulletin of the Seismological Society of America, v. 82, p. 1821–1839.

Lees, J.M., and Wu, H., 1999, P-wave anisotropy, stress, and crack distribution at Coso geothermal field, California: Journal of Geophysical Research, v. 104, p. 17955–17973.

Lees, J.M., and Wu, H., 2000, Poisson's ratio and porosity at Coso geothermal area, California: Journal of Volcanology and Geothermal Research, v. 95, p. 157–173.

Leslie, B.W., 1991, Decay series disequilibria applied to the study of rock-water interaction in the Coso geothermal field, California [Ph.D. thesis]: Los Angeles, California, University of Southern California, 324 p.

Lou, M., and Rial, J.A., 1997, Characterization of geothermal reservoir crack patterns using shear-wave splitting: Geophysics, v. 62, p. 487–494.

Nur, A., 1971, Effects of stress on velocity anisotropy in rocks with cracks: Journal of Geophysical Research, v. 76, p. 2022–2034.

Nur, A., and Simmons, G., 1969, The effect of saturation on velocity in low porosity rocks: Earth and Planetary Science Letters, v. 7, p. 183–193.

Nur, A., Ron, H., and Beroza, G., 1993, Landers-Mojave earthquake line; a new fault system?: GSA Today, v. 3, p. 253, 256–258.

Pickett, G.R., 1963, Acoustic character logs and their applications in formation evaluation: Journal of Petroleum Technology, v. 15, p. 650–667.

Reasenberg, P., Ellsworth, W., and Walter, A., 1980, Teleseismic evidence for a low-velocity body under the Coso geothermal area: Journal of Geophysical Research, v. 85, p. 2471–2483.

Roquemore, G.R., and Simila, G.W., 1994, Aftershocks from the 28 June 1992 Landers earthquake; northern Mojave Desert to the Coso volcanic field, California: Bulletin of the Seismological Society of America, v. 84, p. 854–862.

Sanders, C., Ho, L.P., Rinn, D., and Kanamori, H., 1988, Anomalous shear wave attenuation in the shallow crust beneath the Coso volcanic region, California: Journal of Geophysical Research, v. 93, p. 3321–3338.

Schön, J.H., 1996, Physical properties of rocks: Fundamentals and principles of petrophysics, *in* Helbig, K., and Treitel, S., eds., Handbook of geophysical exploration: Pergamon Press.

Tatham, R.H., 1982, Vp/Vs and lithology: Geophysics, v. 47, p. 333–344.

Walck, M.C., 1988, Three-dimensional variations in shear structure and Vp/Vs for the Coso region, California: Journal of Geophysical Research, v. 93, p. 2047–2052.

Walck, M.C., and Clayton, R.W., 1987, P wave velocity variations in the Coso region, California, derived from local earthquake travel times: Journal of Geophysical Research, v. 92, p. 393–405.

Walter, A.W., and Weaver, C.S., 1980, Seismicity of the Coso Range, California: Journal of Geophysical Research, v. 85, p. 2441–2458.

Wu, H., and Lees, J.M., 1992a, Application of the pseudo-spectral method for calculation of synthetic seismograms [abs.]: Eos (Transactions, American Geophysical Union), v. 73, p. 340.

Wu, H., and Lees, J.M., 1992b, Synthetic seismograms using finite elements for local earthquake data: A comparison with analytic and finite difference methods [abs.]: Eos (Transactions, American Geophysical Union), v. 73, p. 193.

Wu, H., and Lees, J.M., 1996, Attenuation structure of the Coso geothermal area, California, from pulse width data of P-wave: Bulletin of the Seismological Society of America, v. 86, p. 1574–1590.

Wu, H., and Lees, J.M., 1997, Boundary conditions on a finite grid: Applications with pseudo-spectral wave propagation: Geophysics, v. 62, p. 1544–1555.

Wu, H., and Lees, J.M., 1999a, Cartesian parameterization of anisotropic traveltime tomography: Geophysical Journal International, v. 137, p. 64–80.

Wu, H., and Lees, J.M., 1999b, Three-dimensional P and S wave velocity structures of the Coso geothermal area, California, from microseismic traveltime data: Journal of Geophysical Research, v. 104, p. 13 217–13 233.

MANUSCRIPT ACCEPTED BY THE SOCIETY MAY 9, 2001

Geological Society of America
Memoir 195
2002

Seismotectonics of the Coso Range–Indian Wells Valley region, California: Transtensional deformation along the southeastern margin of the Sierran microplate

Jeffrey R. Unruh
William Lettis and Associates, Inc., 1777 Botelho Drive, Suite 262, Walnut Creek, California 94596, USA
Egill Hauksson
Seismological Laboratory, California Institute of Technology, Pasadena, California 91125, USA
Francis C. Monastero
Geothermal Program Office, Naval Air Weapons Station, China Lake, California 93555, USA
Robert J. Twiss
Jonathan C. Lewis*
Department of Geology, University of California, Davis, California 95616, USA

ABSTRACT

Space-based geodetic observations show that the Coso Range and Indian Wells Valley lie along the southeastern margin of the Sierra Nevada–Central Valley (i.e., "Sierran") microplate, which moves ~13–14 mm/yr northwest with respect to stable North America. Detailed kinematic analysis of seismicity indicates that active crustal extension in the Coso Range occurs in a right-lateral transtensional regime along the eastern border of the Sierran microplate. The Airport Lake fault in the northern Indian Wells Valley and the Owens Valley fault are the major strike-slip faults along the eastern margin of the Sierran microplate south and north, respectively, of the Coso Range. Patterns of seismogenic deformation and Quaternary faulting indicate that dextral shear passes through the Coso Range in a right-releasing stepover between the Airport Lake and Owens Valley faults. Extension within the stepover region is accommodated in part by opening of Coso Wash as a pull-apart basin. The stepover is bounded on the east by a blind, northwest-striking dextral fault that is well expressed by patterns of microseismicity. Comparison with analogue sandbox models of pull-apart basins suggests that the Coso stepover is a relatively immature structure, consistent with models for a westward step in the locus of dextral shear along the eastern margin of the Sierran microplate to the Indian Wells Valley and Owens Valley in the past 2–3 m.y.

INTRODUCTION

The Indian Wells Valley and the Coso Range border the southeastern margin of the Sierra Nevada (Fig. 1). Space-based

geodesy has shown that the Sierra Nevada and Central Valley of California together constitute a discrete microplate within the 1200-km-wide Pacific–North American plate boundary (Minster and Jordan, 1987; Argus and Gordon, 1991). The Si-

*E-mail: unruh@lettis.com. Current address, Lewis: Department of Geosciences, University of Massachusetts, Morrill Science Center, 611 North Pleasant Street, Amherst, Massachusetts 01003-9297, USA.

Unruh, J.R., Hauksson, E., Monastero, F.C., Twiss, R.J., and Lewis, J.C., 2002, Seismotectonics of the Coso Range–Indian Wells Valley region, California: Transtensional deformation along the southeastern margin of the Sierran microplate, *in* Glazner, A.F., Walker, J.D., and Bartley, J.M., eds., Geologic Evolution of the Mojave Desert and Southwestern Basin and Range: Boulder, Colorado, Geological Society of America Memoir 195, p. 277–294.

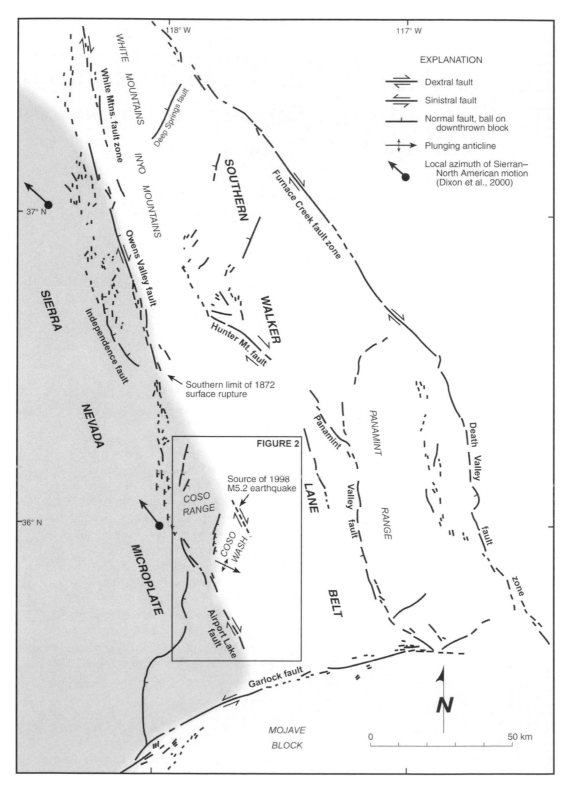

Figure 1. Major active faults of the southern Walker Lane belt (fault traces from Jennings, 1994). The Sierra Nevada–Central Valley (i.e., "Sierran") microplate is indicated by the shaded region. The Airport Lake fault in Indian Wells Valley is the geodetically defined eastern margin of the Sierran microplate south of 36°N (King et al., 1999). The Owens Valley fault is the major eastern tectonic boundary of the Sierran microplate north of the Coso Range. Integrated geologic and geodetic slip rates indicate that ~80%–85% of the total northwestward motion of the Sierran microplate with respect to stable North America is accommodated within the southern Walker Lane belt (Dixon et al., 2000).

erra Nevada–Central Valley (i.e., "Sierran") microplate moves ~13–14 mm/yr in a northwest direction relative to stable North America (Dixon et al., 2000), and the azimuth of motion becomes more toward the west at progressively farther north positions along the eastern margin of the microplate (Argus and Gordon, 1991). At the latitude of Owens Valley (Fig. 1), most of the Sierran–North American motion is accommodated within an ~100-km-wide zone of active strike-slip and normal faulting that borders the eastern Sierra Nevada (Reheis and Dixon, 1996; Dixon et al., 1995, 2000). This zone has been referred to in the literature variously as the Walker Lane belt (Stewart, 1988), eastern California shear zone (Dokka and Travis, 1990), and Sierra Nevada–Great Basin boundary zone (Van Wormer and Ryall, 1980). We use the term "Walker Lane belt" to describe this zone because it has precedence in the literature and is in current usage (e.g., Dixon et al., 2000).

Although geodetic studies have clearly documented distributed northwest-directed dextral shear in the southern Walker Lane belt, Quaternary deformation in the Coso Range is dominated by extensional tectonics. Previous workers have noted that the Coso Range and adjacent Coso Wash to the east are bounded by Quaternary-active normal faults (Fig. 2) and that extension has been accompanied by Pliocene-Pleistocene magmatism (Duffield et al., 1980). The central Coso Range hosts a geothermal field, and surface manifestations of hydrothermal activity locally are associated with Holocene normal faults (Roquemore, 1981). The spatial association of normal faulting and geothermal activity prompted some workers to attribute Quaternary deformation in the Coso Range to basin-and-range-style crustal extension (Duffield et al., 1980). Other workers, noting the predominance of strike-slip focal mechanisms and the en echelon geometry of Quaternary normal faults, have argued that extension is a component of distributed dextral shear (Walter and Weaver, 1980; Roquemore, 1980; Whitmarsh et al., 1996).

In this paper, we present a kinematic analysis of seismicity in the Coso Range–Indian Wells Valley region, with emphasis on interpreting active extensional deformation in the context of northwest-directed dextral shear along the southeastern margin of the Sierran microplate. We synthesize the results of our analysis with geologic, geodetic, and other geophysical data to develop a kinematic model for active deformation in this region, and we discuss the implications of the model for the presence of the Coso geothermal field.

NEOTECTONIC SETTING OF THE COSO RANGE–INDIAN WELLS VALLEY REGION

The Coso Range–Indian Wells Valley region straddles the tectonic boundary between the Sierran microplate and the southern Walker Lane belt. Geodetic data collected by the U.S. Navy Geothermal Program Office and analyzed by King et al. (1999) show that this boundary is characterized by a sharp velocity gradient. When Global Positioning System (GPS) station

velocities are displayed relative to a site in the southern Sierra Nevada, a northwest-trending zone is apparent that separates (1) sites in western Indian Wells Valley that are not moving with respect to the Sierra Nevada from (2) sites to the east and southeast that are moving in a right-lateral sense (i.e., southeast) with respect to the Sierra Nevada. From south to north, this zone passes through the central Indian Wells Valley and Coso Wash, then crosses the northern Coso Range and projects northwestward into the southern Owens Valley (Fig. 1). The velocity gradient across this zone is the geodetic expression of active dextral shear along the eastern margin of the Sierran microplate at this latitude and specifically locates this tectonic boundary in the central Indian Wells Valley and Coso Range.

King et al. (1999) reproduced the observed GPS station velocities in the Coso Range–Indian Wells Valley region by modeling the deformation as a single northwest-striking dextral fault that obliquely crosses Indian Wells Valley, terminates at or near the edge of the eastern Sierran escarpment in southern Rose Valley (Fig. 2), and slips at a rate of ~5 mm/yr below a shallow locked section. The modeled fault of King et al. (1999) generally coincides with a 4–7-km-wide zone of Quaternary faulting (Fig. 2) and active seismicity (Fig. 3) that trends northwest across Indian Wells Valley. At the surface, the fault zone is expressed as a series of short, left-stepping en echelon fault scarps (Duffield and Bacon, 1981; Fig. 2). The fault zone is a locus of background seismicity and swarm activity, and it produced a M 5.8 earthquake in September 1995 (Hauksson et al., 1995; Fig. 3). The northern reach of this fault zone is called the Airport Lake fault, and it is mapped as extending northward to the southeast margin of the Coso Range (Roquemore, 1980) (Fig. 2).

Surface faulting associated with the Airport Lake fault zone splits into two branches at the southern end of the Coso Range. A western branch, called the Little Lake fault, curves west, crosses the southwestern edge of the Coso Range and continues northward into western Rose Valley (Fig. 2). Roquemore (1981) documented structural and geomorphic relationships consistent with late Quaternary right-lateral displacement on the Little Lake fault in the southern Coso Range. Another branch of the Airport Lake fault extends northward, breaks into several splays across the Pleistocene White Hills anticline, and continues north along the western margin of Coso Wash (Fig. 2). Fumaroles, hot springs, and steaming fissures are associated with this fault zone at the north end of Coso Wash (Roquemore, 1981). For convenience, we refer to this branch as the Coso Wash fault. In detail, the Coso Wash fault is a series of left-stepping en echelon normal-fault segments.

The Coso Wash fault joins the north-trending Haiwee Springs fault zone at the northern end of Coso Wash (Fig. 2). Walker and Whitmarsh (1998) characterized this structure as a zone of northeast- to northwest-striking normal faults and north- to northwest-striking strike-slip faults that disrupt Pliocene volcanic rocks. On the basis of the offset of a Mesozoic dike swarm in the northern Coso Range, Walker and Whitmarsh

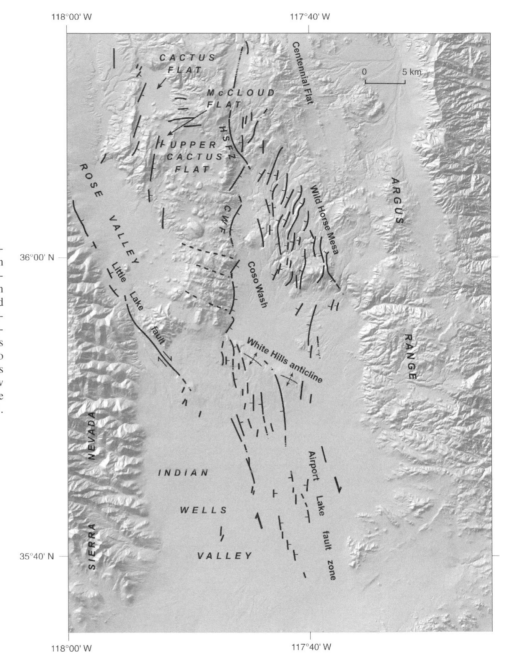

Figure 2. Known and inferred late Quaternary faults and folds along the eastern margin of the Sierran microplate between Indian Wells Valley and southern Owens Valley (modified from Duffield and Bacon, 1981; Walker and Whitmarsh, 1998). Only structures with discernible geomorphic expression at this scale are highlighted. CWF—Coso Wash fault; HSFZ—Haiwee Springs fault zone. Paired bold arrows show dextral shear along the Airport Lake fault zone. Other symbols as in Figure 1.

(1998) estimated that the Haiwee Springs fault zone has accommodated ~5–6 km of right-lateral slip.

The east side of Coso Wash and the adjacent Wild Horse Mesa are deformed by a series of north-northeast–striking, west-dipping normal faults that form dramatic scarps in Pliocene volcanic flows (Fig. 2). This region was referred to as a "step-faulted terrain" by Duffield and Bacon (1981). The displaced surfaces of the volcanic flows progressively step upward to the east along the faults, which terminate along a northwest-trending escarpment at the western edge of the Argus Range. Moderate-magnitude earthquake sequences occurred along this escarpment in 1996 and 1998 (Fig. 3). Aftershocks of the 1998

event formed a northwest alignment of epicenters along the eastern margin of the step-faulted terrain, and focal mechanisms indicated primarily right-lateral slip on northwest-striking nodal planes.

Late Cenozoic faults also have been mapped in the northwestern Coso Range (Duffield and Bacon, 1981). These structures have two major preferred orientations: (1) North-northeast–striking normal faults associated with prominent east-facing, left-stepping escarpments along the margins of Cactus Flat and McCloud Flat and (2) east-northeast–striking faults in Upper Cactus Flat and McCloud Flat with inferred left-lateral displacements (Fig. 2). The northern Coso Range is an

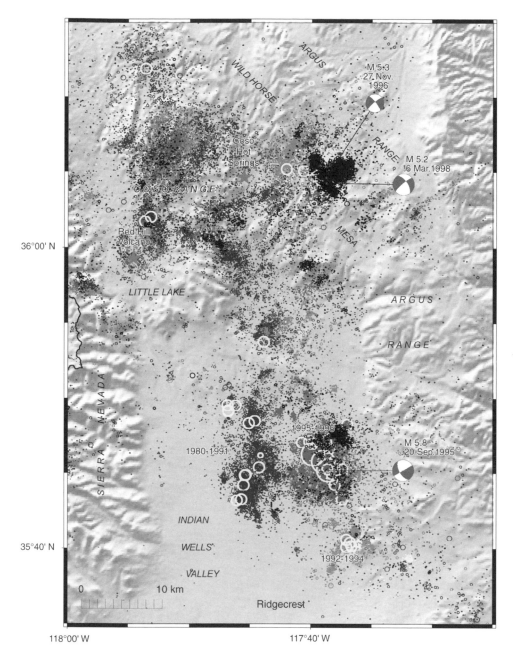

Figure 3. Epicenters of earthquakes in the Coso Range and Indian Wells Valley recorded by the Southern California Seismic Network (SCSN) from 1980 to 1998. Events have been relocated via joint hypocentral inversion. Note prominent clusters of activity in the northern Coso Range and in Indian Wells Valley.

area of elevated background seismicity relative to Rose Valley to the west (Fig. 3), and clusters of small-magnitude events occur in the vicinity of Cactus Flat.

North of the Coso Range, the major active structure along the eastern margin of the Sierra Nevada is the Owens Valley fault (Fig. 1), which was the source of the M 8 1872 Owens Valley earthquake (Beanland and Clark, 1994). Surface rupture associated with the 1872 earthquake extended as far south as the western margin of Owens Lake, within 10 km of the Coso Range (Beanland and Clark, 1994) (Fig. 1). Coseismic surface displacement during the 1872 event was predominantly dextral with a subordinate component of east-side-down normal separation. On the basis of modeling of GPS station velocities, King

et al. (1999) inferred that the Owens Valley fault currently slips ~6 mm/yr at depth below an upper locked section, which is comparable to the 5 mm/yr secular rate estimated for the Airport Lake fault south of the Coso Range. These relationships thus suggest that Quaternary faults in the Coso Range transfer dextral slip along the eastern margin of the Sierran microplate northward from Indian Wells Valley to the southern Owens Valley.

ANALYTICAL APPROACH

The microseismicity in the Indian Wells Valley–Coso Range region provides a detailed snapshot of active deformation along the eastern margin of the Sierran microplate. Most earthquakes recorded in this region have small magnitudes ($M \leq 3$) with rupture dimensions on the order of a few tens to a few hundreds of meters. We evaluate the average brittle deformation of volumes of crust that are much larger than the rupture radius of these small events, such that the distributed coseismic displacements can be assumed to approximate a continuous deformation. When averaged over time, the seismogenic deformation accommodates a "seismic flow" of the brittle crust (per Kostrov, 1974) that is analogous to cataclastic flow of rocks at smaller scales. Our approach to evaluating this "seismic flow" is to invert patterns of coseismic slip on faults within given volumes of crust for the components of a reduced deformation-rate tensor (Twiss et al., 1993; Twiss and Unruh, 1998). The orientations of the principal strain rates can be determined over large areas to depict the regional seismogenic deformation field and assess local fault kinematics (e.g., Unruh et al., 1996).

We use a micropolar continuum model (Eringen, 1966, 1967) as a basis for inverting earthquake focal mechanisms for components of a reduced deformation-rate tensor. The micropolar model assumes that the brittle crust deforms like a granular material, where the "grains" are rigid, fault-bounded blocks with dimensions of hundreds of meters to kilometers (Twiss et al., 1993). The micropolar theory relates the instantaneous direction of shear along the boundaries of the "grains" to the larger-scale deformation of the material and to the local rotation of the fault blocks (Twiss et al., 1991). We make the explicit assumptions that coseismic slip occurs in the direction of the maximum resolved rate of shear on the fault surface and that the shear rate is the net result of the large-scale strain-rate tensor and a large-scale average of the local relative block rotation rates (Twiss et al., 1993). Detailed examples of this approach applied to the analysis of earthquake focal mechanisms are presented in Unruh et al. (1996, 1997) and Unruh and Lettis (1998).

The data used for the inversions are phase picks for earthquakes recorded by the Southern California Seismographic Network (SCSN), a joint project of the California Institute of Technology and the U.S. Geological Survey. The earthquakes were relocated by using three-dimensional V_p and V_p/V_s velocity models (Hauksson, 2000). The take-off angles were also determined by using the three-dimensional velocity model to calculate focal mechanisms. Because of the high seismicity rate in the Coso region, the SCSN has a dense station distribution, making determination of accurate hypocenters and focal mechanisms possible. Over 10 000 focal mechanisms with more than 12 first motions were obtained for the kinematic analysis. The medians of the misfits in the strike, dip, and rake of this data set are 10°, 22°, and 25°, respectively. Histogram plots of the strike, dip, and rake misfits show that the misfits form tight distributions with 50% of the data within 10° for strike, 18° for dip, and 15° for rake. Thus, these focal mechanisms are of high quality compared to mechanisms from other regions of southern California.

We defined subsets of focal mechanisms based on (1) clusters or alignments of earthquakes associated with discrete seismic sources and (2) distributed seismicity within distinct structures or structural domains. We plotted seismic P and T axes (the principal shortening and extension directions, respectively, associated with each focal mechanism) from each subset on lower-hemisphere Kamb contour plots to assess data homogeneity. We then used an automated grid-searching algorithm (FLTSLPVXT98; R. Twiss and L. Guenther, University of California at Davis) to find the values of the parameters for a micropolar model that minimize the misfit between the theoretically calculated P and T axes and the observed seismic P and T axes for each domain. The five parameters of the micropolar model that we use are described next.

1 to 3. Three independent parameters, such as three Euler angles, uniquely define the orientations of the three principal axes of the strain-rate tensor d, the symmetric part of the large-scale velocity-gradient tensor (d_1, maximum lengthening; d_3, maximum shortening; d_2, intermediate principal axis).

4. A scalar parameter D (the deformation-rate parameter) is defined by a ratio of the differences in the principal strain rates and it characterizes the shape of the strain-rate ellipsoid:

$$D \equiv (d_2 - d_3)/(d_1 - d_3). \qquad (1)$$

The parameter D is independent of volumetric deformation, but the geometric interpretation of its values is not. For a constant-volume deformation, the values of D define how the deformation departs from a plane strain. For example, a value of $D = 0.5$ means that d_1 and d_3 are of equal magnitude but opposite sign and that there is no length change parallel to d_2 (i.e., the deformation is a plane strain in the d_1–d_3 plane). Values of $D > 0.5$ imply a component of lengthening parallel to d_2, and values of $D < 0.5$ imply a component of shortening parallel to d_2. If d_1 and d_3 are horizontal, then $D > 0.5$ describes a "transpressional" deformation and $D < 0.5$ describes a "transtensional" deformation.

5. A scalar parameter W characterizes the relative vorticity (i.e., relative incremental rotation) of rigid, fault-bounded blocks about an axis parallel to d_2 (Twiss et al., 1993):

$$W \equiv (\omega_{13} - w_{13})/[0.5(d_1 - d_3)], \qquad (2)$$

where w_{13} is a component of the antisymmetric part of the large-scale velocity-gradient tensor that describes the average large-scale rotation rate about d_2 (i.e., the macrovorticity) and ω_{13} is an independent component describing the local block-rotation rate about d_2; the terms w_{13} and ω_{13} are components in the principal coordinates of d. Zero values of W imply that fault-bounded blocks are rotating at the same rate as the macrovorticity; if the axis of macrovorticity is parallel to the positive d_2 coordinate axis, positive and negative values of W imply local block-rotation rates greater than and less than the macrovorticity respectively. As a first approximation, we ignore components of the relative vorticity about the other principal axes, d_1 and d_3. Twiss et al. (1993) discussed systematic relationships between W and fault-block geometry for various kinematic block-rotation models.

Our inversion used a five-parameter downhill simplex search algorithm called "amoeba" (Press et al., 1990, §10.4) to find a best-fit solution to the fault-slip data. The misfit for each datum is taken to be the mean of the cosines between the observed and the model P and T axes, which for small angles approximates the unique rotation angle that brings the model P and T axes into coincidence with the observed P and T axes (discussed in the appendix to Unruh et al., 1996). The average of these misfits over all the focal mechanisms in the data set defines the mean cosine misfit, which increases toward a maximum of 1 as the model approaches the data. Thus, the search algorithm finds the model parameters that maximize the mean cosine misfit. The average misfit is reported as the angle α whose cosine is the mean cosine misfit (i.e., $\alpha = \cos^{-1}$[mean cosine misfit]) (Tables 1 and 2).

To evaluate uncertainty in the best-fit micropolar model parameters, we performed selected bootstrap analyses on three subsets representing a range of data-set sizes and model misfits (Fig. 4). Each plot in Figure 4 presents the 95% confidence limits determined from 2000 bootstrap models for the orientations of d_1 and d_3 (areas shaded dark and light gray, respectively, in Fig. 4) as well as the Kamb contours of the density of bootstrap solutions for each axis. The 95% confidence limits for D and W are listed below each stereogram. It is apparent that the resolution of the model parameters for the small data set (EUCF) is considerably worse than for the larger sets (NWIW, CAPK). The solutions, however, are highly concentrated in relatively small areas, even for the small data set, as indicated by the contours of bootstrap-solution density for which the contour intervals vary from 20 to 50 times standard deviation (σ) from a random distribution (Fig. 4).

For this study, we focus on the geometry of the strain-rate tensors obtained from the inversions. The significance of the net-vorticity parameter W in the Coso Range is the subject of

TABLE 1. SEISMOGENIC DEFORMATION IN THE COSO RANGE–INDIAN WELLS VALLEY REGION

Domain	d_1 (trend, plunge)	d_3 (trend, plunge)	D	W	$\cos^{-1}$ (Mean Cos Error)	Vertical component	Number of data
SSWI SE Sierra Nevada and SW Indian Wells Valley	128, −3	39, 11	0.5	0.3	5.4020	0	56
RIDG Ridgecrest Area	94, −13	5, 2	0.5	−0.3	6.1863	0.1	250
SWIW SW Indian Wells Valley	91, −23	19, 37	0.5	0.5	6.8368	−0.2	192
NWIW NW Indian Wells Valley	103, −10	15, 12	0.6	0.1	6.3725	0.1	78
EIWV Eastern Indian Wells Valley	97, 2	7, 0	0.5	0.2	6.7727	0	79
SARG Southern Argus Range	81, −22	3, 28	0.4	0.1	6.4217	−0.1	54
WHIL White Hills	106, −2	16, 12	0.5	0.1	6.5561	0	94
COBA Coso Basin	114, −22	29, 13	0.4	0.6	5.3546	0	146
SWLD Southern Wild Horse Mesa	101, −5	185, 48	0.4	0.1	6.5114	−0.5	83
SRNV Eastern Sierra Nevada	112, −4	22, 11	0.5	0.0	6.2990	0	65
RHVO Red Hill volcano area	116, −35	41, 21	0.5	−0.2	6.3275	0.2	48
WROS Western Rose Valley	126, −7	35, −11	0.5	0.3	5.2696	0	37
CACT Cactus Flat area	99, −13	14, 20	0.4	0.3	7.4430	−0.1	46
CAPK Cactus Peak area	106, 5	11, 40	0.5	−0.2	7.6567	−0.4	82
WHCF Wild Horse Mesa–Cactus Flat area	92, −16	356, −19	0.7	−0.1	5.4962	0.1	56
CFHF Coso geothermal field	103, −3	14, 14	0.4	0.0	7.8324	−0.1	240
SUGR Sugarloaf Mountain	129, 1	4, −11	0.5	0.6	4.0944	−0.1	42
NARG Northern Argus Range	90, −15	353, −21	0.5	−0.2	6.3224	0	67
NOCB Northern Coso basin and southern Coso Wash	92, −5	2, −5	0.4	0	6.3742	−0.1	67

TABLE 2. SEISMOGENIC DEFORMATION IN THE CENTRAL COSO RANGE

Domain	d_1 (trend, plunge)	d_3 (trend, plunge)	D	W	Cos^{-1} (Mean Cos Error)	Vertical component	Number of data
WROS Western Rose Valley	126, −3	36, −8	0.5	0.4	3.6598	−0.1	26
SNEV Eastern Sierra Nevada	109, −4	20, 12	0.5	0.1	6.1693	0	48
RSPR Rose Spring area	111, 24	358, 41	0.6	0.7	2.4904	−0.3	11
SNEC NE-trending alignment of epicenters, Coles Flat	94, 5	5, −7	0.5	0.4	3.7883	0	24
RHVO Red Hill volcano area	111, −2	20, −13	0.5	0.1	6.1214	0.1	47
EROS Eastern Rose Valley	115, 4	26, −10	0.6	0.6	5.9178	0.1	281
SWSG SW flank of Sugarloaf Mountain	96, −3	7, 19	0.4	−0.2	4.2771	−0.2	22
SESG SE flank of Sugarloaf Mountain	117, −18	29, 7	0.4	0.2	4.9317	0	44
NWCB NW Coso basin and southern Coso Wash	101, −4	23, 42	0.4	0.0	6.4021	−0.5	91
NOCB Northern Coso basin and southern Coso Wash	97, −2	7, −1	0.5	0.0	5.5924	0	96
SFWH Step-faulted terrain, Wild Horse Mesa	100, −3	101, 87	0.6	0.1	6.2981	−1.0	74
DEVK Devil's Kitchen area, Coso geothermal field	117, −19	28, 2	0.4	−0.2	4.8686	0	19
NOWH Northern Wild Horse Mesa	114, −19	40, 38	0.4	0.4	4.5758	−0.3	46
SLPK Silver Peak area	82, −20	343, −23	0.6	0.0	6.1498	0	99
PVDE Pleistocene vent near Deadman Cabin	102, 6	7, 37	0.5	−0.1	6.2714	−0.3	23
NWWH NW-trending epicenters, 1996–98 earthquake sequence	96, −6	4, −21	0.5	−0.1	6.0714	−0.1	346
NEWH NE-trending epicenters, 1996–98 earthquake sequence	106, −19	17, 4	0.5	0.2	6.6591	0.1	223
NMCC Northern McCloud Flat	63, −43	332, −1	0.5	−0.7	4.6787	0.5	30
SMCC Southern McCloud Flat	84, −23	348, −14	0.6	0.8	4.4045	0.2	26
UCFL Upper Cactus Flat area	113, −40	209, −8	0.2	−0.3	7.9567	0.2	25
EUCF Eastern Upper Cactus Flat	109, −45	21, 2	0.2	0.2	7.8637	0.3	22
RSPR Rose Spring, upper Rose Valley	111, 24	358, 41	0.6	0.7	2.4904	−0.3	11
WCPK Western Cactus Peak area	114, −26	36, 24	0.4	0.0	5.5025	0	51

an on-going investigation and is not assessed here. To illustrate the seismogenic deformation field, we plot the horizontal projections of the principal incremental strains d_1 and d_3 from each inversion; we then draw smooth trajectories through the strain orientations to illustrate regional trends (Figs. 5 and 6). When d_1 and d_3 are horizontal, their respective trajectories are orthogonal. In addition, if the value of the intermediate principal strain rate is zero (i.e., $D = 0.5$), then the deformation is a horizontal plane strain. When one or both of the d_1 and d_3 strain rates have a significant plunge, the bulk deformation may include a component of vertical thickening or thinning, and when both have a significant plunge, the horizontal d_1 and d_3 trajectories are no longer orthogonal. To evaluate the vertical com-

ponent of the deformation field (V_D), we first express the principal values of the strain-rate tensor in terms of the parameter D (see the Appendix), then we transform the tensor from its principal coordinate system to a geographic coordinate system X'_k (with axes oriented east, north, up for $k = 1, 2, 3$, respectively). The value of the component d'_{33} of the transformed tensor parallel to the X'_3 direction is then the magnitude of the vertical extension rate. For a constant volume deformation, V_D is this vertical component of the extension rate normalized by the magnitude of the maximum principal extension rate d_1. A V_D value of zero implies zero vertical deformation. Positive values of V_D indicate net crustal thickening, and negative values indicate net crustal thinning (see the Appendix).

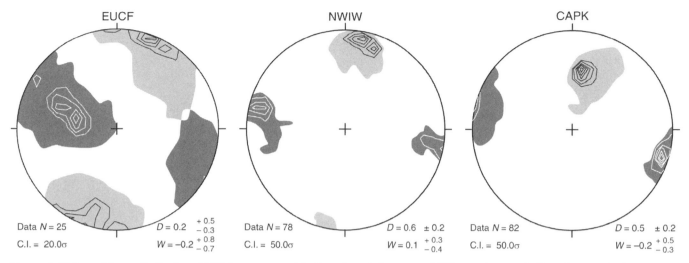

Figure 4. 95% confidence limits from 2000 bootstrap models for selected data sets of different sizes, as indicated for each diagram (see Figs. 5 and 6 for locations of kinematic domains; best-fit model parameters are listed in Tables 1 and 2). Dark gray and light gray areas show the 95% confidence limits enclosing 1900 bootstrap models for d_1 and d_3 axes, respectively. White contours and black contours are Kamb contours for the density of d_1 and d_3 bootstrap solutions, respectively; contour intervals are in multiples of standard deviations above random, as indicated for each diagram. The 95% confidence limits for D and W are listed with each stereogram. Lower-hemisphere, equal-area projections. (See also Fig. 10.)

INVERSION RESULTS

Seismogenic deformation field

Because the period of time sampled by the seismicity data is essentially instantaneous relative to the scale of geologic time, the strain rates and rotation rates that form the basis of the micropolar theory also can be viewed as incremental strains and incremental rotations, which is the interpretation we adopt hereafter. The seismogenic deformation field in Indian Wells Valley and Coso Range is characterized by north-south to north-east-southwest shortening (d_3), and east-west to northwest-southeast extension (d_1; Fig. 4; Table 1). The subhorizontal orientation of the principal incremental strains in all domains directly adjacent to and within the eastern Sierra Nevada favors strike-slip faulting to accommodate the deformation. The principal strain trajectories are oriented ~45° to the eastern Sierran escarpment, implying that seismogenic deformation along range-front faults primarily accommodates northwest-directed right-lateral shear at this latitude.

The inversion results in Figure 4 can be used to assess the direction of maximum incremental dextral shear strain associated with seismogenic deformation. In general, planes of maximum incremental shear strain are parallel to the intermediate principal strain (d_2) and are oriented 45° to d_1 and d_3. In the study area, therefore, planes of maximum right-lateral shear are subvertical and strike northwest. Because d_1 and d_3 in Indian Wells Valley and the Coso Range trend west-northwest and north-northeast, respectively (Table 1), the average direction of macroscopic dextral shear is rotated several degrees clockwise of N45°W. For comparison, the azimuth of Sierran–North

American motion in Indian Wells Valley predicted by the preferred Euler pole of Dixon et al. (2000) is N42°W. We thus interpret that a seismogenic deformation in this region primarily accommodates Sierran–North American motion.

A more detailed map of the principal strain trajectories in the Coso Range (Fig. 6 and Table 2) based on a finer spatial subdivision of focal mechanisms shows that the principal strain trajectories in the Coso Range are less smooth and exhibit distinct changes in orientation over distances of 5–10 km. For example, note the local counterclockwise deflections of the principal incremental strain trajectories near McCloud Flat (domains NMCC, SMCC, and SNEC; Fig. 6). In general, however, the average orientations of the principal strains in the Coso Range are similar to trends exhibited by the regional map (Fig. 5), including a modest clockwise rotation of the trajectories at progressively farther west locations from the Argus Range across the Coso Range to the Sierran escarpment. These relationships suggest that, although the seismogenic deformation field is relatively smooth at a regional scale (Fig. 5) and consistent with the geodetically observed deformation, variations on a scale of 5–10 km are present and may reflect local kinematic adjustments to motions along the boundaries of larger crustal blocks. Given the limited observation period of the seismicity data, we cannot preclude the possibility that these adjustments vary in time as well as space.

Because the principal extensional and contractional incremental strains for individual domains generally are subhorizontal and the value of the deformation parameter D is close to 0.5, the vertical component of the regional deformation field (V_D) is negligible (Table 1). The major exception is the southern Wild Horse Mesa area (domain SWLD; location in Fig. 5; Table

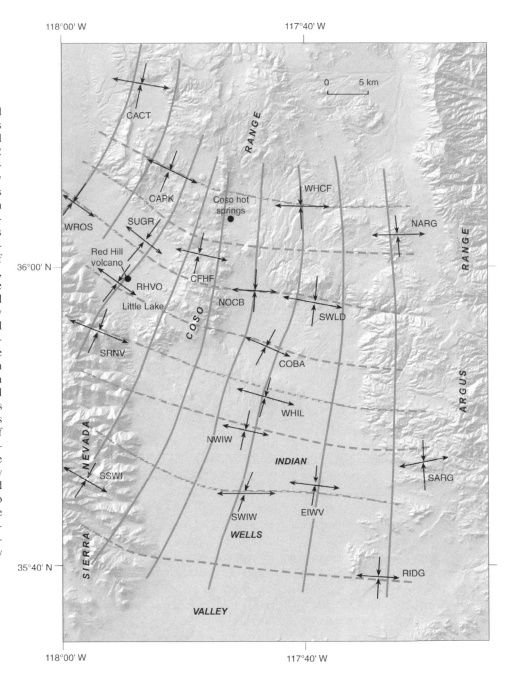

Figure 5. Seismogenic deformation field in the greater Coso Range–Indian Wells Valley region (Quaternary faults and folds are omitted for clarity; see Fig. 2 for a version of this map with Quaternary structures). Pairs of arrows show the trend of the incremental strain axes for individual domains obtained from kinematic inversions of focal mechanisms (d_1 and d_3 trends shown on this map are reported in Table 1). Outward-pointing arrows indicate the direction of maximum incremental extension (d_1), and inward-pointing arrows indicate the direction of maximum incremental shortening (d_3). Arrows only show trends of the principal incremental strains; where one or both of the principal strains plunge significantly (Table 1), the arrows are not orthogonal in plan view. Domain names described in greater detail in Table 1. The regional field is depicted by smooth trajectories drawn parallel to the local orientations of d_1 and d_3 (dashed lines—trends of maximum extension; solid lines—trends of maximum shortening). Note that normal faults are approximately perpendicular to d_1 trajectories, fold axes are approximately perpendicular to d_3 trajectories, and strike-slip faults are ~45° to the d_1 and d_3 trajectories, indicating that the mixed styles of deformation are compatible with a relatively uniform regional field.

1), where the principal incremental shortening strain d_3 is moderately plunging and the seismogenic deformation locally accommodates a component of crustal thinning. We further assess the kinematic significance of crustal thinning in the vicinity of Wild Horse Mesa in the next section.

As previously noted by Roquemore (1981), the diverse orientations of Quaternary structures and styles of faulting in the Coso Range can be reconciled with deformation in a strike-slip regime. In general, normal faults such as the Coso Wash fault and the step faults on Wild Horse Mesa strike at a very high angle to the trajectories of maximum extension (Figs. 5 and 6). The axes of the folds that compose the White Hills anticline

are approximately normal to the trajectories of maximum shortening (Fig. 5). Thus, both normal faults and folds are optimally oriented to accommodate extension and contraction, respectively, in the modern seismotectonic setting. The en echelon geometries of these structures in the Coso Range are characteristic of a transcurrent regime (Roquemore, 1980, 1981).

Localized crustal extension

Values of V_D in the Coso Range and Wild Horse Mesa (Table 2) range from −1.0 (domain SFWH) to 0.4 (domain NMCC; Fig. 7). With the caveat that minor departures from

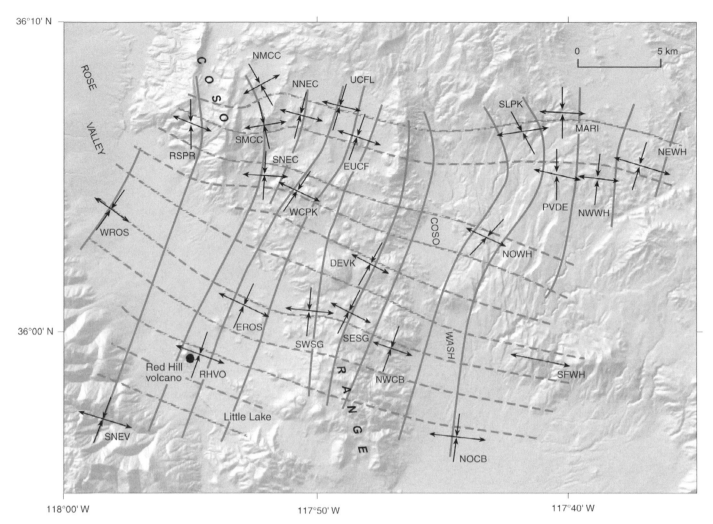

Figure 6. Detailed seismogenic deformation field in the Coso Range. Symbol conventions are the same as for Figure 5; d_1 and d_3 trends shown on this map are reported in Table 2 and explained in the caption for Figure 5. Domain names described in greater detail in Table 2. For clarity, faults are not shown; however, prominent topographic scarps associated with normal faults in Wild Horse Mesa, Coso Wash, and Cactus Flat are readily apparent on the hill-shade map (illumination from the northwest). See Figure 7 for a version of this map with location names and major faults.

zero (± 0.2) may not be statistically significant, several trends are apparent. Areas of Coso Wash and the step-faulted terrain on Wild Horse Mesa are consistently characterized by negative values of the vertical component (Fig. 7; Table 2). In contrast, the central Coso Range and Rose Valley generally exhibit V_D values ranging between -0.2 and 0.2, which we infer to reflect negligible thinning or thickening of the seismogenic crust. Values of V_D in the northwestern Coso Range near Cactus Flat vary between -0.5 and 0.4. These variations, if significant, probably reflect thinning and thickening of the crust associated with local fault kinematics, but exhibit no systematic pattern across a broader region. The vertical component in domains directly associated with the Coso geothermal field generally is zero (Fig. 7; Table 2).

The most significant and laterally extensive departures from horizontal plane strain occur in the vicinity of Wild Horse

Mesa and Coles Flat (Fig. 7), where negative values of V_D indicate that the deformation includes crustal thinning. These inversion results are consistent with the presence of the extensional Coso Wash, the step-faulted terrain of Wild Horse Mesa, and small, fault-bounded alluviated valleys or basins mapped in the Coles Flat area by Duffield and Bacon (1981). Most of the values of V_D in these extensional regions are intermediate (between 0 and -0.5), indicating a large if not dominant component of strike-slip faulting in the seismogenic deformation.

The largest absolute value of V_D in the study region is associated with the step-faulted terrain on Wild Horse Mesa (domain SFWD; Table 2 and Fig. 7). The best-fit tensor for inversion of all focal mechanisms from this domain has a V_D value of -1.0 (Fig. 8), implying uniaxial northwest-southeast extension with an equal and opposite magnitude of vertical

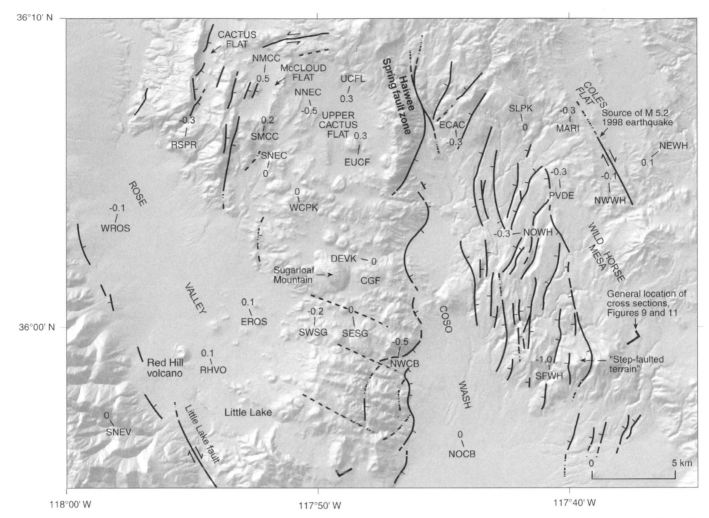

Figure 7. Values of the vertical component (V_D) of the incremental-strain tensors for seismotectonic domains in the Coso Range (Table 2). Base map is the same as for Figure 5, but faults with clear geomorphic expression at this scale are indicated. Note that values of V_D in the Wild Horse Mesa area consistently are negative, indicating that the seismogenic deformation accommodates a component of net crustal thinning. The −1.0 value for the vertical component of domain SFWH is discussed in detail in the text. CGF—Coso geothermal field.

shortening (i.e., crustal thinning). An inspection of the distribution of seismic P and T axes from the focal mechanisms reveals, however, that the data include two distinct groups of events: (1) strike-slip earthquakes, associated with horizontal P axes, and (2) normal-faulting events, with vertical P axes (Fig. 9). Further subdivision of the earthquakes in domain SFWD indicates that normal-faulting events generally are confined to the upper 5 km of the crust and that strike-slip faulting primarily occurs below 5 km depth (Fig. 9). Bootstrap analysis indicates that the horizontal extensional and vertical thinning strain associated with events in the upper 5 km is distinct from the horizontal plane strain in the 5–8 km depth range at the 95% confidence interval (Fig. 10). A cross section of the hypocenters in domain SFWD viewed looking northwest shows that the extensional events are diffusely distributed within a shallow crustal volume (Fig. 9). The strike-slip events define a deeper northwest-striking plane that dips ~65° southwest.

A cross-section interpretation of the relationship of the seismogenic structures at depth to surface faults is presented in Figure 11. Coso Wash is interpreted to be an asymmetric graben bounded on the west by the Coso Wash fault. The west-down step faults of Wild Horse Mesa are interpreted to be antithetic structures that terminate downdip against the Coso Wash fault. The blind, seismogenic strike-slip fault defined by the hypocentral alignment in Figure 9 underlies Wild Horse Mesa and eastern Coso Wash. We infer that seismogenic extension is confined to the volume of crust bounded by the Coso Wash fault and the updip continuation of the blind strike-slip fault (Figs. 9 and 11).

The extensional deformation represented by opening of Coso Wash is driven by a releasing transfer of dextral slip from the Airport Lake fault to the blind strike-slip fault beneath Wild Horse Mesa. Coso Wash graben is a negative flower structure associated with the releasing stepover and specifically is tied to

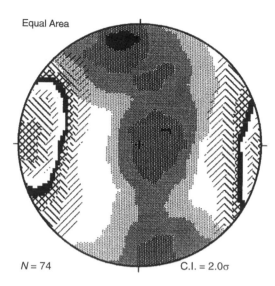

Equal Area

N = 74   C.I. = 2.0σ

Step-faulted terrain, Wild Horse Mesa (SFWH)
P axes shaded; T axes striped

Inversion Results:

d_1 (trend, plunge) = 100, -3
d_3 (trend, plunge) = 101, 87
D (deformation parameter) = 0.55
W (relative-vorticity parameter) = 0.12
Inverse mean cosine error = 6.2981

Figure 8. Kamb contour plot of seismic P axes (shaded) and T axes (striped) from earthquakes beneath the step-faulted terrain on Wild Horse Mesa (domain SFWH; see Figs. 6 and 7 for location). The T axes form well-defined subhorizontal clusters trending northwest. In contrast, the P axes form two discrete maxima: (1) a group of events with subhorizontal, northeast-trending P axes, indicating predominantly strike-slip faulting, and (2) a group of events with steeply plunging to subvertical P axes, indicating predominantly normal faulting.

the blind strike-slip fault beneath Wild Horse Mesa. The blind strike-slip fault projects updip to the eastern edge of the step-faulted region, where a moderate-magnitude earthquake occurred on trend to the north on a northwest-striking dextral fault in 1998 (Figs. 3 and 7). This structural interpretation is consistent with analysis of GPS data by King et al. (1999), who modeled active deformation in the Coso Range north of the Airport Lake fault as reflecting a combination of strike-slip faulting and extension.

Kinematic model for transtensional deformation in the Coso Range

Kinematic inversions of focal mechanisms presented in this paper show that active extension in the Coso Range occurs in the context of distributed northwest-directed dextral shear along the eastern margin of the Sierran microplate. The Airport Lake fault and Owens Valley fault are the primary strike-slip faults

bordering the Sierra south and north, respectively, of the Coso Range. Geologic relationships documented by Roquemore (1980) indicate that the long-term average slip rate on the Little Lake fault in western Rose Valley is ~0.25 mm/yr; thus this fault does not accommodate the majority of the geodetically determined 5–6 mm/yr of dextral shear on the Airport Lake and Owens Valley faults (King et al., 1999). Instead of strike-slip faulting, we propose that northwest-southeast extension in the Coso Range is a significant mechanism for transferring northwestward motion of the Sierran microplate from Indian Wells Valley to Owens Valley.

Given the geometry of the major strike-slip faults and the Sierran range front, a transfer of northwest-directed dextral shear from Indian Wells Valley to Owens Valley requires a right step across the Coso Range. The northwest strike of the Airport Lake fault is subparallel to the N42°W azimuth of Sierran motion, but is oriented more toward the west than the north trend of the Sierran escarpment (Fig. 1). If the Airport Lake fault continued on strike past the southern end of the Coso Range, then it would intersect the Sierran escarpment ~30 km south of Owens Valley. In order for dextral shear on the Airport Lake fault to be transferred to the Owens Valley fault, the locus of deformation must step right across the Coso Range.

At least some of the slip transfer is accommodated by the opening of Coso Wash as a pull-apart basin between the northern Airport Lake fault and the strike-slip faults bordering Wild Horse Mesa. Although neither the strike-slip fault along Wild Horse Mesa nor that fault's possible northward continuation has been evaluated in detail, we infer that such a structure would ultimately exit the northern Coso Range and transfer dextral slip to the Owens Valley fault. Walker and Whitmarsh (1998) interpreted the Haiwee Springs fault zone to be the fault that transfers dextral shear from the Coso Wash fault into the northern Coso Range and possibly northward into southern Owens Valley.

The association of faults and structures in the Coso Wash-Wild Horse Mesa area is similar to patterns of deformation in analogue sandbox models of dextral pull-apart basins (Dooley and McClay, 1997). In these models, extension and basin formation are driven by a discrete right stepover in a dextral shear zone (termed the "principal deformation zone" by Dooley and McClay) along the bottom of the model. An asymmetric, rhombic basin typically forms above the stepover in the principal deformation zone, and one side of the basin generally is bounded by a system of en echelon normal faults (i.e., the "terraced sidewall" of Dooley and McClay) that step downward toward the basin. Related structures ("borderland structures") may develop adjacent to the basin and accommodate a minor component of total distributed shear. Such structures include anticlines and thrust faults, which may transfer minor amounts of slip in a restraining geometry around the extensional region. The White Hills anticline may be an example of a "borderland structure."

The relationships of faults beneath Wild Horse Mesa and

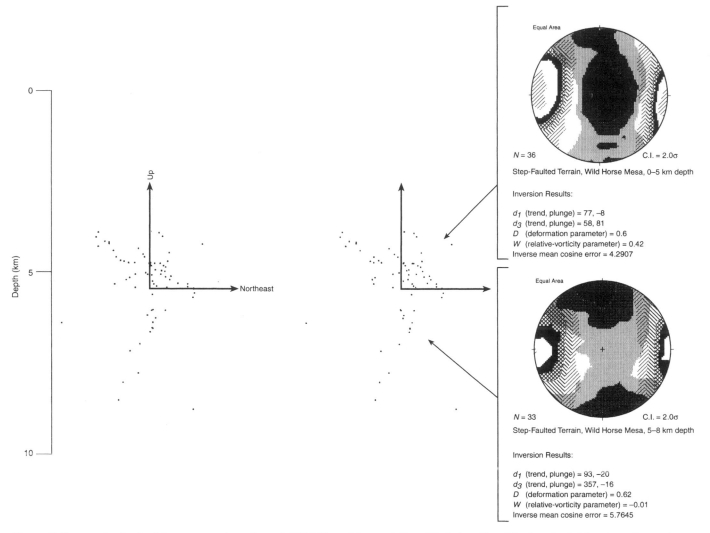

Figure 9. Stereopair of seismicity cross sections through Wild Horse Mesa and Coso Wash (see Fig. 6 for location). View is to the northwest (coordinate arrows point up and to the northeast). When viewed in stereo, the southwest-dipping alignment of hypocenters below ~5 km depth can be seen to form a northwest-striking plane. The Kamb contour plot of P axes (shaded) and T axes (striped) from events associated with the northwest-striking, southwest-dipping plane indicates predominantly strike-slip faulting. In contrast, the Kamb plot of P and T axes for events within the volume of distributed seismicity above 5 km depth shows predominantly normal-faulting events that accommodate a large component of vertical crustal thinning.

the northern Coso Wash (Fig. 8) resemble some cross sections through the sandbox models of Dooley and McClay (1997). Specifically, normal faulting and extension may be confined to shallow crustal levels and detached from strike-slip faulting at depth by moderately dipping faults that act as decoupling horizons or transfer zones (e.g., Fig. 9 in Dooley and McClay, 1997). Seismicity from the northern Coso Wash and Wild Horse Mesa shows partitioning of normal and strike-slip faulting into discrete depth domains (Figs. 9 and 11), kinematically analogous to the sandbox models. The tendency of shallow decoupling structures to form may be enhanced by high heat flow associated with magmatic and geothermal activity in the central Coso Range.

In the sandbox models, the "borderland structures" become

inactive once a throughgoing strike-slip fault develops across the pull-apart basin (Dooley and McClay, 1997). Given that there is no well-defined, integrated strike-slip fault through Coso Wash and that "borderland"-like structures in Rose Valley are seismically active, we infer that entire system is less mature than the final sandbox models described by Dooley and McClay (1997). Dixon et al. (1995) proposed that the western limit of dextral shear in the Walker Lane belt north of the Garlock fault has progressively stepped westward during the past 4 m.y., with the most recent step from Panamint Valley to the Coso area occurring as recently as 2 Ma. If this interpretation is correct, then the extensional Coso Wash graben is relatively youthful and thus may not exhibit some of the characteristics of "mature" structures in the sandbox models (Dooley and McClay, 1997).

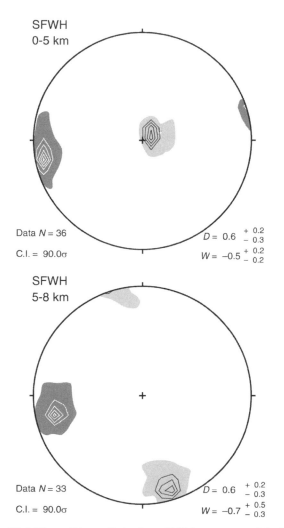

SFWH
0-5 km

Data $N = 36$

C.I. $= 90.0\sigma$

$D = 0.6 \begin{smallmatrix} +\ 0.2 \\ -\ 0.3 \end{smallmatrix}$

$W = -0.5 \begin{smallmatrix} +\ 0.2 \\ -\ 0.2 \end{smallmatrix}$

SFWH
5-8 km

Data $N = 33$

C.I. $= 90.0\sigma$

$D = 0.6 \begin{smallmatrix} +\ 0.2 \\ -\ 0.3 \end{smallmatrix}$

$W = -0.7 \begin{smallmatrix} +\ 0.5 \\ -\ 0.3 \end{smallmatrix}$

Figure 10. 95% confidence limits from 2000 bootstrap models for the step-faulted terrain on Wild Horse Mesa (domain SFWH; see Fig. 6 for location). Same plotting scheme as used in Figure 4. Upper and lower stereograms are for events in the 0–5 km and 5–8 km depth intervals, respectively.

SUMMARY AND CONCLUSIONS

Upper-crustal and seismogenic extension in the Coso Range is driven by a releasing stepover between the dextral Airport Lake and Owens Valley faults along the east side of the Sierran microplate (Fig. 11). The footwall of this system (i.e., the Coso Range) is attached to the Sierra Nevada and is effectively being pulled to the northwest from beneath Wild Horse Mesa, which is moving as part of the Walker Lane belt (Fig. 12). The kinematic relationship we infer between normal faults and strike-slip faults beneath Wild Horse Mesa (Figs. 9 and 11) implies that horizontal extension is confined laterally and vertically to the stepover region. We suggest that brittle upper-crustal extension may be accommodated at depth by ductile stretching and emplacement of igneous bodies, the presence of which have been inferred in the middle to upper crust from

analysis of teleseismic P waves (Reasenberg et al., 1980) (Fig. 12). Late Cenozoic intrusions within the stepover region have been interpreted by Duffield et al. (1980) to be the source of heat for the Coso geothermal field.

ACKNOWLEDGMENTS

This work was funded by the U.S. Navy Geothermal Program Office (contract number N68936-98-M-0621). We thank Michael Hasting of the USN GPO for logistical assistance and discussions about the seismotectonics of the Coso Range. David Benner (University of California, Davis) assisted in the preparation of Figure 9. The manuscript was improved by critical reviews from Timothy Dixon, Joydeep Bhattacharyya, and John Bartley. Stereograms were produced by using R.W. Allmendinger's "Stereonet 4.9.6." Caltech, Division of Geology and Planetary Sciences, publication number 8744.

Appendix. Vertical component of the reduced strain-rate tensor

This appendix presents a derivation of the vertical component (V_D) of the reduced strain-rate tensor obtained from a micropolar inversion of fault-slip data.

Let d_k be the principal values of the strain-rate tensor d_{kl}. Let ζ_k be the principal values of the deviatoric strain-rate tensor ζ_{kl}, where

$$d_k = \zeta_k + \beta \qquad \beta \equiv \frac{1}{3}d_{kk} \qquad (A1)$$

and β is the first scalar invariant of the strain-rate tensor and thus the volumetric strain rate (summation over repeated subscripts is assumed).

The first scalar invariant, the trace, of ζ_{kl} can be shown to be zero as follows. Rearranging Equation A1, we get

$$\zeta_k = d_k - \beta. \qquad (A2)$$

The first scalar invariant of ζ_{kl}, the trace, is

$$\zeta_{kk} = \zeta_1 + \zeta_2 + \zeta_3$$
$$\zeta_{kk} = d_{kk} - 3(d_{kk}/3) = 0, \qquad (A3)$$

where we used the second equation from equation A1. ζ_{kl} is the deviatoric component of d_{kl}, where the components may be defined in any rectangular Cartesian coordinate system.

As defined in the text, the deformation rate parameter D is a ratio of the differences in the principal strain rates:

$$D = (d_2 - d_3)/(d_1 - d_3). \qquad (A4)$$

Substituting (A1) in (A4) and simplifying, we get

$$D = (\zeta_2 - \zeta_3)/(\zeta_1 - \zeta_3), \qquad (A5)$$

which shows that D is independent of the volumetric strain rate β. From (A3),

$$\zeta_1 + \zeta_2 + \zeta_3 = 0. \qquad (A6)$$

Equations A5 and A6 allow us to express ζ_2 and ζ_3 in terms of ζ_1 and D. From equation A6,

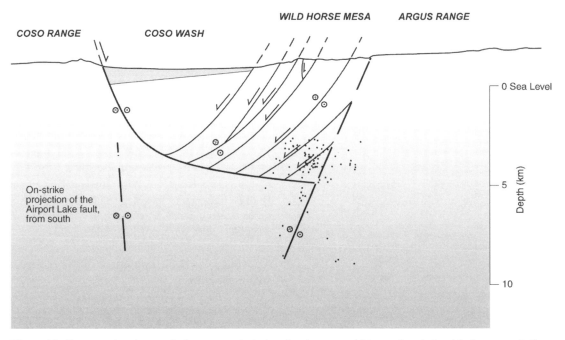

Figure 11. Cross section (no vertical exaggeration) showing interpreted kinematic relationship between shallow normal faults and a deeper strike-slip fault or faults beneath Wild Horse Mesa and the northern Coso Wash, respectively. Hypocenters are the same as those in Figure 9, but projected differently. The strike-slip fault projects updip to the escarpment along the eastern margin of Wild Horse Mesa, where a moderate-magnitude earthquake occurred on a northwest-striking dextral fault in 1998 (Figs. 3 and 7).

$$\zeta_2 = -\zeta_1 - \zeta_3 \tag{A7}$$

$$\zeta_2 - \zeta_3 = -\zeta_1 - 2\zeta_3. \tag{A8}$$

From equation A5 and A8,

$$D = (-\zeta_1 - 2\zeta_3)/(\zeta_1 - \zeta_3) \tag{A9}$$

Solving equation A9 for ζ_3 gives

$$\zeta_3 = \zeta_1[(D + 1)/(D - 2)]. \tag{A10}$$

From equations A7 and A10, we solve for ζ_2:

$$\zeta_2 = -\zeta_1[(1 - 2D)/(D - 2)]. \tag{A11}$$

From equations A1, A10, and A11, the components d_{kl} in the principal coordinates are

$$d_{kl} = \zeta_1 \begin{bmatrix} 1 & 0 & 0 \\ 0 & \dfrac{(1 - 2D)}{(D - 2)} & 0 \\ 0 & 0 & \dfrac{(1 + D)}{(D - 2)} \end{bmatrix} + \begin{bmatrix} \beta & 0 & 0 \\ 0 & \beta & 0 \\ 0 & 0 & \beta \end{bmatrix} \tag{A12}$$

Assuming the volumetric strain rate (β) is zero, then d_{kl} can be expressed as

$$d_{kl} = d_1 \begin{bmatrix} 1 & 0 & 0 \\ 0 & \dfrac{(1 - 2D)}{(D - 2)} & 0 \\ 0 & 0 & \dfrac{(1 + D)}{(D - 2)} \end{bmatrix} \tag{A13}$$

where we used the fact from equation A1 that

$$\zeta_k = d_k \quad \text{if} \quad \beta = 0. \tag{A14}$$

To evaluate the magnitude of the vertical strain, we transform the components of d_{kl} in equation A13 from their principal coordinate system to the geographic coordinate system with axes (X'_1, X'_2, X'_3) (oriented east, north, up). The values of the new tensor components d'_{ij} in geographic coordinates are related to d_{kl} in principal coordinates by the orthogonal transformation $\mathbf{Q}$

$$d'_{ij} = d_{kl}Q_{ki}Q_{lj}, \tag{A15}$$

where

$$Q_{kl} \equiv \mathbf{i}_k \cdot \mathbf{e}'_l, \tag{A16}$$

and where $\mathbf{i}_k$ are the three unit base vectors parallel to the principal axes for d_k, and $\mathbf{e}'_l$ are the three unit base vectors parallel to the geographic coordinates X'_l; the dot indicates the scalar product of each pair of vectors. Thus the components of $\mathbf{Q}$ are the direction cosines for angles between the principal coordinate axes for d and geographic coordinate axes (Means, 1976), and the three components ($l = 1:3$)

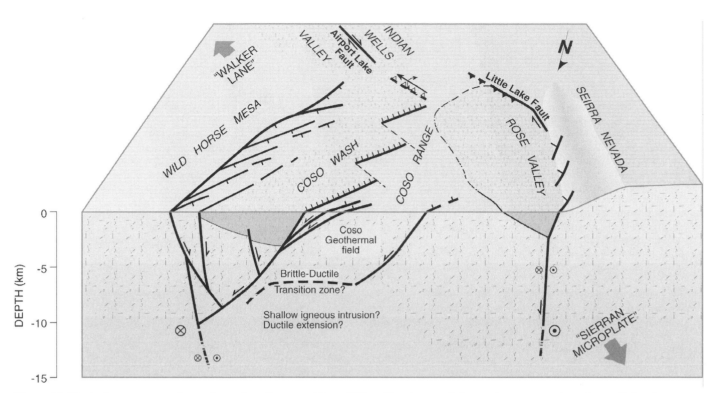

Figure 12. Block diagram across the northern Coso Range and Rose Valley. View is toward the southeast, approximately parallel to the eastern margin of the Sierran microplate. The locus of northwest-directed dextral shear steps right from the Airport Lake fault zone across Coso Wash, resulting in opening of the asymmetric Coso Wash graben. Horizontal extension at depth may be accommodated by ductile stretching of the crust and shallow emplacement of igneous intrusions.

in the kth row of Q_{kl} are the components of the three principal base vectors $\mathbf{i}_k$ ($k = 1{:}3$) in the geographic coordinate system X'_j. The vertical component of the deformation is now nothing more than the extension rate of the transformed tensor in the vertical (i.e., X'_3) direction. From equation A15,

$$d'_{33} = d_{kl}Q_{k3}Q_{l3}. \qquad (A17)$$

Because all of the off-diagonal values of d_{kl} in equation A13 are zero, we use equation A13 in equation 17 and expand to define the vertical deformation ratio V_D for a constant volume deformation:

$$V_D \equiv \frac{d'_{33}}{d_1} = (Q_{13})^2 + \left[\frac{1 - 2D}{D - 2}\right](Q_{23})^2 + \left[\frac{D + 1}{D - 2}\right](Q_{33})^2 \qquad (A18)$$

Equation A18 is an expression, assuming a constant-volume deformation, for the vertical component of the strain-rate tensor, normalized by the maximum extensional strain rate, and expressed in terms of the deformation-rate parameter D and the orientation of the principal strain-rate axes relative to geographical coordinates, as defined by $\mathbf{Q}$. V_D can take on the values $1 \geq V_D \geq -2$. Positive values $1 \geq V_D > 0$ indicate that the deformation accommodates net crustal thickening; $V_D = 0$ implies no component of vertical deformation, so that one of the directions of zero extension rate is vertical; negative values $0 > V_D \geq -2$ indicate net crustal thinning. Values $-1 > V_D \geq -2$ characterize deformations in which, for example, d_1 and d_2 are both extensional and both subhorizontal.

REFERENCES CITED

Argus, D.F., and Gordon, R.G., 1991, Current Sierra Nevada-North America motion from very long baseline interferometry: Implications for the kinematics of the western United States: Geology, v. 19, p. 1085–1088.

Beanland, S., and Clark, M.M., 1994, The Owens Valley fault zone, eastern California, and surface faulting associated with the 1872 earthquake: U.S. Geological Survey Professional Paper 1982, 29 p.

Dixon, T.H., Robaudo, J.L., and Reheis, M.C., 1995, Constraints on present-day Basin and Range deformation from space geodesy: Tectonics, v. 14, p. 755–772.

Dixon, T.H., Miller, M., Farina, F., Wang, H., Johnson, D., 2000, Present-day motion of the Sierra Nevada block and some tectonic implications for the Basin and Range province, North American Cordillera: Tectonics, v. 19, p. 1–24.

Dokka, R.K., and Travis, C.J., 1990, Late Cenozoic strike-slip faulting in the Mojave Desert: Tectonics, v. 9, p. 311–430.

Dooley, T., and McClay, K., 1997, Analog modeling of pull-apart basins: American Association of Petroleum Geologists Bulletin, v. 81, p. 1804–1826.

Duffield, W.A., and Bacon, C.R., 1981, Geologic map of the Coso volcanic field and adjacent areas, Inyo County, California: U.S. Geological Survey Miscellaneous Investigations Series Map I-1200, scale 1:50 000.

Duffield, W.A., Bacon, C.R., and Dalrymple, G.B., 1980, Late Cenozoic volcanism, geochronology, and structure of the Coso Range, Inyo County, California: Journal of Geophysical Research, v. 85, p. 2381–2404.

Eringen, A.C., 1966, Linear theory of micropolar elasticity: Journal of Applied Mathematics and Mechanics, v. 15, no. 6, p. 909–924.

Eringen, A.C., 1967, Theory of micropolar fluids: Journal of Applied Mathematics and Mechanics, v. 16, p. 1–18.

Hauksson, E., 2000, Crustal structure and seismicity distribution adjacent to the Pacific and North America plate boundary in southern California: Journal of Geophysical Research, v. 105, p. 13 875–13 903.

Hauksson, E., Hutton, K., Kanamori, H., Jones, L., Mori, J., Hough, S., and Roquemore, G., 1995, Preliminary report on the 1995 Ridgecrest earthquake sequence in eastern California: Seismological Research Letters, v. 66, p. 54–60.

Jennings, C.W., 1994, Fault activity map of California and adjacent areas: Department of Conservation, California Division of Mines and Geology, Geologic Data Map No. 6, scale 1:750 000.

King, R.W., Hager, B.H., McCluskey, S.C., and Meade, B.J., 1999, Reduction and utilization of GPS data from the Navy geothermal crustal motion network: Final technical report prepared for the Geothermal Program Office, Naval Air Warfare Center, China Lake, California, Contract No. N68936-95-C-0371, 30 p.

Kostrov, V.V., 1974, Seismic moment and energy of earthquakes, and seismic flow of rock: Izv. Acad. Sci. USSR Phys. Solid Earth, (English translation), no. 1, p. 23–44.

Means, W.D., 1976, Stress and strain: New York, Springer-Verlag, 339 p.

Minster, J.B., and Jordan, T.H., 1987, Vector constraints on western U.S. deformation from space geodesy, neotectonics, and plate motions: Journal of Geophysical Research, v. 92, p. 4798–4804.

Press, W.H., Flannery, B.P., Teukolsky, S.A., and Vetterling, W.T., 1990, Numerical recipes: The art of scientific computing (FORTRAN version): Cambridge, UK, Cambridge University Press.

Reasenberg, P., Ellsworth, W., and Walter, A., 1980, Teleseismic evidence for a low-velocity body under the Coso geothermal resource area: Journal of Geophysical Research, v. 85, p. 2471–2483.

Reheis, M.C., and Dixon, T.H., 1996, Kinematics of the eastern California shear zone: Evidence for slip transfer from Owens and Saline Valley fault zones to Fish Lake Valley fault zone: Geology, v. 24, p. 339–342.

Roquemore, G., 1980, Structure, tectonics and stress field of the Coso Range, Inyo County, California: Journal of Geophysical Research, v. 85, p. 2434–2440.

Roquemore, G., 1981, Active faults and associated tectonic stress in the Coso Range, California [Ph.D. thesis]: Reno, University of Nevada, 134 p.

Stewart, J.H., 1988, Tectonics of the Walker Lane belt, western Great Basin, *in* Ernst, W.G., ed., Metamorphism and crustal evolution of the western United States, Rubey Volume 7: Englewood Cliffs, New Jersey, Prentice-Hall, p. 683–713.

Twiss, R.J., and Unruh, J.R., 1998, Analysis of fault-slip inversions: Do they constrain stress or strain rate?: Journal of Geophysical Research, v. 103, p. 12 205–12 222.

Twiss, R.J., Protzman, G.M., and Hurst, S.D., 1991, Theory of slickenline patterns based on the velocity gradient tensor and microrotation: Tectonophysics, v. 186, p. 215–239.

Twiss, R.J., Souter, B.J., and Unruh, J.R., 1993, The effect of block rotations on the global seismic moment tensor and patterns of seismic P and T axes: Journal of Geophysical Research, v. 98, p. 645–674.

Unruh, J.R., and Lettis, W.R., 1998, Kinematics of transpressional deformation in the eastern San Francisco Bay region, California: Geology, v. 26, p. 19–22.

Unruh, J.R., Twiss, R.J., and Hauksson, E., 1996, Seismogenic deformation field in the Mojave block and implications for the tectonics of the eastern California shear zone: Journal of Geophysical Research, v. 101, no. B4, p. 8335–8362.

Unruh, J.R., Twiss, R.J., and Hauksson, E., 1997, Kinematics of post-seismic relaxation from aftershock focal mechanisms of the 1994 Northridge, California, earthquake: Journal of Geophysical Research, v. 102, p. 24 589–24 603.

VanWormer, J., and Ryall, A., 1980, Sierra Nevada-Great Basin boundary zone: Earthquake hazard related to structure, active tectonic processes and anomalous patterns of earthquake occurrence: Bulletin of the Seismological Society of America, v. 70, p. 1557–1572.

Walter, A.W., and Weaver, C.S., 1980, Seismicity of the Coso Range, California: Journal of Geophysical Research, v. 85, p. 2441–2458.

Walker, J.D., and Whitmarsh, R.S., 1998, A tectonic model for the Coso geothermal area: U.S. Department of Energy Proceedings Geothermal Program Review XVI, April 1–2, Berkeley, California, p. 2–17 to 2–24.

Whitmarsh, R.W., Walker, J.D., and Monastero, F.C., 1996, Structural domains within the Coso Range of east-central California: A case for right-oblique extension: Geological Society of America Abstracts with Programs, v. 28, no. 7, p. A-116.

MANUSCRIPT ACCEPTED BY THE SOCIETY MAY 9, 2001

Geological Society of America
Memoir 195
2002

Geologic map of northern Mojave Desert and southwestern Basin and Range, California: Compilation method and references

J. Douglas Walker
Adrian K. Berry, Patrick J. Davis
Joseph E. Andrew, and John M. Mitsdarfer
Department of Geology, University of Kansas, Lawrence, Kansas 66045, USA

INTRODUCTION

Included with this volume is a compilation geologic map of the southwestern Basin and Range province and the northern Mojave Desert (Plate 1). This map is presented at a scale of 1:250000 in paper form and as a geographic information system (GIS) database on the included CD-ROM. The map represents a compilation of new geologic mapping around the area combined with parts of the Death Valley, Trona, and San Bernardino 1:250000 maps prepared by the California Division of Mines and Geology (CDMG). A full list of map references follows at the end of this paper; Plate 1 includes an index map showing the sources.

The CDMG maps are the most useful compilations of the geology of this region. However, owing to budget constraints, these maps are not being regularly updated. This circumstance is unfortunate, because a large amount of new geologic mapping and a vast number of new age determinations for rocks in the region have been made since the current series of maps was published.

We have attempted to compile as much of the recent mapping in this area as possible. Much of the updated geology comes from unpublished student thesis maps focusing on the pre-Quaternary bedrock of the area, which are invaluable contributions to the geologic community, but are usually difficult or impossible to publish. We have included many of these maps as graphic files and GIS files on the enclosed CD-ROM. A description of the CD-ROM and the methodology of generating the GIS data are given in a separate paper (Walker, Black, Berry, Davis, Andrew, and Mitsdarfer, this volume).

METHODS

The compilation map was constructed in three main steps beginning with initial digitizing of the background CDMG maps and all of the new, larger-scale geologic maps that superseded areas on the CDMG maps. Digitizing was done by using the GIS programs Arc/Info and ArcView, written by the Environmental Systems Research Institute. (See Walker, Black, Berry, Davis, Andrew, and Mitsdarfer, [this volume] for a more complete description of methods used.) In all, we digitized all or parts of three CDMG 1:250000 sheets and over 15 separate detailed map studies. Once digitized, the GIS were fully attributed for geologic information.

The second step was to simplify the larger-scale geologic maps and merge them into the compilation map. Most of these detailed maps were made at a scale of 1:6000 to about 1:12000, requiring great reduction of the geologic detail in getting them to 1:250000 while attempting to keep the main geologic information and structures emphasized by the original mappers. These maps were then merged into the compilation map. Most of the simplified maps merged easily into the compilation map (especially for areas of older rocks surrounded by alluvium). In some areas, however, edge matching proved difficult, especially for almost all areas adjacent to the Garlock fault (mostly because of inaccessibility of Fort Irwin and China Lake military bases). Thematic Mapper imagery was used to edge match maps in these areas. Standard band combinations (e.g., 2, 3, 4) and band-ratio images (mineral index 5/7, 5/4, 3/1) were used to extract and extend the geologic match between a given detailed map and the more general map.

The third and final step in compilation was to check the final map for accuracy and completeness. This step was done in a number of ways. The map was examined by most of the workers who contributed larger-scale maps. This check identified gross errors and misguided simplification. We also attempted to evaluate undeniably dated interpretations for areas not covered by the new maps. One example of this process was the elimination of units labeled "gr-m" and "m" on the CDMG

Walker, J.D., Berry, A.K., Davis, P.J., Andrew, J.E., and Mitsdarfer, J.M., 2002, Geologic map of northern Mojave Desert and southwestern Basin and Range, California: Compilation method and references, *in* Glazner, A.F., Walker, J.D., and Bartley, J.M., eds., Geologic Evolution of the Mojave Desert and Southwestern Basin and Range: Boulder, Colorado, Geological Society of America Memoir 195, p. 295–296.

Trona sheet (a designation used previously to denote metamorphic rocks of unknown affinity and age). We accomplished this procedure by assigning a specific rock unit based on literature surveys, inquiries to regional experts, or from our own examination of outcrops.

OTHER MAP INFORMATION

Also appearing on the compilation map are topography and cultural data generated in several ways. The topography was made from a digital elevation model (DEM) for the study area obtained from the Mojave Desert Ecosystem Program database (see www.mojavedata.gov) contoured to make the topographic map. Hydrology was downloaded from the U.S. Geological Survey geospatial data repository (http://nsdi.usgs.gov/). Roads, towns, and place names were digitized from the CDMG maps.

ACKNOWLEDGMENTS

Support for this project was provided by a grant from the Geothermal Program Office, Naval Air Warfare Center, China Lake. We thank John Bartley, Allen Glazner, and all of the contributors for careful reviews of this map.

REFERENCES CITED

Albee, A.L., Labotka, T.C., Lanphere, M.A., and McDowell, S.D., 1981, Geologic map of the Telescope Peak quadrangle, California: U.S. Geological Survey Map GQ-1532, scale 1:62 500.

Andrew, J.E., 2001, Unpublished mapping.

Boettcher, S.S., 1990, Structure and petrology of Iron Mountain, central Mojave Desert California [M.S. thesis]: Chapel Hill, University of North Carolina, 94 p.

Bortugno, E.J., and Spittler, T.E., 1986, Geologic map of California, San Bernardino sheet: Department of Conservation, California Division of Mines and Geology, scale 1:250 000.

Carr, M.D., Christiansen, R.L., Poole, F.G., and Goodge, J.W., 1997, Bedrock geologic map of the El Paso Mountains in the Garlock and El Paso Peaks 7½′ quadrangles, Kern County, California: U.S. Geological Survey Map I-2389, scale 1:24 000.

Cox, B.F., and Diggles, M.F., 1986, Geologic map of the El Paso Mountains wilderness study area, Kern County, California: U.S. Geological Survey Miscellaneous Field Studies Map MF-1827, scale 1:24 000.

Fletcher, J.M., 1994, Geodynamics of large-magnitude extension: A field-based study of the central Mojave metamorphic core complex [Ph.D. dissertation]: Salt Lake City, University of Utah, 109 p.

Glazner, A.F., 1988, Stratigraphy, structure, and potassic alteration of Miocene volcanic rocks in the Sleeping Beauty area, central Mojave Desert, California: Geological Society of America Bulletin, v. 100, p. 424–435.

Jennings, C.W., Burnett, J.L., and Troxel, B.W., 1962, Geologic map of California, Trona sheet: Department of Conservation, California Division of Mines and Geology, scale 1:250 000.

Linn, J.K., 1992. Kinematics of Late Cenozoic deformation, the Kramer Hills, southern California [M.S. thesis]: Lawrence, University of Kansas, 94 p.

Loomis, D.P., 1984, Miocene stratigraphic and tectonic evolution of the El Paso Basin, California [M.S. thesis]: Chapel Hill, University of North Carolina, 172 p.

Martin, M.W., 1992, Stratigraphic and structural evolution of the Shadow Mountains, western Mojave Desert, California: Implications for the tectonic development of the central and western Mojave Desert [Ph.D. dissertation]: Lawrence, University of Kansas, 266 p.

Miller, J.S., 1994, Geochemical and isotopic investigations of Mesozoic magmatism and crustal structure in the central and western Mojave Desert, California [Ph.D. dissertation]: Chapel Hill, University of North Carolina, 130 p.

Moore, S.C., 1976, Geology and thrust fault tectonics of parts of the Argus and Slate ranges, Inyo County, California [Ph.D. dissertation]: Seattle, Washington University, 128 p.

Schermer, E.R., and Busby, C.J., 1994, Jurassic magmatism in the central Mojave Desert: Implications for arc paleogeography and preservation of continental volcanic sequences: Geological Society of America Bulletin, v. 106, p. 767–790.

Schermer, E.R., Luyendyk, B.P., and Cisowski, S., 1996. Late Cenozoic structure and tectonics of the northern Mojave Desert: Tectonics, v. 15, no. 5, p. 905–932.

Spencer, J.E., 1990, Geologic map of southern Avawatz Mountains, northeastern Mojave Desert region, San Bernardino County, California: U.S. Geological Survey Miscellaneous Field Studies Map MF-2117, scale 1:24 000.

Streitz, R., and Stinson, M.C., 1974, Geologic map of California, Death Valley sheet: Department of Conservation, California Division of Mines and Geology, scale 1:250 000.

Walker, J.D., Martin, M.W., Bartley, J.M., and Coleman, D.S., 1990, Timing and kinematics of deformation in the Cronese Hills, California, and implications for Mesozoic structure of the southwestern Cordillera: Geology, v. 18, p. 554–557.

Walker, J.D., and Martin, M.W., 1995, Unpublished mapping.

Whitmarsh, R.S., 1997, Unpublished mapping.

MANUSCRIPT ACCEPTED BY THE SOCIETY MAY 9, 2001

Geological Society of America
Memoir 195
2002

Geologic maps of the northern Mojave Desert and southwestern Basin and Range Province, California: Explanation of maps on CD-ROM

J. Douglas Walker
Ross A. Black, Adrian K. Berry
Patrick J. Davis, Joseph E. Andrew, and John M. Mitsdarfer
Department of Geology, University of Kansas, Lawrence, Kansas 66045, USA

INTRODUCTION

Included with this volume is a CD-ROM containing numerous geologic maps for areas in the southwestern Basin and Range Province and the northern Mojave Desert. These maps represent new and significant revisions to the geologic understanding of the area. Many of the maps come from student theses; some are from unpublished mapping by the authors, and some are more detailed versions of published simplified maps. In addition, a map of aeromagnetic data for the Indian Wells Valley and surrounding areas is also included.

The geologic maps are presented in a variety of formats. In compiling these data, we constructed a geographic information system database for each geologic map. This database was then used to make graphic files that reproduce each map in color. A description of the data for each map area is included on the CD-ROM.

METHODS

A general description of methods used to make the maps included on the CD-ROM is given below. For further background the reader is referred to Walker et al. (1996). The first step in making each map was to digitize contacts and point data (e.g., strikes and dips). For most maps, this was done by scanning the map at relatively high resolution (typically 300–400 dpi) and digitizing lines and points using the ArcEdit module of Arc/Info. Some maps, however, were provided to us in a vector format, either postscript or DXF. These maps were imported directly into Arc/Info as vector files and then manipulated using Arc/Edit. All scans and vector data were projected into real-world coordinates prior to digitizing.

The lines forming the contacts and all point data were as-signed attributes once each map was digitized. Attribution followed the methods of Walker et al. (1996) and was done using the ARCVIEW program. We have written a script that runs under ARCVIEW to do all the contact, point, and rock unit classification. This script, GEOEDITOR, is included on the CD-ROM. Once classified, the contacts were built into rock units (a rock unit is defined by its bounding contacts). The rock units were then classified using the same script.

Topography and cultural features also needed to be incorporated into each map. Many areas had such data available online from the U.S. Geological Survey (USGS) (http://nsdi.usgs.gov/). For these areas, we downloaded DLGs (digital line graphs) for 7.5′ topographic maps. Several areas, however, had no such data. For these maps we scanned and autotraced the 7.5′ USGS topographic maps. These were then manually edited to eliminate errors and enhance clarity.

The GIS databases were then plotted into layers using the ArcPlot module of Arc/Info. Each data type (contacts, points, rock units, topography, etc.) were plotted into individual files. These files were then converted to postscript files and imported into Adobe Illustrator for final map preparation. Each layer was checked and manipulated so that labels did not overlap and were easy to read. In addition, a legend for the map was created at this step.

The maps were checked for digitizing and attribution errors. Then all maps were sent to the original mapper for checking. The maps contained on the enclosed CD-ROM went through at least three stages of error checking.

DATA FORMATS

Maps on the CD-ROM are mostly available in four formats. These include a raster graphic format, a GIS format, and two scalable vector graphic format. (Note: the aeromagnetic map is only in TIF format and was generated by point data; the Lava Mountains map is only in a vector graphic format.) The graphic format included is the GIF graphic interchange format. This file format is ideal for geologic maps because it very efficiently compresses graphics files with a limited number of colors. Geologic maps typically contain from 10 to 200 colors. The GIS format is Arc/Info exchange format (e00). This format can be imported into all ESRI programs and most major GIS and geologic modeling packages. Files in e00 format contain all of the vector information as well as all of the GIS and geology attributes. Metadata on attributes for the maps are included in files labeled "readme." Finally, the maps are included as postscript and PDF vector graphics files. Both formats are included because each has certain advantages for the user. Postscript files can be read and edited by a large number of programs. The various geologic layers (e.g., topography, contacts, etc.) in each file are also contained as separately addressable layers. Thus, customizing output of the files is simple. PDF files are included because of their ease of viewing and use in many packages: these files can be read by many graphics packages, Acrobat Reader (a freeware product of Adobe), and by most Web browsers.

MAPS ON THE CD-ROM

We have included maps for 15 areas on the CD-ROM in folders compressed using WINZIP on a Windows-based PC. These folders can be expanded using either WINZIP on a PC or a program such as STUFFIT Expander on a Macintosh. Maps included cover the following areas.

Aeromagnetic data for the Indian Wells Valley area

An aeromagnetic map for the Indian Wells Valley and surrounding area in east-central California is included on the CD-ROM. This map is listed as **AEROMAG** and was prepared by Allan M. Katzenstein, Francis C. Monastero, and Robert C. Jachens. The survey consists of more than 9033 line-kilometers, covering approximately 4150 km^2 in the northeastern Mojave Desert and the southwestern Basin and Range. It was flown at a 250 m drape (height above average terrain) with a principal line spacing of 0.54 km and 10% cross-lines. The principal line orientation is N65°E. The map was constructed using Oasis Montaj software from Geosoft, Inc. of Toronto, Canada. More than 480,000 corrected data observations to produce a gridded and contoured map. The product was then converted to the tagged image format (TIF) at a resolution of 300 dots per inch.

The Buttes

A single geologic map is included and is listed as **BUTTES** on the CD-ROM. This is geologic mapping done by John Fletcher, Mark Martin, and John Bendixen, and covers part of the central Mojave metamorphic core complex (see Chapter 2). The map is described in Fletcher (1994) and Fletcher et al. (1995).

Coso Range

This is geologic mapping done by Richard S. Whitmarsh. This mapping covers part much of the Coso Range. The map will be described in Whitmarsh's Ph.D. dissertation at the University of Kansas once completed. Several geologic maps (organized by 7.5′ quadrangle) are included. These maps are listed as **COSO** on the CD-ROM.

East Sierran thrust system

The East Sierran thrust system map included on the CD-ROM is from a compilation map by George C. Dunne. This mapping covers this system from the Inyo Mountains southward to the Garlock fault. The map is listed as **ESTS** on the CD-ROM.

El Paso Mountains

The El Paso Mountains map included on the CD-ROM is from the M.S. thesis of Dana Loomis completed at the University of North Carolina (Loomis, 1984). This mapping covers mostly Miocene rocks in the western El Paso Mountains. The map is described in Loomis (1984) and is listed as **ELPASO** on the CD-ROM.

Fremont Peak

This is geologic mapping done by John Fletcher, Allen Glazner, Jonathon Miller, Drew Coleman, and Mark Martin. The map is described in Fletcher et al. (this volume) and is listed as **FREMONT** on the CD-ROM. This mapping covers the northwestern-most part of the central Mojave metamorphic core complex.

Hinkley Hills

This is geologic mapping done by John Fletcher and Mark Martin. This mapping covers part of the central Mojave metamorphic core complex and is described in Fletcher (1994) and Fletcher et al. (1995). This map is listed **HINKLEY** on the CD-ROM.

Iron Mountain

This is geologic mapping done by Stefan Boettcher as part of his M.S. thesis at the University of North Carolina. This map covers part of the east Sierran thrust system as expressed in the Mojave block. The significance of the mapping and further background information is given in Boettcher (1990) and

Boettcher and Walker (1993). This map is listed as **IRONMT** on the CD-ROM.

Kramer Hills

This is geologic mapping done by Jonathan Linn as part of his M.S. thesis at the University of Kansas. This mapping covers an area of the central Mojave metamorphic core complex. Structures on the map include evidence for Cenozoic contraction. The map is described in Linn (1992) and Linn et al. (this volume). The map is listed under **KRAMER** on the CD-ROM.

Lava Mountain

This is geologic mapping done by Deborah Keenan and Eugene Smith. This mapping covers the western part of the Lava Mountains. The geology is described in the paper by Smith et al. (this volume). The map is listed under **LAVAMT** on the CD-ROM.

Mitchel Range and Waterman Hills

This is geologic mapping done by John Fletcher, John Bendixen, Robert Fillmore, Doug Walker, Allen Glazner, and John Bartley. This mapping covers part of the central Mojave metamorphic core complex. The map is described in Fletcher (1994) and Fletcher et al. (1995). The map is listed as **MITWAT** on the CD-ROM.

Shadow Mountains

This is geologic mapping done by Mark Martin as part of his Ph.D. dissertation at the University of Kansas. This mapping covers an area of primarily Jurassic deformation in the western Mojave block. The map is described in Martin (1992), Martin and Walker (1995), and Martin et al. (this volume). The map is listed as **SHADOW** on the CD-ROM.

Sleeping Beauty area

This is geologic mapping done by Allen Glazner. This mapping covers the Sleeping Beauty area of the southern Cady Mountains. The map is described in Glazner (1988) and is listed as **BEAUTY** on the CD-ROM.

Southwestern Basin and Range and northern Mojave Desert

This is a geologic compilation map for the southwestern Basin and Range and northern Mojave Desert. This compilation is described in Walker et al. (this volume) and the map is also included as a paper copy (Plate 1) enclosed with this volume. The map is listed as **COMPMAP** on the CD-ROM.

ACKNOWLEDGMENTS

Support for this project was provided by a grant from the Geothermal Program Office, Naval Air Warfare Center, China Lake. We are particularly grateful to Liz Schermer, John Spencer, John Bartley, Allen Glazner, Stefan Boettcher, Jon Linn, Dana Loomis, Mark Martin, and Richard Whitmarsh for providing maps or other information for this project. Special thanks goes to Frank Monastero for guidance through this work.

REFERENCES CITED

Boettcher, S.S., 1990, Structure and petrology of Iron Mountain, central Mojave Desert California [M.S. thesis]: Chapel Hill, North Carolina, University of North Carolina, 94 p.

Boettcher, S.S., and Walker, J.D., 1993, Geologic evolution of Iron Mountain, central Mojave Desert: California: Tectonics, v. 12, p. 372–386.

Fletcher, J.M., 1994, Geodynamics of large-magnitude extension: A field-based study of the Central Mojave metamorphic core complex [Ph.D. dissertation]: Salt Lake City, University of Utah, 109 p.

Fletcher, J.M., Bartley, J.M., Martin, M.W., Glazner, A.F., and Walker, J.D., 1995, Large-magnitude continental extension: An example from the central Mojave metamorphic core complex: Geological Society of America Bulletin, v. 107, p. 1468–1483.

Glazner, A.F., 1988, Stratigraphy, structure, and potassic alteration of Miocene volcanic rocks in the Sleeping Beauty area, central Mojave Desert, California: Geological Society of America Bulletin, v. 100, p. 424–435.

Linn, J.K., 1992, Kinematics of late Cenozoic deformation, the Kramer Hills, southern California [M.S. thesis]: Lawrence, University of Kansas, 94 p.

Loomis, D.P., 1984, Miocene stratigraphic and tectonic evolution of the El Paso Basin, California [M.S. thesis]: Chapel Hill, North Carolina, University of North Carolina, 172 p.

Martin, M.W., 1992, Stratigraphic and structural evolution of the Shadow Mountains, western Mojave Desert, California; implications for the tectonic development of the central and western Mojave Desert [Ph.D. dissertation]: Lawrence, University of Kansas, 266 p.

Martin, M.W., and Walker, J.D., 1995, Stratigraphy and paleogeographic significance of metamorphic rocks in the Shadow Mountains, Western Mojave Desert, California: Geological Society of America Bulletin, v.107, p. 354–366.

Walker, J.D., Black, R.A., Linn, J.K., Thomas, A.J., Wiseman, R., and D'Attilio, M.G., 1996, Development of geographic information systems oriented databases for integrated geological and geophysical applications: GSA Today, vol. 6, no. 3, p. 1–7.

Manuscript Accepted by the Society May 9, 2001

Index